the
outdoor
encyclopedia

the
outdoor
encyclopedia

compiled by

TED KESTING

editor

Sports Afield

Magazine

A. S. BARNES AND COMPANY • New York

Published on the same day in the Dominion of Canada
by THE COPP CLARK COMPANY, LTD., TORONTO

Library of Congress Catalog Card Number: 56-5555

foreword

THE REDISCOVERY of the out-of-doors in the past decade is one of the greatest phenomena of our modern way of life. Each year since World War II the numbers of people enjoying participant outdoor sports have soared. The United States now has over thirty million licensed hunters and fishermen—millions more fish our oceans and bays without the need of a license. Over 600,000 outboard motors are now sold annually, most of them for small pleasure craft. Every year half our entire population visits America's 200 million acres of national parks, forests and wildlife refuges. A quarter of them spend some time there to camp, fish, go boating, skating, skiing or just to look.

The tremendous upsurge in outdoor interest is not hard to understand. The pressures of twentieth century civilization are enough to make any sane person want to get close to woods, waters and mountains to retain whatever sense of reason he has left. The shorter working hours and greatly increased leisure time we now enjoy have made it possible for more and more to go afield. Better roads, improved air service and speedier trains have all brought the out-of-doors closer to the average man.

Everything points to continued booming outdoor activity. The economists are predicting a four-day work week in the near future, with greater pay. The move away from metropolitan centers increases every year. Industry is going more and more to rural areas because it knows that employees with bigger families do not want to raise their children on city streets. The mammoth new highway construction program now under way is bringing huge wilderness areas no more than a day's drive from the homes of millions of Americans.

All of the foregoing seems to be good reason for *The Outdoor Encyclopedia*. The purpose of this book is to make it possible for those who want to spend their free time out-of-doors to get the very utmost in enjoyment from their leisure hours. There are numerous books and hundreds of magazine articles on all of the subjects covered in this volume, but we have collected the best of what we know to be in existence so that basic information could be made available between two covers on all of the principal activities of woods, fields and waters.

The writers whose works are represented in the 22 chapters of this book are considered to be among the top experts in their various fields. My heartiest thanks to them and their publishers for allowing us to use their material in *The Outdoor Encyclopedia*. Without them there would be no such publication, for no one man can hope to know all there is about the vast out-of-doors.

Ted Kesting

acknowledgments

COMPILING THIS encyclopedia would not have been possible without drawing upon many experts whose knowledge and experience cover every phase of outdoor sports. I am deeply appreciative of the contributions of each.

Readers of *Sports Afield* Magazine and the *Sports Afield* Annuals will recognize such well-known writers as:

Erwin A. Bauer, Pete Brown, Lou S. Caine, Arthur H. Carhart, Willard Crandall, Byron W. Dalrymple, Henry P. Davis, Verne E. Davison, Weston Farmer, Paul A. Fluck, M.D., Jerry Geerlings, C. W. Gillam, C. E. Gillham, Robert D. Hall, Michael Hudoba, Ellsworth Jaeger, John Jobson, Cal Johnson, Wayne Judy, A. M. Libasci, M.D., Jason Lucas, Horace Mitchell, William Byron Mowery, Robert M. Ormes, Jimmy Robinson, W. L. Searle, Shep Shepherd, McGregor Smith, Jr., Bob Stewart, Col. Townsend Whelen, Bill Wolf, Lee Yeager.

I am also indebted to the writers whose works have appeared in other books previously published by A. S. Barnes and Company, Inc. They are:

Cora, Rose and Bob Brown	*The Country Cook Book*
Ivan S. Ivanovic	*Spearfishing*
Harold McCracken and	
Harry Van Cleve	*Trapping*
Frank G. Menke	*The Encyclopedia of Sports*
Harold Putnam	*The Dartmouth Book of Winter Sports*

I am also grateful to the following publishers and writers who allowed us to use portions their works:

Horace Coon	*Hobbies for Pleasure and Profit*
	A Signet Key Book
	The New American Library
Vlad Evanoff	*Surf Fishing*
	The Ronald Press Company

Adrian Eliot Hodgkin	*The Archer's Craft*
	The Ronald Press Company
Carl D. Lane	*How to Sail*
	W. W. Norton and Company
Walter Prager	*Skiing*
	The Ronald Press Company
Eric Sloane	*Eric Sloane's Weather Book*
	Duell, Sloan and Pierce, Inc.
Ormal I. Sprungman	*Photography Afield*
	The Stackpole Company

I am also indebted to The American Red Cross for their section on safety on ice and The Winchester Arms Company for their section on the care of firearms.

A special thanks must go to L. E. Wilde, who contributed countless hours in researching material to be included in this work, to Zack Taylor for his painstaking editing assistance, and to Bill Harris for his careful proofreading.

Ted Kesting

contents

7. FISHING

8. HUNTING

9. MAPS AND COMPASSES

10. MOUNTAIN CLIMBING

11. NATURE

12. OUTDOOR ACCESSORIES

13. PACK TRIPS

14. PHOTOGRAPHY

15. PUBLIC LANDS

the
outdoor
encyclopedia

CHAPTER 1

archery

ARCHERY CONTINUES to hold the headlines as one of America's fastest growing outdoor activities. There were less than 1,000 bowhunters in New Jersey in 1950; in 1956 there were over 11,000. In 1937, 194 bowhunters took advantage of Michigan's special season for archers. In 1956, with the entire state open to archers, more than 38,000 bowhunters purchased licenses. The same story of phenomenal increase in the bowhunting fraternity can be told of New York, Pennsylvania, Wisconsin, Minnesota, Kentucky, California and almost any other state you wish to name.

Why this explosive interest in a sport that predates the invention of gunpowder? Probably there is no single reason, but one reason certainly lies in the weapon itself. Modern bows descend from the long bows of the 5th century and archery today, while utilizing modern techniques and material, still holds the charm of olden days. The pages that follow will give you all the basic information you need to know about this delightful new phase of outdoor activity.

THE BOW

DEFINITIONS

Archers use technical language like other professional people and craftsmen. Here are some terms you will want to remember.

The back is that side of the bow that is farthest from you as you shoot. It is flat or slightly rounded.

The belly is the side of the bow nearest to you as you shoot. In the longbow it takes the form of a Roman arch; in the flat bow the arch is drastically flattened or indeed there may be no arch at all, the belly being quite flat.

Stack. A bow is said to be "high-stacked" when the arch of the belly is deep in proportion to the width of the bow. The higher the stack the more readily will the bow break.

The handgrip (or handle) is just that. It is *not* in the centre of the bow.

Riser. A modern term applied to a piece of wood fixed to the belly of a flat bow to increase the depth and to strengthen it at the handgrip.

The tips are the last four or six inches at each end of the bow.

Whip-ended is when the tips are weak relative to the rest of the limbs.

The limbs, upper and lower, are the halves of the bow above and below the handgrip respectively. Measuring from each end of the handgrip the lower limb is shorter than the upper by 1½ inches.

Set back in the handle is when the whole of each limb has a slight forward inclination, i.e. toward the back, when the bow is unstrung.

The nocks are the grooves at each end of the bow which receive and retain the loops of the string.

The dips. When the belly of a bow dips sharply from the full depth at the handgrip to a lower level it is said to have "dips." A modern innovation said to make for less jar in shooting. The old longbow had no dips; the line of the wood ran in an even taper from handgrip to tips.

The arrow-plate is a little piece of ivory, shell or fiber inlet stuck on the side of the bow immediately above the handgrip on the left-hand side as you shoot. It prevents the arrow from damaging the surface of the bow in its passage across it. For hunting, a buckskin arrow-plate has the advantage of being noiseless.

Backing is anything glued on to the back of the bow either to preserve it from accidental damage or to reinforce its ability to stand tension when the bow is drawn. Archers will never cease to argue about the utility of this.

To tiller a bow is to observe the shape and character of the limbs when the bow is drawn, fully or in part, and to correct irregularities where they show themselves.

The weight of a bow is that number of pounds which, if attached to the centre of the string, would draw the bow to the full draw of the archer who owns it.

To brace a bow is to set the string in position ready for shooting.

Fistmele is the distance between the handgrip on the belly side and the string when the bow is braced. If you place your clenched fist on the handgrip and stretch up your thumb, the tip of the latter should just touch the string. Hence the name. A bow which is highly strung, i.e. where the distance is more than ordinary fistmele, will shoot more cleanly, if with slightly less power, than one which is not.

Cast is the way a bow causes the arrow to fly. A bow which has a good cast will send the arrow in a flatter trajectory than one which has not. An important characteristic since a bow with good cast helps to reduce an archer's main difficulty: the estimation of distance and hence of aim.

BOW WOOD

The bow is essentially a spring. The material of which it is made must therefore have the necessary characteristics. It must endure being bent repeatedly and to an extreme degree, and must then return, faithfully and with great rapidity, to its original shape when the strain on it is released.

Notwithstanding the diversity of materials of which bows can be made, in regard to wood archers are agreed that only three varieties can properly be called first class.

These are Osage Orange (*Maclura Aurantiaca*), Yew (*Taxus Baccata,* or *Canadensis*), and Lemonwood (*Calycophyllum Candidissimum*).

Osage Orange is a very tough wood. Those who know it say that it is just a little bit better than yew.

Yew is the classic material for the English longbow. Irregular and difficult to work, it makes a bow lovely both to shoot and to look at.

Lemonwood, is a hard, heavy, yellowish-buff wood without any apparent grain. It makes first class bows and is easy to work.

In wider vogue today than the all-wood bows are bows that use wood (usually maple) for their core only and are lapped on back and belly with fiber-glass cloth. Other bow construction materials are all fiber glass, aluminum and steel.

LENGTH OF BOWS

Here is a subject on which only a bold man will dogmatize. The old rule for the longbow was that it should be at least equal to the height of the archer. However the longbow was used principally for warfare in open fields. You, on the other hand, are not going to war but to hunt. A bow of six feet or more will be clumsy in the woods and will prevent you from shooting comfortably. What you want is a bow that is at once short and durable.

Wood cannot be bent without limit; there comes a point at which it will snap. Everybody knows that but nobody can tell you just when that point will be reached. So a given piece of wood tends to decide the length of the bow it will make. Another deciding factor is the length of your reach or draw.

To measure this, stand up sideways so the line through your two shoulders points toward your target. Stretch out your left arm toward this target holding a thick stick in your hand as if it were a bow. Your arm should be straight but do not lock your elbow joint. Hold your head up, turn it to the left, and look directly over your left shoulder at the target. Now get somebody

to measure the distance between the back of your left forefinger and the point on the angle of your jaw vertically below your right eye. That is your "draw." It is more usual to measure from the jaw to the back of the bow. Some prefer taking the longer length to the back of the forefinger. Your draw, if you are a "Long Man," may be 28 inches or more: if a "Dwarf" 26 or 27 inches.

Inches are important things, both in bows and in arrows; do not think of them as trifles.

The longer your draw, the longer must be your bow.

For flat bows (wide and short) authorities recommend 5 feet 3 inches to 5 feet 6 inches for draws of 27 to 28 inches and over, respectively. An average of 5 feet 3 inches is quite satisfactory. You can, of course, go shorter if you like to experiment. A wooden bow shorter than 5 feet is not to be relied upon for a man, of, say, 28-inch draw, if it is to be used continually.

THE WEIGHT AND CAST OF BOWS

Your bow must be within your compass and under proper control. The temptation to have a bow too strong for you is one which it is very difficult to withstand. It is easy enough to work up to a strong one, but do not begin with it, or you will never learn to shoot properly. For an average grown man whose muscles of fingers, arm and body are not yet accustomed to this unusual exercise a weight of 45 pounds is not too low. Anything heavier will be a struggle. Work up gradually. Bows of 60 to 62 pounds are about average; 70 pounds is about tops.

It does not follow at all that the heavier the bow the faster and longer will the arrow fly. A heavy bow can, and indeed after 70 pounds or so must, project a heavier shaft; but it may not have the cast of a bow two-thirds of its weight. For every stave there is a weight at which its cast will be a maximum. A 60 pound bow will have a point-blank range of 70-odd yards with birch arrows and 75 to 80 yards with bamboos. "Point-blank" range is that range at which the center of the target will be hit when aim is taken in such a way that the arrowhead seems to rest on that center. Do not let yourself be unduly worried with theory. If your bow is sweet to shoot and strong enough for your purpose, surely that is all that matters.

ARROWS

The choice of target arrows is a very exact business; for hunting arrows you need not be quite so meticulous. After all, in hunting you never know exactly the range at which you shoot. Any miscalculation of the distance will far outweigh some slight variation in the arrows' behavior one from another and by the laws of chance this variation is just as likely to correct any miscalculation as not. Moreover, no good sportsman will shoot at long range and the shorter the range the less will be the effect of variation in individual arrows. So, while it is nice to have all the arrows precisely uniform in all respects, it is less important than you might think at first. At a fixed and known distance of course, as in target shooting, it is fatal not to have them all as nearly identical as you can make them.

Arrows consist of four parts: the shaft itself, or stele; the head; the shaftment where the three feathers are; and the nock into which the bowstring fits.

THE STELE OR SHAFT

This is not only the body of the arrow, but its mind as well. Upon its qualities (and sometimes, apparently, its temperament also) depends the whole behavior of the arrow in flight. Two seemingly identical shafts, of the same dimensions and substance, may behave quite differently. These vagaries cannot be predicted. The only test is that of shooting.

Whatever the shaft may be made of it must have three properties: be of a suitable weight; be sufficiently rigid to withstand the sudden push of the string; be sufficiently springy. The scarce Port Orford cedar is probably first choice for arrow shafts. Following that are Sitka spruce, also hard to get; white birch, tough but with a tendency

to warp; fiber glass, strong, straight and impervious to moisture; and aluminum, practically indestructible but noisy and expensive.

THE NOCK

This is ⅜ inch deep, and of such a width that the whole arrow will just hang on your particular bowstring without falling off. The base of the nock may, with advantage, be just a shade wider than the jaws. If your nock be too wide you will have difficulty in keeping your arrow on the string as you go through the woods; if too narrow, your string will likely split it at the loose.

FEATHERS

There is no substitute for these wonderfully intricate and beautiful mechanisms. It is possible to use arrows without feathers, but only for very short distances. Beyond these, the shaft requires guidance. You cannot use just any feather; you require something at once stiff, durable, flexible and irrepressible. Goose feathers are good, but nowadays more archers use turkey. Both are readily obtainable, so make your choice. White feathers are a great help in finding arrows after the shot. Also they look nice, but the common gray-barred-black turkey is more usual.

ARROWHEADS

What is required from your arrowhead? Very simply that it shall cut deep and wide. Cutting without penetration gives merely a surface wound. Penetration without cutting gives a deep and grievous wound indeed, but not a merciful one since there is little bleeding.

You can insure a wide cut by choosing a suitable width for your blades; you can ensure depth of penetration by a suitable shape, by the keenness of the point and edges, by the strength of the bow and the weight of your shaft.

The power of an arrow never ceases to astonish. Here is a very light thing, flying most leisurely as speed is counted nowadays, which yet will deliver such a blow as would skewer two men together were they so foolish as to stand one behind the other and offer themselves for a mark. It can penetrate chain mail and plate armor. It can be shot through a door without any arrowhead at all and it will slay almost everything that walks or crawls upon the earth. Compared scientifically with a rifle bullet the arrow is nothing. Compared by its results it is in a lot of respects superior. Consider just a few figures. A modern cartridge for a game rifle may carry a bullet which weighs 180 grains and discharge it at an initial velocity of 2,700 feet per second. Such a bullet, after it has gone 100 yards, will have a remaining energy of some 2,500 foot pounds; or, in plain language, it will deliver upon the mark a blow equivalent to that which would be given by more than a ton weight dropped from a height of one foot.

The steel blank; corners broken off; roughly shaped; drilled, bevelled and tempered

A riveted broadhead   *A tanged broadhead*

An arrow, on the other hand, will weigh approximately twice as much as the above bullet, but will only have a velocity of some 150 feet per second, and an energy of 25 foot pounds.

Broadheads, big and little

Since it is the energy that counts, you might conclude that the bullet would be one hundred times as effective as the arrow. It is not so. Then what do you conclude? Simply that you are not at all comparing like with like. Now if you were to compare the effect of an arrow, of the broadhead sort, with that of a sword-thrust you should be on firmer ground. Both penetrate deeply, both cut widely. The bullet is outside the picture; it is a different thing.

As to actual killing power, anything, be it bullet, arrow or sword, which reaches a vital part will be effective. The arrow kills by the depth and extent to which it severs the organs of an animal, not by the shock of the blow it delivers.

BOWSTRINGS

A bowstring is made up of a number of threads laid side by side and twisted together with a loop at one end. The ends, both of them, are thicker than the middle and are twisted differently.

The strength of the string must be related to the "weight" of the bow. Not only that, but there must be a large margin of strength to take care of the tremendous momentary strain to which the string is subjected as the bow snaps back at the instant when the arrow leaves it. Allow, therefore, a factor of about five; that is, use a string which will break only when subjected to a tension in pounds weight of five times the "weight" of the bow.

Thus, for a 60-pound bow, the string should just be capable of supporting a trifle under 300 pounds. Since each strand of linen breaks at five pounds weight, 60 strands will be about right; and, indeed, this makes a string of very convenient thickness to take the nock cut in an arrow of $5/16$ inch diameter. For weaker or stronger bows the calculation is simple. But, although the thinner the string the faster the bow is said to cast, do not use one too thin. A broken string usually means a broken bow; and anyway you are making hunting gear, which should be robust and reliable. If in doubt, err on the thick side.

SUNDRY GEAR

Certain things are part of the traditional equipment of the archer. They are the bracer or armguard; the shooting-glove or, alternatively, the tab; and the quiver. Whether you will want all or any of them you can decide for yourself. The quiver certainly, unless you propose to carry your arrows in your hair as some wild peoples are reputed to do. The glove or tab most certainly at first, but not so surely later on. The bracer, perhaps. This is dependent upon your own anatomy and the height to which you string your bow.

The tab   *The tab in position*

THE BRACER

When you loose the string it may, or will, catch you a hard whack on the inside of your left forearm. It all depends on the shape of your arm and how you hold the bow. A highly-strung bow will hit you less severely than one which is low strung; it may, indeed, not touch you at all. If you shoot in an ordinary jacket the sleeve will take the blow —and deflect the shot.

So people lash or buckle a piece of stout leather on the part of the forearm just above the wrist, the lashing coming on the outside so the bowstring has a smooth surface to strike on. Practically, it is as good to tie up the wrist of your jacket with a piece of string or tape. Some never want any bracer at all. The "stripe" of the string is not so severe that it cannot be endured on the bare arm for a dozen or so practice shots. For the occasional shot in the woods, it is quite superfluous. But if you are going to practice in real earnest at a target then indeed you may want something.

THE QUIVER

This holds your arrows. It should be about 22 inches long; five inches wide at the top and four inches at the bottom; flat-sided, soft and collapsible. If you like a hard, rigid, tubular affair then of course your diameters will not be so great as the above figure, but don't take such a thing with you into the woods. For hunting, a quiver must have certain indispensable characteristics. It must be noiseless. This rules out hard leather, wood and canvas, which all either cause the arrows to rattle as you move, or make an intolerable noise as you push through undergrowths. It must be roomy enough so arrows can be easily withdrawn, and so that the heads do not rub together too much and destroy their cutting-edges. It must have no projections whatever on the inside to catch the arrowhead as you withdraw the shaft. And, finally, it must keep out the wet. The best material for the quiver is a heavy, oil-tanned moosehide or horsehide. Failing this, good, stout buckskin, or some similar thick, soft leather. Reinforce the bottom with a double thickness. As an accessory, in case it rains while you are out, procure an oiled-silk or plastic bag with a drawstring. Slip this over the feathers. It is true they are secured with waterproof glue, but wet does them no good and at the least makes the feathers soft and liable to be crushed out of shape.

The quiver

THE SHOOTING-GLOVE

This, or its much more satisfactory substitute the "tab," is quite indispensable while you are learning to shoot, or when you intend to shoot more than a very few shafts.

The string is drawn with the tips of the fingers and, as you draw, the tip of the forefinger, on its inside surface will get severely pinched in the angle between the string and the shaft. This can be avoided, but not altogether, by making the forefinger do more of the work of drawing than it is naturally inclined to do. Moreover, the surfaces of all three finger-tips cannot withstand for long the rub of the string unless they are protected.

The shooting-glove, or the tab, will not avoid the former ill, but will effectively ensure against the latter.

Do not bother about a glove, or even a modified one; they are hot and always either too large or too small. Use the simple, an-

cient tab. This is a piece of supple leather, about $\frac{1}{16}$ inch thick, cut with two holes to slip over the fore- and third fingers, and projecting so as to cover all three of the working fingertips. A slot is cut between the fore- and second finger so the shaft may come through. It is easy to make, always fits if made right in the first place, never falls off and is completely effective. It also has the great advantage that, if turned back, it frees the hand at once for any other work.

After a little, when your fingers have hardened up, you may be able to dispense with this protection. But one cautionary word. Should the inside of your forefinger get sore, as described above, particularly in the neighborhood of the nail, stop shooting at once, and do not go on until it is properly healed.

SHOOTING

Now far be it from me that I should attempt to teach anyone how to shoot with the bow. I have not succeeded in teaching myself with any great success, although from time to time I am astonished at the sight of my arrow in the mark. By the laws of chance this must necessarily happen occasionally. If it did not no one would continue with his archery. For, have no doubt about it, to shoot well with the bow is very difficult. It is easy enough to discharge arrows in the general direction of what you want to hit and when you walk up to look at them it is also easy to persuade yourself that some of them have landed pretty near. But no miss, near or far, will bring any game to bag. So you must learn to hit. Good field archery is a very skilled business. At first nothing goes right. Then will come a day (yes it will) when you surprise yourself, when your arrows one after the other fly straight and true and when it all seems the easiest thing in the world.

TARGETS

The regulation archery target is a thick disc of straw, at least four feet in diameter, propped up about two feet above the ground on a tripod and has a cloth stretched over it painted in bright-colored rings. It is expensive to buy, most laborious to make and not necessary.

If you want a circular target, a very serviceable and easily-made one can be contrived out of corrugated cardboard, the stuff used for lapping round parcels. This can be bought in long rolls, and is about 15 inches wide. If you roll this up very tightly, to any diameter you please, and then tie the circumference with string or wire, you will have a very durable and cheap target which holds arrows well. Do not roll it as this loosens it; carry it, and store it flat. It needs no tripod but will stand up on the ground by itself.

It is also easy to construct a deer of straw. A few sticks or battens lashed together to form legs, backbone and neck; some wisps of straw bound on to this skeleton with string; and you have a very lifelike object.

Easier yet; a handful of dry grass or hay just put on the ground. That represents your hare or rabbit.

Anthills and molehills are also good marks, but the former are usually much honeycombed and do not hold arrows well. Whatever your mark may be, you will find it a great advantage to have behind it something to catch arrows which have skidded. Long bundles of hay or straw serve quite well—or a low bank of earth or sand. Let this stop be of a good width to catch your bad shots. Without it, some of your arrows will be found to have skidded as much as 50 or 60 yards and may be troublesome to find.

Let us remind ourselves first of all *how to string the bow*. Grasp it by the handle, back up, in the left hand. Put the tip of the lower limb into the angle between the instep of the left foot and the ground. Slide the palm of the right hand up the bow till the loop of the string is reached by the thumb and forefinger. Then, pulling up strongly with the left, and pushing down and out with the right hand, slip the loop into the nock. Make sure it gets properly into both sides of the nock; and do *not* get your fingers under the string.

STANDING

There is an easy rule for this: Be comfortable and stand as suits you best. The accepted rule nowadays is to stand with your shoulders in line with the flight of your arrow, or very nearly so, and to place your feet somewhat apart, and firmly. This is excellent for target shooting; but what about when you are in the woods and do not want to stand up like a telegraph pole? You must be able to shoot kneeling, or squatting; even perhaps from the back of a horse like the Indians used to do. So find out how you can most comfortably shoot from unorthodox as well as orthodox positions and having found out, stick to it. The great thing in archery is constancy, to eliminate as many variables as you can.

Whatever positions you do finally decide

Standing and nocking

on they must be stable ones. When your bow is drawn you are under very considerable exertion. There is nothing left for any balancing feats.

NOCKING

Bearing in mind that the arrow lies on the left side of the bow, there are two other points only in this: to nock so the cock feather is outwards, pointing away from the string; and to nock in the right place on the string, neither too high nor too low. This will require no thought and hence waste of time when your game is in sight, if you have already made two little lumps in the serving on the string that show you immediately where to nock.

DRAWING

The bowstring is drawn by the tips of the first three fingers of the right hand. Mark you, the tips. The fingers should not be hooked round the string; but with a heavy hunting bow perhaps some slight approach to a hook may be tolerated both for security and ease. The less hook the better the loose.

Drawing

The nock of the arrow passes between the fore- and second fingers, so that there is one finger above and two below it. This is known as the Mediterranean Release, and is the most practical of all the possible methods. Make the forefinger do its full share of work. It is apt to shirk, and the more it does so the more will its inside get painfully compressed against the arrow.

In drawing keep the right elbow up, so at full draw, and indeed all along, the forearm is in line with the shaft. Any other position doubles your work and cramps your freedom. Keep the right thumb doubled up out of the way, so that it will not touch your face or jaw.

Today archers do not draw to the breast or to the ear. But either to the middle of the chin, or to a point on the jaw directly beneath the right eye. You will find the latter "anchor-point," as it is called, much more natural and easy than the former. Choose which you like and stick to it. Every shaft, whether your mark be at your feet or 200 yards away, will be drawn full to this point.

The arrowhead will just touch the back of your left forefinger when the bow is full drawn.

And now, having learned the orthodox doctrine, forget it. To hit anything much nearer than 15 or 20 yards by this method is desperately difficult; and in a thick wood you often gets shots at rabbits and squirrels which appear suddenly almost at your feet. Then cast orthodoxy to the winds and draw direct to your eye. This cuts out all mental calculations, and the arrow is directed straight at the mark. If you cannot quite manage the full draw in this position, at so short a range it makes no practical difference.

With this learned, go on to the actual act of drawing.

Here you have again to contend with diverse views; whether one should grip the handle tightly or loosely; whether you should extend the left arm fully and then draw with the strength of your right arm, or "lay the body in the bow" as they did when archery was in its prime. It all depends upon the weight of the bow. A light bow requires no particular effort, a heavy one may tax your strength to the utmost if you are to draw it at all. Most archers hold the handle without any deliberate grip, and at the full draw fingers only encircle it lightly and can be stretched out at full length with the bow's thrust taken in the crotch of the thumb and forefinger. Start with the arrow pointing downward, as nocked, and the left arm extended straight, but not so straight that the elbow-joint is locked. Then, draw back the string, the left arm is steadily raised, until at the full draw it is in position with the bow vertical. But halfway through this simple, and indeed natural, performance, when the left arm is almost up and the right hand partly back, there comes an opportunity to use, apparently, your body weight: and this is the explanation of what is meant by laying the body in the bow.

If at this stage of the draw, when the bow is beginning to show its strength against you, you square your shoulders, cock out your chest and advance it as if to get inside the bow between it and the string, you will accomplish the rest of the draw without trouble. It feels as if you were forcing your hands apart by the weight of your body.

The whole draw must be a steady, continuous motion from the beginning to the end. The left arm, the bow and the right hand all move together and arrive in their final positions simultaneously. The grip of the bow must be in such a position that the arrow comes against the arrow-plate and not on part of the handle. The bow must be vertical. A slow, deliberate draw makes for accuracy; a quick draw, followed by an almost instantaneous release, makes a strong shot, but probably not an accurate one. At the beginning of the draw you will have fixed your gaze on the mark, both eyes being open. Keep it there, and on no account let it wander. Never glance at or along your shaft, and then back to the mark again, nor look at your arrowhead. If you do, your concentration will go all to pieces and you cannot make a good shot. When you come to full draw you will find that your arrowhead will swim into your field of view (but do not focus on it) quite distinctly enough for you to aim it. It is a thing that wants a

little practice, since it rather goes against one's instinct. But it is not difficult to learn, and once learned becomes a habit.

HOLDING

This is the moment between the attainment of full draw and the loose—the instant when you coordinate your mark and your arrowhead, making necessary allowances for range and wind. The shorter you can make this moment the better your shot. The longer you hold, the more tired both you and the bow become.

Range is the principal thing which is settled by this holding. Before you draw at all you will have estimated the range and will have thought where, in relation to the mark, your arrowhead must come. At point-blank range the head will seem to rest on the middle of the mark. Beyond that range it will have to come above it, and your bow-hand will partly or wholly obscure it. This

Holding

is an "underhand" shot. Below that range your head will be aimed below the mark and this is a "forehand" shot. How much in each case is a matter for you to determine according to the characteristics of your bow and shafts. The variations are much larger than you would expect, particularly at long ranges. Nor is it at all easy to hit something which lies almost at your feet—unless, that is, you break the rules as you have already learned.

Allowance for a side wind is a tricky business. An arrow is not much affected by wind at the short ranges used in hunting. Be content with the fact that you can for practical purposes neglect wind, unless it be very strong indeed, up to a range of 80 yards or so.

To sum up: the instant of holding is when you settle all these matters in your mind and adjust your arrowhead accordingly. The quicker you do it the better.

LOOSING

This is the act of letting the string go—apparently very simple, in reality most difficult to do well.

Loosing

The fingertips just slide off the string. There must be no backward pluck, or your arrow will fly into the next county. There must be no weakness, or forward creep, or your arrow will fall short.

With a strong bow the loose is easier to do well than with a weak one since the string is so very ready to tear itself away.

At the loose, there are two things which must *not* happen. The right hand must not move from the anchor-point on the jaw; and the left hand and arm must not move at all. Both should stay in position until the arrow has done its flight. The greatest difficulty is with the bow arm—it requires a conscious effort to remember that, once the bow is drawn and aimed, the left arm has done its job and from that moment takes no part in the proceedings other than as an inert support for the bow. It takes no part in the loose and it cannot affect the flight of the shaft by being waved about after the arrow has gone. More shots are spoiled by movement of the bow arm than by anything else at all. Keep it still. It is the right hand only which is the active agent at this moment. And let this latter stay against the jaw, do not move it backward or outward.

The loose, then, should be imperceptible. Your whole position, both before and after the arrow has gone, should be unaltered until the mark is hit.

When you have perfected your loose you will have done something which no other archer has yet accomplished.

HUNTING

The notes that follow are in no sense meant as instruction given by a skilled hunter to the new entry. On the contrary, they represent simply the cogitations of one who has had some experience hunting game both large and small, but who is comparatively new to the use of the bow for the purpose. Regard them, if you will, as a disquisition on the elementary principles of getting up to your game, but with particular application to the peculiar and additional difficulties which beset the solitary archer.

The fox, deer and rabbit hunters, plus the shooters of pheasants and partridges, often pursue their object with energy, noise, a complete absence of concealment and usually in large company. They do actually pursue it. They go after it, literally, and it is the exhaustion of the beast they chase, or the forcing of it to go in a given direction, that enables them to do what they want.

As an archer, you must go to work quite differently, there is no use chasing in the ordinary sense. The method you must use is known as *still-hunting*. The thing that distinguishes still-hunting is that you do not run after your game. At most you move very slowly and quietly, at best you let the game come to you. The underlying principle is very simple. All wild creatures are afraid of man, therefore you must let them neither hear you, nor smell you, nor recognize you for what you are, even though you may actually be in plain view. Simple to describe, but abominably difficult to do.

Let us consider this matter in analytical fashion. Every wild creature is ruled by four emotions, or senses, or whatever the correct word is. These are fear, hunger, curiosity and sex.

Man, in hunting the creature, can make these feelings work for him. But, in doing so, he is countered by the animal's three powerful defenses. These are the animal's ears, his eyes and his nose. Perhaps also form and color, although naturalists hotly dispute the last. All game animals do not have these defenses equally well developed. But it is not safe to rely on this, as an archer has to approach so close. Much better assume that everything is in first-class working order. It most likely is.

Your problem divides itself into two parts; first, how to make use of the wild thing's emotions; and second, how to avoid or nullify its defenses.

Fear you do not make use of, unless one archer is driving game to another, which is not what is being considered. On the contrary, your whole aim in still-hunting is to avoid alarm of any kind.

Hunger, also, is not a thing upon which you want to play. No one wants to shoot over baited grounds, but it is quite a proper thing to lie for a beast at the edge of his normal feeding ground. That presupposes some skill, care and observation.

Curiosity is a well-marked trait in many creatures. No one who has ever pitched his tent in a field of cows needs be told this. So long as an object cannot be identified without doubt as a man, anything strange is likely to attract notice at once. If it moves oddly, but not alarmingly, it may even induce the watcher to come nearer for a better view.

Sex is an emotion which can be played upon in the mating season. Every boy has read about calling for moose. The hunter makes a trumpet of birch bark, and with it imitates the call of the cow. Another method is based upon the habit of the bull moose of thrashing about in the bushes with his antlers. So you do the same with a stick. He hears a rival, he thinks, and will come to polish him off. If you try this, remember, the moose is as likely to approach you from behind as from the front, and will certainly circle to get your wind as he gets near. It is as well to remember, also, that any large animal is liable to be dangerous during the rut. He is then bold, defiant and looking for trouble.

So much for the mind of the game. Now just a little about its equipment.

The *ear* in animals is an incredibly efficient instrument. Three things you must avoid. Talking, coughing and sneezing, of course; noise in making your way through the brush; and cracking sticks underfoot.

Man is ideally equipped by nature for going silently, only if he goes naked. His skin makes no noise against the twigs and branches, his feet fall without sound and can feel everything underneath that might crack. But a variety of reasons make it impractical to follow our natural inclinations and you must adopt some outer garments. The question is what?

Wearing the skin of something else is logical. Leather or buckskin will be fine as long as the weather is good, but when you get wet you will look and feel as slippery and as clammy as an eel.

Cotton, unless it be soft like a shirt, is noisy in brush. Most rucksacks are of hard-woven cotton and this is one disadvantage of carrying your kit in one.

On all counts wool is the best; good home-spun for a jacket and flannel for trousers. The short type of "battle dress" blouse is good, and does not catch on things.

As for your feet, rubber soles or rubber boots are moderately quiet but take away all feeling for what is underfoot. If you really want to get as nearly as possible to the feeling of bare feet and go silently without breaking twigs, wear moccasins. The real article is of moosehide or thick buckskin; but if you can't get this, then ordinary soft chrome-tanned leather which does not go hard after a wetting would do just as well. With moccasins that have no hard sole attached, as some do, you can go in absolute silence and feel your way almost by touch alone. The drawback is that your feet will always be wet if the ground is at all damp. That makes little difference as long as you keep on the move and it isn't too cold.

Moving through brush, go slowly and watch where you put your feet. Bend under branches, or push them out of the way quietly with a hand. In brambles, lift your foot up and tread on them. Avoid muddy places, liable to produce loud squelching noises. Dry leaves, especially if frozen, make it quite impossible to hunt quietly.

For quiet shooting, bind a thick piece of buckskin round the bow where the arrow passes, or fit a buckskin arrow-plate in place of the more usual bit of fiber or horn. It is also said to be a good thing to bind some fur round the bow, just below the nocks, to avoid the snap of the string against the wood as the bow straightens.

As you move, the arrows in your quiver will rustle loudly against each other. Keep a hand on them to stop this.

If, in spite of all your care, you do make a sudden loud noise, stop and stay stopped for several minutes. The things you have frightened may by then have recovered their equanimity.

And while you are thus going carefully and quietly and slowly, hoping to avoid being heard, listen yourself. Sometimes it is easier to hear game than to see it.

As to the *eye*, and being seen, there is little to be said that is not obvious. A man looking like a man is a sight that no truly wild animal will stay to investigate, unless it feels aggressive. But a man looking like a hummock or a tree stump, or just a piece of a man, is a different matter and may promote investigation. The most difficult thing in the world is to see before you are seen.

If you sit down, and stay still, in some likely and convenient place you are more likely to see before being seen than if you move about. But unless you are more or less in cover as well, you will give yourself away when you prepare to shoot.

If you are seen first, you will not know that it has happened, and you are not likely ever to see that particular animal at all. But if it should still be looking at you when you spot it, try not to let your eyes meet directly. An animal that thinks it has not been seen may stay to watch you further. If it knows it is being looked at it will go at once. Try this on the next squirrel you meet. It is quite easy physically, but most tantalizing mentally, to pretend you are not looking at an animal, and all the time to watch him out of the corner of your eye. If, at the same time, you seize any opportunity to advance, do so diagonally, not directly, and you may get within range.

Avoid sudden movements. They catch the eye immediately.

As to disguise, we all know the value of camouflage. Let your clothes be of such a color that they blend with the surroundings, but lighter rather than darker if there is any choice. Let the back of your bow, if it has a vellum backing, be broken up with color, so it does not show as a long white, disturbing streak; and cover up the feathers of your arrows if they are conspicuous. You can gain immense advantage by painting the face and hands. Even the best-looking man has a face which stands out in the woods like a full moon!

Train yourself, then, to see quickly, remembering that you will seldom see the whole of an animal at once and that it is not likely to be in the picture-book attitude unless it has already seen you. And train yourself, also, to keep out of sight. Both are equally important—and difficult.

In the matter of *nose*, man is not a competitor at all. It is occasionally possible to smell game, if very close indeed. In general one can say that man's nose is quite useless to him. To an animal, on the other hand, loss of his powers of scent would be an irreparable and shattering calamity. His nose is usually his principle defense, far more so than his ears, and certainly, in thick cover at any rate, more than his eyes. The degree to which the power of scent is developed is amazing.

Therefore when you enter the woods you must assume you advertise yourself loudly and inevitably to every creature downwind of you for hundreds of yards. It follows that you must know the general direction of the wind and hunt against it. If the wind is very light, you can discover its trend by throwing up a little dust or some small bits of dry grass, or by watching your tobacco smoke. Wind is, however, a fitful thing, easily deflected by obstacles of any sort and by variations in the contour of the ground. It then forms eddies, the behavior of which cannot be predicted. Thus, unless you know your ground intimately, your most careful precautions may be in vain. In a really dense wood there will be little or no wind, however hard it may blow overhead. There will, nevertheless, be a slow drift and if you are moving, you may be able to keep pace with your own scent. Here, again, the smoke from your pipe will tell you whether you are doing this or not. Few now believe there is any harm in smoking while hunting. Tobacco has a strong smell, certainly, but it has not the terrifying smell of man and it cannot travel farther or faster than the latter, since scent is air-borne. The strong prejudice against smoking, where it exists, is due to a confusion of ideas. The danger of setting the woods on fire is quite another matter. Hunters cannot be too careful to avoid doing this.

Scent has a tendency to rise. If, therefore, you can get above your game you have some advantage.

Habit is as much ingrained in animals as it is in man and all creatures have their habits, their roads and tracks, their feeding-

and drinking-places, their playgrounds and their homes. Making proper allowance for their nature, they lead regular, if not blameless, lives.

If you wish to hunt intelligently and successfully, you must make it your business to find out all these things. You will find it fascinatingly interesting. Read up your natural history and apply to your own ground the lessons learned. Once you realize that all the creatures you meet are on business, and not (or seldom) just taking the air, you can really begin to plan your hunting. It is the absence of this "local knowledge" which makes it so difficult when you go to a strange territory. Should you do this, remember the military maxim: "Time spent in reconnaissance is seldom wasted."

Apart from these questions of place, there is also time to consider. Game moves at more or less regular times, and favors the very early morning, the very late afternoon, and, of course, the night. You cannot shoot in the dark, so dawn and dusk are your best times.

Bracing the bow

If you are in position then, at the place your observations have recommended to you, you will be hunting intelligently and will have much more chance of success than will come from any casual invasion of a wood or other hunting ground.

An archer must be a naturalist first and a shooter second, if he is to fill his bag.

The actual act of shooting requires a little consideration and some revision of ideas if you have been used to hunting with a rifle.

How the arrow lies

The Mediterranean release

Range, of course, is very much reduced. In the open, your effective range for any game, is not likely to exceed 80 yards. In the woods it will be much less. Not that the arrow will not kill at greater distances. It will, up to the limit of its flight. But you cannot hit with certainty, and therefore will not shoot. It is not range so much as the restricted "field of fire" which is the principal difficulty. With a rifle, at say 80 yards, you can shoot between two close branches or through a hole in the bushes 30 or 40 yards away or take aim at a head, or a shoulder, that just shows through a small gap. You

know that the rise of your bullet above the line of sight will be inappreciable at this distance, less than an inch, probably. With an arrow, the corresponding rise is a matter of feet, six or 12 of them according to your tackle. The arrow requires more space, and plenty of it, in a vertical direction—much more, usually, than you would think. There is, therefore, no sense in hunting where the growth is too thick or in hiding-up in a place overhung with branches.

Note that the soles of the feet, and the heels, are flat on the ground

Familiarize yourself with the trajectory of your shafts at various ranges, and get the hang of things by shooting practice in an actual wood.

It is a great advantage to be able to shoot from a squatting position, both to diminish the effect of the high trajectory and to improve concealment. There is nothing difficult in it, provided that your bow is short enough (as it can easily be), and that you are limber enough to be able to get right down on your heels. The soles of the feet must be flat on the ground, firmly. It is impossible to be effective if you are just perched precariously on the forepart of your feet. You can have no control over anything in that position. Kneeling is just as good; right knee on the ground, left knee up. The drawback is that a wet knee is an abomination.

Talking of squatting reminds hunters that it is much more convenient to carry the quiver slung at the left hip. The usual place is on the other side. This way when you want to extract an arrow, it is necessary to wave the whole of the right arm in the air, away from the body, as you do it. Moreover, the arrow comes up on the wrong side of the bow. Slung on the left, the arrow-nocks are comfortably close, particularly when squatting, and a shaft can be withdrawn easily and without any exposure of the arm. Also the arrow comes up on the proper side and can be nocked at once.

Carry the bow in the left hand, pointing fore and aft, braced, back down and string up, with an arrow on the string ready for use. The arrow is kept in place by pressing it against the bow with the left forefinger. The left hand can also keep the arrows in the quiver quiet as you move, leaving the right free for moving branches, or anything else.

In your quiver there should be big broadheads for deer and large game, smaller ones for little creatures and perhaps some blunt points for birds; a dozen or more in all. The different colors of the nocks indicate quickly which is which.

From the book THE ARCHER'S CRAFT
By Adrian Eliot Hodgkin
Published by The Ronald Press Company
Copyright 1953

CHAPTER 2

boating

IT WOULD not be far wrong to say that we have gone "boat crazy." During the past several years almost every phase of the boating world has shown a spectacular rise in interest. Water conservation projects have opened new sprawling lakes all over the country in areas that formerly knew only small sluggish streams. Historic boating centers have also felt the surge of interest, and the boat population of these waters too has soared. The outboard industry alone today is producing about a half a million units yearly. The same vigor can be shown for every other phase of the sport. It can be truly said America's families have taken to the water.

FOR THE BEGINNER

Here are the fundamentals of the various types of small boats and the motors that power them.

Pleasure boats are broadly classified into three groups according to what makes them go—sail, motor or hand power. Some boats combine these, as rowboats fitted for oars but with a squared stern for an outboard motor, and canoes that can either be paddled or pushed with a small outboard or fitted for a sail. Some boats, called auxiliaries, are designed as sailboats but have a motor to assist them. These are usually large craft on large waters.

The gasoline motor is the most popular choice for boat engines. Diesel power is becoming increasingly popular for big craft, 30-footers and over, and electric outboards, simple to run and quiet, drive small fishing boats at slow trolling speed.

Gasoline motors are of two types, inboard and outboard. The inboard is always installed inside the boat, the propeller shaft running through a hole in the bottom. An outboard motor is a removable unit clamped to the stern, no openings through any part of the boat are required as the shaft is entirely outside the craft. Outboards have an advantage in that the propeller will tilt up and over underwater obstacles. They can escape with minor damage from groundings that would severely damage a fixed propeller and shaft. This makes them the choice for shallow and obstructed waters. But they must be comparatively small, as there is a limit as to what weight and horsepower can be set on a stern, seldom are outboards over 50 hp, and usually a lot less, down to less than two hp. They are a high-speed type of engine, designed to produce a lot of horsepower with a minimum of weight. They are self-contained units. In the smallest motors, steering handle and gas tank are integral parts. Medium and large models have separate fuel tanks for easier carrying. Most outboards start by hand—you pull the flywheel over with a cord that rewinds itself. Electric starting is popular with large models where the extra weight is of less account and the motor harder to turn over by hand. Steering wheels replace the steering handle for larger faster models. These give safer smoother control and are less tiring than holding the handle of a powerful motor. Outboards are not steered by a rudder, but by moving the whole motor. While nearly all outboards employ a water propeller, there are small models with an air propeller enclosed in a guard.

In general, inboards resemble a car motor. While most outboards are lubricated by oil mixed with the gasoline, inboards usually have an internal oil pressure system. Inboards are usually mounted out of sight under hatches. Gas tank or tanks, steering apparatus, batteries and the like are separate installations.

As lots of cool water is always available, most boat engines are water-cooled. Some models are air-cooled, particularly those small enough so that air can reach all parts.

Small boats are classified in fairly defini groups. Canoes must be narrow to facilita paddling. They must be light for portagin

Canoe

and built with a rather flat bottom carrie well into the bow and stern to make up fo lack of width. The flat bottom tends t make them float in very shallow water. Row boats are designed for oars or small ou boards or sometimes various hand-propulsio devices are attached to the stern. To mak

Duck Boat

for easy rowing, these boats are narrow rowing a wide boat is more work. The aut top boat is just what the name implies. The are sometimes built to take small outboar motors. They are usually short, for con venience ashore and to help keep weigh down, and wide in proportion to length, give maximum stability in a boat that ma be used on various sorts of waters.

Utility boats are those with little or n decking; the crosswise seats are generall

A 12-foot Car-Top Boat

without attached backs. Anglers, the chief users of these craft, have the freedom aboard they need. Often they are called fishing boats. In outboard utilities, about 14 to 17 feet are the most popular lengths. Ample width and high sides are desirable qualities for a boat that must meet various load and water conditions.

Portable Runabout, Glass Covered

Runabouts, especially outboard ones, are often the same basic hulls as utilities. They have more deck and comfortably backed seats, often upholstered. The bottom design

A 16-foot Outboard Cruiser

must be such to combine an interesting degree of speed and smooth riding in waves, and to provide for safe easy handling. High sides and spray rails on round-bottom boats help keep occupants dry. Larger runabouts—or utilities—may be equipped with convertible tops.

Outboard Cruiser for Offshore Fishing

Cruisers are boats with overnight accommodations. As these craft are larger and heavier and often are used on long trips into strange waters, their motors frequently feature economy rather than speed. Bigger motors and consequent higher speeds may be preferred for big-water trips where there is no scenery variation, and no danger of striking underwater objects. Carefully planned

A 42-foot Cruiser with Convertible top

cabin interiors are very important in a cruiser—accommodations and space are limited enough as it is. Strength is also important, for a cruiser on large waters may get a pounding from high seas, and damage or weakness in the hull is not so readily detectible as in a small open boat.

Sailboats can be any size. They have a design of their own, are usually wide or deep, to prevent tipping too far in a strong breeze. In general, the more sail area, the faster they are. Ones that are "stiff," that is don't tip as readily because of design or proportionately small sails, are less likely to go fast and less likely to go all the way over. Because of the necessary impediments like masts, ropes and stays and their dependence on wind direction, sailing boats are not used much for fishing.

Why do boats vary so much in size and style? There's a simple answer—there is no reason why they shouldn't. Waterways are of all sizes and each has its own wind and wave characteristics. Boats don't have to fit in bumper to bumper on standard-laned highways or in standard-length garages.

What makes a boat good (or bad) is harder to answer. Features often vary according to size and type. It's impossible to list all the desirable features of the perfect boat, but the trio of stability, seaworthiness and strength are important in any vessel. Stability is, simply, a lack of tippiness; seaworthiness, as we use the term, is ability to ride out waves safely. Ample beam is important in securing both these desirable qualities, and correct bottom design has a marked effect on seaworthiness particularly at high speeds. Beam, incidentally, merely means width, not width measured in any special way.

Narrow boats propelled by paddles can be quite seaworthy, for, to put it in a very simple way, the paddles in the water substitute in a way for more beam. To an extent this is true of oars, too. Strength means durability under use, hulls must be able to withstand the pounding of waves. Strength depends largely on construction, weight and type of materials used—and to some extent on design.

Over the years, wood has been the favorite material to use in boat construction. With all the varied wood constructions—plywood, planked, canvas- and plastic-covered, there is not a single type or size of pleasure boat that cannot be built well of wood. Fiberglass boats are a popular new development.

Metal boats have been on a fast increase, particularly portable boats of aluminum.

It is impossible to try to summarize here all the good and bad points of metal for boats, any more than with wood, but any beginner should keep in mind his choice of material depends on many things. How much he plans to keep his boat in or out of the water, what he plans to use the boat for and what he'll power it with. Also to a fair extent on personal ideas and desires. Here are a few random observations: Metal is a good choice for arid regions; dry heat can take the "life" out of wood. Aluminum boats take the changing conditions of outdoor storage well, at least in fresh-water areas. Metal craft do not take much upkeep. If their appearance cannot be "freshened up" as with a wood boat, if they are more difficult to work with than a wood craft, neither is their utility ordinarily affected by this failure to work on them. They also resist the scraping damage that may occur in trailer loading and unloading.

If a boat is to be kept out of water between each use, it must not be a wood type that leaks after such a drying. Some wood boats require a "soaking up" period to close the seams. Plywood and canvas- and plastic-covered constructions are examples of leakproof types of boat.

Canoes and others of the lightest boats are carried overland by trailer or, usually, with a suction-grip carrier, on the car top. Larger boats, up to outboard cruisers and small inboards, are carried by boat trailer. The best trailer for the boat is one that fits it most exactly, that supports it well at all the vital points. Boat trailers are small-wheeled and low, for easy loading and to carry the load well down. As they are springed and bedded for a boat load, almost the poorest of them is better than an unconverted utility trailer. A hand winch to pull the boat from the water to trailer on land is a popular feature of many boat trailers.

Perhaps the most important fundamental any beginner should learn about outboard boats is that each is designed for a certain range of speed. The tables included in the following article will help you in getting this essential combination of power and hull.

Remember, we said boating was really a simple sport, and it is. If the beginner will mix common sense with a reasonable amount of caution, he'll be all right. Let your ambitions be modest at first, while you're learning. Before you know it, another beginner will be turning to you to help him get started.

By Willard Crandall

WHICH BOAT FOR YOU?

Choosing the right boat, in most cases, is not simple. Too many prospective sailors get off on the wrong foot by considering boats so all-purpose that lines and size don't matter. To the uninitiated, boats appear enough alike so that they choose one only on the basis of material, construction, price, weight, arrangement and looks—and what size fits their convenience.

The better way to pick an outboard outfit is to take into consideration the waters you plan to use it on and the loads you'll want the boat to carry. Select a boat that meets these requirements, *then* buy the motor to fit the boat. That way, you buy seaworthiness, stability, safety, good handling, real comfort and speed. Remember, some boats are called all-purpose because they work well for varied types of fishing and other boat sports, *not* because they are built to take all, or even most, waters, loads and motors. Although it is a fact—sometimes a misleading one—most of the outboard utility hulls have a remarkable ability to perform on various waterways, under all kinds of loads and engine sizes.

Even the person who understands the prime importance of choosing a boat according to the dictates of where he'll use it and what he'll use it for may have difficulties when he starts shopping. He'll be confronted with V-bottoms, round-bottoms, "semis" and "modifieds" of both. Boats labeled "semi-V-bottom" by one manufacturer may seem to have more "V" in them than the boat another manufacturer calls a regular V-bot-tom. To the unpracticed eye all may look more flat than anything else.

Look at the diagrams of typical outboard planing boats, elsewhere in this section. Note that V-bottoms and round-bottoms are essentially much the same. Especially is this true if the V-bottom has beveled chines. There is likely to be much more difference, so far as actions on the water is concerned, between a good V-bottom design and a poor one; and between the usual round-bottom and one with markedly more "round" in it. The sailor should never forget this general rule about planing boats: the flatter the bottom from side to side, the faster and the harder riding the boat; the more round, *or* V, the slower and softer riding.

The fact that good outboard planing boats are so much alike in design allows the purchaser to make width and length a deciding factor in his choice. The following table shows suggested beam-length combinations for various motors, with accompanying material on suitable loads and waters. Using it, and considering the other points in this article, the uninitiated with all-purpose use in mind *can* make a good choice. Though it should never be forgotten that apparently minor points of design can always be important.

	Approx. Min. Beam (inches)	Approx. Max. Beam (inches)	Speed (mph)
12-Footers, 2 or 3 Persons*			
7½ hp	50	54	16
10 hp	52	58	20
14-Footers, 3 or 4 Persons*			
7½ hp	52	58	13
10 hp	54	62	17
16 hp	56	66	21
30 hp	60	70	28
16-Footers, 4 or 5 Persons*			
16 hp	58	67	17
30 hp	62	74	25
40 hp	64	78	29
18-Footers, 6 Persons or Equivalent*			
30 hp	66	78	20
40 hp	68	82	24
60 hp	72	86	29
21-Footers, 7 or 8 Persons or Equivalent*			
30 hp	70	86	16½
40 hp	72	90	20
60 hp	76	96	26

* Maximum load.
Speeds are for loads given. In some cases, speed with one person may be as much as 10 mph greater.

Boats with more beam than those listed on the chart can be excellent on almost all scores except speed. Boats for use on big waters should have more beam, even if speed definitely drops. Generally, 12- and 14-footers are for smaller bays, inland lakes and rivers, where wakes of large boats are not a problem. The 16-footers are also for inland lakes and larger bays, where sky may meet water in the distant view, and for use in good weather near shore on the Great Lakes and oceans. The husky 18-footers and larger craft can go farther and more safely on these big waters. Top loads should be carried only on smaller and calmer waters than these. Remember, too, when considering boat size for inland waters, that the larger models give a less jarring ride in a chop.

Boats that tackle the big open waters must have additional features. These include high sides with flare, particularly forward, and a high stern with a long shaft motor. All boats with the more powerful motors should have steering wheels for safe, smooth control.

It is interesting to note how the all-purpose pattern continues into the large outboard planing cruisers. This is true whether the sport is fishing, family cruising or what, sunrise to sunset or overnight. Shallow draft and tilting motor make the planing outboard cruiser a good choice for shallow spots in rivers and bays. Some 20-footers that sleep four can ride out high seas nicely, speed across the bay, then slip over foot-deep bars in an estuary.

How fast a boat and motor to buy depends on how well the sportsman and his family like speed and how many dollars they're willing to pay for it. However, just what sort of fishing or other sport is planned has some part in the decision. For instance 30 hp motors troll remarkably well, but not as well as smaller motors. Less than 25 hp is no longer recommended for water skiing. A 15 hp will certainly pull one skier, but today the sport has developed till all the kids try single-ski riding, pulling two skiers at once and other variations. For all these, 25 hp is really needed.

For general use, no 12- or 14-footer should have less than about 7½ hp; no 16-footer less than about 12; no 18-foot or over cruiser or similar craft less than 25. The minimum is low in each case if loads run heavy. With less than this horsepower, the boats will not plane properly.

Inboard-powered planing boats can be labeled all-purpose, less accurately, but there are more varieties and sizes of them than there are of outboards. Many of them have a surprisingly wide range of usefulness. The inboard's big advantage, of course, is the more power it can handle. More power gives more speed. Big inboards have the ability to take real seas better and carry more of a load well.

Round-bottom design is especially popular for open inboard planing boats designed for big-sea angling—the sea-skiff types. They are seaworthy at high speeds, and make the top speed a flat-V design can, but without as much slapping on various waves.

Inboard or outboard, a planing boat must have the strength to keep its lines, handling qualities and speed, under the pounding of waves hit sharply at high speed. You can do best if you choose one of the models that have the most fastenings and the thickest planking and the most frames, if the construction style calls for framework. (Some, like molded plywood, do not.)

Anyone putting together a kit boat can always put in extra screws and frames over those furnished. As good and strong a kit boat can be built at home as any factory can turn out completed.

By Willard Crandall

BASIC BOAT TYPES

Here are the basic types of small boats that have been developed and used by America's sea-going sportsmen. Over the years these boats have been tested under all kinds of conditions on all sorts of waters from Maine streams to the California coast.

Only the average types are shown. Remember from these are drawn thousands of variations. An example of one development from the basic types illustrated is the canoe, kayak or duck boat with stern squared for an outboard motor. However, there are very nearly as many variations as there are boatbuilders.

All boat bottoms fall into one of the two classes you see illustrated in the accompanying drawings. This is true even of larger craft such as sailboats, ocean cruisers and racing motorboats. The two classes are displacement and planing. As the diagrams show, the form of the bottom (round, V-bottom or flat) does not divide the classes. Rather, it is the way the boat sits and rides on the water that differentiates them.

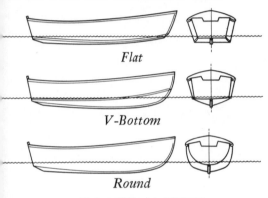

Flat

V-Bottom

Round

BOAT BOTTOM TYPES
(Displacement Boats)

The bottom of a displacement boat is shaped in such a way that the craft cuts through the water. It shoves the water aside, "displaces" it. On the other hand, the bottom of a planing boat is shaped so that when the throttle is advanced the power of the motor first lifts the bow, then the stern, until the boat skims, or "planes," over the surface. Only a minimum of water is shoved aside at full speed.

Generally speaking, a displacement boat sits and rides somewhat deeper in the water than a planing craft. Because the water must be pushed aside by the power of the engine or sail there is a point where increasing the power does not appreciably increase the speed of the boat. Too much power in a displacement boat merely causes the stern to sink and drag a gigantic wake, showing a loss of efficiency. The best example of a displacement boat is the deep-hulled offshore dragger. Duckboats, kayaks, rowboats and sailing auxiliaries are always displacement boats.

The planing boat is lifted out of the water by the thrust of the propeller. At full speed these boats ride only on the tips of their hulls. An extreme example of the planing hull is the so-called "three-point" racing hydroplane. At top speeds, these boats ride only on a small area of two outboard sections in their hulls and the blades of their propeller.

15 Ft. Outboard Utility

Obviously, planing boats go best with medium- or high-powered motors since low-powered engines lack the thrust to lift them.

11 Ft. Auto-Top

A displacement craft, on the other hand, needs only a low-powered engine since large motors make them try to rise and plane which they cannot do because of their shape.

Many modern outboards combine the best qualities of these two types. At low speed the hull sinks into and grips the water, making the boat seaworthy and stable. As the speed is increased the boat lifts on her broad aftersections and flashes over a calm surface with almost no wake.

15 Ft. Outboard Runabout

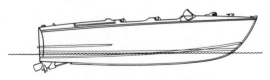

19 Ft. Inboard Runabout

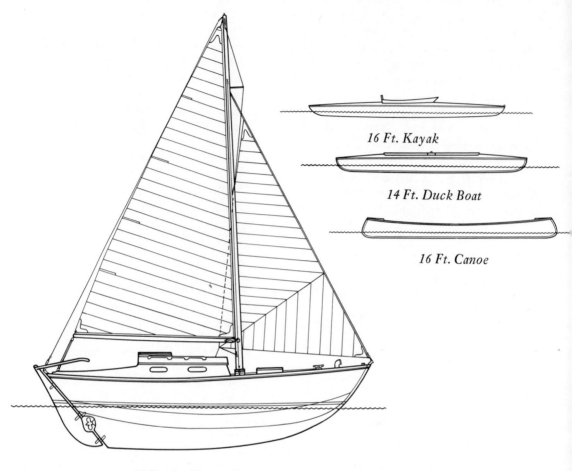

16 Ft. Kayak

14 Ft. Duck Boat

16 Ft. Canoe

20 Ft. Auxiliary (Sloop)

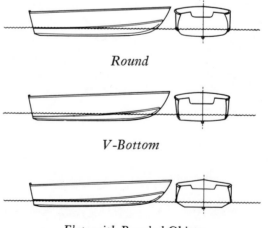

Round

V-Bottom

Flat, with Beveled Chines

Boat Bottom Types (Planing Boats)

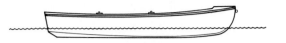

13 Ft. Rowboat

*21 Ft. Cruiser, Trunk Cabin Type
(Outboard or Inboard)*

21 Ft. Sedan (Outboard or Inboard)

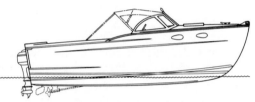

*21 Ft. Cruiser, Raised Deck
(Outboard or Inboard)*

17 Ft. Outboard Convertible

By Bruce N. Crandall

OUTBOARD MOTOR CARE

There's a new way in outboard motor care.

Remember Sunday work on the car a generation back?—crawling under with wrenches for a dark, grease-smeared afternoon. Today, it's a hosing or coat of no-rub wax, done in an hour.

Like automobiles, outboard motors have come of age. The modern motor runs better left alone. Dealers are better equipped to do all under-hood work.

Motors are blossoming out in bright colors and resistant finishes. It's worth keeping them looking new—and not hard to do. Hosing the complete outside is simple, and if done regularly will keep down grease, dirt and scum (algae on submerged parts) that can work in and deteriorate finish. Remember, polishing is more of a prevention than a cure; give the motor its first wax coat before it is ever put into use. Here's the polishing procedure:

Wash off all foreign matter with a mild detergent in warm water. Unless it's the motor's first polish application, take off all old wax with naphtha or benzene. Then apply the wax coat: Use a silicon-base wax, for it will dry to a hard, high-gloss finish— it's especially good for a surface that may come in contact with water. Polish any stainless steel or chrome trim with metal-base chrome polish. Go over the lower unit with a rag soaked in a gas-oil mixture; that's the ticket for parts that will be constantly submerged.

Touch-up painting is no real problem now that matching paint is available. For scratches and small spots, a water-color brush can be used. Pay particular attention, in painting, to blending the new paint in with the original finish near edges of the damaged portion.

Paint in push-button spray cans is becoming widely available now. Simple to use, they are excellent for repaint jobs as redoing the fuel tank or lower unit. Spray only in dead calm.

Some careful precautions help preserve the utility as well as the appearance of the motor. Avoid, for instance, bumping or slamming it around. Pad or wrap the engine well for an overland trunk trip in car. If it's carried on a boat transom on a trailer, keep the clamps tight, tie it down so it can't tilt and put a cover over the powerhead.

Then don't leave the motor unnecessarily outside in the weather. Covers are important, but tight covers have been blamed in some climatic conditions for causing damaging condensation in the motor, especially if the cover is left on a long time.

Any new motor deserves the correct breaking-in. Modern motors are built to tolerances not thought of years ago. This means less break-in and, therefore, less excuse for not doing it right. Tolerance standards can vary from make to make, as well as the composition of the metal parts involved. As only the manufacturer has accurate data on this, give primary attention to his instructions on the break-in.

Using extra oil at first is not a bad idea even if the manufacturer doesn't suggest it. Avoid a lot of very slow running during the break-in, and many, abrupt changes of throttle position too. Stopping the motor occasionally to let it cool off is a good practice. Always break-in a motor on a boat, never on any sort of barrel.

Extending the break-in period sensibly can do no harm, and may give you a nearly perfect job.

It is important to include some short fast spurts in your break-in. Just be sure they are quite short—about 10 seconds each—till breaking-in is well advanced. The spurts burn out excess oil that may cause carbon. Prolonged high-speed running, with excess heat, could "bulge" some fast-moving part. Don't make these spurts completely full throttle, or too often, the first two hours. Just before you reduce oil, they can be done every five minutes.

All fuel lines should be carefully checked and tightened at the fuel pump and carburetor. All connections must be leakproof.

After the vent screw and filler plug have been removed and the old grease drained, the gear case should be filled with new outboard gear lubricant.

What amount of what oil you feed your motor, and how well it is mixed, is important. Of less consequence is your choice of gasoline. Marine white gas is the best, "regular" about as good. Use good 2-cycle (often called outboard) oil. Invariably use the exact amount recommended for your model. Mix fuel *completely*, *each* time. Strain the mixture before use. If your motor is one that takes gas and oil separately, follow manufacturer's instructions carefully. Change or check lower unit lubricant as the manufacturer suggests; don't skimp or put off here. Follow the instructions carefully, and you'll do more toward keeping your motor running sweetly into that distant "forever" than any amount of tune-ups, overhauls or parts replacements can ever do.

The starter rope should be checked for wear and abrasions, and replaced if necessary.

Salt-water use is no longer an excuse for a dingy, rusted motor. Don't skip flushing off the outside with fresh water when you're through for the day. If the motor has a neutral gear, the cooling system can be flushed by running the motor with the propeller in a pail of fresh water. Or, for many motors, regular hose flushing-nozzles are available. Otherwise, internal flushing must be on a barrel or tank. The last step is to wipe the outside with an oily rag. Check the lower unit lubricant twice as often as general or fresh-water instructions call for; oil or grease forced in drives salt water out. Occasionally

put a dab of grease on all external moving parts—that's not a bad idea for fresh-water areas, either.

The remote fuel tank fuel line and connector should be carefully examined and checked for tightness of fittings and chafing of the hose. All connections must be leakproof.

Spark plug wires should be carefully examined and replaced if chafed or cracked. Poor spark plug wires can mean the difference between a rough running or a smooth running motor.

Nearly all manufacturers' instructions cover adequately the important, if simple, procedure of preparing the motor for putting it away, during a season of idleness. Never let the lower unit be higher than the rest of the motor, even briefly. You don't want to try to drain water into the powerhead.

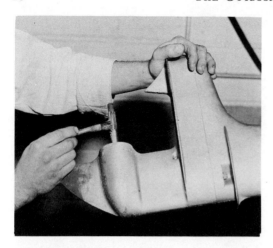

A light coating of waterproof grease on the propeller shaft spline will make later removal of the propeller easy.

A word about the care of boats. Boat washing is simple. It can be done right in the lake before you tie the boat up, or with a hose when trailer, boat and motor are home. A key point in cleaning the craft is an old housework rule—don't use a cleanser or detergent stronger than needed for the particular job. Too powerful a cleanser can make the finish appear lighter where used.

There are many products and compounds that will help keep your boat in brand-new condition. Wood dough is only one of these that will quickly enable you to touch up any scratches or checks in wood boats.

By Willard Crandall

SAILING

A sailboat is a boat with sails.

But a sailboat is also a cat, sloop, cutter, yawl, ketch, schooner or, as with some salty enthusiasts on the Chesapeake, a diminutive square-rigged brig or bark. A cat may be a cat-schooner and a schooner may be a schooner-cat as well as stays'l schooner, bald-headed, fisherman, tops'l, Marconi, wishbone or bug-eye!

There are complications, you see, in this matter of blithely calling a sailboat simply a sailboat. A sailboat to a Maine man is a schooner, to a Cape Codder a cat and to a

Boulder Dam sailor a sloop. So the experienced skipper never says he owns or sails a sailboat—invariably he names it by rig, calling his boat a sloop, yawl, ketch or whatever.

Should you be asked about *your* boat, say you have a sloop.

That's the correct and best answer, and this is why.

A sloop is the best possible type of boat in which to study and learn the art of sailing. When you can sail a sloop well, be it in calm or dirty weather, you can, with a little further experimenting, sail anything that's rigged fore-and-aft. The sloop rig, which is a simple two-sail rig, can alone give you that all-important sense of balance which is the basis of good sailing. The cat rig, or one-sail rig, does not do this. In the small-sized cat rig, like the dinghies and so-called "Frostbites," you have a tender and sometimes treacherous little boat that challenges the talents of even experts. In the large cat-boat, you have an enormous single sail with a very long boom, an outfit which often requires unusual seamanship to keep it from rolling the boom into adjacent billows and from jibing. A single sail does not necessarily denote simplicity in handling. Single-sailed boats have their legitimate places in the sport, and in racing and cruising—but do your "learning" in a sloop-rigged boat.

Your first boat should definitely be of such size that you experience the "feel" of a large craft. Length is not the sole factor making up size; beam, model, rig and ballasting methods also contribute to size. For a center-board boat, having only inside trimming ballast or none at all, something of moderate beam, say a beam about one-third of the length, between the over-all lengths of 18 and 25 feet, is recommended. For a boat with a ballasted fixed keel, the length can be somewhat less, say 17 to 21 feet.

The question of centerboard or keelboat must be determined by local conditions. In general shoal waters such as rivers, lakes and salt bays call for centerboarders. Boats with fixed keels require generally deep waters.

While safety is an important consideration in selecting the ideal type of hull, there

KEELS

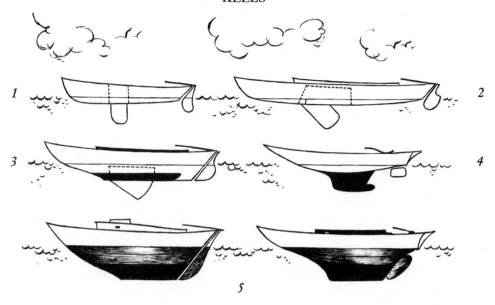

1. Dagger Board   2. Centerboard   3. Combination Keel   4. Fin Keel   5. Full Keels

is also another factor to be considered. *Your sailing waters are always limited to those deeper than your own draft.* A deep fixed keel sometimes closes many miles of pleasant waters to you, or keeps you from entering interesting little shallow bays or coves.

If you are not familiar with the waters you intend to sail, try this. On a Coast and Geodetic chart of the area, encircle with a red crayon all the areas, large and small, which show a depth less than two feet greater than the extreme fixed draft of your boat. The areas remaining are those which you can safely use; all else is closed to you. Only *you* know if this is sufficient "sea room" for your proposed life afloat. Then buy, build or find the boat with the extreme fixed draft that will permit you to sail in the areas you wish to.

Try to forecast the major uses of your boat. If you like to afternoon sail alongshore, or picnic on islands and beaches, take your family with you and *for the most part* avoid open waters, by all means get yourself a centerboard boat. If you like to cruise, take

long offshore slants from cape to cape, or if you are sure that you will never want to land for a beach roast or to clam or to camp, get a keelboat. If you like to race, the hull type will be dictated by the class you race in and the matter taken out of your hands.

The sloop rig is of two types, gaff-headed or jib-headed. By all means, try to make your first boat one with a modern jib-headed sail rig. She will not only sail and handle better and faster but she will retain her value for much longer than the old-fashioned gaff-headed rig.

The type of boat—open, decked cabin, wide, narrow, clinker-built or carvel, keel or centerboard—is fairly indicated by observing the classes in use in the sailing waters around you. These are undoubtedly the best types for you to consider. They are in use for sound reasons—the chief one is that they are safe and ideally suitable for the waters they sail in, which should be reason enough for you to follow suit. Another reason is that your boat investment will be somewhat guaranteed by having your dollars in what

SLOOPS

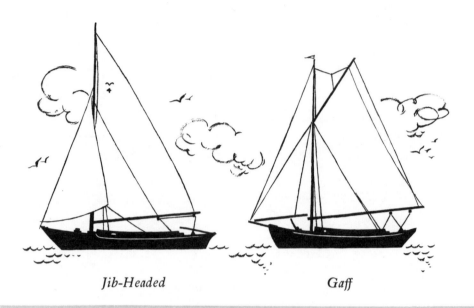

Jib-Headed　　　　　　　　　　*Gaff*

your locale accepts as an ideal boat. A used Star boat is worth more in a Star boat area than in a region which races six-meters or Comets.

In selecting this first boat you will need to exercise more care than necessary for any subsequent boat. All sailors advance through the yachting scene in a fairly regular pattern —they eventually want a bigger boat. Soon your own experience and matured judgment will be able to appraise a boat correctly on its apparent merits and potentialities. But for now, you will have to rely upon the advice of others and upon demonstrations—which, after all, won't mean very much to you since an experienced skipper is probably doing the advising and demonstrating. Beyond recommending size and rig, it would be foolish indeed to attempt to define your first boat. However, here are some thoughts to keep in mind as you study the beautiful folders of the builders or tramp the yacht storage yards in search of a used boat.

1. Avoid extreme racing machines, like the Star boats. Safety factors have been omitted in the design to achieve speed; they are strictly for experienced sailors and, in their hands, perfectly safe.

2. Class boats, especially if the class is popular and large, may be considered safe; the speed factors have been given secondary place. Such a class boat may race, of course, but it races like a saddle horse, not like Man-o'-War.

3. A boatbuilder, who shows evidence of having built and *sold* small stock or custom boats, especially if the boats have been designed by known naval architects, may be trusted to give you the boat he and his advertising says he will. The stock boat is more than wood and canvas. In it is a great deal of experience, of trial and error; all the bugs have been eliminated from the design. Beware, however, of the boat dealer who tries to sell you a boat of a type which you have decided is too large, too small or too deep. If you want a new 20-foot boat, consider only builders who offer this size or very close to it; turn a stony heart to the nice salesman who tries to sell you a 14-footer or a 26-footer.

4. Beware of used-boat bargains. Often

they are bargains, but seldom to the novice owner. Usually they require repairs, refinishing, rerigging and/or recanvasing. Boatyards can do this work for you, of course, or possibly you can do it yourself, but you will always be surprised that the total cost is not very far from a brand new boat. Above all, do not be tempted by the obvious "wreck"—the nail-sick, rot-gutted, basket that, aided by shores, pitch, low price and that powerful springtime urge to get afloat, seems to be an ideal boat for you. Never, never, buy her! Buying a new boat is obviously safest but economic reasons sometimes permit only the purchase of a used boat. Insist that such a boat has a known history, and, by all means, have the boat passed upon by a professional marine surveyor, a naval architect, a disinterested boatbuilder or a nautical friend of long experience.

5. Look with favor upon modern innovations of tried and true worth. Sheet and halyard winches, light modern patent anchors, wood preservative treatment, plywood correctly used, stainless steel standing rigging, linen or nylon running rigging, streamlined and handy cleats, turnbuckles and chandlery—all these contribute toward the factors of safety, seaworthiness and handiness and leave your mind and your body free to concentrate on the important first consideration of learning to sail.

6. Do not, at this stage of the game, consent to try out boats representing new or radical design, construction methods or materials. Stick to what has been proved a safe, popular type of boat, rig and design. You must have, if you are to learn plain sailing, a boat without kinks, hitches or special handling problems.

This boat will cost you a pretty penny, plus a few more pretty pennies. She will probably come to you "bare." Depending upon the uses to which you will put her, she will undoubtedly require some extras. For day sailing and racing, you will have to procure life preservers, charts, compass, foghorn, dock lines, fenders, bilge pump, deck mop, anchor and anchor warp, mooring gear, possibly lights, oars or outboard engine, a dinghy or tender, storm clothing, flags, sail covers, boathook, name and port of hail. For cruising you will need in addition, mattresses, stove, cabin lights, and icebox, fresh-water storage facilities, a john, simple or complicated, possibly an engine and its auxiliary equipment, much of which is included in the stock cruising boat.

If you have $1000 in the budget don't spend more than 90 per cent of it for the boat itself. The rest will be required to make the boat completely useful, safe and secure while afloat.

Another cost to be reckoned is marine insurance, which, while not compulsory, is certainly advisable. Insurance firms and their agents, who are often yacht brokers or yacht yards, offer protection from loss by fire, theft, storm, collison and stranding, damage to rigging, spars or the boat itself, or to, or by, other boats. The cost for the few months the boat is in commission is not excessive. While in winter storage, only fire and possibly theft insurance (called Port Risk) are desirable. The storage yard *does not* carry insurance on your boat during storage unless so instructed by you.

There are no charges of any kind for anchorages and mooring places in public waters. However, there may be a charge for use of another's mooring gear, or for lying in a berth at a public or private wharf.

Any yard will cheerfully give you an approximate estimate of costs before buying. If you must watch the dollars closely, you should very thoroughly investigate the question of costs. More sailors founder on the reef of financing than on those gentler ones inside the channel buoys.

It is strongly recommended that the novice commence his sailing life under the burgee of a well-organized, active yacht or boat club. Most yacht clubs are a strong group of boat-minded men. They have combined for fellowship and for community objectives of anchorages, harbor improvement, locker and storage space, launch, steward and boat services, in aggregate too expensive for the individual. The novice, especially the one who wishes to go in for racing, can greatly increase the challenge and adventure of boat ownership by becoming identified with a club. He will learn sailing more quickly and will take greater pride in learning it well. Boating will become a true hobby and pastime, even during the long winter when many clubs sponsor seamanship and navigation courses, fellowship affairs, winter dinghy racing and the like.

The combined voices of American yacht and boat clubs, the U.S. Power Squadrons, class sailing clubs such as the Snipe, Star, Moth and dinghy clubs, each with its local chapters, the yacht racing associations, the Off Soundings and other cruising clubs, and the boating journals, are lusty and powerful. By all means, give serious consideration to becoming identified with one or more of these organizations.

From the book HOW TO SAIL
By Carl D. Lane
W. W. Norton and Co., Inc.
Copyright 1947

CANOEING

Half of North America is blessed with gorgeous canoe waters and cruising country. Some of our rivers, it is true, have been so industrialized that they are little more than drainage ditches. But there are routes without end, long and short, where you can launch a good little canoe, load it with a sufficient outfit, and casting aside all worries and responsibilities, be footloose and free. You live on the grub she carries, and game and fish you get en route. And you can paddle and glide from the breakup of the ice in the spring until the fall freeze. The canoe, indeed, is the poor man's yacht.

The original canoe of our Northeast was of course the birchbark. The good Indian builder made it on certain very closely prescribed lines. And except for durability, these lines have never been surpassed. But the birchbark is now a craft of the past.

Canoes of numerous types, sizes and construction are built in America. Some are good, some indifferent, and some bad. A few are excellent. Since the pleasure and

success of your cruise, and indeed your *life* may depend on your little craft, you'd better know how to choose a suitable one.

Canoeing on Duncan Lake in Superior National Forest, Minnesota

The largest demand for canoes is by the summer resort trade. Most of these are too narrow, not deep enough amidships and the bottoms are too rounded. They are tippy in rough water and won't carry the weight of passengers, camp outfit and grub, and have enough freeboard.

Freeboard is the distance from the surface of the water to the gunwale amidships, and it should be at least six inches with the canoe loaded to safely navigate large lakes and rough waters. The wilderness canoe should *never* be narrower than 36 inches, nor less than 13 inches deep in the center. It should have a *flat* bottom, and the ends should not be so high that the wind striking them will make control difficult.

Canoes are ordinarily made in lengths from 13 to 20 feet. Their ability to carry weights and to run safely in heavy seas depends on their length as well as their lines. One writer stated that one man and his light outfit could go anywhere in a 12-foot canoe. That might be true for quiet rivers and small lakes. But in high seas, a short canoe plunges its bow or stern into the crest of the waves when the wind is ahead or astern. A short canoe, though, certainly is easier for a lone cruiser to paddle than a long one.

For wilderness cruising, two fellows

should choose a canoe at least 16 feet long. You can usually figure that your outfit, including tent, sleeping bags, cook-kit and personal items will weigh about 100 pounds. Grub will weigh 125 to 175 pounds per month, depending on whether the country can be counted on for game and fish. To this you must add the weight of the two canoeists, say 350 pounds, that's a total of about 600 pounds.

Twenty-foot canoes are really freight canoes, and are seldom used by sportsmen unless there are three passengers and outfit. Two men to a canoe is best, then both can use their paddles to maximum effect. A third man is usually just dead weight, for he can put little effort into his paddling when seated in the center.

As to construction, canoes are made of wood, of a light wood shell and ribs covered with canvas; of plywood; and of aluminum. The all-wood canoes are heavy and difficult to repair if a hole gets knocked in them, and are seldom seen these days. Canvas-covered canoes are most common, and the well-made ones are topnotch. They've easy to repair with a patch of canvas and canoe glue or spruce gum. Their weight runs from about 50 pounds for the 13-foot craft to about 90 pounds for the 18-foot prospector type.

Aluminum canoes are receiving considerable approval by many experienced canoeists and woodsmen. On the other hand, many still feel the canvas-covered canoe is superior.

The aluminum crafts have air chambers under the decks so they will float if overturned, and these air chambers are so located that when capsized the canoe will automatically right itself. This is important if you ever get turned over and have to climb into your canoe when it is afloat.

In almost all accidents aluminum canoes dent instead of puncturing. And they're as easy to straighten out again as an automobile fender. They are made in lengths from 13 to 30 feet, and in two weights, the standard running from 55 pounds for those 13 feet long to 83 pounds for the 18-foot craft. The lightweight models run similarly from 45 to 71 pounds. The bow and stern seats are placed about four inches lower than in similar craft, which increases their stability greatly.

Of course, aluminum canoes are not affected by weather, and do not warp or become waterlogged. The 18-footer is a very fine craft for a long cruise in a wilderness where you would encounter many large lakes and rapid-filled rivers.

The weight of your canoe is of some importance where your route includes many portages. But most inexperienced persons place too much importance on weight. Weight is of less importance on a long carry than a comfortable way to keep your load on your shoulders. If you do not ship a carrying yoke, paddles tied to the center thwart and front seat will serve perfectly.

You can get all makes of canoes with square sterns for use with an outboard motor. But almost always it is best to select the standard type, pointed at both ends, and use the motor with a side bracket. It is more comfortable and convenient for the man in the stern to control the motor if mounted with a bracket, and the standard canoe is faster, lighter and much easier to paddle.

With a 13-foot canoe, the motor should not be greater than one and one-half hp, and for the 18-footer, for safety, not more than three hp.

The motor about doubles your speed as compared with paddling, but it does not increase your cruising radius if time is not a factor. Roughly speaking, your canoe might be fully loaded for a 400-mile cruise with motor, gas, outfit and grub for two weeks. Without the motor and gas, you can carry enough grub for two months, and make that 400-mile trip at your leisure.

Two paddlers in a canoe not too heavily loaded, and in lake travel without adverse winds, can average 30 to 40 miles a day. But with only one or two short portages to make and no head winds you better not count on more than 15 miles a day.

Eliminate weight and bulk as much as consistent with comfort, not only to insure a safe freeboard, but for ease and rapidity of portaging. Most of your outfit had best be packed in the Duluth type of packsack with tump line, no pack to weigh over 60 pounds. Your lighter loads of rolls of tent and sleeping bag can easily be portaged on top of one of these packsacks.

If you have three packsacks, and two rolls, everything including the canoe can be taken over a portage in just two trips. Load the weight of your cargo as much as possible in the center of the canoe, heaviest articles in the bottom.

Portaging is usually looked on by the novice as hard, disagreeable work. But the old-timer thinks of it as a break in the monotony of paddling, and a chance to limber up and stretch his legs. Portages are usually around falls and rapids, below which you usually find the best fishing, with a chance to add to your grub supply for the next day.

In the popular canoe country of the North —Minnesota, Michigan, Ontario and Quebec —there are many outfitters and camps that will rent you a canoe and outfit, sell you the necessary grub and provide you with a map on which they have marked your route. However no party should start on a cruise without having been in a canoe before. The bare essentials of safe canoeing and paddling are not difficult to learn, but you should always have four or five days of practicing on a lake or river near home.

By Col. Townsend Whelen

OUTBOARD MOTOR RACING

In 1926 modern outboard racing was born. That year a six hp motor appeared on the market. It was the largest motor to date and had enough power to make a boat rise up and skim over the water. The outboard hydroplane was introduced; the day of sporadic outboard races with canoes was ended. Thousands of the new racing boats, about 14-footers in those days, were built, and races staged from coast to coast. Horsepower of motors went up until racing models were developing over 50 mph. Then the

depression slowed racing; next, World War II stopped it.

Now racing is back, with faster motors, smaller, still faster hydroplanes and with more entries than at any previous time. National championships draw over 300 boats. About 3,000 stock-racing outfits are registered with one of the two national governing bodies of racing, and many outfits raced only locally are registered with neither.

Outboard racing, Florida

Back in the late 20's, rules called for stock motors, as they do today. All competition was with engines labelled "racing models," but these usually differed from service models in having shorter, more streamlined lower units, no underwater exhausts and in other minor ways. Soon, though, stock-motor rule enforcement became increasingly lax and the rules constantly more "liberal." With the coming of the war, sale of parts by the original manufacturers was discontinued, never to be resumed with some models, and rules were relaxed to keep the motors going.

A new stock division was established for engines built since the war, in which the rules are tighter than in the old days. Stock motors raced today are essentially the same as their nonracing brothers except lower units are shorter, there is no shift, and the gear ratio is low for top speed on light, fast boats.

Motors, racing and stock, are not classified for racing according to horsepower. They cannot be because horsepower is only a rating, not something that can be definitely proved to be any certain or exact figure, and different manufacturers may use different ways of arriving at ratings. Instead, motors are classified according to cylinder size—piston displacement, to put it exactly.

Class A is for motors under 15 cubic inches piston displacement; Class B, under 20; Class C, under 30; Class D, under 40. There are larger classes: F, under 60, for which no stock motors are made and few racing motors left; and X, in which absolutely any outboard motor can compete. There are also smaller classes: M (Midget) for racing motors, and J (for Junior) for stock. One national association sets the limit for J and M at 7½ cubic inches, and lets only drivers under 15 in J. The other association ups J to 12½ cubic inches but puts the age limit on both classes, with this exception—no limit if the driver is female. There have been, and are, a few women outboard racers.

B is the most popular stock-racing class. Motors this size develop somewhere over 18 hp. Excellent modern stock motors for racing are available also in A, and in D, where the four-cylinder stocks compete. J is the other class being raced with generally available, modern stock motors; regular lower units are used with them.

Boats for racing are of two types, and generally they do not race against each other. First, there are regular one-man racing hydroplanes, usually called hydros. As there are no restrictions on these boats except weight minimums they are small, only about eight or nine feet, and ride on two or three surfaces, generally on the stern and two "pontoons" forward. This three-point riding, as it is often called, allows the boat to have the very fastest sort of bottom for calm-water straightaways and still handle well on turns.

The other racing group consists of the so-called utilities or runabouts. They are generally quite different from the utility you use for fishing, or the runabout for water skiing; actually they are a special class of racing boats, a little larger than the one-man hydros, averaging over 11 feet, and with no breaks in the bottom surface (pontoons, not

quite so much needed with the larger boats, are not allowed).

Boat size increases with the size of the motor and, of course, so does weight. Weight restrictions are imposed to prevent the entry of boats so fragile they would be battered out of competition after two or three events.

In the majority of outboard races you see most winners make between 40 and 50 mph. D's go around 10 miles per hour faster than A's. Hydros make only about two or three miles more than utilities. The difference between racing and stock motors is a little greater, but the gap is closing here.

Some races are marathons—100-mile auxiliary fuel-tank events up- or downriver, and across lakes. But most events are on oval or round courses, the finish line being also the starting line. Standard distance is five miles, usually five laps over a mile course.

Starting clocks are now generally used, even at small regattas. A six-foot clock faces the drivers on the starting line, and its one big hand moves to show the seconds remaining until the start. The exact split instant the hand reaches zero, or any time after that, any driver can make a fair start. But cross it before, and he's disqualified. Experienced champ drivers can often start their craft across the line at 50 mph almost as the clock hand stops moving.

Are most outboard racers professionals? If so, how much money do they make? Most of them are, and none of them makes any money. All races are held week ends; the average driver can hit about 13 during the summer. Even to enter a small, unsanctioned race he usually has to trail his outfit 100 miles or more (round trip) over the highway. Such races may pay only $20 cash for first place; there is probably only one event for his class, although he may be eligible for other, faster classes.

Bigger, sanctioned events usually offer two heats in each class, with perhaps $30 or $50 for first; occasionally it is quite a bit more for each heat but competition here is much keener. Some races offer only merchandise or trophies. (One or the other is always offered to amateurs in lieu of cash.)

There are expenses for at least two because unloading, tuning up and emergency repairs are too stiff for one man alone to tackle. You need several racing propellers; spark plugs, which wear fast at "hot" speeds; all sorts of motor parts replacements, because one only slightly worn may cut speed; life vests; water speedometer; crash helmets; knee pads; association dues; and so it goes. A new racing boat may cost $300 or more, less if a kit, still less if built from plans. Class A stock motors for racing cost about $325, Class B, around $400.

Winners don't make money; they just make racing expenses. Whatever you think of outboard racing, the drivers are in it for the sport, and that only.

What's the best way to get started in outboard racing? You simply buy an outfit and enter the first race you can find. No license, no particular experience, no special physical qualifications are necessary. For official races you just have to be over 14 years old for Class B or larger, over 12 for Class A.

Know the rules. Write the American Power Boat Association, 700 Canton Avenue, Detroit 7, Michigan, and the National Outboard Association, 707 Market Street, Knoxville, Tennessee, for the national rules. But these aren't universally followed, especially in small, unsanctioned regattas which are often the real place for beginners. Find out all about the rules where you will actually race—that might be hard because they may be unwritten, but try it. You want to buy the fastest boat and motor those rules will allow.

There's nothing to being a champion driver you can't learn. It's a sport open to all on an equal basis. You don't have to be born tall, muscular or with any special physical advantages to reach the top. There is no sport quite like it.

By Willard Crandall

WATER SKIING

Nowadays it is no longer startlingly unusual for a beginner to make his first take-off on water skis with no more instruction than a glance at the skis and a hitch in his bathing suit. This doesn't mean that the take-off isn't still the hardest part (the only hard part) of simple skiing; nearly all novices take several dives learning it. But water skiing is vastly simpler than it was with the converted snow skis of only a few years back. Today water skiers in the hundreds of thousands, from coast to coast, ride in rough water and calm, do straight riding, do stunts, ride behind slow boats and fast boats.

Seven-year-olds water ski. Men with more white hair than black have tried it and kept it up because they like it. You can have fun without having to learn stunts, or be pulled at high speed.

It is probably unfortunate that getting away on the skis is the hard part, for those who give up at this point never know what they're missing. So, although most learners start with little knowledge except what they've picked up watching, it's best to learn and follow beginners' instructions. Otherwise, you're more likely to tumble your first few attempts, and then give up.

Practice on land first. Put the skis about eight inches apart; put your feet in toes first, then pull up on the heel binding. Now sit on the rear of the skis, your knees against your chest and seize the towrope handle.

Next have someone take hold of the rope itself, brace against the forward tips of the skis and pull you up. Don't you help. You concentrate on keeping your knees bent, arms straight and body slightly forward.

Then get in no more than 2½ feet of water and do this with a boat. The driver should start off reasonably fast, at steady speed. Let the boat pull you up, as practiced on land. Keep your crouched weight balanced over your feet. Don't wave or pull up with your arms.

Some recommend the first take-off be a deep-water one. The disadvantage here is that a beginner may have more to do than he can handle in getting and keeping himself in position for the take-off, particularly with no bottom to touch. However, with a deep-water start the take-off is more gradual, with

This sequence of photographs shows how to take off from deep water: skis about a foot apart, knees bent to your chest, elbows straight. Keep that crouch for balance as the boat pulls you up. In seconds you'll be skimming on the surface at full speed. If you think you're going to fall forward or backward, quickly pull or release the tow-rope a bit. If you spill, let go of the rope at once.

a constant acceleration to full planing, instead of practically jerking the skier up.

In the deep-water start, try to handle yourself and your skis much as you would in the shallow water. Elbows straight, crouch the same for balance and let the boat pull you up. Keep the skis not more than a foot apart at the start; remember that while they are plowing toe-high, their direction can be controlled by banking the ski slightly with the foot in the direction you want to go. Bank both inward and you'll cross your skis. Bank outward and you'll spread-eagle. If you tend to lose your balance forward or backward—very common—quickly pull or release the rope a small amount. In some cases it is a marked help if the driver will run at a speed that leaves you mostly in the water with the skis' toes way up, until you get on to controlling them in that position. Sometimes a start in about five feet of water, so the skier will have some help from the bottom in getting set, works best.

There are variations. Certainly, anyone having trouble with one kind of start should switch to another. There is no sense in taking flops over and over again.

If the take-off is throwing you, there's no reason to believe that you'll have trouble

skiing underway. There is no necessary connection, and anyway slow learning can mean good learning.

Once you're off, planing behind the boat, you'll soon automatically learn turning and wake-crossing. How to turn is variously described, but anyone learning simple skiing can merely lean in the direction he wants to go, naturally banking the skis as he does. If you go into a spill, let go of the rope quickly.

To land in reasonably deep water, simply let go of the rope. You will glide about 20 yards at 25 mph, maybe 40 at 35 mph, before sinking to a stop. Don't try a landing on the beach. Skis will stop abruptly when they hit sand, and you don't want to go flying over the nose of them.

A good driver adds a lot to skiing. One who knows boat handling, and especially who knows the boat to be used, will catch on to most of what's necessary in ski-pulling almost automatically. Here are salient points the driver should keep in mind:

Don't start from a bathing beach if anyone other than the skier is in the water.

Don't make long looks back, only quick ones are necessary. Give all other boats and obstructions a wide berth. Keep your turns broad with a beginner.

Use reverse sparingly and for very short periods, and never when anyone is in the water near the stern—always stay in neutral then. Watch the rope when you do reverse—winding it on the propeller is no fun.

To get the rope to a spilled skier, go by him slowly, a little over five feet to the right; once you've cleared him, turn left and keep going slowly. This will pull the rope to him. To land a skier, drive near the landing spot at normal speed. The skier can let go the rope about 25 yards from the dock and glide on in, banking if necessary.

Various size skis are on the market; those not much under six feet are as popular as any for general skiing. The more weight to be carried, the larger the skis should be for steady riding. Skis long in proportion to weight are easier to get up on, but more sluggish and harder to control underway. The shorter, the more maneuverable. Shorten them much, though, and they can get too maneuverable for the amateur. Within limits, the longer the skis, the less power needed to get a rider up and pull him.

Slick-bottom skis are easier to pull, and easier on the skier's arms.

Standard towrope length is 75 feet; ropes a bit shorter are often used. A ¼-inch three-strand Manila rope is recommended. Experts propose it for stunting and for beginners because it is weak enough to break if a foot gets caught in it. Never use nylon, because of its elasticity.

Always fasten the rope to an outboard transom in two places, one on each side of the motor and rather close to it. During turns a rope pulling on the stern way at one side of the boat may try to tip the craft over.

Life jackets (there are some made especially for skiers) are a good idea for beginners and anyone whose swimming is so poor he does not feel entirely home in the water. Experts seldom suggest skiing for nonswimmers—most of them don't enjoy it too much. Life vests must always be well-tied on.

A 10 hp outboard is about the minimum that can pull an adult skier. A 16 hp is much better; 25 is recommended.

Inboards are often preferred because of their reserve power. The skier on a turn, with even a slow boat, can hit a speed 10 mph faster than the craft makes, so drivers of fast inboards must always keep the danger of falling in mind. Drivers of the top-power outboards or with dual big motors should also take it into consideration. Hitting the water in a spill at 30 mph can hardly do more than knock some air out of the lungs; however, danger of possible injury increases rapidly as ski-speed rises above 40 mph.

By Willard Crandall

BOAT SAFETY

KNOW YOUR BOAT

Every boat has its limitations. Learn what you can expect from your boat.

HEAD *INTO* THE WAVES

If waves are high, head your boat at an angle toward the waves at slow speed.

BALANCE YOUR LOAD

Distribute weight evenly in the boat — from side to side and from bow to stern.

WATCH THE WEATHER

Head for shore before a storm breaks. If caught out, seat passengers on floor.

DON'T OVERLOAD

Seats do not indicate capacity. Two or three adults may be a full load under many conditions.

USE THE RIGHT MOTOR

Too much power can damage your boat — may even swamp it. Look for OBC recommended horsepower plate.

The best nautical "law" of all is the "law" of Common Sense Afloat. Basic "clauses" of that "law" are illustrated above. Others include: Avoid sharp turns—they are hard on people and sometimes on equipment; keep low—and step in the center when boarding the boat and changing seats.

From Outboard Boating Club, 307 North Michigan Ave., Chicago, Ill.

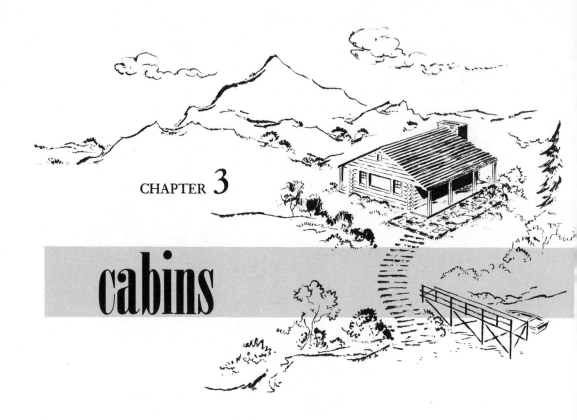

CHAPTER 3

cabins

THERE ARE so many good reasons for having a cabin that it is unnecessary to list even some of them. Whatever your reasons have been in the past, there will be even better ones in the present and future. Over the last 20 years life has become increasingly complex and tense, and indications are it will continue so in the future. The consensus of the medical profession seems to be that one of the means of avoiding the harmful accumulative effects of daily tension, is to have a retreat where life can be simple, quiet and relaxed, but with plenty of temptations to engage in a sport or hobby.

It often alarms us to find that perfectly sensible business men do not apply the same principles of sober consideration when acquiring a campsite or building a cabin, which they habitually follow in their daily business. Granted that a brisk, sunny autumn day after a sultry summer, or a warm, soft spring day after a bitter winter, are heady stuff to overcome when tantalized by an intriguing campsite and an astute seller. We can understand the all too-quick decision to buy and build, but we want to prevent regrets if possible. We have therefore assembled data on the following pages which should be helpful from the time you begin site hunting, until you determine on the final details of your cabin.

These pages are by Jerry Geerlings, Registered Architect.
From the 1955 SPORTS AFIELD CABINBUILDING ANNUAL.
Copyright 1955 by The Hearst Corporation.

CHOOSING THE RIGHT CABIN

WHAT DO YOU MEAN BY "CABIN"?

Your definition of "cabin" will determine where it will be, what type of construction it should be, how you'll use it and when you'll use it. It's good to be open-minded, of course, like first tramping over new hunting territory to find out what kinds of quarry there are before actually hunting. But eventually in hunting you have to decide what you are going to aim at if you expect to bag any game. It's that way with cabins, too. Fix your sights on a reasonable target that isn't too distant. You want to be relaxed to enjoy your cabin, and that's tough if it's a financial nightmare.

Is your dream cabin compact and rustic, with only the bare necessities? Will you build it in the deep woods?

Or maybe your dream cabin is on a river or lake. Does it have a large screened porch and other conveniences?

Perhaps you go for a rambling cabin with a view of hills or mountains.

Then again your dream cabin may run toward a more contemporary sort of design. Maybe you'd like to have it on the sea or a lake bluff.

FIND OUT BEFORE YOU BUY

Once you've bought the land it's too lat to change your mind. Before you buy is th time to check these points:

1—Do you get a guarantee that you wi not eventually be part of a crowde development?

2—Can your view and privacy be pro tected?

3—Beyond what point will you have t pay for extensions of road and electri power?

4—What are water, fishing and huntin rights?

5—Is there a clear title? Are taxes paid up

6—What building restrictions are there—any minimum construction cost, or an required setback distances from prop erty lines?

7—What is history of flooding, and wher is high-water mark or highest know tide?

8—Are local prices reasonable for buildin materials, labor, fuel and the like?

9—Is there well water that's fit to drink

WHEN WILL YOU USE THE CABIN?

Occupancy in only the hot, dry season means you save on construction costs by *not* having to build a draftproof, insulated cabin, or a road with a good rock bed. But if you expect to use your camp in spring and autumn, remember that frost coming out of the ground in spring, or continued autumnal rains, can bog your car on the same road that was fine in summer. Winter usage may involve snowplowing problems, or reliance on skis or snowshoes. Visit the prospective sites in all seasons, so you have firsthand knowledge.

IMPORTANT LOCATION FACTORS

Good hunting? Good fishing? Invigorating climate? Or an extensive view? Do you insist on being on the water (stream, river, small or large lake, sea) or do you prefer the hills or mountains? To get what you want in your cabinsite, are you willing to pay for a long road or trail to reach the property? How will isolation, lack of neighbors and no doctor in case of emergency, affect your decision? Make a list of the pros and cons for each site you seriously consider, assign values to each element, and deliberate before buying.

START OFF WITH A MODEL

Before you buy, camp on the site. Before you build, make a model of the property, showing its relation to lake, river, best view, and so on. Mark points of compass, and locate trees you want to save. Cut out shapes of cardboard to correspond with contour lines.

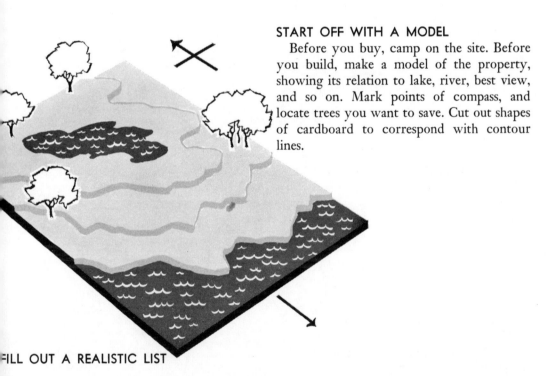

FILL OUT A REALISTIC LIST

	Land	Road and Clearing	Over-all Cabin Size	Bunk Rooms	Galley	Fireplace	Electric Power Unit
Dream Specifications— What Do I Want?	about 12 acres on water	good road for all-year access	60' x 30' = 1800 sq. ft. $10,000?!	4 rooms— 2 large, 2 small	sink, range, refrigerator, cabinets	1 indoors, 1 outdoors	yes—to supply light, run refrig.
Hard Facts— What Do I Need?	1 acre on water	summer + autumn access	1 all-purpose room + bunks and galley	bunks for 6; some on porch?	(family decision necessary)	would like inside fireplace!	(must find out about costs)
What Can I Afford To Spend?	$600?	$200?	30' x 20' = 600 sq. ft. $2,500?	3 double-decker bunks	oil-stove, ice-box, shelves	Franklin stove, pre-fab chimney	not at present (?)

DON'T SPEND MONEY ON DISAPPOINTMENTS
WHEN YOU BUY A CABINSITE

Find out about difficulties of hauling building materials to site. Get written agreement for cost per truckload if special road or trail conditions make trucking uncertain or hazardous.

Find out about possible road tax assessments and location of any planned through-ways or other state or county highway developments, and locations of any railroad, power or gas line right-of-ways.

Find out about actual tempe ture and humidity range the entire year from the st weather bureau. Don't depe on local hearsay. Temperat and humidity both affect ca construction cost.

Find out about long-ra flood control or power plans, and how water le would affect your site. V watershed plans for drink water reservoirs prohibit fut swimming and fishing?

Find out about noise nuisances such as auto races, boat races, proximity of probable new airport, county fair or public picnic grounds. Are there any restrictions against roadside taverns?

TEMPERATURE   HUMIDITY

Find out about poison ivy, poison oak or other growth which will be costly to eradicate. Also determine whether there are erosion-prevention measures which are necessary along cliffs or riverbanks.

Find out about cost of artesian well, if that is sole drinking water source. Before relying on spring or stream, have water tested and find out if there is a dependable flow throughout the summer.

Find out about your water rights on any stream or lake. Also explore stream to determine whether its course may shift and either cut into your site or deposit silt. What is its flood history?

Find out about low, swam areas, and whether you v have to do your own pest-co trol spraying. Are there a quicksand areas? Will any s cial foundations be necessa as driving wood piles?

Find out about cost of cle ing trees and underbrush cabin construction and a vie If cabin is located in most sirable spot, will there be a trees left to provide shade p a windbreak?

HERE ARE SOME IMPORTANT CONSIDERATIONS
AFTER BUYING CABINSITE BUT BEFORE PLANNING

You'll want the cabin to reflect your personality and your special requirements, but don't make it too special and tricky. If you do, it may pall on you and it may be difficult to sell. On the other hand if you observe sensible, currently accepted practices of planning and construction, your cabin is much more likely to be a potentially salable property in any season. Make your cabin as contemporary as you wish, but also make it comfortable to use in all seasons. Select stock materials and utilize the talents of local labor.

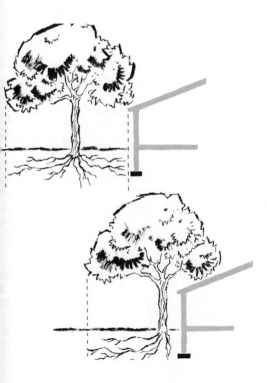

Trees adjacent to the cabin will provide shade and serve as a windbreak, but remember that the roots of a tree extend about the same distance from the trunk as do the branches. Use this as a gauge when locating cabin near trees so that roots are not so damaged and weakened that the tree may blow over on the cabin after a wet spell.

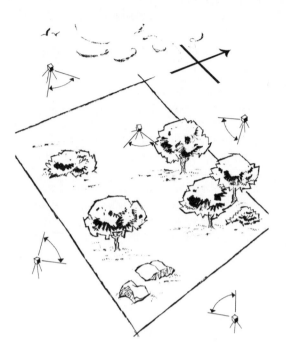

The most successful cabin is one which looks as though it grew out of the site. This is not a matter of luck, but the result of careful planning. You'll want to get advice and maybe some professional help, so take the time necessary to make a survey of the site with enough contours and locations of important trees, rock outcroppings and any other natural assets, which will help you when planning at home. Take photos from all property lines and close-ups of cabinsite and make a diagram to show photo viewpoints plus the points of the compass.

Light and sunshine come with the land, so make the best possible use of them. It would be a pity if you bought a fine cabinsite in order to get a wonderful view, or you wanted to enjoy an entirely different life from your accustomed one, and then built a cabin which produced as much of a "closed in" feeling as a city apartment. Take advantage of the view, the immediate surroundings and sunshine, by having at least one side or one corner of the cabin sufficiently open to create a gradual transition between indoor and outdoors.

GOOD PLANNING MAKES IT COMFORTABLE

There is no charge for making your house-keeping chores light, except the time necessary to plan carefully. In the cabin to the right the galley is open to the all-purpose room, but it can be closed off by a curtain hown at the end of the dual-purpose bunk seat. The nearby table with an impervious op can be used for dining and games. Conveniently located cupboards and closets for clothes, personal equipment and amenities will encourage automatic tidiness. Floors, walls and ceiling of stained wood require practically no upkeep.

Both mildew and that characteristic musty mell can be prevented by inducing air to circulate while the cabin is unoccupied. The drawing to the right indicates how to create controlled air movements independent of windows. At left (A) the air enters the cabin through floor registers and escapes through roof ventilators, because heated air rises. Another method is shown (B) on the right wall of the cabin, with air entering grilles near the floor, and escaping near the eaves. Hinged, solid panels over grilles can regulate air flow.

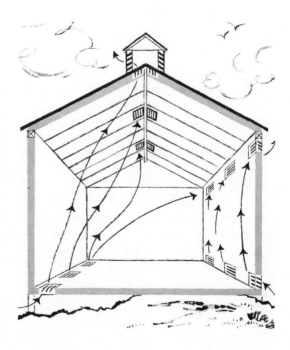

A cabin needn't be big and expensive to have the qualities which appeal to every camper: a cheery interior, a relaxing atmosphere and a convenient arrangement. Take the compact cabin to the left—windows above dual-purpose bunks provide ample light; the galley is located in the two cupboards at the sides of the fireplace.

No matter how large a cabin is, it will seem small and cluttered unless there is a convenient place for everything. Every occupant should have near his bunk sufficient closet and shelf space to stow his belongings. As shown to the right, there can be pull-out drawers under the bedspring, open shelves above and facing the end of the bed, and a closet just beyond the shelves. In laying out your plan, allow six and a half foot for bed, one foot for shelves, two and a half foot for closet, for a total of 10 feet. This space is also satisfactory for a double bunk unit.

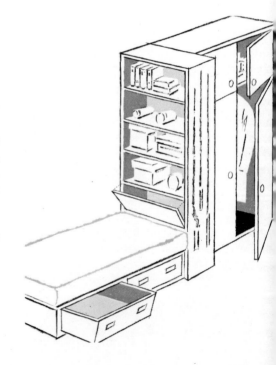

GOOD MATERIALS ARE GOOD ECONOMY

FLOORS

There are two types of "rough" or "underflooring" commonly used over wood joists: tongue-and-grooved boards (A), preferably laid on the diagonal for improved rigidity, or plywood panels (B). Select a finish floor which will require the least upkeep and won't show abrasive marks if sand tracked in. For example, settle for an oil-stain finish on wood flooring (1) and forget about city polish. If you prefer linoleum (2), or any of the tile materials (3) as asphalt, vinyl, rubber or cork, use these over plywood underflooring for the best results. The latter requires nailing along *all* edges, to provide two by fours between joists wherever sheets abut.

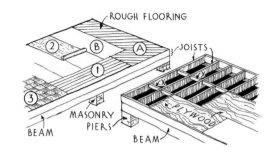

WALLS

There are two general types of sheathing for a frame cabin as indicated in the left half of the drawing. The first is wood sheathing (1) which produces desirable cross bracing when used on the diagonal. The second is insulating sheets (2) which are easy to apply and increase all-year comfort.

Building paper should be nailed over either wood sheathing (1), or insulating sheets (2), as shown in the right half of the drawing, before applying the exterior materials. The latter should be your choice of regular siding, "shiplap" siding (good if you want a smooth effect), shingles, plywood, or sheets of cement-asbestos. Vertical boards (3) (either with square edges and batten strips, or tongue and groove) require wood sheathing underneath to allow nailing.

ROOFS

Tin or copper can be used on all roofs, but shingles (wood, asphalt, cement-asbestos), slate or tile, should be used only if the roof slope is at least five in 12 (see diagrams to right), unless the manufacturer specifically guarantees any flatter slope. For a pitch of less than four or five in 12, a "built-up" roof is recommended, as indicated in the "detail" of the drawing to the right. Generally some type of sheathing paper or saturated asbestos felt is nailed over the wood roof boards (1), then coal-tar pitch is mopped on (2), just before a gravel-like roofing is rolled on (3). Be sure to follow the manufacturer's directions in all respects.

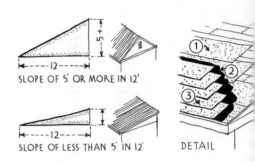

SLOPE OF 5' OR MORE IN 12'

SLOPE OF LESS THAN 5' IN 12'

DETAIL

WINDOWS

A recent and ingenious development is a basement-like window which can be used singly or in groups, vertically or horizontally, as shown in the left half of the adjacent drawing. Used horizontally it is called a "hopper" type if it swings in from the top, and an "awning" type if it swings outward from the bottom. You'll find it convenient to swing them in, rather than out, and so use stock screens on the exterior. In the right half of the drawing are shown double-hung sash (each half slides up or down), and casement sash (hinged on the side and swung out). A fairly recent development is the sliding type.

HOPPER OR "AWNING"

DOUBLE-HUNG

CASEMENT

SLIDING

BEFORE YOU START SPENDING, WORK OUT A BUDGET THAT INCLUDES ALL EXPENSES. YOU'LL SAVE MONEY AND AVOID DISAPPOINTMENT. HERE'S YOUR CHECK LIST OF THE COSTS THAT YOU'D BETTER COUNT ON MEETING

1 ACCESSIBILITY OF SITE.............$200.00

Make a deal to have trail or road work done during the contractor's dull season. Check his reputation. Also check cost of turnoff from main road if there are special conditions like a steep bank. Concentrate effort on low or swampy areas. It's better to spend money on a good job there, than to pay repeatedly for being pulled out during the wet season. Be highly skeptical that a ford will be okay the year around. Avoid a site that requires you to build a bridge. If you pay for a right of way, have a written agreement with owner so you get definite amount refunded if others use the road you built.

2 LAND AND RIGHT OF WAY........$500.00

Be wary of an unexpected "bargain"; maybe owner believes value will depreciate. Be *sure* to have title searched. Have property surveyed, and markers located along boundaries. Your lawyer should examine all documents, contracts, title and so on in advance of any down payments, and should represent you at the final "closing." Know where your property rights extend into the water so any dock you build will be yours. Don't be satisfied with a statement that your property ends at the "water line"—this is far too indefinite.

3 ELECTRICITY AND FUEL............$300.00

Check how much it will cost to bring in electricity from the nearest power line. Get a guarantee for a refund if others tap power from poles you paid for between main line and your property. If you decide on a generator that runs on gasoline, get complete data on costs and how to start the unit after it has been idle for several months. The unit needs a little shed of its own—it's noisy. Kerosene for the cook stove and wood for the fireplace require a small shed that will also be handy for other things such as tools.

4 TAXES, CARRYING CHARGES, INSURANCE $100.00

Taxes may not be much, but find out for certain. Carrying charges equal interest you'd get investing money. Get fire and theft insurance if it's available, and buy some good fire extinguishers, plus the carbon tetrachloride glass-bomb type that operates automatically when the temperature reaches 160° F.

TOTAL FOR ITEMS 1, 2, 3, 4.........$1,100.00

From the highway to your boat wharf are places where you'll have to spend money.

AMOUNT CARRIED FORWARD...$1,100.00

5 CABIN MATERIALS
AND LABOR $2,400.00

This is the big item. Find out how much you can spend on it, by subtracting from your total available cash, the four items listed on the preceding page, as well as furnishings and equipment.

The amount available for cabin-cost only, divided by $5 (the estimated cost per square foot), gives you a rough idea how many square feet you can afford. If you intend doing all the work yourself, then divide by $3 (the estimated cost per square foot for materials only). Or do it the other way around: say you want a cabin 20 ft. by 30 ft., or 600 sq. ft.: multiply 600 sq. ft. by $5 (for labor and materials) = $3,000.00, or multiply 600 sq. ft. by $3 (for materials only) = $1,800.00.

Let's say you'll do all the work yourself, except for $600 for footing piers and masonry. This $600, plus $1,800 for materials, adds up to $2,400 for a 20 ft. by 30 ft. cabin.

These estimates on a square-foot basis ($5 with labor and $3 for materials only) are bound to vary from one section of the country to another. Also, they are based on the assumption there will be no plumbing, no heating system and no electric wiring. If you want all these in a "cabin," then the price will be about the same for any all-year house, plus the increased cost of transportation.

The cost of any type cabin will also vary according to the distance and difficulty of delivering materials, the type of materials, the availability of local labor and the simplicity or complexity of the plan and design. Look into two possibilities: hiring local labor during its slack months (late autumn and winter), and prefab construction.

TOTAL FOR ITEMS 1, 2, 3, 4, 5.....$3,500.00

6 EQUIPMENT AND FURNISHINGS.$300.00

It's tempting to disregard the cost. "We'll raid the attic and use a few old battered pans," has often been said, but tried without much success. Base your cost estimate on a list of items that are not castoffs but which must be bought—such as springs, mattresses, galley equipment, eating utensils, crockery, chairs and lamps.

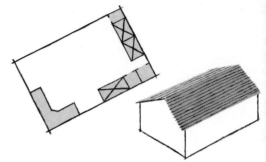

Keep your plan a simple rectangle.

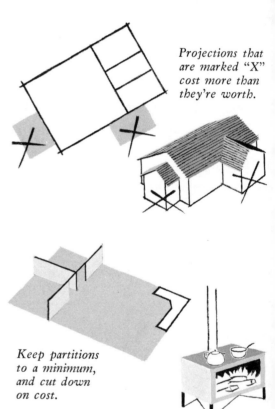

Projections that are marked "X" cost more than they're worth.

Keep partitions to a minimum, and cut down on cost.

Old Franklin stove comes in new forms; good to cook, heat.

Equipment and furnishings cost more than you'd guess.

7 UPKEEP AND IMPROVEMENTS ...$200.00

Strictly speaking, these costs shouldn't be included in your first-year building budget. But you should have a sinking fund for annual upkeep, such as unforseen repairs, and for conveniences not included in the original construction. Include this sum in your initial budget as a reserve fund.

8 TRANSPORTATION $200.00

Unless you have a flying carpet, transportation costs more than you think, and reduces what you can spend on the cabin.

GRAND TOTAL $4,200.00

Even if you do much of work yourself, lumber, nails, paint and tools add up surprisingly.

Don't ignore travel cost. It leaves less to spend on cabin.

DECIDE WHAT YOU WANT AFTER YOU HAVE MADE OUT THE BUDGET AND BEFORE YOU START PLANNING

1   HOW MUCH WILL YOU SPEND ON CABIN?   (Refer to budget you made out).

2   What has priority in locating cabin on site?

Do just as you would *after* deciding to go hunting but *before* you get down to details. First general decisions—where to go, who will go, what kind of game. That's the way to go about planning a cabin too. Use this check list to help get a clear idea of what game you are after and what ammunition you'll need.

☐ View   ☐ South sun   ☐ Summer breezes   ☐ Trees

☐ Privacy   ☐ Near road   ☐ Near water

The ideal orientation of your cabin would be as shown, with view and ground sloping away toward the south, trees to the west for shade from the hot afternoon sun, and prevailing summer breezes from the north. You probably will have to make some compromises, depending upon what is of chief importance to you. Weigh all the factors and write down the reasons for your choice. If this is the first cabin you ever built, get advice from several sources.

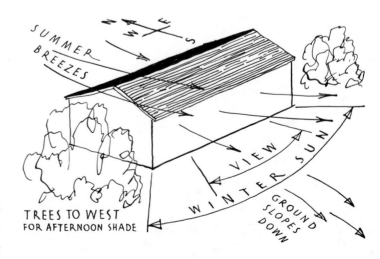

SUMMER BREEZES

TREES TO WEST
FOR AFTERNOON SHADE

VIEW

WINTER SUN

GROUND SLOPES DOWN

3 WHO WILL USE THE CABIN MOST?

☐ Your family
☐ You, your wife and friends on week ends
☐ You, your wife and occasionally business associates
☐ Men only: ☐ Fishing ☐ Hunting ☐ Business entertaining
☐ Tenants—perhaps

Visualize who will use the cabin, what they will require as a minimum, and make decisions accordingly. If you plan to provide sleeping accommodations for your children so that they can get to bed early and not be bothered by adult conversation and games, then you can be reasonably sure those same sleeping quarters will be satisfactory for friends, business guests and hunting or fishing pals who are light sleepers. Private bedrooms will appeal to tenants too, and bring a higher rental than lack of sound barriers. However, dividing your cabin into small sleeping cubicles has its disadvantages too. Not only does it increase construction costs, but it becomes very similar to building a suburban house in the woods. Obviously if the cabin is to be a hunting or fishing lodge for men only, there are fewer requirements.

4 WHAT TYPE OF "LIVING"?

☐ Much the same as all-year house
☐ More relaxed than all-year house
☐ Entirely different from all-year house
☐ Medium housekeeping duties
☐ Minimum housekeeping duties
☐ Indoor bathroom
☐ No indoor bathroom

Many a cabin starts out to provide a simple way of living, entirely different from the year-round home, but ends up with the same complexities and luxuries. If you are genuinely interested in living the simple life in a cabin, but your family has never done so, rent a cabin to find out what the minimum comfort requirements actually are. It would be a pity to go to the expense of building a primitive log cabin with no plumbing or heating facilities, and discover all too quickly that your family was disappointed after one short trial. So find out what type of "living" is going to make its users not merely uncomplaining, but eager to return. Having this information will make it easier to check a number of the items which follow.

5 WHAT GENERAL TYPE OF PLAN?

☐ *All-year type with living room, dining area, kitchen, bedrooms and bath.*

The plan to the right is similar to a typical prefab or home-builder house, except that it is only 16 instead of 18 or 20 feet wide. An overall width of 16 feet was selected because this is an economic floor joist and roof rafter length. Keep costs down by making partitions of single thickness plywood, and only door height. These will afford visual but not acoustic privacy. If bunkrooms only six feet deep are too small, make cabin 18 feet wide.

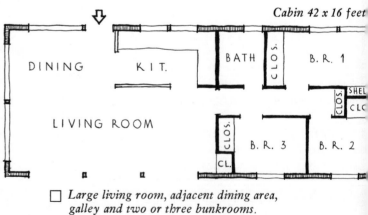

Cabin 42 x 16 feet

DINING　　KIT.　　BATH　CLOS.　B.R. 1

LIVING ROOM　　CLOS.　B.R. 3　B.R. 2　CL.

SHEL　CLO　CLOS.

☐ *Large living room, adjacent dining area, galley and two or three bunkrooms.*

This plan is 16 feet wide for the same reasons given for the one preceding. For economy's sake it could be built without separate bunkrooms. Dual-purpose seat-bunks in the living-dining room could serve as sleeping accommodations, or there could be bunks on a porch. The galley is conveniently located for serving food indoors or outdoors, regardless if porch or terrace be toward the front, rear or side. The galley could be closed or semiopen toward the living room; it could be screened from the dining area by curtains if desired. Notice that bunkrooms get cross-ventilation.

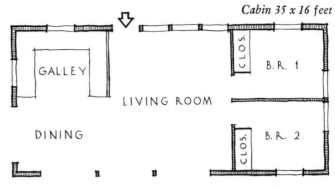

Cabin 35 x 16 feet

☐ *Large all-purpose room with bunks, galley and closets along the outside walls.*

Here's an economic plan for a cabin with 448 square feet. At a cost of $5 per square foot for both labor and materials, it would be $2,240. However, since it's about the same size as a two-car garage (20 x 22 feet, or 440 square feet), and need not be any more elaborate at the outset, the price might be considerably less. There is but scant closet space, unless the cabin were used only for week ends. If the floor space of one of the four bunks could be given over to storage, this might be a possible solution, particularly if there were one or two double-decker bunks for a total of five bunks. This plan would lend itself to making a bunkroom addition by extending the cabin to the left, or by a wing toward the right rear. One single door, three pairs of double doors, and three double windows, are required, plus 53 lineal feet of wall surface.

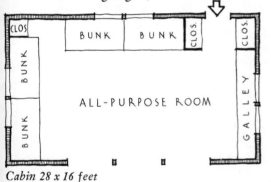

Cabin 28 x 16 feet

6 WHAT MATERIALS?

☐ Do you have any preconceived ideas about the exterior design you will insist on, regardless of the availability of the necessary materials? If so, cost will be high.

☐ Will you choose materials according to their local availability, and familiarity of local labor to use these? If so, you are sure to save money and trouble.

☐ Will you choose materials on the basis of low initial cost and high upkeep, or quality materials with low upkeep? Over a 10-year period latter will cost less.

7 WHAT TYPE MATERIALS?

(a) Foundations

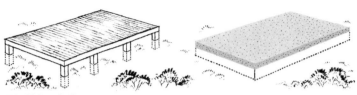

☐ Wood floor on masonry piers usually least expensive, but allow one foot between surface of earth and wood members.

☐ Concrete slab on ground. More expensive but good. Footing and foundation walls must extend below the frost line.

(b) Walls

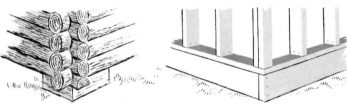

☐ Logs
Investigate supply and type of logs, available labor and upkeep of chinking between logs.

☐ Wood frame
Uprights of two by fours or four by fours lend themselves to family labor and the use of standard materials.

(c) Roof

☐ Shed roof
Least expensive type for small cabin; one man can build it.

☐ Gable roof
Best type for ventilation between ceiling and roof.

☐ Hip roof
Most expensive of three types. Roof ventilation difficult.

(d) Windows and doors

☐ Many single openings
This traditional design results in greater labor costs than cabin with grouped openings.

☐ Few but multiple openings
Take advantage of view by having several large groups of stock windows or stock doors.

8 WHAT TYPE KITCHEN OR GALLEY?

☐ Separate room

Typical plan suitable for an all-year house.

☐ Semiopen to dining area

More in character with informal cabin life.

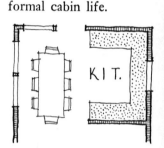

☐ Open—in corner of all-purpose room

This could be screened off with curtains.

☐ Open—along one end of all-purpose room

Also economic and well suited to cabin life.

9 WHAT TYPE CLOSETS AND STORAGE?

☐ Standard closet with doors
These need not be more than 22 inches deep. Rear and sides can be of wallboard or plywood. Doors can be stock, or made of vertical boards nailed to horizontal boards top and bottom. Line up top with other doors.

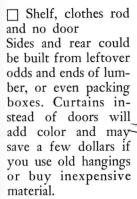

☐ Shelf, clothes rod and no door
Sides and rear could be built from leftover odds and ends of lumber, or even packing boxes. Curtains instead of doors will add color and may save a few dollars if you use old hangings or buy inexpensive material.

☐ Shelves above bed, wood strip with hooks
Shelves above a bed do not provide easy access but are better than none. Here they are shown parallel with the bed, but there could be shelves above one or both ends of bed instead. Curtains over shelves would add color.

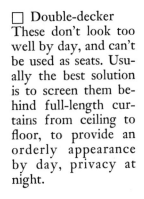

☐ Open shelf, clothes rod and/or hooks
This may be necessary on outside wall surfaces between windows, to get sufficient closet space. The effect can be fairly pleasing if curtains made of burlap are dyed same color as adjacent wall surfaces.

10 WHAT TYPE BEDS?

☐ Standard
These occupy considerable space and are appropriate only in bedrooms. For all-purpose rooms the suggestions below are more suitable for conserving cabin floor space, and for securing dual usage from beds.

☐ Double-decker
These don't look too well by day, and can't be used as seats. Usually the best solution is to screen them behind full-length curtains from ceiling to floor, to provide an orderly appearance by day, privacy at night.

☐ Fold-away
You can buy standard units, or make them. Bed is hinged on one side to be in vertical position when not in use, and to swing down to horizontal position at night. Hang curtain from shelf to cover bed during daytime.

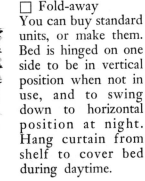

☐ Dual-purpose
This is one of the most useful ideas for a cabin: the bed remains in a horizontal position, but has a hinged wood back. Latter serves as a seat backrest, but swings up and away when bed is used for a bed at night.

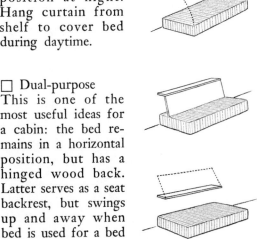
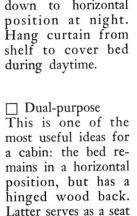

11   WHAT TYPE FIREPLACE?

☐ **All masonry**
Be sure to get a mason who will guarantee fireplace won't smoke.

☐ **Steel prefab shell plus masonry**
A steel unit veneered with brick. Cold air is heated and circulated.

☐ **All prefab**
Good combination: Franklin-type stove plus a prefab chimney.

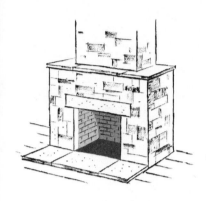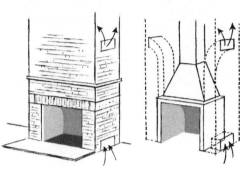

12   WHAT TYPE PORCH?

☐ **Glass-enclosed**
Space uprights so stock storm sash can be used.

☐ **Screened**
Useful for sleeping, dining and general living.

☐ **Open**
Build foundation piers so you can add a roof.

☐ **None**
Locate cabin so there is room for porch addition.

USE CUTOUTS TO PLAN THE BEST ARRANGEMENT OF BUNKS, EQUIPMENT AND FURNITURE YOU CAN USE IN THE LEAST SPACE. IT'S MUCH EASIER AND QUICKER TO MOVE MODELS THAN WINDOWS, DOORS, PARTITIONS

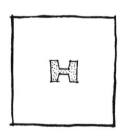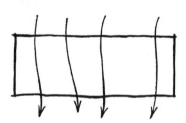

SQUARE FOR COLD CLIMATE
AND ELONGATED FOR HOT

You'll be money ahead if at the outset you choose a square or rectangular shaped cabin, because it will be the cheapest to build, saving you time and money; and it is easiest to heat.

Keep your objectives in mind from first to last if you want to insure a good cabin plan. This means making an itemized list with assigned priorities, and keeping it propped up in front of you as you work. It might read something like this:

1—Must be within budget:
    a) Have rectangular shaped plan
    b) Have unbroken roof
    c) No indoor bathroom; wash-up shelf instead
    d) Concentrate windows and doors rather than having lots of singles

2—Take advantage of site:
    a) View has first priority, next—south sun
    b) Locate cabin so future additions can be made in rear or at ends without altering roof
    c) Retain trees to west, but clear out to south
    d) Utilize slope by having garage under cabin
    e) Locate cabin so breezes provide natural cross-ventilation

3—Cabin requirements:
    a) Two double bunks plus one single, screened with curtains on ceiling tracks
    b) Galley to be U-shaped and in a corner
    c) Locate most windows on two sides (view and air)
    d) Fireplace, if budget permits
    e) Closet, shelves or row of hooks near each bunk
    f) All-purpose table for cooking, dining, play; good lamp needed

Beautiful scenery is part of your cabin. Regardless of cabin style or the type of roof, plan for additions to be put at the rear or side so as not to spoil the view.

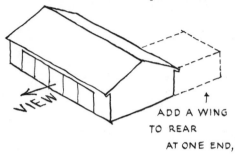

ADD A WING
TO REAR
AT ONE END,

OR ALONG
ENTIRE REAR,

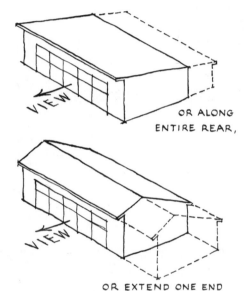

OR EXTEND ONE END

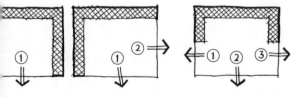

Plan a concentration of windows or doors to take advantage of the view, which may be in one, two or three directions, as shown in the drawings at left. The criss-cross lines indicate location of closets, bunks, galley, fireplace along the walls.

Here are two plans (see next page) which illustrate how cutouts can help you quickly visualize alternate layouts. The relative advantages and disadvantages can be judged between separate bunkrooms and liberal closet space in the plan above, compared with more sleeping accommodations but less closet space below. Make cardboard cutouts figuring a quarter inch on paper to equal one foot in reality. Label each with name and size: bunk (six and a half by three feet), chairs (one and a half by two feet), closets (two feet deep), fireplace (seven by two and a half feet), galley equipment (two feet deep).

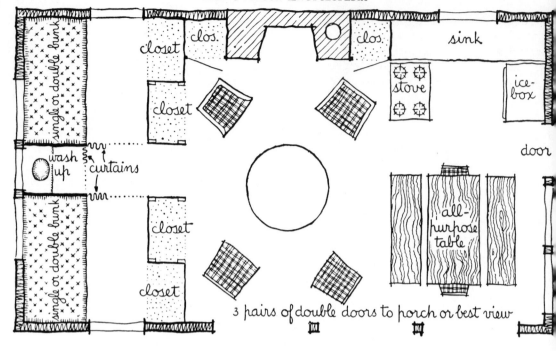

Both cabins on this page measure 28 feet by 16 feet overall, and are shown at a scale of ¼ inch equal to one foot.

This cabin, same size as one above, sacrifices privacy but gains an additional bunk, plus effect of being more spacious.

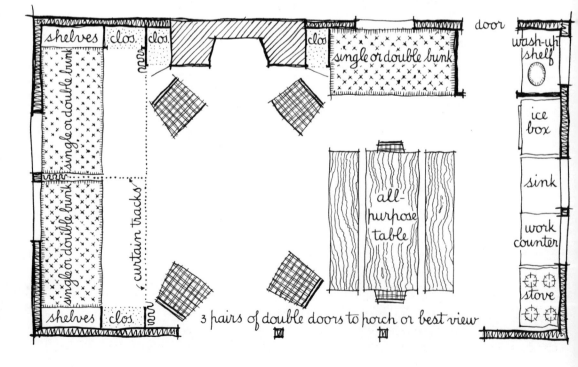

THE COMPLETED CABIN

This cabin is designed to be built almost singlehanded, with a plan that makes it possible to enjoy cabin life in an all-purpose room 32 feet by 12 feet. There is a fireplace in the center, a galley to the left of it. Windows and doors on three sides take advantage of light, air and view. Later on the balance of the cabin (the rear half) could be added, with bunkrooms at a level six steps up, and with a garage, storage or washroom eight steps down. In the interests of economy vertical posts are spaced eight feet apart in one direction, and 12 feet in the other.

The front of the all-purpose room opens out on a terrace located to take advantage of the best view. At one end of the room a single door opens on an outdoor platform which has steps leading down to the garage level, and up to an outside door which opens to the bunkroom level. The two doors are useful because when bringing in food supplies from the car to the galley, you'd want to enter directly on the all-purpose room level. At other times it may be desirable to get to the bunkroom level without going through the living room.

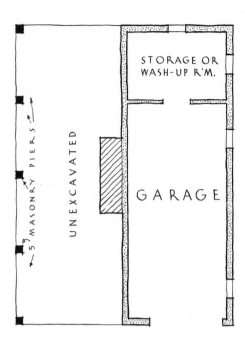

Plan at lower level showing garage.

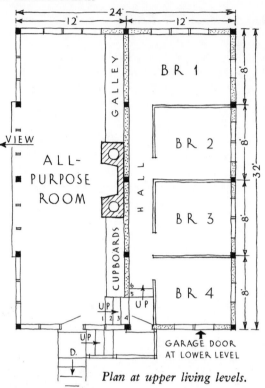

Plan at upper living levels.

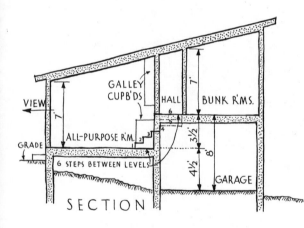

Try out a room width of 12 feet with a length of 32 feet, by laying out such an area in your garage or basement, before building a cabin room to these dimensions. Maybe you'll decide in favor of a 14-foot width for the all-purpose room, as well as for the bunkroom portion. While this will increase the cost of lumber and other materials, the additional living space may be well worth it.

The washroom is located beyond the garage on the assumption there is no running water for a regular bathroom. However, if you can substitute a bathroom for one of the bunkrooms, obviously that would be the most convenient location.

Interior perspective of all-purpose room.

CHAPTER 4

camping

ONE OF the most appealing things about camping is the very real comfort an experienced camper can enjoy with so little equipment and such a minimum of effort. True, it isn't the comfort of overstuffed chairs and indirect lighting. But it is the comfort of good food cooked over a live bed of coals, the comfort of a warm and private tent, the satisfaction of a soft bed and casual conversation when the embers burn low. Added to this is the wonderful feeling of freedom and independence that making your own camp gives. This chapter is a guide to the many different and exciting kinds of camping. It covers, among other things, tents, including the famous Indian tepee, sleeping facilities, camp foods, cooking methods, camp stoves and the important, but often overlooked, essential little things.

CHOOSING THE RIGHT TENT

Which is the best tent? You're right—*no* tent is ideal for all purposes. Like all items of outdoor equipment, tents are compromises. No single type of tent is "the best." There are tents for semipermanent camps, for automobile camping, for canoeists, for backpackers and horsepackers. There are tents for the tropics and for the arctic, tents for summer and tents for winter, tents for alpine conditions and tents usable only in forest country. Nothing in the outfitters' catalogs comes in more varieties than tents. Each has its own purposes and its own limitations.

But, for obvious practical and financial reasons, most of us would like to settle for just *one* tent—the one tent which represents the best possible compromise among the varying conditions under which it will be used. The best tent is the tent that is satisfactory in all the different situations in which it will be used. Instead of being ideal for one certain set of conditions such as the clear, still, bug-free October night or the June rainy-day-in-camp, it is designed to meet a wide variety of conditions satisfactorily. It is frankly a compromise, not a special-purpose item.

The average man does most of his camping in the summer and fall, and his tent should be chosen with this fact in mind, though he will want a tent that can be used in winter and early spring as well. The most important use for the tent will be his annual trip to the mountains or the north woods, but the tent's usefulness should not be limited to wilderness conditions if it is to give maximum enjoyment. The average man goes on a camping trip with one or two companions; it follows that his tent should be large enough for two or three people, and that larger parties should use two or more tents. A light tarp is suitable for one-man trips, and also serves as a highly useful accessory to the basic tent.

The best tent for all-round use will have these qualities:

1) It will be easy to erect and easy to take down and pack. Ease of pitching the tent is emphasized here not only because it is essential but also because it usually is given too little thought. At the end of a long day's ride or paddle you don't want to spend half an hour cutting poles. You want to get the tent up alone while your partner works on dinner, and you want to get it up fast. Your tent should have the bare minimum of poles, stakes and ropes.

2) It will be easy to carry. The tent will be light in weight, and will pack into a small space. For most purposes weight is not quite so important as ease of pitching, but it still is one of the first things to consider.

3) The best tent is big enough—just big enough. Too much room is as bad as too little, for it will make the tent hard to pitch

and hard to carry. But the tent must be minimally adequate in size, which some very popular tents certainly are not. Have you ever taken a pup tent on an extended trip? If you have, you know that your tent must have sufficient headroom; preferably, you should be able to stand inside to dress. A tent with a steeply pitched roof has more usable room than one with more sloping angles; tents with walls are out because of the additional difficulty of pitching them under adverse circumstances, although they have advantages.

4) The best tent is flexible. It can be used successfully at different seasons and in different kinds of country. It is insectproof, of course. But it can be opened up wide to be warmed efficiently by an open fire on those cool and bug-free fall nights. It sets well on uneven ground, and can be used with rough, crooked or weak poles, or only one pole, or no poles at all. It is well ventilated, yet turns rain and snow efficiently. It is easy to handle in windy locations and is stable in windstorms. It affords privacy when privacy is desired.

5) Subject to all these requirements, the best tent is the cheapest—which means either that its first cost is low or that it lasts a long time. You'll have to evaluate this.

The miner's tent is one compromise. The miner's tent is shaped like a pyramid—square on the ground, with each side sloping up at a steep angle to a sharp peak. One side is slit from ground to peak to form a door, and there is enough extra material on this side so that the door flaps overlap six inches or so when closed. The common sizes are from six and a half by six and a half by seven feet high to ten by ten by eight and a half feet high, the former being adequate for two persons and the latter ample for three. Weight, without floor, varies from under six pounds to about 15 pounds, depending on size and material.

The miner's tent is the easiest of all types to pitch. You merely stake down the four corners and then suspend or prop up the peak. The easiest way to do it is to spread the tent under a suitable tree, stake down the corners, attach a rope to the peak, toss its free end over a low limb, pull the rope snug and tie it to anything handy. You can do this in about as much time as it takes to explain it. Give some thought to the selection of a tree, though. If it is dead or not firmly rooted, or has large dead limbs, it will be dangerous in a windstorm. The swaying of a large tree or limb can loosen the stakes or tear the tent if the suspending rope is too taut or shrinks when wet. On the other hand, a springy limb will keep the tent trim and still "give" enough to be safe. If there are no large trees handy, a bush or sapling can be bent over and the tent peak tied to its top; the springy tension of the sapling will suspend the tent perfectly.

Lacking a tree, the tent can be pitched with just one pole. One end of the pole is thrust into the peak of the tent, and the other end rests on the ground in the center of the tent. The corners of the tent act as guy ropes, and you have a very stable setup. Only one short pole, as long as the tent is high, is needed. A telescoping aluminum pole of this length weighs only a pound or so, or you can insert a telescoping extension in the shaft of a spare canoe paddle to make up the necessary length. The only disadvantage of the single-pole pitch is that the pole breaks up the floor space in the center of the tent, just where you have the most headroom.

This disadvantage is overcome by using two somewhat longer poles. Tie them together near their tops to form a scissors or bipod, erect them over the staked-down tent, and suspend the peak of the tent from the point where the two poles are tied together. This gives you a stable pitch regardless of where the trees happen to be growing, and without obstruction of the floor space. A further advantage is that you can tie out two sides of the tent to the poles by means of light lines extending from small webbing loops (called "parrels") sewn into the sides of the tent at the center of each side. This takes all "belly" out of the tent, but is rarely done since the steep slope of the sides allows very little sagging. Sometimes it is worthwhile if you are going to leave the tent pitched for several days.

If your tent has a webbing loop about a foot long sewn to the peak, you don't even have to tie the shear poles together. Just hook a crotch on each pole into the web loop and lift the peak into the air as you catch the bottom ends of the poles in the ground. It's just like propping a clothesline. One man can do it easily.

The double-shear-pole method is the most elaborate way to pitch a miner's tent, but in forest country it shouldn't take one man more than five minutes, including the cutting of the poles. Compared to pitching any kind of tent having a horizontal ridge, it's child's play. Any old pole that is long enough and strong enough will do—since the poles don't touch the tent, they don't have to be straight or smooth. The poles can be pretty light, perhaps only an inch thick, because the thrust on them is at an acute angle, not at right angles.

In forest country, you will pitch the miner's tent under a tree about two times out of three. If you have to carry poles, take a collapsible center pole or two shear poles, depending on your means of transportation.

When the peak is suspended, shove the corner stakes firmly into the ground and stake down the sides between the corners. Most miners' tents have either one or two stake loops on each side, beside the corner loops. For one-night stands in settled weather, it often is sufficient to stake down the corners only. If the ground is rocky or frozen, tie the stake loops to rocks or logs instead of using stakes. This is the best plan in very sandy soil, too. If you use stakes, very light ones are sufficient because of the very low wind resistance of the tent and its balanced design, which puts an equal strain on all stakes. When you carry stakes, use steel-wire pins with rings formed into one end, the kind used by the army for pup tents. These are about six inches long and weigh less than an ounce apiece. They cost one cent each in a surplus store. They may bend in rocky soil, but can be straightened easily.

To strike the miner's tent, drop the peak, pull the stakes and roll it up.

Single-point suspension explains the ease of pitching the miner's tent. It requires a minimum of stakes and poles, and no guy ropes at all. But the advantages of the pyramidal shape only begin with ease of pitching. Since the slope of the roof is steeper than in any other tent, rain is shed with maximum efficiency and the danger of leakage is at an absolute minimum. The tapering shape, closed on all sides and braced equally in all directions, gives minimum wind resistance and maximum strength against the most contrary gusts. A miner's tent is more stable in the wind than any other tent, with the possible exception of certain highly specialized tents used by mountaineers at extreme altitudes. The steep slope of the roof provides maximum usable inside space, short of the use of cumbersome vertical walls. The floor space is covered with a minimum of material, making for light weight and economy. Since the tent is a closed one, you can have privacy when and if you want it; this costs almost nothing extra in weight or expense of material, since the door is also an essential wall. And, luxury of luxuries, you have headroom to stand up comfortably inside!

In some situations, however, a closed tent is neither necessary nor desirable. If the campsite is insect-free and protected from high winds, nothing is quite so satisfying as a tent open to the warmth and cheer of the campfire. The versatile miner's tent is easily pitched as an open-front, ridgeless lean-to, and is just as efficient an open tent as the Whelen lean-to with horizontal ridge or the forester's tent.

To pitch the miner's tent as an open lean-to, peg down the two rear corners of the tent first, then peg down the front corners about four feet farther apart—keeping the bottom edges of the rear and side surfaces of the tent taut, of course. Next, suspend the peak of the tent by whatever method is most convenient. Readjust the position of the front corners if necessary to make the tent trim, and peg down the intermediate loops on the rear and sides if there is any prospect of wind. The result is a lean-to with a floor plan in the shape of a "W" or trapezoid, open to the fire on the wide side and shaped to reflect the fire's warmth efficiently from all three sides. The front opening is vertical, and will be about five feet high and nine feet wide for a six and a half by six and a half by seven foot miner's tent, or proportionately larger for the larger sizes. The rear width is, of course, unchanged.

A miner's tent pitched as a lean-to has all the advantages of the conventional lean-to, except that there is less headroom at the sides. The disadvantages of the regular lean-to also are present, except that the miner's tent is easier to pitch. Its sides slope at a gentler angle, and do not shed rain or snow quite so efficiently. It is almost impossible to secure the tent against a strong wind blowing directly into the open side, but it is easily turned around or changed to conventional pyramid shape if a contrary wind comes up.

When the miner's tent, pitched as a lean-to, is supported at the peak by shear poles, a front guy rope is necessary only in windy weather. Otherwise, just lean the shear poles toward the front of the tent, so that they cross at a point just above the peak (front) of the tent but rest on the ground at a point about midway between front and rear. The weight of the poles, leaning forward against the tension of the rear side of the tent, keeps the tent trim and automatically compensates for any shrinkage of the material in rainy weather.

The miner's tent is easily made insectproof by means of a zippered netting sewn inside the door. The netting is sewn to the front inside corners of the tent from ground to peak, and separated at the center by a full-length zipper. It has a tent-material border at the bottom, to be tucked under the tent floor or ground cloth. The netting can be tied back out of the way, when not needed, by means of short cloth tapes sewn into the front corners of the tent, inside, at intervals of a foot or so.

A sewn-in floor gives perfect insect protection and makes it easy to stake out the corners of the tent to a perfect square, but prevents a neat pitch on uneven ground and of course makes it impossible to pitch the tent with the open trapezoid-shaped floor plan so desirable for use with a reflector fire. Therefore it is best to order a miner's tent without floor, but with a sod cloth sewn around the bottom edge of the tent. The sod cloth tucks under a separate ground cloth floor for effective insect protection. Instead of the usual nine-inch sod cloth, however, get one about twice as wide. This adds very little to weight or cost and makes a certain seal on uneven ground.

The best material for a miner's tent is closely woven, cotton cloth waterproofed by the green copper process. This material is as waterproof as cotton can be made without becoming airtight; does not rot or mildew if the tent is thoroughly dried out every 10 days or so when in use; and does not support combustion—that is, sparks will not spread. It has given complete satisfaction for decades. The weight and quality of the material will be chosen according to your needs and pocketbook. Tent fabrics may be fireproofed; the process adds weight to the cloth. Aberlite, the cheapest and next-to-lightest, will last many years if not seriously abused and is entirely satisfactory. Egyptian and Copperyacht are even more durable, especially in large tents or under very hard use, but are more expensive, and heavier. Extra Light offers a slight weight saving over Aberlite at considerably greater cost.

This material is porous to air, and even a small closed tent made of it does not become stuffy. For additional ventilation and vision outward, a small hooded window, screened with mosquito netting, may be sewn into one or more sides of the tent. The hood may be held out at an angle to the tent for ventilation during a rain; just run a cord from the hood to a limb or stake. The hood should have a loop or ring in its lower edge for this purpose and should be cut very full.

The ground cloth is best made of plastic-coated nylon. This material is very light and strong and absolutely waterproof. Get it about six inches larger each way than the floor space of the tent, to allow for wrinkles and uneven ground, and have grommets in the corners and midway of each side so the ground cloth can be used as a tarp or fly. The material is expensive, but sometimes can be salvaged from war-surplus life-raft sails or gun covers at slight cost.

The tent must be very carefully made if the light material is to give good service. All seams should be triple-sewn and lockstitched, and all lines of tension from stake loops to peak should run along seams or be reinforced with cloth tape. Parrels should be anchored to seams and tape patches. Machine-set grommets should not be used; brass or galvanized-iron rings, sewn in by hand, are much stronger. Stake loops are anchored to such rings, and are made of light rope, preferably nylon. The suspension loop at the peak should be of heavy webbing, and the entire peak area should be well reinforced with a double or triple thickness of tent material. A sewn-in ring at the peak anchors the suspension rope and receives the tip of an inside pole. The tape ties for the door flaps and mosquito netting should be carefully sewn to seams or hems and end-whipped to prevent raveling.

Obviously a tent of this sort is utterly different from the usual cheap, heavy, short-lived, leaky affair. Yet the miner's tent is the cheapest of the high-quality tents, except for pup tents, open lean-to's and plain tarps; and it costs very little more than these. Compared to explorers' tents and similarly exotic (and inefficient) designs it is dirt cheap. The reason for this is the simple design of the miner's tent. It uses and wastes a minimum of material. All seams are straight. There are no complicated doors, ridges and the like. It is made largely of identically shaped pieces. The happy result is that the best possible combination of desirable characteristics is available at relatively low cost.

For example, an Aberlite miner's tent, six and a half by six and a half by seven feet, with sod cloth and mosquito netting, weighs less than seven pounds (packed in the desir-

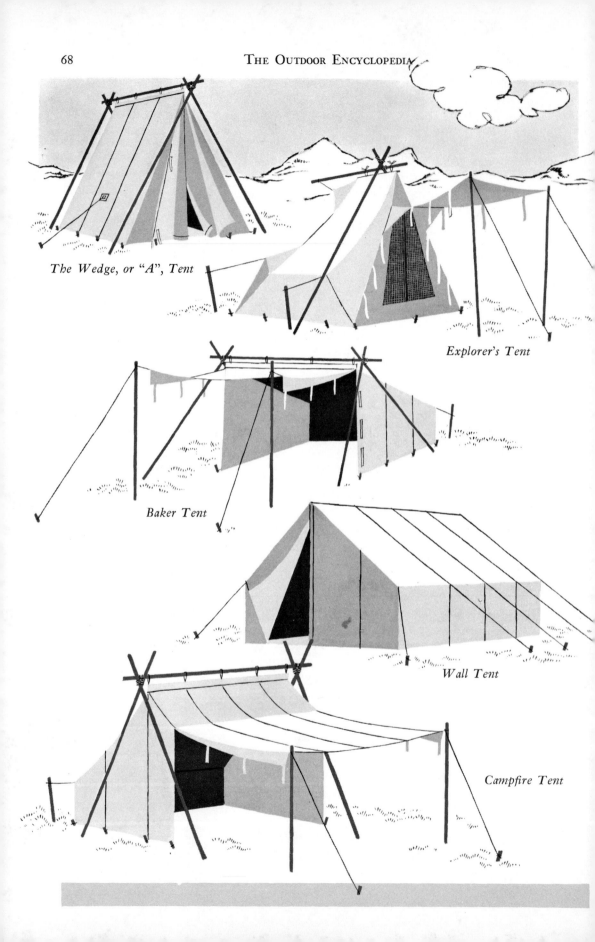

The Wedge, or "A", Tent

Explorer's Tent

Baker Tent

Wall Tent

Campfire Tent

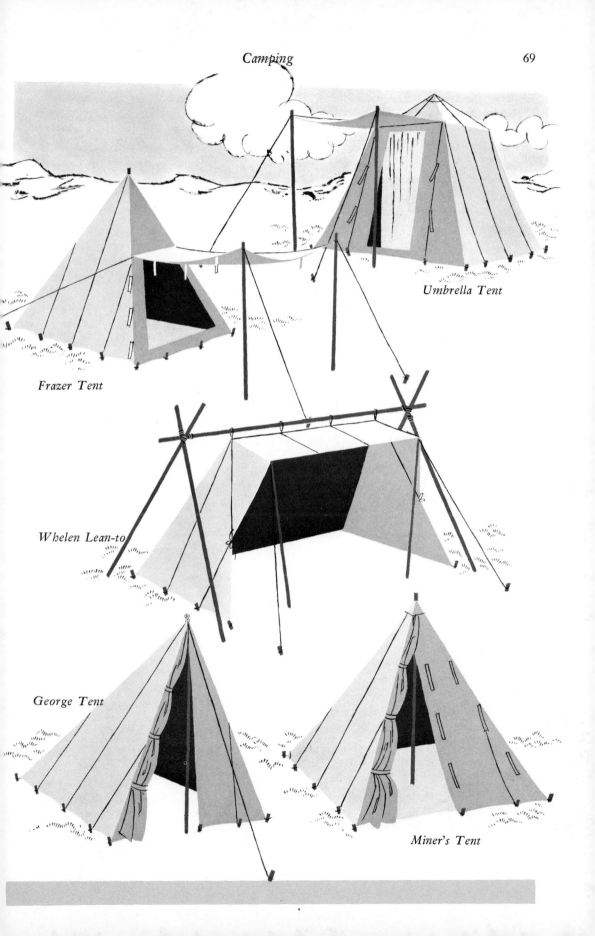

Umbrella Tent

Frazer Tent

Whelen Lean-to

George Tent

Miner's Tent

able protecting drawstring bag supplied by the manufacturer) and costs about $40. It should last 20 years or more if well cared for, and is an ideal light tent for two. (The eight by eight by seven and a half foot size is better for tall people and is roomier for anyone who doesn't mind the additional two pounds' weight.) In canvas or muslin, waterproofed with a commercial preparation, a practical miner's tent can be made for $10 or $15.

The miner's tent has only one serious disadvantage: The door, which slopes back to the peak, has to be kept closed during a rain. With the porous cotton material recommended, this does not present a ventilation problem; hooded windows make the tent even more airy. But you must pitch a fly over the entrance for rainy-weather cooking.

Various modifications have been suggested to overcome this disadvantage. The Pinkerton miner's tent has very wide door flaps, which overlap three feet or so. By tying the flaps halfway down from the peak in such a way that most of the overlap is eliminated, enough slack is created so that the flaps can be staked out, leaving a vertical doorway three or four feet high, from the shelter of which cooking can be done. This also adds to the usable room inside the tent—and adds to weight and cost. To a limited extent, the flaps of the plain miner's tent can be handled in the same way, but the effect is less pronounced because of the smaller overlap of the door flaps.

The Frazer tent is another modification designed to overcome the disadvantage of the sloping door. It substitutes for the sloping door of the plain miner's tent a narrow doorway, with a flap sewn to the top of the doorway only, like the door of an umbrella tent. This flap can be staked out, with the use of two poles, to form a fly or porch. But the horizontal fly catches water, and the door construction makes it impossible to open the tent to a warming fire. A sewn-in floor is appropriate with the Frazer tent; the result is a good tight shelter for use during the mosquito season. However, the plain miner's tent is just as good a summer tent

and a far superior all-round tent for use in all seasons and climates. There is something to be said for the Pinkerton tent if an extra pound or two is unimportant to you, but the Frazer tent, with its too-small fly and lack of flexibility, creates more problems than it solves.

A light separate fly with a plain miner's tent makes a more flexible rig than either the Pinkerton or Frazer modifications. A nylon poncho, or a nylon tarp the size of the ground cloth, shelters the tent entrance and cooking area efficiently during a rainy spell, has many other uses and can be left at home when you must go light.

The George tent is somewhat like a miner's tent cut in half—a half-pyramid with a vertical front wall. It is almost as easy to pitch as a miner's tent, but requires a front guy rope in the most inconvenient location, unless the peak is suspended from a tree limb. The headroom is less usable, the rear slope sheds rain less efficiently because of its gentler angle, and it is less stable in a contrary wind. The George tent is light, readily warmed by an open fire and easy to cook from in rainy weather. With the addition of a low rear wall, it is roomier, heavier and harder to pitch. The miner's tent, pitched as a lean-to, is roomier than the George tent, easier to pitch, more convenient and more versatile, more effectively warmed by a reflector fire because of its efficiently flared reflecting angles and generally better. The one real advantage of the George tent is that it can be closed after the fire has died down without restaking the front corners. But when conditions favor a reflector fire, there is no need to close the tent.

By C. W. Gillam

THE REAL INDIAN TEPEE

Ever since man learned to build a fire, the aborigines of the northern hemisphere the world around, have lived their whole lives, have raised families, and have prospered in health and vigor in a certain general type of shelter or tent. Everywhere it has consisted of a round shelter, made of animal skins, bark or, in later days, of fabric.

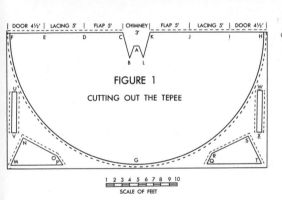

FIGURE 1

CUTTING OUT THE TEPEE

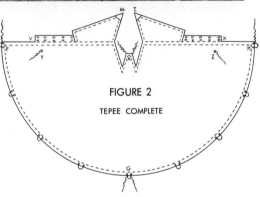

FIGURE 2

TEPEE COMPLETE

This is the pattern you will need when cutting out your tepee. It is designed for a 16-foot tepee.

Sew the smoke flaps and lacing pieces to the semicircular portion exactly as is shown in Figure 2.

A wood fire used for heating, cooking and lighting is built in the center. And a hole in the center of the roof lets the smoke escape.

In the Far North, the tent was usually erected on flexible poles such as willow which were stuck in the ground in a circle and bent inward at the top to form a dome-like structure. Even today you find these dome-shaped tents all the way from Tibet to Lapland.

But it was in North America that this form of tent reached its ultimate development because of the availability of straight pine and spruce poles. The straight lodgepole pine of the Rockies made perfect poles on which to erect the tent. The structure of

our nomad Indians was conical instead of dome-shaped.

The woods Indians covered their pole structure with bark, moss and partly with animal skins. Here it was generally known as a "wigwam." The plains and mountain Indians originally used a covering of the skins of buffalo and moose which made the tent more portable and better suited to their wandering life. And here it was generally called a "tepee," although the old white plainsmen and mountain men generally referred to it as a "lodge."

The plains Indians cut their poles from the lodgepole pines growing in the foothills of the Rockies, and in their journeys follow-

Here is the way that you go about wrapping tepee around the cone of poles.

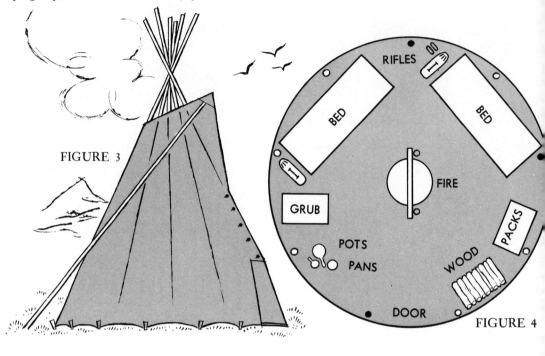

FIGURE 3

FIGURE 4

AAA–THREE INITIAL TRIPOD POLES

FIGURE 5

Pitching tepee. Place three of the poles on the ground and parallel, the butt of the center one six inches below the butts of the outside ones. See text for full details.

ing the buffalo herds dragged the poles behind their ponies in the form of a travois with the skin covering lashed on top. But the mountain Indians found their poles everywhere they camped, just for the cutting.

The superiority of this form of shelter for northern living lies in the wood fire burning in the center. This fire furnishes adequate and adjustable warmth even in blizzards and arctic cold, facilities for cooking under shelter even in rain and snow. Also the fire gives light during the dark hours, providing perfect ventilation, and always the joy of living before a wood fire with its cheerfulness and romance. Today you can heat a modern tent with a stove, and can cook over it. But you have no light, no ro-

mance, no cheer. And that stove is just a heavy, dirty thing to pack around.

But make no mistake. The tepee is hardly satisfactory for a camping trip where you do much traveling and pitch your camp at a different site every day or two. First, the tepee is too heavy, weighing from 30 to 50 pounds when made of canvas, and thus needs adequate transportation—pack horse, canoe or auto. And then, there is too much labor entailed in cutting the 11 long, straight poles every time you shift camp.

But for a more or less permanent camp in a cool or cold country where mosquitoes are not troublesome, it is the finest tent ever devised.

Today the modern tepee should differ

from the original Indian type only in being made of canvas instead of buffalo or moose skins. It should be made of a good grade of *white* canvas or duck, about eight- or 10-ounce material. It should *not* be waterproofed. White, so the fire will illuminate the interior at night; heavy, so the small knots on the poles won't tear or wear holes in it; and *not* waterproofed because the steep pitch sheds water perfectly, and no waterproofing material would long remain in the mild heat the canvas receives from the fire.

The ideal diameter on the ground is 16 feet. That's sufficient for two or three campers. If made smaller it would place the beds too close to the fire. And if larger, it would be heavy, difficult to find straight poles long enough for it, and rather expensive. But for a boy's camp it might be made 20 feet in diameter, then a whole lot of kids can get in it to sit around the council fire.

If you're an amateur builder, you will find the tepee easiest to construct by first sewing your canvas into a rectangle approximately 33 feet by 17 feet. Then cut out the pattern as shown in Figure 1. This for a 16-foot tepee. Notice the cuts at the peak, the two smoke flaps and the pieces for the front lacing above the door. In this way you waste very little material. Sew the smoke flaps and the lacing pieces to the semicircular portion exactly as shown in Figure 2, and hem up the bottom as shown by the dotted lines. Also work in the five double sets of pinholes, each an inch in diameter, in the two lacing strips, and sew on and reinforce the pockets at the top of the smoke flaps.

Add grommets, pinholes and the short tie-ropes at A and G, as shown. This completes the canvas portion of the tepee, and is fairly simple. It just involves a little sewing and some buttonhole stitching to reinforce the pinholes in the lacing strips.

To pitch the tepee you need 11 poles, as straight as possible, 20 to 22 feet long, three and one half to four and one half inches in diameter at the butt, and one to two inches at the top.

Scratch a circle 16 feet in diameter on the ground where the tepee is to be erected. Place three of the poles on the ground and

parallel, the butt of the center one six inches below the butts of the outside ones, as shown in Figure 5. Over these poles lay the tepee, inside down, the back tent peg loop (G, Figure 2) at the butt of the center pole, and the peak. A pulled out as far as it will go toward the tip of the center pole.

Tie the short lash ropes at A and G to the center pole. With a strong piece of rope, lash the three poles together at a point two and a half feet above the point where peak A is tied to the center pole. These three poles are to form the tripod upon which you lean six other poles to make the cone of nine poles around which the tent is stretched and wrapped.

Erect these three poles as a tripod. The butt of the center pole, with the tepee tied to it is to be placed just about where the back of the tent will come. One of the other poles is to be placed with its butt where one side of the door will come, and will form one of the door poles or posts. The third pole is placed on the circumference of the 16-foot circle, making a firm tripod.

Against this tripod you now lean the other six poles, butts equidistant around the circumference, one of these poles being located for the other door pole as shown in Figure 4. The butts of all these poles should not be planted quite up to the 16-foot circle you have drawn on the ground, but about a foot inside it. They will be moved out to, or nearly to, that circle later when you make the entire tent sit taut.

Around this cone of poles you now wrap the tepee, the peak of which has already been stretched to its full height by being attached to the back pole. To get it high enough all around you just take hold of its upper portion and fling it up on the cone of poles. The two door ends (F and H, Figure 2) come around to the butts of the door poles, and are tied to them. To assist in getting the tent high enough on the cone you take the 10th and 11th poles (which should be about a foot longer than the nine other poles) insert their top ends in the pockets in the smoke flaps, and poke the flaps and peak of the tent upward as shown in Figure 3. Then you cut five little pins about one-half inch in diameter, eight inches long and point them at both ends. With these you pin the front of the tent together above the door, poking the pins through the holes in the two lacing strips. This keeps the front of the tent together.

Your tepee is now up, but it is a rather baggy, sad-looking thing because the butts of the poles have been located on about a 14-foot circle. Go inside the tent, and one at a time push the butts of the poles out about a foot, and relocate them slightly, and separate the two door poles slightly, or bring them together, until the whole tepee stands taut and shipshape as shown in Figure 3. Usually these door poles should be about four feet apart at the butts, and the other poles equidistant around the circle. Raise the smoke flap poles enough to make the peak of the tent smooth.

Then cut nine tent pegs, and peg the bottom of the tepee down to the ground all around. The sides must be up an inch or two off the ground all around to allow air to get in under the walls, or your fire will not draw properly and your tepee will be full of smoke.

The tepee should be pitched so that if possible the door is at right angles to the prevailing winds. Generally the smoke flap on the windy side of the tent is raised and the other lowered. The only time you will have any trouble with smoke is when the wind blows in the door, and only when the door is open. Since the walls of the tent must not quite meet the ground all around, check this when it is snowing, as the snow must be dug out a little to preserve this air space.

Now take any small tarp—about five feet square is most convenient—and tie the two upper corners to the two cords at Y and Z, Figure 2. Tie a pole across the bottom corners of the tarp, then the tarp will hang down to form the door. To enter, just lift the pole, stoop down and walk in.

The fire, whenever needed, is built in the center of the tepee, and should be about two and a half feet in diameter, a round rather than elongated fire, with small, split, dry logs pointed towards the center. It is convenient to place a ring of stones around the fire to limit it to this diameter. A crosspiece above

the fire and pothooks may be used to hold pots over the fire as with any outdoor wood fire. Try to use wood that does not throw sparks, as the beds are placed rather close to this small fire, and sparks might ignite the bedding. To reduce this chance, keep sleeping bags covered with the heavy canvas pack covers.

Usually the fire will draw perfectly no matter how the smoke flaps are arranged, so that there is no smoke inside for five feet above the floor. Above this it will probably be a little smoky so that ordinarily you don't stand completely erect inside. If you have any trouble, raise the smoke flap on the side from which the wind is blowing, and lower the other side. If the wind blows toward the door, raise the flaps and bring their peaks to meet in front and keep the door closed.

Figure 4 shows the most convenient arrangement of your beds and duffel within the tepee. The beds should be arranged to get the benefit of the fire's heat, occupy less room and not come too close to the fire. It's easier to get in and out of bed, too. Only tenderfeet sleep with their tender feet towards the fire.

A slight draft does come in around the slightly raised bottom of the tent. This is necessary, and 29 days in the month will not be noticed. If this flow of fresh air over your bed becomes objectionable, take a pack cover or small tarp, tie its upper edge to the poles about three feet above the bed, and tuck its lower edge under your bed on the side away from the fire. Air will then still come in between the tarp and the tepee wall, and the fire will still draw well.

Keep some shavings and small split wood close to the head of your bed when you turn in, and in the morning before you get up reach out of your sleeping bag, place these on the fireplace and touch a match to them. In five minutes you get up and dress in a nicely-warmed and illuminated tent.

In hot weather, build your fire out in front of the tepee, and roll the walls up two feet all around just as you would roll up the walls of a wall tent, and you will have a comfortable, cool tent in muggy weather.

By Col. Townsend Whelen

CAMP BEDDING

There's a moralistic old saw to the effect that "you've made your own bed, now lie in it" which is applied by the more righteously smug types to their less fortunate brethren who have gotten into a mess and can't get out of it. It could often apply to campers, too, in a more materialistic sense.

Next to substantial and appetizing meals, a good night's sleep is the most important thing in a camper's life. The easiest way to insure it is to start with the best equipment you can buy, and then learn the few tricks necessary to achieve comfort. If you must economize in camping gear, don't start with your bedding. This does not mean you must purchase the most expensive equipment. It only means that the camper should spend whatever is required to get the sleeping gear best fitted to the kind of camping he will do.

For instance, it would be foolish to buy a down bag costing $100 for ordinary summer camping. You would be comfortable, yes, but such a bag is made for subzero weather, is fairly bulky and too expensive for summer use. On the other hand, it would be just as ridiculous to take a $15 kapok sleeping bag into the winter woods and expect to be comfortable. Buy what you need.

Your sleeping equipment outdoors is basically the same as at home, although different in construction and appearance. You need something over you and something under you, with more under than over, just as in a bed. You'll probably want a pillow of some sort. You will want something adaptable to changes in temperature. Unlike home bedding, however, you must carry yours with you by whatever way you travel, a factor which will determine many of your selections. Let's see how you can go about making a bed in the outdoors, and sleeping in it comfortably.

IN GENERAL

When traveling light, carrying everything in a pack, you are arbitrarily limited to the lightest sleeping bag you can use for the weather you will encounter. Anything else is superfluous weight, although some hiker-campers will make sacrifices in other gear to include a small air mattress. You might get by with a very light woolen blanket in the warmest weather, but you can't trust it.

If canoe-camping, without too strenuous portages, you can tote a few more luxuries, such as a pillow and a mattress, but they must continue light in weight.

If horses carry the pack, you are limited only by the number in the train and the portability of your gear. The pack horses can even manage folding cots.

Auto camping allows almost any equipment within reason, so long as you have space for it. You can use larger and more comfortable sleeping bags and mattresses, carry pillows and folding cots and make yourself quite comfortable. Some cars and station wagons are designed to be turned into beds, either as auxiliary sleeping quarters for large tenting parties, or used alone. Most persons are acquainted with these, but not too many know there is a conversion unit available that will transform a stock model car into a double bed. This Make-a-Bed kit is manufactured by an Ithaca, New York, firm (M. H. Ripley) and will fit most recent models of Fords and Mercurys.

MATTRESSES

Whenever possible, mattresses should be used, and not only for the extra comfort they provide. The greatest problem in sleeping outdoors is to provide warmth and insulation *under* the body, whether sleeping on the ground or on a cot. A mattress furnishes this insulation. It's amazing how the ground chill can creep up through even a good bag, or how the circulation of cold air under a canvas cot can give the sleeper gooseflesh—if he can sleep at all. You have your choice of natural mattresses, rubber air mattresses, plastic mattresses and those filled with down, wool or other substances.

Natural Mattresses. Least dependable because building material is not always available in all parts of the country, and it is often far from perfect when it is available. It is better than nothing, though. You can make a bed out of balsam and spruce boughs, or any springy twigs, even very *dry* grasses and leaves will do. Some protection under you is almost a necessity if the ground is damp and you have no ground cloth.

Rubber Air Mattresses. These mattresses, in which rubber and fabric are vulcanized into an airtight unit, are most dependable if made by a reputable firm. The camper must remember that the lighter the weight, the more likelihood of puncture. Thus, rubberized nylon is extremely light, but not as tough as some other cloths. On the other hand, punctures usually are the camper's own fault and can be prevented. The lightest mat-

The shear poles of the tent can be used to air sleeping bags or other bedding.

tress made is of nylon, full length of 73 inches, and weighs only two and a half pounds. Other rubberized cloth will weigh at least twice that much—but is more durable. The cost is about the same—so let your carrying method dictate the kind. Get the tubular or tufted mattress so you don't roll off.

Plastic Air Mattresses. Usually these are lighter in weight than cloth, but not as punctureproof. Both rubberized cloth and plastic mattresses are available with built-in head-

rests or pillows, a somewhat dubious advantage since most people like to shift a pillow around.

(Note: If possible, get the kind that can be inflated by pump *or* mouth. A pump can be lost or damaged. Don't inflate too hard or you will have trouble staying on the mattress. *And don't fail to carry a repair kit.*)

Other Mattresses. Slightly bulkier than the foregoing, but light in weight, are kapok mattresses which give good insulation on cots, and are less expensive than air mattresses. Some mattresses with wool batting are available.

PILLOWS

An inflatable pillow is one of the handiest things around a camp. Its first and most obvious use is as a headrest in bed, but it doubles as a seat or backrest. Did you ever try to find a dry spot where you could sit on a rainy day? A pocket-sized air pillow, not much larger than a handkerchief, solves that problem nicely.

Air pillows are available in both rubberized cloth and plastic.

Air Pillows. These are made of both rubberized cloth and plastic. Easy to inflate. Get the tufted or divided type and don't inflate hem too hard unless you want the exciting adventure of trying to keep your head from rolling off the pillow.

Other Pillows. You can buy a pure down pillow, 14 by 22 inches, weighing six and a half ounces, as a most comfortable luxury item if you wish. Or you can make a good pillow for auto camping by cutting foam rubber to size and covering it with cloth. On backpacking trips, you can carry a cloth bag in which to stuff loose clothing, and use it as a pillow.

BAGS AND ROBES

There is a slight distinction between sleeping "bags" and "robes," but all will be referred to here as bags. That's what they all are—bags into which you lower the body and are more or less comfortable. The slide fastener probably is the greatest single contribution to sleeping bags in the last 50 years. In the old days, when you had to use buttons or snap fasteners, there always seemed to be spaces where cold crept in—but even the slide fastener is no guarantee against preventing this if the bag is poorly made. An exposed slide fastener that touches the body is cold in itself, and admits cold from outside. Good bags overcome this with a tube of fabric and filler that runs the length of the zipper seam.

Double bags to accommodate two people, or single bags that can be zippered together for two persons, are available. It may sound cozy, but a lot of cold air can enter between two heads and bodies. Use only in warm weather.

The zipper should be at the side, except in the cocoon- or mummy-type bags where the construction (designed to reduce weight to an absolute minimum) makes this impossible. The usual argument against top slide fasteners is that the bag can't be reversed, and the permanent underside will mat down eventually. A much more important consideration is that the side fastener enables the user to sleep on his favorite side. Built-in pockets for air mattresses can be ignored. Put the sleeping bag on top of the mattress.

Evidence that manufacturers are becoming more practical is shown in the attention to the head part of bags. That's where most cold enters. Adjustable hoods are now available even in moderately priced bags. Good bags made for cold weather always did have a head cloth, or some arrangement for stopping the drafts that blow down the neck. Head flaps, like a little tent, look good, but serve no useful purpose. One firm, however, has carried the idea to the ultimate, and elongated the head flap into a complete tent, so that the sleeping bag is bag and tent combined. Very practical as an overnight shelter for one person.

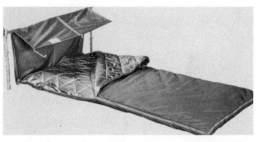

Among modern aids to more comfortable camping are sleeping bags such as this.

Some bags are built with ties for the insertion of a sheet or blanket. Unless they are so built, don't try to use a blanket inside because it will cramp your quarters. Some heavy-duty, cold-weather bags are lined with pure wool blankets which increase their warmth. If you wear *dry* woolen clothing (shirts, pants, etc.) when sleeping in a bag you will be much warmer than without it, but *don't* crawl into a bag with the clothes which you have worn all day because the dampness from body moisture will chill you. And keep the bag dry, airing it whenever possible in the sun. In all camping, remember this: Dampness means coldness.

Down Bags. Science has labored overtime, but there still is no completely satisfactory substitute for pure goose down. It is the lightest, warmest material available for sleeping bag filler. It also is expensive. You can buy a bag weighing only four pounds, 14 ounces, that will keep you warm down to 20-below zero, but it will cost about $60. A three-pound down bag suitable for temperatures as low as freezing will cost $35 to $40.

Those, by the way, are just about the lightest bags made in the world. In the more-than-$100 class are the all-down, wool blanket-lined heavyweights from 10 to 16 pounds, designed for the coldest weather and for carrying in dogsled, airplane or car. Bags containing a combination of down and chicken feathers are cheaper. It is not especially surprising that waterfowl down is the best lightweight material for warmth in sleeping bags since it has been keeping ducks and geese farm for thousands of years without handicapping their flight.

Wool Bags. Where space and transportation do not prohibit, bags filled with prime quality wool batting are not to be despised. It is excellent, in fact, and a wool-filled bag is much warmer than blankets of similar quality wool and weight.

Dacron Bags. Considerable curiosity has been aroused by the introduction of this "scientific" insulating material. This Du Pont fiber is warmer than wool or kapok, not so warm as pure down, but is moderately bulky and heavy. That is, a Dacron bag will run larger in size and weight than the equivalent protection in down or virgin wool, but it is less expensive.

Kapok Bags. Least expensive, least warm, but perfectly good for ordinary summer camping under nonrugged conditions. A kapok-filled bag is fine for ordinary summer auto camping.

Other Bags. The onetime famous Fiala sleeping roll is no longer on the market. This was a complicated, but practical, system of folding covers designed to anticipate any temperature. Bedding rolls to accommodate blankets are still available. Or you can buy a sleeping bag shell and use whatever blankets you want. A word of caution: Don't try to use the Army or Navy blankets because they were designed for durability as well as warmth, and are too closely woven to give real warmth. If you use blankets, either on a cot or in a bag, buy the best quality *fluffy* wool you can afford.

COTS

Considerable ingenuity has been spent on designing folding cots for campers, and the choice today is wide. There are many kinds: all-metal, metal and canvas, wood and canvas. About the only new development in many years of camp cot use is an Eddie Bauer product called Nestle Down in which a canvas cot on a metal frame has an underlining of down-filled tubes, which goes back to the original statement here that the outdoor sleeper needs more under him than over him. You can take your choice of such a product, which has underneath insulation, or you can provide your own with something under the sleeping bag or blankets that cover you. In any case, you still need insulation for a cot. There is nothing colder under the moon than sleeping on a cot without insulation in cool weather. Just as a suggestion, if caught in an auto camp by cold weather, and you have no cot insulation, buy newspapers and line the bottom of the cot with them. A good mattress, of course, will eliminate such emergency measures.

All-Metal Cots. These are really folding beds, complete with springs, which fold into compact units. Come in single or double size, excellent for auto camping.

Metal and Canvas Cots. Canvas cover over aluminum or other metal frame. The new concept is a low frame, since height is not useful.

Wood and Canvas Cots. The sturdy and reliable old-timers, like the metal-and-canvas, but with a wooden frame.

In all cots for tents, be sure to get those which are wide enough for the user. A narrow cot is an abomination, especially for a large man, since you find yourself sleeping partly on the frame sides.

By Bill Wolf

CAMP FOODS

Most camp food lists are drawn from an arbitrary "norm" that demands so many pounds of this and that for so many people, so many days in camp. If the campers involved don't happen to like this or that, they can learn to eat it or, presumably, starve.

A better system might be called the multiplication method. It makes allowances for individual tastes and preference. (You like cream in your coffee, your partner takes sugar.) It also takes into account the occasional guest, animal or human, who may wander into your camp to share its hospitality. The system works like this:

Take three sheets of paper and a pencil. Mark one sheet "Meals," another sheet "Food Quantities," and the third sheet "Utensils Required." Start with the very first meal you will eat in camp. This is usually lunch or the evening meal, since a trip ordinarily is started after breakfast, but, for the sake of simplicity begin with breakfast.

Put down on your Meals sheet "First Day, Breakfast—" and you list "bacon, eggs, breadstuff, coffee," or whatever you plan. Then, on your Food Quantities sheet, you list the foods and amounts needed for that one meal, like this:

Bacon: ½ lb. Eggs: 4. Bread: 4 slices. Coffee: 8 tablespoons

But you go beyond that. Eggs require salt and pepper. Most persons like butter on bread. Some drink coffee black, some use cream only, some sugar only, some sugar and cream. So, still bearing in mind everything that will be used for that one breakfast, you continue your food headings across the sheet:

Salt: ? Pepper: ? Butter: 2 oz. Milk: 1 oz. Sugar: 1 oz.

You will fry the eggs and bacon in a frying pan, you will spread the butter with a knife, make the coffee in a pot, drink it from a cup, stir your cupful with a spoon and eat the eggs and bacon with a fork. Therefore, you start on the Utensils Required page and list:

1 Knife, fork, spoon per person
1 Frying pan
1 Coffee pot
1 Cup per person

The eggs and bacon can be cooked and turned with the eating knives and forks, and the coffee can be measured with one camper's individual spoon since anything smaller than a tablespoon makes no sense in a camp anyhow. Teaspoons are a luxury.

That isn't all, however. You must have plates to eat from, and then you must wash the utensils. You will have leftover bacon fat. So your Utensils Required list grows:

1 Plate per person
1 Cake soap
1 Metal sponge
1 Empty sealtight can

You would be foolish to throw away the tried-out bacon fat, which is so useful in other cooking, hence the empty can for saving such fats. The kind with the press-on lid is handy.

The same procedure is followed for "First Day, Lunch—" and "First Day, Dinner—" Then you begin with the "Second Day, Breakfast—" and, for the sake of this illustration, assume that you are going to have exactly the same breakfast you had the first day. Your Food Quantities list will read thus after you have marked the amounts required for two exactly similar breakfasts:

Bacon: ½ lb. Eggs: 4. Bread: 4 slices. Coffee: 8 tablespoons. Bacon: ½ lb. Eggs: 4. Bread: 4 slices. Coffee: 8 tablespoons.

You also must add 2 ounces to your Butter, 1 ounce to your Milk, 1 ounce to your Sugar under those headings. The utensils remain exactly the same.

It doesn't matter whether you are going to stay two days, one week, or several weeks. Plan each meal in advance and set down the quantities of everything for each meal, including utensils needed. You will have rows of items reading Flour, Canned Beef, Potatoes, Beans, Biscuit Mix.

When the quantities for every meal are set down and the list is complete, add up each row and you will have precisely the amount of each thing required for the entire trip. Obviously, the two similar breakfasts above will require 1 pound of Bacon, 8 Eggs, 8 slices of Bread, 16 tablespoons of Coffee, plus 4 ounces of Butter, 2 ounces of Milk, 2 ounces of Sugar when they are added up. Salt and pepper are left with question marks, because it would take a genius to figure the precise amount required for each meal. Play it safe by taking plenty of both. The loaves of bread required can be determined by learning the average number of slices in each loaf, and translating total slices into loaves.

Finally, having attained the precise total quantity of each food, add a bit extra for safety's sake. If your coffee total is 1¾ pounds, add an extra ½ pound or so for that cool evening when you make another pot. If your Flour total comes out to 2 pounds, add ½ pound for the fish you might catch and want to flour before you fry them, or for the amount you might need to flour your hands before handling sticky biscuit dough. Assume that you will ruin at least one meal, by accident or carelessness, and make allowances for it, as well as for possible guests. And add a few luxuries. A chocolate bar never tastes better than when the body demands the energy it supplies.

MEATS

Except for use the first day or two, fresh meat is out of the question. Most reference here, by the way, is to back-packing, and not to automobile or boat camping where refrigeration and weight are no problems—although auto and boat campers will find the suggestions helpful.

The first day out will find the camper tired, hungry and impatient with elaborate cooking by evening mealtime. That's when a steak or some chops taste best. Pack one large steak, frozen hard, per person, well-wrapped and insulated, for that first dinner. The meat thaws by the time you are ready to broil or fry it, and it is no trouble to cook it. That's the only fresh meat you need to take along.

Meats that keep well fall into several classes —smoked, air-dried, sugar-cured, highly seasoned or canned. And it might as well be made clear immediately—your chances of finding what you want at your favorite grocery and meat shop are poor. You are going to have to hunt for it. In some cases good preserved meats are easiest to get through the mail. Especially if you live in a small town or rural area.

Persons who live in large cities, surprisingly, can find meats for camping more easily than in smaller towns. The German, Italian, Greek, Jewish and similar sections of big cities are wonderful hunting grounds for camping meats.

Sliced meat (bacon, dried beef, bologna) doesn't keep as well as the same product will in bulk. No meat will keep perfectly if wrapped in paper and stored all the time in a packsack. Buy cheesecloth, wrap the meat in it sufficiently well to discourage flies, and hang it in the air occasionally. Sunlight and air discourage mold, and delay spoiling.

Bacon. Buy a flitch, or slab side, of bacon and slice it as needed. The rind is extra weight, but use it to grease the griddle for pancakes. Ordinary store bacon is worthless except for very short trips, because it is not well cured. The drier the bacon through curing and/or smoking, the better because its weight is reduced and it keeps well. Really good bacon almost invariably is quite salty. Unless you expect to use the tried-out fat, bacon has too much waste to be a perfect camp meat; but it is an excellent source of frying and cooking fat. Best buys, although expensive, are American country-cured, hickory-smoked lean bacon, Irish and European bacons. *Canadian bacon* (called "back bacon" in Canada) is nearly all meat with little fat and entirely unlike side bacon. Some Canadian bacon is encased in a protective coating of ground meal and is then called "pease meal" bacon. Some German bacons have a similar protective coating of paprika. These keep well. Bacon goes well with breakfast eggs or pancakes, of course, but it is also flavorsome in other dishes. Try boiling lima beans with salt, pepper and some strips of bacon.

Ham. Avoid "store" hams. These moist, under-salted, tenderized hams spoil quickly. What you want is a dry, hard, salty ham that has been sugar-cured or hickory-smoked. The Virginia, or Smithfield, type is good. Westphalian ham is excellent, as is Italian *prosciutto.* Country-cured hams (as opposed to meat packers' types) generally are all right. A great favorite is the black, dry, hickory-

moked kind. Unless you intend to use the
one for bean soup, it is unnecessary to carry
ts extra weight. Trim the meat from the
one as much in a single piece as possible,
vrap in cheesecloth. One of the best buys is
well-smoked, *boneless* pork butt, in a net-
ing bag. A lean one is all meat, no waste.
And don't feel that frying is the only way to
ook ham. Ham and beans, either baked or
oiled, are natural affinities. Or pare and quar-
er potatoes and boil half an hour in the
roth in which a chunk of ham has been
lowly cooking for an hour or more. Crush
he potatoes on your plate and pour some
roth over them. Cook edible wild plants in
am broth for greens. Make satisfying, tasty
oups of split peas, navy beans, lentils or
ma beans, cooked with ham, adding dried
nion, parsley and celery flakes if you wish.

Beef "Bacon." This is a new product on
he market. It is just about what its name
ndicates—flitches of beef with alternate fat
nd lean, cured like pork bacon, used like
acon. Keeps considerably longer than fresh
eef, of course.

Pork Roll. Ground pork in a bag. Keeps
onger than fresh pork, especially if hung up
ightly, but not as long as smoked pork
roducts. Tasty when fried. "Summer sau-
age" of Pennsylvania-German country is
milar.

Salt Pork. This is the backbone of fish
howders and baked beans. A pound goes a
ong way. Make sure it is really salted,
hough, rather dry and firm. This insistence
pon plenty of salt is not due to extreme lik-
ng for it, but because of its preservative
owers.

Corned Beef. If weight isn't too great a
onsideration, corned beef is now available
acked in tough vinyl plastic bags in its own
rine. Keeps longer than fresh beef without
efrigeration.

Dried Beef. This is best known to most as
aper thin shavings, "chipped beef," but those
havings come from a solid piece of beef
vhich has been cured in brine and dried. Buy
t in the solid piece, and slice as needed. Most
ommercial dried beefs are too moist. Coun-
ry meat processors smoke it thoroughly to
reduce the moisture content to a minimum
and to flavor it. Sauté some shredded dried
beef in butter in a frying pan to bring out its
taste, then scramble eggs with it for a hearty
breakfast. Or make brown creamed dried
beef like this: Sauté half a pound of the
shredded beef in butter until almost crisp.
Then sprinkle a handful of flour into the pan
with the beef and brown it thoroughly *without burning it*. Start adding milk gradually,
stirring all the while as it cooks over the fire
until you have a creamed dish as thick or thin
as you like it. Season with pepper, and extra
salt, if needed. Serve over toasted bread, or
with fried potatoes, for a strengthening
breakfast, or a different dinner.

Canned Meats. Campers usually are advised to avoid canned foods because of the
tins' weight, but it is not a bad idea to carry
a few extra ounces and be sure of some meat
in edible condition than to depend entirely
upon preserving uncanned meat, or living off
the land. A tin of corned beef in the pack is
good insurance against hunger. There are 12
ounces of beef in the standard can, and the
metal weighs an extra 2¾ ounces. One can
of beef, boiled in a quart or more of water
with four large potatoes cubed, dried onion
and parsley flakes, salt and pepper to taste,
makes a handsome stew for two men. The
various canned pork products like Spam,
Prem, Mor can be eaten as they are, fried or
used in various dishes. Canned bacon, when
obtainable, is excellent.

Bolognas and Sausages. Here is a field that
is seldom mentioned in a camp cookery discussion, yet it is filled with interesting possibilities. Many "foreign" kinds of bolognas
and sausages keep indefinitely without refrigeration. Some are dry and firm, some heavily
peppered, some redolent with garlic, some hot
with crushed red peppers—but just right for
an outdoor appetite. A good, genuine Italian
salame is a salted and spiced bologna; buy in
one piece and slice for lunch meat. *Cervelat*
is a *salame* without garlic. Italian *peperoni*
(sometimes spelled *pepperone*) is a spicy,
hard sausage. Parboil it in a bit of water in a
covered frying pan, then brown it. The German *landjaeger* is a small sausage or bologna,

about eight inches long. It comes in linked pairs, which are invariably hung over a rope or wire above the counter of a German delicatessen. They are flat, hard, flavorful and their name ("country hunter" in English) indicates their use—a meat that could be stuck in the pocket and carried on a hunting trip without further care. The *landjaeger* has a bigger brother called *schuetzenwurst* ("shooting sausage") containing the same meat, but as big as a *salame*. Both are ideal for campers.

CHEESE

Like bolognas and hard sausages, cheese is generally overlooked as a long-keeping, valuable source of proteins. Most men like cheese, but seldom think of it for camping. Except for an inevitable small amount of moisture in even the driest cheese, there is no waste weight. Cheese can be used as it is, with macaroni, fried with bacon or baked into biscuits. It's ideal for camping.

Bulk Cheese. Best buy is a good, sharp, dry cheddar, both for flavor and keeping qualities. Wrap securely in cheesecloth, pressing cloth against cheese, then wrap in parchment paper to keep oils from soaking through. If any mold forms, simply cut it away. It does no harm. Some cheeses, like *provolone* (piquant Italian cheese) come in protective wax cases of their own. So do Edams and Goudas, but they are rather mild for camp use. To make a creamed cheese macaroni without baking: Cook desired amount of macaroni 12 minutes in boiling, salted water; drain off water, add milk up to top of macaroni in pot, add small pieces of cheese, cook slowly and gently, stirring frequently, until cheese is melted. Remember: High heat makes cooked cheese stringy.

Packaged Cheese. All of these keep very well, better than bulk cheese; but watch the label. If it says "cheese food," it isn't all cheese, but has milk solids added. There's nothing wrong with this—some are delicious —but you will be carrying extra moisture per protein content.

DEHYDRATED FOODS

During World War II, dehydrated foods were common in stores because of the short-age of metal for cans. You could buy any kind of dehydrated soup, and even such things as dehydrated applesauce, and they were excellent. Now, only a handful of firms package dehydrated foods for campers, but their products generally are of good quality. Chief advantage is cutting down weight (15 pounds of raw potatoes reduce to two pounds dehydrated), but some of the dishes are better than the average camp cook could prepare from scratch if he tried to duplicate them. Most dehydrated soups are very good, dehydrated potatoes can scarcely be told from their original form, powdered milk and eggs make carrying these necessities feasible and there is nothing wrong with good powdered coffee.

In the Far North, where there are no cows or gardens, people live quite happily using dehydrated milk, eggs and vegetables. The second most important advantage to foods packaged especially for campers is the packaging itself. The packets are waterproof, usually tough, of convenient size. Food spoilage is almost unknown, although powdered *whole* milk and eggs might turn strong over a long period of time—as from one year to the next—in packets. Powdered *skim* milk won't do this, but it also is less nutritious, less appetizing on cereals or in coffee. Powdered cream is available. Some dehydrated potatoes and vegetables require soaking before use, but this can be done while setting up camp, and before getting the evening meal ready. Present-day dehydrated foods add immeasurably to the pleasure and convenience of outdoor living.

BREADSTUFFS

It is possible to carry baked bread for the first several days; after that, you bake biscuits or use other breadstuffs. A modern loaf of bread contains a lot of air. Reduce the bulk by taking a loaf in its waxed paper wrapper and slowly press both ends toward the middle, forcing out the air. The result is not the lightest bread in the world, but it is squeezed down to size and perfectly edible. You can make up your own biscuit mix, or buy the kind packaged by dehydrated food supply houses. If you mix your own, be very careful to carry it in an absolutely water-proof bag because it's worthless if moisture gets to the baking powder it contains. The same holds true for pancake mixes. It isn't safe to depend upon the boxes in which such mixes are sold in stores. When obtainable, hardtack and pilot's biscuits are a satisfactory substitute for baked bread or biscuits.

BUTTER

Butter is not a luxury when camping, but close to a necessity for the fats it provides (especially in cold weather) and its aid in cooking, as well as for spreading on bread-stuffs. Not easy to carry in warm weather except when canned, and even canned butter does not keep indefinitely.

DRIED BEANS, ETC.

Here are the standbys of outdoorsmen for centuries. Dried navy beans, lima beans, green peas, lentils and rice can replace potatoes in camp, supplying bulk and starches; but too steady a diet of them induces indigestion. Wherever possible, get precooked beans, rice and peas to save time on the trail. Fancy dishes are not necessary. There is no better-tasting bean dish than dried limas boiled until tender in a minimum of water, seasoned with salt and pepper, and with a dab of butter over them. A good gravy (available in dehydrated form) poured over cooked rice helps make it a meal in itself.

DRIED FRUITS

Be sure to take plenty of sugar along for these, but also be sure to take some of these along. Dried apricots, peaches, prunes, raisins, apples add a tartness to the menu that cuts the grease of camp cooking, supplies the demand for sweets if sugared well.

CONDIMENTS, SEASONINGS

Most men like mustard, most hesitate to carry it because it comes in heavy glass jars. You can buy dry mustard and mix your own by adding water whenever you need it. It's available in most stores. Pepper can be toted in the shaker-top containers in which it is sold; salt is transferred to shaker tins or other containers. There's no need to go camping without dried onion, parsley and celery flakes to vary your food's tastes. These are also available in grocery stores. Most camp cooking has a common fault—it is too insipid. Spice it with the foregoing articles, a bit of curry or chili powder or bouillon cubes.

BEVERAGES

Tea is the lightest to carry, as invigorating as coffee. Coffee should be coarse-ground for "boiling"—but don't boil it. Put coffee into cold water in pot, bring to boil, pull it aside, bring to boil again, remove and let it stand briefly, add a dash of cold water to settle it. Cocoa and chocolate are nourishing drinks, and somewhat soporific if taken before bedtime. Beef and chicken bouillon cubes or powders make stimulating warm drinks. Orange and lemon crystals make a good cold drink, and satisfy a civilized craving for something other than just water.

MISCELLANEOUS

When camping where fish are not available for the catching, carry some salt cod. If parboiled and the water is poured off to get rid of the salt, it is a hearty base for chowders, fish cakes, etc. Salted, smoked fish (like the herrings sold in small packs, and often called "blind robins") are a fine camp food, as they are, or cooked in a bit of water. There's no waste to such fish. Except for the weight of the container, peanut butter is all food, and rich in oils. Jams are good additions to camp diets. Oatmeal is the standard breakfast cereal. If you expect to do much frying, or need shortening, don't depend entirely upon bacon fat, but take along one of the vegetable shortenings available.

By Bill Wolf

CAMP COOKING OUTFITS

Caught unexpectedly in the woods you can usually improvise some sort of shelter against the elements, or make a fairly comfortable bed out of things at hand. But did you ever try to boil water without some kind of pot?

Sure, it can be done by making an Indian-type bark receptacle to hold the water, into which very hot rocks are dropped. But that's for the birds and Indians.

Furthermore, no sane Indian would dream of making hot water that way today unless paid well to perform such cute tricks. And even then the lecturing Indian would have to read some white man's book on quaint wood-craft to find out how to do it.

A skillet, and a can or kettle to "boil up" with, constituted the basic cooking outfit of the pioneer woodsman, trapper or explorer in this country. Some even dispensed with the skillet, and broiled or roasted their fish and game on spits, and wrapped their bread dough—if they had flour—around sticks to bake it over the coals. You can do the same, if you wish. In fact, most persons who camp much reach the point where they want to try such lightweight going just as an experiment. In that case, you can reduce the total weight of your cooking outfit to whatever one light kettle weighs.

However, it is safe to assume that the average camper is not a pioneer striking out into the wilderness, a trapper in uninhabited

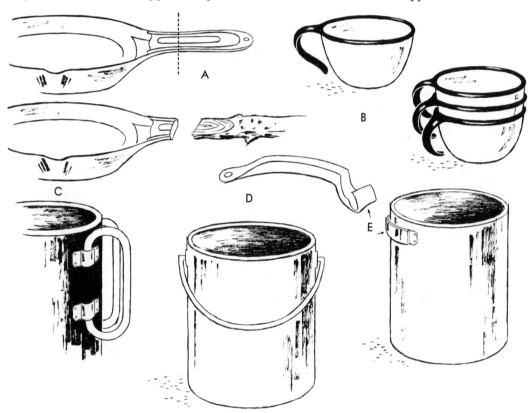

Handles are quite important where stowing away the cooking outfit compactly in a packsack is necessary. The metal handles of some frying pans are hollow. Such a handle can be cut off as in dotted line in Figure A, and a heavy stick can be inserted for use over the fire. The stick handle can be thrown away after use. The porcelain cups in Figure B have open handles, for nesting together as shown, and also because open handles do not conduct heat to burn lips and hands as closed ones do. The handles in Figure C fold flat against the coffeepot, out of the way when in the pack. The bale wire handle in D is best for kettles. The detachable handle shown in Figure E is common in most nested kits, and fits all pots and all pans.

mountains, nor an explorer: He's an ordinary camper who doesn't want to take along any more than he will need, but who doesn't want to need something he's left at home.

A sharp distinction must be made between two kinds of cooking outfits—the one where weight and space don't matter, the other designed for carrying by pack or canoe. Another distinction must be made between the person who does a lot of camping and wants a permanent outfit, and the one making a single trip of a few days.

Where it is possible to travel on a fairly large boat, as on float trips requiring no portage, or where camping can be done from an airplane, automobile, auto-and-trailer or by pack horse, it would be foolish to skimp on the cooking outfit. This does not mean that the contents of the kitchen at home should be dumped into a piano box and carried along; but you can include a good gasoline stove, a nested cooking outfit and small luxuries.

If you do not have to carry your cooking equipment more than a short distance from a trailer or plane, by all means, get one of the efficient gasoline stoves. You'll find them a pleasure to use, especially the big three-burner type. Nearly each manufacturer has some outstanding feature—one make will light

Some form of cooking grate is practical and handy when it can be carried. The grill type of strong wire, shown in Figure A, gives a firm, level surface for pots and pans. Such grates can be purchased. Those pictured in Figures B and C must be handmade. B is simply a piece of light iron, about 24 inches long, bent in shape of a U. The grate in C is made of flat, iron horizontals to accommodate several utensils. The hunter-trapper fire in Figure D is built between logs or stones which support pots and pans. This, of course, is a natural grate and needs no carrying. Flatten top of logs to support pots and pans—and keep space between logs rather narrow.

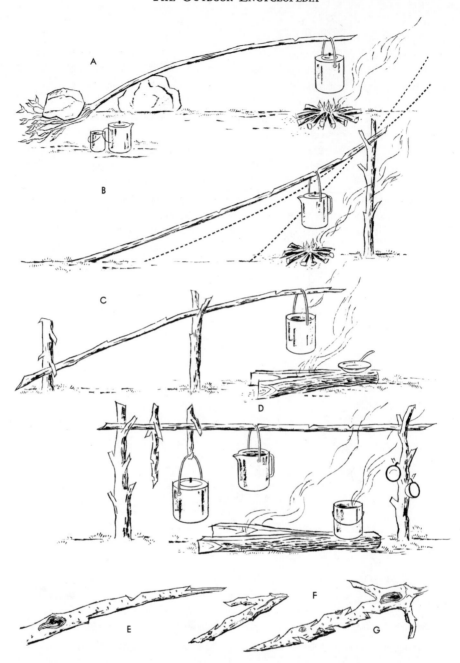

Dinglesticks and cranes are devices for suspending pots and kettles above a fire. Branches were left on the end of the one in Figure A to provide some purchase for the rock holding it down. More adjustable are the ones shown in B and C, the former by moving the angle of the stick, the second one by raising or lowering the anchor end of the dinglestick. Cranes, as in D, are adjustable, too. They usually are built in a more or less permanent camp. Figure E is an enlargement of the end of a dinglestick, showing way notch cuts can be made to hold bale wire handles. Figure F is a single-notched pothook for use on a crane; G is one with multiple notches for adjusting height of kettles above the flame. All such devices spill foods if insecure.

instantly without any preliminary warmup, another uses any kind of gasoline, a third has wings and top which open up to form working trays, or act as shields against the wind.

The nested cooking kit fits right into this sort of camping. It is compact and complete, storing easily into the back of a car, a trailer, boat or plane. In one of the best kits on the market, everything fits into the largest seven-quart kettle, which is covered by the largest frying pan, making a kit exactly nine inches in diameter and seven and a half inches high. Inside are a smaller frying pan of seven and a half inches in diameter, one five-quart kettle, one two and a half-quart kettle, a six-cup coffeepot, four plates and four cups.

Such an outfit, made of moderately heavy-gauge aluminum, weighs only a little more than five pounds, costs about $15, and will serve the needs of four persons, with exceptions that will be noted. A waterproof carrying bag will add another pound to the weight, but is worth it. The kettles have bail wire handles, and both pots and pans have a slot for attaching a detachable handle.

The same kit can be carried in a packsack, but there are some objections to it for such use. Some of the objections also apply if it is carried where weight is no object, but there the objections are easily overcome. For instance, four coffee drinkers in camp are seldom satisfied with a six-cup coffeepot. Also, four plates aren't enough for four persons. A couple of extra plates are needed in cooking, if not in eating. A larger coffeepot should be added to the kit, as well as a plate or two. Better still, one of the kettles can be used for making coffee—but, in any case, even the carefully planned nested kit must be modified to be practical. But any added items probably won't nest.

If the kit is to be used by only two persons, more modification is necessary unless you want to carry unnecessary items. The kit can be cut down for two by eliminating two of the kettles, or one of the kettles and one of the two frying pans, one plate and two cups. The large kettle and large frying pan cannot be eliminated, since they are the outer shell of the kit, unless you don't mind some loose

odds and ends. The spare space made available by discarding items can be utilized when packing the food.

A very compact outfit, consisting of a small gasoline stove, two pots and two frying pans, has certain uses when traveling through country where campfires are not permitted at hazardous periods of the year. This Primus stove carries one half pint of gasoline which will burn one and a half hours. It heats one pint of water to boiling in five minutes. The whole outfit nests inside the largest pot, which has a three and a half-pint capacity. Carrying fuel and a stove definitely is *not* recommended for most hiking trips, except under unusual circumstances.

The small personal kits are useful only for heating things, and are valueless for actual cooking since nothing is large enough. They usually consist of a frying pan, a dish which can be used as a sauce pan, a tiny kettle and a cup which nest in a cloth cover. Such kits can be used to fry one egg and two pieces of bacon, and to heat one can of beans. Hardly enough for camp appetites.

So much for the nested kits. The better ones are made of heavy-gauge aluminum, or, less frequently, of light stainless steel. Both metals are good for camp cookware, with some exceptions.

Many campers prefer to put together their own cooking outfit for the back-packing trips, rather than buy nested kits with standardized items. There are many good reasons for this, chief among which is the fact that you can get exactly what you want, although it sometimes requires a long search.

Since few men are solitary campers, it is best to consider putting together an outfit for two persons. This can be expanded for four by the addition of two more plates, another frying pan, another kettle. Odd numbers of persons pose problems camping because of tent space, room in a canoe and so on. Two in a canoe with luggage in the center, or two in a small tent are ideal—a third person is a sore thumb.

Sizes and materials will be discussed later. The following is a basic cooking outfit for two men:

1 Large frying pan *with* lid
1 Smaller frying pan (or substitutes which will be noted)
1 5-quart kettle *with* lid
1 2½-quart kettle
2 Large spoons
2 Forks
1 Spatula
1 Salt container
1 Pepper container
1 Coffeepot, or pail

It will be noticed that knives are not included. That is because each man should carry a knife. A big pocket jackknife with a four-inch blade for everything from cutting meat and fish to spreading butter and whittling is good. A sheath knife, not too large, serves the same purpose. Why have a small teaspoon along when the two big spoons (the old army style, about twice as large as a tablespoon and available in surplus stores) will serve for stirring cooking food, serving it. You can always stir sugar in coffee with the handle or a cut stick?

The spatula is included because most campers don't like to stir things in the hot frying pan with their good knife. A spatula doesn't take up much room. It is about six inches long and one inch wide. Buy one in the five-and-dime. If you *really* want to go light you can yank it from its wooden handle, and have a wisp of metal that can be fastened easily into a split stick in camp. No weight at all.

The five-and-dime, and similar shopping spots, are great places for hunting camping material because the inexpensive cooking equipment they sell often is just right for back-packing because it is light. Take lids, for instance. They carry the nearly flat—light lids with a wire ring for lifting which can be flattened for packing away. Don't buy lids with knobs for lifting. The fewer projections the better. And don't forget lids. It is best to have one for each utensil—failing that, get two large ones to cover any size frying pan or pot. Water boils much more rapidly when the kettle is covered, and foods can be parboiled in a covered frying pan instead of fried.

The coffeepot is a problem. Unless you can acquire exactly the right kind—with practically no spout, and with folding handles—it is far better to buy a pail with a bail wire handle. The average household coffeepot with projecting spout and handle is a nuisance.

All kettles and pots should be broad, rather than high and slender, because they catch the heat better. A camping party of two could get by with one kettle, but an extra is good to have along. A stew can be cooking in one, while prunes or some dried fruit can be cooking in the other, or the second can be used to heat water. Ditto with frying pans—one can be made to do, two are better. However, there are substitutes for the second frying pan. For example, sometimes a flat cookie tin is a good and light substitute. This is a rectangular metal item with a raised edge, and on it you can cook potatoes and fish at the same time, although they require watching since the metal isn't heavy and burning is a hazard.

Such a tin weighs much less than another frying pan, and, if packed right next to the back, it serves the same purpose in the packsack as a pack board does—it keeps rough items from gouging the back. Since they are cheap, they can be discarded at the end of the trip if desired.

The much-despised army mess kit with the divided lid actually has its uses in replacing the second frying pan, although not many things can be fried in it. In two-man camping use the divided lid for baking biscuits, and the pan part for frying certain foods, keeping other foods warm or as a soup plate for the noontime lunch. The divided lid is just right for making two nice long biscuits. You can fill the two divisions, which are sort of half ovals, with dough, fry it for a while on top of the fire to bake the bottom, then lean it at an angle to the hot coals to bake and brown the top.

Strong aluminum probably is as good as any material for the kettles, and even the frying pans, although lightweight steel frying pans have gone along on many camping trips. A big aluminum pan a foot wide comes in handy when four go camping. If you must make a choice, always remember that one really large pan is worth two small ones.

Salt and pepper containers are essential. It's all right, perhaps, to dive a hand into a cloth or plastic bag to get salt, but a shaker beside the fire gives the camp a more civilized air. Large shakers of aluminum (which look like a can with a shaker top) can be found in five-and-dimes or household departments of other stores. Fill with salt, put waxed paper in the shaker top and screw down. The salt won't come out until you remove the paper. A similar device is all right for pepper, but black pepper usually comes in a sturdy box with shaker top.

The buyer should pay close attention to handles for the reason mentioned earlier— you don't want anything that projects in your pack. Bail wire handles are fine for pots and kettles, but make sure the bail ears don't project too far from the side. The folding wire handles, found on coffeepots, as a rule cause no trouble. In cups, don't take any handle but the one *open* at the bottom. With this kind of handle, the cups nest easily in each other, occupying little space and they won't burn your fingers from hot coffee.

The frying pan handle is a problem. Some big aluminum pans have detachable handles, but you're out of luck if you lose a detachable handle. Light steel pans come with heat-proof handles, which are hollow. By sawing this off, the metal handle can be discarded and a wooden one whittled and inserted on the spot. This saves space and weight. Some frying pans for outdoor cooking are made with handles that fold inside the pan, some with handles that fold over the outside. These are good. The ring-type handle, which folds down flat, is the only kind for pot and pan lids, just to emphasize something mentioned earlier.

Brawny he-men who don't mind scorching the hair off the backs of their hairy hands, or raking their food out of the ashes and eating it with relish, cook without the aid of grates. More sensible campers take some simple form of grate to make *sure* that they have at least one level, stable surface for at least one cook pot or pan.

The simplest form of grate is the hunter-

trapper fire between two logs (or stones laid in similar manner), but this is none too ideal although it doesn't require carrying anything extra along. It's usually too wide for the rather small pots or pans used. A better choice is the U-shaped rod of light metal. This is 24 inches long before it is bent into a U shape, which is then about 10 inches long, four inches wide. One of these on stones or flattened logs gives the cook a firm base for a pot. Two or more practically create a stove.

Grates of the grill pattern are available with legs that theoretically sink into the ground and hold things above the fire. Don't depend upon them too much, however. It is better to remove the legs and use the grate across a rock fireplace because it gets too wobbly if the spikes are stuck in the ground. It, too, like the flat cookie tin, can be packed into the bag right against the back to act as a packboard and prevent gouging.

Nessmuk (George Washington Sears, a shoemaker who lived at Wellsboro, Pennsylvania, and probably influenced outdoor living more than any other man in the past century) is credited with the design of the other grate, the one shaped like a V standing on three legs. In effect, this is a prefabricated hunter-trapper fire without sides. If carried in a pack, it should be no longer than the pack is deep—say, 28 inches. Nessmuk used flat pieces of iron for the horizontal bars, $\frac{1}{4}$-inch thick, $\frac{7}{8}$-inch wide. The spikes were of the same weight. The spike at the closed end of the V was held by a bolt two inches long to allow some play in spreading the V. The two spikes at the other ends of the horizontals were bolted on more tightly, but still loose enough to allow folding up for carrying. Chief drawback to this, as well as the grate held on spikes, is the fact that much of the fire's heat is wasted at the open sides. A good blacksmith or metal-worker can whip up this, and the U-shaped iron, in a few minutes. You can't buy them ready-made.

The dinglestick is a time-honored campfire accessory. And, like lots of time-honored things, it is open to some question. The dinglestick is a branch used to suspend a cooking utensil over a fire, easier to picture than to describe. In its most elementary form, one end is held down by a rock or log while the other end is raised above the fire by leaning the stick on another rock or log. It is inclined to roll when thus, however, so the anchored end should have some limbs and leaves left on to give the anchor rock a grip. The two other forms pictured are better variations.

The crane in Figure D is in much the same class. It's too much trouble for its worth. However, it does have an advantage in holding pots and kettles handy near the fire, and it is useful for some kinds of cooking. You can change the height of the pot above the fire at will by raising or lowering one or both ends of the horizontal bar.

If camping for the first time, you are bound to make mistakes in choosing and using your cooking outfit. You will learn through experience, and form your own conclusions. For instance, some experienced woodsmen everywhere use the dinglestick as a cooking aid, especially to "boil up" at noontime, or in the evening—that is, to heat water quickly in a pail for coffee or tea. You will have to decide many things for yourself through the trial and error method, including the use of the dinglestick and the crane. It all boils down to using your own head, and correcting on the next trip the errors made on the preceding outing.

By Bill Wolf

CAMP STOVES

For camps in the open, where firewood is available, what camper wouldn't build an open wood fire A real "campfire" appeals to our primitive inheritance which is perhaps the chief urge that sends us into the open. In fact, a camp without a wood fire seems to be no camp at all.

With the wood campfire there is romance, the delicious smell of the smoke, the cheerfulness and the glow of embers in the evening. Food roasted, broiled or baked over wood coals has a special allure.

And the campfire also shows its superiority when it comes to toasting yourself or drying wet clothes. Such a fire costs nothing, and there is nothing to transport but your ax.

But in spite of all that can be said for an open fire, there are times when a stove is indicated by common sense. You cannot heat a closed tent adequately with an open fire—you need one of lean-to or open-front type. Yet with an open tent, in weather well below zero, you would be chopping wood all day and hugging the blaze to keep warm. At many public and roadside campgrounds no firewood may be available, and if women are in the party privacy makes a closed tent desirable.

Cooking in a heavy rain can be an awful chore and sometimes impossible over an open fire, and cooks whose whole experience has been in a kitchen take more naturally to the stove. So let's explore the problems and advantages of the camp stove.

Today the most popular camp stove is one that uses gasoline for fuel, with two or three burners. Some of the new ones burn white and leaded gasoline. The gasoline stove solves the cooking problem admirably, particularly for boiling or frying, and a separate oven can be had for it. But there is no way you can broil tastefully with gasoline.

This type of stove is ideal, and often a must for public camping grounds, and also for certain states where nonresidents are prohibited from lighting a wood fire except when accompanied by a resident or guide. Such a stove should have at least two burners so boiling and frying can go on simultaneously.

For any territory where firewood is available, the sheet-iron, wood-burning stove has decided advantages. You'll seldom see one today in city stores, and they're unfamiliar to campers with little experience. But on the frontier where you meet the old-timers, the sheet-iron, wood-burning stove is about the only type ever considered.

Such a stove usually weighs a little more than the gas stove, and is usually bulkier. But there is no gas to transport, and the sheet-iron stove is not difficult to carry, even over a portage or on a pack horse. You can cook on it in the rain, safely warm closed tents and cabins, dry clothing around it and broil and toast over an open pothole.

If it has an oven, it is perfect for baking and roasting. Without an oven, a folding reflector baker faced against its hot side can be used.

The standard A-wall tent seems best adapted to a wood-burning stove. Such a tent seven by nine feet is about the smallest that is suitable, and the nine by 12 size is better for two men, because your beds will not be too near the stove. The stove should not be closer than 18 inches to the wall of the tent, which should *not* have a sewed-in floor.

The telescoping stovepipe had best go straight up through the roof, rather than have elbows to angle it through the back wall, and it should extend at least six inches above the peak of your tent outside so wind won't blow sparks directly against the canvas. There should be a fireguard where the pipe goes through the roof or wall. This guard can be had from most any tentmaker.

An asbestos guard is better than a tin one as it does not rattle on windy days. The guard separates the pipe from the canvas by about three inches. If the stove has no legs, and you'd like to raise it to a more convenient height, just drive four stout stakes in the ground and cap each with an old tin can.

Such stoves are provided with an adjustable draft hole so you can make them burn as fast or as slow as you wish. But you should never fill the stove full of wood and then go away and leave it with the draft wide open. If you do, it's liable to become red hot in a hurry, and then you may have the stage set for a conflagration.

We read a lot in fiction about the "Yukon" stove that's used in tents and small cabins in the North. You'd hunt a long way trying to buy one, for a Yukon stove is merely made of anything from old tomato and condensed milk cans to a gasoline drum.

The most famous, and one of the best stoves for tents and small cabins, is the Sheepherder stove of the West. It is a rather large stove of box type with capacity for cooking a meal for five or six campers. It is about 27 inches long, a foot high and wide, and has an oven five by eight by 11 inches, and weighs 27 pounds.

Any sheet-iron stove will burn out in time, but the Sheepherder stove has the reputation of lasting longer without burning out than any other made of sheet iron. Some have been in almost continuous use for four years.

The only place I know of where you can get the Sheepherder stove is the Smilie Company, 536 Mission Street, San Francisco 5, California. These large camp outfitters also have a smaller and lighter stove, 20 by 12 by 12 inches with a small oven, weighing only 12 pounds, and less expensive. This is fine for two or three campers, does not have the long life of the Sheepherder. Both types come with telescoping pipe.

Many of the small stores near hunting and trapping country in the West and in Canada also have stoves of the box type, without oven, about 20 by 12 by 12 inches, with a door to the firebox which also has an adjustable draft hole. Four or five joints of stovepipe, not telescopic, come with them. They also are very satisfactory, and if you have a folding reflector baker you can use that faced against their hot side.

There used to be a few folding box stoves on the market, but all but one seem to have disappeared. The only one available now is made by Sims Stoves, Lovell, Wyoming. It folds flat to about three inches thick, and has a stovepipe. This is a splendid, well-made little stove, and because it folds so flat it is easy to pack.

One drawback to the stoves mentioned is that they are both bulky and heavy, and cannot be sent by mail. So if you live far from their source of procurement you have a large express bill which, added to their cost, makes them a little expensive. Herter's of Waseca, Minnesota, make a little midget of a stove that is remarkable in several ways. This small stove, which Herter calls the "French Canadian Ice Fish House and Duck Blind Stove," is well made of heavy sheet iron, and yet is light in weight.

Because of its light weight and size they are able to sell it at slightly less than five dollars postpaid, largely because they do not include a stovepipe with it.

Still it will warm up a small tent or a small trapper's cabin very nicely, and there is capacity on top for both a kettle and a frying pan at the same time.

This stove is so small, takes up so little room, that it ought to make things very snug and comfortable in a small tent, and it looks like just what the trapper needs for his line cabins.

The small "Knapsacker" folding reflector baker furnished by the Smilie Company would be a "natural" for baking and roasting with this stove.

By Col. Townsend Whelen

CAMPING'S ESSENTIAL LITTLE THINGS

The major planning on a camping trip is focused on the tent, the grub lists and bedding—the major necessities. The minor things—which can assume major proportions when they're missing—are likely to be overlooked.

It's possible to improvise shelter if there's no tent, make a bed without blankets and live off the land for food if you have to. But what camper can whump up an aspirin tablet, or create any but the most primitive fishhook when he's miles back in the bush?

Neither is any man so clever that he can replace the dry kindling for the morning fire that he forgot to take into the tent the night before—when the worst rainstorm of the year just happened to put in its appearance. Of course, you can always go out in the soaking woods and find kindling, but . . .

Over a period of years of living out of a packsack on camping trips chances are you'll come to the conclusion that it is the little essentials that make the difference between just a camping trip and a memorable experience in the outdoors.

There will be days of drenching rain when life inside cramped quarters of a tent will become mind-numbing without a small pocket-sized book. You can't sleep all the time. There may be a night when it is too early to go to bed, and the downpour outside discourages sitting around the fire. One plumber's candle inside the tent makes everything cheerful, and encourages conversation.

Since immediate personal care comes first, let's start there. Whether you shave, brush your teeth, wash your face or comb your hair when you're on a camping trip is entirely up to you. However, if you intend to do any of these things, you'd better plan ahead.

You probably won't forget a razor, but how about a mirror? Some geniuses can shave without consulting one, but the average man likes to make sure what he is cutting. And how about soap that will lather, and a pocket comb?

You needn't pack your razor and blades in a box. Take the bare razor and enough blades to last. A metal razor needs no protection, and you can afford to use a new blade for each shave since you won't be doing that often.

An untended beard gets itchy during the first week (the usual length of a camping trip) and uncomfortable until the second week or so. So if you shave at all, plan on doing it with moderate frequency.

The small metal mirror that you can hang on a twig is sufficient, and nearly weightless. As for soap, suit yourself. A tiny, five-and-dime store tube of brushless cream is good. So are the small tubes of lather cream. But, the soap you carry for doing dishes, washing socks and scrubbing your face will suffice. Just wet your beard, rub on the soap, use water to work up a lather and start the surgery.

If you don't want to use the same soap for both dishes and your personal hygiene, take a cake of Packer's Tar Soap. It lathers in almost any water and can be used for bathing, shaving or shampooing.

Although two men could share all things except a toothbrush, they seldom do. Your personal ditty bag will probably start out with these items:

1 Razor and sufficient blades
1 Metal mirror
1 Tube shaving cream, or cake of soap
1 Small comb
1 Toothbrush, and tooth powder or paste

Although it doesn't go into your ditty bag, a towel is a natural accessory. It need not be a heavy bath towel. The small, lightweight hand towels found in hotels, but seldom in homes, are ideal, though this is not to suggest stealing them from hotels because they can be purchased in stores.

But don't take a new towel of this type on a trip, because they are not very soft or absorbent until they have been laundered several times. If you want to carry a washcloth on a back-packing trip choose any kind you wish—but they are always wet when they shouldn't be, and mess up a pack.

The other things that go into a personal kit aren't easy to list, because the individual's needs differ. Some men have more aches and pains than others. Some have corns, and some don't. Some use cigarette lighters and require fluid and flints. Some need laxatives, some don't. Some are inclined to get distressed stomachs, especially if the cook uses too much grease. Some can anticipate tooth trouble.

You are the best judge of such needs for yourself, so go prepared—but don't load yourself down.

The only remedy recommended for all campers is a small, flat tin of aspirin, or some other pain-inhibiting tablet. Anyone is likely to catch a cold, suffer from neuralgia or have other aches. The need for a laxative is much overrated, but some persons think they can't live without them.

Into your personal kit, then, go these additional items (eliminate those not applying to you):

1 Flat tin of aspirin, Acetidine or Bufferin
1 Can lighter fluid and extra flints
1 Container of soda mint tablets, or other digestive and antacid aids
Laxatives
Toothache drops
Corn plasters.

One word about lighter fluid: the cans it comes in are impractical because the pouring spout is too easily bent or even broken off in your pack. Some kinds come in bottles, and they are too heavy and may smash. Try to find a small tin with a flat, screw-down top and transfer the lighter fluid from its original container to this.

By this time, it must be apparent that you need some sort of checklist. One is necessary, not only for these things, but for *everything* that goes into your packsack.

And don't make the mistake of checking off an item against the list when you purchase it, because it is easy to forget to put a new purchase into the bag. Check it off when actually packing for the trip. Keep this checklist from year to year right in the packsack, then there is no need to figure out a new one for each trip.

There's no harm in keeping certain items in the packsack from one trip to another. You're doubly sure not to forget them. Some have to be replaced or replenished at the end of a trip, but they are always there, ready for the next expedition.

Nails may seem a curious thing to take along camping, but they're handy, especially in the semipermanent camp where you may stay several days. For example, they can be used to fasten down securely the two saplings that are suspended between logs to form a stretcher-type bed. When driven into the flat top of a pole, they form a point over which a tent grommet can fit. Several nails driven into a tent pole can be used for hanging up clothing and other articles that shouldn't be on the ground or ground cloth. You wouldn't do this on a long-term camp tent where you carry poles, for the nails would punch air-conditioning where you don't want it.

Blanket pins perform obvious services where large pins are required, and less obvious ones such as helping suspend meats and other supplies from a line between trees where it will keep better than in the pack, and be safe from varmints.

A plumber's candle, that short, fat, long-burning candle, can help *warm* an enclosed tent as well as light it. The campfire is fine as a source of illumination except that it flickers too much.

So add these odds and ends to the list:

4 Large blanket pins
2 Plumber's candles
8 or 10 nails, several sizes
1 *Filled* waterproof match container, to be used only in emergencies when the regular supply of matches is wet or exhausted
1 Sewing kit, with needles, threads, buttons
1 Small roll of Mystik Tape, or small cut patches, for quick but permanent repairs to tears in sleeping bags
Toilet tissue

Some of these things might seem unimportant, when viewed from comfortable home surroundings. But they can be major items when you're many miles from nowhere. Tears in sleeping bags, allowing the "innards" to escape, are especially annoying if you have no means of repair—and the only way to repair them is to sew the ripped part, or use something like Mystik Tape. Useful for tent repairs, too. Adhesive tape is, at best, only a temporary repair medium. As for toilet tissue, leaves are an unsatisfactory substitute. Half a roll will last two campers for a week.

Even if you are no fisherman a few coiled leaders, a short length of line and a few lures appropriate for the fish that inhabit your camping country can provide a welcome change of diet.

There are lots of campers who try to wash camp pots, pans and dishes with sand, or they hunt around for scouring rush. It's so much easier to carry one of those metal sponges which are nearly weightless and bulkless. One of these and a bit of soap (but not for the frying pan, which shouldn't be touched by soap any more than the interior of a coffeepot should) will clean all pots, metal dishes and cutlery. The soap isn't even necessary if you add some wood ashes from the fire to a greasy pot. The lye and grease form a crude soap, if used with very hot

water, or if brought to a boil together in the pot to be cleaned.

The "permanently-packed" bag therefore receives such additional items as:

1 Very compact fishing kit
1 Metal sponge for dishwashing
1 or 2 extra keys for opening tins (such as corned beef) so you don't have to ruin an ax or knife blade
1 White cotton glove, usually for left hand, for cooking over fire
Several pieces of fine rope of varying lengths, which will come in mighty handy

All this looks like a lot when put down in a list. But it takes up very little space or weight in your pack. And it can mean the difference between comfort and discomfort.

Then there are always such things as a pencil flashlight, or a pair of the thin leather "pullman slippers" that crush up into almost nothing. The slippers are useful to put on at the end of day when you're sitting around the fire, when it is a relief to get out of your walking shoes or when you have to go out of the tent at night. They are much lighter than moccasins. The flashlight will come in handy when you need light in a hurry.

LITTLE THINGS AROUND CAMP

And how about "small" things to remember when you're actually camping? Like taking in the kindling at night. Even when it doesn't rain, kindling is apt to be wet with dew and slow starting if left outside without cover overnight. So take your dry, firm twigs and branches to bed with you. They usually wind up as part of your pillow, covered with odds and ends of clothing. But when morning comes, you can start a fire instantly in any kind of weather. It isn't a bad idea to keep kindling inside the tent even during the day.

A small piece of waterproofed cloth—*not* a standard tarpaulin material because that is too heavy—will serve the same purpose in keeping moisture off fine firewood, and anything else that must be kept dry, where tent space is at a premium.

Among other small things to make camp living easier and more pleasant:

Keep clothing off the ground even in dry weather, because it absorbs moisture from the earth, especially if made of cotton. Use as little cotton material in camp as possible. Wool is far better.

Air your bedding, whether blankets or sleeping bag, each morning if weather permits. If rain gets bedding wet, dry it out *thoroughly* in front of the fire, even if it means siting up half the night to do it. There's nothing colder or more uncomfortable than wet bedding, and you won't sleep in it anyhow. You might as well dry it out.

Go without clean shirts, clean pants, clean handkerchiefs or even clean thoughts, but don't go without clean socks if the day involves much walking. A good *woolen* sock (even in hottest weather, it should be wool), is spongy and alive, and kind to the feet if kept clean. If sweated and matted down, it loses its virtues. Carry spares and wash socks at every opportunity, even if it means pinning them outside your pack when they're partly dry and toting them through the day. The aforementioned blanket pins will come in handy for this. This suggestion is not based upon cleanliness, but just plain comfort.

Try to find a large flat stone, or hew a log to a flat upper surface, or clear some space beside the fire, and place all cooking utensils and ingredients there. If you put down a spoon, a fork, the pepper, the knife, at any old place around the fire, you are going to waste time finding things, and get them dirty in the bargain. Also pick one clear spot to put all loose odds and ends that have to be taken from your packsack, even if it is only an overnight stop. Grass and leaves hide small but important items too well to ignore this precaution.

You can beat anybody bringing water to a boil from scratch—if they start with cold water from a brook or lake while you get your water several hours in advance. Considerable cooking time can be saved in a semipermanent camp by keeping a pailful of water standing in the daytime sun (covered, of course, to keep out the flavoring ingredients blown about by the wind). Since the sun takes as many as 20 to 30 degrees off its temperature, it comes to a boil much more quickly than ice-cold water fresh from the source.

The most wearisome thing about camping is not the hiking, nor the pack-carrying, nor the labor involved, but the constant squatting or sitting flat on the ground. It is unfortunate, but modern man is used to chairs.

Where it's at all possible, try to simulate a chair, especially in the semipermanent camp where time allows. Build up stones, logs or take advantage of contours of the ground, and relax.

Another hint on comfort: a hot drink, or a bit of food, taken before turning in helps bring on sleep which is important on a camping trip.

These suggestions could go on for considerable space. You will learn a lot in actual practice if you're making your first trip. If you're a veteran camper, you already have some good tips of your own.

By Bill Wolf

CHAPTER 5

cooking

FISH AND GAME IN GENERAL

THERE IS no mystery to fish and game cookery. With a few exceptions, meat and fowl can be handled in almost exactly the same way as beef, veal, domestic chickens, ducks and turkeys—if the cook will remember that wild meat usually is drier than the store-bought kind and care must be taken to keep it moist while cooking. It also often is tender enough to require less cooking time than beef or poultry. Its so-called gaminess has been exaggerated, and most of this gamy flavor is in the fat, which can be removed.

The only mystery about preparing game has been created by would-be gourmets, who like to call their dishes *à la Something or Other*, and add exotic ingredients not obtainable at the corner grocery. Our first settlers, and country people who depended upon game for fresh meat, made simple dishes with what they had at hand and called them Brunswick stew, burgoo, jugged hare and hasenpfeffer. The gunner who wouldn't hesitate to try cooking "rabbit, hunter's style," might shy from the same thing if he encountered it under its fancy hotel name of *lapin à la chasseur*, or turn from squirrel stew if he found it masquerading as *salmis d'écureuil*.

Pheasants are so much like domestic chickens that they can be prepared from any good cookbook recipe for fowl. If roasted, however, their dry meat must be moistened by strips of bacon or thin slices of salt pork laid across them, or by constant basting with butter. Roasting them in a *covered* pan, taking off the cover only in the last minutes to brown them, helps retain their scant moisture.

The same thing applies to wild turkeys. Handle exactly as domestic turkeys.

To a lesser extent, grouse of all kinds can be cooked as would breasts of chicken.

Speaking generally, as much game is spoiled in the field as in the kitchen. Large animals (deer and such) should be cleaned and bled when killed, then hung from 10 to 15 days, in *cold climates*, but much less in warm. Green venison is as undesirable as green beef. You should clean rabbits and squirrels soon after they are shot, and quail, grouse, pheasants and similar birds at least on the day they were killed. One school of thought says birds should not be cleaned until ready for use, after hanging some days to age. Few subscribe to that. Never use water in drawing game. Put an old cloth in your hunting coat for wiping out the body interior, or use dead grass.

In cooking, salt draws moisture from meat and should never be added until the last few minutes in baking, broiling or fying, unless you are roasting a bird or small animal whole, in which case salt can be rubbed into the body interior with the pepper. In stews and like dishes, where extraction of the meat juices to flavor the whole is desirable, salt can be used from the start.

By Bill Wolf

FIELD CARE

DEER

To many hunters the fun of deer hunting ends when the shooting stops. Field dressing is considered a chore and butchering too complicated to try. The truth is the fun of deer hunting can carry right through until a sirloin of venison is on the table before you.

All butchering requires is common sense and knowledge of a few rules. Most inexperienced butchers process their deer before it's properly aged which makes it tough and flat tasting. With proper aging, even the meat of an old buck becomes tender and delicious.

The temperature of the storage space should be maintained between 32° and 38°F.

Freezing should be avoided until the meat is properly packaged and ready for the freezer. Hang the carcass in a chill room at least a week, and two weeks is better.

Clean the body cavity thoroughly before aging. Some say this practice is detrimental to the meat but professional packing houses even scrub the cavity with water. After washing, allow the cavity to drain and hang the deer by the back legs with the head down. The skin should be left on during the aging process.

When the meat is aged, skin the animal and butcher. Make your big cuts first and your little cuts later and you'll have no trouble.

By Wayne Judy

RABBITS

Proper field care is essential if your rabbits are to be fit to eat. Properly prepared, they are superb fare—perhaps the finest of all wild foods. Preparation for the table begins right after you bag a bunny. Handling on the spot is the difference between mild, tender meat and a strong, stringy carcass that isn't worth cooking. Remove the entrails immediately. It's popular to stuff the eviscerated bunny into a hunting coat, but a rabbit carried outside, tied to the belt, is easier to skin later on. When temperatures are high, skin the rabbit as soon as the hunt is over and store it in the refrigerator. In cold weather (under 45° F.) hang rabbits outdoors for several days; freezing may improve the flavor, but alternate freezing and thawing over a period of days has the opposite effect.

By Erwin A. Bauer

DUCKS

Most duck hunting is done during week ends. The hunter pulls out on Friday, possibly shoots a few birds that same night and returns home Sunday with his spoils. Using the word "spoils" accurately hits the nail right on the head. Tens of thousands of ducks are spoiled during the hunting season and there are many reasons why. After you have killed your ducks, try to keep them separated as much as possible, and then hang them to dry for a few hours as soon as you return to camp. Never toss your ducks in the back of your car where they have no air.

Keep your game birds hung on the north side of your shack and be sure they are protected from flies. Clean your ducks as soon as possible and get them to a freezer. If you have no freezer and no ice, dig a hole and fill with fresh moss or grass so your birds will be fresh when you start for home.

Some hunters hang ducks by the feet, others by the head—either way is all right. Some don't like to draw a duck until it is plucked. If your game is badly shot up, clean as soon as possible. A good duck strap is much better than carrying your birds in your game pocket. Birds soon "ripen" in your shooting jacket, especially on a warm day. It isn't wise to freeze in the field ducks if you can avoid it.

There are several ways to clean the feathers off ducks. After years of experience at our duck club, where we clean all of our ducks, I have found a patented compound to be by far the best on the market. It is a mixture of rosin and wax and after dipping the ducks into it the pinfeathers can be shelled off when it hardens. This compound was designed to take the drudgery out of picking wild waterfowl, though it can be used to advantage in plucking domestic ducks and geese. It is scientifically formulated to penetrate to the base of the feathers, pinfeathers and down without injury to the skin of the bird.

A blowtorch is also a good finisher. Simply pick your duck dry and then singe with the torch. A blowtorch has more intense heat than blazing paper. However, the torch method does not take out stubborn pinfeathers.

Some use paraffin. First pick the duck dry and chop off the wings. Heat a kettle of water until it is boiling, then drop in the paraffin. When the paraffin is melted, dip your duck and pull it up and down slowly. Hang it until cool, then scrape. This method will take out most of the pinfeathers. One pound of wax is enough for several birds and can be used over and over again, if strained.

After you have removed feathers, down and pinfeathers, draw the bird, being sure to save the liver and gizzard for the dressing or gravy.

By Jimmy Robinson

FISH

Here are some hints to help you keep fish fresh and prime, so that you may savor the joys of eating them as fully as those of catching them.

If you are camping and want to get fish home in good shape, better clean each as you catch it. Be sure to get all blood out along the backbone. Wipe the fish dry, with grass if nothing else is available, but do not wash in water if you intend to keep the fish even for a few hours. Fish cleaned, wiped and hung on a bush for a few moments will dry nicely.

Never put green grass or leaves in your creel. It heats. Dry grass is all right but see that the fish are dry, too. And lay them in grass in your creel so they won't touch. Ever notice how trout touching in a creel get streaked? They soften as well! Dry grass lets dry air get around each fish.

Low-altitude fishing means wet air; high-altitude fishing will be in dry air. Fish keep better and longer at the high, dry altitudes. Same goes for wet or dry weather regardless of altitude.

Never put dead fish in a pail of water. It's a good way to spoil your catch. Never clean a fish and leave it soaking in a pan of water. You might better hang it on a bush to dry, with some cheesecloth around it to keep flies away.

If you cannot discipline yourself to clean fish as you catch them, do it as quickly as possible afterward. Stomach contents, gills and blood will quickly start deteriorating and taint the fish. Never put uncleaned fish on ice. Be sure any icebox has a drain, so melted ice doesn't flood the fish. Whenever possible, try to avoid having fish touch in an icebox, put cracked ice between them. Be sure the icebox is not airtight, and that it is clean.

To keep trout in high mountains, draw, dry and wrap in dry grass in the creel. In camp, put salt and pepper along the backbone (inside) and hang the trout all night on a string between trees. Don't let them touch. During the day keep them in dry grass in a cool place. Trout can be kept quite a few days this way. Then soak half an hour before using—and they'll look and taste like fresh trout.

By Byron W. Dalrymple

COOKING FISH

Fish would no doubt be America's most popular food if our 17 million licensed fishermen had as many skillful fish cooks to serve up their catches. For to get the most out of a fish, the cook must be nearly as wily as the angler, and at least as understanding of its habits and nature.

Roughly generalizing, species from clear water are more delicately flavored than those taken in salt water, and with a few exceptions, require less complicated seasoning. The character of the fish should govern its treatment in the kitchen: trout and salmon which furiously battle the angler are like game birds, with a high gusto of their own easily spoiled by too much fussing over; cod which fights like an old boot needs the help of oysters, shrimp or other seafood to accentuate the tang of the sea. Their eating habits must be considered too, since there are vegetarian fish, insect feeders, shellfish eaters and cannibals, all with their distinctive savors.

Then there are the fat and the lean, the latter needing much better. Fresh-water fish are usually lean, notable exceptions being lake and salmon trout, whitefish, catfish, eels and those two fat fish, salmon and shad, which are sea fish coming into fresh water only to spawn. In the last class is also the mullet which ascends rivers during the breeding season.

Among lean sea fish are the cod and its relatives, the ling, cusk, pollock and hake; the croaker, the weakfish and the tautog;

likewise the flounder and related flat fish, except the giant halibut, which is fat.

Another dividing line is between scaly fish and the scaleless ones you skin, some of the latter, including eels, skate and the entire catfish family, are distinctly improved by marinating. Eels, skate, blacks and the carp (which loses most of its scales when domesticated) are about the only fish that combine well with red wine, all others requiring white wine to enhance their more delicate flavor.

The young of all varieties have finer and more tender texture than the old. Besides there is that simplest of classifications, the large and the small, from pan frys to those which are so big that they must be butchered into oven or pot-sized cuts.

Besides, there is perishability to consider. Some fish begin to deteriorate the minute they have given their last flop and should be kept alive until ready for the fire. Others improve by being wrapped in cloth and matured in the refrigerator for one or two days. A general rule applying here is to eat at once those taken from the top of the water. Deep sea bottom dwellers and feeders are better the next day, for their meat ripens like beef.

The only way to untangle the intricacies of cooking fish, unless you catch them yourself and learn their culinary characteristics, is to talk with anglers and then make use of all the wisdom stored up since Izaak Walton began to record it three hundred years ago.

Boil no fish unless you wish afterward to mask it in mayonnaise, use it in a salad or put it in a pie. And then never cook it in plain water, but in a well seasoned courtbouillon. Is there a dish more tasteless than boiled cod with a gluey white sauce and a badly boiled potato?

COURTBOUILLON FOR BOILING OR POACHING FISH

Liquid to cover fish	6-10 peppercorns
1 onion, sliced	Salt
1 garlic clove	Bouquet of herbs
1 carrot, sliced	(Bay leaf, parsley
½ celery stalk,	and another herb
sliced	of your choosing)

For liquid use the water in which other fish or seafood has been boiled. Or use plain water and include some cut up, lesser fish with the other ingredients, or a fish head and backbone. Mix half dry white wine with the cold liquid, or add the juice of a lemon, or just a couple of tablespoons of vinegar. Bring all to boiling point and cook for a half hour; strain through cloth, and bring to boiling point again preferably in an oval fish kettle. Put in the fish, either wrapped in cloth or laid on a rack and simmer until done, allowing six to seven minutes to the pound for soft and medium-sized fish, and nine to 10 minutes for hard-fleshed or large fish. If eaten hot there must be a rich sauce made from some of the reduced broth, with lemon juice, plenty of butter and minced herbs, and egg yolk for thickening, in any variation to suit the fancy and kind of fish. A good strong courtbouillon, if it has had enough heads and backbones cooked in it, can be boiled down until it jellies when chilled, forming a natural aspic which is grand on a hot day with fish fillets imbedded in it, and a garnish of cucumber salad surrounding it.

If brook trout are so plentiful that you tire of them when prepared in the simplest manner, here is an old country recipe which would be good in any state where the trout season stays open until apples are ripe.

BROOK TROUT IN CIDER

To 8 trout:

1½ quarts cider	6 scallions, sliced
1 small carrot,	(or 1 small onion)
sliced	3 sprigs herbs
1 celery stalk,	Salt and pepper
sliced	to taste

Bring all to boiling point, add the trout and slowly simmer, but do not let boil, for 10 minutes or less. Drain, keep hot, quickly reduce liquid to three cups. Heat two tablespoons butter, add two tablespoons flour and stir; then add liquid and stir until it thickens. Pour over fish, and sprinkle with minced parsley or chervil. Or use less cider, arrange all in a covered dish and poach in the oven.

PAN FISH

Small fish are best for the pan. But many people prefer this frying method for some of the lean larger fish, which must, of course, be cut into convenient pieces. Dry thoroughly in a folded towel. Mix flour, salt and pepper. Lay fish on a plate, dredge thickly on one side and then turn over and dredge the other side. Have plenty of butter or bacon fat well heated in pan, put in the fish so they do not touch each other and fry rather slowly until half done and crusty. Turn and cook on other side. Take up on a hot platter and garnish with grilled tomatoes or stuffed peppers. Eat with tartar sauce or mayonnaise.

A neat way to fix small fish is to lay them in the pan, heads toward the center, tails pointing outward. Fill the open spaces with smaller fish and when ready to turn, place a plate over them and invert the pan. The fish will come out whole on the plate in the original pattern. Add more fat to pan, quickly heat and slide the fish from the plate back into the pan in the same wheel formation. Finish frying. Set plate over them again, invert pan and they are on the plate ready for the table.

PERCH

The lovely flavor is enough to make us forgive perch for all their bones. They grow larger in the South than in the North and are a favorite fresh-water fish in the rich gourmet market of New Orleans, where they are always broiled, or poached in lightly seasoned courtbouillon—never fried.

It is a German custom to rip off skin and scales together, but the meat is so delicate that the Louisiana way of merely cutting a small letter S on the back with a sharp knife, is better. Even this breaking of the skin must be followed by wrapping the fish with twine before poaching. Great care must be taken in lifting the fish onto the platter, either from grill or pan. Melted butter is poured over them then, and lemon slices and parsley are the classic garnish.

CATFISH

These are another variety of the finny tribe likely to be slighted, although they can't be classed with the dainty perch. If taken in clear water, however, catfish are good eating, but if from muddy bottoms they should be kept alive in a tub of clean running water for a day or two, to get rid of that earthy taste. Then skin your cat and marinate as for conger eel. When ready, dredge with seasoned flour and fry in bacon fat.

DEEP FAT FRYING

This is the last resort for fish that are too small for any other purpose, and for whitebait. Dip in crumbs, and then in egg beaten with a tablespoon of milk, then in crumbs again. Or dip in an egg batter. Be sure to test temperature of fat before beginning to fry. Put fish in frying basket, immerse and serve at once when done. The traditional accompaniment is potato chips.

BROILING

Season with salt, pepper and a sprinkling of lemon juice. Brush fat fish very lightly with oil, spread on the thin ones all the butter they will take and then add melted butter while grilling. Unless too small, all grill better if split open. Lay on a well greased rack or in a double wire toaster, and cook flesh side first. Don't overcook or they will dry out and harden. Brush with melted butter, sprinkle with herbs and serve with lemon quarters. Most suitable for broiling are brook trout, herring, kingfish, mackerel, pompano, sea bass and trout, Spanish mackerel, blacks and weakfish, and the steaks of cod, haddock, halibut and swordfish.

BAKING AND POACHING IN THE OVEN

Leave the skins of fat fish whole but score the skins of lean ones by cutting diagonal gashes across. Fill gashes with butter. Fill insides of the meagerly flavored ones with highly seasoned stuffing of seafood and heavily buttered crumbs and sew up. Spread all of them with softened butter. Baste the dry ones with courtbouillon which should be put into the pan hot after baking has begun, or poach in courtbouillon under a closely fitting cover. A pretty trick for additional seasoning is to lay on the prepared fish a row of overlapping onion rings, large rings at the head tapering to small ones at the tail, or use tomato slices in the same way, or alternate tomato slices with onion rings. Following these suggestions practically all sizable fish can be baked. But it is a favorite method for bluefish, carp, hake, lake trout, salmon, shad, snapper, sturgeon and whitefish.

PIKE BAKED WITH SOUR CREAM

3-pound pike	½ teaspoon sugar
4 tablespoons butter	Buttered bread
Salt and pepper	crumbs
1 onion, minced	2 tablespoons grated
1 bay leaf	cheese
1 tablespoon flour	1 tablespoon grated
1½ cups sour cream	horseradish

Clean the fish and split open, the two halves being held together only by the skin. Remove backbone, and other visible bones. Wipe dry with a towel. Rub with salt and pepper; lay in buttered pan, skin-side up. Spread with softened butter, and place in hot oven. Meanwhile work the flour and sugar smooth with a little of the cream, and add to the rest of the cream. Fry the onions in butter until golden. After fish has been baking 10 minutes add onion, bay leaf and cream. Bake 10 minutes longer, basting several times. Sprinkle with crumbs and cheese, and let brown. Slide fish onto a hot platter. Add horseradish to contents of pan, and pour around the fish.

This recipe serves for pickerel and other lean fresh-water fish.

STUFFED COD OR BLACKFISH

Make stuffing as follows: Mix ¾ cup chopped ham, two tablespoons melted butter, parsley, thyme, marjoram and a few oysters. Add two eggs and enough fine bread crumbs to bind together. Stuff, sew up, dredge with flour and bake about one hour, basting with butter, lemon juice and oyster liquor. Make a sauce of pan contents.

FISH AU GRATIN

(For bass, kingfish, trout, flounder and big smelts)

3 mushrooms, chopped	1 teaspoon minced chives
1 carrot, sliced	½ teaspoon herbs, minced
1 celery stick, sliced	
1 small onion, chopped	Salt and pepper
1 clove, minced	Paprika
Melted butter	½ cup fish broth
1 teaspoon minced parsley	½ cup white wine
	1 tablespoon lemon juice
Cracker crumbs	

If dried mushrooms are used, soak several hours before chopping and be sure to use the water in which they soaked. Mix vegetables and fry in three tablespoons hot butter. Season, add herbs, seasonings and broth and simmer ½ hour. Spread in bottom of baking dish, lay fish on top, cover and bake 15 minutes, adding wine (or more fish broth) when necessary. Baste frequently. Uncover, sprinkle with crumbs, dot thickly with butter and brown. When fish is done make a sauce of pan contents, and strain over fish. Serve a dish of sautéed mushrooms, either fresh or dried, with it.

FISH BAKED WITH SPINACH

Cook any ordinary fish in courtbouillon. Make a spinach purée and a cream sauce, as follows:

1 quart spinach	2 tablespoons onion juice
2 tablespoons butter	
2 tablespoons flour	2 cups milk or cream
Paprika	Salt and pepper

Press water from hot cooked spinach and pass through a sieve. Melt butter, stir in flour, add milk, heat and stir until smooth and thick, adding seasonings. Spread seasoned spinach on bottom of a baking dish, lay fish freed of skin and bones on top of spinach, mask all with cream sauce and brown in oven. A sprinkling of grated cheese may top the dish to assist in browning.

MACKEREL WITH GOOSEBERRY STUFFING

2-3 pounds mackerel	1 carrot, minced
Salt and pepper	1 young turnip, minced
½ pound fresh herring, chopped	
	1 herb bouquet
Unripe gooseberries	6 peppercorns
1 onion, chopped	

Clean mackerel, salt and pepper inside and out. Mix seasoned herring with sufficient stemmed and seeded gooseberries to fill. Stuff mackerel with mixture and sew up. Lay in fish boiler with vegetables, bouquet and peppercorns; cover with salted boiling water or fish broth, and slowly simmer. Take up, saving broth for fish soup or for boiling other fish. Serve with a dish of gooseberry sauce.

PLANKED FISH

A fish plank should be a part of the equipment of every fisherman's kitchen. It is nothing more than a thick piece of hardwood, oak, hickory or ash, cut across the grain. It should be at least a foot and a half long and a foot wide, for the best fish to plank are sea trout, shad, blues and lake bass of fair size. Department stores carry these planks, of course. Like the wooden salad bowl, the plank improves with use.

Clean the fish and cut off head and tail. Split it full length, lay on the plank, skin side under. Season with salt, pepper, minced parsley and a dash of lemon juice, and brush well with melted butter. Place under the grill, or tie fish to plank and tilt up before live coals. Grill for 15 minutes. Have ready some hot well beaten mashed potatoes, freshly cooked peas, baby carrots or other vegetables such as Brussels sprouts, cauliflower flowerets, sliced beets, whatever the garden supplies. Make a ring of mashed potatoes around the fish, brown them for five minutes. Decorate the space between the potatoes and fish with little piles of the other vegetables.

COOKING FURRED GAME

While the savor of feathered game is overpowered by strong seasonings, furred game, on the contrary, is usually enhanced by spices and herbs. Methods for cooking young and old wild animals differ, just as they do for domestic livestock, so first judge the age of your kill before deciding on your recipe. Old tough meat is tenderized by longer hanging, and by marinating in sourish cider or wine, or in lemon juice or vinegar mixed with water, or by adding one of these mild acids to the cooking liquor.

RABBIT AND HARE

The rabbit has light or lightish meat and the meat of the hare is dark, which leads to the general rule that hare is treated with heavier cooking liquid and seasoning than the paler fleshed bunny. The young of this entire family have sharp unworn claws and tender ears. All must be thoroughly cooked, never rare.

Hang by the hind legs in a cool place for several days. Some folk think freezing improves them, but this is a matter for argument as is the removal of the kernels from under the forelegs and the small of the back.

If very tender they may be quartered and grilled like spring chickens, only use more pepper and the lightest dusting of spice or cayenne, and a little of your favorite herb either on the meat or in the butter poured over before serving. This may be the easiest method, but it is not the best for it yields no gravy.

SADDLE OF RABBIT IN PAPER

If you have brought home a full bag, roast only the backs saving the rest of the carcasses for soup, stew or jugging. If you are impatient you can eat the livers at once; just cut out the galls, wash, dry, slice and season them, dip into egg and then into crumbs, and fry them.

FOR FOUR RABBIT BACKS

¼ pound bacon, minced	½ teaspoon grated nutmeg
½ cup bread crumbs	⅛ teaspoon cayenne
1 cup strained tomato	Salt
	Minced parsley
1 garlic clove, minced	Minced tarragon or fresh sage

Salt the meat. Mix all other ingredients except herbs and mash to a paste. Lay each back on a long oval of well buttered paper. Fold paper down the middle to make an envelope, double the edges together so no steam can escape and secure with paper clips. Lay packages overlapping in a roasting pan and bake until thoroughly done. Either open the papers at the table, passing little dishes of minced herbs; or open in the kitchen and make a gravy of the juices which have collected in the papers, adding a little butter, lemon juice or wine, and either sprinkle the minced herbs over the meat or drop them into the gravy.

STEAMED RABBIT

Pioneer Americans had another way of holding in the juices and flavor. They wrung a cloth out of cold water, covered it with all the flour that would stick, wrapped the seasoned rabbit, either whole or jointed, in the floured cloth, sewed it shut and sealed the stitching with wet flour. Then they steamed it one to two hours, depending on age, and browned it in frying pan or oven. Rice cakes and apple sauce, once served with this dish, still survive as accompaniments to rabbit in some sections of the South.

If your rabbit is old and you think it will be very tough, there is an old reliable American pickling mixture which will soften it, and season it at the same time.

MARINATING MIXTURE FOR GAME

¼ cup vinegar	1 chopped onion
1 cup water	1 bay leaf
8 peppercorns	

Mix all ingredients together, bring to boiling point and cook five minutes, cool, pour over jointed rabbit and let stand 12 hours, turning the pieces over once or twice so all will be equally soaked. Rinse in cold water, dry, season with salt and cook as you will.

The French marinade requires wine instead of vinegar as do nearly all French game recipes.

POSSUM

Possum and woodchuck should have the glands or kernels taken out from under the forelegs and the small of the back. Many people also remove some of the layer of fat that lies under the skin. If the animal is to be baked, a favorite stuffing is equal parts of boiled chestnuts, apple sauce and bread crumbs. The best possum we ever ate was left unstuffed, but its outside was stuck full of sassafras twigs until it looked like a porcupine. An Ozarks woodsman roasted it for us before an open fire, in sight of its skin which he had tacked up on the wall to dry. There is an old recipe from the Deep South, however, which is the classic. "Place an ax handle across the possum's neck, hold the tail and pull until the neck is broken. Meanwhile have ready a pot of boiling oak lye, made of a quart of oak ashes and a gallon of water. As soon as the neck is broken, put the possum in this, for a minute; take out and scrape clean, open down the breast, remove entrails and wash thoroughly. Hang in a cool place. Rub inside and out with salt and black or red pepper; place in a roasting pan, with a teacup of boiling water, one of vinegar, a tablespoon of butter and a half dozen or more small peeled potatoes (sweets, of course). Baste the meat frequently. When tender remove to a dish and garnish with potatoes and parsley."

WOODCHUCK OR HEDGEHOG

Soak overnight in a weak solution of vinegar with a sliced onion and salt. Wash. Parboil 20 minutes, drain, put into fresh boiling water with a sliced large onion, four or five cloves, and a stick of celery. Cook until tender. Thicken the gravy wih flour.

PORCUPINE

Toss into fire and leave it there until quills burn off, wipe clean, split skin down the stomach and take it off, chopping off the ends of the legs; empty and season lightly, for the flavor is delicate. Stew or roast, whole or cut up. The skin is considered the best part if the beast be first salted, peppered and marinated for a day, and then broiled.

FRICASSEED SQUIRREL

Scald 15 minutes in just enough water to cover; skim well, then drain, season, dip in egg and crumbs and fry in butter. Reduce water in which the meat boiled. Add more butter to pan, brown a tablespoon of flour in it and add the reduced broth.

Their gamy flavoring, however, is better brought out by preparing them according to any of the recipes for rabbit.

VENISON

Deer meat, even though fat, is dry and is best when patiently basted with wine or fruit juice. The age is ascertained by the condition of the hooves which are widely spread in the old. It should be hung in the hide at least a week before cooking. A doe is preferred to a buck. And if you would like to have venison out of season in safety, be sure to invite the game warden to go hunting with you.

VENISON STEAKS, CHOPS AND LOIN CUTLETS

Cut one and a half inches thick, brush with oil or butter and grill under or over a hot fire five minutes on each side, seasoning while cooking. Serve with a mixture of lemon juice and melted butter, and pass currant jelly. Or, dredge with flour, brown in butter, take up and keep hot; add more butter to pan and a tablespoon of flour; stir and brown. Add water or meat broth, stir and cook until it thickens. Replace meat, cover and simmer until done. Add currant jelly and a tablespoon of wine to the gravy at the end.

HAUNCH OF VENISON

For hunters the well cleaned hoof and the hair just above it is left on, thickly wrapped in buttered paper, and tied to keep it sightly. Season and lard meat with bacon or salt pork strips, make little incisions all over it and insert triangular bards of bacon or salt pork, lay in a pan and place in hot oven. When the fat begins to run commence to baste, and cover with buttered paper. Pour heated wine or fruit juice into the pan by the half cupful as basting proceeds. When done unwrap the hoof and slip a frilled paper cuff over it

etween hair and meat. In carving cut off a
ortion of the tenderloin for each serving.
at with currant sauce.

DRIED CURRANT SAUCE

2 tablespoons dried currants	2 cloves
1 cup water	1 glass port (or similar homemade wine)
1 scant cup sifted crumbs	Butter

Boil currants in water five minutes, or more
f very dry. Add crumbs, cloves and port and
immer, working smooth with a wooden
poon. Thin with pan gravy, stirring until
vell mixed.

COOKING FEATHERED GAME

All game birds should be strung up in their
eathers as soon as possible after being shot.
The English, meticulous in the treatment of
eathered game and the source of most of our
wn traditions, like their birds high and hang
hem for 10 days or longer in the cool cli-
nate of the British Isles. In some households
trings are tied to both head and feet so they
an be reversed every day. In others they are
ung by the heads until sufficiently cured.
They are never scalded, but dry-picked, the
eathers being pulled downward, in the direc-
ion they grow, not upward since the skins
re often tender and will tear. All shot must
e removed.

Choose the youngest and plumpest for
rilling. Use the old ones for bird soup, game
ies and casserole dishes.

Rub small birds with salt and pepper, truss
with small sticks or wooden skewers, wrap
ompletely in bacon and broil under slow
lame or over low coals, turning often for 15-
20 minutes. If bacon is too charred to eat, remove. Lay on toast and pour pan-dripping
ver. Slices of lemon and sprigs of parsley
r cress may garnish. Or, roll in vine or cab-
age leaves or just buttered paper and bake;
r lay close together in a pan and bake, bast-
ng frequently with fruit juice or wine. And
f you must take out their insides replace

them with an oyster and a tablespoon of
butter in each tummy. With few exceptions,
the simpler the seasonings, the better, since
nothing should detract from the wild flavor.
As to cooking time, the general rule which
applies to all meats holds good—white-fleshed
birds, like veal, should be well done but not
dry; and dark fleshed ones, like beef, should
be rare and rosy.

And all game calls lustily for wine, both
in the kitchen and on the table, so the hunter
who shoots to eat just naturally becomes a
wine maker, unless he can afford to stock a
cellar with imported vintages.

WINE SAUCE

1 cup port (or similar wine, homemade)	Salt and pepper
1 cup pan liquid	Piece of mace
1 teaspoon minced shallot (or onion)	Grating of nutmeg
	1 tablespoon butter
	1 tablespoon flour

Simmer liquids with seasonings 10 minutes.
Knead butter and flour together, stir in and
keep on stirring until mixture has boiled two
minutes.

WILD DUCKS

Wild ducks should be hung by the necks
in a cool dry temperature for at least two
days after being shot, but unlike some of the
other game birds they should not be allowed
to get high. They should not be washed with
water. If the cloth that wipes them must be
wet, then dampen it with applejack, whiskey
or any other strong spirits, even just plain
grain alcohol.

Young mallards and canvasbacks should be
split down the back, wiped well, rubbed with
salt and pepper and then with butter or oil,
or spread with slices of bacon. They are then
ready to be trussed open and broiled under
or over a hot fire, turning at least once. Ten
minutes will serve for canvasbacks and a little
longer for mallards which are larger.

The old canvasback needs no celery stuffing if he has been eating his favorite food, the
tape grass or so-called wild celery, nor does
the redhead, providing he has had plenty of
vallisneria roots to dive for. The latter grows
so fat on this diet that the breast sometimes

splits open if a shot brings him down from a height to fall on the water.

The famous old Creole way with a pair of redheads is to mix any liquid from the grill pan with the juice of two Bigarade or sour oranges; heat but do not allow to reach the boiling point, and pour over the ducks after they are laid on toast.

And if you are a gourmet and a duck hunter, too, you will invest in a duck press, and eat the breasts only of your ducks, pouring over them the juice which your press will squeeze out of the rest of the carcasses. Or you will even go so far as to baste one duck in the juice of another half-roasted one.

Dainty teal should be left whole, only plucked, drawn, seasoned and wrapped in bacon. They require a slower fire, like grouse, so they will be evenly heated through, and are done in about half an hour. Remove bacon and pour over them melted butter snapped up with lemon juice and minced parsley.

Ducks are very tricky to cook in any fashion since they dry out and harden in a few seconds after reaching perfection.

MALLARDS ROASTED IN THE OVEN

Pluck dry, singe, empty and truss with each neck turned back and fastened with a skewer. Wipe clean inside and out, rub with a little salt and black pepper. Lay inside each a whole small celery stalk and a tablespoon of butter—another of wine if possible. Close the vents with small skewers. Place close together, breast sides up, in roasting pan, and cover each breast with a generous slice of salt pork, thinly sliced, making slits lengthwise in the pork over the breast bones. Put in a hot oven (450°F.) and begin to baste as soon as fat runs out of the pork. Roast 25-35 minutes depending on size, turning them over once and back again so the juices can baste the insides. The flesh should be dark carmine in color and the dish-gravy deep red. Serve very hot with slices of hot toast. About half a cup of liquid will have collected on the inside of each duck which should be poured over the choice breast slices laid on toast. The backs are delicious picking, but

the legs, unless the birds are young, are likely to be tough and should be used next day for duck soup or hash.

WATER BIRDS OTHER THAN DUCK

The sora, crake or Carolina rail whose ruddy flesh tastes like duck but is sweeter—a sort of cross between snipe and teal flavor, should be simply trussed and broiled.

The corn crake of the dry field and the little black rail should be both emptied and skinned, their skins replaced by an all-over covering of bacon. The Bartrimian sand-sniper or papabotte of New Orleans is so rich it may even be baked with a stuffing mixed with its giblets. Or it may be broiled. Be sure to discard the gizzards. The rest of the trail may be minced, cooked in butter and spread on toast with the bird laid on top.

The reed bird or bobolink is never emptied or there would be nothing left of it after cooking. Wrap in bacon and string a number of them on a pair of skewers and grill. They are so sweet they need almost no seasoning. Pile on a hot platter and pour their own drippings over them.

Moor hens or American coots are sometimes very fishy. Smother in cabbage and simmer; or roast with sliced onion and a few tablespoons of wine or fruit juice in baking pan, removing onion at the finish.

BRAISED GROUSE

Prepare as for grilling; lay in pan on strips of bacon; place bits of celery around, and for each pair an onion stuck with four cloves, a thick slice of carrot and eight peppercorns. Fry a sliced onion light brown in butter, add a cup of meat broth or water, and, if tough, a tablespoon of whiskey or applejack; cut a circle of buttered paper a little larger than the pan and lay over the birds, tucking it in around the edges so no steam can escape, cover tight and simmer or put in the oven. Add a very little wine to the pan gravy before serving.

PARTRIDGES

Young partridges, those with dark bills and yellowish legs, may be split down the back, dipped in oil and bread crumbs and grilled.

There are innumerable recipes for old ones, most of them of French origin.

Boiled Partridges. Put in a floured cloth and then in boiling water, boil rapidly 15 minutes then reduce heat. For the sauce add butter, flour, cream and some of the cooking liquor; add minced parsley at the end.

Roast Partridges. Roast like chickens ½ hour, chop livers into the gravy. Eat with currant or grape jelly. Or braise like grouse.

PHEASANT

The pheasant and woodcock must be well matured on their strings and the problem of the amateur is to decide just when to take them down if they are to be in full flavor and not past that perfect point.

Split young pheasant down the back, truss open, brush well with melted butter and grill. The age may be determined by the last big wing feather which stays pointed while the bird is young and grows rounder with the seasons.

The old males which have long sharp spurs, can only be grilled if parboiled first; then drain, dry, dot with butter, season and broil. Reduce parboiling liquid to a few spoonfuls, add to pan drippings and pour over after laying the birds on toast. Or, season birds and brown in butter; lay in a casserole on a bed of chopped apples which have been browned in butter, and surround with the browned chopped apples. Bake well covered.

QUAIL

Season and rub young quail thickly with butter before completely covering with bacon and grilling. The flavor and odor of quail is evanescent and quickly evaporates if exposed to the air in cooking, so they should never be split, but must be kept whole and covered up with something, preferably not a liquid. French cooks fold each one in an oval, buttered paper, doubling the edges of the paper tightly together so no steam escapes. The papers are not opened until they are on the table. Each package contains a little natural gravy which is emptied over the bird after it is laid on hot toast. In England grilled

or poached beef marrow is spread on the toast just before the grilled quail are put to bed.

Braise old quail like grouse; or smother in green peas like pigeons; or just simmer in butter in a closely covered pan, add a tablespoon of wine to the gravy and garnish with green grapes.

WOODCOCK

Here is the problem of the trail again for the squeamish non-gourmets. If you must remove any of it take out only the lower end, then season your bird, rub thickly with butter, wrap completely in bacon slices, fastening the ends of the slices together with toothpicks, and slowly grill or roast, turning often, for 15-30 minutes. Lay on toast, pour pan drippings over and then pour over melted butter mixed with a little minced parsley and lemon juice.

Woodcock in Blazes. Split half-roasted woodcocks, lay in a casserole, saving the trail; cover with ¼ cup or a little less of applejack, rum or brandy for each bird and light. Baste with the burning liquid. Push to one side and add the minced trail with a tablespoon of butter for each bird, heat and stir, add a squeeze of lemon juice or a dash of good vinegar. Pour gravy over toast and lay bird halves on top.

A Frenchman would be shocked if the heads of either woodcock or snipe were cut off, for he likes to pick the brains of that last delectable tidbit. The long neck is twisted, the head is turned so the bill points forward and is held in that position by the bacon wrapping.

From the book
THE COUNTRY COOK BOOK
By Cora, Rose and Bob Brown
A. S. Barnes and Company
Copyright 1937

MISCELLANEOUS FOODS

SPOON BREAD

½ cup corn meal
2 cups milk
3 eggs
½ teaspoon baking powder
1 tablespoon melted butter
1 teaspoon salt

Heat the milk to nearly the boiling point, stir in the corn meal very gradually and continue cooking in the kettle for several minutes while stirring so it will not scorch. Then add the baking powder, salt, melted butter and the yolks of the eggs beaten until light. Fold in the whites of the eggs beaten stiff. Pour into a buttered baking dish of such size that the mixture will be about two inches deep, and bake for 30 minutes or more in the reflector oven until it gets a golden brown crust on top. If you do not have fresh milk make it of powdered whole milk, and in the absence of fresh eggs stir in three tablespoons of powdered egg. Eat with butter as a vegetable, or with syrup as a special treat for your dessert.

HUSH PUPPIES

2 cups yellow corn meal
¾ cup flour
2½ teaspoons baking powder
1 teaspoon salt

Mix ingredients and add one cup of water to make a medium thick dough. Drop big gobs of the dough into deep hot lard, or better still hot peanut oil, and cook until a golden brown. (The original recipe called for cooking in lard in which fish had originally been fried, which makes fine dog food in camp.) Very good to eat with fresh fish. Canned hush puppies can also be purchased.

DEHYDRATED FOODS

In years past old-timers did not have much use for the dried and condensed foods. They were not appetizing, and they did not give you energy or staying power. But there has been a tremendous development and improvement in dehydrated foods since the last war, and everyone going into camp in country where transportation is difficult, and ice not obtainable, should certainly look into them for they now offer very desirable additions to the staple foods.

Particularly they offer a greater variety of tasty dishes than the average camp cook is able to prepare, and this means a lot to outdoor appetites. They are extremely easy and quick to prepare, in most cases requiring only the addition of water, and heating. Few need pre-soaking, and most of them take not more than 10 to 20 minutes to prepare. Above all there is the greatest economy in weight and bulk. Dehydrated foods usually come in durable waterproof envelopes, each envelope containing enough to serve two to four persons, and with complete instructions printed on them in such large type that it can be read by the light of the campfire. No other containers are necessary, and freezing does not spoil them. No utensils other than kettle or frypan are necessary.

A great variety of these foods are offered. Powdered eggs, dehydrated potatoes, Spanish rice, pre-cooked beans, cereals with milk and sugar added, griddle cakes, ginger cookies, concentrated maple syrup, beef gravy, beef broth, vegetable and meat stews, hot biscuits, many thick and creamy soups, beef or chicken pot pie (to be prepared in the frypan), lemonade, fruit punches, macaroni and cheese, chili and beans, tinned bacon, butter and countless others.

SMOKING GAME AND FISH

When fishing or hunting away from civilization, there is often the problem of preserving the fish or game impossible to consume at the next meal or two.

In dry seasons and climates where the nights are cool, you can keep game much longer if you keep flies away from it and open it up to cool at night. The best arrangement is a rough frame closet covered with cheesecloth, in which the meat can be hung and the fish placed on shelves. It must be located in the shade.

Another method is to store meat in an iron bucket, almost completely immersed in a cold mountain brook. A tight cover keeps bugs and flies out.

SMOKING WILL KEEP IT

Smoking will preserve game and fish almost indefinitely in most any climate, and when so preserved it is delicious and as good eating as if fresh. Smoking meat is relatively simple

INDIAN TEEPEE SMOKE HOUSE

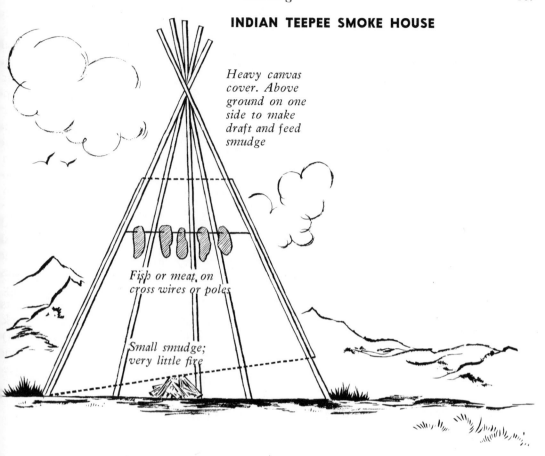

Heavy canvas cover. Above ground on one side to make draft and feed smudge

Fish or meat, on cross wires or poles

Small smudge; very little fire

ut it does require attention to the fire or mudge four or five times a day during the rocess, which takes from two to four days. The principle is to keep a fairly steady flow f warm but not hot smoke flowing over and round the meat, at least during the daylight ours when flies are abroad, and to shelter it rom dew and rain.

Some kind of smokehouse is necessary, but : does not have to be elaborate. The simplest rrangement is to rig up some kind of chimey, say 30 to 40 inches square, made of /ood or sheet metal, with a trench below it r slightly to one side. A smudge is kept oing in the trench with draft arranged so the moke will go up the chimney, somewhat like he accompanying sketch. The chimney has wo or three shelves, which may be wires rung several inches apart or removable ames made of chicken wire.

A simpler smoking apparatus is an Indian pole tepee, covered with heavy canvas (pack covers will do) except at the top, as in the other sketch.

Suppose you have a big catch of fish. Any species can be smoked, just so they are large fish that will fillet into slabs a half an inch thick. Smaller fish dry out too much. Large trout and salmon are fine. Clean the fish, remove the heads, and split in two pieces in line with the backbone. Lay the halves skin side down on a log, sprinkle salt over them and cover with canvas. Do this in the early evening when the flies are gone.

BURN ONLY HARDWOOD

In the meantime, you have rigged up your smokehouse. In the very early morning, build a fire in the flue or under the tepee, just enough to make a small bed of coals. Then feed it on rotten, punky or wet wood so it will smolder and smoke, with little or no flame. You must use only hardwood—birch, maple, aspen. Never any pitchy wood like spruce, pine or hemlock that would give a disagreeable taste to the smoked food.

When you have the smudge going well, with a column or even just a wisp of smoke going up the chimney, wipe the salt off the fish with a clean cloth, and lay the fillets, skin side down, on the shelves, and close up the chimney. Keep the smudge going all day so smoke is constantly circulating around and over the fish. You want only warmth, not heat. Neither the fish nor the chimney should ever get so hot you cannot place your bare hand on them. The chimney must have some smoke in it all the time during daylight to keep flies off, so you probably will have to

tend the smudge every two or three hours. Build it up fresh when you go to bed, and again very early in the morning.

It probably will take from two to four days to smoke your fish properly, depending on the weather and the volume of warm smoke. After two days try a small piece of fish. It should be well done; that is, not like kippered herring, but more like smoked herring or smoked salmon. If the fish is smoked too long, it will dry out and crumble.

At the proper time take the fillets out and lay them flat, skin side down, perhaps in a box, away from flies and insects and where they will keep dry. You don't have to keep them cold. Do not place in a refrigerator or any damp place or they will mildew. Smoked fish will keep for weeks. It is mighty fine eating dry, just as it is, without any cooking.

SMOKE CHIMNEY

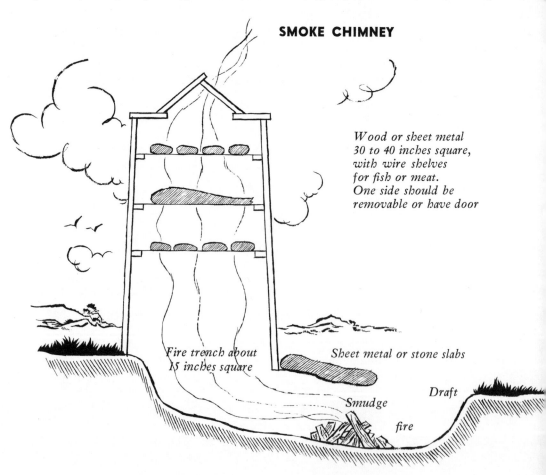

Wood or sheet metal 30 to 40 inches square, with wire shelves for fish or meat. One side should be removable or have door

Fire trench about 15 inches square

Sheet metal or stone slabs

Draft

Smudge fire

GAME BIRDS AND ANIMALS

You can smoke game birds such as quail or grouse in exactly the same way, splitting them, slightly salting them overnight and laying them flat on the smokehouse shelves. Deer, moose, caribou, tongues, even sheep and beef, may be similarly smoked, cutting fat-free meat in flat strips not over about an inch thick, and either laying flat on the shelves or hanging. Smoke meat until quite.dry; it will turn almost black. This makes jerky. It may afterward be cut into cubes and stewed, but it is much better eaten cold and raw. Just bite off a chunk and chew.

It is the most concentrated emergency food there is. Old-time hunters often kept a hunk of jerky in their pocket, and would "bite off a chew" every couple of hours. Jerky makes a fine lunch for the hunter. It keeps indefinitely in cloth bags, anywhere away from insects and dampness. Smoked tongue is a great delicacy.

You can make pemmican out of jerky. Pound it into shreds and mix with it warm lard that you have fried out from the fat of deer, or any of the hoofed animals, until the mixture has the consistency of sausage meat or raw hamburger. Do not use salt. Then pack in tin cans or even in canvas sacks. It also will keep indefinitely away from insects and dampness.

Pemmican is good eaten raw, or it may be made into a stew. It is a nourishing and sustaining food, far better as an emergency ration than anything else that has been devised by man. In the old days in the North, and on our own northern plains, the Indians and whites alike lived for months at a time on nothing but jerky, pemmican, and when they could get it, a little tea. So long as no salt was used on the jerky or pemmican, scurvy was unknown.

By Col. Townsend Whelen

COOKING WITH FOIL

More and more outdoor cooks are preparing their meals in aluminum foil. With aluminum sheeting you can practically get rid of

Reynolds Metals Co.

Foil is easily formed into shape by a frying pan.

dish washing on a camping trip. And your meats and vegetables will have a sealed-in flavor that makes them even more taste-tempting than before.

Cooking camp food in aluminum foil is simple from the start. You need nothing to hold the foil-wrapped food package together, since foil molds to any shape, then holds it. When you crimp the edges of the foil, you seal your food package against moisture, air light and odor. And when you "zip" down the crimped edges, your meal is ready to eat —complete with a dish made from the same foil it was cooked in.

For cutting "kitchen" time to a minimum, you can even prepare your meals before you set out, wrapping each one in a foil package. Then just stick the right packages in the coals when you get to your camp. But you'd better make sure you know which package is which, for various foods take different cooking times. There's nothing quite like a well-cooked chicken dinner turning out to be well-burned bread.

Most foil uses call for regular weight foil, which comes in rolls 12 inches wide. This weight is best for wrapping food to be cooked on coals, since you use two layers of foil. If one layer punctures or tears, you still have another protecting the food.

But for making pots and pans, or wrapping meat on a spit, heavy-duty foil is best. This comes in rolls 18 inches wide, and is about double the thickness of regular aluminum foil.

RIGHT KIND OF FIRE

The fire you need for foil cookery is actually no fire at all, but hot coals. You never want a flaming blaze except when using a reflector oven or, if you like, when you're cooking in a foil pot.

To get hot coals, it's best just to let your campfire burn down. But that takes time. If you need a good bed of coals in a hurry, get dead—though solid—hardwood such as the white oaks, sugar maple, hickory or birch. Split it into small sticks two inches around and 12 inches long. Then stack the wood in "log cabin" style until you have walls about a foot high.

Start your fire inside this pen, and cover the top of it with several layers of parallel sticks, each layer at right angles to the other. Build up this "thatching" for another foot.

The draft will give you a roaring fire, which burns down entirely to coals. Add bark from hardwoods, if you want, which helps make coals even sooner. And if you need to keep your bed of coals, add more bark, which quickly burns to ashes and covers the coals.

WRAP IT UP

After there's a hot bed of coals, put in your foil food package. Wrapping the food in foil is simple, but each step in important. Here's a check list:

1. Put your uncooked food on a single sheet of foil, which you've cut big enough to allow a fold-over and a three-fold crimping of each of the three open sides.
2. Fold over the foil and crimp in the open sides, folding over each at least three times to make sure of an airtight seal.
3. Then take another sheet of foil the same size and wrap your package again. The fold-over and open edge should come on the same sides, but reversed top and bottom so you crimp on the opposite surface from the first time.

Clear a hole in the coals with a stick, and bury the foil package. Then rake the coal back over the package, so heat will get to a sides. After it has cooked the right time, tak the package out of the coals and let it sit minute on a rock. Then the foil will hav cooled off enough for you to zip down th crimped edges and open the package, makin it into a foil eating dish. And there's one mor dirty dish you won't have to wash. Jus throw it away when you're through eating

A reflector oven is easily made of foil.

WHAT YOU CAN COOK

The list of cook-in-foil camp menus practically endless. Foil wrapping makes you own pressure cooker or miniature bakin oven, giving you almost as many possibilitie for meal variety as the kitchen range.

Here are some menu ideas, with cookin times. These times vary with wind strengtl firewood, age of coals and other factors, s they are only approximate. After all, you campfire has no thermostat.

With each dish, wrap it twice as explaine before. Also always add shortening, fat, but ter or bacon—or, when cooking vegetables, few drops of water—to the package befor cooking. This completes the pressure cooke idea, and keeps food from burning or stick ing to the foil.

MEATS

Hamburger. Wrap with sliced onion an shoestring potatoes. If the meat doesn have much fat in it, add ½ pat of butte or its equivalent of shortening or fat. Coo 12-15 minutes.

Elkburger or Venisonburger. If you saved some of the meat from your last hunting trip in the home freezer, it will provide another grand meat dish. Cook it as you would hamburger. But just taste the difference.

Steak. Use a one-pound piece of meat, either beef brought from home or game meat bagged on the trip. Lay the steak on a sheet of foil with a little butter underneath.

An old picnic favorite, "Pigs In Blanket" are baked in foil.

Add potatoes and onions if you like. Steak can also be cooked on an open piece of foil, with the corners folded up to hold the gravy-makings inside the foil. Cook 10-15 minutes, depending on how well done you want it. If on open foil, let each side of the steak have about six to seven minutes.

Game Fowl or Chicken. Wash a piece of the bird (leg or breast) to add water. Put a slice of bacon under the meat, and add washed vegetables, if desired, to make a New England dinner. In hot coals, the meat will cook in half an hour.

Fish. Clean and wash the fish, then put it on the foil with half a slice of bacon underneath or rub the fish with butter. Wrap and cook about 12 minutes. For sizes up to a pound, cook whole. For larger fish, cut into one-pound steaks and bake each separately.

Chops. Wrap as usual, and let the package cook fully 20 minutes in hot coals. Pork must be thoroughly done, so if the meat is at all pink on the inside, wrap it up

again and stick it back in the coals for more cooking.

Whole Bird. Here's a real outdoor treat. Roast a small game bird or chicken on a spit, wrapping it with foil to seal in the flavor. Turn every 15 minutes. Let a one-pound bird cook about an hour and a half, putting the spit eight to 10 inches above hot coals. If you like it browned, peel off the foil (being careful to save the cooking juices) and turn the bird for a few minutes directly over the coals. For duck or large game bird, cook in the same way, but your roasting will take considerably longer. Allow an hour and a half for the first pound, half an hour for each succeeding pound. Take off foil at a couple of places to check cooking after two hours.

Roast Venison or Beef. Cook this also on a spit, wrapping it with foil. Allow half an hour per pound, turning every 15 minutes. A four- to five-pound piece of meat is best.

Rabbit. Roast on a spit, and wrap with aluminum foil. Cooking takes about an hour when the spit is eight to 10 inches above hot coals.

Franks in a Blanket. Mix prepared biscuit flour, and "roll" it out as thin as you can—preferably about ¼ inch thick. To roll the dough, run a tin can or glass jar over it until it's flat or press it with your hand. Use a piece of foil under the dough to protect it from the ground. Sprinkle a little flour on your hands first to keep dough from sticking. Cut the dough in large enough pieces to surround the frankfurter, but still letting the frank stick out of the dough ½ inch at each end. Wrap and cover with coals. Cooks in 15 minutes.

VEGETABLES

All vegetables should be washed just before you put them in the foil. This gives them needed moisture for that pressure cooker effect. In most cases, you can cook vegetables right with the meat, saving foil and adding flavor. Dice or slice them beforehand to cut cooking time. If you like, use frozen vegetables. They'll keep well for a weekend in most weather, and there's no cleaning or other preparation needed before cooking. To bake a whole potato, wash it, then cut out a few deep holes in it and wrap in foil. Cook 15-20 minutes, and then test. If not done, cook longer. Cooking time depends on the size of the potato.

BREAD

Mix prepared biscuit flour, adding a little water at a time. Be careful not to get in too much water. Use a pan made out of foil for mixing, or pour about a tablespoonful of water into the box of flour and twist dough around a stick until it reaches the right consistency for baking. To bake biscuits in coals use two feet of doubled foil, greasing the inside with butter. Wrap loosely to allow for rising, and set at the edge of hot coals, putting it in the center of the coals for only the last couple of minutes of the total baking time of 15 minutes. While it's at the edge of the coals, turn frequently to get heat at all sides. Even if you like to bake with a reflector oven, you can also use foil for this job. Choose heavy duty weight or a doubled thickness of regular weight foil. Bend a sheet in the center to form a 90-degree angle, and put a stick or rock under the bottom at the back to tip it up toward a flaming fire. Let biscuits brown on top, then turn them over to bake them all the way through. Test to see if they're done by poking one with a sharpened twig. If the biscuits are done, the twig will come out clean without dough sticking to it. Baking takes about 10 minutes if the fire is hot.

FRUIT

Baked Apple. Take out the core with a pocket knife, then add two tablespoons of brown sugar (or white sugar if you didn't pack any brown sugar).

Dried Fruit. Soak overnight in heavy-foil "pot" with enough water to cover the fruit. Add a tablespoon of sugar in the morning if you prefer your breakfast fruit sweet. Put the pot over the edge of your fire (coals are not needed for this but are preferable). When using a foil pot, always put your food in it *before* you put it on the fire.

Fresh Fruit. Stew in a foil pot and add sugar to fit your taste.

Baked Banana. Cut off both ends, leaving the banana in its peeling. Slit down the center and sprinkle with sugar (brown is best). Fold and wrap twice, then bake in hot coals for 10 minutes. Serve right away.

AFTER YOU'RE THROUGH

Usually it's not practical to save your used foil for more cooking, since it has been zipped down at the three crimped corners and is rather crumpled. So burn off any food then cool the foil and roll it into a small ball.

Foil doesn't disintegrate in fire or air, so you'll have to bury it. Dig a hole with your heel, drop in the foil ball and cover it with earth.

With these menu ideas, your foil cooking problem should be wrapped up rather well. But it's still a good plan to try out some of these recipes at home before you use them on camping trips. The backyard fireplace—or even the kitchen oven—will get you familiar with the way it's done. You'll probably end up using foil for all your family backyard cook-outs, once you've found how easy—and tasty—foil makes your outdoor cooking.

OTHER USES FOR FOIL

You'll find that foil can be used for more than cooking on your outdoor trips. You can shape a drinking cup from it, use it to cover pocket articles (such as matches) to keep them dry and even wrap an iced catch with it to keep the fish cool until you get home.

Also foil can seal your tackle, gun or other outdoor gear from off-season dampness in storage.

In short, aluminum foil cuts down your work in camp and gives you better cooking results. And that gives you more time for hunting and fishing.

Sound like an easy solution for many of your camp chore problems? Well, it is!

By Bob Stewart

CHAPTER **6**

first aid

DESPITE ALL precautions and care, accidents sometimes do happen. And when one happens out-of-doors, far from a doctor, quick first aid is essential. The following section explains what you should do in case of a broken bone, gunshot wound, insect or snake bite, frostbite, heat- or sunstroke and how to pack your own first-aid kit.

BROKEN BONES

A broken leg or arm can present quite a formidable problem when you're hundreds of miles from the nearest doctor. So you owe it to yourself and your fellow sportsmen to learn how to treat fractures in an emergency. This knowledge may spell the difference between a well-healed arm or leg and a permanent deformity!

A fracture is simply a broken bone. Doctors classify fractures as either "open" or "closed."

An open fracture is one in which the broken bone pierces the skin and protrudes or one in which the object broke the bone after piercing the flesh. An open fracture is more serious because of the greater chances of infection.

In a closed fracture there is no break in the skin, and so no chance for infection from outside.

How do you determine if a bone is broken? Here are the four signs to look for:

(1) Tenderness over the injured part, and pain when movement is attempted.

(2) Swelling and "black and blue" discoloration.

(3) An unnatural shape of the limb.

(4) The victim either cannot move the injured part or suffers great pain if he can move it.

All of these signs are not always present in every fracture. But if you're in doubt, treat the injury as though it *were* a fracture. No harm will result. Don't take chances.

The first and most vital rule in treating fractures is this: *Do not move the patient until you have effectively splinted the fracture!* If you remember only this one rule you will do a lot of good.

"Splinting" sounds formidable to the average layman. It need not cause any confusion. Splinting simply means applying any material that will *prevent* or *lessen* movement of the broken bones. Only after you have done this should you start to move the patient.

If you move him before splinting, you are doing him great harm by increasing the damage produced by the broken bones. The jagged and sharp edges will tear and lacerate the delicate surrounding tissues, producing nerve and blood vessel injury, great pain and possibly serious permanent paralysis.

Applying a splint does not require skill or experience. *But don't attempt to "set" a broken bone.* Merely straighten out the arm or leg before applying the splint. If the fracture is in or near a joint, do not try to straighten it out. Apply the splint to make the joint immovable in whatever position you find it. If the skin is broken, treat that as you would any wound.

No special apparatus is needed for splinting in the field. Knowledge of what to do and improvisation is all that is necessary. The basic principle in splinting arm or leg bone fractures is to make the limb immovable not only over the fracture, but also at the joints above and below the fracture.

Boards, oars, rifles, tree branches or anything similar can be used as splinting material. For padding—pillows, blankets, shirts, coats

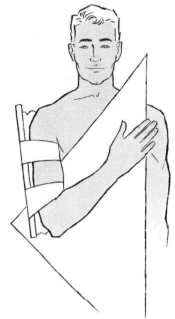

Boards, tree branches, oars, rifles—many things can be used as splinting material.

or even folded newspapers are acceptable. For wrapping the limb to the splint, you can use—for example—strips of clothing, belts, gun slings.

Here are the four requirements of a good splint:

(1) It must have rigidity and strength enough to immobilize the limb.

(2) It must extend above and below the broken bone.

(3) It must not be too heavy.

(4) It must be well padded with soft material.

A very effective and quick way to splint a broken leg is to tie it to the *uninjured* leg. Use any material available and tie both legs together in two places below and two places above the fracture. Do not bind too tightly.

A suspected broken back should be treated with utmost care. Any movement may cause the sharp fragments to cut the spinal cord. *At least three* men should be used if you *must* move the patient. Do not bend his back or raise his head or neck. He may be carried face down in a blanket.

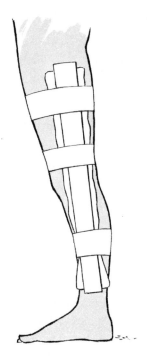

A good splint must have rigidity, be padded, extend above and below broken bone.

A broken neck is even more dangerous. Keep the patient's head and neck *straight and still.* Any movement may kill him! If he must be moved, wrap a folded shirt, coat or other material around his neck and tie it. One man should handle the head and keep it straight during movement.

These then are the few rules you need to know. And the most important principle of all is: "Do not move your patient until you have applied a splint!"

By A. M. Libasci, M.D.

GUNSHOT WOUNDS

Fatalities due to accidental gunshot wounds while hunting are all too common. And the tragic fact is that in the vast majority of these cases the most elementary knowledge of how to stop serious bleeding would have saved the victim's life. Every sportsman who is around guns or handles guns should learn the proper emergency treatment of gunshot wounds. Not only to help others. This knowledge may save his own life.

Each year approximately 2,250 people die of accidental gunshot injuries. Deaths due to firearms rank seventh among the list of accidental deaths. Only one fourth of all firearm accidents occur while hunting. Twice as many occur in the home. About 80 per cent of all firearm accidents are nonfatal. Of those that are fatal a goodly percentage die needlessly because of faulty or inadequate emergency treatment. Many of these bleed to death.

There is nothing mysterious or complex about the emergency treatment of gunshot wounds. The first thing to remember is that you must be quick and you must be cool. You may save a life if you know what to do, and what not to do; and if you are speedy and calm. If you yourself are the victim keep your head. What you do within the first few minutes may mean the difference between life or death, or saving an arm or leg.

There are three vital steps to indelibly fix in your mind in the emergency treatment of gunshot wounds. Memorize these so you will never, never, forget them: (1) stop the bleeding (2) protect the wound (3) prevent shock.

Your first and immediate concern is to stop the bleeding. Uncontrolled bleeding results in shock and death. You will have to work fast. Examine the wound and quickly make a decision as to its seriousness. If there is only oozing and dripping of blood place a large dressing (improvise if none available) over the wound and apply pressure. Use the palms of both hands against the dressing and apply a steady, unreleasing pressure. Continue the pressure until you are sure the bleeding has stopped. Then wrap a firm bandage around the dressing to keep it in place.

If your examination reveals serious bleeding—spurting and gushing of blood from the large arteries—or if you have tried pressure and bleeding continues, you will have to apply a tourniquet. This is, of course, used only for limb injuries.

Very few people know how to apply a tourniquet effectively. The principles are simple. You must apply it where it will cut off the entire circulation to the arm or leg.

This means high up where the main artery enters the limb. The tourniquet should be no lower than one handbreadth from the armpit or from the crotch.

Use any suitable material at hand for a tourniquet; a belt, strips of cloth or, best of all if you have one, a rubber tourniquet. Apply the tourniquet over the clothes to avoid cutting the skin. Place a small pad under the tourniquet on the inside of the upper arm and on the inside of the thigh so that it can wedge against the main artery and block it off more effectively.

All first-aid manuals caution you to loosen the tourniquet for five minutes every half hour. Don't do this if the bleeding is serious. Your patient will bleed to death. Leave the tourniquet on tightly if great bleeding occurs when you loosen it. You'll save the patient's life.

The illustration shows you the proper location for tourniquets of various types. Study these well and don't ever make the mistake of applying a tourniquet on the forearm or calf. Always place it high up as illustrated.

If you are quite sure there is no fracture, elevate the limb as high as possible. This will lessen bleeding. Immobilize your patient and keep him quiet and comfortable. Don't let him walk around or run for help.

Your second step, to protect the wound, is to keep your hands and fingers off it. Cut off the clothes around the wound and cover it with a sterile or clean dressing. Use anything you can get in an emergency. Keep the wound covered at all times.

The third step is to prevent shock. Shock is a great weakness of the body and can result in death. Any wound can cause shock.

Various types of tourniquets showing correct sites of application

This is a belt that is being used as a
A *tourniquet. Apply the tourniquet over the clothes to avoid cutting the skin.*

The improved windlass type of tourni-
B *quet. If the bleeding is serious, don't loosen the tourniquet every half hour.*

A rubber tourniquet applied to a leg
C *and arm. Remember—the first thing after accident is to stop the bleeding.*

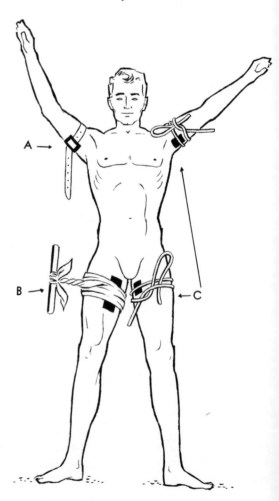

Severe bleeding will cause shock. A person in shock is very pale, cold and clammy, trembles, has a very weak pulse and may be unconscious. The best way to treat shock is to prevent it. Prevent shock by (1) making your patient comfortable (2) keeping him warm (3) lowering his head and shoulders to increase flow of blood to the brain.

These, then, are the three lifesaving measures to remember for all gunshot wounds. There are two types of wounds that require additional special attention—chest wounds and abdominal wounds.

Chest wounds through which air is sucking in and out are very dangerous. The air squeezes the heart and lungs and death will result. You must plug up the wound and make it airtight. Pack the wound with a dressing and then cover it with a piece of raincoat or other available material. Bind this tightly by belts or strips of torn clothing around the chest. Have the injured man lie on his wounded side.

For a belly wound, only two things can be done: (1) cover the wound and (2) treat for shock. Use a sterile or clean dressing and fasten it securely. If the intestines are protruding don't touch them or try to push them back. Don't give anything by mouth—no water, no foods.

When assembling your equipment for a hunting trip it will be very wise to include two items of first-aid equipment: (1) a tourniquet and (2) a compressed first-aid dressing. They will occupy space equal to about two packs of cigarettes and may help save a life or limb.

The best type of tourniquet is simply a strip of rubber band two inches wide and five feet long. When rolled up the roll is just two inches in diameter.

The first-aid dressing best suited for field use is the one carried by our troops. It is packed in waterproof foil inside a waterproof pasteboard container. It measures four inches by two inches by one inch. When opened it consists of a thick gauze dressing with four "tails" to use for tying. Carry this in your hip pocket at all times like our soldiers do.

It is hoped that every outdoorsman will study the few simple instructions given in this short article. If you apply the measures described here you will be doing someone (perhaps yourself) a great service. After you have given this emergency treatment, transport your patient as carefully as possible to a doctor.

By A. M. Libasci, M.D.

BITES

One of the "occupational" hazards of the outdoorsman is the possibility of being bitten by insects, animals or snakes. We are here presenting the symptoms and treatment of each of these three types of bites. Untreated bites may prove fatal. An understanding of this subject is of vital concern to all sportsmen.

The bites of ordinary insects such as mosquitoes, ants, bees are not unduly serious. Symptoms usually are those produced around the bite—swelling, itching and pain. Relief in most cases is prompt by the local application of baking soda or dilute ammonia.

Bites of poisonous spiders and scorpions are more serious. Spiders actually bite with fangs through which the poison is squirted. Scorpions sting by means of a stinger located in the tail.

The symptoms of poisonous spider and scorpion bites are both local and systemic. Locally, around the bite, there is pain at the instant of being bitten. The sting of the scorpion is much more painful than the bite of the spider. A slight swelling follows. The systemic symptoms occur within one half to two hours. The patient develops shock. Extreme thirst, nausea and vomiting are common. The symptoms of shock are pallor, cold skin, weak and rapid pulse and unconsciousness. In spider bites, muscle cramps may develop. In scorpion stings, numbness and paralysis develop near the sting. Death is not usual although the patient may become extremely ill.

The treatment is aimed at prevention of spread locally and treatment of shock systemically. To prevent spread, if the bite is on a limb, apply a tourniquet above the bite, i.e. between the bite and the heart. Do not apply it too tightly. Just enough to distend the veins. For treatment of the shock, have the patient lie quietly at rest and keep him warm. The cramps of spider bites are sometimes relieved by warm baths. Transport the patient to a doctor for further treatment.

Animal bites can be extremely serious. There is a twofold danger: (1) the bites are usually roughly lacerated and the danger of infection from the many infective bacteria in the animal's mouth is extremely high; and (2) there is always the possibility of rabies.

Rabies occurs in dogs, cats, wolves, horses, sheep, goats, etc. The disease is transmitted through the saliva during the bite. There is no cure for rabies. Once the disease develops, mortality is 100 per cent! However, it can be prevented by instituting the Pasteur treatment.

The treatment of animal bites can be divided into three phases: (1) treat the bite locally (2) observe the suspected animal and (3) institute the Pasteur treatment.

The best treatment of the bite locally is to wash it thoroughly, using soap and warm water. Wash both the wound and surrounding area, removing all dirt and saliva. The wound should then be cauterized. This had best be done by a doctor. If the wound is cauterized within a few hours, the patient may be protected against rabies. If no doctor is available, cauterize promptly with a red-hot needle or other metal object. Cover the wound with a dry, clean dressing.

The animal should not be killed. Capture it alive, if possible, and shut it up in a pen for three weeks for observation. If the animal has rabies, death will occur in seven to 10 days. Meanwhile, the time required for rabies to develop in man is three to eight weeks. If the animal is killed or dies, its head should be removed for examination. The Pasteur treatment should be taken if the animal is definitely rabid, if the animal escapes after biting, or if the animal develops symptoms of rabies during observation.

Do not attempt to treat animal bites without medical aid. If you are bitten far afield, it is best to cut short your hunting trip and return to the nearest available medical facility. Even if not rabies-infected, all animal bites are extremely dangerous and likely to develop a serious infection. Don't take this chance!

Snake bites may be of two types, poisonous and nonpoisonous. Unless you are an expert on snakes, every snake bite should be treated as though it were poisonous. If you are an expert you probably won't need this advice.

As with insect bites, the symptoms of snake bites are local and systemic. Locally, severe pain develops, and swelling. Systemically, severe shock develops within 15 minutes to two hours. Nausea, vomiting, diarrhea, faintness and unconsciousness occur. The skin becomes cold and clammy, the pulse feeble and rapid, there is difficulty in breathing. In the later stages come muscular weakness and coma, and death finally occurs in untreated cases. All these things don't happen at once. They occur as the venom is slowly absorbed.

Treatment is aimed at accomplishing the following: (1) prevent absorption of the venom (2) remove the venom (3) treat for shock and (4) give antivenom.

Absorption of the venom can be prevented by applying a tourniquet above the snake bite, if it is on a limb. Apply this just tightly enough to swell up the veins. Every 15 minutes loosen the tourniquet for one minute.

To remove the venom, make several crisscross cuts over each fang mark and over the swollen area. These cuts should be about ½ inch long and ¼ inch deep. There should be free oozing of blood and lymph. Use a flame-sterilized sharp knife or razor blade for this operation. Apply suction over these cuts. Use a suction syringe from a snake-bit kit if you have one. If necessary use your mouth. The venom will be destroyed in your stomach if you accidentally swallow it. There is danger *if you have a cut* on your lips or in your mouth. The suction should be continued at least 20 minutes out of every hour.

To treat for shock, have the victim lie down at complete rest; give him plenty of water to drink, keep him warm. Do not give any alcoholic drinks or other stimulants. That's the worst thing you can do!

Antivenom is now available for the venom of most poisonous snakes. For this treatment the patient will have to be transported to a place where medical facilities are available.

If you follow these instructions carefully you will minimize the hazards of bites considerably. There is no other field in which a sound knowledge of first aid can do more than in the emergency treatment of bites. Study these few instructions. They may save a life, perhaps your own!

By A. M. Libasci, M.D.

COLD-WEATHER CARE

Too many outdoorsmen return from their winter trips with frozen fingers, toes, ears or other parts of the body. In most cases proper preparation can prevent such injury.

Let's take a look at what the Army does about frostbite. The Army's methods are based on years of research plus the experience in three wars.

Just what is frostbite, anyhow? It's an injury to tissues caused by exposure to temperatures below freezing. The damage happens because the blood vessels close down either partially or totally, cutting off nourishment to the tissues affected. This results in either partial or total death of the tissue. Severe frostbite cases become gangrenous with total loss of parts affected.

The first sign of frostbite is a grayish or whitish patch on the skin, a sort of blanching. This is usually numb. Watch for this sign on yourself and on your companions. It may show up after only a very short exposure. If you detect it, you should apply first aid at once.

Proper clothing, of course, will prevent most frostbite. But to be adequately protected you should understand a few basic principles. The most important of these is that clothing, by itself, cannot generate warmth. Clothing keeps us warm by trapping our body heat and preventing it from escaping. It's an insulator.

The best insulator in clothing is air. So take advantage of this in two ways: (1) wear clothes that trap many small pockets of air in the weave or pile of fabric and (2) wear multiple layers of clothing so you'll get air spaces between layers.

Two medium-thickness layers are more effective than one thick layer in retaining body heat. The air spaces between the layers do the trick. Make sure clothes fit loosely to provide about ¼ inch of air space between layers.

To take full advantage of the air pockets in a fabric, you must keep it clean. Grease and dirt will clog air pockets and so reduce the insulating properties.

Another important point is to avoid overdressing. Too much clothing makes you sweat. Sweat clogs up the air pockets, reducing the insulating effect. If you're sweating profusely, ventilate by loosening clothing, or remove an *inner* garment.

Wet clothes conduct heat away from the body. So keep the inside dry by avoiding overdressing and sweating. Keep the outside dry by using an outer layer of water-repellent material.

Here's an example of how the layer system works:

Layer One. Next to the skin wear long underwear of half wool and half cotton. A loose, two-piece suit is best.

Layer Two. Wear medium-weight wool pants and a wool shirt tucked inside pants. Fit must be loose.

Layer Three. A pair of water- and wind-repellent pants and a medium-weight, loose-fitting wool sweater. Both pairs of trousers should be supported by suspenders.

Layer Four. A pile- or fur-lined, light-weight, loose jacket.

Layer Five. A Mackinaw, parka or short overcoat.

This gives you three layers on the legs and five layers on the upper body. The legs need less covering because they're exercised more.

The same layer principle works on your hands and feet. Mittens should consist of a wool inner liner, and a separate outer wind- and water-repellent shell. Get the type with an "escape hatch" for your trigger finger. Make sure they are loose fitting!

On your feet, wear two pairs of wool socks. The outer pair should be at least half a size larger than the inner pair. Your shoes should not fit tightly. You should have plenty of room to wriggle your toes. Tie your trouser leg around the shoe top by means of a draw string or rubber band. Special insulated footwear is very effective if you expect to hit extremely cold weather and ice and snow.

If, in spite of everything, you do get frostbite, here are the basic first aid measures you should remember:

(1) Get out of the cold and into warm shelter.

(2) Use body heat to warm the part. Never use external heat warmer than body heat. If the frostbite is on your face, ears or trunk, cover it with your warm, ungloved hand. If your fingers are frostbitten, place the affected hand inside your shirt, up against your body. If a foot is frostbitten, remove your shoe and sock and place your foot within the shirt and against the body of another individual. *Never rub snow or ice on frostbite.* Never rub at all.

(3) If your skin is broken, cover the area with a sterile dressing. Don't use strong antiseptics.

(4) Take warm food and drink.

(5) Get medical aid.

When you're hunting in cold areas, use common sense. Keep moving, avoid long periods of inactivity, don't touch metal with bare hands. If you must stand still for long periods select an area on rocks or twigs rather than bare, wet and colder ground.

If you clothe yourself as recommended and use a little common sense, frostbite is far less likely to sneak up on you.

By A. M. Libasci, M.D.

FIRST-AID KITS

First-aid equipment can be purchased far more economically when it is selected item by item than in a prepared kit, and the thought that goes into its selection is good training for the time when you have to use it. Actually, it's surprising how little equipment you need.

One 10-yard roll of one-inch adhesive is sufficient to provide for a number of injuries, and to serve in other emergencies as well. Adhesive tape can pinch-hit for a missing reel seat, it can bind guides fast to fly rods, and it can cover the splintered edges of a boat seat. A roll of adhesive then should be your first purchase.

Next you will need a good antiseptic to prevent germs from multiplying on the surface of wounds. Tincture of iodine did a great job in its day but medical research laboratories have developed far better germ killers. Tincture of Metaphen is probably the best, although Merthiolate and a number of modern antiseptics are equally effective.

Cotton swabs are included in most every first-aid package. But in the heat of the first hectic minutes immediately following some personal catastrophe, the cotton swabs are used up. A few toothpicks, serviceable in their own right, will speedily become cotton swabs (although they won't be sterile ones), if a small package of cotton is included in your kit. But keep the cotton clean by keeping it wrapped carefully in its own blue wrappings and placing a rubber band tightly around it.

Include at least three rolls of two-inch bandage and a couple rolls of one-inch bandage in your kit. Buy a dozen three-inch squares of sterile gauze in envelopes, and the best pair of scissors you can afford.

Practically all field wounds, and especially puncture wounds, carry with them the danger of lockjaw, what doctors call tetanus. Every splinter, every misguided knife blade, every rusty nail, every wire fence barb, every bullet, every grain of shot, every burn wound, whether from campfire, gunpowder or brush friction, can carry billions of lockjaw spores into the human body. There, in the absence of air, these spores become living tetanus bacilli which create a toxin that is quite capable of ending the life of the most rugged man on earth.

Two injections of tetanus toxoid by your own doctor will protect you from tetanus, which is at least one of the 10 worst diseases afflicting man. Those who served in the armed forces have had these injections. Every year or two, just to keep their immunity in shape for any emergency, they should have a "booster" shot.

But how many sportsmen take this precaution? How many go into the wilderness *protected* against a disease which follows them to the corners of the earth? Most wounds of this nature reach a local doctor's office several days after they occur, too late to benefit much from the injection of tetanus antitoxin the doctor administers. This form of protection is quite a different matter from the permanent protection afforded by the toxoid, but it is the best available if you have forgotten to lock the stable door.

When you pack your first-aid kit, give a thought to your personal ailments. Are your teeth in good condition? If they are not, arrange to see your dentist before you leave. Otherwise you may spoil the best days of your life by suffering with a toothache. Your doctor can provide you with pills that will check a diarrhea or a headache, and give you any other remedies he thinks you should carry. You should also take along some water-purifying tablets if you are traveling through a region where your water will come directly from streams, lakes and springs.

In the wilderness, the old law of the survival of the fittest still operates. So pack your own first-aid kit and give some serious thought to how and when to use it. It's the best way possible to insure that you or your friend's name keeps off the casualty list.

By Paul H. Fluck, M.D.

EXPOSURE TO HEAT

Every time you go afield in hot weather, you're a potential victim of three ailments: heat cramps, heat exhaustion and heatstroke (sunstroke).

Your body has a very sensitive and very effective heat regulatory system. When your body is subjected to excessive heat, you perspire profusely. This perspiration evaporates from your skin, and in the process of evaporation heat is lost from your body.

Unfortunately, though, in profuse perspiration, your body loses much salt. Prolonged exposure to heat, with profuse loss of salt in the sweat, results in heat cramps.

The symptoms of heat cramps are severe, painful cramps involving the muscles of the abdomen, legs and arms. The intestines also cramp up and there's vomiting. Severe weakness results.

To treat these heat cramps, keep the victim warm and quiet, and have him lie on his back with his head low. Apply hot water bottles to abdomen and other cramp areas. If no hot water is available, rub afflicted areas gently. If victim is conscious, give him plenty of water to drink, and salt either as tablets or plain table salt.

Heat exhaustion also results from overheating the body. In this condition, although there's profuse sweating, evaporation and cooling are interfered with. Heavy, tight-fitting clothing, very high humidity, poor ventilation and other external conditions may be to blame for inadequate evaporation.

The symptoms of heat exhaustion are pale, sweaty skin, weak and rapid pulse, shallow breathing, normal or below normal temperature and faintness. The patient is usually conscious.

The treatment for heat exhaustion is to loosen clothing and remove patient to a cool comfortable place keeping his head low. If he's conscious, give him plenty of water to drink. (Add one teaspoonful of salt per quart.) See that patient is kept warm, and give him warm liquids to drink.

The most serious of these conditions is heat stroke. It frequently causes death. In this condition, your body's cooling system breaks down completely. Though your body is very hot, there's no perspiration. There's no cooling possible, and the body heat rises, reaching dangerous and often fatal temperatures.

The symptoms of heatstroke are sudden complete collapse, sometimes accompanied by unconsciousness, the skin is red, flushed, very hot and dry, and breathing is very deep. Mouth temperature is very high—from 105°F to 110°F. Death frequently occurs.

The treatment: Remove the patient to a cool place and place him in cold water making sure there's no danger of drowning. Rub and massage the skin briskly. When mouth temperature is down to 102°F, remove the patient from the tub. If you can't get patient into cold water, spray or splash him with water and fan him. Electric fans are the best answer when you're in civilization.

For this fanning, the patient should lie flat in the shade, with his clothing loosened. If no stream of water is available, apply wet cloths to his body and fan him continuously with a wet cloth such as a shirt.

When you're fishing, hunting, working or playing in overheated surroundings:

Increase your salt intake. Take one salt tablet with each glass of water, or add one teaspoonful of salt to each quart of water you drink.

Increase your fluid intake. You may need four or five or more quarts of water per day.

Avoid heavy, nonporous clothing.

Take short rests often.

Eat moderately. Avoid fats and greasy foods.

Don't overindulge in alcohol.

HOW TO RECOGNIZE HEAT CASES

	CRAMPS	EXHAUSTION	STROKE
UNCONSCIOUS	usually not	usually not	frequently
SKIN	pale, cold	pale, cold	flushed
PERSPIRATION	profuse	profuse	none
PULSE	weak and rapid	weak and rapid	strong and rapid
MOUTH TEMPERATURE	normal or below	normal or below	very high 105°F to 110°F
BREATHING	shallow	shallow	deep, snoring
DEATH	very rare	rare	frequent

By A. M. Libasci, M.D.

CHAPTER 7

fishing

MORE PEOPLE enjoy the out-of-doors by fishing than through any other single participant or spectator sport. On the following pages, you will find pictures to help identify the most popular fresh- and salt-water fish, information on how, when and where to catch them and the proper fundamentals for the use of fly rod, casting rod, spinning gear and salt-water outfits.

BAIT-ROD CASTING

Don't try to use casting tackle unless you know you'll take the time and trouble to assemble it properly and learn to cast correctly with it—and will do a bit of practicing before going on a fishing trip.

The casting rod should never be under five feet, and some experts prefer one of six feet or even two or three inches over that. For ⅛-ounce lures (which few learn to handle comfortably on casting tackle) it may be even six and a half feet or longer.

You sometimes hear it said that straight reel seat and handle are preferred only by old-timers who learned with that type. This is not the case. Many learn with a sunken reel seat, and use one for several years before deciding they like a straight one better—discover it perhaps by joining a tournament casting club and using rods belonging to other members. A reel seat (fly-rod type) and grip built onto the blank are much lighter than those of the usual sunken-seat type; also, they have a live feel and action running clear down through the hand. Still, there's nothing wrong with a sunken reel seat, if you prefer it.

Flexibility of your rod must match the weight lure you use with it. With a bamboo rod, you haven't over about ⅛-ounce leeway on either side, if you wish to do comfortable casting. Most hollow-glass rods allow a wider range, some of them a surprisingly wide range of weights, and still permit casting comfortable enough for practical fishing purposes.

Even if your rod is meant for ⅝-ounce plugs, you can handle ⅛-ounce lures with it. For instance, if you're bass fishing, run onto a bed of crappies, and want to try them for a change—but your casting will be jerky since the rod won't bend enough with this light lure.

But for the last word in delicate, artistic casting, you'll probably have to get a rod listed for considerably lighter plugs than you mean to use with it. This because most makers—not all—list rods as for the heaviest plugs not likely to break them when inexpertly handled.

Experts recommend lighter rods strictly on the supposition that you will *not* attempt very long casts with lures heavier than those for which the rod is listed (or even with lures for which it *is* listed if it's called a "tournament accuracy" blank) since to do so is just begging for a broken rod. Long casts waste half your fishing time anyway.

Some, who lob a plug out, prefer a rod with all-over bend, slow in action. Others like one with fast tip action, bending mainly near the tip during a cast; these "shoot" the plug fast. It's a matter of taste as a rule.

Most prefer rods with action about halfway between the two types mentioned—one that's quite stiff in the lower half, bending nicely in all the upper half. Since this is midway between the two extremes, it is advised for those who haven't yet formed opinions on the subject. It should suit most.

Some experts also most strongly recommend getting a longer casting rod of two-piece construction, with the ferrule preferably some distance below the middle where the blank is stronger, and is called upon for less action in casting.

The whole heart of good casting is a light reel spool. And remember that the weight of line—wet when fishing—is as important as weight of the spool itself. A large spool full of wet line has too much inertia to start or stop easily and smoothly. And having a large spool only half full of line won't help, since then it—and all the other mechanism—must travel twice as fast as a full one to get out the same amount of line. Which means that one must use a smaller, narrow-frame reel, of what was formerly known as the "skish" type. Finding one will give no trouble; all such reels made by the standard companies are fine for practical fishing, though contest casters may argue over the merits of various ones.

Here is one great reason why so few ever become good with casting tackle: *they simply will not learn to oil their reels often enough*, and the best casting outfit ever made will cast poorly and backlash, if the reel runs dry.

Occasionally, take the reel apart and clean the gears thoroughly. Then grease them very lightly—much grease will slow a reel greatly, especially in colder weather.

Some of these small reels have no anti-backlash device. Most have, but try to learn to cast without it, to use the reel "free-running." This means that a slight click should be felt when the spool is taken in the fingers and shaken endwise. However, it takes a good deal of practice to use a reel when it's running so fast, but at least learn to use the antibacklash device as lightly as you can.

For practical, pleasant fishing with a fast reel, the softer the line, the better it will cast. A hard, wiry line is inclined to spring up in coils, to cause backlashes; but it becomes better in this respect when it's been used a good deal.

For good casting, the rule is that the lighter the plug, the lighter the line should be. For ⅛-ounce lures, a five-pound line is about right—lighter is impractical in landing fish, as a rule.

By Jason Lucas

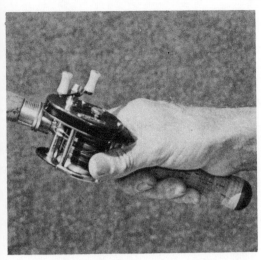

The right way to cast: Hold your rod loosely —"strangling the grip" causes bad casting; the reel handles are up.

Snap rod straight up, the grip barely past vertical; the forearm shouldn't move—let your wrist do all the work.

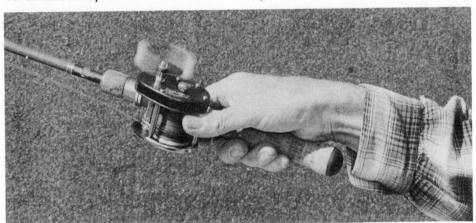

The power for forward cast comes from immediately below forefinger knuckle. Don't try to "drive" with your thumb.

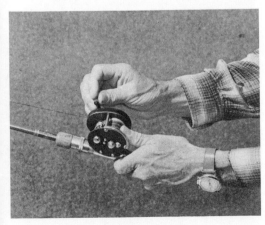

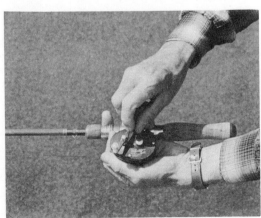

To retrieve, the thumb should rest on rear pillar, just brushing the line, ready to drop onto spool if fish hits.

Veterans "palm the reel" to retrieve, as shown here. If fish strikes, thumb is quickly slid back to rear of spool.

HOW, WHEN AND WHERE FOR FRESH-WATER FISH

FISH	DESCRIPTION	LOCATION	NATURAL FOODS
LARGEMOUTH BASS Pugnacious battler. Food value: good.	Dark-green back and sides, lighter green below. Blackish stripe along sides. Darker splotches sometimes along and above lateral line. Upper jaw extends beyond eye.	Nearly every state. Warm, sluggish water. Lakes and ponds; around lily pads, rushes, reeds, sunken weed beds. Rivers and streams: pockets in banks, alongside logs, submerged tree trunks.	Minnows, frogs, mice, worms, crawfish, hellgrammites and other larvae; grasshoppers, crickets, other insects, flies.
SMALLMOUTH BASS "Pound for pound, the gamest fish." Food value: good, usually better than largemouth.	Basic color bronze or brassy green. Darker markings sometimes appear as vertical bands. Eyes usually marked with red spots. Upper jaw ends below eye. Dorsal fin not so deeply notched as largemouth.	Almost every state. Faster-moving streams than largemouth; in lakes, rocky shore lines—in clear water, sand or pebble bottom. In streams, behind boulders, at foot of riffles or rapids, deep, clear pools.	Minnows, frogs, worms, crawfish, hellgrammites, other larvae; grasshoppers, crickets, other insects, flies. Prefers live bait.
WHITE CRAPPIE BLACK CRAPPIE King of Pan Fish, striking almost any artificial lure or natural bait. Food value: excellent.	Dark olive green, with darker spots sometimes almost black. Silvery cast over lower part. Black crappie markings: irregular, numerous. A school fish.	Nearly every state except some on Pacific coast. White crappie abundant in the South, black crappie in North. Primarily lake fish, congregate in deep holes; close to shore or quite a distance out. Let boat drift until you get a bite, quietly anchor.	Flies and other insects, small minnows, worms, shrimps, crawfish, other crustaceans.
BLUEGILL Fish of boyhood days, caught with cane pole, bent pin. Food value: excellent pan fish.	Back: dark greenish olive, purple luster. Chainlike greenish bars downward, dorsal fin to belly. Belly is often brilliant red, cheeks iridescent bluish green. Fins greenish cast, gill cover rich black.	Nearly every state, Canada. Inclined to "school" around edge of weed beds, pond lilies, brush piles, stumps, bridges, docks, deep holes and pockets.	Small minnows, worms, grasshoppers, crickets, other insects and flies.
BROOK TROUT Game, vigorous. Favorite of fly fishermen. Food value: excellent.	Back mottled with dark olive green, black; small red spots on sides, lighter whitish spots. Dorsal and tail fins mottled, lower fins dusky with white on forward edges. Belly reddish. Scales scarcely visible. Tail square.	Originally from Labrador west to Saskatchewan, thence south through Alleghenies to northern Georgia—but not west of the Mississippi, excepting Iowa and Minnesota. Now found in cold streams from California north through British Columbia to Alaska. Found on downstream side of rocks—close to bottom, heading upstream.	Under ½ pound, feeds on nymphs, insects, worms, small crustaceans; when larger, diet includes small fish, larger crustaceans such as crawfish and mollusks, frogs.
RAINBOW TROUT (Steelhead) Furious runs, spectacular jumps, make it gamest trout. Food value: excellent when from wilderness streams.	Bluish or olive green above lateral line, silvery green on sides. Sides, tail, dorsal fins have small dark spots. Wide lateral purplish-red band on sides from head to tail. Lower fins dusky whitish. When rainbow migrates to sea it becomes a "steelhead" and color fades to light blue, silvery sheen.	All states except southern part of those bordering Gulf of Mexico. Larger, swift-flowing streams of West and smaller streams of East in fast water. Edge of strong currents, head of rapids, overhanging banks in swift current.	Insects in larval and mature state, worms, flies, minnows, crustaceans, salmon eggs.
BROWN TROUT Wary and crafty, survives in waters where brook trout cannot exist. Food value: good.	Upper body dark brown, lighter brown sides. Black spots on back, red and black spots on sides. Older fish have overshot hooked underjaw characteristic of salmon.	Every state except southernmost, also Canada. Streams, rivers, lakes, submerged obstructions, overhanging banks. Lower end of pools, beside or just ahead of rocks protruding from the current.	Flies and insects. As it grows, diet includes snails, crawfish, worms, minnows.
LAKE TROUT One of the our largest fresh-water fish. Food value: excellent unless too fat when flesh has oily taste.	Grayish: from very dark to pale. Covered with pale spots often tinged with pink. Forked tail. Teeth on roof of mouth. Flesh varies, almost white to deep pink.	New England states westward through Great Lakes to British Columbia, north of this area to Labrador, Hudson Bay and Alaska. Water temperatures between 40° F. and 50° F. Summer: waters from 40 to 100 feet and deeper. Early spring and late fall: on reefs or shoals, 10 to 20 feet or less depth. In deep water, near bottom.	Late fall and early spring, in shallow water. Feeds on flies, insects. In deep water, on small whitefish, herring, smelt, other small fish and minnows.
WALLEYE Good, though not spectacular, fighter. Food value: excellent.	Dark olive mottled with yellow, forming indistinct bars. Belly, lower fins pinkish. Eyes large, whitish, glassy. Two dorsal fins.	Most states, excepting far western and extreme southern. Nocturnal feeder around the shallows. Prefers moderately deep, clear-flowing water with rock, sand bottoms. Found in schools in deep holes, rivers and lakes. In pools under falls and below rapids, and bottom of reefs, ledges.	Small fish and minnows of all kinds, frogs, crawfish, worms, aquatic insects.
NORTHERN PIKE Vigorous striker at all kinds of artificial lures. Food value: fair to good, although bony.	Greenish or olive gray, at times a bluish cast. Lighter on lower side, yellowish cast on belly. Many whitish or yellowish elongated light spots against darker sides. Fins, spotted.	From Lake Champlain westward, Great Lakes region to upper Mississippi Valley, Lake of the Woods, northward to Alaska. Plentiful in Canada. Sunken weed beds, holes along edges; among lily pads, edge of rushes in deep holes, near sunken logs; in hot weather, deeper water, rocky channels.	Minnows, frogs, insects, all kinds of smaller fish, including its own young.

HOW, WHEN AND WHERE FOR FRESH-WATER FISH   *by Lou S. Caine*

ARTIFICIAL LURES	METHODS AND TACKLE

ARTIFICIAL LURES

Floating and diving plugs, underwater plugs, top-water plugs, deep-diving plugs, spoons, pork-rind lures, wet and dry flies and bass bugs.

METHODS AND TACKLE

Bait casting: Rod not shorter than 5 feet, action suitable to weight of lure to be cast. Braided silk or nylon line 9 to 12 pounds for 1/4- and 3/8-ounce lures; 20 pounds or heavier for lures over 7/8 ounce. Reel: quadruple multiplying level-winding bait-casting reel, holding 100 yards of line. Light aluminum spool. *Fly casting:* Rod about 8 1/2 or 9 feet, balanced with proper line. Reel: single-action or automatic.

Midget underwater lures weighing 3/8 ounce. Floating and diving plugs, deep-diving plugs, spoons, pork-rind lures, wet and dry flies, bass bugs, spinner-and-fly combinations. Surface lures in smaller sizes.

Bait casting: Rod not less than 5 feet, with "light" action. Reel: light with "fast" spool, 100 yards of 15-pound silk or nylon line. With light lures, use line of 9- to 12-pound test. *Fly casting:* Rod 8 1/2 or 9 feet built on 2 or 2 1/2 ferrule. Line, E or D level or HDH or HCH tapered, depending on rod. Single-action or automatic reel.

Flies, fly-and-spinner combinations, bugs and fly-rod lures. Small spoons, spinners, pork-rind lures, 1/4- and 3/8-ounce bait-casting plugs, other small lures.

Bait casting: Midget bait-casting lures, rod 5 to 5 1/2 feet. 100-yard size level-winding reel; silk or nylon line not over 10 or 12 pounds. *Fly casting:* 8 1/2- or 9-foot rod, bass-trout action, 2 or 2 1/2 ferrule, weight 5 ounces. E or D level line or an HDH or HCH tapered line. Gut or nylon leader 3 to 6 feet; wet flies, fly-and-spinner combinations, artificial bugs. *Trolling:* Casting rod, midget lures. *Still-fishing:* Old-fashioned cane pole, 8 to 10 feet, line of equal length, black silk or nylon casting line about 9- to 12-pound test. Lightweight cork or float, very small sinker—split shot or strip lead. No. 3 or No. 4 hook. Live minnows, 1 1/2 inches long.

Small spinners with fly attached, sponge-rubber spiders, small trout flies, deep-hair surface bugs, small popping fly-rod lures.

Still-fishing: 8-foot cane pole, limber action, line long as pole, light bobber, split-shot sinker, Size 3, 4, 5 or 6 Carlisle hook, can of worms. *Spinning:* Rod light action, 7 1/2 feet long. *Fly fishing:* Light trout-action rod 8 1/2 feet long. Split bamboo, 1 3/4 ferrule, weighing 5 ounces. F level fly line. Leaders 7 feet long, testing 6 pounds. Dress lure to keep floating. Reel, single-action or automatic. Cork and plastic-bodied bugs, spinner-and-fly combinations, small bucktails with tiny pork-strip streamers.

Wet and dry flies, spinner-and-fly combinations, artificial bugs. Wet flies most effective, fished as deep as possible. Larger trout taken on small underwater bait-casting plugs, spoons.

Fly casting: Most favored. Rod varies 7 1/2 to 9 feet, good tip action. For small, bushy streams, light line and flies, short rod with small ferrule size. On larger water, heavier line and bugs and longer casts, longer rod with more backbone. A line size balancing properly with rod; rod length 7 1/2 feet; ferrule size 1 1/2 inches; level line F; tapered line HEH. The smaller the lure, lighter the leader. Reel: in proportion to rod, line.

Large streamer flies, salmon flies, bucktails and, on small streams, dry flies; spinner-and-fly combinations, spoons, salmon eggs, fly-rod lures; casting-rod lures—especially those weighing 3/8 to 1/2 ounce.

Fly casting: For rainbow, rod 7 1/2 to 9 feet. For steelhead, split bamboo rod of 9 feet, built on 2 3/4 ferrule—with D level line or HCH tapered. Larger reel for steelhead, 100 yards 6-thread linen line; heavier leader. *Still-fishing:* Same rods with salmon eggs, worms. Special "steelhead" rod, 7 1/2 to 9 feet for casting spinners, plugs, bait. *Bait casting:* Rod 5 feet, light-medium action. *Trolling:* Special steelhead rod above.

Wet and dry flies, streamer flies, spinner-and-fly combinations, floating bass bugs, fly-rod lures. Larger brown trout strike midget-sized bait-casting lures.

Fly casting: Lightweight rod, 1 3/4 ferrule, 8 feet long, 5 ounces, with HDH tapered fly line or E level line. Larger brown trout: rod 9 feet long, 2 1/2 ferrule, HCH tapered or D level line. *Bait casting:* Rod 5 feet long. Lightweight "fast" level-winding reel, 50 yards 9- to 12-pound-test silk or nylon line. A 3-foot light nylon or gut leader. *Still-fishing:* Above rods, but when large baits are cast, with more backbone, HCH or GBG tapered line, D or C level line.

Shallow water during fall and spring; strikes flies, spinners, spinner-and-fly combinations, plugs and pork-rind lures. Deep water during summer, large spoons and wobblers, large giant-sized plugs.

Trolling: Summer months, get the lure or bait near bottom, using metal line or heavy sinkers. Salt-water trolling rod, 6-ounce tip, 5 feet long, 18-inch butt. A 3/0 size salt-water reel, star drag. Large spoons of wobbling type, plugs with wobbling motion. *Bait casting:* Spring months, rod 5 to 6 feet long, medium or stiff action. 100-yard size level-winding casting reel. Underwater plugs in small, medium size. *Fly casting:* Rod 9 feet long, 2 3/4 ferrule, weighing 6 ounces. Back fly line with linen or casting line. *Still-fishing:* Bait-casting rod and reel. Deep hole, sand or rock bottom, fish off the bottom with live baits.

Underwater plugs, especially deep-diving baits, spoons and pork-rind lures. Surface lures at late evening, night. Flies, bass bugs for early morning, late evening.

Trolling: Rod stiff, medium action, 5 feet long. Multiplying level-winding bait-casting reel, 100 yards 15- to 20-pound-test silk or nylon line. Short 9- to 12-inch wire leader. Lures that will go deep or sinker tied on 2 feet ahead of lure. Troll slowly. *Bait casting:* During the day, deep-diving lures. Evening or night, shallow-running or surface lures. Light or medium-action rod, same reel and line for trolling. *Fly casting:* Rod 8 1/2 feet long, heavier leaders. *Still-fishing:* Rods for bait casting, above. Keep bait close to the bottom.

Floating and diving plugs, underwater plugs, top-water plugs, spoons, pork-rind lures, flies, bass bugs.

Bait casting: Rod 5 and 5 1/2 feet long, light, medium and stiff actions. Quadruple multiplying level-winding reel, line 20-pound test. Wire leader 9 to 12 inches. *Trolling:* Stiff-action rod, reel holding 100 yards line. Spoons and wobblers, trolled to edges of weed beds, rushes. *Fly casting:* Rod 9 feet long, powerful action, 2 3/4 ferrule, shade under 6 1/2 ounces. D or C level line, very fine wire. No. 2 leader a yard long—fasten one end of leader to lure, other to very small-size swivel.

HOW, WHEN AND WHERE FOR FRESH-WATER FISH

FISH	DESCRIPTION	LOCATION	NATURAL FOODS
MUSKELLUNGE Largest American fresh-water game fish except lake trout. Crafty striker; when hooked, tremendous battler. Food value: fair.	Great Lakes type: olive-green back. Great Lakes Basin and St. Lawrence River. Chautauqua, Ohio, type: bronze back. Ohio River drainage. Mississippi type: bluish-gray cast. Hudson bay and Mississippi drainage.	Principally larger lakes and rivers. Sheltered spots around weed beds, sunken logs; edges of channels, around bars, reefs.	Minnows, suckers, small fish including its own. Frogs, snakes, mice, squirrels, young of muskrats.
ATLANTIC SALMON World's greatest fresh-water game fish. Prefers flies to all other artificial lures, fights furiously. Food value: excellent.	When fresh from sea, steel blue with silver sides, black spots on head, body, fins. Red spots, patches on sides of males. After being in fresh water, brownish-red cast.	Nova Scotia, New Brunswick, Quebec, Labrador, a few in Maine. Clear, open streams, lying at lower end of pools.	In the sea, small fish such as herring, smelt. Entering fresh water on way to spawn, feed little—at spawning ground, not at all. When young, parr feed on larvae and insects. Entering the sea, as smolts: sand flies, small crabs, shrimps, other small fish.

HOW, WHEN AND WHERE FOR SALT-WATER FISH

FISH	DESCRIPTION	LOCATION	NATURAL FOODS
WEAKFISH SPOTTED WEAKFISH A most popular East Coast salt-water fish. Savage striker but tender mouth. Food value: fine.	Brownish-cast back, sides silvery with irregular lines forward and downward. *Spotted weakfish:* Bluish gray along back, sides silvery, spotted. *Weakfish:* Soft rays of dorsal and anal fins scaled.	*Weakfish:* Atlantic coast, from Cape Cod to the east coast of Florida. *Spotted weakfish:* New York to Texas. Inshore waters such as tides, rips, surf, inlets, bays, in tidal rivers, lagoons.	Shrimps, squids, herring, scup, menhaden, butterfish, mummichog, small mullets, shiners, spearing and needlefish; also sandworms, bloodworms.
CHANNEL BASS "Bulldog of the Surf." Fished in or just beyond breakers, a tacklebuster. Food value: good.	Iridescent silver sides, copper red toward back. Larger fish, reddish shade, black spot at tail.	Atlantic coast from New York to Florida, and western Gulf of Mexico. Protected shallow waters of tidal rivers, bays, lagoons, sloughs near ocean, gulf, breakers close to shore.	Crabs, sand fleas, shrimps, clams, squids, small fish such as mullet and menhaden.
STRIPED BASS Fine fighter in fresh or salt water. Food value: excellent.	Olive-green back, greenish silver sides. Light silver belly. Dark horizontal stripes, greenish from head to tail along back. Two dorsal fins. Lower jaw extends beyond upper.	Atlantic coast from the Gulf of St. Lawrence to Florida into Gulf of Mexico. From Cape Cod to North Carolina. Monterey, California, to Coos Bay, Oregon; San Francisco Bay. Rock-bound shore lines, beaches. Winter and spring, rivers, inlets, sloughs.	Bloodworms, crabs (especially shedder crabs), shrimps, clams, mussels, squids, eels, small fish such as mullet, whiting, herring and menhaden; on Pacific coast, sardines.
BLUEFISH One of fiercest salt-water fighters. Food value: a supreme table fish.	Dark, iridescent greenish blue to silvery blue sides. Handle carefully as it has strong, sharp teeth in each jaw.	Almost world-wide. Atlantic, central Brazil to Nova Scotia. Erratic migration, usually appearing off Virginia coast about middle of May, New York most of summer. Follows coast line, sometimes miles offshore or right in surf. Also inlets, tidal lagoons, rivers.	Menhaden, spearing, mullet, small fish, squids, shrimps, sand eels, cut bait.
BLUEFIN TUNA One of the world's largest game fish. Catching tuna is grueling battle, lasting hours. Food value: excellent.	Iridescent all over, dark-blue black bluish gray above lateral line. Silvery gray sides, lighter on lower sides, belly. Tail, dorsal fins dark blue. Finlets along back, dorsal fin to tail and from anal fin to tail.	Both sides of Atlantic, Pacific. Atlantic, Newfoundland south to Bahamas. Pacific coast, Columbia River to Lower California. Open seas, but at times in channels and tide rips flowing in and out of bays—sometimes within few hundred yards offshore.	All kinds of smaller fish, in schools, such as flying fish, herring, mackerel, menhaden, sardines, bonitos, anchovies.
BONEFISH Considered fastest fish that swims. Supreme catch of light-tackle angler. Food value: rarely eaten.	Burnished-silver sides. Darker back, olive tinge; at times indistinct stripes on sides. Snout overlaps small mouth, suckerlike appearance. Powerful forked tail.	All tropical seas, Florida Keys, Gulf of Mexico, Pacific. Bahama Islands off Florida coast. Shallow water to feed with rising tide, on mud and sand flats.	Small crabs, hermit crabs, sand fleas, shrimps, small crawfish and conches.
TARPON One of the world's great game fish. Savagely strikes flies, plugs, spoons, other artificial lures, many kinds of natural bait. Food value: poor.	Gleaming silver sides shade to coppery-greenish cast along back. Last ray of dorsal fin greatly prolonged. Extremely bony mouth.	Famous locales: lower east and west coasts of Florida, coasts of Louisiana and Texas in the Gulf, waters adjacent to Canal Zone, Mexico's Panuco River. Follows coast line in schools, ascends freshwater rivers, frequently in brackish water. Mouths of rivers, passes and cuts, tidal bays, creeks, lagoons.	Mullet, catfish, pinfish, other small fish, crabs.

HOW, WHEN AND WHERE FOR FRESH-WATER FISH
by Lou S. Caine

ARTIFICIAL LURES

Surface and underwater baits, spinner-and-bucktail combinations and spoons. Bass bugs, large-sized streamer flies.

Wet and dry flies. Large streamer flies, occasionally a spinner-and-fly combination, even small plugs.

METHODS AND TACKLE

Bait casting: Rod with enough backbone to forcibly set hook; 5 feet long, medium or stiff action. 100-yard level-winding reel, silk or nylon line testing 20 pounds. Lure fastened to metal leader 9 to 12 inches long. *Fly casting:* 9-foot rod, plenty of backbone, on 2¾ ferrule. Metal leader, No. 2 to No. 5 wire. *Trolling:* Rod, like above for bait casting. Oversized level-winding reel, 150 yards 25-pound-test silk or nylon line. Underwater lures, spoons and large chubs or suckers.

Fly casting: Rod 9½ feet long, size 3 ferrule, weighting 6½ to 8 ounces, 6-inch rear grip. GBG tapered line, single-action reel with adjustable drag—holding 100 yards of 6- to 9-thread linen spliced to fly line. Light terminal tackle, tapered leaders of at least 9 feet. Salmon flies large, gaudy.

HOW, WHEN AND WHERE FOR SALT-WATER FISH
by Lou S. Caine

ARTIFICIAL LURES

Spotted Weakfish: Sinking plugs, jerked when retrieved. Surface lures, spoons, squids, feathered jigs. Fly-rod fishermen: spinner-and-fly combinations, streamer flies, bass bugs.

Trolling: Spoons, feathered jigs, large sinking plugs. *Surf casting:* Large plugs, surface and sinking, metal squids. *Bait casting:* Bass-size plugs, in sinking, floating-diving, surface types. Feathered jigs.

Squids, feathered jigs, spoons, spinners, spinners and bloodworms, eelskins, strip bait, pork-rind lures. Large floating-diving surface, underwater plugs. Fly-rod lures—bass bugs, streamer flies.

Trolling, casting: metal and eelskin squids, feathered jigs, underwater plugs. *Bait casting:* sinking and surface plugs.

Strip bait, various types of jigs, especially feather jigs.

Formerly, bonefish rarely struck artificial lures. Catches reported now on sinking and surface plugs, feathered jigs and streamer flies.

Trolling: Large floating-diving baits, spoons, feathered jigs, cut strip bait. *Bait casting:* Surface baits, floating-diving baits, underwater baits. *Fly casting:* Bass plugs, surface fly-rod lures, large streamer flies.

METHODS AND TACKLE

Bait casting: For spotted weakfish, rod stiff or medium action, about 5 feet long. Level-winding reel holding 100 yards of 15-pound test nylon or 6-thread linen line. *Fly casting:* Weakfish, rod 9 feet long, 2¾ ferrule. Size HCH tapered or a D level line. Streamer flies, 1/0 hook size together with size 3 spinner; floating, popping bass plugs.

Surf casting: Surf-casting rod with tip 6 feet long, butt 30 inches. Free-spool reel, drag handle, 200 yards 9-thread linen line. Leader 18 inches long, No. 8 wire. Pyramid-shaped sinker of 4 ounces, 7/0 O'Shaughnessy hook, tinned finish. *Bait casting:* A 5 or 5½-foot rod, musky type. Oversized casting reel, 150 yards 9-thread linen or 20-pound-test nylon line. Bass-size fresh-water lures, wire leader 9 inches long. *Trolling:* Outfit above for bait casting.

Surf casting: Surf rod with tip 6½ feet long, 30-inch spring butt. A 3/0 free-spool reel, adjustable drag, 300 yards 12-thread linen line. Wire leader 18 inches long. Hook, 9/0. *Trolling:* Rod tip 5 feet long, weight 4 ounces. Butt 18 inches long. A 3/0 free-spool reel, adjustable drag, 400 yards 6-thread line. *Bait casting:* Rod 5½ feet long, medium or stiff action. Level-winding bait-casting reel, 150 yards 20-pound-test silk or nylon line. A 9- to 12-inch wire leader, underwater, floating-diving bass lures. *Still-fishing:* Bait-casting outfit described, no sinker. Baits: soft-shelled or shedder crabs on Atlantic coast; sardines on Pacific. *Fly fishing:* Rod with backbone, 9 feet long, 3 ferrule. D level or HDH tapered line backed with 100 yards of 6-thread linen or 20-pound-test nylon. Streamer flies.

Trolling: Fish edge of school, a rod with 4-ounce tip and 6-thread line. *Surf casting:* Surf-casting rod, 9 feet long, 30-inch spring butt, wire leader. *Bait casting:* Medium-weight rod 5 feet long. Level-winding reel, 100 or 150 yards nylon or linen line. Metal squids, feathered jigs, underwater plugs.

Smallest size, so-called "school tuna": Rod with 9-ounce tip, 4/0 wide reel, 400 yards 15-thread linen line. School tuna take bait close to boat. Feather jigs, with wire leader made from No. 8 leader wire 12 feet long. *Larger Pacific coast tuna:* Rod with 12- to 16-ounce tip, a 6/0 reel, 300 yards 24-thread line. *Giant tuna of North Atlantic:* Rod with tip weighing 20 ounces, a 12/0 reel holding 600 yards of 39-thread line.

Still-fishing: Wading or poling in skiff, incoming tide. Fish with no tension on line when bonefish strikes. Rod with tip 5 feet long, weight 4 ounces. Detachable butt, 17 inches long, 1/0 free-spool reel, 300 yards 6-thread linen line. Half-ounce sinker with snelled hooks 3/0 size. *Bait casting:* Procedure same. Small sinking plugs, surface lures, feathered jigs. *Fly casting:* Rod 9 feet long, a 2¾ ferrule, plenty backbone. Much 6-thread linen line for backing as reel holds.

Trolling: Rod tip not less than 5 feet long, weighing 6 ounces. Detachable butt 18 inches long. A 4/0 reel, 450 yards 9-thread linen line. Wire leader, 6 feet long, No. 9, 10 leader wire. *Still-fishing:* Same tackle. Bait, 10-inch mullet. *Drift fishing:* Same outfit. *Bait casting:* Rod medium or stiff action, 5 feet long. Level-winding casting reel, 100 yards 20-pound-test silk or nylon line. Wire leader 9 inches, just ahead of bait. *Fly casting:* Rod 9 feet long, No. 2¾ ferrule. D level or HCH tapered line. Leader of No. 2 stainless-steel wire. Bass bugs, lures, streamer flies.

HOW, WHEN AND WHERE FOR SALT-WATER FISH

FISH	DESCRIPTION	LOCATION	NATURAL FOODS
BLUE MARLIN One of the world's great larger game fish, aerial display a marvel. Food value: excellent, but rarely used by sportsmen.	Deep-blue back, bluish silver sides, silver belly. Spear short, rounded; dorsal fin, sickle-shaped in front almost length of back.	Atlantic coast from New York through West Indies; off coast of Cuba. Offshore, where reefs drop into deep water; at the edge of Gulf Stream.	Mullet, mackerel, barracuda, other kinds of small fish, squids.
WHITE MARLIN Pound for pound, has no equal as a game fish; aerial acrobatics, walks on its tail. Food value: only tasty when smoked.	Bluish-green back, purplish cast, silvery sides. Lavender-gray narrow bands top of back to below lateral line. Dorsal fin bright blue with darker spots; smaller, lower dorsal fin than sailfish.	Atlantic Ocean, Cape Cod to Florida, waters of West Indies. Strictly offshore, alongside reefs, around waters of Gulf Stream.	Menhaden, mullet, mackerel, flying fish, other small fish, squids.
SWORDFISH Greatest game fish, rarely caught with rod and reel. Food value: one of the finest.	Purplish blue, brownish cast, on back; lighter sides, belly grayish. Fins dusky purple; sword almost black on top—flattened, narrow-edged. Dorsal fin higher than marlin, also shorter—never extending past middle of body.	Open seas of world, coasts of Atlantic, Pacific oceans. Atlantic coast, Labrador to south of Cuba; Pacific, Santa Cruz Island off California to Chile. Deep offshore waters. Feeds at considerable depths, reluctant to strike offered bait.	Smaller fish like mackerel, bonito, dolphin, barracuda, flying fish, herring. Also squids and fish found at great depths.
PACIFIC SALMON King, or Chinook, salmon is largest, game qualities of the highest. Other salmon: coho, humpback, dog, sockeye. Food value: excellent.	Silvery, with bluish-olive tinge on upper sides, darker on back; head dark slate color; body with metalliclike sheen. Upper body with small dark spots, plentiful on dorsal, caudal fins. Spends life in the sea, entering fresh water only to spawn, then die.	Both coasts of northern Pacific; Bering Strait south along coast of North America from Alaska and British Columbia to Monterey, California. King and coho salmon caught by trolling in open sea. Majority taken leaving the sea to start migration to fresh water; caught at mouth of rivers emptying into sea, brackish waters above mouths.	Young salmon, before migrating to sea, feed on flies, insects, crustaceans, worms. Reaching salt water, feed on herrings, anchovies, sardines, shrimps, squids, crustaceans.
PACIFIC YELLOWTAIL Great Pacific game fish, fighting ability second to none. Food value: excellent.	Bright metallic blue above, greenish cast; bluish silver sides. Irregular brassy or yellowish stripe along side from eye to tail. Belly silvery, fins and tail bright yellow.	Coast of Chile to Monterey, California; also Gulf of California. Deep-water fish; channels around islands, kelp beds, open sea.	Anchovies, sardines, herring, smelts, other small fish; crabs, shrimps, other crustaceans.

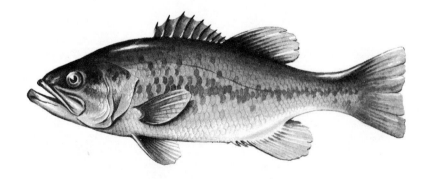

LARGEMOUTH BASS
Micropterus salmoides

HOW, WHEN AND WHERE FOR SALT-WATER FISH   *by Lou S. Caine*

ARTIFICIAL LURES	METHODS AND TACKLE
No artificial lures. Whole fish bait.	*Trolling:* Rod of hickory or laminated woods. Size 36-thread line. 14/0 reel. Outriggers which hold angler's line high, keep bait out of propeller wash, give lifelike skipping motion.
Taken by trolling whole fish or strip bait, but they will strike artificial lures. Feathered jig; sometimes caught on diving-wobbling lure.	*Trolling:* A 6/9 outfit, rod with detachable butt 18 inches long, tip 5 feet long when seated, weight 6 ounces. A 4/0 reel, 500 yards of 9-thread line. The strike startles angler, so allow fish to take bait before setting the hook.
No artificial lures.	*Trolling:* Heavy tackle. Rod with tip weighing 26 ounces, 12/0 reel, 1,000 yards 39-thread line. A 14/0 size hook. Once a fish is sighted, bait is put overboard. Taking swordfish requires patience of Job.
Spoons, spinners, feathered jigs. Large and medium-sized wobbling plugs. Flies, especially large streamer flies.	*Trolling:* Rod with a tip not less than 5 feet long, not over 4 ounces. Butt detachable, 18 inches long. A 2/0 or 3/0 free-spool reel with star drag, ample supply 6-thread linen line. *Stripping:* From skiff. Salmon or steelhead rod. Line: 200 to 300 yards of knotless gut or nylon leader testing 30 pounds. Bait is strip cut from herring, fastened to hook to spin and wobble. *Bait casting:* Rod 5 feet long, medium or sturdy action. Level-winding bait-casting reel, 15-pound-test silk or nylon line. Wobbling spoons, small underwater plugs with lips to give swimming motion. *Fly casting:* Rod with backbone, a No. 2¾ ferrule in lengths of 9 and 9½ feet.
Metal or bone squids, feathered jigs and strip bait, occasionally plugs, spoons.	*Live-bait fishing:* From live-bait boats, southern California coast. "Chum" thrown overboard, fish begin feeding, anchor dropped. Live-bait boat rod, tip 7 feet long—fitting into butt 18 inches long. Free-spool reel, automatic drag, 250 yards 9-thread linen line. Baits: anchovies, sardines. *Trolling:* Outfit, ultralight 3/6 means rod with over-all length of 6 feet, weight 6 ounces. A 6-thread linen line. Alongside kelp beds, deep channels next to rocky shores.

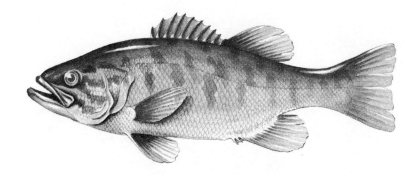

SMALLMOUTH BASS
Micropterus dolomieu

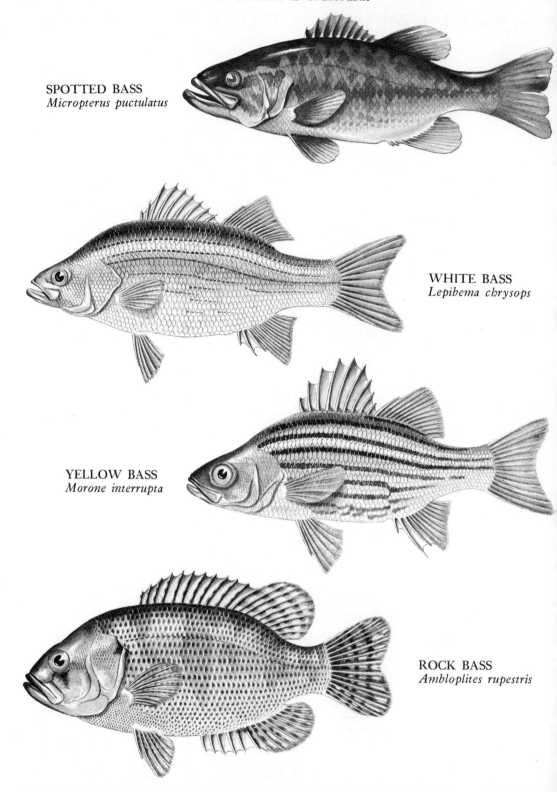

SPOTTED BASS
Micropterus puctulatus

WHITE BASS
Lepibema chrysops

YELLOW BASS
Morone interrupta

ROCK BASS
Ambloplites rupestris

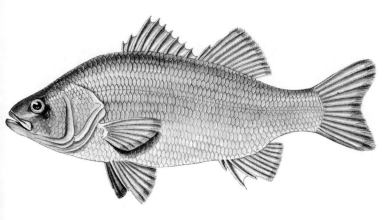

WHITE PERCH
Morone americana

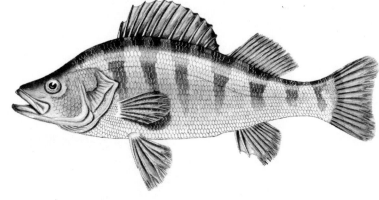

YELLOW PERCH
Perca flavescens

MUSKELLUNGE
Esax masquinongy

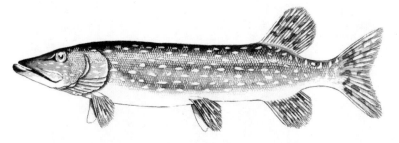

NORTHERN PIKE
Esox lucius

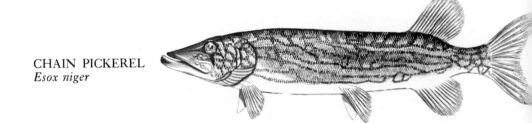

CHAIN PICKEREL
Esox niger

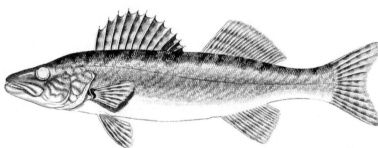

WALLEYE
Stizostedion vitreum vitreum

WHITE CRAPPIE
Pomoxis annularis

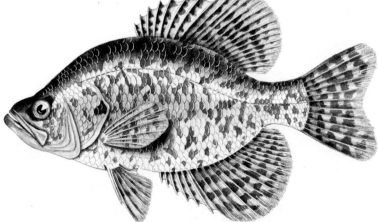

BLACK CRAPPIE
Pomoxis nigro-maculatus

BLUEGILL (SUNFISH)
Lepomis macrochirus

UMPKINSEED (SUNFISH)
epomis gibbosus

ATLANTIC SALMON
Salmo salar salar

KING SALMON
Oncorhynchus tshawytscha

LANDLOCKED SALMON
Salmo salar sebago

OUANANICHE SALMON
Salmo salar ouananiche

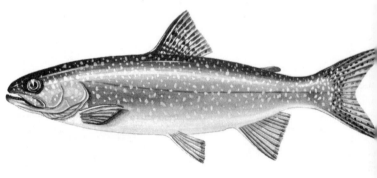

LAKE TROUT
Cristivomer namaycush

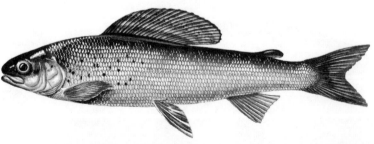

MONTANA GRAYLING
Thymallus signifer tricolor

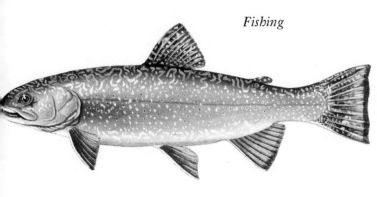

BROOK TROUT
Salvelinus fontinalis

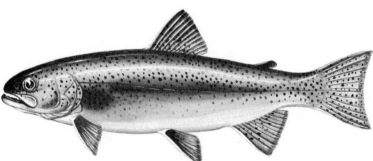

RAINBOW TROUT
Salmo gairdnerii

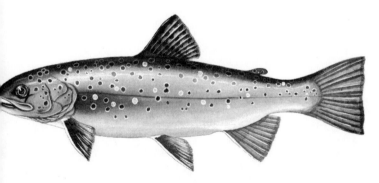

BROWN TROUT
Salmo trutta

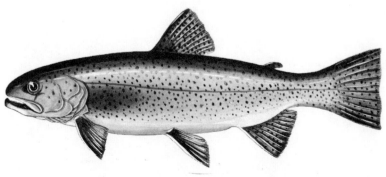

CUTTHROAT TROUT
Salmo clarkii

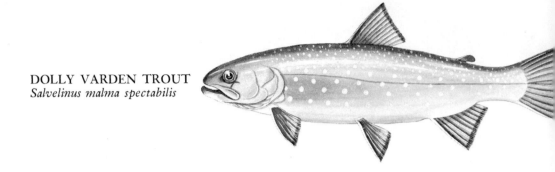

DOLLY VARDEN TROUT
Salvelinus malma spectabilis

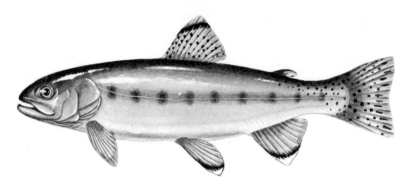

GOLDEN TROUT
Salmo agua-bonita

BROWN BULLHEAD
Ameriurus nebulosus

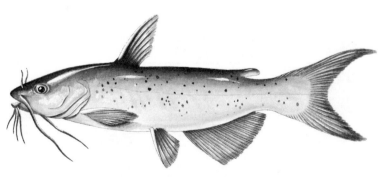

CHANNEL CATFISH
Ictalurus lacustris

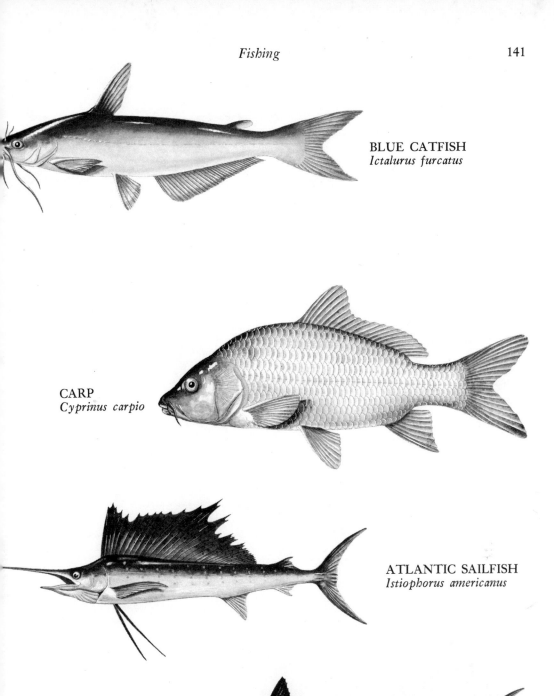

BLUE CATFISH
Ictalurus furcatus

CARP
Cyprinus carpio

ATLANTIC SAILFISH
Istiophorus americanus

WHITE MARLIN
Makaira albida

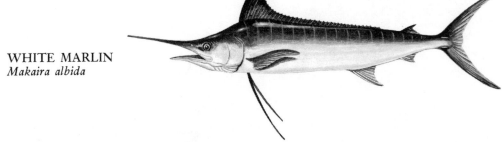

BLUE MARLIN
Makaira nigricans ampla

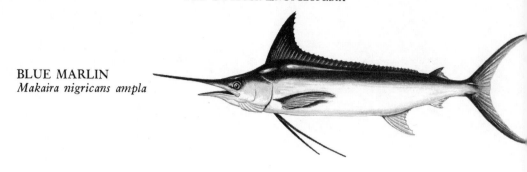

SWORDFISH
Xiphias gladius

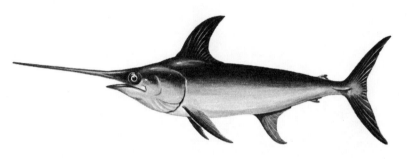

TARPON
Tarpon atlanticus

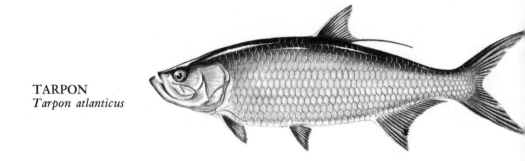

DOLPHIN
Coryphaena hippurus

GREAT BARRACUDA
Sphyraena barracuda

PACIFIC BARRACUDA
Sphyaena argentea

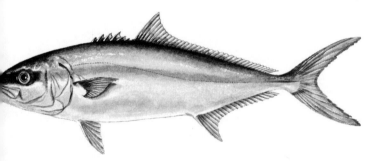

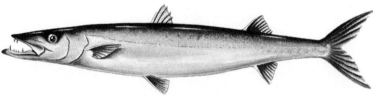

PACIFIC YELLOWTAIL
Seriola dorsalis

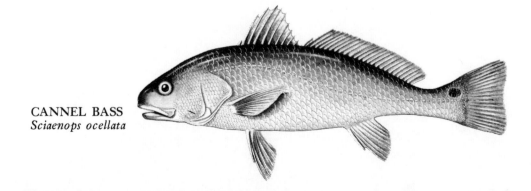

CANNEL BASS
Sciaenops ocellata

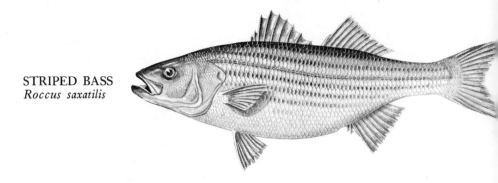

STRIPED BASS
Roccus saxatilis

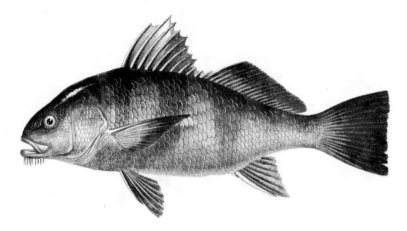

BLACK DRUM
Pogonias cromis

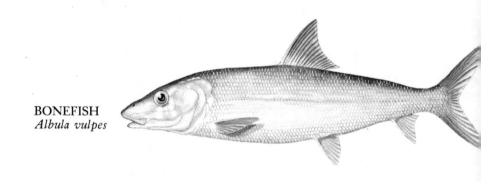

BONEFISH
Albula vulpes

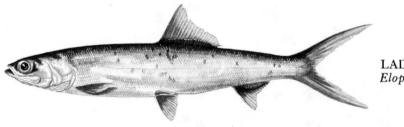

LADYFISH
Elops saurus

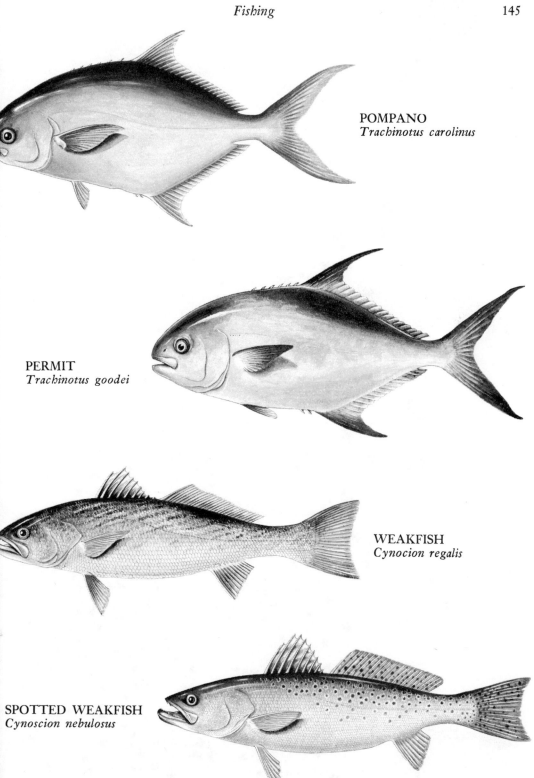

POMPANO
Trachinotus carolinus

PERMIT
Trachinotus goodei

WEAKFISH
Cynocion regalis

SPOTTED WEAKFISH
Cynoscion nebulosus

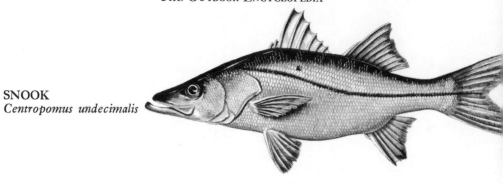

SNOOK
Centropomus undecimalis

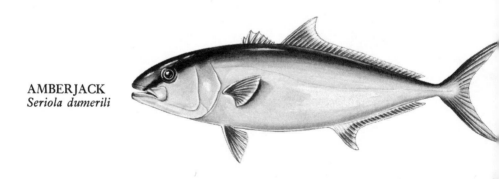

BLUEFISH
Pomatomus saltatrix

AMBERJACK
Seriola dumerili

WAHOO
Acanthocybium solandri

ATLANTIC BONITO
Sarda sarda

JACK CREVALLE
Caranx hippos

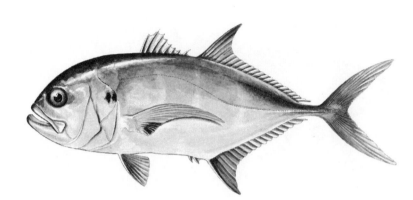

KING MACKEREL
Scomberomorus cavalla

SPANISH MACKEREL
Scomberomorus maculatus

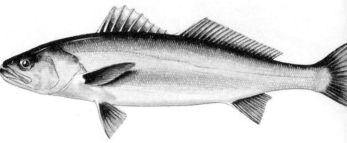

CALIFORNIA WHITE SEA BASS
Cynoscion nobilis

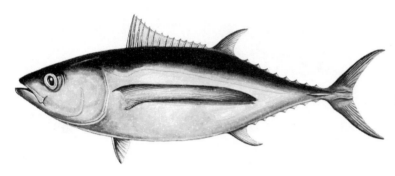

ALBACORE
Thunnus germo

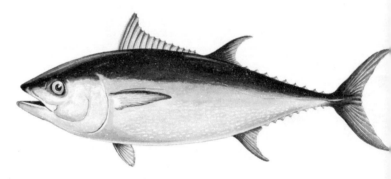

BLUEFIN TUNA
Thunnus thynnus

SPOTTED JEWFISH
Promicrops itaiara

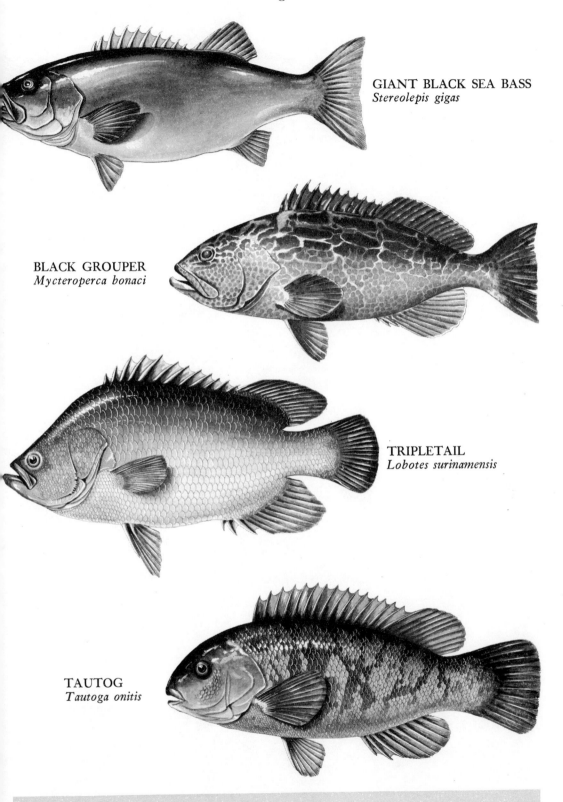

GIANT BLACK SEA BASS
Stereolepis gigas

BLACK GROUPER
Mycteroperca bonaci

TRIPLETAIL
Lobotes surinamensis

TAUTOG
Tautoga onitis

MANGROVE SNAPPER
Lutjanus griseus

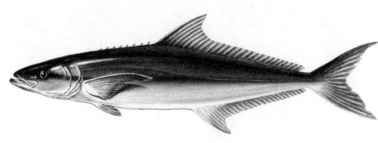

COBIA
Rachycentron canadus

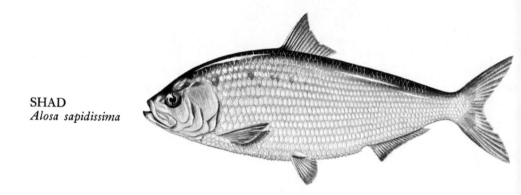

SHAD
Alosa sapidissima

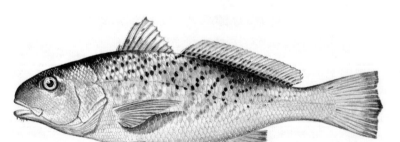

CROAKER
Mocropogon undulatus

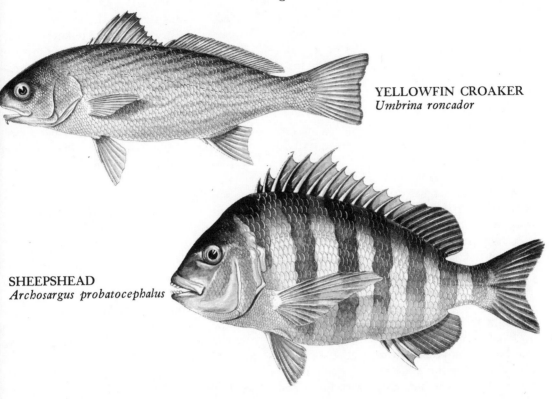

YELLOWFIN CROAKER
Umbrina roncador

SHEEPSHEAD
Archosargus probatocephalus

FLY-ROD FISHING

What explains the great fascination the fly rod has for all who learn to use it reasonably well?

For one thing, it gives most sport, most pleasure, in playing the none-too-large fish we find in most places nowadays; it makes big fish out of little ones. Not that it isn't suitable for big ones too; in Florida, old pros use a fly rod almost exclusively for quite large snook, tarpon and such.

In spite of a common notion to the contrary, it is much easier to learn to cast with a fly rod than with a casting rod—*if* one will take a little pains in learning how to assemble the right outfit, and how to use it. Nor does it call for nearly the constant practice that plug casting does; fly casting is somewhat like swimming—having acquired the knack, one never quite loses it.

Fly-rod fishing is simple, but it is simple only when three things are right: one must

have a suitable rod; one must get a line to match it; and one must learn correct casting technique. So let's consider today the problem of selecting a rod.

The number and variety of rods shown in catalogues is frightening—long rods, short rods, light rods, heavy rods; rods with actions described as nymph, wet-fly, dry-fly, bass-bug, parabolic, hyperbolic. Experts advise a rod somewhere between seven and a half and eight feet, and usually weighing between three and a half and four ounces. (Not that weight means anything, since the grip and reel seat has much to do with that, but nothing to do with the action or strength.)

You wonder if there isn't danger of breaking such a light rod? Certainly, but anyone who is likely to break it would be almost as likely to break a heavy rod. In the whole history of fishing, a fish has never yet broken a rod; it's the user who does it.

Of what material should the rod be? For one of moderate means, and especially for the beginner, hollow glass is advised since it will require less care than bamboo and won't take a set if improperly handled or stored—not that it won't have some limits in these respects, too. And in the lower price ranges, it will be stronger than a bamboo, though not unbreakable if badly mistreated.

How can one tell if a rod in a store has dry-fly action? The best way is to run a line through the guides, fasten it well out in front and pull a reasonable amount with the butt about at right angles to where the line is attached. Or, you can make a pretty good guess by flipping the rod gently and quickly. The butt part should remain quite straight, the front taking a nice, graceful bend.

Nobody living can do good fly casting with mismatched rod and line. About 99 times in 100, the troubled fly caster has a line much too light to bring out the action of his rod.

On any given rod, you should use the same size line for anything from small trout and bluegills up to the largest sea fish—you use the one line that will do the best casting with that rod.

So when you buy a rod, how do you know what size line to get for it? You might hunt up a friend who is a really good fly caster. He is likely to have lines in a couple of sizes, to try on your rod. If you don't have such a friend, get a C level, an HCH double-taper, or a GBF three-diameter.

This choice is based on the fact that a high percentage of fly rods bought nowadays are of hollow glass, and that a great majority of these work best with lines of those sizes—almost regardless of lengths or weights. Remember that a limber nine-foot rod will take a lighter line than a rather powerful one of only seven feet, though the nine-footer weighs much more—and nearly all the shorter fly rods now are quite powerful.

The beginner may do best to get a level line since it is somewhat easier to learn with. A double-taper is practically necessary for dry-fly fishing, and is quite satisfactory for wet flies too. The advantage of a three-diameter line is that it will cast farther than any of the others. You can use a three-diameter for everything but dry flies.

The new long-floating lines are so superior to those of the older types as to render them obsolete. Start from the first with a floating fly line. It is impossible for anybody to pick up a fairly long piece of drowned line for a good backcast—and a good backcast is the whole heart of a good forward cast. Silk or nylon? Well, the one real difference between them is that nylon won't rot or weaken when damp. Whichever you decide on, dress it daily. No line will shoot well through guides without dressing on it.

By Jason Lucas

Here's the first step. Keep your thumb stretched on top of the grip. Get about 20 feet of line out in front—doing it in any way you can. Relax—taut muscles will ruin your casting. Straighten line in front by pulling some of it in with left hand—and slowly raising rod tip. At this point, start to accelerate the upward motion.

Now end with a sharp flip, stopping suddenly—with the rod no farther back than is shown in this picture. Try to toss the line straight up. The line won't go there but you will get the necessary high backcast. Pause until line is almost straight behind—practice will show you how long.

Now bring rod tip forward with a smooth, gradually accelerating motion that suddenly loses speed at about the point shown. If the rod was stopped a little behind the vertical, the backward-flying line (if it fits the rod) will have pulled a bend—a spring—in it, to make this movement an easy one.

There's a slow follow-through that should not go lower than about the point shown in this picture. By aiming high above your target, the line will straighten in the air—and then it will settle gently down on the water. You must remember, in order to cast a straight line, even your faster movements should never be jerky ones.

Here's what not to do! The rod is brought back, as shown here, only in an entirely different style of casting—using the "double haul" for extreme distance. This is very difficult to learn, may break a good rod not meant for such a strain—and is useful perhaps to only one angler in hundreds.

The roll cast is shown in this picture and the one below. It is used when trees or other obstacles leave you no room behind for a backcast. It is also a very convenient method for straightening line out for an overhead cast. Raise the rod to the position shown here, and let the line sag back until it has just passed it—but has not "gone dead." Try this out.

SPINNING

When a man's fly or plug casting is consistently bad, there's a good chance that the trouble lies not with the tackle but with himself—that he hasn't learned the proper technique of casting. But spinning is so intrinsically simple that if after your first couple of hours at it you're still having trouble, it must be the fault of wrong tackle, not of anything you're doing.

The unfortunate fact is that there are on the market some spinning reels, and some rod-and-reel combinations, of erroneous design. Fortunately, it is a simple matter to avoid buying a misbegotten cross between a spin-

ning and casting reel. With a properly designed spinning reel the spool does not revolve in retrieving; there is a device to wrap the line back around the spool in the exact opposite of how it came off, so when the line is all back on it's as straight and untwisted as before you cast. You just make sure, when selecting a spinning reel, that some pickup gadget is wrapping the line back on and that the spool does not revolve.

In spinning reels many prefer manual pickup to automatic. They think a manual pickup much simpler and more pleasant to use after getting used to it.

As for rods, most who are experienced with this type of fishing seem to prefer the seven-foot length, although many advocate shorter ones. The rod must be flexible enough to bend well in casting lures from ⅛ to ¼ ounce. Bamboo and hollow glass rods work about equally well for spinning. Solid glass rods are fine in lengths up to around six feet, but in longer lengths they tend to become top heavy and slow in action.

Some experts maintain that it's a trifle easier to learn spinning with braided line, but practically all now use monofilament. For really good casting with fresh-water spinning lures, one shouldn't use line over four-pound test. But when it's necessary to hold larger fish from dense weeds, snags and boulders, a six-pound test works quite well, and an eight-pound can be used. Anything heavier is just begging for short, difficult casts, snarls and other troubles.

One more important point—proper adjustment of the drag. Set the drag when you have line way out in the water and are retrieving. This way you allow both for guide friction and for a small diameter of line on the spool. Set the drag at what you consider safely below the test of the line. You can get a good idea of what that is by first breaking a piece from the end with your hands.

By Jason Lucas

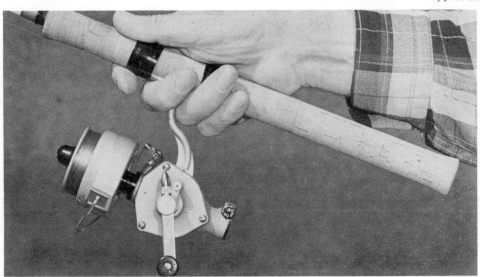

Hold the rod loosely with your thumb on top; you can't cast correctly with a tight grip. Most hold the rod with the reel post this way; some prefer it between first and second fingers.

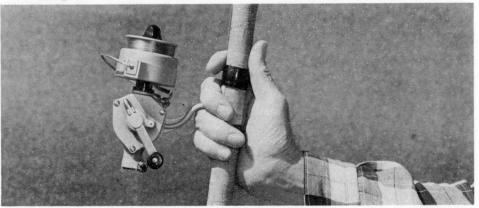

The whole cast should be done chiefly with your wrist; the forearm helps slightly, the upper arm not at all. The rod is driven forward by push from thumb.

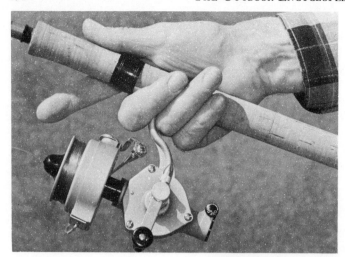

As the tip comes forward, release line from under your right forefinger, letting lure fly out. A few experimental casts will soon teach you how to do this properly.

At first, you may stop the lure by beginning to crank if you find that is easiest, but you will get much greater accuracy by stopping the line with your forefinger on the spool.

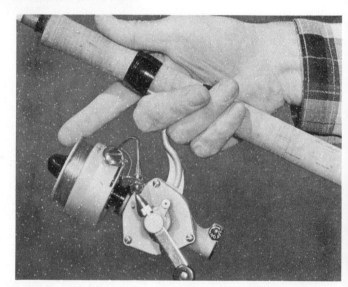

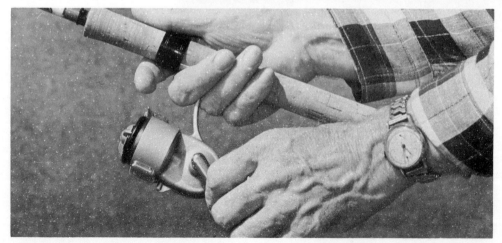

With manual pickup, the left hand does nothing but crank. After a cast bring it back on forefinger, and roller picks it off; back reel handle a bit before the next cast.

SURF FISHING

It takes a long time to become an experienced surf angler. The period of apprenticeship which must be served in order to transform the novice into a veteran surf caster can be discouraging and often runs into years. About the nearest thing to a short cut is to have an old-timer take you under his wing and let you accompany him on fishing trips. Since surf casters are noted for their reticence and refuse to part with their hard earned secrets, this road is open to only a handful of lucky anglers. The next best step is to join one of the many surf fishing clubs, but even here gaining knowledge is apt to be a long, drawn-out process.

TACKLE

Surf fishing tackle is divided into light, medium and heavy classes. A light outfit is used for metal squids or plugs as well as very light sinkers. The split bamboo or glass rod tip should be five and a half or six feet long and weigh from six to nine ounces. It can have a single guide or several guides, whichever you prefer. The proper butt for the light tip is the spring type, about 20 to 22 inches long.

The reel for the light rod should be a 150 or 200 yard model, depending upon whether you use six- or nine-thread line. Most surf reels made today have a star drag and a free spool. Other features are: the lightweight spool, which helps prevent backlashes, and a gear ratio of three to one. This ratio enables an angler to bring in his lure much faster—a necessity when fishing among rocks.

When it comes to lines, a good line of six or nine thread is used for the light outfit. The beginner should use a nine thread, until he has acquired skill in casting and playing a fish. In recent years many nylon lines have appeared on the market. While in certain respects they are better than linen, they're far from perfect. A nylon line doesn't swell or absorb water and it runs out smoothly during a cast. But some of them are too elastic. The best nylon lines are the braided type, which have less elasticity than the twisted kind.

One word of caution on the use of the light outfit described above. This tackle is intended for light lures and sinkers. The use of three-ounce metal squids or four-ounce sinkers would quickly ruin the light tip.

The medium weight outfit is suitable for all-around use. The tip for the medium rod should be from nine to 12 ounces in weight and from six to seven feet in length. The butt can be from 22 to 28 inches, depending on the angler's arm length and preference.

A reel that holds 200 yards of nine-thread line is ideal for the medium rod. The nine-thread line is best for squidding and only occasionally you'll need a 12 for bait fishing. The medium weight rod will handle all the artificials used in surf casting, and can also be used for bait fishing. But don't strain the tip by using too heavy a sinker and bait.

The heavy weight rod is used mostly for bait fishing. The tip weighs from 12 to 16 ounces. The length can be anywhere from six and a half to eight feet. The butt would be 26 to 30 inches long and should be faiirly heavy in order to balance the rod.

The reel should be the 250 yard type. That is, it would hold 250 yards of nine-thread line, but only 200 yards of 12.

In choosing the butt for any of these rods the angler should take the one that feels most natural in his hands. The general rule is short man, short butt; tall man, long butt.

The medium weight outfit is best for the angler who can afford to buy only one rod. But you may find yourself handicapped when fishing under certain conditions. When the surf is heavy and there is a strong undertow, you'll need at least five or six ounces of lead to hold on the bottom. If you're fishing for striped bass or channel bass, the bait may weigh an additional two or three ounces. This constant casting of a half-pound weight won't do your medium tip any good.

Most surf fishermen like to have two rods, one either light or medium weight, and the other heavy. Then, if they decide to go squidding, they use the light or medium rod. If bait fishing is the thing, they switch to the heavy rod. This also gives them a spare rod in case one is accidentally broken.

Surf Fishing at Delray Beach, Florida

Generally speaking, the longer the tip, the more action it has. A long tip usually has a gradual taper and the action extends right up to the butt. A short rod with a sudden taper has the action in the tip section only. The long flexible rod is preferred in fishing with artificials. It is better for casting light lures and tires out a fish more quickly than a short stiff rod.

SURF CASTING

Words are really inadequate when it comes to describing the correct procedure in casting. The best way to learn how to cast is to go down to the beach and watch an expert at work and try to do likewise.

One of the most important considerations in casting is the proper weight sinker or lure for the rod. In casting, the rod tip does all of the work. Therefore a sinker or lure that is heavy enough to bring out the action of the tip is the right one to use.

The overhead cast is used by the majority of surf anglers. This is the one for the beginner to learn, because once he has mastered it, he can easily acquire the other styles. You can practice anywhere the ground is flat and there are no obstructions nearby. At the beach your line is always wet and there is little friction. When casting on dry land, you'll have to wet your line at regular intervals or wear a thumb stall. Also, use a round sinker instead of a pyramid, so it can be reeled in along the ground after each cast.

To start the cast, first strip off enough line so that the stinker is about three feet from the tip guide. Throw the lever on your reel into free spool, which allows the spool to turn without the handle moving. Grasp the butt grip directly under the reel with your right hand, the thumb resting on the spool. The left hand holds the other grip at the end of the butt. Then twist the rod so that the face of the reel (the side with the handle) faces toward the ground. Swing your sinker back and let it fall on the ground; making the line run towards the tip guide on the same angle as the rod is held, which is slanting downward.

Your left arm is slightly bent and almost even with the shoulder, while your right arm extends backward and down. Now bring the rod up and over your head in an arc. Do this quickly, but smoothly. Your body which was facing to the right now turns to the left and bends forward at the trunk. Just after the rod reaches the perpendicular, directly over your head, you release the thumb from the spool. This is done only for an instant and the thumb is soon brought back into position to apply pressure until the sinker hits the water.

The novice quickly masters the correct form in casting, which is easy. His greatest difficulty will be in thumbing the spool. Too much or too sudden a pressure on the spool causes the sinker to fall at the caster's feet. If too little pressure is applied, the line will backlash, which often results in a lost rig. There's no short cut in learning how to thumb a reel. The only advice is constant practice until the novice gets the "feel" of the spool. In the beginning, the angler should try only short casts until he has acquired this feel.

Another difficulty is caused when spooling the line on the retrieve of the cast. This is very important, in order to avoid trouble in future casts. If the line is spooled unevenly, it fails to run out smoothly when a cast is made and a backlash is almost certain. The proper way to spool the line is to have it run between your thumb and forefinger. The remaining three fingers grasp the rod directly above the reel. As you reel in, the line is spread evenly by working your thumb and forefinger back and forth. If despite your efforts the line does "bunch up," take it easy on the next cast and you will avoid trouble.

When you fill your reel with new line, make sure the spool is not too full. Linen line swells when wet and if you have too much on your reel it will rub against the metal bars.

Distance in casting is obtained by applying power at the proper moment. Both arms play an equally important part. As you push forward with your right arm you pull back with your left. If this is done smoothly with an extra snap to bend the tip to its fullest, you will get the most force. At the same time aim at a point just above the horizon and not at the spot you expect to hit.

There are several ways in which you can retrieve your line after the cast. When using a bait rig, the tip should be worked up and down from the horizontal to the vertical. Turn the reel handle only when the tip is being dropped to the horizontal position. This method brings in your rig faster and is less tiring to the user. Artificial lures can be retrieved with the rod tip in the horizontal or the vertical position. The rod tip held the horizontal causes the lure to ride deep. Holding the rod in the vertical makes it travel near the surface.

Finally, practice casting whenever you get a chance. If you are on a beach and the fishing is poor, spend the time perfecting your casting technique. Then, when the fish are in, your casting will be smooth and efficient.

SURF CONDITIONS

Three factors that play more of a part in surf fishing than any others are: the food supply, the wind and the tide. The most important of these is the food supply. The presence of food in the surf will often bring in

the fish even if the other conditions are unfavorable.

The movement of bait-fishes depends on the temperature of the water and their own food supply. Thus we have the migration of vast schools of bait-fishes during the various seasons. On the Atlantic Coast, this migration north usually begins in February or March and continues until July and August. Some of the bait-fishes come in from the deep offshore waters; while others follow the coastline north. Schools of mossbunker, anchovies, mullet, sand eels and spearing will appear in the surf during April, May and June. Striped bass, channel bass, weakfish, bluefish and mackerel follow right behind them. This furnishes the surf angler with his first sport after a long winter of inactivity. Metal squids, plugs as well as bait will take fish during this time.

The bait-fishes enter the bays and inlets during the summer, making July and August poor months for surf fishing. Some large fish are taken at night while bait fishing and a few are caught on metal squids, plugs and eels. However, the best fishing during the summer months is found in the inlets, the bays and the canals.

The first big northeast storm or north winds in September seem to act as a signal for the fish to begin schooling again. As the water cools, the bait-fishes leave the bays and inlets to gather in huge schools.

This activity makes the fall of the year the best season for surf fishing; September and October being two good months with the fishing lasting well into November. Then as winter sets in, the larger game fish disappear, leaving the waters to the cod, the ling, the frost-fish or whiting and the skate. Of course, the angler can always follow the fish south and be assured of further sport, but the great majority of surf anglers are contented to lay away their "stick" and await the return of the fish.

Winds also affect surf fishing in many ways. A southwest wind is one of the most favorable for surf fishing along the Atlantic Coast. This wind brings warm water and food into the surf. It is usually strong enough to cause plenty of white water, which is needed to wash out the variety of food that the surf fish feed on, and at the same time conceal the big fish. The southwest wind with its choppy waves also serves to break up the schools of bait-fishes. It may make casting very difficult at times, since it comes in at an angle causing a belly in the line. The slack line also makes it hard to detect a strike from a fish. The best thing to do is to cast very low and directly into the wind. If that doesn't help, then wait a few hours as southwest winds usually moderate at sunset.

South or southeast winds are also good if they're not too strong. These winds tend to make the surf roily if they blow for any length of time. With dirty water the surf fishing is poor.

East or northeast winds bring rain and storms. If the wind is light, fishing may be excellent in the surf. Since these two winds are also accompanied by clouds they create good fishing throughout the day. When a northeast storm reaches its height, the wind may make fishing impossible, but as soon as the blow dies and the wind shifts, head for the beach.

The winds that generally follow a storm are north and northwest. They cause ground swells and murky water. As long as the water isn't too dirty the fishing is likely to be good. Several days of a north or northwest wind, however, will calm the ocean and clean the water. Then the water grows cold and crystal clear causing the fish to stop biting.

The question of tides never fails to start an argument among surf anglers. One man will say that he fishes only at high water, and then go on to tell of the excellent catches he made during this tide. Another man will be just as emphatic about low water, and also furnish proof for his argument. The point is that fish feed whenever and wherever they can reach their food, and the tide helps them in this respect. At low tide the sand bars and reefs where food is concentrated are too shallow to float the bigger fish. Thus, the game fish may lie in the deeper water until the tide is high enough to enable them to swim into such places. This is the chief reason why most bait fishermen prefer the high tides to the low ones.

Low water is a favorable tide for the surf angler fishing with artificials. The bait-fishes seem to be more concentrated in deeper water during low tide, whereas, during high tide they scatter and feed over the shoals and flats.

The best surf fishing occurs when all three factors combine and result in what is known as "perfect conditions." This happens when there is plenty of bait in the water, plenty of white water and the proper tide for the locality. There have been times when perfect conditions failed to produce a single fish. Nevertheless, surf fishing is far better under perfect conditions than if one of the above factors is unfavorable.

More and larger fish are taken during the night than by daytime anglers. The reasons for this are obvious. Darkness enables the game fish to approach the bait-fish without being detected. Also, there is more bait present, since eels, crabs and other sea creatures come out of hiding during the night to feed.

The days when there are no gulls, bait-fish or fish showing, will require a study of beach formations and other conditions. To locate bars or holes (always good fishing spots), study the color and action of the water. Watch the waves as they come rolling up to the beach. You will notice a wave build up to a peak until it hits a bar, where it breaks up. The color of the water on a bar is a much lighter green than over the deep holes and channels.

Wood or rock jetties are also very good locations because they harbor the small animal life upon which the larger fish feed. The backwash of the waves creates a rip alongside of the jetty which catches the small creatures, sweeping them to the waiting fish.

When fishing a rocky coastline each cove presents an individual problem which must be solved. Locating fish in a rocky area is simple compared to a sandy beach. Moreover, once you take some fish from a certain spot, you can be fairly sure of having further luck there in the future. Rocky areas seldom change and the fish seem to follow the same feeding habits in such spots year after year.

Sunken or exposed boulders produce excellent fishing. The waves crashing against the rocks wash out food and turn the water white. The boulders also cause the bait-fishes to follow a definite course in swimming past these obstructions. The bigger fish are there to meet them. Your lure should be cast just short of the boulder, on the side nearest to the shore. You can also cast beyond the boulder, reeling in on either side of it as close as possible without fouling.

Small rocky peninsulas are usually productive areas since they generally jut out into deep water. You can fish a large area here by casting in an arc on both sides of the point.

Finally, one of the best ways to locate fish is to keep moving.

By Vlad Evanoff
From the book SURF FISHING
The Ronald Press Company
Copyright 1948

SALT-WATER BOTTOM FISHING

There is a very specialized group of gentlemen who love the spectacular battle of giant-size fish and the song of a singing line. But the most numerous, without any doubt, are the bottom fishermen who enjoy the solid strike and the tug of a deep-water fish.

Deep-sea party fishing boats, some holding 25 or 30 anglers, others well over 100 fishermen, sail from nearly every important fishing area along our coasts.

The average fishing boat has no reserved seats, so the first arrival has the choice of location from which he may fish. The best spot is usually the stern of the boat, unless the skipper can bridle his boat sideways to the tide or current, thus giving a wider area to the anglers. This can only be done when there is no danger of capsizing the boat. Some captains insist that every angler move about 10 feet every 15 or 20 minutes to insure all fishermen an equal opportunity of fishing from the best location.

The most popular rig to use for most deep-sea bottom fishing is the two-hook rig, with one hook fastened about 19 inches to two feet above the lower hook and sinker. It is a good idea to use a 1/0 hook near the sinker, and a larger size as the upper hook. The bank-style sinker, which is as near nonfouling as possible, should vary in weight from five to 12 ounces, depending upon the depth of water, current and tide. At certain times and at various locations, the tide and currents may be working in opposite directions, and it becomes very difficult to keep your line taut enough to feel a strike. This is one particular time when you will be more successful if you work your bait by raising and lowering your rod tip.

The vast army of salt-water anglers who indulge in bottom fishing prefer to dunk a baited hook in bay or offshore waters. But there are anglers who love to troll over the rolling offshore ground swells with spoon, squid or feather jig.

The salt-water angler, who does not have the stomach for the heaving offshore waters, can have a record day by drifting in the more quiet bay waters near the inlets. There is a style of fishing for every taste.

By Robert D. Hall

SHELLFISHING

Oblivious to the general opinion that it isn't even a sport, a contented group of Americans fish for crabs, oysters and other shellfish. All they get out of it is a lot of fun—and some of the best eating the waters of our continent provide.

CRABS

Although several edible crabs exist on the East and West coasts, the number one favorite is the blue crab which is found from southern New England down to Florida and all around the Gulf Coast. When the tide goes out, you'll find hand netters near the channel and weeded patches in the bays. The crabs are exposed in the shallows and are simply dipped out with a net which has a handle of six feet or so. On the West Coast the Dungeness crab takes the place of the blue crab as the one most likely to be caught as recreation.

The old-time crab trap is still used in some places. The other amateur method of catching crabs is to lower a bait on a line which may or may not be attached to a pole. When it is drawn up, the crabs cling to the bait and, if you're lucky, you hand-net them at the surface.

Crab baits lean toward the smelly type because crabs are scavengers. A rich, ripe piece of menhaden (mossbunker or fatback, as it is known in some sections) is good. Professional crabbers use horse meat which has been salted and set in the sun for awhile.

CRAWFISH

Call these crawfish, crayfish, crawdads or mudbugs, they are appreciated only in the Mississippi Delta country. That is the rest of the nation's loss. The crawfish (which is almost strictly a fresh-water crustacean and is not to be confused with the salt-water crawfish known as the spiny, or rock lobster) resembles a small lobster, even to its claws. It is familiar to bass and trout fishermen and a good bait, in its smaller sizes, and is considered a nuisance by everyone who fishes bait on the bottom. It will cling to the bait, eating it even when drawn from the water. In fact, that's one of the simplest ways that you can catch crawfish.

This simplest method consists of taking a piece of string tied to a pole, and baiting with a chunk of meat. The more professional method consists of using a square of net with four wires coming up from the corners. Place the meat bait in the center, lower the trap to the bottom and later collect it by pushing a stick through the wires.

CLAMS

Gathering clams is mostly a matter of using a rake, a narrow and long spade or a long-tined fork, and working at the job. It is difficult to imagine clam-digging being exciting, but it can be.

Usually you beat on the sand as you advance. The vibration causes the clam to withdraw its siphon (neck), and thus expose its position. You scoop out a shovelful of the hard sand, then plunge hand and arm into the soft, watery sand beneath and grab the clam, if you can.

In the East, both hard and soft shells usually are dug out with clam hoes on the tidal flats when the water is low. A primitive method is "treading," in which the barefooted wader feels for the clams in the mud with his toes, and then picks up the clams by hand. Visitors to the Jersey coast, where treading is common, swear the natives have developed abnormally long toes just for this purpose. Clam rakes are much used in New England, usually with a net attached to pick up the clams loosened by the rake from the soft bottom.

OYSTERS

"Wild" oysters, as distinguished from those cultivated by commercial growers, are found in nearly all our coastal waters. The amateur collector has to guard against encroaching on some commercial outfit's oyster beds. And beware of oysters from polluted areas.

The amateur usually collects a few oysters for his table from rocks and other objects partly exposed at low tide. In some Florida waters, you can collect oysters from the roots of trees. About the only equipment you need is something to pry them loose from their beds.

FROGGING

States usually have laws governing frog catching, so check before you go out. Frogs are most easily obtained at night, partly because they are most abroad then, partly because a bright light blinds and hypnotises them so that they can be speared, netted or whacked with a flat paddle. You can walk along the banks, wade the water or push and paddle a boat around. The flashlight picks up the two eyes and the white throat of the frog. A burlap bag for carrying the catch is the only equipment you need besides the spear, paddle or net.   *By Bill Wolf*

FISHING TACKLE CARE

At least five times as much good tackle is ruined by lack of reasonable care as by its use. It is astonishing how remiss most anglers are in this respect, and for their thoughtlessness they pay a huge bill.

The proper care of tackle is simple and takes little time.

The following applies to tackle used in fresh water, but care of salt-water tackle is exactly the same except for one added precaution: Immediately upon coming in from fishing, the residue left by sea water, which has a strong corrosive action, should be washed off with fresh water.

THE CARE OF RODS

Some hold that keeping bamboo rods in metal cases will ruin them. This is pure nonsense, for there is no safer place to store or carry one. However, before closing such an airtight case on a rod you must be sure that rod, cloth bag and inside of the case are *bone dry*. A trace of moisture in there will cause the rod to disintegrate—though a weak spot caused thus may not show up until the rod breaks in playing a fish or attempting a long cast.

If there is a particle of exposed metal on a steel rod shut up thus, rust will attack it eventually causing a break. Glass rods are not supposed to be subject to damage from moisture, but their ferrules can corrode and cause poor appearance and fit. So steel and glass rods should be dried as thoroughly as bamboo rods before putting them away in airtight cases.

Fishing camps are generally in damp spots, subject to heavy dew. Leaving rods outside all night is poor policy. And things get damp while out fishing, so if you put your rod safely in its metal case when coming in, take it out again when you reach camp. The cloth sack may have a small tape loop to hang on a nail on the wall, and if it hasn't, it will take but moments to sew one on, or to make one of string. Casting rods, if not taken down, can stand in a dry corner of the cabin where nobody can trip over them.

However, it is during winter storage that most bamboo rods disintegrate. In most cases, storing in a basement causes the trouble —few basements are dry enough for safe storage of rods. A dry closet is a good place, or perhaps the attic will do. If the angler will give the matter a little thought, he can soon find a suitable place.

When a bamboo rod has been used much during the season, it will need a fresh coat of varnish before storing. Clean the surface with high-test white gasoline on a rag—a good lighter fluid is about the same thing, and easy to obtain. (Of course be careful with such stuff; it's highly explosive when mixed with air—better do it outdoors.) Use a rod varnish of reliable make; ordinary varnish simply won't do.

Luckily, the best way of varnishing a rod is also the simplest. Apply a light coat with the tips of the thumb and forefinger, too-heavy varnish will deaden the action. A tiny brush may be used to work under the guides —but the varnish there is probably in good condition so that more will not be needed.

If the rod has been used so little that it does not need varnish, it is an excellent plan to give it a coat of good floor or auto wax— and frequent coats of such wax during the season help preserve both finish and appearance. The same is true of steel and glass rods; frequent waxing is fine for them, and waxing before storage especially desirable.

REELS—AND WHAT TO DO FOR THEM

The man who won't often oil his casting reel—fresh-water or surf—simply can't expect to cast well. He'll spend about as much time picking backlashes as fishing, and he can't get even reasonable distance. Every hour or so is none too often to apply a little oil on the level-wind mechanism.

How often the end bearings need oiling varies with reels of different designs, and with how worn they are. If the end caps of your reel are removable, occasional visual inspection will soon show how long oil stays there, and how often fresh is needed. If they aren't removable, experiment will tell you how frequently oiling is necessary to keep casting smooth—but there are few reels that won't work more smoothly if the end bearings are oiled for each half day's fishing.

The gears inside the headplate need peri-

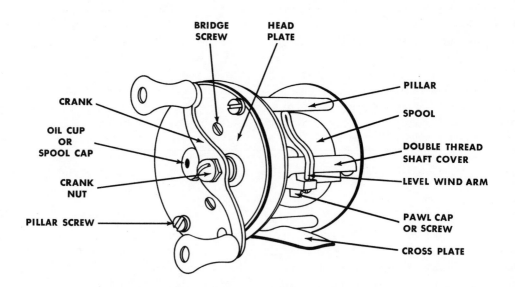

odic cleaning and greasing. How often they'll need it depends partly on the user. Once a year will do for the man who fishes only occasionally—and before storing for the winter is a good time to do it, to remove anything that might cause corrosion.

Taking a reel apart and reassembling it is no trick for one with the least mechanical ability. An instruction sheet for this comes with every reel.

Kerosene or gasoline and an old toothbrush are fine to clean the insides of a reel. And when they are clean, inspect to see if any parts are sufficiently worn to require replacement; if so, order the new parts in early winter, to be sure of having them in plenty of time for next season. About the only ordinary repair calling for a trip of the reel to the maker is replacement of worn end bushings.

Most use vaseline on the gears. This will do, but it's better to use a good reel-gear grease—and that sold by the maker of your reel should suit best the material he uses for gears. Here, again, do not overdo.

Fly reels do not require nearly so frequent lubrication as casting reels. Few men fish so much that their fly reels need it more than once a season. But never lubricating one is

throwing good money away, in causing the reel to wear out very rapidly. Clean the insides as you would a casting reel. But since a fly reel has nothing to do with the cast, the exact type of lubrication used isn't so important. The main thing is to see to it that there's always some sort of reasonably clear oil or grease in there, to permit smooth operation and prevent undue wear.

YOUR LINE NEEDS ATTENTION

A silk casting line should be removed from the reel and dried thoroughly at the end of each day's fishing, or it will soon weaken greatly. This drying is unnecessary with nylon lines, which are not subject to rot. But whenever one is not to be used for some time, it is well to remove it and dry it, largely to prevent corrosion of the aluminum spool.

Fly lines are a very different proposition. In use, regular application of a good dressing is necessary not only to float the line and to allow good shooting, but to prevent undue wear. However, a line with dressing just smeared on will cling to the guides and will shoot worse than a line with none—for best results, leave only a little and polish it in well.

WHAT TO DO WITH WADERS

Waders, even more than rods and fly lines, are far more often ruined by improper storage than by use. Nearly every angler believes that it is best to store waders by hanging them up in the air.

Don't do it! With soap and water, remove any oil or grease that may be on the waders—these are natural enemies of rubber—then rinse and dry thoroughly. Roll the waders up tight, wrap them heavily with brown paper and store them in a cool place. To preserve them still better, wrap the paper package with something airtight, such as cellophane or pliofilm.

This, too, is the best way to store other articles of light rubber, such as inflatable boat cushions, or the fish pocket from the back of a wading jacket.

THESE ALSO NEED CARE

Hooks and other steel articles generally will not show noticeable rust if stored during winter in a very dry spot. Still, it is a good precaution, and takes little time, to wipe all such articles with a greasy rag before putting them away.

Spoons and spinners of plain copper or brass dull quickly in use, which lowers their attractiveness for fish. The simplest and fastest way to polish them is with a little wad of fine steel wool kept in the tackle box for the purpose; for highest polish, always rub back and forth one way.

Each time a fly leader of natural gut is wet and dried, it becomes more brittle and weak; when one has been wet, it should be kept wet, between moist felt pads. But pads kept damp with plain water will mold and rot. A 50 per cent mixture of water and glycerin, with a pinch of baking soda, helps prevent this, and the glycerin keeps the leaders flexible. Still better to prevent mold is a half-and-half mixture of water and ethylene glycol—antifreeze.

At the end of the season, it is well to throw away all gut leaders that have been wet—unless you want to pay particular attention to storing them damp with some good leader-soak, and then test them carefully before use next season. Nylon leaders need no particular attention.

Flies and fly-tying materials seem the favorite food of moths. Put such things away without moth repellent, and when you next look at them you'll probably groan at the sight of a pile of dusty rubbish.

It would seem to me that DDT or similar stuff would be ideal, being permanent, to keep moths from flies and materials. But the largest fly and material firms favor the use of such older preparations as naphthalene flakes or paradichlorobenzene crystals. These must be replaced rather frequently.

By Jason Lucas

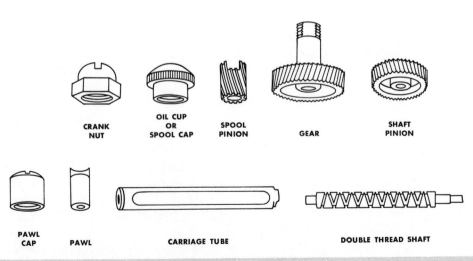

CRANK NUT   OIL CUP OR SPOOL CAP   SPOOL PINION   GEAR   SHAFT PINION

PAWL CAP   PAWL   CARRIAGE TUBE   DOUBLE THREAD SHAFT

CHAPTER 8

hunting

HUNTING IS a sport as old as the history of man. Nearly 2,000 years ago the Egyptians hunted waterfowl out of blinds, over decoys, in a fashion amazingly similar to the way it is done today. Although hunting has at various times in the past been basically a means of survival, it was more than that to the ancient Egyptian—and it is more than that today. As the population of this and other lands has increased, it would seem logical to presume that game populations would show a corresponding decrease. Such is not the case. America's deer herd, to cite just one example, is larger today than at any other time in the nation's history. Modern conservation techniques are producing more game for more hunters. In the chapter that follows you will find basic information on hunting big game, deer, upland game, ducks and geese, and varmints.

BASIC PRINCIPLES

Why does anybody go hunting? If they need the meat for survival, then almost any means of obtaining it is probably justified. But survival meat is usually not the motivating factor any more. The average hunter spends far more money on a pound of meat taken from the field or woods than he does getting it over the counter.

When we speak of a way to hunt in this day and age, we are primarily concerned with the individual who enters into the hunt because he enjoys the spirit of the chase and possesses, in his make-up, the basic principles of sportsmanlike conduct. He doesn't want to shoot something that doesn't have a sporting chance of eluding him. He doesn't want his game to suffer, and he respects the land that is his privilege to hunt on.

In referring to the sportsman, we are not thinking solely of the hunter who has the latest and best of equipment. It's not the equipment that makes the sportsman. One sportsman may have an old beat-up gun that was handed down by his grandpappy. This fellow may be as good a sportsman, get as much game, enjoy the hunt and do as clean a job of it as the man with a custom-made gun that set him back a few hundred dollars. A hunter who stalks his deer with the low-powered .25-20, gets within close range and places his shot in a vital spot will make more clean kills and spoil less meat than the high-powered gunner who shoots wild with a 30-06, .270 or .375 H & H Magnum—with no consideration for anatomy.

It behooves every hunter-sportsman to first know his gun.

Then, too, a man can become a better hunter by learning something about the bird's or animal's inner working parts. A big factor in making a good kill is placing the shot in a vital spot and this is impossible to do unless you know the vital spot—and can hit it.

We can have the most fun and satisfaction out of hunting and preserve it for the future if we appreciate the outdoors by learning all we can about it. With this knowledge comes a realization of why a lot of money and study goes into establishing our laws concerning hunting seasons, bag limits and hours of shooting. We are paying the bill, and if we don't respect these well-founded laws we are only defeating ourselves.

We won't feel that everything is lost if we don't bring home game every time—even though we are disappointed. We can take satisfaction out of knowing that we gave the game a sporting chance, because this is the American way of doing things.

BIG GAME

If your heart is set on a big-game hunt, you'd better make your plans and line up your equipment well in advance. If you want your hunt to be a success, you can't start off on just a couple of days' notice. A big-game hunt is very different from a trip for upland birds or waterfowl.

Big-game forests are seldom visited in closed season except by an occasional warden. So a locality where game was plentiful last year, and where you planned to hunt, may be almost destitute this coming fall because of food conditions, or perhaps because of a new road and a corresponding influx of hunters. You ought to choose a really promising location, and you usually need time to discover it.

Most any good shotgun shoots about the same—delivering a wide killing circle of shot right on your point of aim. But a rifle, even a brand-new one, at 100 yards may not place your bullets within two feet of where you aim—unless you have personally sighted it in with the particular ammunition you will use.

Also, almost any decent footwear will do for bird shooting. But big-game hunting often involves many miles of noiseless tramping over wet, snow-covered or rough country. Unless you have proper, well-broken-in shoes, your first day may cripple you for two weeks. It will pay you to look into all these things—place, time and equipment—long in advance.

Maybe this is your first hunt. Well then, what species of game do you want to hunt? Where would you like to go?

In the United States our big game consists of white-tailed, mule and Columbia black-tailed deer, elk, antelope and black bear. Moose, sheep, mountain goats, grizzly bear and peccary are also found but in isolated spots. The season on them is usually open for a short time and, in many cases, the number of hunters is regulated by "drawings" weeks in advance of opening day.

Canada and Alaska offer moose, caribou, sheep, goat and grizzly bear. Alaska has the big brown bear as well, but successful hunts in these northern fields take lots of time and are fairly expensive.

Do you plan to go alone, or with a more or less experienced companion, or will you hire a guide for your first hunt? If this is

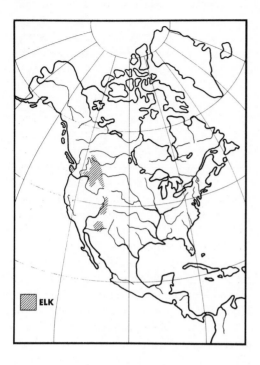

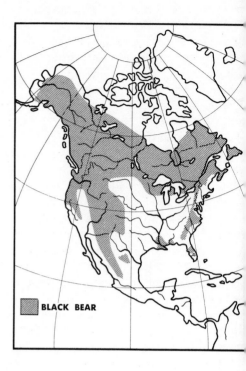

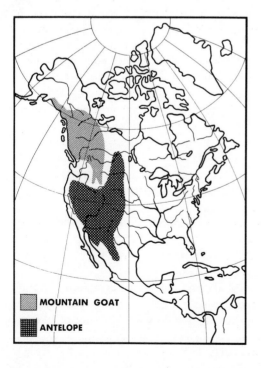

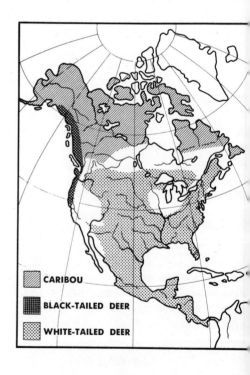

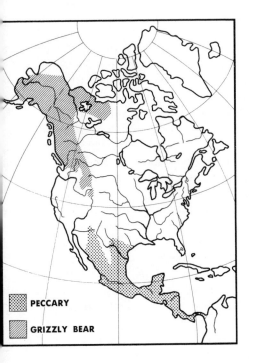

PECCARY

GRIZZLY BEAR

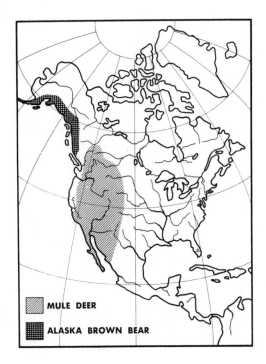

MULE DEER

ALASKA BROWN BEAR

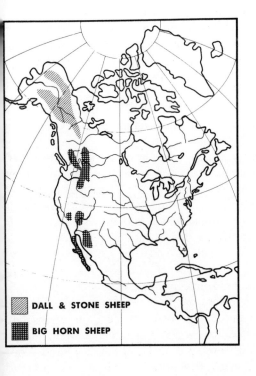

DALL & STONE SHEEP

BIG HORN SHEEP

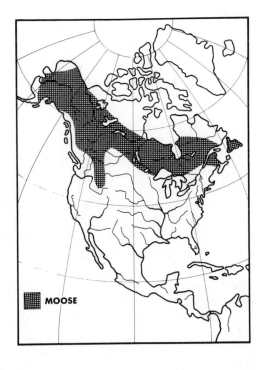

MOOSE

your first hunt you don't stand much chance going alone. There are too many things you need to know that only experience can teach. It is best to go with a friend who has been there before, who knows a good location, and more or less how and where to hunt. You and he may plan to hunt from an established hunting or sporting camp, you may board at a farmhouse on the edge of the deer forest, or you may make your own auto camp at the end of the road. In the West you may pack into the back country, and hunt from your tent camp. In this case you'll need a complete camp outfit and grub. In any event, you'll provide your rifle, personal outfit and clothing. Often it is also advisable to take a sleeping bag.

Undoubtedly your best bet, if you're a novice, is to hire a good registered guide. He knows the best country, will show you where and how to hunt, and may even find the game for you, thus saving you lots of time. Also he makes a fine instructor, enabling you to go alone successfully on later hunts. In several states non-residents are required by law to have a registered guide for big-game hunting.

Successful hunting always involves a lot of hard physical work. If you are in good shape, it is the finest of all physical exercises in a glorious climate and country. If you are not it is anything but, and you may have a rather harrowing time that you will not wish to repeat.

The young athletic fellow who plays a lot of tennis and golf has nothing to worry about. Other city men should train for their hunt, particularly in long-distance walking off pavements. You should train your eyes too. See how many gray squirrels you can see in a three-hour walk through the park.

Then there's the all-important matter of footwear. After an hour's walking over rough ground, your feet get longer and wider than normal from the exercise and the increased supply of blood drawn to them. Your easy, soft shoes must be of a size to allow for this—generally a size longer and wider than your everyday shoes. Your hunting shoes should also be light in weight.

Among the best all-around footwear for hunting dry or wet ground, just so it is not exceedingly steep mountains, is the lumberman's rubber—it has a rubber bottom with corrugated sole, and leather uppers, not more than six to eight inches high. It is comfortable, noiseless, waterproof and takes less breaking-in than any other shoe.

This shoe should be big enough so you can wear it with a felt insole and one pair of heavy wool socks in moderate weather, and with felt insole and *two* pairs of socks in cold weather.

But these rubber shoes won't do for the steep grass, rock- and snow-covered slopes of western mountains. You would slip and break your neck in them. What you need for rough western mountain hunting is sharply hobnailed alpine boots, or loggers with small calks, not over seven inches high, for they must be light.

Another type of shoe, which is perhaps even better because it is noiseless, is the soft, oil-tanned light sportsman's leather shoe that's soled with deeply cleated rubber soles—the kind that have rubber cleats on both sole and heel about half an inch thick.

Get either kind to wear with one pair of nylon socks under one pair of wool socks.

Your clothing should not be extra-heavy; no heavier than you would wear for golf in the late fall. But there will be times in hunting when you will stop for more than a few minutes, and then, unlike golf, you have no warm clubhouse to go into. So usually you should carry also a warm shirt or jacket, perhaps one lined with goose down. When you are moving, it is best carried in a small rucksack on your back, which also holds your camera, lunch and the other little gadgets we all like to take along.

You will be perspiring when you're moving, and then when you stop you will quickly get cold unless your clothing is wool. Also, wool does not scratch audibly when you're going through brush. Except for an absolute wilderness where you are the only hunter, your shirt, coat and cap should be red. Your rucksack will probably be just the color of a deer's back, but you can fix that for hunting by sewing a red bandanna handkerchief over it. Game is not alarmed by red more than any other color. What does alarm them are movement and noise.

On your person you always have a compass, a map of the area, a waterproof match safe, your sharp hunting knife, a whetstone and your watch. Make sure you never leave any of these when you start off for a day's hunt. For the butchering of game larger than deer, you also ought to have a very small hand ax or a small meat saw.

Your rifle probably looms up large on your equipment list. Hundreds of articles have been written, and will continue to appear, on the proper rifles and cartridges for various species of game. Most of these articles are excellent guides to selection. But hardly any of these articles give sufficient emphasis to the extremely important detail of sighting-in your rifle for yourself with the ammunition you will use, so it will hit where you aim.

In this connection, note another little detail that is scarcely ever mentioned. Do your sighting-in with a cold rifle. That is, fire not more than three shots, then wait until the rifle gets fairly cold before shooting again in the sighting-in process. Rifles may shoot to an entirely different spot when they get hot from firing, and of course in hunting you are always shooting from a cold or fairly cool rifle. In many hunts you will have only one chance and you want to be ready.

By Col. Townsend Whelen

DEER

Deer hunting is a fine, clean sport. It is matching one's knowledge, skill and instincts against the guile and unexcelled woodcraft of a big buck.

First of all, deer are browsing animals. They do not graze on grass, but browse on leaves, buds, young growth of bushes, certain wild flowers and weeds. Around farms they will eat apples and garden products. Mostly today they feed almost entirely by night. Their bedding grounds where they lay up during the day and their favorite feeding grounds are in entirely different country, different particularly as far as vegetation is concerned. Commonly they leave their bedding grounds about an hour before sunset, spend the night in their feeding grounds, and wander back to bedding grounds about an hour after sunrise. This indicates the country in which hunters should look for them.

The feeding grounds of white-tailed deer are often in old slashings where the heavy growth has been lumbered off, and bushes, high plants and young aspens, poplars and willows have sprung up. Or in and around abandoned farms or unfrequented parts of backwoods farms, particularly in and around apple orchards, and on hillsides with a southern rather than a northern exposure. The mule deer of the West feed in similar country, but generally along rougher hillsides and draws high up in the mountains. The Columbia black-tailed deer find much of their food in the more open country opening out from the beaches of the Pacific Coast.

Used feeding grounds can be identified by the tracks that wander around through the grassy and bushy places, and among the young tree growth; by the marks of tender branches and buds bitten off; and by bruised and broken branches and trunks of the smaller trees where bucks have been hooking and rubbing with their antlers.

Shortly after sunrise deer commonly leave such ground and wander into their bedding ground where they lie up for the day. The bedding grounds are usually in much thicker brush, and in the denser forests of larger trees; particularly in spruce, hemlock or pine thickets, and in country where there are many fallen trees and blowdowns. Quite frequently these bedding grounds are above or uphill from the feeding grounds. Usually, when deer stop feeding they will wander into a bedding ground that is upwind from their feeding ground so that their noses will warn them of any danger. The direction of the wind figures importantly in their daily wanderings, and may cause them to use different feeding and bedding grounds on different days.

Thus, if there is evidence of fresh feeding in a certain locality, the deer probably are bedded down in the thick growth that is upwind. Weather must also be taken into consideration, for on many early mornings there is no wind at all, or it may be a foggy, rainy morning and the deer will likely go to their favorite shelter. Bucks in particular like to bed down high up or on the top of ridges.

Deer approaching their bedding ground upwind will look for a thick place to lie down for the day, likely in some thicket or blowdown where they can watch their back tracks. Their noses warn them of any danger in the opposite direction—upwind. Deer also have exceedingly acute hearing.

As you hunt, watch not for a whole deer, but for parts like feet, antlers, ears, tail. You may discover the deer still in his bed. Stop often in places where you have a good lookout and just wait and listen.

There are numerous gun and cartridge combinations, old and new, on the market which are suitable for deer hunting. It is not necessary to get the most powerful cartridge made. The biggest factor in getting a deer, after you find it, is to put the bullet into a vital zone. This depends more on the man behind the gun than on the weapon itself.

By Col. Townsend Whelen

RABBITS AND SQUIRRELS

The first rule in hunting is *know where to go!* It's just as true for rabbits and squirrels as it is for grouse or turkeys or white-tailed deer. Take squirrels: No woods is good at midday during hot, humid weather, the squirrels are panting in the shady treetops. And you would be foolish to spend October hunting time on a maple flat. On the other hand, when squirrels are hunted in the spring, a maple grove is one of your best bets. It is that way with every game bird and animal.

Cottontails are great "holers" during severely cold weather—but they don't hibernate. They have to come up to feed, regardless of temperature. Bunnies are night feeders, however, and are likely to be back under-ground when it is light enough for you to shoot. So, when it's bitter cold, work on the ducks, and wait for the thaw. But watch the weather. When the mercury goes from way below to way above, take your hounds and cover the brushy wood lot and the bluffs along the creek.

That's for cottontails. Snowshoes are different. It doesn't get too cold for these big-booted bunnies—the true hares—and most hunters wait for a few inches of snow before getting down to serious "snowshoeing." Then, a pair of pups will serve you best, because no hunter can work through cedar swamps or alder thickets without driving the snowshoes ahead or aside. Turn the hound loose, find an open stand nearby, and wait. Soon a white-furred ghost will come circling by. That is the standard formula from Wisconsin to Maine, and south through the Appalachians.

In the West, rabbit hunting has been somewhat overlooked. There are good reasons, of course, with all the deer, elk, antelope and generally, far less hunting pressure. But rabbits are building up in the wide open spaces. During recent years they have become farm game species number two (pheasants first) in several states west of Kansas and the Dakotas. And it is cottontails that count in the West, although snowshoes take over in the high country.

East or West, rabbits are shotgun game and they make sporty shooting in front of the hounds. But stalking with the .22 is not out. Rabbits like to sit tight, and will, if you move cautiously. Both cottontails and snowshoes are hard to see against their native backgrounds. But the cottontails on snow, and snowshoes before snowfall, show up all right. The snowshoe's habit of sitting on top of the snow, usually under a log or close to a tree, gives the sharp-eyed hunter a chance to stalk small game in deer cover. For the rifle addict it's a good way to get through the long, cold months after putting the high-powered gun away.

In rabbit hunting there are two or three points that you can put down as solid. First, cottontails will hole if dogged—snowshoe

THE COTTONTAIL RABBIT
AND ITS RELATIVES

DISTRIBUTION: *Rabbits are something like minnows; they're everywhere. The ubiquitous cottontail, alone, is found in every state in the nation. Any attempt to estimate its numbers is the wildest guesswork, so its abundance could be indicated by simply tracking up the entire map with rabbit prints. It does thrive best, is most abundant, and hunted most in fertile farmland country, but it also is found up the sides of high mountains, in wooded lowlands, big timber, arid wastes and prairie land. It is runty in some of these places where food .isn't plentiful, and scarce in others, but it's always there. Its relatives, like the swamp rabbit, even inhabit watery places; others, like the snowshoe hare, get along well in the cold regions; the jackrabbit, also a hare, lives where there is room to stretch its legs. The cottontail is the most important game animal in America, barring none, furnishing more hunting and pounds of eating than any other.*

ever. Second, both of these rabbits circle, making it possible, with trained dogs, to shoot them from stands. Finally, bassets or beagles make any rabbit hunting good—and good rabbit hunting is tops in the small game field.

Rabbits and squirrels offer great contrasts in upland hunting. This is largely because rabbits are active at night, and to be seen by hunters they have to be *disturbed*. Squirrels are daytime animals, and are hunted successfully only if they are *not disturbed*. There is no substitute for going slowly and quietly in the squirrel woods. But when the leaves are too dry to walk quietly, it must be a waiting game. At such times, choose a strategic position—a white oak or hickory grove, a tangle of fruiting grapevines, a bottomland cornfield—and wait. It may be five minutes, or 30, but sooner or later a squirrel will frisk into range.

This waiting technique is good for both fox and gray squirrels. There is no basic difference in the habits of the two, except that grays shun open wood lots and are most common in the great hardwood forests of the Appalachians and Ozarks. The big reds, because of their fondness for open cover, often give you longer shots—and for this reason a scoped rifle is a bit more useful for them than for the smaller grays.

The most essential skill in squirrel hunting is the trained ear. As long as leaves are on the

THE TREE SQUIRRELS

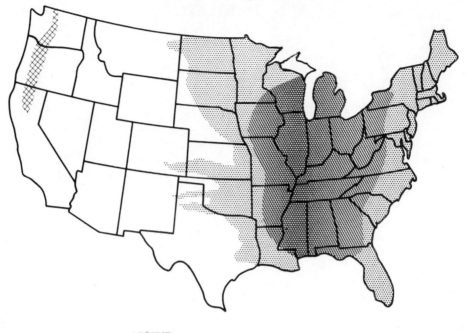

LEGEND

Range of the eastern gray squirrel

Range of the fox squirrel, overlapping
that of eastern gray squirrel

Range of western tree squirrels

DISTRIBUTION: *Only a few kinds of the tree squirrels are hunted, but two—the gray and the fox squirrels—provide almost as much shooting as rabbits, and cover much the same range as cottontails east of the Rockies, except they must have trees as part of their environment. The fox squirrel is more limited in its range than the gray, being uncommon in the easternmost part of the gray squirrel's domain; but, generally speaking, both inhabit the eastern deciduous forests and reach as far west as the borders of the treeless Great Plains. The gray (silver) squirrel hunted on the west coast is not the eastern gray squirrel, and not even closely related to it. The eastern gray squirrel has two color phases—the one which gave it its name, and a melanistic phase producing a black squirrel. The fox squirrel is often called the "black" squirrel in the south because of the startling difference in its coloring from that of the rusty-yellow fox squirrel of the Ohio basin and upper Mississippi valley. It is a handsome, dark animal in its southern range. Only a relatively small part of the northern Pacific coast country provides squirrel hunting.*

trees, the hunter can, on the average, hear squirrels farther than he can see them. But he hears other noises, too—falling nuts, sapsuckers tapping, jays cracking acorns, a thousand more sounds! Out of this whole forest symphony he must detect, amid the calls of birds, planes overhead and whispering breezes, the half-dozen sounds made only b⸱ squirrels themselves. And, even so, there ⸱ great similarity in the crash of squirrel an⸱ crow on a leafy branch—but the crow si⸱ and the squirrel crashes again into a neigh⸱ boring tree. To the experienced hunte⸱ nothing sounds quite like the patter of wa⸱

nut cuttings on leaves below, the scrape of teeth on a nut, the scamper of feet on bark. And when he can distinguish these sounds with certainty, he is saved the embarrassment of stalking redheaded woodpeckers going *slur-r-r*, or lowly chipmunks feeding on the forest floor.

"Pass" shooting is a squirrel hunting natural. Find a narrow strip of timber connecting two nearby wood lots, or a wood lot and cornfield. Then make a simple blind on the south or west side and on warm, sunny November afternoons take out after passing squirrels instead of the raft of mallards far out from shore.

Rabbits and squirrels can be hunted on any pocketbook; and they are hunted by far more people than any other American game species. They are the *people's* game. Sportsmen all over the country are coming to appreciate these two that are capable of living in field or wood lot and able to stand a lot of shooting. In the face of increasing hunting pressure, rabbits and squirrels are two of our stand-by game animals.

By Lee Yeager

VARMINTS

The name varmint is possibly of mountain-folk origin, but it has been generally accepted among a certain shooting fraternity that goes afield for small animals and birds that are considered harmful or otherwise undersirable. These animals may prey on game that is protected at great cost, or they may be unpopular with farmers because of the damage they do to livestock or crops.

This general classification could include the black bear in some states, but the name varmint somehow isn't quite befitting an animal of this stature. The coyote, lynx and bobcat are sometimes referred to in the varmint class but this is about the upper limit in size.

The mountain lion is also a trifle large to be considered a varmint—although he is classified as a predator wherever he lives.

The most widely hunted varmint is the woodchuck, known in some parts of the

U.S. Field & Wildlife Service

The Woodchuck—our most widely hunted varmint.

country as a ground hog, whistle pig and so on. In Canada where the chuck goes French-Canadian, he is referred to as a "siffleur." Officially the chuck is a marmot and wherever he may be he is not a pig at all for the chuck is a member of the squirrel family. A terrestrial squirrel.

There is a strip down through the prairie states, the Dakotas, Nebraska and Kansas, where the woodchuck leaves the lesser greenery to its terrestrial squirrel cousin the prairie dog.

The chuck usually has more than one entrance to his subterranean quarters—at least two and probably three. One of these will be clean of loose telltale dirt around the edges, and it is apt to be located in a spot that's shielded by vegetation or rocks. Chucks hibernate underground when the weather starts to get cool. This depends on the climate; their hibernation lasts four to six months. They wake up and stagger topside when it gets warm in the spring.

The chuck himself has a keen eye and may be studying you while you are waiting for him to pop his head out of another hole. He digs his hole close to his source of food—whether it be grass, alfalfa, clover or a truck garden. So he seldom wanders far from home. The chuck feeds in the daytime and his favorite feeding hours are early morning and evening. He may come out between these times to nibble or sun himself. He enjoys lying stretched out on a nearby rock, log or fence rail while the sun warms him through. You can frequently spot him in this repose if you look close.

Next to the chuck, the most popular pest target is the crow. Here is another smart operator. Unless you give him some study, he will outsmart you every time instead of just most of the time. A crow at 200 yards or more out in a field may see you and stand still while you take a shot. But if you want to pick him off at closer range, you will generally find it necessary to use a concealed approach or be hidden from view before he comes in for a landing. Approaching crows on the ground to get them within practical range of a light gun is no easy matter. You can feel you've really done something if you are able to stalk a crow.

Even when they're feeding in a wide-open field, crows will post a sentinel who will warn the other crows of your approach if you look the least bit suspicious. You can be sure that if you are trying to get within shooting range with a gun you will look suspicious to the sentinel. His eyesight is famous and he doesn't miss much.

By observing crow flights in the late afternoon you can frequently locate a roosting area. In the morning the crows scatter far and wide to feed. In the evening they are winging a direct flight to the roost and they gather there by the thousands to spend the night.

If you conceal yourself under a roost and wait for a large gathering late in the evening, you can sometimes shoot crows as long as the ammunition holds out. To hide, you must construct a blind or get well in under a tree in the shade where they won't see you on their approach or when they get directly above you. Wearing clothing that blends in with the foliage or brush gives you a tremendous advantage. Crows are quick to pick up any movement so you must also remain as motionless as possible.

Crows are highly gregarious and members of the flock communicate freely. Equip yourself with a good call and learn to imitate their many calls. Flocks will band together to drive off their enemies. A stuffed owl and some crow decoys may better your chances as the crows lose their caution at the sight of an owl if he looks authentic and your call is effective.

The prairie dog is an interesting little varmint to hunt and can be used as a long-range target. They have always been considered somewhat of a nuisance on the plains because they take over good pasture land. They also invade alfalfa or clover fields and the more succulent foods when available. They can also be omnivorous and have been accused of eating young burrowing owls.

The coyote is rather large for the name varmint, but shooters sometimes refer to him in this class. The coyote, a predator of the highest or lowest order—depending on your point of view, is a noble animal in some respects even if he doesn't look the part. If you catch him unaware, which is seldom, you will see him slinking along like a shabby, unkempt shepherd dog. Once alarmed, he will take off in an amazing burst of speed with his long bushy tail held down between his hind legs. None but the fastest breed of dogs can come close to outrunning him. Unless you seek him out, you will usually see him at daybreak or late in the evening. This is when he does most of his hunting. In spite of civilization closing in about him he has demonstrated remarkable staying ability. He is cunning enough to den up within a half mile or so of a farm, raid the farmer's chicken yard in the early morning hours, and get away with it while he grows old.

A lynx or bobcat will weigh 20 to 25 pounds against 35 to 40 pounds for a good sized coyote. Individual specimens of either animal may run considerably more or less in weight. For their weight, the lynx and bobcat are probably as destructive to game as the coyote, but they do not always inhabit the same range. They are more of a wood animal and are primarily nocturnal. On occasion, though, they get about in daytime.

The lynx is a cold-climate animal while the bobcat is found more in the warmer sections

Bobcats have not given up where civilization has pressed in on them. As long as there is a reasonable expanse of timber cover, they manage to hang on. In the southwest desert country the bobcat has adapted himself well and this is one of the hunter's favorite spots to hunt him. Hunting is customarily done with trained dogs. A hunter out on his own has to be awfully good or awfully lucky to even see a bobcat, let alone get a shot at one. Bobcats do sometimes follow old roads or trails in the woods but they are extremely shy and careful about not coming face to face with a human.

Foxes are a controversial animal. It is usually admitted that they destroy a lot of game, but there are two other considerations. In some states it is a sport to run foxes with hounds, and pressure is brought to bear to save the fox. In some states the fox is classed as a fur-bearing animal and is protected for this reason.

Hawks and owls are generally considered in the predator class but stop and familiarize yourself with the law before you shoot. Not all hawks and owls are considered harmful, and their hunger for pests like mice usually more than offsets any harm they may do to game or farmyard poultry.

The hawk's reputation varies in different states and localities. In the first place some states have more hawks or owls than others, and there are other factors to be taken into consideration. It is generally conceded that the most harmful hawks are the Cooper's, sharpshinned and goshawk and these infamous three are unprotected in practically every state in the country.

When it comes to most of the other small animals, there may be a question about just how the authorities in your state regard them. In some states certain animals are classified as fur bearers and therefore they are an economic factor in these particular states. Most states offer some protection to the raccoon in the form of a closed season and/or trapping regulations. In a few states the raccoon is considered a predator and is offered no protection.

The opossum, too, offers a subject for a difference in treatment in various states. A large number of states protect the opossum with a closed season and/or trapping regulations.

Most states pay no attention to the porcupine. The poor old slow-moving rodent pretty well takes care of himself and does little damage except to dogs, predators and any material that contains a trace of salt. This latter trait makes him a nuisance to campers and he may even chew up a canoe paddle that contains only the salt that works its way into the wood from perspiration on the paddler's hand. Porcupines also destroy a number of trees in some places by removing too much bark from around the tree's girth. There is little, if any, sport in shooting a porcupine and they cannot rightly be considered in the varmint class.

By Pete Brown

DUCKS

Many hunters spend a few days in the field or duck marsh each fall, then hang up their guns until the following year. They wonder why they can't hit ducks. The answer is simple: They're rusty. Duck hunters should get in plenty of practice on clay targets before the season opens. Hand-trap practice is also practical. Skeet is great practice for the decoy shooter, but trapshooting is better for training pass shooting, the most difficult form of duck shooting.

If you are missing your ducks, chances are you are shooting behind them. You are making the most common mistake of the amateur wing shot—you are stopping your gun and not getting enough lead. Some good duck hunters say you should lead a duck two to three duck lengths at 40 yards. That may be correct, but the lead on a canvasback coming down with the wind should be at least double that.

Protected by their superb insulation, ducks are hard to kill and you need to use a heavy load, No. 6 shot or larger, for all duck shooting and put your faith in a 12-gauge gun, for all-around shooting it is the best.

THE DUCKS AND GEESE

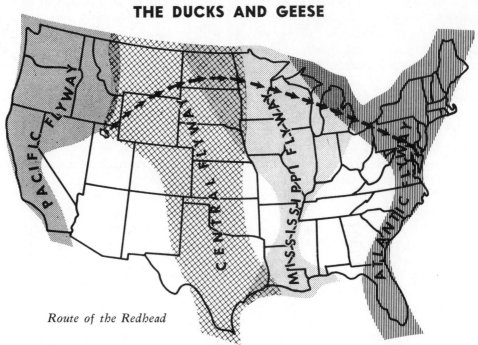

Route of the Redhead

DISTRIBUTION: *Although native ducks, which breed and often remain the year around in one locality, furnish some hunting, the bulk of the ducks—and nearly all of the geese, brant and sea coot—sought by gunners in the United States come down from the vast summering grounds in Alaska and Canada. They travel four main flyways, the Atlantic, Mississippi, Central and Pacific. Only the Central flyway is relatively simple and not complex, being a more or less straight north-and-south route. The others are more like funnels, at the upper end of which the birds come from many directions to be channeled into narrower confines as they near their southern terminus. Several important feeder lines run into the Atlantic flyway, giving it a great variety of species. Greater snow geese and Atlantic brant follow the seaward channel into the funnel from the eastern Arctic islands and Greenland, to be joined by Canada geese and black ducks from the Maritime Provinces, Labrador and Newfoundland. Blacks and honkers follow another route from interior Canada. Canvasbacks and scaup come from the northwestern feeder into this flyway.*

The most extraordinary route of any migratory waterfowl probably is the flight of redhead ducks from the Bear River Marshes of Great Salt Lake in Utah to reach the Atlantic flyway. They further the reputation of redheads for being headstrong, and fly northeast to the Dakotas, then east to Wisconsin, New York, Maryland, and Virginia, crossing at right angles the southern flights of their cousins in the Central, Mississippi and Atlantic flyways. The Mississippi flyway, which looks like a slightly cockeyed champagne glass in outline, is sometimes called the "mallard route," although it gets heavy concentrations of Canada geese, pintails, blacks and ring-necked ducks. Most birds using this flyway winter in a small area in Texas, Louisiana and Mississippi, and are heavily concentrated there. The Central flyway overlaps the Mississippi and merges with the Pacific in the north. Cackling geese, black brant and sea ducks enter the Pacific flyway on the seacoast side. From the interior of Canada and Alaska come the bulk of Pacific flyway pintails, widgeons, and baldpates.

There are experts who believe that a duck hunter should start out with a full-choke gun and they have arguments to back up their opinion. However, the average duck hunt who fires only a few hundred shells or l each year will be quite happy with the mo fied choke because he will have the wide pattern he needs at the distance he can kill.

DUCKBLINDS

A good duckblind that is well placed can be as important as a good gun. You can't expect to kill ducks if they flare 100 yards from your blind. Ducks have sharp eyes—they can see and they can hear. Just move an eyelash and that old drake pintail will see you and keep out of gun range. The same applies to mallards and all dipper ducks. While the divers are more careless and, in most cases, easier to decoy, there are times when they, too, are as jittery and wary as a crow.

Your blind must resemble natural cover. For instance, a green blind might be suitable at the opening of the season, but would not be as the vegetation changes with the season. If you are shooting in a marsh, pick out a piece of thick cover and push your boat in at right angles to the flyway. Your boat will make a hole when you push in, so be sure to build up the cover at this end. You can do this by cutting a few reeds or rushes and sticking them up at the end of your boat. Remember that the ducks are overhead so be sure to tilt your blind inward so you have good concealment. The most important thing is to remain motionless once you're set.

There are many kinds of blinds. A waterproof barrel sunk into the marsh edge, with the top about a foot above the water's level, is excellent. A cover to shed rain can be improvised. And the platform blind covered with branches that they use in the Arkansas woods is not only dry and comfortable but effective, and about the only kind you can use in this wooded area. Some stubble hunters on the western prairies dig pits, while others merely use barley or wheat shocks.

DECOY SHOOTING

Pass shooting is a game for the experts and few indeed are the hunters who can come in with a duck for every five shells expended. Shooting over decoys is much easier, still it is tricky. You must be quick as a cat to get results, since you don't have as much time to point out your ducks as you do on the pass.

You must swing on those ducks that come down with the wind outside your blocks, much the same as pass shooting. You must be alert, keeping an eye peeled for incoming birds, right or left, front or behind.

How can you hit the duck that bores right into your blind? You won't have too much trouble with mallards, pintails or other dipper ducks because generally they flare when they swing over your decoys or blind, but the cans, bluebills and redheads seem to be afraid of nothing and will bore right in. Stand up when you see them coming in at about 50 yards. Then they put on the brakes, start climbing, and permit you to get in your shot at the right range.

It takes two to do business if you expect to jump ducks on a lazy afternoon on the marsh. The shooter must be ready in the bow of the boat while his companion rows or paddles as silently as possible around the edges. When you flush that big mallard, he will swing skyward and you had better swing your gun right with him because the *lead* is *up*. He is rising much faster than you think.

DECOYS

The Federal ban of 1935, prohibiting the use of live decoys, makes the artificial decoy a necessity. The decoy manufacturers have the right decoy for every type of shooting. The heavy wooden blocks of yesterday, in most cases, have been replaced with lighter types. A dozen or two dozen blocks is sufficient to get the small limits of today. The duck decoy that you use in Arkansas or Louisiana may not be suitable for use in northern Minnesota or Canada. When the drake drops into the southern marshes in late November and December, he is in full plumage. But it is difficult to tell a young mallard drake from a hen bird during the month of September in the North. It would be unproductive to set out a stool of blocks in full plumage for these early drab birds.

Use no more than 10 decoys at the beginning of the season in the North. Increase this number as the season advances and the flocks become larger and more wary. Big stools, as many as 100 or more, are still used in the canvasback and scaup waters on the Great Lakes, Chesapeake Bay and as far south as the Carolinas. Deep-water giant redhead or canvasback decoys with plenty of white showing are standard. In Louisiana a favorite is the sheet-metal profile type, clamped in the ends of split canes and stuck in the mud.

Make sure your decoy cord is heavy enough so it won't tangle. The lead weights that you can twist around the duck's head are good, and there is a very practical iron weight shaped like a horse collar that can be dropped over the head.

DUCK CALLING

Duck calling is an art. A duck caller gets more satisfaction from bringing a flock of mallards in to his decoys than he does out of shooting them. An inexperienced duck caller is a conservationist—he scares away the ducks. There are days when ducks respond readily to a duck call. There are times when the birds pay no attention to a call. The best duck call is really a musical instrument. It should be designed to imitate the mallard hen. Most of the dipper ducks will respond to the call of the mallard hen. The purr of the diving ducks is easily imitated on any duck call.

The best way to learn duck calling, after securing a high-grade call, is to buy a record and practice the calls. Personal lessons from a good caller will help. Forget all about the fancy calls and learn to imitate the feed call you hear a mallard hen so frequently make on the marsh. After you have progressed to where you have learned the mallard "chuckle," you can consider yourself an expert.

By Jimmy Robinson

GEESE

The great thrill in hunting geese is outwitting the big, smart birds. A successful goose hunter experiences the same sense of self-satisfaction as a speculator who outguesses the market, but what's money compared to a couple of big Canada geese hanging over your shoulders?

Regardless of the number of geese, a hunter must know how to hunt them if he expects to get a shot—unless he is just plain lucky. Geese rest in big water at night and feed during the day. Most geese come out to feed in the early morning and you better be in your pit at dawn.

There are several methods of hunting geese. One method is pass shooting as geese come out to feed. You build a natural hide where you think the flock will pass and shoot them as they fly overhead.

Lead a goose as you would a duck. Use heavy shot—at least No. 4's. If the cover is thick, a good retriever will come in handy.

Pit or field shooting with decoys is the most fascinating method of taking geese. Here is where you get the thrill of watching a flock of Canadas set wings over your decoys. They will fool you time after time. To get them within range is difficult. They will flare at the smallest sign of danger. You must be properly concealed in your pit and you must not move an eyelash. Don't smoke or raise your head above the rim of the pit. Don't get discouraged and leave your pit in the middle of the day. Geese may come in at any time, even just before dusk.

It is necessary to find the feeding grounds of the geese. Binoculars will come in handy here. When a new flock of geese comes out, they are very cautious. They will probably circle the field several times looking for the best feeding place and for any signs of danger. Geese that have been feeding for several days in one spot will head in as if they owned the field. If you have plenty of time and the field abounds with food, let the geese feed a day or so before you hunt them.

Do not spot geese on a windy day. Geese do not like to buck a heavy wind. They will more than likely drop into the first field that looks desirable for feed. But you can bet they won't feed there the next day when the wind has died down.

Now that you have located the geese, ask permission of the farmer to hunt. Promise him that you will fill up the pits after you have used them and offer him a goose or two if you are successful. Do not disturb the geese but come back at night to dig the pits.

Or, if the geese have left the field in the morning and your time is limited, dig your pits at once and get into them. These same geese may come out before dusk. Don't pit in where the geese have gleaned all of the food. They will start to feed about where they left off on their previous visit.

There are two kinds of pits. The best are single holes, dug waist high, about 15 to 20 yards apart. They should be dug equidistant from the decoys. If you have a large party of hunters, dig several large pits, each big enough to hold three or more hunters. They should be dug as narrow as possible, yet big enough for elbow room to stand up and shoot. These pits can be built 50 or 60 yards apart. Often geese will circle the edge of your decoys and either pit might get a shot. Sometimes geese light outside of your decoys. This is unfortunate because new geese coming into the field will head in with the live birds. Here is where your guide or another hunter who is posted along a fence will come in handy. This is the only time you should flush geese. He can flush them toward you so you may get a chance shot as they fly near or over the pits. Then you will have to wait for another flock.

After you have dug your pits, carry away the fresh dirt. Don't leave big mounds of dirt, even if you have covered them with straw, near your hide. Place a couple of decoys at the edge of the pit. They serve as a protection for the hunter who watches the flock. Make the pit as natural as the surroundings. After you have dug the pits, mark them well so that you can find them in the dark of the early morning. Everything must look the way it did before you dug your pits.

The most popular goose decoys for field shooting are silhouettes or stuffed decoys. There are some new rubber Canada goose decoys on the market which are just as good. In scattering your silhouettes, be sure you do not have them all facing the same direction because the geese may not see them when they circle in. They can see stuffed decoys at any angle. Blue and snow geese decoys are simple. Here you use either a newspaper or white table napkins. Fold them over hunks of dirt so they resemble a live goose.

Goose hunters have their own definite way of setting out decoys. But it is most important that you make your decoys look like feeding geese. Place decoys upwind so that when the geese come in against the wind, they won't have to come in over the decoys. They may light short of the decoys. Place your blocks about 35 or 40 yards from the pits—do not bunch them too closely.

When you first sight the flock, get out your goose call and start squawking. Now is the time to check your gun. See that it is ready and free from grit or dirt. If the geese decide to visit you, they will come in with the wind, circle a time or two, then set their wings. This is the moment that separates men from the boys—what you do now will mean success or failure. Be sure the geese are within range and keep down, down, down. Let one shooter give the word "fire," then spring up. Keep cool and pick out your bird. Knock over the leader if possible, and others may be confused and swing back. Never jump out of your pit when you fire the first shots unless the geese have left the field. Geese often circle back to see what has happened.

By Jimmy Robinson

PHEASANTS

When it comes to pure cussedness of action the ring-necked pheasant bows his red-wattled head to no game bird. No one can predict what he will do at any time under any given circumstances. In the comparatively short time since he has become an important factor in the hunting scheme in this country he has given more dogs running fits and caused more hunters to break the Second Commandment than any other feathered quarry. Often reckless to a suicidal extent, the ringneck, despite his brilliant plumage, can do a fade-away act, right before your eyes, in short cover that would be envied by any Houdini. He can also carry an astonishing amount of lead and can stage an amazing recovery from what has all the appearance of an instantly fatal gunshot wound.

THE RING-NECKED PHEASANT

DISTRIBUTION: *The first attempts to introduce pheasants into the United States were made around 1790, but success wasn't achieved until 1881 when Chinese ringnecks were planted in Oregon and multiplied beyond the wildest dreams of the importers. There is still a heavy concentration of pheasants in Oregon, Washington and up into British Columbia, making this one of the top-notch hunting sections. A fertile hybrid of English ringnecks and Chinese ringnecks was introduced in the East and began to thrive early in this century. Mongolians, Japanese green pheasants and mutants of several kinds were stocked by various states, crossbreeding occurred and today we have a mongrel which we call the ring-necked pheasant. It thrives best where there is good farmland, but not where cultivation is right up to the fences, leaving it no cover. Hence, it is found in varying abundance in the East, where it is nevertheless a major game bird; it is plentiful in the upper Midwest, and reaches its peak of abundance in the Kansas-South Dakota-Nebraska-Iowa-Minnesota-Wisconsin country wherever food and shelter coincide. Most peculiar thing about pheasants is that they are damyankees. If the Mason-Dixon line were extended across the country, pheasants would be found north of it, seldom south of it. They get along best roughly between the 40th and 50th parallels. They can live in the South, but don't reproduce there. Hand-reared birds make controlled shooting possible in the South. Some southern states raise and stock a few pheasants for put-and-take shooting.*

The pheasant is essentially a seed eater, although grasshoppers and other insects are favorite foods too, and he thrives on wild and cultivated fruits. The young eat a high percentage of insect food. Severe weather holds no terrors for pheasants if generous amounts of food and ample cover are available.

South Dakota is the most populous pheasant state and at one time was the mecca for thousands of pheasant huners from all over the country. Here the hunters deploy, some walking abreast through the long rows of corn, while others known as "stoppers" skirt the field and take up positions at the end.

This forms a sort of drive, the birds either flushing immediately in front of the moving gunners or flying over the heads of the "stoppers" at the end of the field. No more than 12 persons are permitted to hunt in a group.

At the beginning of the season these fields are fairly well populated with pheasants and retrievers are valuable assets in this type of hunting, especially when the drive is over, for the shooting is sometimes fast and furious. And when pick-up time comes, a retrieving dog is worth his weight in gold.

Not all pheasant hunters, however, have

access to this popular and productive prairie-state type hunting of the wily ringneck. In other areas he is not so plentiful and putting him in the bag takes a bit of doing. He has a fairly regular daily routine that the pheasant hunter will do well to learn. At sunup he usually leaves his roosting cover to replenish his food supply along roadsides, byways and country lanes, where he also picks up what grit he needs. If corn is available, there he will soon be found, and some may stay nearly all day. Others, getting their fill of this favorite grain, will move into other types of cover, weed and brier patches, vine-grown, brushy tangles and along waterways. During the heat of the day, the pheasant will seek the closest, coolest cover available, with dust-bathing places handy. Here he is apt to "lay" tight until the brush-breasting gunner almost treads on him.

Along in the afternoon the pheasant will feed again, and it is best to look for him then where you know food is to be found.

The best equipment a pheasant hunter can have consists of a good pair of legs and a lot of patience. Travel light, for you'll get plenty of exercise. And by all means go comfortably shod. Dress according to your own climate and terrain, but don't burden yourself with uncomfortable or unnecessary clothing.

While smaller guns are used by experts, the best all-around pheasant gun is a 12-gauge, light enough to carry all day. Express loads with an ounce and a quarter of No. 6 chilled shot; barrel bored either full or modified choke are good shot size and choke. But the shooter must remember about pheasants that on any shot the rear two-thirds of the target is his long tail. Hitting only this appendage won't put him in the bag.

By Henry P. Davis

QUAIL

Telling someone how to hunt quail is like telling a general how to carry on a major campaign. They can offer almost as many variables as smart troops afield.

Naturally, to shoot quail you must find birds, or your dog must find them. Dogs are a must. Without a pointer or a setter or some breed proficient in locating and pointing bobwhite, you would be almost as much off base as a gourmet eating jello with chopsticks. Any kind of a dog that can locate coveys and hold them for you and then find the birds you shoot is a good one.

Next to a dog of good hunting ability, there is no greater asset than having with you someone who knows the area where you are hunting and where particular coveys of birds are to be found. If you hunt hard all day you might be able to hunt some 1,000 acres of cover if the going is not too tough. If you put up six coveys in a day you are going away above average on ordinary farmlands. Quail preserves might hold 20 coveys in this area and show a population of possibly one bird to five acres. Quail, then, are not like ducks in a good marsh. They are never abundant—and they must be hunted.

Quail love the edges of good escape cover. If you are in a bobwhite state, frequent the edges of woodlands where poorly farmed weedy fields furnish corn or soybeans. Ragweed and lespedeza are bread, butter and dessert to these birds.

Look for birds where food is adjacent to cover. Often this is in creek bottoms. This has led some to the idea that quail must have free water. Usually this is not true, the possible exception being in a period of prolonged drought. Many quail undoubtedly live out their lives without dipping their bills in pond or stream. They get their water from their food, and from dew, rain and snow. They like wet creek bottoms because these furnish more succulent food and close and heavy cover in which to hide.

Wherever possible you should hunt into the wind. Dogs do not overrun birds so easily if they get a whiff on the breeze coming toward them. You should be out early, especially if you have the day before you. Frost will still be on the ground and if the weather promises to be warm and bright, birds will be out early on their feed. If the night has been cold, gloomy or wet, it's possible the covey will not be abroad so early. At such

QUAIL

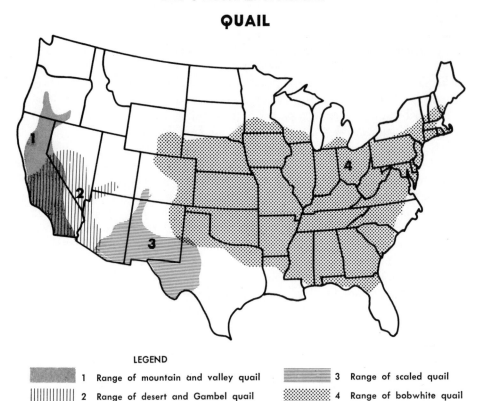

LEGEND

1 Range of mountain and valley quail   3 Range of scaled quail

2 Range of desert and Gambel quail   4 Range of bobwhite quail

DISTRIBUTION: *The many different kinds of quail cover very nearly the entire lower portions of the United States. The range of the desert and Gambel's quail extends from the southeastern part of California and southern Utah through New Mexico to Mexico. They are numerous in the valleys of the Colorado River. Scaled quail are found in the arid chaparral and mesquite country of southern Colorado, Arizona, New Mexico and west Texas. Mountain quail are birds of the high slopes of the Pacific west, living at altitudes of 2,000 feet and higher. Valley or California quail scurry through dense covers along the West Coast from southern Oregon to central California. A southern species of valley quail is found down into Mexico and as far east as Nevada. All quail are gregarious, as many as 20 or 30 or more living in a covey, sharing the same range. They are seed eaters, able to live on a minimum of water and through hot weather. The familiar bobwhite of the East and South is far and away the hunter's number one choice, if for no other reason than his abundance. Bobwhite's call, which gave him his name, can be heard from the salty shores of Cape Cod down to the heart of Dixie—where plantation living and horseback hunts with the dog wagon trailing along behind have made bobwhite hunting an American institution.*

times, they are hard to find. They are still in a huddle and a dog can almost step on them without knowing they are there.

Maybe you'll find the birds are rather widely dispersed and a ragged bevy may rise. Look out here, maybe all of them didn't get up—and these shots should be the easiest if you are set and on balance.

In the afternoon, around three or four

o'clock, bobwhite move out to feed. Actually, from sundown until it is too dark to shoot, the most quail are taken. Here, weather may interfere to some extent. The birds seem to know if a storm and cold weather is approaching. They may feed earlier to store additional food for fuel.

Many birds are lost by novice hunters, or those overly courteous, because they do not immediately walk in behind the dog on point. Step in briskly. If you delay, the birds may run if they are shy or at least move away and confuse your dog. As you walk up the birds be ready to shift your balance. You will need to face your bird whichever way he goes. When he bursts forth, *face* your target. This is essential. At the same time, if you are a right-hander, get your left foot forward so you can pivot and swing freely. With a left-hander, vice versa. Keep your gun high. This is a safety factor for your dog or a shooting companion who might inadvertently step in front of you.

If you are a slow shooter, one who shuts an eye and takes some time in singling out a bird, your gun should be bored modified choke. And remember, your target is a rising one—a slow shooter is apt to undershoot. If, on the other hand, you get into action promptly, an improved cylinder bore is best. Also, you need little lead and you seldom will undershoot your bird. Really fast shots will use nothing but a full cylinder bore, and often will down two or three birds before the slow fellow takes his first one. They will shoot point-blank at the target, and because of their closeness, open bore and speed of swing need no lead whatever.

The size of gauge is your business. Unless one is an excellent shot, guns smaller than 20 bore are a menace and will cause the wounding of many birds.

Quail hunters use all shot sizes from No. 6 to No. 9. If you are a fast shot, the smallest may be the best. Better for the average man are No. 8 or standard No. 7½ trap loads. Also, use low-velocity shells. They give evener patterns and are ideal for such close shooting and do not punish you with recoil or blast your dog's ears.

By C. E. Gillham

DOVES

To be a great sporting bird, one that demands real skill with a shotgun, a feathered target must be fast, uneven of flight and small enough so that tight-bored guns need be used

in taking it. In addition it is to the bird's credit, if it is good to eat. Doves embrace all of these requirements and some 10 million of them are shot yearly in the United States. Their popularity is outranked only by quail, pheasants and ducks. A resident of every state, the mourning dove is legal game in about half of them, and in certain southern states he ranks tops in populariy of all feathered game.

The food of doves is almost entirely vegetable and they have a great preference for small grains. They will eat corn and weed seeds and in winter months they readily eat acorns and beechnuts. Look for them then in good feed areas. Stubble fields, peanut fields and buckwheat are very attractive to them. They must have gravel and always want water at the end of the day.

Doves sometimes nest in big trees and are found at the edge of heavy growths, but more often build their homes near clearings because they feed in fields. Look, then, for doves at the edges of timbered areas or in large fields, far from heavy cover. A scouting expedition, prior to the opening of dove season, is really in order to find where birds are feeding. Fields with all the makings of good dove shooting may be entirely barren of birds and others entirely similar may be loaded with them.

Once a good dove field is located, watch the flight of birds approaching or leaving it. Such a flyway will be productive just so long as there is scattered grain left in the field or until the shooting pressure has become so heavy that the birds are "burned out" and seek another location.

For such pass shooting, a shotgun of tight boring is in order. A full-choked pump or automatic will prevent many of the small swift-flying birds from slipping through your pattern. While many gunners prefer small shot such as No. 8 or even No. 9, a high-velocity load of No. 7½ is preferred by many top gunners and some even shoot No. 6's. If you use a double-barrel, a modified and full choke is recommended. Here again the hot-stove league will argue into the night, some contending that an improved cylinder

THE MOURNING DOVE

The mourning dove occurs in every state, but the density of lines in the above map indicates where it is most abundant—in the great valleys of the Appalachian Range from New England south, and along the West Coast into the Southwest. It may occur locally in considerable numbers between these extremes, but these two areas on opposite sides of the continent are what might be termed natural flyways that the doves follow in their southern migration each fall. The Pacific route is shared by band-tailed pigeons. The flights converge on Mexico, if the doves migrate that far. Many winter in the southern and southwestern states.

DISTRIBUTION: Persons who do not hunt them may find it hard to believe, but the mourning dove probably is the most widely distributed game bird in the United States. It is found in every state, although some are more favored than others from a shooting standpoint. When the autumnal migratory flights south take place, Georgia, South Carolina and other southern states enjoy outstanding dove shooting—but a state so far removed from them as California considers the mourning dove its most important game bird. Both the western dove, and the eastern dove are subspecies of ZENAIDURA MACROURA. They differ primarily in range and only slightly in size and color. In addition, the west coast has another member of the pigeon family whose southward flight line is much the same as the mourning dove—the band-tailed pigeon. Reversing the flight pattern, white-winged doves come up from Mexico into the southwestern states. All are considered "doves" from the shooter's viewpoint, but doves mean the mourning dove to those who love to hunt for this slightly smaller, but close relative of the extinct passenger pigeon. Bird hunting seasons seldom come in early enough in northern states to give hunters there much chance at doves, which flock up early in the fall and move south before really cold weather arrives, but the gunners below the Mason-Dixon line benefit. Since many birds converge on Mexico from east and west for winter quarters, it follows that Mexico offers superb "pigeon" shooting. However, doves' migratory habits are not as fixed as those of waterfowl, and mourning doves might winter anywhere in the South where the climate pleases them.

and modified is the proper barrel combination. The more open boring is satisfactory if birds are not taken beyond 40 yards.

By all means use a dog in dove hunting. It will save you endless time in looking for birds that are dropped in heavy cover. All of the retrieving breeds are good. Pointing dogs may be used, but they are not quite as efficient in locating dead and wounded birds.

Another sporty form of dove shooting is jump shooting. Hunters walk up the birds in stubble fields, while they are on the ground feeding. Doves suddenly burst forth, usually singles—two or three at the most. Their first flight is low and often erratic and they are not easy targets.

At certain times of year, doves fly in rather scattered flocks but they are rarely close bunched as are their relatives, the pigeons. Usually doves are shot as singles though pairs frequently travel together. In attempting to make a double, never shoot the lead bird first. Always take the back one. If the front bird is dropped, his companion usually zooms downward with him, twisting and dodging and skimming away low, presenting a most difficult shot.

Doves are not as man-conscious as ducks, geese and pheasants. However, it does pay when you're on a stand, waiting for birds to fly by, to have some concealment.

Frequently hunters sit down behind a tree or fence post and in open fields often small blinds of weeds or cornstalks are thrown up for concealment. Care should be taken here that you remain motionless when a bird approaches or he will spot you. Neutral-colored clothing at such a time is an advantage.

For some reason, probably because of the coolness involved, dove hunters frequently wear white shirts. When birds are at all wild, such clothing should be avoided.

By C. E. Gillham

RUFFED GROUSE

Picture a piece of grouse cover as follows: A small, dense lowland cedar thicket with an open, poplar-studded ridge beside it. You approach from the lowland where the cedars grow. Your bird is feeding on the sunny slope up which you climb. When he flushes, he dives straight toward you, passing very close and sweeping with bullet speed behind you, into the thick cedars. This very common grouse act is often used to illustrate the contention that the bird is wild, wary and shrewd. Actually it proves no such thing. This tactic is the ultimate in simplicity and directness of reaction. The cedar thicket is his "house," the slope his feeding ground. Startled, he hurries for the safety of his castle, not cannily attempting to confuse you, only trying to save his skin. Under comparable circumstances, you'd do likewise, without even pausing to plan a course of action.

No, if there is one thing the ruffed grouse is *not*, it is wild or crafty. Actually, the entire grouse family is by nature a trusting, friendly bird group, not given to complicated thought or action processes. When our country was young, and ruffed grouse were amazingly abundant throughout the East, they were commonly called "fool hens," because of their staunch refusal, at first, to believe that humans were to be taken seriously as predators. That fact is not commonly known, since in our day the term "fool hen" has been wished upon the spruce grouse.

The same is true of the sage hen, just as it was true, in the beginning, of the eastern ruff. It happened, however, that the ruffed grouse was unwilling to go on forever trusting those bent on killing him. Had he been any less abundant and less widely distributed, his slow decision to accept retreat would have been his undoing.

In reality, a grouse's friendliness and utter simplicity are responsible for his action. He hears a movement in the woods. When it gets close enough to make him uneasy and interfere with his acorn gathering, he flies away, more annoyed at the interruption, no doubt, than concerned. If you shoot at him, and the cover is reasonably thick, he won't fly more than twice as far as he would away from your footsteps alone.

His daily routine is simplicity personified. At sunup he leaves his evergreen bedroom,

THE RUFFED GROUSE

DISTRIBUTION: *The ruffed grouse is traditionally a bird of the colder climates and evergreen forests and his favorite haunts are the abandoned apple orchards and wild grape thickets that grow along the deep forest edges. With various related species such as pinnated grouse (prairie chickens), sage grouse and sharp-tailed grouse, the family is widely distributed throughout the United States, with the exception of the deep southern and southwestern states. The New England states, Wisconsin, Michigan and the states of Washington and Oregon are those places where the ruffed grouse has ruled the upland bird scene for as long as hunters have gunned for him. Grouse are generally omniverous, but the bulk of their diet is berries. They adapt readily to changing conditions and can suit their appetites to food found in various localities. The uncanny wisdom of the ruffed grouse coupled with the startling roar with which he takes wing in the thick, tangled cover where these birds are usually found, has earned them accolades from hunters everywhere. Like most game birds, grouse are subject to violent fluctuations in their population, but due to their enormous survival capacity and adaptable diet, enough of a breeding population is carried over each year to insure a continued crop.*

walking, as a rule. He trudges up the slope, feeding as he travels. He goes for a drink, always to be found near his chosen larder. Presently he tires of feeding, rests in the sun for a time, or takes refuge in a thicket if the weather's bad. In late afternoon he feeds industriously back toward his bedroom, taking on fuel to tide him through the night.

Clearings and swales attract the grouse for there they find food and a place to sun themselves. Also hunt hollows and fields where there is plenty of second growth and hemlock, birch, alder. You will also find grouse in abandoned orchards where there are berry bushes and briers. The wild cranberry bog, for example, is a fine spot to find him. Don't pass up fern beds, patches of brier and slashing piles—explore them thoroughly before going on. You may find birds almost under your feet.

If you live in Pennsylvania, a wood lot is apt to contain ruffed grouse. In Vermont or New Hampshire, you may flush him from a resting place in the hedgerows.

Early in the day, hunt eastern and southern slopes where the sun has made a warm area for him to rest. Later, look for him on the western and northern slopes.

Flush a grouse when he is among big trees and chances are you'll have to take him as he angles off into still deeper woods. But if you surprise him on the edge of a clearing, he is apt to head straight out into the clearing affording you an open shot. His location, before he is flushed, is apt to dictate the direction of his flight. In rough mountain country, no one can tell how he will flush or in what direction. The best tip for all grouse hunting is to go slowly and as quietly as possible.

The type of cover you can expect to find ruffed grouse in dictates the kind of gun you should use. It should be light and it should be fast. Open bores are preferred since most shots will be close. Shot size should be small— No. 6 to No. 8.

By Byron W. Dalrymple

WILD TURKEYS

Shooting wild turkeys is more than a sport —it's a great American tradition. It's a game that requires all the craft, cunning and patience you can muster. A wild turkey is the mightiest of all upland game birds. He is the sole ruler of a lonely pinnacle—the most wary and secretive of winged creatures.

Despite his wisdom and sagacity even the smartest old gobbler can be fooled. One fatal flaw gave him his name. He talks—and you can learn to listen for him and even out talk him. A gobbler gobbles because he wants hens to hear. This gives away the direction he is taking, and allows you—with luck and expert management—to get in position for a crack at him.

His hens talk with a soft p-er-t-t, p-er-t-t, which excites the gobbler. You can learn to imitate it. And if you have the good sense not to overdo it, you can talk a gobbler within gun range. Since he mates in the spring, the gobbler will be more succeptible to your calling at that time.

Your best all-around bet for a gun will be a 12-gauge shotgun. A smaller gauge is all right if you don't shoot a 12. One box of

shells is plenty; shot size No. 6. You can use a rifle if it is not illegal in the state you are hunting. The .22 Hornet or any light rifle is good. But *you* had better be mighty *good*. If you happen to have a shotgun and rifle combination, this is perfect.

For clothing you will need everything absolutely drab. No light-tan outer garments, no white T-shirt showing at the neck. No colors of any kind. A well-dirtied jungle camouflage suit makes an excellent outergarment. Dark olive drab shirt, jacket, britches are best otherwise.

Dawn until around nine or 10 a.m., and then four p.m. until dark are the "working" hours. Seldom is a turkey killed during the middle of the day. The reason is simple. Gobblers gobble most during early morning, sometimes again just before going to roost.

Of course, weather makes a big difference in how much gobbling the males do. If it is too cold, or too wet, or too windy, or too this or that you may get out at dawn only to find that not one gobbler lets out a peep all morning.

A bright, windy day is the bane of every turkey hunter's existence. You can't hear the gobbles plainly, nor spot their direction well enough. And you can't hear a turkey walking—they make plenty of noise when not suspicious.

When a gobbler starts toward you, no matter from how far away, ease your gun, half an inch at a time, into actual shooting position, and slip off the safety. Hold the gun right there, even if it's for an hour. Unless you've hunted turkey's you've no idea how marvelous their eyes and ears are, how quickly a gobbler can disappear.

The body of a gobbler looks mighty big. But don't shoot at it. His *head* is your target. Body-shot gobblers seldom go down and stay down, and they're seldom caught. Same goes for a gobbler with a broken leg or wing. A rifle shot is all right in the body, but isn't considered very graceful. It spoils too much meat.

Another thing—don't run up to a fallen, flopping gobbler and pick him up carelessly. He weighs anywhere from nine to 25 pounds,

THE WILD TURKEY

LEGEND

▰ **ESTIMATED 70,000 POPULATION.** Texas, Pennsylvania.

▨ **25,000-PLUS TO 40,000.** Arizona, New Mexico, Alabama, Florida, Georgia.

▩ **5000-PLUS TO 25,000.** Colorado, Arkansas, Louisiana, Mississippi, North Carolina, South Carolina, Tennessee, Virginia, West Virginia.

▥ **1000-PLUS TO 5000.** California, South Dakota, Maryland, Missouri.

▦ **LESS THAN 1000.** North Dakota, Oklahoma, Utah, Wyoming, Kentucky, New York, Ohio.

DISTRIBUTION: *The wild turkey, from which our domestic bird is descended and which is difficult to distinguish from its farmyard cousin, is enjoying an upswing in numbers, and hunters are enjoying some of the best turkey hunting seen since pioneer days. From near-extinction to a national flock numbering nearly half a million, the number of birds has increased to the point where hunting is allowed in many of the states possessing turkeys, and the annual kill is around 50,000. It is considered "big game," and many hunters feel it is the noblest quarry of them all, since it is wary, inhabits isolated country, and is not so plentiful as other "big game." The hunter's chances are best in two widely-separated states, Pennsylvania and Texas, where the U. S. Fish and Wildlife Service estimates the flocks at 70,000 birds each. Other states in the wooded sections along the Great Lakes, noticing Pennsylvania's success in the rehabilitation of wild turkeys, are striving to re-establish them. There are about four distinct strains in this country, although they differ only slightly in physical characteristics. Arizona and New Mexico in the Southwest, and the Alabama-Georgia-Florida triangle furnish the best hunting outside of Pennsylvania and Texas.*

and is awesomely strong. His big spurs can cut you badly. The usual procedure is to hold him down and finish him with a quick knife thrust into the brain. Of course, a well-placed head shot at good range will drop him motionless.

You can buy turkey-calling recordings, and a call, and learn beforehand to call your own gobbler. But it is wise, at least on first hunts, to have a guide who is an experienced caller. It takes a lot of know-how and experience. Some callers use a cedar box yelper, and ome use a yelper made from a turkey wing bone.

Perhaps you're wondering how you're going to tell which is a gobbler and which a hen. The head of a hen looks smaller, more slender and often bluish. A gobbler's head will appear big, mostly white, with red wattles below. But always, to avoid mistakes, look for the beard. A gobbler has a "beard" anywhere from three to 12 inches long sticking out of and hanging down from his breast. It's coarse as horse-tail hair, and always easily visible. You can see it whether he walks, roosts, runs or flies.

By Byron W. Dalrymple

CLEANING TROPHIES

Trophies cost a lot—a lot of money, time and effort. Too many sportsmen let them deteriorate because they don't know what to do to keep them looking as sharp as when they came from the taxidermist. When so little effort will keep these exciting reminders of your hunting and fishing in top shape, it is well worth expending.

The prime and most common enemy of trophies is dust. It is not nearly so easy to get off as it seems to be to get it on. Dust seeps down in, dulling gloss and making a mounted game head or bird look disheveled and dingy. If left to collect long enough, particles of grease and oil and moisture from hundreds of unseen sources may permanently ruin the trophy. Thus, you should spruce up all trophies at least once a year.

Handle your prize with extreme care when taking it down from the wall, and while doing the cleaning. All trophy parts become more and more brittle with age. Because they are constantly exposed to the hottest air in the room, they dry out badly even in rooms with good air insulation.

The dust on them may be taken off with a vacuum cleaner. But if at all possible you should use one of those small hand vacuum cleaners—large cleaners have such strong suction they are apt to damage the trophy. If you must use a standard-sized vacuum, be sure to use the brush attachment, and don't press down hard.

On trophies where hair or feathers have been poorly fixed by the taxidermist, too strong an application may pull them out in chunks. So, just keep lightly brushing the trophy, going over it several times. Be sure you brush with the grain of the hair, otherwise you'll rough it up badly.

On spots which will not come off with the vacuum, a mild soap solution can be applied lightly with a soft cloth or a sponge wrung almost dry. If you do this, however, you must then make sure the trophy has a chance to dry completely before you brush the hair smooth again.

Shiny places, such as eyelids, glass eyes and nostrils, can be brightened up by brushing on clear shellac with a water-color brush. A brush of this kind, dipped in turpentine, can be used to clean up beak, feet and legs of birds. When cleaning antlers and horns it is best simply to polish them by rubbing. No oil of any kind should ever be applied to true *horns*, for they are porous and the oil will seep in, darken the horns and gather more dust. *Antlers*, however, may be oiled very lightly with fine oil, and then polished.

Fish, as a rule, can be cleaned by wiping them free of dust. They can then be touched up with oil paints. Make sure the colors match perfectly. Then give the trophy a thin coat of colorless lacquer and it will look like new. Never do this, however, unless it is really needed. If lacquered too frequently, the colors will darken.

By Byron W. Dalrymple

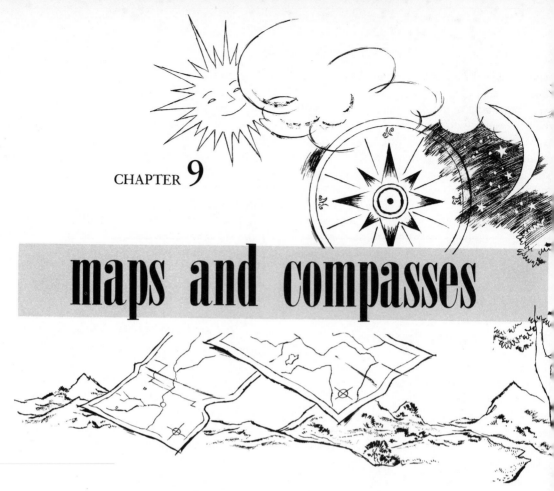

CHAPTER 9

maps and compasses

THERE IS one faculty above all others that distinguishes the real outdoorsman. This is his ability to find the way, to travel surely, though unfamiliar country. A real outdoorsman can go on a day's tramp and find his way unerringly back to his starting point. He can wander for a day or a month, and always know just where he is. This chapter tells you how to do just that: how to read the signposts of the outdoors and how to use your two most vital direction finders—your map and compass.

In the outdoors you have the sun, moon and stars to keep you straight. In cloudy weather you have your compass.

NAVIGATING OUT-OF-DOORS

Navigating (which means only to direct one's course) is simply using them. Any fairly educated person can find his way surely if he just obeys one rule.

It has been proved scientifically and practically, times without number, that neither civilized nor primitive men have any homing instinct or a compass in their heads such as displayed by migratory birds and fish. There is no such thing as a "bump of locality" except by observance of this rule.

An Indian cannot find his way through country he does not know, and is therefore afraid to enter such country. On a one-day trip he might be able to find his route back by following his trail home. Occasionally we hear an old woodsman say he can find his way anywhere, that he never gets lost and does not need a compass. He may honestly think so, but on careful investigation we find that he subconsciously obeys this one rule.

What is this rule? It's as easy as falling off a log: Always keep track of the directions and distances of your wanderings. You know where you have gone, and therefore where you are. At first this requires that attention be given to directions and distances, but after a time it becomes automatic.

Actually, this rule may be translated: Use common sense.

First of all this involves always taking the precaution to keep yourself oriented, meaning that you are sure of your direction at all times—know where north, south, east and west are. Second, it involves remembering how far you have gone in a certain direction.

A compass is essential on a cloudy day or night, when there are no recognizable landmarks. Put one of those characters who boast that they have a compass in their heads adrift in a small boat on a large lake in a fog, and see where he comes out! Being on a lake or in a thick forest or on a flat plain on a cloudy day is analogous.

Knowing how to gauge distance is very important if you are not to get lost. In most rough countries the distance you travel in any recorded direction is best kept track of by time. On level ground and a good trail you can expect to cover about three miles in an hour. As the going gets harder your time-distance becomes less. In very steep, rough country it may be not more than half a mile in an hour. On this basis you soon get to gauge your distances close enough.

Perhaps you can keep directions and distances in your head—that is, you keep a *mental map*. This is the way the experienced outdoorsman does it, and it is the way the old boaster does it, whether he acknowledges it or not. Such a man will also boast to you that he never misses anything on a day's hunt. He sees wildlife, every animal track and sign, he notes the tree growth and peculiar formations, and each twist and turn in his day's travel.

You can learn to do this in steps. At first you make little maps of your "home country." Pretty soon you'll find you can make a pretty good map of country you have been over several days previously. You're now making "mental maps" that answer perfectly. As you continued these wanderings, the time comes when your routes are impressed on your memory like a mosaic with scarcely any thought at all. Occasionally you will sense a situation that requires unusual care, and then you may want to sketch an actual map as you go along. This is particularly necessary in flat, monotonous, wooded country when the sun is not shining.

You can learn all this easily once you realize the common sense of it. Start making rough sketch maps. First draw an arrow to show which direction on the paper is north, and another line showing the scale of distance or time. If you go straight in a certain direction for three miles or an hour, get out your sketch, turn the north on the paper to correspond with the north by sun or compass, and beginning at the starting point, draw a line the correct direction and distance you have just traveled. Continue in the same way for each similar lap of your trip. Make a note along the lines of such things as the kind of wood, hills, streams, cliffs, each in its proper location.

It is not necessary to take a lot of pains, or to spend much time over it. After you do this on three or four jaunts you'll realize that most of it has become unnecessary because you will be able to remember just how you go, and all the features of your travel. You will be making a mental map.

In open hilly country all this is a cinch. You just keep track of the obvious landmarks. If there is a hill with a peculiar shaped top, tree or cliff on it that you can see from all directions, and your camp is two miles south of that, there may be nothing else to remember. This is also true if your route lies along a fairly straight valley or ridge.

A good outdoorsman notices and remembers many things as he goes along, and particularly he will remember the character of the country and the vegetation. In a thick country be careful of your orientation. Draw your courses more frequently and more accurately on your map.

The times the real outdoorsman looks back on as the happiest are those when he is wandering free in strange country, with a good rifle in his hands, and a little pack on his back, going in any direction he wants through beautiful, unspoiled land.

Then you can bed down wherever night overtakes you, sheltered mostly by the limbs of trees; subsisting on the little store grub you brought along in your pack and such grouse, rabbits, porcupines or muskrats as you might come on, or what trout you can snag out of the small streams.

Nights before your little warming fire are the pleasantest of all. The smell of balsam and burning aspen is in the air and far off the hoot of an owl or the laugh of a loon echoes off a nearby lake.

Lonely? Not on your life. You'll enjoy every minute of it, for you have Nature to keep you company. Thank goodness there are lots of places where you can still wander free in this way.

And so the old mariner whistles as he puts out to sea in his little bark, knowing that by dead reckoning he can always come back to his home port.

By Col. Townsend Whelen

COMPASSES

There are many questions asked about using a compass. Some people think a compass will point the way back home or to your camp. It will do no such thing.

All a compass will do is to tell you in what direction north lies—and of course, the other points, (clockwise) east, south and west. But if you use your bean along with your compass, you can keep from getting turned around and bewildered. Because one true direction is all you need to know, from one direction that always stays the same you can reckon all others.

For example, the country you want to explore is east of your camp. The compass shows you north—you sight in an easterly direction and walk off. Choose an object to

keep you on course—a mountain peak or even a tree will do. Keep repeating this until you arrive at your destination.

To return reverse the procedure. Find west from your compass or the stars and keep steadily on that bearing. Trust your compass rather than your "sense of direction" and you're back in camp before you know it.

There are two forms of compasses—the heavenly compass and the magnetic compass. The heavenly compass consists of the sun, moon and stars. Everyone knows that the sun and the full moon rise in the east and set in the west, and are in the south at midday and midnight. Likewise the two outer stars that form the Big Dipper bowl point to the North Star which is about seven times the apparent distance from these stars than they are from each other.

When the sky is clear, you have little need for a magnetic compass. But when the sky is clouded, your pocket compass is an absolute *must* in unfamiliar territory.

If you place a magnetic compass on a flat surface, and let the needle settle down, it will point north. That is, it points to the magnetic north, and not to the true north. The magnetic pole is in extreme northeast Canada, or almost due north of the center of Ohio, and only in that longitude does the needle point to the true north. In the state of Washington the needle points about 20 degrees east of true north, and in Alaska about 30 degrees. This *declination* as it's called must be taken into consideration when you're reading a map, for most maps are laid out with true north at the top.

Your compass need not be an expensive one, but choose one in which the north end of the needle is unmistakably marked. Many cheap compasses simply have one end of the needle bright and other end black, and when you're mixed up you can't remember which is which.

By Col. Townsend Whelen

MAPS

There are two kinds of maps, the mind map which you keep in your head as you go along, and the more or less accurate published map. It is your mind map, plus just common sense that will keep you from getting turned around or lost. If you can't trust yourself to keep a mind map in your head, then sketch it on a piece of paper as you go along. Here's how you use it.

You are camped in a level or slightly rolling piece of country that's entirely unknown to you. There are no prominent and easily seen landmarks. In the morning the wind is from the north so you decide to hunt in that direction. As you move along, you constantly check up on your direction of travel with the sun, or with your compass if the day is clouded.

You hunt north for three hours, then you find the wind has shifted to the east, and you decide to turn in that direction, keeping fairly accurately on that course by referring to the sun or your compass. You travel east for three hours. Then it is time to turn back to camp. Naturally if you now take a course straight southwest by sun or compass for about four and one-half hours you will be back at camp.

There are a great many variations of this, all easily figured out by common sense. But the point is that if you keep a mind map you always know just about where you are. If you don't keep such a map, you had best keep out of the woods or stay within sight of a guide.

Let's take a few fine points that also are just common sense. Suppose your camp is in dense woods in more or less level country. Steering your course back to it you might arrive at a point 200 or 300 yards from it and never see it. In such a situation you should previously have memorized the country within half a mile of the camp, so when you arrived within that radius you would recognize it and could walk right into camp. Or in country where it's allowed, you can previously spot a line of blazes on an east-and-west line through camp for a half mile or so, and striking that blazed line, you can again walk into camp. Two blazes on the side of the tree toward camp, one blaze on the side away from camp.

Or suppose again your camp is on a tote road, a stream or a lake shore running east and west. If you hunt north all day, then toward evening all you have to do is head south and you will surely strike that line. But when you strike this line, which way is camp, east or west? You could easily turn in the wrong direction, and at dark you had gotten nowhere. So again you can do two things. You can run a line of blazes along that line as already suggested, or in traveling south you can deliberately take a course that will surely take you to one side or the other of camp, and then, striking the line, turn in the right direction.

In some parks and reserves there is a decided objection to blazing trees. Instead you can break down the upper branch of a small bush toward camp so the light underside of its leaves will be a prominent mark. The Appalachian Trail has white paint on trees instead of blazes.

In more or less open country, with easily recognized prominent features, like much of the mountain country of our West, your problem is relatively easy. You fix in your mind the appearance or outline of a certain mountain that lies, say, just three miles northeast of your camp. That mountain will remain in sight from almost every little elevation all day long, although it may change its outline slightly as you travel around it, and you must keep track of this. Then you always know just where your camp is. And as you travel, keep looking back, and note the appearance of things, so you can easily travel back over the same route.

Now let's consider published maps. No sportsman should enter strange country without the best available map of that region. The map makes your trip safer, more successful and interesting, and it saves you a lot of time.

The best maps obtainable for any portion of the United States are the standard topographic maps of the U.S. Geological Survey. They are published in *quadrangle* sheets covering about 15 minutes of latitude and longitude. The maps themselves are about 14 by 18 inches, and the scale is half an inch or an inch to the mile. Each quadrangle is designated by the name of some city, town or prominent feature in it.

You can get these maps from the Geological Survey, Washington 25, D.C. for areas east of the Mississippi River. And for states west of that river, including Louisiana and Minnesota, you can get maps from the Geological Survey, Denver Federal Center, Denver 15, Colorado.

Write first for a free index sheet of the state you're concerned with. This shows the quadrangles, their names and locations. Then you order the quadrangle maps you need, enclosing 20 cents for each by money order or check payable to the order of Director of the Geological Survey. Stamps aren't accepted.

The back of every map shows the conventional signs and how to interpret the contours that show height, shape and slope of hills and mountains. An arrow shows the declination of the compass.

These maps are extremely accurate, but some were made 50 years ago and may not show recent roads, trails and new small towns. So you'd better get an ordinary auto road map to use with them. Also from the U.S. Forest Service, you can get maps of our national forests and from the National Park Service those of the parks, showing recent trails and so on. The address for both of these services is Washington 25, D.C.

For Canadian maps write to Map Distribution Office, Department of Mines and Technical Surveys, Ottawa, Ontario, Canada, giving the exact location or latitude and longitude limits for which you wish maps, and asking for the price of the best available maps. Many of these maps are based on recent air photographs and are absolutely accurate, but do not always show features that are not visible from the air. So it would be well, when arriving on the ground, to have a ranger, game warden or local sportsman mark the trails, portages and so on, on your map.

As a rule the best maps of other countries are those published by the National Geographic Society, 16th & M Streets N.W., Washington 6, D.C.

On almost all maps, the top indicates the true north. To orient a map, place your compass on the map, and turn the map until the compass needle is parallel with declination line on the map. Make sure that true north and magnetic north on your compass are the same number of degrees apart as they are on the map.

Now from your position on the map, you can note the direction to all other points on the map. If you get a little befuddled, and don't know exactly where you are, you can easily find your location on the map if you can see two prominent features such as hills, mountains or towns that are approximately a right angle apart. Orient your map by compass as just indicated. Place a small pebble or twig on the map over one of these features, and move another along the near edge of the map until it is in a line with the first pebble or twig and the prominent feature. Draw a line between the two pebbles or twigs. Do the same with the other prominent feature. Where these two lines cross is your location on the map, and you know the direction of every other feature from where you now stand.

By Col. Townsend Whelen

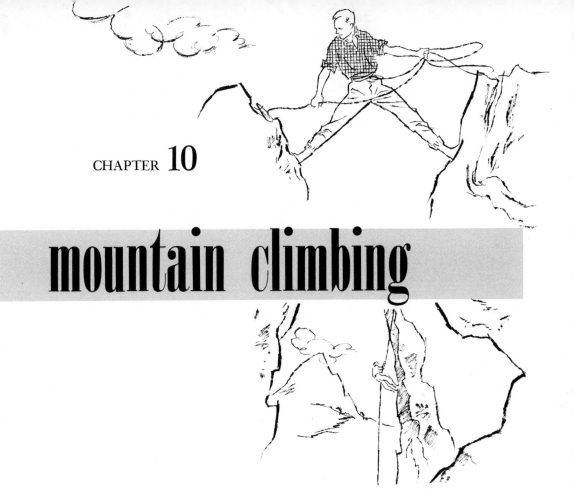

mountain climbing

ALL OUTDOORSMEN can appreciate the majestic grandeur of the mountains. But to some these peaks, by nature of their formidable terrain, are an irresistable challenge. Climbers are drawn by the "shattering of fears that slowly evolves into conquests," to use the author of this chapter's words. The greater the obstacles, the more exhilarating the successful climb. But you do not have to attempt Everest to profit from the lessons mountain climbing techniques have developed. Campers, hikers, fishermen and hunters can put these techniques to practice and assure themselves of safer, easier sport.

BALANCE CLIMBING

Everyone who ventures into the mountains, whether in search of new pools for his trout fly, new vistas for his camera or new summits for his boots, must learn by experience the fundamental skill of mountaineering—balance climbing. Its principles are as useful to the man who scrambles around in rough terrain looking for butterflies as to the boldest cliff climber.

The first principle has to do with the choice of footing. Most people soon learn that it is easier to step over a log than to climb up and jump down, that wet logs can be slipperier than ice, that a sprinkling of sand or gravel on a frozen hillside or a rock acts like roller bearings underfoot. There are fewer who realize that in uphill work it is better to have the ball of the foot on a level and the heel unsupported than to have the whole foot supported on a sloping surface.

The upper side of a grass hummock, the upper side of a loose stone, even a stick, can provide the little platform which holds the weight in balance. Where the hillside is loose or wet and wants to give underfoot, a good climber will seem almost to screw his foot into place. On a snow slope, he levels his stance by kicking a platform for his toe. The result is twofold. He does not often have to go through the tiring act of floundering for balance; while his weight is poised securely on one leg the other has an instant of almost total rest. It is the sum of these continual relaxations which keeps the muscles free from aching.

The second principle involves avoiding hurry—lunging ahead throws the body off balance. The pace to learn is the one which does not lead to panting and frequent rests. There is a tendency, especially when you are tired, to charge the objective—camp, lake or mountaintop—so as to get there before all your strength is gone, as if it were the passage of time instead of the expenditure of energy that caused fatigue. On talus (slopes of broken rock) and in timberfall this haste does not allow sufficient time for the choice of footsteps, and leads to barked shins and more serious injuries. In any kind of terrain it causes spasms of exhaustion which delay and demoralize the traveler far more than a deliberate pace.

In the growing fraternity of cliff enthusiasts, one learns that balanced posture and deliberate timing are all-important.

Any new climber has a natural fear of falling that causes him to lean in toward a slope and cling to it with his hands. There are mischievous results. In the first place, he overworks the muscles which are at rest when he is standing erect. In the second place, since most of the footholds you find are either level or outsloping, he lessens the frictional force which keeps his feet from sliding. In the third place, he is teaching himself to depend upon his hands and arms for lifting power. If the climb is at all long, he can't take it. Not even if he is in top-flight condition. In the fourth place, the position keeps him harried and uncomfortable. He is missing the psychological

kernel of climbing, which is like moving through an ocean of peril on an almost invisible chain of islands, each a resting place where the confidence is restored, the muscles are relaxed and the eyes have leisure to make a judicious selection of the next move.

To appreciate the nature of balance climbing, you can make a simple experiment. Set up a fairly steep ladder and climb it: The first time lean your body so you are almost parallel with the ladder. The second time stand erect touching the ladder with your fingers only enough to preserve your balance.

In the first experiment you will be cramped and under strain; the balanced way seems more daring but you'll see it allows you to straighten your legs. It is deliberate—and therefore relaxing.

With balance climbing there is little tendency to hurry through a bad place in the hope, usually false, of finding a better place beyond. One learns, often without being told, the rule that only one hand or foot is moved at a time. The other three members are kept on the rock.

With a minimum of specialized equipment you can make a mountain camp at high altitudes.

ROPE CLIMBING

Rope climbing is on the increase, yet the impression still prevails that there is a trick to it, like the old gag of India—toss the rope up and climb it. The primary function of the rope is to make climbing safe. Only in certain fancy applications is it used as a direct aid.

Climbing ropes are generally 120 feet long by 7/16- to ½-inch in diameter. Hemp, linen and silk were used before the war, today nylon has the advantage of being stronger, more resistant to both rot and wear, and is capable of far more stretch—a feature which tends to ease the impact of a fall.

In a two-man party, the fastest climbing team, the climbers tie in at the ends of the rope with the bowline; or if they don't want to have it all out they may coil some up and use the bowline on a bight. They proceed like a measuring worm, the first moving up to a place of safety and waiting while the other climbs to him.

When the first man reaches his position, he passes the dangling rope over a rock knob and takes up the slack. If there is no knob, he passes the rope over his shoulders or behind his hips, depending on whether he is leaning back from a standing position, or sitting. He must be well braced against the possibility of a sudden wrench from below. The rope should be just taut enough to prevent a fall.

When the latter reaches the leader's position, he takes over the braced position and feeds out the rope as the first proceeds. His responsibility is far greater. He must be prepared to check a fall from a point somewhere above him to an equal distance below. For this reason, the lead distance is kept as short as possible where the going is thin. If a fall does occur, the belay man can ease the impact.

The procedure is far safer than it sounds. In the course of training more than 2,000 men for the Army, countless second-man slips were checked, and of the dozen or so first-man falls I know of, every one was held to a minor injury or a mere experience in fright. The despondent impression—that a rope merely guarantees both will die if either falls —has little corroborating evidence.

For the sake of added strength and companionability, many parties are made up of three. These proceed in the same manner as two, except that the measuring worm now has a medial foot and must lumber along more slowly. At each stance, the second man belays the leader first and then brings up the third man, so as not to crowd the belay position.

When more than three go on a climb, it is customary for the party to be split up into ropes of two or three each. They may spread out over the cliff in parallel routes to save time and lessen the danger of dislodged stones, or they may follow the first rope in tandem and call for a lifeline over the difficult pitches.

The rope techniques used for rock apply to ice and steep snow climbing, except that the ice ax is driven into the surface and serves in place of a rock knob. On the gentler slopes of a glacier and on snow which is soft enough for kicking steps, the whole party often moves simultaneously. When anyone slips, the others drive the point or blade of the ice ax head into the snow and ride the fall to a stop.

The descent of a cliff is always more difficult than the ascent. Footholds are below the climber and must be tested or searched out often without being seen. If the climber makes a false start and must retreat, gravity is against him. There used to be a fast rule: Never climb up what you can't climb down. It still applies to a leader who is up ahead trying to make a difficult pitch, but difficult descents are generally negotiated by rappelling—sliding down the doubled rope in a body sling.

The rope is untied from the climbers. Its middle is looped around a rock projection, a large boulder or tree, and the free ends flung out over the cliff. To get into the rappel sling, the climber faces up the rope, straddling it. He reaches behind with his right hand and picks up both strands, bringing them around to the front side of his right hip and diagonally across his chest to throw them over his left shoulder. He faces right, and again takes the strands from behind with his right hand.

He leans out over the cliff far enough to give his feet traction on its surface and walks down, supported by the rope friction of his body. He can govern his speed or check it entirely by a very slight grip of the right hand.

With the Army, the rappelling technique was begun on gently sloping rocks. Before the end of the first day the instruction supervisors had a problem to prevent the classes from sneaking off to ride down overhangs!

Rappels assume exaggerated importance to the beginner. They are at once easy and sensational, but should be looked on as a convenience only. It is the sharing of fears that slowly evolves into conquest that constitutes the heart of the sport. The rope acts not only as the physical means by which belayer supports climber, but also as the transmission line of their mutual trust. Mountaineers become so fond of their ropes that they will take them along even when there is no likelihood they will be used.

PITON CLIMBING

The piton, like the rope with which it is used, is primarily a safety device. It might be termed a rock nail. It is made of soft iron in lengths from two to five inches and has either an eye or a ring at the pounding end. There are at least four different kinds that are used in various types of cracks in the rock and there is a larger, tubular one for ice climbing, made of a light alloy.

One of their chief purposes is to strengthen the process by which climbers alternately belay one another. When the leader of a roped party moves up to a position he may find it too precarious for him to hold the second man from falling in case of a slip. He can drive a piton with the light hammer carried for the task and use it in either of two ways—either lash himself to it with the sling rope and belay with his hips or shoulder, or belay from it directly, as he would from a rock knob. When the second man has reached the position he in turn uses the piton to belay the leader progressing toward the next stance.

In addition to making the anchoring stations safer, the piton may supply a series of substations where the leader must advance a long way over sketchy holds between one position of security and another. Suppose that one anchorage is a full rope length—over 100 feet—above another. If the leader falls when he is just short of reaching the upper one, he may drop 200 feet before any checking is done. His anchor man would try to take in slack as he came down, but his main concern must be bracing himself for the terrific impact. Such a fall would be disastrous in most cases.

The leader places pitons, on the trickiest sections, around 10 feet apart. He laces his rope to each one by means of a snaplink, an oval ring of steel which opens and locks on the safety-pin principle. His maximum drop is thus limited to 20 feet.

This involves nothing like the hazard of falling 20 feet to the ground, where the body strikes a hard surface at right angles to its line of drop. The impact is taken by a supple and elastic rope, made more elastic by the muscular give which is imparted by the belayer.

In climbing, the leader leaves a snaplink on each piton, and these are brought up to him later by the second man. His rope is thus laced to the mountain in several places, so that even if the top one gives away there is more support under it.

On ice, the piton is used in the same way as on rock. The driving pressure melts the ice for an instant with each stroke, and the subsequent quick-freeze helps keep it in place. But on a hot day the piton tends to melt the packing of ice around it by conducting the sun's heat. The piton is not safe for more than a few minutes under some conditions. Unlike rock pitons, which are usually regarded as expendable, ice pitons are unharmed by repeated pounding. They can easily be taken out by the last man and brought up to the leader, who uses them again.

The piton is an invaluable aid to speedy descent from a mountain. In rappelling on a doubled rope it is necessary to have something to loop it over. There are often no trees or boulders, and sometimes no knob which can be depended on not to bind the rope and prevent its recovery. But a little looking will usually reveal a suitable crack for a piton. A sling rope is often threaded through the eye and tied into a short loop, which serves as the pulley necessary for retrieving the climbing rope.

SNOW CLIMBING

In all the great mountain regions of the world the valleys are paved with snow-covered glaciers; even the lesser mountains have snow fields and long feeder arms running down into them from the steep couloirs or ravines above. In many mountains the major part of the climbing is done on snow which may run all the way from powder to the hardness of ice. Winter climbing on snow is rarely practicable except on skis, since in the timber where wind and thawing have not compacted it, one often sinks in waist deep. In the spring, the timber is pretty well melted out and offers no obstacle. Near the head of the valley there are still patches of snow in its floor. After the night's freeze they may be hard and precarious to walk on. A little later they begin to mush on the surface so that the footing is better. But by midday they are difficult; the traveler goes through the under-crust and wallows hopelessly. Proper timing is vital to a successful snow climb.

One of the feeder arms—a long snow couloir—is selected as the route to the higher reaches of the mountain. The party moves up to its lower end on a concave snow slope which grows steeper as it rises. If the snow is not hard, they can kick steps into it which will be deep enough to support the ball of the foot. The lead is changed frequently, as the first man has to make steps for all.

The course may be directly up-slope, or zigzag. With the zigzag it is easier to maintain a good rhythm of motion as resting is not often necessary. But this process cuts out two sides of a triangle and precipitates any tendency the surface may have to avalanche. The direct attack places all the climbers in a straight line, one above another, so that their combined efforts can be used in checking anyone who slips. Furthermore, the toe can make a deeper step than the side of the foot, and the hands are also more useful to a climber facing in-slope.

As the angle increases, the party ties into a climbing rope. The end men use the bowline, those in the middle the butterfly knot. Unlike a rock party, they move simultaneously and there may be more than three on the rope. The rope between climbers is allowed no slack; any slip is stopped before it develops momentum. But each climber climbs carrying two or three loops of the section ahead of him, so that he can stop the next man without jerking. The leader has no loop. Both his hands are free to drive home the shaft of the ice ax if he or anyone below him slips.

Once they are between the confining walls of the couloir, they may meet much steeper snow than would lie on the open mountainside. The climb grows more exacting, and at the same time more fun. The leader may have to slash out his steps with the point or adze of his ice ax to make them deep enough. The slower method of moving one at a time is adopted. Two climbers may detach themselves and tie into a new rope. If they lead the way it is a simple matter for them to alternate step cutting and belaying for each other. In very steep snow the leader can make finger holds for those who follow by jabbing the point of his ice ax in at right angles to the slope. These should be used only to maintain balance; erect stance is even more important on snow than on rock. The floor of a step in snow will support a downward push, but not an outward one caused by leaning forward.

Snow climbing requires discretion in two matters. Snow can avalanche whether it is wet and heavy or dry and powdery, if there is a frozen crust below to which it does not adhere. There are instructions on riding avalanches—a tread-water motion with the legs, elbows high, erect stance. Couloirs are often a natural route for rocks pried loose by the freezing action and thawed and dropped.

There are slopes which are constantly rattling with little ones, and occasionally roaring with big ones, during the warm part of the day. A couloir which is grooved with stone falls should be avoided unless the weather is very cold.

ICE CLIMBING

The snow which falls through the air, and the ice which forms when a pond freezes, seem as different as sugar and glass. On a glacier the one grades gently into the other; there is sometimes no line of distinction. The water of melting surface snow runs down into deeper snow and freezes into a mixture of snow and ice. The immense weight in the depths of a glacier, and the abnormal pressures as it slides like slow lava over the undulations of its bed, cause temporary liquefactions. The main mass becomes blue ice, sometimes of astonishing hardness. Yet it differs from the refrigerator article in being granular rather than crystalline. This is fortunate, for it does not split and shatter under the blows of the ice ax; niches for the fingers and the boot toes can be cut in it and relied on.

As snow graduates into ice, snow climbing graduates into ice climbing. A snow field may have sheet ice under it; the snow blanket on a glacier may have merged into the ice beneath; snow itself may become so hardened by wind or thaw and freeze that it requires the more careful techniques of ice climbing.

Ice slopes and hard snow slopes require crampons. These are strap-on bottoms for the shoes which have six or eight sharp spikes an inch long. They don't slip, but on vertical ice, steps must be cut which are deep enough to hold more than the two front spikes.

As in rock climbing, pitons may be driven into the ice either as security or as direct aids to the climber. The leader connects his rope to the eye of the piton by means of his snap-link, thus raising his protection to a point higher than the belay man and shortening the distance of possible fall. As a direct aid, he can drive a series of pitons to use for hand-holds and footholds.

Glacial ice forms are among the most weird and curious in nature. The river of ice moves along its bed anywhere from a few inches to a mile or more every year. As it flows over a hump in its bed or changes from a gradual slope to a steeper one, the top is cracked open and yawns with crevasses, which are widened by the penetration of the sun and air. Blizzards form snow bridges over crevasses when they would otherwise be impassable. Flowing into a depression tends to close them up again.

When the glacier turns downward very sharply, to leave a high flat valley floor for a steep section, the crevasses are so numerous and wide that only standing blocks of ice separate them. These are carved into shapes like nothing ever seen before. They are called seracs until they lean too far over or are undermined and topple in a roar of crashing ice. The ice fall, a chaos of these broken seracs, presents the most difficult kind of obstacle to the mountaineer. Some of the chunks he climbs over, some he goes around and some he must climb or crawl under. The only successful route may take hours to find, and require him to cover five times the airline distance.

There is little serious glacier climbing in the United States outside the region of Mount Ranier, yet the climber who starts up a snow couloir anywhere in the Rockies may be glad to have his crampons and will certainly need his ice ax.

CHIMNEY CLIMBING

One of the most welcome features in the climber's landscape is the chimney. This is a rock crevice, vertical or nearly so, which is wide enough for a climber to enter, and narrow enough so that he can maintain contact with both sides at once.

The most comfortable width is that which allows him space to keep his hips on one wall and the balls of his feet a little lower on the other with the knees slightly flexed. While apparently sitting on air, he has the security of a powerful crossbrace. The walls are vertical and generally far too smooth to let him climb either of them alone, but by walking his feet up one and squirming his back higher on the other he can rise as far as the combination will take him.

Narrower chimneys are no less secure, but harder to climb in unless they have good footholds. The climber tries to find irregularities for his feet as always, but he often can rest in curious jammed positions—for instance with both back and feet on one wall and knees and forearms on the other. The hands may be used for an upward pull if their purchase is good, but in a smooth chimney they are often more effective placed flat against the rock. Hands and shoulders can hold a crossbrace while the hips are forced up to a new level. In a very tight chimney, hands may be worked against elbows in the same way; even an expanded chest may form a momentary holding aid while hard-pressed arms and legs are trying to swim the body upward.

In a widening crevice, the chimney technique may have to be abandoned at some point for a face climb on one wall, but there is one wide-chimney combination that is good for a thrill. As soon as the legs are at full stretch across the chasm, the climber works himself around until he is face down. With hands on one wall and feet on the other, he walks up backward. There is a happy surprise in the holding strength this position gives. The body has become an arch and has tremendous frictional force. This is a refinement which would almost never be necessary to the success of a climb, but once in a while it seems more convenient than anything else for a short pitch.

More often than not the most difficult part of a chimney is the process of getting out of it at the top. The majority of chimneys are roofed over with large chock stones which force the climber out to the exposed and curving lips of the crack for the final pitch. In this case, and others as well, the right hand and foot are often used on one wall, and the left on the other. In this stance the climber can face the chock stone and use it as soon as it presents him with a good handhold.

The chimney often gives the only way of passing through a vertical cliff band on a mountain and is nearly always easier than anything else approaching it in pitch. For the beginner, who has a tendency to shy away from anything which does not have hoe-handle grips on it, nothing is better than chimney work to teach the lesson of security by friction. The experienced climber finds it a sheltered interlude on a long climb in which much of the time is spent on exposed faces.

By Robert M. Ormes

CHAPTER 11

nature

In MANY ways there are no more interesting facets of the outdoor world than the smaller "special" sections. Any outdoorsman is a nature lover—or he wouldn't want to be outdoors. But how much more interesting to the skier or hiker is his trail through the forests if he can name the animals and plants of the woods he roams. What boatman doesn't enjoy his sport more if he knows the life that goes on under the keel of his craft. A study of natural history enriches our pleasure no matter what our outdoor interest is. In this chapter you will find a variety of avenues in which to get acquainted with these "special" sections. Two are devoted to gathering wild plants and mushrooms, the superb foods of the wild. Other sections tell how to raise game birds and build and manage your own fishpond. Another important group of outdoor enthusiasts like to observe wildlife and a section on birdwatching offers a look at this interesting sport. Still another section tells you how to recognize and imitate the many sounds animals make in their communications with one another.

NATURAL HISTORY

Natural history can be approached in so many ways, and investigated from so many angles, that there is a choice for every individual, an avenue of exploration which you can make peculiarly your own. You do not need to go to the Galápagos Islands like William Beebe, or to the frozen North with Vilhjalmur Stefansson, or to Patagonia with W. H. Hudson. You can ay at home like Henry Thoreau by your eighborhood pond; you can sit in your own oom like Gustav Eckstein, or just stay in ed like Charles D. Stewart. The bugs, birds nd animals will come to you. You need no quipment but an inquiring mind and an lert eye, unless you insist on looking at nicro-organisms and want a microscope.

You can find natural history in Times quare or in Central Park, in the streets of Washington or the sands of any lake, gulf, cean shore. However, if you want to get way from it all, the study of natural history an be a better excuse than most to climb nountains, wade through swamps or travel o wild and lonely places. Within the scope f what is called natural history reside a host f sciences: insects, flowers, animals, fishes, irds. You can go back into the past with he geologist and the paleontologist, or into he future with the astronomer.

Every child is a born naturalist who loves collecting and wants to know the names, habits and purposes of everything that moves or doesn't move. We love nature out of imple, animal, primitive curiosity to find out into what sort of an astonishing place we have been born and what is all this around us, anyway. We love nature because it is ight there, or right here, in front of us and within us, and we expect, or hope, it always will be.

The healthy, human, natural instinct of the normal human being is to want to know more than he does about nature. For modern nan it is a retreat and at the same time a way of examining reality, it is a hobby which gives him pleasure and if pursued intensively will add to human knowledge. At the same ime it is an enjoyable recreation. Sometimes a writer on nature, however, will deflect you by his manner, his vocabulary or his personality. Some of them, it must be admitted, are unnecessarily florid or sentimental or cute.

You cannot go far into the literature of natural history without encountering some wonderful personalities who are new, fresh and stimulating; people you have never met before or writers you have had forced upon you at a time when you were not yet ready to appreciate them. Henry Thoreau has suffered at the hands of schoolteachers. Questions about Walden have needled you on exam papers. It is necessary to come back to him at some time, however, in a more receptive frame of mind. If we do not cotton to him as a lover of nature, we admire him as an independent individual who loved freedom of expression, who lived as he wished regardless of the conventionalities of his time.

You may discover a kindred spirit in a gentle English curate named Gilbert White who liked to watch birds and was fascinated by bats. Louis Agassiz may open your eyes to the purpose or the scientific reasons for collecting, for collections that add up to something. Maurice Maeterlinck will introduce you to the social life of the bee and lead you on to Jean Henri Fabre. If you like ironical, satirical writing you will be delighted by William Morton Wheeler who had the imagination to compose a letter from the king of the termites criticizing the organization of our human society.

As you go through the history of the writers on nature you may be surprised, although you shouldn't, how many of them have been amateurs, not professionals, in the field of natural history. Some of them have been chemists or engineers or literary men who have investigated nature because it appealed to them, because they enjoyed such study and did it as a recreation. Theodore Roosevelt, if he could have been kept out of politics, would have been one of our greatest field naturalists. He communicated the joy of the out-of-doors.

Many first-rate naturalists use photography as a part of their study, and a number of top-notch photographers have made a name for themselves by their nature shots. From the hobby of photography you can easily move into the field of natural history. Tropical fish might make a good ichthyologist out of you as birdwatching will turn you into an ornithologist. Gardening leads to botany; hunting, by a stretch of the imagination, into biology; and hiking can lure you nowhere better than straight into the midst of nature's wonders.

Any interest in your environment, the relationships of man or the animals to each other and their environment, is a part of natural history.

From the book HOBBIES FOR PLEASURE AND PROFIT
By Horace Coon
A Signet Key Book
Published by The New American Library
Copyright, 1955, by Horace Coon

BIRDWATCHING

Hamlet may have been a birdwatcher because he claimed he could tell a hawk from a handsaw. If he was not, then John Kieran could certainly have sold him on the hobby, for he sells it to everybody who comes near him, including Clarence Budington Kelland, whom Kieran persuaded to look for owls in the middle of the Arizona desert. That is really spreading the virus to others.

Once infected, you never stop looking for birds. You see more and more of them, get to know them well, and invite them to dinner. To non-birdwatchers it may seem silly, or slightly indecent to be so curious about the private lives of such helpless creatures. People are apt to laugh at you; it is not simple to explain easily to unsympathetic friends why you get up at the crack of dawn with your binocular to stare at your feathered comrades on the wing. It is not a habit you can hide from your family. But the better you know your birds the less you care what your friends say.

Birdwatching is a hobby that can be enjoyed for an entire lifetime. It is not something completely useless or impractical. In small ways persistent birdwatchers are adding to our scientific knowledge about birds and their habits. To do it right requires a lot of study, but you soon become so fascinated in the new worlds of life opened to you by close observation, that you learn to do it correctly, and you are eager to plunge into the vast literature about birds. Eventually you may add a little to this tremendous body of knowledge. Meanwhile you are immersed in a hobby you do not need to apologize for no matter how much fun your friends make of it. You improve your health, and you achieve a lasting and blessed peace of mind.

It is something you can do anywhere, at any time of day.

Ideally you should be introduced to the hobby by such an enthusiast as John Kieran. It is possible an experienced birdwatcher is a neighbor of yours and you don't know it. You may find bird students through the magazine published quarterly by the American Ornithologist's Union, called *The Awk* or *Audubon Magazine*, a bi-monthly publication of the National Audubon Society.

You will need a pair of binoculars. With the help of these books mentioned, and others, you will start recognizing more birds than you thought you ever knew. Then you begin to take notes on each trip you make, giving the place and date you saw the birds. One way to save yourself trouble is to carry a field card giving a list of birds in your locality. Bird clubs publish such cards, but you will also need a notebook. You're then ready for a field trip.

The next step is the lure of migration watching. Counting birds or estimating their numbers is another fascinating problem. The distribution of birds north of the Rio Grande is another. Birdwatching can be a contribution to science. Watchers represent the eyes of the conservation movement; they can if they assert themselves see to it that conservation becomes a major force in politics and public opinion.

Before you devote yourself to that, however, learn how to look and what to look for. Ask and answer about a bird: what is its size, its shape, how does it act, how does it fly, what are its field-marks, its voice, where and when is it found?

Take gulls, for example: Most gulls are larger than pigeons, with wings that are much longer in proportion. They are largely white with pearly-gray backs. The young ones are dappled browns. The things to look for on a gull are: Its wing-tips, the color of its feet, the color of its bill. Never call them sea gulls. Call them Herring-gulls, laughing gulls, or whatever they may be. Sea gull is inappropriate, for flocks can be seen on the prairies.

How much more it means if you know

all about the species you watch; if you know where it breeds, how its children learn to fly and why it is where it is.

From the book HOBBIES FOR PLEASURE AND PROFIT
By Horace Coon
A Signet Key Book
Published by The New American Library
Copyright, 1955, by Horace Coon

MUSHROOM HUNTING

Any one who uses common sense can gather mushrooms afield with perfect safety. In fact several million people do, year after year.

The few people who get into trouble—and they are very few—are those who don't know what they're looking for. We don't let highway and hunting accidents keep us from automobiling or hunting. Neither should we let uninformed mushroom hunters keep us from the enjoyable and fascinating outdoor recreation of gathering mushrooms.

Wild mushrooms are as common today as ever—some species even more so—and gathering them can be as fine an outdoors recreation as hunting or fishing. As a mushroom hunter you never come back skunked—well, *almost* never. You need only a dime-store basket and a kitchen knife. And from snow-spitting April till long after hickory-nutting time, you never lack an excuse for an outdoors jaunt.

The way to become a mushroom hunter is to start with just one species, and then gradually add other kinds till you have a repertoire of about half a dozen. There are hundreds of mushrooms, many edible ones and many that are inedible because they are leathery, woodlike or bad tasting, some that are moderately poisonous, and a few that are deadly poisonous. Learning this whole field would be laborious, and entirely unnecessary. Four species are so abundant and so well spread out through the season that they're all you need to be familiar with. And each of these kinds has some feature so distinct that identification is easy and simple.

As a matter of fact, the "Big Four" among mushrooms make up the bulk of mushrooms gathered by the expert hunters.

Bill Wolf

Wild mushrooms are as plentious as ever.

The puffball is by all means the mushroom you should start with. These white, roundish, conspicuous objects, some a bit flattened like a Kentucky pumpkin, others pear-shaped, others as round as a basketball, can't possibly be mistaken for any other mushroom provided they have no stem running through them. In fact, they're like nothing else outdoors. The different species range from marble size to as big as a bushel basket. Those the size of an apple or larger are the most prime. These larger ones, belonging to a family called Calvatias, are always delicious.

The one and only rule you need to know about puffballs is simple and infallible: *If it's white all the way through and there is no distinct stem running through the meat, eat it.*

When the spores inside a puffball begin to ripen, the "meat" turns brownish, and though it is not poisonous at all, it tastes somewhat bitter. Incidentally, a puffball will remain fresh in the refrigerator for a week or more, and often you find a Calvatia so big that it takes you a week to eat it up.

In preparing a puffball, simply remove the rind or peridium, which is about orange-peel thick, and then slice the meat with a sharp knife, as you'd slice a dish of mush. That's all there is to it. Frying is the traditional way of cooking puffballs, and the fried slabs are so delectable that most people never go on to any other way, but diced puffball goes fine in soups, stews and gravies. It is a little too delicate in flavor to make good sauces.

Where do you find puffballs? You'll find the larger ones in the late summer—mid-August in the central states—and their season extends till the first hard freeze. You can go back and gather them at the same place year after year. The Calvatias, the big puffballs, often grow in fairy rings, and a fairy ring of these large "moon melons" is a spectacular sight and a prize find.

So much for the puffball. If you remember that one simple rule—*white all the way through and no distinct stem running through the meat*—you can add puffball hunting to your list of things to do outdoors.

The meadow, pasture or pink-gilled mushroom is the identical species (*Agaricus campestris*) that is grown commercially. So you can learn this mushroom by simply buying a few at the grocery store, and examining them. Buy specimens at different stages of development.

Notice that in the "button" stage the gills are covered by the "veil." At the next step, when the veil has broken, notice the pinkish color of the gills. This is the mushroom's distinctive feature. As the cap expands until it is nearly flat and the spores ripen, the gills turn dark and at maturity they are a pastel black, with a tinge of purple.

Because it's a fungus, a mushroom doesn't need sunlight, as chlorophyll plants do. So the pasture mushroom is grown mostly in caves and other underground spots where temperature and moisture can be kept just right. It is harvested in the button stage partly because it stays salable longer that way

and partly because customers seem to prefer it that way.

But most think the flavor is much better when the cap is about three-quarters expanded and the gills are starting to darken, and most hunters agree on this point. However this is a fine mushroom at any stage. And more people gather the pink gill than any other kind of mushroom.

It occurs mostly in the open—pastures, lawns, golf courses and along the roadside—from July till late October, and in good year it grows very abundantly indeed. It is not unusual to gather a bushel of them within an acre.

Whenever your cookbook says "mushrooms" it means the pink gill or pasture. So you can look there and find the different ways of cooking it. This mushroom is quite versatile and can be used for soups, gravies, sauces and stews, besides frying.

Now we come to that mushroom master piece, that delight supreme of the gourmet that visitor to apple blossom time—the morel. To the scientist it's the *Morchella esculenta*, to foolish souls it's a toadstool; to our forefathers it was the "sponge mushroom," as it is to many people today. And to everybody who eats it, it's the ultimate in foods. You don't have to get used to it, as with raw oysters or green olives. With the first taste of it you're hooked.

The unique morel has no gills. The spores are borne in microscopic pouches that are distributed all over the surface. Notice the elongated, cone-like form of the cap. Notice the broad, irregularly shaped pits and the network of narrow ridges that run more or less up and down. When you pick one, notice that the stem and cap, both equally good to eat, are hollow. Altogether, no other mushroom looks anything like it, and all morels are good.

Only trouble is the morel season is brief. You find the earliest ones, perhaps no bigger than a thimble, around mid-April, and by the first of June they all are gone.

When the very first apple blossoms appear, start looking, so you'll miss none. The height of the season comes when the warblers re passing through, or just a few days later. You look down and see a morel in the young grass or pushing up through a drift of last-autumn's leaves.

If you live within driving distance of high ills or mountains, where the march of spring vill be maybe a fortnight later than in the alleys, you can extend the morel season a it. But otherwise resign yourself to the act that about four weeks each year is all he good morel hunting you'll have.

Like gold, morels are where you find 'em; here seems to be no rhyme or reason about heir occurrence. But they are "repeaters"; hat is, they are found at the same place on accessive seasons. But beyond that there are o rules that hold water. Morels occur in he deepest woods and in wide-open fields, black muck soil and in acidy clay, and greatly differing habitats.

When you find morels, cut them off close the ground, taking care not to waste an ota of the stem. At home slice them length-vise into inch-wide strips. Soak these in salt vater for about half an hour. Remove, drain, ust lightly with flour and then fry them in noderately hot grease. It would be cuisine lasphemy to use them in stews or gravies r as a sauce for steaks.

In recent years some surprising discover-es have been made about mushrooms as ood, and research now in progress may turn p facts even more surprising. Many people em to think that mushrooms are merely a asty flavorizer for various dishes. That isn't ue; mushrooms are a good food on their wn. Besides their minerals and other nutri-onal factors, the species commonly gathered ontain protein. This protein is the reason hy a meal of mushrooms "satisfies" you ke a meal of meat. Besides this food value, ushrooms contain a battery of strong en-ymes, in the nature of tenderizers and gestants. The discovery of this fact led to eir being recommended for the diets of ertain invalids, and the results have been enerally good.

But now one line of research is digging ill deeper—into the possibility that mush-oms may contain substances of an antibi-

otic nature. In various folklores and "native medicine" practices, mushrooms have long been thought curative or at least helpful for certain illnesses. Before we dismiss this as witch-doctor stuff we should remember that mushrooms are closely akin to, and some-times grow in helpful association with, those molds and soil fungi that are the source of penicillin, the different "mycins" and others of our "wonder drugs."

We should also remember that folklore in several European countries had it that a poul-tice of moldy bread was good for external infections, and pellets of moldy bread were good for internal infections. In pre-penicillin days a few doctors, here and abroad, surrep-titiously tried out this home remedy by giving moldy-bread pills to critically ill pa-tients, and they saved lives by it. But they didn't know why the remedy worked and they were afraid of getting laughed at if they publicized their results, so penicillin had to wait till Fleming discovered it properly.

The last of our Big Four is the oyster mushroom, so called because of its shape. Some people call it the log oyster or the woods oyster, because that's where you find it; others refer to it as the oystershell.

With mushroom hunters the oyster mush-room is Old Dependable. It's a repeater; the same log will produce a fresh crop about every 20 days all summer, and will keep doing this for two or three years. It's one of the most prolific of mushrooms, and its season is the longest of all, beginning in early April and lasting till December.

The oystershell is so easy to identify that any beginner can recognize it at a glance. In the first place it grows only on wood—an old stump, a fallen trunk, a dead branch of a live tree. The stem is not attached to the center of the cap but laterally—to one side. But the most unique and distinctive feature is the fact that *its gills run down onto the stem*. This feature of "decurrent gills," is an important help in identification in the oyster mushroom and its relatives. These gills are white. When you find a mushroom that is growing on wood and has a lateral stem (or none) and white gills running down on the base, it's an oyster mushroom; it can't possibly be anything else.

Many trees—apple, maple, elm, ash and others—are host to the oyster mushroom but it never grows on their living wood, only on their dead stumps, trunks or branches. Its mycelium, or what we might call its root system, is a mass of whitish threads which penetrate the dead wood and digest it. Like many other mushrooms, it "buds" during the coolish spells in summer, when the temperature dips into the 60's for a day or two. When the weather warms again, these buds grow into the fruit caps.

When you find a batch of oystershells, remember the place. You can harvest them there half a dozen times during the summer.

There's a special wrinkle, and a dandy one, that you can work with the oystershell. When you find a log that's growing them, a log of a size you can handle, you can take it home, put it in the back yard, wet it with a hose now and then, and it will keep on bearing there just as well as in a woods. A fresh-fallen log will be good for two or three seasons. As a matter of fact, you can bring a couple of oystershell logs in each fall and put them in the basement, with a slow drip-bucket arrangement to keep them moist, you'll have fresh mushrooms at intervals right through the winter.

In nature's scheme of things, the appointed work of the fungus legions is to keep the earth clean and fresh. Consider what happens when a tree, a maple let's say, dies. The oystershell starts working on it and continues for two or three years, till it has exhausted its particular food substances. Then some other mushroom takes over and "reduces" the dead wood further. This process may be repeated three or four times, each successive mushroom being lower in the fungus scale, till at last the log is little more than crumbly rot. Then the molds and slimes take over and reduce the log to black, rich humus.

If it were not for this fungus activity, trees and plants would die, fall over and persist for decades or even centuries. Soon the surface of the earth would be a piled-up mass of dead vegetation, impossible to traverse, subject to gigantic fires and blanketing any new growth. You get a faint glimpse of this sort of thing at certain places in the Canadian subarctic. There you'll sometimes find deep valleys where the windfall has piled up to a depth of 30 or 40 feet, because the wood-destroying fungi are mostly of the "shelf" kind and very slow growing.

Besides the mushroom Big Four, which a beginner can gather with complete safety, there are dozens of other kinds, such as the shaggymanes, corals, most of the Clitocybes, the common Coprinuses, the big, snow-white hedgehog and the fawn-colored Pluteus. All these and still others are very common.

Estimates have been made of the amount of edible mushrooms that go to waste each year country-wide, and these estimates are quite staggering. Far exceeding any simple crop we grow, the total runs into millions of tons. Sometime perhaps we will get around to making use of this excellent and abundant food. But meantime you can go hiking through the fields and woods and bring back a basketful of morels or pink gills, log oysters or melons of the moon.

By William Byron Mowery

RAISING GAME BIRDS

If you want to raise game birds try to get started in the spring because June, in most states, is the last month when you can safely begin. See if you can get game-bird hatching eggs free from your state game farm. Most states have some sort of arrangement for this. Find out how many you can get and when. In case there is no chance of obtaining any that way, you will have to buy them from your nearest commercial game farm.

Ringneck pheasants, bobwhite quail or mallard ducks are the best species to start with. The pheasants and ducks are practically as easy to raise as domestic chickens if they are handled right. The quail may be a little harder, but not too much so.

The only equipment you will need is all at hand on the average farm as it can be

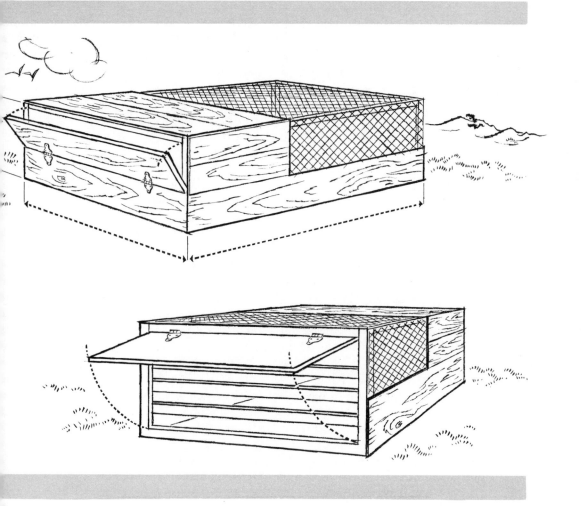

asily and inexpensively made. You will also need a broody hen that is not too heavy in weight, and is steadily broody when the ggs arrive; a nest box, any old box that is ig enough to give the hen enough room ut not too much room; and, later, a coop.

The nesting box should have a cover that ives the hen plenty of fresh air. Be certain here are no holes in the box or cover that re over half an inch wide or high.

Wash the box with disinfectant and line with clean hay or shavings. Prepare the en by setting her on some dummy eggs a ew days before the game-bird eggs are due o arrive. The hen should be dusted with igh quality louse powder. Follow the direcons on the package and have the last dustg come at least a day before the hatching

eggs are given to her. Let her off the eggs for feed and water once or twice a day every day. For feed give her cracked corn. She'll like it if a dish of grit is where she can pick up a little now and then. Keep the box where the hen will not be disturbed. She'll like privacy and quiet.

When the game-bird eggs arrive slip them under her easily and take out the dummies. The number of eggs a hen can cover thoroughly depends on her size and the size of the eggs. On an average, a hen can take care of from 10 to 15 pheasant eggs or seven to nine mallard duck eggs. You may find it wise to deal out your eggs in different numbers than these. It is best to have too few eggs under a hen than too many. If there are more than she can cover it will mean that all the eggs will be chilled in a few days as the hen turns and shuffles them around the nest.

If you are hatching quail eggs, be especially careful that you have very lightweight hens for them. Quail eggs are easily smashed. Bantams are the best foster mothers for them.

Ringneck eggs hatch in from 21 to 23 days, or, at times, a day less or a day more than that. It depends on the strain of bird and on the age of the eggs between laying and setting. Quail eggs are closer to an even three weeks. Mallards are pretty regular with 28 days.

To be extra sure the eggs are properly turned during incubation, it is wise to run the palm of your hand over them every few days. Some hens do a good job of turning their eggs and others do not. This explains some poor hatches. Putting a pencil mark on each egg gives you a good check on whether they are being turned or not. With waterfowl eggs, hens often have trouble turning them correctly because of their slippery shells. When the eggs begin to pip, put the hen back on them and close the cover and leave her alone for 48 hours. Disturbing her then is dangerous. It gets her uneasy and she is almost sure to tread some of the newly hatched birds to death.

Have a secure brood coop ready for the family. Anything that will keep them inside, protected from the weather on one end, and open to the direct sunshine on the other end, is okay. A good model is four feet long by three feet wide by 18 inches high. Making the back end of the boards of matched lumber is best if you can get it. The top board should be hinged at the bottom for a door. You'll need to reach inside to feed and water the brood. On the sides have a seven- to nine-inch board run the entire length. For a third to a half of the rear length, put boards clear to the top. They meet boards making a roof for a third or a half of the length.

For the remainder of the sides and the top use wire netting. Either the ½-inch hexagonal mesh or the ½-inch square mesh "cellar window wire" is good. At the front end, put slats about two inches apart. These are for later use in keeping the hen confined while the brood gets out. If the slats are on the inside of the corner posts (two by three's are best) then a solid wooden door can be hung on the outside. Hinge this at the top. It is useful later if hung that way for it can be propped up with a stick and, if it is desired to catch the brood, a line to the stick can be pulled to close the door when the brood is all inside.

About 48 hours after hatching, carefully examine the brood. Slide your hand gently under the hen to see if all the eggs have hatched and all the chicks are dried off well. Be sure the chicks don't escape. If they get lost, it is almost impossible to get them back because they have not been with the hen long enough so each has learned the other's language. After the brood has completely hatched and dried, leave them with the hen in the box for another day. This gets them acquainted.

Then into the coop with them. The coop should be on a dry spot where the sun will strike it. Or if the climate or the weather is hot, put it in the shade. Have a watering fountain that keeps the water clean and cool and is not so big that the chicks can get into it bodily. Mix the best brand of baby chick starting mash so it is crumbly-wet—use water, or sweet or sour milk. Feed this on clean plates four or five times a day for the first few days. Give them only what they will clean up in a few minutes. A can set too high for the chicks to reach, containing cracked corn, gives the hen the extra nourishment she may need. At 10 days or two weeks, the brood has wings and is able to fly a little. Open the front door on a day when the weather is good, always keeping feed inside the coop.

If the coop is gradually moved toward the open fields the brood will be automatically liberated. Gradually the birds will forsake the hen and spend the nights outside the coop. Once they are able to care for themselves the hen can be taken away. For a few days leave food in the vicinity of the coop and then discontinue that.

Be careful about expecting too much

Hatches of 100 per cent and the rearing of 100 per cent of birds hatched has happened, but it isn't normal. At times there will be complete failure of all eggs to hatch. But where 50 or 100 eggs are involved, this is very unlikely unless the eggs were badly shaken, badly chilled or badly over-heated in transit.

By Horace Mitchell

ANIMAL CALLS

Those of us, who travel the forest trails, often wish that we might know the multitudinous languages of the wildwood and the wild folk. We can turn to the woods Indian as our mentor in this art for he has long been a linguistic expert in woods talk. In forest conversation he uses at least two methods. One is with voice equipment and lips alone. On other occasions he often employs instruments such as our duck and crow hunters use.

The time of year often influences the subject of conversation in the wild. Spring is the favorite season for love songs among the birds and some other animals. However, we must wait until the falling-leaf moon before some animals, such as those of the antlered families, succumb to cupid's arrows.

In the fall bull moose roam over hill and dale listening for the love songs of their ladies, who then become most loquacious. While the bull seeks, the lady moose sings, and her song is so potent at this time of year that even a man-made imitation will frequently be answered by amorous swains.

Long ago the woods Indians learned the art of woods conversation and for centuries have called moose in the autumn. Their equipment is a bark megaphone, which is rolled from a piece of bark peeled from the canoe birch and sewed together with watap, stringy roots (A). The Indians say the moose-calling megaphone should be as long as the forearm, the large opening as wide as the palm of the hand, the small opening two fingers wide (B). With this simple instrument they give several different sounds

that spell romance to the listening ears of these big fellows of the forest. At times the Indians give a coaxing cow call, which gradually increases in volume until a bellow echoes over forest, lake and barren land—and then gradually subsides again to the coaxing notes.

Another cow moose rendition seems to ask the question, "Where are you?" Starting on a very high, violinlike note *eeeeeeee* it continues on with a *u-u-u-u-uh yuh* ("Where are you?"). Since cow moose usually call between twilight and early morning, the Indian caller often sings his moose love song several hours after midnight.

The Indians wait before calling, listening for any sounds of a bull who may be close. It is often difficult to spot the presence of a bull moose—he is able to sneak as quietly through the thick brush as a moccasined Indian. The first call is just about a half minute long and the megaphone is moved in a circular motion, pointed toward the ground (C). If an answering bull is heard, the coaxing call may be given again and then everyone is as quiet as the grave until a few hours before sunrise. Just before daybreak another lovelorn call is given, with the megaphone pointed straight into the woods. Toward the close of this call, the megaphone is pointed earthward.

As light comes to the eastern sky, the Indian caller holds the megaphone about a foot from the leaf-covered ground and gives the squealing "Where are you?" call. The bull may answer with a trampling of undergrowth and a slashing of antlers against the brush. The latter sound often resembles a hollow crash, as if a canoe had been dropped upon the rocks. The Indians sometimes imitate this sound—to put in a note of competition—by slashing the undergrowth with a small moose antler. The bull, if not too far distant, may also give an answering grunt or challenge, a sort of *oo-wuh*.

In a canoe, the hunter paddles very quietly and he may call directly into the forest. Another trick he may use is to dip the megaphone into the water, holding his hand over the smaller end and then pouring the water

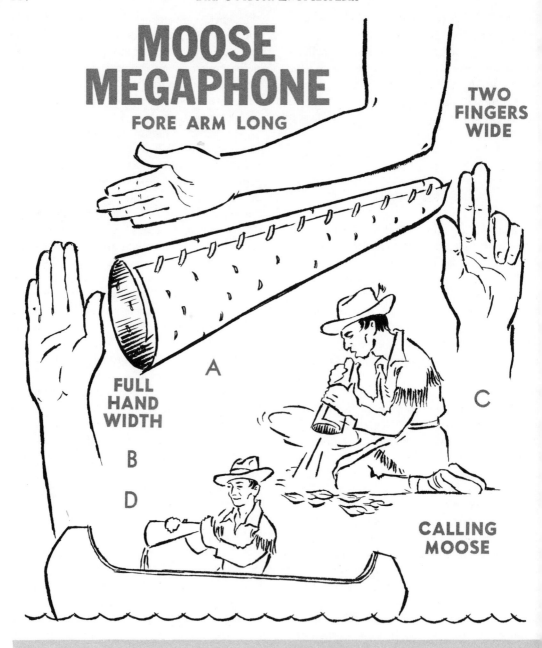

MOOSE MEGAPHONE

FORE ARM LONG

TWO FINGERS WIDE

FULL HAND WIDTH

A

B

D

C

CALLING MOOSE

Here are the method and means utilized by the Indians for calling to the moose.

back into the lake (D). This sounds as if a feeding moose is lifting its head out of the water. Should the bull emerge from the brush and see the blurred, shadowy form of the canoe and hunter, he is all the more convinced that a cow is feeding, provided of course, the wind is in the right direction.

Moose conversation varies greatly. On occasion, the Indian uses a smaller megaphone about eight or nine inches long. With this he makes the grunting *oo-wuh* sound and shuffles his feet among the dried leaves—as if a rival bull, spoiling for a fight, is making his way through the underbrush.

MOOSE TRACKS

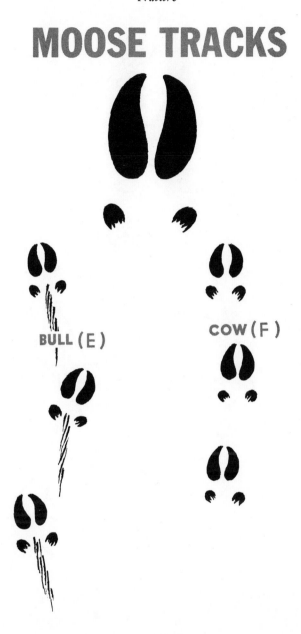

The moose, in love, often drags his feet.

A bull moose in love does strange things. He may drag his feet like any schoolboy and his tracks will indicate his feelings (E). Then, too, he often makes a wallow, irrigating it with his urine excretion and trampling the earth into sticky mud. He then rolls in this odoriferous mess and the resulting odor can be detected at quite a distance. The cow's tracks are clear (F).

The Penobscot Indians called caribou in much the same way. However, they used a smaller megaphone. This too, was made of birch bark rolled in the same manner as the moose-calling instrument. The dimensions,

CARIBOU CALLS

Indian caribou caller into which are made their strange, coughlike grunting sounds.

however, were different. Most were about 11 inches long, three inches at the large opening and one inch at the smaller end (G). A coughlike grunt is made with this instrument, similar to one of the sounds made by the caribou. The old hunters gave this coughing sound, as they moved about in the dry leaves, in imitation of caribou moving through the woods.

Caribou sometimes make a double grunt. The first part of the sound is loud and deep and seems to be made as the animal takes a

OJIBWAY FAWN CALL

Ojibway imitating bleat of fawn with a caller made of softwood, vibrating reed.

deep inhalation. This is followed by an explosive cough. At times the bull caribou gives a rumbling deep within his throat. A very characteristic sound, made by caribou when moving about, is the strange crackling in the region of the hoof.

The foregoing calls were made with the voice itself amplified by the megaphone. However, in some instances the Indians made calling instruments which created the sounds. The Ojibway make a call of this kind, imitating the bleat of a fawn. This is made of

CHEROKEE DEER CALL

SPLIT STICK

K

L

RHODODENDRON LEAF

J

Deer caller which is blown upon from the side—and then will produce buzzing sound.

four hollow, cone-shaped pieces of softwood that fit into each other. A small vibrating reed is fastened in the smaller end of the middle section (H). The caller places his cupped hands over the mouth, opening one hand as he makes the call (I).

Another deer call made by a Cherokee, Kaloski Standing Deer, collected by Dr.

Frank Speck, was made from a piece of rhododendron wood (J). The twig, a little thicker than a pencil was split at one end (K) and a rhododendron leaf inserted (L). When this call is blown upon from the side, it makes a buzzing sound which attracts deer.

Muskrats of our cattail marshes and swamps have a number of communication

MUSKRAT CALLS

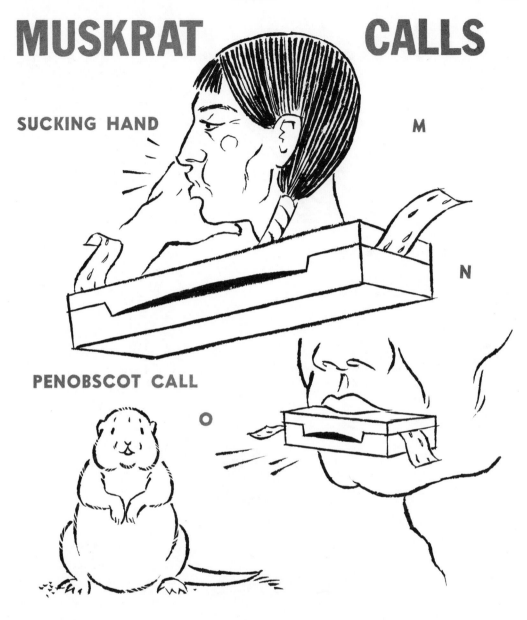

SUCKING HAND

M

N

PENOBSCOT CALL

O

Two ways used by Indians for muskrat calls—with the bare hand and a caller.

sounds. In times of danger they may give alarm splashes. One of the common bits of muskrat conversation, however, is a low squeak. The Indians make this sound by sucking the back of the hand (M).

A simple muskrat call is made by the Penobscots of two rectangular pieces of softwood about three inches long, mortised to-

gether (N). An opening is made between the two blocks by cutting away a small section so that the caller can blow through it. A very thin strip of birch bark is placed between the blocks, which is stretched taut, when the wood sections are fitted together. As the caller blows through the opening, the bark strip vibrates and produces a reso-

TURKEY CALLS

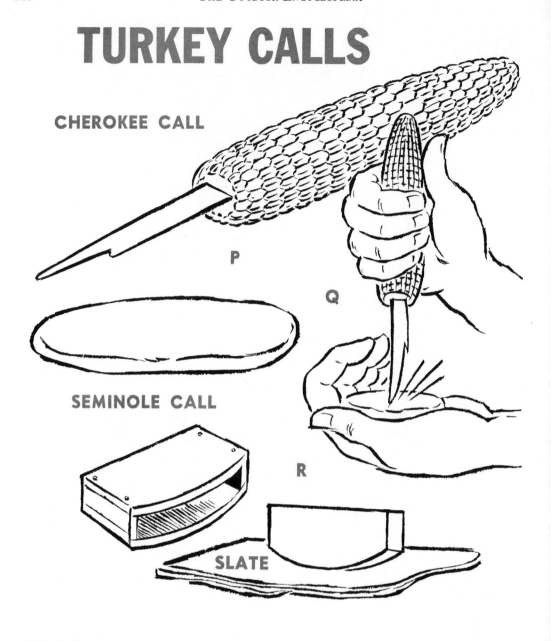

CHEROKEE CALL

P

Q

SEMINOLE CALL

R

SLATE

Here are interesting devices of Cherokees and Seminoles for calling turkeys.

nant buzzing similar to that made by drawing the lips tightly and sucking in air through the corner of the mouth in short intakes of breath (O).

The Cherokee of the Great Smokies make an interesting turkey call (P). The materials needed are an old dried corncob, a sharp piece of bone and a flat pebble. The bone is driven into one end of the corncob, so that it fits securely. To make the soft, throaty sounds of the turkey, simply hold the corncob tightly in one hand and rub the sharp, pointed end of the projecting bone upon the flat pebble, which is held horizontally in the other hand (Q).

The Seminole of Florida make another type

CALLING BEAVER

Beaver will often respond to this sound.

of turkey call—a small rectangular box made of pieces of wood, about cigar-box thickness. The base of the box is open and rounded (R). Its dimensions are four inches wide, two inches high and about half an inch through. The rounded base of the box is lightly scraped over a piece of slate, which makes good turkey talk.

Sometimes in calling an animal, its curiosity has much to do with its response. This is true with beavers and the Indians long ago discovered a way to attract them. They found that the beaver will often respond to the sound made by rapping the gunwale of a canoe with a knife or paddle. Tapping a gunstock or the *plunk* of a small stone tossed

WHITE-THROATED SPARROW CALL

How to imitate this musical bird's song.

into the pond may also lure them close (S). Some woods Indians call beavers by making a hissing sound.

One of the most beautiful theme songs of the North Woods is the "Old Sam Peabody, Peabody, Peabody" call of the white-throated sparrow. In Canada the Canadians say he sings, "Oh! Sweet, Sweet, Canada, Canada, Canada!" While this song can be whistled by anyone who can hit the high notes necessary, it can be successfully imitated on a small twig whistle developed by Professor William Harlow of the New York State College of Forestry at Syracuse, N.Y.

ELK CALL

WOOD PLUG

FF

EE

CC

3/4"

HH

GG

5/8" INSIDE DIAMETER

6 OR 7 INCHES LONG

DD

Breath pressure regulates this call's tone.

This instrument can be made from the twigs of red maple, willow or basswood, a little less than pencil thickness and eight or nine inches long. Two inches from the thicker end, cut through the bark all around the twig (T). The twig is then carefully pounded over the whole bark surface above the girdling to loosen the bark so it will pull away from the wood in a complete cylinder (U).

A notch is cut a half inch from the smaller end on the topside of the twig (V) and a small piece is also cut off the end on the bottom side (W). This is the mouth end of the whistle. The wooden core is then pulled out of the loosened bark cylinder (X) and at the mouth end the wood is cut off (Y). A small sliver is sliced off the topside of this wooden plug (Z). The remaining section is placed into the mouth end of the bark cylinder (AA) and the long wood core is inserted at the opposite end (BB). By moving the core back and forth inside the bark, the varied whistled notes of the whitethroat can be imitated, as well as the chickadee.

Autumn is the "Love Moon" of the elk. His martial bugling pours out with a throaty roar, rising higher and higher in bugle tones until it becomes a shrill whistle. Then it fades again into the lower throaty sounds, ending with savage grunts.

According to Frank M. Yale, a simplified bull elk's call is composed of three notes. Beginning at a low note it reaches a middle tone, ending gradually on a shrill whistle somewhat resembling that of the hoary marmot. It is often heard at a long distance. The pitch of an elk's bugling ranges from middle C on the piano, for the lowest note, to C two octaves higher on the second note —going up to E an octave above, and two notes higher for the last and highest note. Thus there is a tonal range of three octaves and two notes for the average elk bugle.

Mr. Yale successfully approximates the elk call with a large whistle made of bamboo or basswood. A bamboo section is used, six or seven inches long and about ¾ inch in diameter. The inside diameter should measure around ⅜ to ⅞ inch. The bamboo is cut so that a solid end of a section remains intact (CC). The open, or mouth end, of the bamboo is cut diagonally (DD). About three quarters of an inch from this end, a notch is made about a third of the way through the tube (EE).

A wooden plug is now whittled from softwood to fit snugly into the open end (FF). The top of the plug is whittled flat. Shave off a little at a time and test it for sound. The plug should be long enough to line up with the notch in the tube (GG). Tone and pitch are regulated by moving the plug forward and backward. In some positions, only one or two notes are produced. When the plug is in the right position, however, all three notes of the bull elk can be made, from the low note to the high-pitch whistle. By experimenting, the exact position of the plug will be found and it should then be fixed permanently in place by boring a hole through the bamboo tube and into the plug and driving in a hardwood peg (HH).

The various tones are produced by the amount of air blown into the whistle. To imitate the call of the bull elk, take a deep breath and blow gently to produce the first low note. By blowing a little more strongly the middle tone is made. The shrill whistle note is produced with a final and greater effort.

In calling elk, calls should be made in about five-minute intervals. If the imitation bugling is too frequent, the bull will become suspicious. Remember that once the bull has heard your bugling and has given an answer, his whole attention is concentrated upon it. If he is the least suspicious, however, he will take his harem and silently move off.

By Ellsworth Jaeger

HOW TO BUILD A FISHPOND

Fishponds can be made by man, as well as by nature. As a matter of fact you can often manage waters *better* than nature does. Here is the procedure, arranged in the proper order. Follow it and you should get fine results.

THE SITE

The size of a fishpond must be related favorably to the size of its watershed. The runoff of rains from a 100-acre watershed is too great for a one-acre pond; but it is favorable for lakes of four to 20 acres. Too much water entering the pond: (1) carries mature fish over the spillway; (2) makes fertilization and high yields of fish impossible; (3) forces the owner to build an expensive dam and spillway; (4) shortens the pond's life too rapidly by siltation. Many ponds are no good—cannot be managed—be-

U.S. Soil Conservation Service

Proper care and management will keep even a small man-made pond producing fish year after year.

cause watersheds above are too big! To select suitable sites, your Soil Conservation Service technician is usually the best adviser.

CONSTRUCTION

The soil inside a proposed impoundment is suitable if it will hold water well. The basin can be improved by taking soil from the pond area—if you leave enough of the watertight subsoil. The washed-in soil and debris at the dam site must be cut through— and a core wall of good clay replaced—to avoid leakage under the dam. A safe dam is obviously essential.

Ten years ago ponds were designed very poorly for fish management. Engineers built safe dams on large watersheds; and both engineers and fish culturists wanted lots of fresh water. Most fisheries technicians recom-

mended considerable shallow water (less than two feet deep) around the edges. But today we know that shallow water means trouble with aquatic weeds; and, happily, fish don't need those once-advocated shallow areas or their weeds.

Today we are not content to design a spillway which is merely safe from an engineering point of view. The spillway should be extremely wide, allowing all but infrequent floodwaters to leave the pond in a shallow stream (one to three inches deep). Catchable-size fish go out with four inches or more of running water. If half or more of them go out at once, your ratio of intermediate-size fish will increase enough to make fishing very poor. However, screens are never successful; if they hold the fish, they hold trash also.

So leave screens out of your spillway design. Widen the spillway instead. If you're still concerned about the loss of fish, build a chicken-wire pen down the branch below the dam and pick up any usable fish which wash over the spillway. The fish still in the pond will grow rapidly, restoring in only a few days the same number of pounds washed out. With a wave of the hand and a good-natured smile, bid the "little" fish *bon voyage* wherever the floodwaters carry them or leave them. New thousands will come off the spawning beds inside the pond.

FLOOD AND EROSION

The land, from which rain waters run into the pond, must not be allowed to erode even moderately—or you will ruin your best pond site without ever producing good fishing. Silty waters have no place in good fishponds.

Soil Conservation Service technicians understand soils, waters and watersheds. They are available for assistance with these soil and water problems of fishponds in every one of the 2,000-odd soil conservation districts in our 48 states. The plans you can make with them are your best guarantee that the next steps in fish management can be taken safely, economically and successfully. By diversions and contours and plenty of vegetation the soil conservationist will show you how to lessen the problems of floods. By every reasonable device of soil and water conservation, you'll make your fishing waters more profitable. Use them all!

STOCK CORRECTLY

Some laymen—and even a few fisheries men —seem to think you can stock pond waters any old way, and nature will overcome all obstacles. It won't. Incorrect stocking is the chief cause of poor fishing in most ponds and lakes. There are a thousand ways to stock fishponds to insure failure but only a few to assure successful fishing.

Your selection of fish must include the kinds which can live and reproduce together under the most adverse conditions to be expected in pond waters. The temperature of water in ponds is considerably higher than that in streams. Oxygen becomes much lower in ponds than in streams—in the heat of a windless, cloudy, summer day.

A pond, having little fluctuation in level or size, exerts no control of fish population through the process of expansion and contraction—a very important factor that usually controls crappies and catfish in bayous and backwater lakes in the valleys of our major streams. In stabilized ponds you must depend on (1) bass and (2) correct numbers when stocking if you want to maintain a fishable population.

A fishable population must be 70 per cent or more of catchable size (by total weight). If you allow the weight of little fish to exceed 30 per cent of the pond's total, you might as well stay at the office instead of going fishing. You can upset this 70-30 ratio in several ways:

By stocking too many fish.
By stocking too few fish.
By leaving bass out of the stocking combination.
By allowing too much cover to grow in the pond.
By stocking the wrong kinds of fish.

There's another thing about stocking correctly. You shouldn't put as many fish in an infertile pond as you'd stock in one with greater fertility.

POND MANAGEMENT

During the first year or more after stocking your pond with fish, leave them alone! Put your efforts to keeping the waters fertile; keep the weeds out; and make the soil stay up in the pasture, the woods and the fields.

If your water gets muddy with every rain, you can't fertilize the pond successfully.

If your pond stays clear—so that you can see two, three or more feet beneath the surface—you'll get a heavy growth of submerged waterweeds in the pond. Weeds interfere with fishing. Weeds protect too many little fish. Submerged weeds and clear waters always indicate moderate to low fertility. Weed control is a major reason why fertilization is recommended so highly.

Fertile water is dark-colored (usually green), made so by vast numbers of microscopic plants and animals which result from high fertility. You do not fertilize all ponds once a month or every three weeks, as some people have suggested. You fertilize at weekly intervals every spring until the color has come up high enough to obscure any bright object held 12 inches beneath the water's surface. Your pond is not fertilized adequately until it reaches this test. Your next application is due when you can see an object 12 inches below the surface. No one can tell you whether your pond will take one application, six or 16. You can learn only by following the instructions.

For weed control at the pond edges, you'd better get Farmers' Bulletin No. 1983 from your county agent, soil conservation technician or the U.S. Department of Agriculture.

There are a lot of chemicals which kill weeds by spraying, but you should get an expert to help you. Chemicals are often harmful. At best they are only temporary. The same weeds will come back quickly again unless you fertilize the water, pull the new weeds or graze the edges. Weed control is easier if you'll make it a part of your soil and water management plan.

Fertilize pond waters when the weather is warm enough to grow microscopic plant life in pond waters. This season is 12 months a year in Florida; eight months a year in central areas and five or six months in northern states.

FISHING

You should have good fishing, years without end, if you take the first five steps toward creating manageable fishing waters. (1) Build on favorable sites. (2) Construct correctly. (3) Protect the fish from silt and floodwaters. (4) Stock with the right kinds and numbers of fish in the beginning, and (5) Establish and maintain high fertility all through the mild seasons. Thousands of pond owners now have such ponds and enjoy excellent fishing. Unfortunately, thousands more have very poor fishing because they failed to follow these good practices.

The extensive experience of the Soil Conservation Service with tens of thousands of fishponds reveals that most pond owners need to learn additional tricks of fishing—not fancy refinements, but basic facts.

"When can we start fishing?" they ask.

Many have begun as soon as the bluegills have spawned, and are big enough to cook. That's too soon.

Wait until the bass, too, have spawned. Bass will reproduce at the age of one year—which means the first spring after stocking—if they reach a size between nine ounces and a pound and a quarter. Bass do not spawn smaller than that. Only when there are too few of them for their food supply of little fishes do they grow above a pound the first year. The overabundance of little bluegills, left when bass are too few, are able to eat all the bass eggs off the beds—thus preventing bass increase.

So, every pond should be checked by minnow seine the first spring after bass are stocked. This is March-April in Florida, April-May in other southern states, May-June in central latitudes, and June-July in northern states. As soon as you find the largemouth minnowlike fingerlings in the seine, your waters are ready for fishing. Take both bass and bluegills as you can, thereafter, by hook-and-line methods.

The reason for leaving the adult bluegills until bass spawn successfully is to allow them to exert their full weight against their own young in competition for food. This assures a low ratio of intermediate-size bluegills—a very important necessity in new ponds.

Fishing needs almost no restrictions—no size limits, no closed season, no creel limit—to protect the fish in ponds and lakes. A creel limit is admittedly an acceptable rationing system where anglers are too numerous for the annual yield of public or club waters; but this is seldom a problem on privately owned ponds.

In any case, no amount of hook-and-line fishing pressure can endanger your pond and its fish. Fish stop biting before you reduce their numbers or poundage harmfully. As you take 10 pounds of fish from lake or pond waters, 10 pounds grow back quickly—in only a week or two. If you take 50 pounds, 50 pounds grow back almost as quickly. Heavy fishing is good for fish and fishermen. The fish grow all the more rapidly as you remove more and more pounds.

By Verne E. Davison

WILD FOODS

The best beginning for a discussion of edible wild plants is a frank statement of facts about them. Too much fiction and semi-fiction has led some persons to believe the woods and fields are one vast larder of delicious wild food which is available at all times for the gathering. This is not true. Other persons, just as misguided, feel that anything not found on a grocery store counter is poisonous, or must have a bad taste. That isn't true either.

There is a medium between these extremes, and the camper who wants to supplement his fare with wild things will find it is a happy medium if he remembers that:

MILKWEED

Young milkweed shoots can be used as a vegetable.

1. A beginner should start with plants, roots, berries, fruits and nuts that are easy to recognize, easy to obtain and pleasant to taste. Branch out later.

2. Some things are edible, but only after considerable preparation to change their natural bitterness, sourness, toughness or other unpleasant characteristics.

3. Few things are poisonous, but some are sufficiently deadly to make it unwise to take chances. Be certain.

4. Some things are not poisonous, but can upset the digestive tract if eaten unwisely.

5. Wild foods should be regarded as a welcome addition to the camping diet, and not as a sole means of sustenance except in an emergency.

6. Book instruction helps considerably, but is only an introduction to practical experience.

Fear of being poisoned keeps many persons from experimenting. Actually, cases of poisoning from wild foods are rare, the greatest number occurring from consumption of poisonous fungi.

The young and tender shoots of some plants are nonpoisonous, whereas the mature stalks are more or less poisonous. Examples: Pokeberry, and even the plants of the common potato and tomato. The application of heat in baking or boiling removes the poisonous properties of certain edible roots. The tapioca you eat comes from a plant that is poisonous in its raw state.

EVERYONE KNOWS THESE

Even the least experienced outdoorsman can recognize some things at a glance because they are almost exactly what he finds on his table. *Blackberries* growing wild differ little from cultivated ones, although the related and equally good *dewberries* might puzzle those accustomed to thinking of all blackberries as growing on bushes. Dewberries trail over the ground. *Purple* and *red raspberries* are as good wild as tame. Look for such berries on abandoned farmland, in open creek bottoms, clearings in the woods or burned-over sections. The same advice holds for many of the things under discus-

POND LILIES

Both the seeds and roots of several kinds of water lilies can be eaten.

ion, because the deep woods are not very productive of ground plants except for ferns and fungi.

Huckleberries and *blueberries* follow the ax and fire in forest lands. They are easily recognized by most persons, and form a delicious addition to the camp diet, either as they are, or baked into pies and muffins. The *low-bush blueberry* ripens first, the *high-bush berry* is late-ripening, so there is fruit from June to September. Caution: Don't gorge on any berries if you would avoid diarrhea.

The *wild strawberry* deserves separate mention. It differs from the tame berry in two major ways—it is much smaller and much better.

Two other berries or fruits commonly recognized by most persons are the *wild cranberry* and the Atlantic Coast *beach plum*. The latter can be eaten as it is when fully ripe, but cranberries require a heavy amount of sugar to be palatable.

There are many other edible, and very good, berries; but they don't belong here because they are not so familiar as the fruits mentioned. Among them are *wild currants* and *gooseberries*, *persimmons*, and *mulberries*.

An old rhyme is a fairly good rule-of-thumb for berries:

> *Berries red, have no dread;*
> *Berries, white, flee on sight.*

Of the various grapes, the northern *fox grape* and the similar southern *muscadine* are most edible in the raw state. If you cannot recognize them, sample any ripened grapes you find—taste will tell. Nearly all wild grapes make good jellies and wines.

The edible nuts belong to late autumn, just as most berries belong to summer. It hardly seems necessary to describe some, such as *black walnuts* and *hickory nuts*, because they are so widespread and well known, but just in case—. Both have hulls. The hull breaks easily in neat sections from the smooth hickory nut; the walnut hull must be scuffed from the corrugated shell. A walnut is about twice the size of a hickory, and better flavored. It is rather difficult to crack and extract the meat from both nuts, but they are worth the trouble. They are nearly unexcelled as emergency foods, each possessing about three times the food value in calories of round steak. There are several kinds of hickory nuts, the shellbark or shagbark being best known, all edible, but varying in quality.

BLACK RASPBERRY

This is a companion to the red raspberry; both edible.

Other edible nuts, not so familiar although anything but rare, include *beechnuts, butternuts* and *hazlenuts*. The western *nut pine*, or *piñon*, with seeds in the cone, usually is included among edible nuts.

Edible seeds, and there are many, don't belong in this easy-to-recognize group with the possible exception of *wild rice*. The long, slender, dark seeds of this native grass, which grows around lakes and rivers, are unmistakable.

The first actual *plants* that come to mind, because they are familiar to most persons, are *skunk cabbage* and *burdock* (surely two of the least prepossessing), *dandelion* and *watercress*. Skunk cabbage has its characteristic namesake odor and isn't pretty, while burdock is a rank weed best known for the troublesome burrs that stick to clothing and dogs' hair. The young, tender shoots of skunk cabbage, however, lose their fetid odor when the water is changed a few times

while boiling them, and there is no trace of it at all when butter and seasoning are added to make a delicate vegetable dish. The *great burdock* (larger than the more widespread *common burdock*) has several virtues. The tender shoots of spring, or the mature leaf stems, can be peeled and eaten like radishes with a touch of salt, or cooked like asparagaus which it resembles slightly in flavor, or cut up into a salad. The flower stalk can be used the same way before the flowers bloom. The root can be baked or boiled and eaten.

Dandelion needs no description. The leaves, gathered when young and tender, are boiled briefly. The water should be changed once or twice if the natural bitter taste isn't desired. It is served with butter and a dash of vinegar. Better still is a sweet-sour hot dressing of vinegar, sugar, bacon and bacon drippings. It is also good when boiled with ham or salt pork.

Watercress can be found in tiny, cold brooks, and even along the banks of larger streams. Its spicy taste is instantly recognizable. The leaves can be eaten as they are with salt, or used in salads. Since it is eaten raw, make sure the water in which it grows is unpolluted.

Perhaps *wild asparagus* should be included in the easiest-to-spot plants because asparagus surely is known to everyone, and that which grows wild is (like watercress) an escape from cultivation. Gather young shoots only, of course, and cook only until soft in a minimum of water.

GET ACQUAINTED WITH THESE

Less easily recognized wild foods, or those requiring more than ordinary preparation, are numerous. Some, like the *yellow water lily* or *spatterdock*, possibly could have been included in the foregoing because they are common enough and easy to identify; but spatterdock's use involves both seeds and roots. The roots can be baked in the fire or boiled, the seeds must be parched by heat before they taste good. The *yoncopin* is somewhat similar in uses, but its edible root is larger and tastier than the spatterdock's,

FOX GRAPES

One of the largest wild grapes, and one of the few sweet enough to eat raw.

RED RASPBERRY

Just as delicious eating wild as in the tame state.

and the larger seeds more filling. The yon-copin has many names—*American nelumbo, American lotus, water beans, wankapin* and *water chinquapin* among them. Usually its seeds are soaked in water, then parched, to make it easy to get the kernels. As some of its names indicate, it is a water plant, with giant leaves and big flowers.

The common *fern* known as *brake* or

bracken is tough when mature, but delicate and delicious when the fronds are just un-folding in early spring. The young stems of other ferns also are good if gathered be-fore the leaves unfurl. Use as potherbs, or like asparagus. Very young *milkweed* plants make good greens if the water is changed several times while boiling them to remove the milky fluid. When well cooked, it tastes

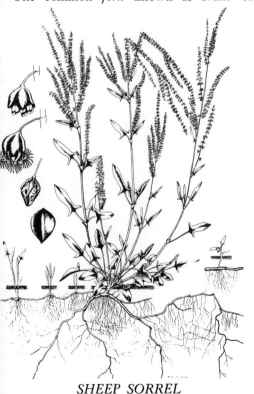

SHEEP SORREL

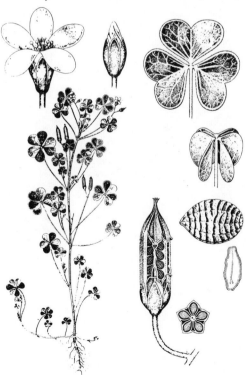

FIELD SORREL

like spinach—if you like spinach. The young pods, pulled before the down fiber forms inside, can be cooked with meat.

Spring is pre-eminently the time to gather edible wild plants, because many things are then tender and green, suitable for potherbs, salads and use in dishes, whereas they turn tough and bitter later in the year. Among these are *sorrel, lamb's-lettuce, marsh marigold (cowslips), miners' lettuce, purslane* and *green amaranth* or *redroot (pigweed)*. The young shoots of *pokeweed* are fine food, used like asparagus, but the mature plant is likely to upset the stomach. The roots are poisonous, so cut off well above the ground line in the spring.

Heat works miracles with wild plants just as it does with domestic ones. A raw potato isn't the best of foods—baked, boiled fried, it becomes delicious. A raw *Indian turnip (jack-in-the-pulpit)* is the most acrid thing you ever tasted, burning the mouth and tongue for a full day; but the acridity vanishes if the bulb root is cut open and roasted (or even heat-treated in the sun before it is boiled like an onion. Some slightly poisonous roots can be rendered harmless by baking in the coals of a fire. Acridity, bitterness and even poison reside in the fluids of a root—eliminate the fluids by heat, and you eliminate the objectionable features.

By Bill Wolf

BRACKEN FERN

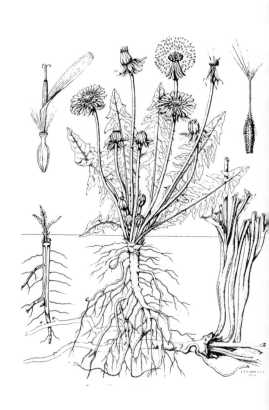

DANDELION

CHAPTER 12

outdoor accessories

SUCCESSFUL TRIPS out-of-doors depend on attention to details and, it may well be said, start next to the skin—with your clothing. A pair of ill-fitting or ill-suited boots can turn the likeliest trip into a nightmare. Clothing that is too light or too heavy can do the same. Certainly one of the most important items in any outdoorsman's kit is a sturdy and reliable knife or ax. It is probably your single most useful tool. But almost equally important is the choice of sunglasses or binocular. And few would argue that comfort at night is paramount to a happy camp. The wise choice of a sleeping bag is insurance for that. In this chapter you will find information to help you in the selection and use of all these.

CLOTHING

There are many factors to consider in outdoor clothing. One, of course, is comfort. Another is durability. Still another is its suitability for wet weather. Warmth, comfort, durability and water-repellent qualities often tie in together, and can be found in a single item, such as a woolen shirt, for example.

It is almost impossible to provide a handy check list of what should be taken along because everything depends upon how long you will be gone, how you will travel, the kind of terrain where you will camp and the time of the year. There will be no attempt here to furnish such a confusing list, although minimums for any kind of camping will be mentioned under the separate divisions. This is a head-to-foot job, so we will start at the bottom.

FOOTWEAR

This can easily be the most important thing in the camper's outfit, if much walking is done. Let us examine the various items that contribute to foot comfort one at a time.

Socks. Foot comfort starts here. For the purposes of comparison, examine a collection of modern outdoor socks with well-known brand names, all made by reputable companies which take pride in their products, against "woolen" socks purchased from so-called Army and Navy stores of the type found in every city and town. Some of these stores maintain a high standard of quality, but many don't. The socks from these stores bear no manufacturer's label, the tag states merely "all-wool," and they are, but it is all reprocessed wool instead of live, virgin fiber. They feel wrong to the touch, and they wouldn't be comfortable; neither would they last long.

A pair of good socks will make even a pair of bad shoes more comfortable. Most outdoorsmen are partial to wool, and fairly heavy wool at that even in midsummer, because wool socks retain their shape, absorb perspiration, are warm even when wet in bad weather and their sponginess absorbs many shocks to the feet.

On the other hand, the major manufacturers are putting out new all-nylon socks that look like wool and feel like wool, and have many of wool's good characteristics. They are well worth trying, and may fit your needs.

A minimum of two pairs of good socks should be carried on a hiking trip—one to wear and one to wash and dry, because clean socks are comfortable socks—and at least four pairs should be taken along when auto or pack train camping.

Slipper Socks. After a day of walking in sturdy shoes, it is a relief to get out of them, but going barefooted isn't too advisable since most of us are tenderfeet in the most literal sense. Slipper socks are an ideal solution, since they combine a soft woolen sock with a leather bottom, and are light enough to be carried even when backpacking. A pair of down socks (made like down jackets) with leather bottoms that are light in weight, are also very comfortable. One other solution is to get a pair of moccasins that are light as gloves.

Boots and Shoes. For the kind of auto camping many people do, little more is needed than a comfortable pair of loafers, or canvas oxfords with heavy rubber bottoms. If your camping involves hiking, however, you should have a pair of shoes or boots that come above the ankle—but not much higher. Don't wear hightops for any kind of walking over any distance. The lacing restricts the leg too much and such shoes often are heavy. Hightops or boots with buckles and straps across the instep and at the top of the calf are all right for horseback camping, or where the terrain or snake conditions indicate their use.

An excellent all-round camping shoe is the Maine Guide Shoe (the name under which it is sold by one manufacturer). It is light but rugged, comes just above the ankle and has a composition sole. Shoes or boots with leather soles are useless for most hiking-camping since they slip too easily on grass, rocks and leaves. Get a good composition sole.

Don't worry too much about the waterproof quality of your footwear in summer. If you have to wade across a stream, you will get wet feet anyhow, no matter what shoes you have. And don't go into the woods without being absolutely certain that your footwear is in good condition. If it is more than a year old, have a shoemaker check the seams and stitching—unless you want to wind up with soles stripping off. It is next to impossible to repair shoes with the means at hand in the woods.

One pair of walking shoes, and something light in weight to change into in the evening, is the minimum for a walking trip. Where transportation is no problem, a pair of all-rubber or rubber-and-leather waterproof shoes can be added for rainy weather.

UNDERWEAR

Underwear is an unimportant item unless you gall easily about the inner thigh, or anticipate cool weather. In fall and winter camping, or at high altitudes, it is most important. A most practical undergarment for cool to moderately cold weather is the two-piece suit of full-length pants and shirt, made of lightweight wool, or part wool and cotton. For a very short trip, one set of such underwear is sufficient.

TROUSERS

Men and women have the same clothing problems when camping, except that it is more complicated for women who, somewhat naturally, also like to look fairly presentable. Most of the following suggestions will apply to both sexes.

The very popular jeans worn by men and women have much to recommend them, but they also have drawbacks. They are inexpensive and durable, which are in their favor; but their pockets are miserable, and pockets are important to the camper who must carry everything he needs with him. The typical slash pockets in front are hard to get into, and they come at a bend of the body when squatting around the fire. The hip pockets aren't much better. Jeans are not much good in briars or bad brush, nor in wet going.

Trousers of any kind which are tight at the knee, as in riding breeches, should never be worn when camping. The amount of squatting done is surprising, and any knee restriction is irritating. The stress also wears the garment at the knee. A popular camping trouser is the Zouave-type of trouser which is full from waist down to the narrow knit cuff bottoms, allowing full freedom for thighs, knees and legs. Use the lightest weight briarproof, water-resistant cloth you can get, summer or winter, depending upon underwear beneath it for warmth if required.

The manufacturers of hunting and fishing clothing provide the best field for finding camping pants. They are available in a wide variety of cloths. There also are some comfortable models that lace below the knee, but are cut full at the knee. Cuff bottoms are dirt collectors and can trip you up. Too many pants have the slash pockets mentioned earlier, but someday bellows pockets may be available in all models.

For high-altitude mountain trips, where very cold weather can be expected, down pants are available. They look bulky, but are very light in weight and nonrestricting. They are equally good, of course, for any winter camping.

For rough camping, your pants should turn briars and the whiplash sting of branches. It helps if they are somewhat waterproof. Shorts are almost worthless except in the easiest kind of camping, and even there they are an open invitation to flies, mosquitoes, chiggers and poison ivy.

SHIRTS

Carry one light and one heavy shirt, and you are equipped for almost any summer camping where you are your own pack horse. Both should be long-sleeved (the sleeves can be rolled up when it's hot) because of protection against insects, cold and poisonous plants. The heavier shirt should be larger than the lighter one so it can be worn over the latter in cold weather. As for materials, wool is preferable for both, although the lighter one can be part wool. It doesn't have to be rough and literally heavy in weight. There are fine wool flannel shirts on the market that are soft on the skin, and yet provide warmth. Wool has several virtues in shirts: It provides warmth, isn't clammy in the rain, doesn't draw moisture and it absorbs body perspiration. One very light cotton sport shirt with short sleeves can be carried for a change, if you wish. Your supply of shirts can grow if you travel by car, pack train or boat.

There are exceptions to the rule against cotton. One is a thick "chamois" type shirt, the other is the better grade blue or tan work shirts. Both are good outdoor garments. Sweat shirts, wool or cotton, are all right, but they seldom have pockets, and once again, the camper needs pockets. Get button-down flaps if you can.

Pull-over and button sweaters fall into the "shirt" category. If there is room in the pack, a good woolen sweater can be a comfort on cold days and nights.

OUTER GARMENTS

By this is meant various jackets and coats. If you want to carry a jacket, and are limited to exactly one, by all means get one of the lightweight, tough rain jackets because it will serve the double purpose of being waterproof and windproof. If you have more choice, get a rain jacket and another one for warmth. Falling into the class of jackets is the cruiser shirt, which is large and roomy, has plenty of pockets, is warm. Don't overlook the standard hunting coat as a good cool-weather camping coat.

If it's warmth you want, the outer coat or jacket must come down over the kidney region. The short jackets that fit about the waist don't do this. Down jackets offer the most warmth for weight, wool is good, and so is the new material known as Thermo-Wear.

HEADGEAR

A duckbill visor cap is good in wet weather, otherwise a rather wide-brimmed hat is best. It keeps sun and rain from the face and neck, protects the head from gouging sticks and branches, and can serve as an emergency "kettle" for picking berries along the way, or the turned up brim makes a drinking cup. For cold weather, you need a hat that can be turned down over the ears and neck.

ACCESSORIES

A large bandanna handkerchief of the old-fashioned small tablecloth size is one of the most useful accessories. It serves so many purposes when worn around the neck to keep off sun or insects, around the forehead to keep sweat out of the eyes or to ease the pressure of a tumpline, or draped down the back of the neck from under a hat as a sort of hood against insects. It can even be used for blowing the nose. Gloves aren't needed except under certain circumstances which can be anticipated. Women campers will find a scarf handy for the head, but

they scarcely need to be told this since they usually carry one.

By Bill Wolf

OUTDOOR TOOLS

The most indispensable tool for an outdoorsman, in fact for any man or boy anywhere, is the knife, a "business" size knife, sharp and keen.

You need a knife constantly for many purposes afield. For example, the camp cook will need one for slicing bread and meat, paring potatoes, and such. Any fair-sized knife will do for such chores; however, it is better to have a special one for kitchen work, an ordinary small butcher knife, because it gets rough treatment and it is a lot of labor to keep it sharp enough for other work. Have a sheath for it, and keep it in the bundle with the knives, forks and spoons.

THE POCKETKNIFE

Afield, particularly in the woods, you will need a knife for whittling more than anything else. All boys should learn to whittle when they are young. You can't do it for shucks with a little vest-pocket penknife.

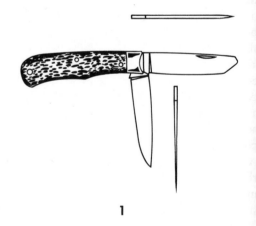

1

The best type is shown in figure No. 1. One blade is for rough work and the other for finer work in closer quarters. The first blade with the rounded point is also excellent for general skinning; the lower for more delicate work around eyes and ears and for small animals—the point is sharp enough to even

ft a splinter out of your hand. This type is
usually called a "trapper's knife," and most
arge cutlery companies make it. Whatever
other knife you have, better have one of
these, and keep it in your pocket always.

SHEATH KNIVES

While the trapper's pocketknife will do
everything needed for the camper or hunter,
many of us, particularly if we hunt big game,
like to have and carry a sheath knife, and
almost all interest in outdoor knives revolves
around this type. There are some who think
it is a sort of "Billy the Kid" weapon, and
that one on the belt marks its owner as a
tenderfoot. But there is no law against carrying it in the rucksack, and that is the best
place for it. Trouble is that most sheath
knives one sees, and that are advertised, are
of the Billy the Kid or Bowie pattern; entirely too large, long and thick bladed to be
of any practical use. The sheath knife is
primarily for the hunter's use, and should
be designed chiefly for skinning and butchering animals, but should also be good for
all purposes. Most old-time hunters prefer to
keep it for hunting alone, and razor sharp.
They usually prefer it with a blade not more
than 4½ inches long, with a straight edge
until it curves to the point, and with the
point rounded for skinning, rather than a
sharp spear point. A thin blade that tapers
all the way from the back to the cutting
edge will take a much keener edge, and you
can work faster and easier with it than with
a blade that is thick from back to middle
and which tapers sharply to an edge like a
cold chisel.

There are several excellent types shown in
this illustration. No. 2 is a favorite of hunters
in the Green River area of Wyoming and its
style is widely copied.

No. 3 is excellent in every way, and anyone wishing a knife of moderate cost would
make no mistake in selecting this type. It
is made by many cutlery firms.

No. 4 is a custom-built knife, fine in every
way but rather costly. The size, the shape
of the bone handle, and the blade are just
about right.

2

3

4

Notice the shape of the point on this
blade. It will make the initial slits up the
belly and down the legs of an animal with
the least danger of cutting into the flesh,
which is a thing you want to avoid doing if
possible. The sharp points on knives 2 and
3 are particular offenders in this respect.
However, there is nothing to prevent your
modifying the points on these, using a file
and a whetstone.

These knives come with suitable leather sheaths to protect them, and you can carry them in your rucksack or your belt as you wish. If the latter, it would be a good idea to reinforce the sheath with copper wire stitching so as to be sure the point of the knife will not cut through the sheath and drive into your leg or hip should you fall on it.

KNIFE STEEL

The first question most anyone asks about a knife is, "Is it of good steel?" Thirty years ago everyone swore by Sheffield steel knives made in England, although some thought that certain German knives had very good steel, particularly those made in Solingen. But times have changed and for many years the United States has led the world in the metallurgy of steel, and practically all our knives made by reputable companies have excellent steel in them.

Anyone who has used and sharpened knives for some time will recognize good steel the moment he touches the blade to a whetstone. There is something indefinable in the way a good blade takes hold and slides on a whetstone, soon recognized when you have tried to sharpen a few good blades and some poor ones.

For a general-purpose knife, and particularly for a hunting knife, avoid all with stainless steel blades. They may be all right for fish and table knives, but they won't take a keen edge, and when they are dull it takes forever and a day to bring them to even half decent sharpness on a whetstone.

SHARPENING STONES

A knife, ax or any edged tool should be kept almost razor sharp for best use. As knives come from the makers they do not usually have a keen edge, and they should be honed before use. It does not suffice to merely sharpen your knife before you start on a trip; it is dulled with use, and will require sharpening many times afield. Skinning an animal takes the edge off a knife very quickly, and in skinning a deer you will probably need to sharpen it three or four times.

The carborundum stone is the best for outdoor use. It is coarse on one side for first quick work, and fine on the other for putting on the keen edge, and it can be used with water only. The finest Arkansas whetstones are perhaps better for producing a very keen edge, but they are slow cutting and require oil.

The best carborundum stones for the field are the round ones, known as the "Sportsman" and "Boy Scout," because they can be held in the hand and do not require a bench or wood base. In sharpening, hold the blade in the left hand, and the round stone in the right, and use the stone with a circular grinding motion. It's best to have two stones, one for your camp kit, and one in your rucksack so that one will be at hand whenever you have a skinning or butchering job.

AXES

The ax is also an almost indispensable tool for most woodsmen, but is a dangerous instrument in the hands of a tyro. It is not really needed in the average summer camp, or on summer backpacking trips where the lighter, short-handled hand ax will serve every purpose. It is rather the tool for heavy work, for getting in heavy wood for warm fires, for building large shelters and for cutting out trees that may fall across roads, trails or canoe streams.

For such work it should have a medium heavy head, about 2½ pounds. Heavier axes bite deeper and are faster, and that is why the lumberman uses them; but they require special skill that the sportsman seldom acquires. Lighter axes do not bite deep and require many more blows. The Hudson's Bay ax has a good reputation, but it was designed for Indian use on the trap line where a light ax was desirable. Its head has a narrow poll (where the handle goes through it) and with heavy work the handle soon comes loose. Double-bitted axes are very dangerous tools in the hands of all but experienced men, and they cannot be used as a hammer for which you will use your ax a dozen times a day.

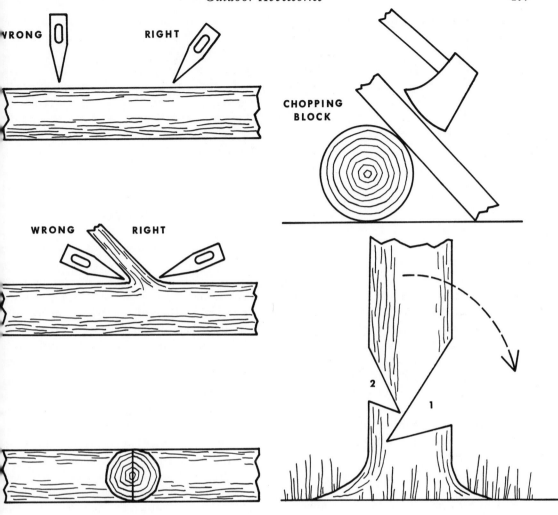

Top—an ax won't cut well across the grain. Center—how to cut limbs off a tree trunk. Bottom—to cut a large log make a notch at least as wide as the diameter of the log, cut half way through; repeat on the opposite side.

Top—to split a short piece of wood, have solid backing where the ax will strike, otherwise the chunk will fly up and may hit you. Bottom—to fell a tree first cut more than half way through the side on which you want it to fall, then cut a little above that.

So get an ordinary single-bit ax with about a 2½-pound head, and a handle or helve about 26 to 28 inches long. If you adopt one length handle and use it exclusively, you will come to do better work, and it will be safer.

The edge on the ax you buy is probably sharp enough for the average two-weeks-a-year camper, but the good axman will probably want to thin this edge for keener cutting. The best tool for this and for rough sharpening is a grindstone, but since you cannot carry one into the woods a 10- or 12-inch flat file does a good job. To sharpen an ax start about an inch back from its edge, and carry out that straight and gradual taper to the edge itself, then finish up with the carborundum stone.

A whole volume could be written on the subject of axmanship. Our best axmen almost all learned as boys on the farm or in the woods, but anyone with practice and care can learn well enough for all the usual camp chores. Don't try to chop at right angles to the grain of a log; the ax won't bite in that way. Use it at an angle of 45 degrees or more. Keep your eye on the exact spot you want the edge to strike, and practice until it does strike there. Don't try to use force; never strike a heavy blow; let the gravity fall of the ax do most of the work. The sketch shows the principal points of good chopping.

HAND AXES

The light one-pound ax with a 12-inch handle will do about all the work that is necessary in the summer or auto camp, and on backpacking trails. The average camper will use it much more effectively and with greater safety than he will a long-handled ax. The "Boy Scout" type, made by many companies, is an excellent model. Have a sheath made for it, but don't carry it on your belt, which is inconvenient and uncomfortable. Stow it in your pack. If you are hunting elk or moose be sure to have an ax in your rucksack. These large animals cannot be packed out whole, and a hand ax is needed for splitting and quartering.

SAWS

It is usually much easier and quicker to saw a fair-sized or large log in two than to chop it. If you are using a wood-burning stove, a saw is worth its weight in gold for sawing the wood the right length to fit the fire box. Buck or Swedish saws are made so they can be taken apart and packed in very small space. See that they have teeth designed for cutting rough timber, not the ordinary crosscut and rip teeth of the carpenter's saws.

REPAIR KITS

Some kind of repair kit should be included in every camp outfit, except perhaps that of a backpacker who has to pare everything down to the last ounce. Don't attempt to carry a whole carpenter shop or machine shop with you, but include only those small articles that you think will be needed, and for which nothing else will serve.

Suggested contents are: A tool handle containing screwdrivers, gimlets and awls. A small flat-nose pliers with wire cutter. A file for sharpening your ax. A box of assorted nails, tacks, rivets and buttons. Spools of thin copper wire and shoe thread. Needles for the shoe thread and large glovers' needle for sewing leather and canvas. A tube of all purpose cement.

By Col. Townsend Whelen

BINOCULARS

The individual preparing to buy a binocular is confronted with a confusing problem. He is faced with hundreds of specifications, makes, models and prices. Even if he sees the binocular and takes a quick look through them he can't detect everything on the inside and unfortunately any difference in optical qualities may not be apparent under the conditions of the brief look across the street. He may consider binoculars made in America, Germany, Japan, England or France. There may be good makes from any one of these countries, but on the other hand there are some poor ones too.

Practically no one can see and test all or even nearly all of the makes and models of binoculars that are on the market. Seeing one binocular is not sufficient to judge a make or model except in regard to construction in general. In addition to the possibility of getting hold of a particularly good one of a generally poor make, and vice versa, there is the possibility that a manufacturer has greatly improved his product since the last one was examined by the man passing judgment. Consequently, it is futile and decidedly unfair to try to list the hundreds of binoculars and evaluate them. Men who are commercially independent experts in optics have indicated that the finest optics in the world have been made in this country for the last few years.

The consensus seems to be that the high standards maintained by our leading lens manufacturers make them supreme in the field today. In the United States there are

Bausch and Lomb binoculars that are made on the highest standards. The Bausch and Lomb know-how is backed up by many years of experience in the field of optics. Wollensak has produced a lot of lower-priced telescopes, but they are also blessed with a lot of know-how in the finer optics field. They have produced some precise optical equipment for the government as well as commercially. The Wollensak binoculars are well made and good glasses. The Kollsman Instrument Company made binoculars during World War II and produced some commercially after the war with the brand name of Sard. Their 6x42 wide-angle made during the war, their 7x50 and the little 6x20 are all of excellent quality.

Some of the German binoculars are very good. Zeiss and Hensoldt binoculars are well known in this country for their good quality. Some Leitz binoculars have been imported into the United States recently and they also are very good. There are other German imports that have quality workmanship and there are some which are not so good.

English binoculars in general are well made. Some Ross binoculars are now being imported. Ross has had a reputation for turning out good stuff.

The majority of the imported French binoculars are cheaply made and are not what you would call good glasses. There are, nevertheless, some manufacturers in France that turn out a good job. For instance, some of the Huet "Miralux" 8x30s imported from France give fine performance and seem to be well constructed.

Japanese binoculars are a very controversial subject. Right after World War II there were imported a lot of particularly poor ones. Some repair people labeled Japanese binoculars in general as junk, but usually make a few exceptions. On the other hand, some praise them very highly. A lot depends on the particular experience of the repairman. The answer is that some of the Japanese imports are good values and give good performance while others are poor throughout. Among some of the Japanese binoculars you will find faulty metal work—including threads that won't hold and tubes bent in to keep the ocular lenses in place. In some of them the prisms are poorly secured and a high percentage of Japanese binoculars are badly out of alignment for one reason or another.

There are some importers of Japanese binoculars who are exercising some control over their imports. They select the better-made jobs. They also have facilities for testing their imports before resale and stand behind what they sell. Through these sources you can get your better values.

When selecting a binocular one of the first considerations is the specifications of the type to meet your needs. The most important specifications are magnification, size of objective lens and field of view. Binoculars are commonly marked with 6x30, 7x50, etc. The first number indicates the magnification and the second number the size of the objective lens in millimeters. The field of view is usually given in the descriptive literature in feet at 100 yards or 1,000 yards. For comparison, you can convert the 100-yard field to 1,000 yards or vice versa. For example: if the field is specified as 39 feet at 100 yards, at 1,000 yards it would be 10 times this much, or 390 feet. You can't get high magnification, light weight and a large field of view all wrapped up in one binocular so it is necessary to compromise in meeting your all-purpose requirements—even if you are not willing to compromise on quality.

Everything else remaining equal, the larger the objective lens, the larger and heavier are the binoculars. Some people make the mistake of thinking that a large objective lens makes a better binocular. This is true for some purposes but it may not be true for the specific use you have for binoculars. The size of the objective lens has nothing to do with the field of view in a prismatic job. The large objective lens does admit more light which you can use under darkened conditions of observing. Under good light conditions you will get no more light to your eye through a 7x50 than you will through a 6x30, 7x35, 8x30 or other glasses with smaller objective lenses.

You should buy a binocular in much the

same manner in which you would make a careful purchase of a good watch. Both are lifetime investments you might say. In the final analysis, you fall back on the reputation of the manufacturer or the dealer. If you don't know of the manufacturer then rely on a dealer who knows his product inside and out and has the reputation for being reliable. It is also worth knowing that you can get repairs and replacement parts in case of breakage. If you are buying a secondhand binocular you should be particularly cautious.

There are a few simple tests that you should make in buying a secondhand binocular or a new one that is of unknown origin:

1. Shake the binocular. If anything aside from the carrying strap rattles there is something amiss.

2. While holding the eyepiece up to the light, look through the objective or wrong end and you can see enough of the inside to determine if it has a chipped prism or a chipped lens. A small chip may not be too damaging to use, but it definitely devaluates the binocular. You can see if it is dirty with dust on the inside surfaces. At any point where the cement binding corrected lenses has broken loose, it will appear frosty and translucent. Bubbles in the lenses or prisms will also become apparent when examining the optics through the objective end. A small bubble won't hurt anything and is not noticeable when normally looking through the eyepiece, but a bubble of any size or several small ones would certainly be indicative of poor optical standards. Look for scratches on the outside surfaces of the lenses. Scratches on the objective won't be visible when using the binocular and a few small ones won't detract to any noticeable degree from the efficiency. Keep in mind that coated lenses make small scratches much more noticeable when looking directly at the lens. These more apparent scratches do no more harm when using the binocular than the unnoticeable ones on uncoated lenses.

3. Look to see if the optics are coated. This can be detected by holding the binocular to catch a reflection from a light such as a window or other light source directly off the lens surface. The reflection, if the optics are coated, will have a reddish purple or bluish tinge. A dark purple doesn't mean anything. It is easier to detect, but is possibly less efficient than a light-purplish tinge. If the outside lens surfaces are coated the inside ones should be also. Otherwise you are not getting the benefit of coated optics. With practice you can catch reflections from the prisms while looking through the objective end and get a pretty good idea if they are coated or not. Any reliable firm coats all optical surfaces if they coat the outside surfaces.

4. Pick out some object like the top of a telephone pole, a television aerial or tower 200 yards or more distant. Then move the binocular away from you while keeping your eyes on the images in the exit pupils. If you see two images, the binoculars are out of collimation. If the object is 200 yards away and the two images appear to be separated by more than about eight inches the binoculars are out of alignment far enough to cause some eyestrain. This test takes some practice and some people don't seem to be able to do it at all. It is the best check you can make by eye if you can do it. Another test for alignment is to rapidly blink one eye and then the other. If the image seems to jump up and down or from side to side the binoculars are noticeably out of alignment. This latter test is much easier to perform.

5. Try turning the eyepieces. They should require a firm pressure from two fingers to turn them, but the movement should be smooth and effortless. If they feel sloppy the machine work is not right or they lack grease. If they are difficult or impossible to turn, the grease has become hardened or the metal parts are binding.

6. If the binocular is a central focus, grip the binocular in both hands and place the thumbs on the edge of the eyecups. Tip them gently up and down. They will have a small amount of give in the bridge holding the eyepieces, but they should not be loose.

7. Rotate the binocular about the hinge

in. Throughout the entire swing, the tension should be firm and uniform. If they are sloppy about the hinge or if there is any side play in the hinge, then beware. The hinge is worn, needs adjustment or was poorly made in the first place.

8. The resolution of a binocular is important. Simplified, the resolution is the measure of the quality of a binocular or telescope to give fine detail in the image. Resolving power is a distinguishing mark of the quality of the optics. Yet resolution is a difficult thing for the customer to evaluate at the counter unless a glass is particularly poor in this respect. Your best out is to look for some printing that might be on a restaurant menu across the street. Try a few of the binoculars available, focus them carefully and try to read the smallest print you can find. The binocular that brings it out with the greatest clarity has the best resolving power under the prevailing conditions. To be fair, you should compare binoculars of equal magnification. The higher-powered binoculars should resolve more at a given distance than the lower-powered.

9. You can make a check of a binocular for bothersome aberrations—not to scientific exactness, but well enough to keep from getting something too far out of line. Pick out two objects of contrasting color, preferably black and white, to focus on. Look for a fringe of color at the dividing line between the two objects as you move the binocular to shift the image from one side of the field to the other. It is extremely difficult to make lenses that are entirely free from chromatic aberration and if you try hard enough you will probably see some color in a good binocular. If there is enough color to be bothersome for normal use the lenses are definitely of inferior quality.

When lenses are accurately ground and properly corrected you should get a sharp image over the entire field of view at one focal point. Pick out a small object and focus on it at the center of the field. Now move the binoculars to bring that point to the top, bottom and sides of the field. It should remain in focus although it may get fuzzy when brought in very near the edge of the field. It should at least stay in sharp focus over the main portion of the field.

Now look at the face of a tall building—the edge of a tall building, a flagpole or something that will serve equally well. As you move the straight edge toward one side of the field it will be inclined to bow outward at the center (barrel distortion) or inward at the center (hour-glass distortion). Most any glass will show this effect to some degree close to the field edge but it will be much more noticeable in the poorer glasses.

By Pete Brown

SUNGLASSES

Your most prized possession is your eyesight. Your efficiency as a wage earner, your safety and welfare and your happiness depend on your ability to see clearly and quickly. You should, therefore, take every possible precaution to protect your eyes from injury at all times.

A potential source of eye discomfort and eye damage is to spend long hours outdoors in bright sunlight without proper eye protection. It is true that man's eyes were designed for outdoor use. However, our eye troubles began when man became an indoor dweller, subjecting his eyes to long hours of close work under relatively poor light conditions. As a result, eye protection is needed in bright sunlight. Those who spend most of their lives outdoors become accustomed to the brighter light and do not need eye protection.

Every outdoorsman and sports lover should know how to protect his eyes under conditions of bright sunshine by the use of effective sunglasses. Sunglasses are spectacles using various types of colored or tinted lenses to protect the eye against damage from strong sunlight. The colors or tints are produced by adding colorant to the batch of optical glass during its manufacture.

The proper choice of a sunglass will make your outdoor hours doubly enjoyable by eliminating all discomfort, irritation, squint and possible damage to your delicate eye tissues, thus giving you better vision. Conversely, poor sunglasses will not only fail to protect but may in themselves cause additional discomfort and damage.

There is nothing mysterious or too difficult to understand about how a good tinted lens protects your eyes. It does so in two ways: (1) It reduces the total amount of light that enters the eye and (2) it filters out certain rays of the sun that are either harmful or not useful for vision. That's all there is to the theory behind the use of sunglasses.

The first requirement for an effective tinted lens for general outdoor use in bright sunlight is that it filters out and protects the eye from dangerous (and useless for vision) ultraviolet and infra-red rays. Filtering out these rays produces two beneficial results: (1) Prevents injury and promotes comfort; (2) increases visual acuity because the vision-blurring ultraviolet rays are screened out.

In addition to removing the dangerous rays, a tinted lens for general outdoor use should materially reduce glare. Glare is merely excessive light or brightness to the point of causing eye discomfort due to blurred vision, squinting, irritation, etc. Tinted lenses remove glare by reducing the amount of light that enters the eye. This reduction depends on the shade density of the lens.

Shade densities are designated by letters or numbers, depending on the manufacturer. Thus the letters A, B, C, D and the numbers 1, 2, 3, 4 designate light transmission of 75 per cent, 50 per cent, 25 per cent and 10 per cent respectively. Thus a "C" or "3" shade admits only 25 per cent of the light; and a "D" or "4" shade only 10 per cent of the light.

Lastly, a tinted lens for general outdoor use, especially for driving, should not seriously impair color discrimination. This may cause confusion in distinguishing colors of traffic signals.

Sunglasses should be chosen as carefully as a pair of corrective spectacles. Do not use the cheap plastic and celluloid or molded-glass type. Get a pair with optically perfect lenses of high-quality optical glass. The cheap ones not only give you poor protection but will cause eyestrain due to distortions produced by the faulty lenses.

There are hundreds of shades and colors of sunglasses available. How can one possibly choose the right type?

By far the most effective, and most popular, tinted lens for general outdoor use is the yellow-green type. This type filters out (that is, refuses to pass) almost all the potentially harmful ultraviolet and infra-red rays. Colors are distorted but little, there being no confusion distinguishing traffic lights. They are manufactured in various degrees of density. Well-known and reliable brands are the American Optical "Calobar" in shades B, C and D, and the Bausch and Lomb "Ray-Ban" in shades 1, 2, 3 and 4. There are many other reputable brands such as the "Ozark Green" of Mitchell Optical Company, the "Contra-glare" of the Titmus Optical Company, the "Aviation Glass" of Willson Products, Inc., and other lesser-known but reliable brands.

These yellow-green tinted lenses in appropriate shade will transform an irritating, uncomfortable and hot scene into a beautifully cool and comfortable view. With these yellow-green lenses you will actually see better because they cut out the blurring ultraviolet rays and because they reduce glare by reducing the amount of light that enters the eye. They pass the greatest amount of light in the green and yellow portion of the visible spectrum, thus following very closely the sensitivity of the eye.

Routine use of this yellow-green lens outdoors in bright sunlight is strongly recommended. If you wear glasses routinely, have your sunglasses ground to the same prescription. "Hook-ons" also are available but are not as desirable as separate spectacles, since they introduce and multiply reflections.

There are many colors of sunglasses other than the yellow-green on the market. The yellow-green is probably the best all-around tinted lens for routine outdoor use in bright sunlight. Select a shade that will give you maximum comfort and visibility for your eyes under the conditions you will meet.

A very fine special-purpose glass is the yellow-green polaroid. This is a "sandwich" lens consisting of two lenses of yellow-green glass with a center insert of "polaroid" material. With this glass, in addition to the protection given by the yellow-green lens, there is a marked reduction in reflected glare. These are wonderful for driving. They materially decrease road glare and the glare from approaching cars. They are available in the various shade densities above described.

The yellow-green sunglasses are also excellent shooting glasses; both for target or game shooting, with rifle, pistol or shotgun. They sharpen up your vision, reduce glare, prevent eyestrain and lessen fatigue. For shooting you may need a shade lighter than for general outdoor use.

An interesting lens being widely exploited is the yellow tint. This lens should not be used as a general outdoor sunglass. It is purely a special-purpose lens for use under conditions where the light is poor. These yellow lenses are wonderful at twilight or on overcast days for routine outdoor use or for shooting. They increase visual acuity and transform a dull, dark scene into a vivid, bright one. Do not use these in bright sunlight.

A word of caution about the use of sunglasses under conditions other than in bright sunshine "à la Hollywood." Do not use any type of sunglass routinely indoors unless your eye doctor has prescribed it. Routine use of dark glasses indoors will seriously harm your eyes. They will become habit forming so that your eyes will become less and less able to stand bright outdoor light. The light indoors is dim enough—so don't make it worse by wearing dark glasses!

Don't be too proud to wear sunglasses. They are an adjunct to pleasant living. You will increase your outdoor enjoyment manifold if you cultivate the use of a good sunglass. If you need help in selecting a good sunglass, consult your physician or optometrist. The results will be worth the effort. Don't take chances with your most valuable possession—your eyesight!

By A. M. Libasci, M.D.

SLEEPING BAGS

No sleeping bag or clothing produces any warmth. In the absence of a fire the human body is the only heat-producing machine in a camp. The normal man, sleeping or loafing, liberates approximately 50 calories of heat per hour. This can be increased (a) By exercise. Violent exercise may increase the output as much as 16 times. Shivering, a form of muscular exercise, will increase the heat output several times, and is nature's method of preventing freezing. (b) By eating. The increase is quick but of short duration for carbohydrates, greater and more lasting for proteins.

The skin automatically shuts off surface blood circulation when exposed to cold, and decreases the heat loss from the skin as much as a fourth of normal. Alcoholic drinks prevent this natural thermostat from functioning properly and result in rapid heat loss. Wind, equally with low temperature, produces chilling and rapid loss of bodily warmth.

Therefore all that a sleeping bag or any article of clothing can do is to prevent or delay the loss of bodily warmth by producing insulation that will retain the warmth inside, and protect from wind. The most effective heat insulation known is dry, still air. Thus the effectiveness of a sleeping bag in enabling one to retain his normal bodily warmth is in direct proportion to its *thickness* and not its weight. The thicker a garment is, and the "fluffier" its nature, the more dead air it contains.

Fifty years ago sleeping bags consisted of several thicknesses of wool blankets sewed into bag form, with an outer bag of canvas. They were merely a convenient way of preventing the kicking off of blankets during sleep. The insulating value of a blanket is in direct proportion to the looseness of its weave when it is sheltered from wind. Army blankets are closely woven for durability and are not nearly as warm as Hudson's Bay blankets.

Modern sleeping bags utilize more effective insulating material that is both thicker and lighter than blankets, therefore containing much more dead air space. The best insulating material is genuine down which is pretty expensive. Some makers mix in a few duck feathers with the down, reducing both the expense and the insulating properties. But you still have a good bag. Next in insulating value probably come the new synthetic materials, such as Dacron, which are light, durable and mothproof. After these, wool in the form of batting, and kapok. The down, feathers or batting must be enclosed in a light but very closely woven fabric from which it cannot escape, and this fabric container should be sewed into tubes so the stuffing will not shift, but will be of uniform thickness throughout.

Outside of this insulating bag is a light but closely woven cover which should be water-resistant, fairly windproof, but *must not be waterproof*. If the cover were waterproof it would confine the vapor that the body constantly throws off, and make the bag cold, clammy and smelly.

Usually there is no inside lining, the sleeper being in contact with the shell that contains the down or other filler. Some of the better bags intended for arctic use have a thin, all-wool flannel inside liner that adds to weight, bulk, warmth and comfort. There is no particular objection to pinning cotton or linen sheets inside any bag for cleanliness.

Now we come to the $64 question. What kind of a bag and what weight (and consequent thickness) of insulating material will a camper need to sleep comfortably at the minimum night temperature he expects? This cannot be answered definitely because individuals differ greatly in the amount of bedding they require to keep in their body heat. However, very generally speaking, the bags filled with wool batting and kapok offered by our leading sleeping bag manufacturers are quite satisfactory for ordinary summer

camping where night temperatures do not g[o] below 40° F. Such bags are much less expen[-] sive than those filled with down.

As yet we lack practical experience wit[h] the new bags filled with Dacron and simila[r] synthetic materials, although the moth- mold- and mildew-proof qualities are ver[y] attractive. The bags containing three to fou[r] pounds of a mixture of down and duc[k] feathers are usually satisfactory down t[o] almost zero.

For fall hunting in the North, and at hig[h] altitudes in our Rockies with temperature[s] of −10° F. to −20° F., about four to fiv[e] pounds of down are required. About five t[o] six pounds of down, a flannel inside linin[g] and some ground insulation under the ai[r] mattress, such as a blanket or an animal skin are needed for arctic conditions. *Provide[d] that* in all the above cases, at the minimu[m] temperature to be expected, the campe[r] turns in, clad in dry wool underwear or dr[y] flannel pajamas; that he have some kind of [a] soft mattress under his bag so that his weigh[t] will not compress the contained still air ou[t] of the underside of his bag; and that his ba[g] is sheltered from the wind under a tent o[r] a tarp spread over the bag.

At the lowest temperatures the campe[r] should sleep with the top of his bag pulle[d] up over his head, and with just a small hol[e] poked through the covering through whic[h] he can breath suitably. The heavier down[-] filled bags will be uncomfortably warm whe[n] night temperatures are above about 45° F[.] but this trouble is easily overcome by sleep[-] ing with the head, arms and chest outsid[e] the bag, and it is always best to choose [a] bag suitable for the lowest expected temper[-] atures.

Several outfitters supply a "Mountai[n] Down Bag" with only two pounds of down[n] and weighing complete about 3½ pound[s] rolling into a very small bundle. Such bag[s] are intended chiefly for alpine climbers wh[o] have to pack all their equipment on thei[r] backs in steep country, but they offer won[-] derful possibilities in "go-light" equipment[.] Our experienced mountain climbers hav[e] found that these are satisfactory down t[o] about −10° F., provided they are used in a small alpine tent with some kind of a soft mattress under them, and at minimum temperatures the camper turns in, clad in all his outdoor clothing which should be dry.

These mountain bags are made coffin shape, that is about 18 inches wide at the bottom, and about 34 inches wide at the top, to economize in weight and bulk. One is thus encased like a mummy, and when he turns over during sleep the whole bag turns with him on top of the mattress or the floor cloth of the tent. This is not objectionable once one becomes accustomed to it. Other bags are usually rectangular, about 34 to 36 inches wide, top to bottom. These also will often cling and turn over during sleep because the inner lining is not as slippery as the sheets in one's bed at home, but this is easily obviated, and the bag will remain upright on its mattress if the camper, when he turns over, will press down with his hands on the two sides of the bag as he turns. After a night or two this comes to be second nature. A large man, six feet or over, will find bags 40 inches wide or over much more comfortable than the 36-inch width.

Maximum comfort is attained when one has an air mattress under his bag, which requires only about five minutes to inflate, while a browse mattress would take about half an hour to make properly, and then would mat down so as to be uncomfortably hard after the first night. Smooth off the ground on which the bed is to be, lay a poncho or ground cloth on the spot, inflate the air mattress only so full that when pressing down hard on it with the fist the ground can be felt under it and then lay the sleeping bag on top.

Good air mattresses are those that are only 48 inches long by 24 to 26 inches wide. These will support the shoulders and hips which is all that is necessary. They are cheaper, lighter (about 3½ pounds) and quicker to inflate than the full-length mattress. Also one is less apt to roll off them during the night. They should be located just under the shoulders and hips, with some browse, leaves, brush or a blanket to level off under the head and legs. The stability given by this last leveling off of the sleeping surface seems always to eliminate all tendency to roll off the mattress during the night, but any kind of a four-inch log, or even a couple of large rocks placed at either side of the bed, will also keep everything in position.

Many sleeping bags are provided with an awning attached to the cover which can be erected as a shelter over the head, and with a pocket on the underside of the bag for the air mattress. You don't need any awning over the head of your bag if you have it in a tent or under a tarp as you should to protect from wind. The awning flap, though, can be used when you're rolling up your bag for carrying, and this eliminates the need of a special sleeping bag container. And the air mattress pocket isn't necessary if your bed is arranged as described earlier in this article.

As a last shot in the dark, you will never know the ultimate in cold-weather sleeping comfort until you adopt a good goose down bag with adequate thickness of filler, a 48-inch long air mattress, a light tarp or poncho to go under both, and turn in in flannel pajamas. My guess is that you will find this combination more comfortable than your bed at home.

By Col. Townsend Whelen

CHAPTER **13**

pack trips

A MAN moving across wilderness country either on foot or on horseback is almost as independent as it is possible to be in this day and age. With all his necessities stowed in his pack or saddlebags he can utilize the materials of the woods to make his home—swiftly and comfortably—when and where he pleases. The steady tramp of his boots or his horse's hooves quickly eat up the miles and the days are long and filled with a thousand interesting incidents of the outdoors. It's no wonder trails all over the nation are seeing more campers heading away from civilization. In this chapter is all the information you need to take off into the wilderness either alone or with your family—on foot or on horseback.

HIKING

Each summer thousands of young people, and oldsters as well, are spending their vacations on the Appalachian and Pacific Coast Trails, in our national parks and forests, or in little pieces of wild country near their homes. In beautiful and healthy localities they wander foot-loose with a freedom that can be experienced in no other way. They pack their entire outfit and food on their backs, and are dependent on no one.

There is nothing particularly new in this. It has been going on for years. But recently new methods and new equipment have been developed that rid it of all the former hard work. In the past many have found backpacking not at all to their liking—too much hard work—all because of improper

At left above is the Bergan's type of frame rucksack, and at the right is the Alaska packboard, the two methods of carrying most advocated by experts for their comfort on lightweight trips. The rucksack has an advantage over the packboard in that its contents are easily reached whereas the entire packboard must be unbound to reach a single item. However, the packboard will carry objects of any shape or dimensions without irritating the carrier's back. Both distribute the weight on straps across the small of the back, just above the hips. The rucksack is more costly.

equipment and methods. Many who attempt it once never repeat it. And yet those who have adopted those best ways formerly known only to a few, are repeating it year after year, taking their children along, and the children now are going it on their own hook. Many are combining the hiking and camping with hunting and fishing in country and at a cost they could not otherwise attempt.

Hiking is not just for the strenuous young men. It is entirely applicable to wives, teen agers of both sexes, and the aged; in fact anyone from eight to 80.

In the past, a lot of hikers overloaded themselves under the impression they needed a lot of stuff to avoid hardships. If you adopt the right articles, and use them in the right way there are no hardships. There are two slogans the backpacker must adopt: "Go light but right," and "When in doubt leave it out." Your basic pack to shelter you, keep you warm, dry and comfortable, and prepare your food need not and should not weigh more than 14 or 15 pounds, even for cold weather. Proper food for such vacations will net just about 2¼ pounds per man per day. If you are a husky young fellow and used to hiking, 35 pounds is a sensible maximum limit for your backpack on rough mountain trails. You can do eight to 12 miles a day with that without fatigue, and that means you can carry 10-days' food in country where no replacement en route is possible. If you can count on game and fish from the country you can extend your vacation almost indefinitely. Ladies and youngsters must grade their maximum pack weights down to about 20 or 25 pounds. These weights are nothing at all if your pack and your methods are right.

THE BEST PACK

It must be right. You will find inexperienced people advising that the pack should be carried high up on the shoulders. All wrong. It unbalances you if carried high, and makes your footing in rough country uncertain. It should sag down and be carried mostly on the broad of the hips. Also it should not overheat or abrade the back, and the shoulder straps, pressing down and not back on the shoulders, should be wide and soft. Those who have had many years of packing, who have studied the subject, and who have been able to get the best, choose between two principal types of packs which they regard as really satisfactory for all-day packing, day after day.

One of the best packs is the frame rucksack of the Bergan's type which is used practically exclusively by all alpinists and mountaineers, and has been so used for the past 40 years. It was also adapted by our Army for mountain packing in World War II. It consists of a durable, waterproof canvas sack about 22 by 20 by eight inches. On the outside of this main sack are two side pockets, about 12 by six by two inches, and a flat outside rear pocket for clothing, etc., about 12 by nine by two inches. A flap covers the main sack, and there are provisions for tying a roll of bedding on the top or under the flap. On the side toward the back, a triangular frame of aluminum tubing is fitted, with the apex of the triangle at the top where the shoulder straps are attached. Across the bottom of the triangle a broad web strap rests on the hips. The rucksack rides low, most of the weight is on the hips, and it hardly touches the back at all so there is constant air circulation between the pack and your back. Bulky articles such as food and cooking utensils go on the large center sack, the heavier ones at the bottom and toward your back. Small articles and odds and ends go in the two side pockets, and clothing is packed flat in the outside back pocket. The bedding, poncho and plastic tarp are rolled into a bundle about five by 20 inches, tied with short cords (which serve also to erect the shelter poles) and tied on top of the whole pack, usually under the flap.

The Bergan's type of frame rucksack is made of very serviceable materials by at least two camping outfitters, and there is also an Army model which is very good and can sometimes be found in Army-surplus stores. The fine commercial ones are rather expensive, but well worth their price.

Another preferred type of pack is the Alaskan packboard, or the commercial type of it known as the Trapper Nelson Packboard. The latter is made in three sizes—get the medium size. There is also a military model, well made of plywood, but it is now hard to find in surplus stores. This packboard is the type preferred by the trappers, prospectors and hunters of our Northwest, Canada and the Canadian Northwest. It will carry unbelievably heavy loads. Hard articles like a sack of ore, or an outboard motor can be packed on it without hurting the back. It consists of a wood frame on which a canvas cover is tightly laced, and on the back side are broad shoulder straps. There is about a 1½-inch space between the taut canvas on either side, and only the canvas touches the back. It sags down on the lower back and hips, feeling much as though a canvas cot was pressed against the back. The load, everything, is rolled up in the poncho, tarp and bedding, into a roll approximately 18 by 12 by 24 inches, and this is tied onto the back of the packboard. The packboard is very good, is much less expensive than the frame rucksack, and is very popular. However, to get at anything in the pack en route the whole bundle must be unpacked, while with the frame rucksack articles are much more accessible in the various pockets.

BEDDING

This is the bulkiest article you carry in or on your pack, and as mentioned above, it is usually rolled and tied on top of the rucksack, or used to enclose the bundle of everything on the packboard. The bedding you need to assure comfortable and warm sleep depends on the night temperature and whether you are one of those who heap on the comforters at home. Not so much is needed for summer camping as you would suppose, except at high altitudes. For summer camping where temperatures don't go much below 45 degrees a three-pound Army blanket with a poncho under it is usually enough if you are a young and rugged individual. On the colder nights you roll up with most of your clothing on. See that bedding and clothing have been dried before the campfire or in the sun. Nothing is worse than trying to sleep in sweaty, damp clothing. If you require more bedding than this, particularly if your vacation is in the late fall or at high

altitudes, the warmest for its weight and bulk which comes within our weight restrictions is the alpine or mountain sleeping bag that contains two pounds of goose down and that with its lining weighs about 3½ to four pounds. This is the bag preferred by experienced alpinists who camp in regions of ice and snow. If you take precautions as to dryness it will keep a sturdy fellow warm almost down to zero when out of the wind. The cover is so light it is not very durable, and it is advisable to have a sheet of light plastic to go under it and protect it from ground dampness and the bough mattress. It also is rather expensive, but like the frame rucksack, is well worth its cost.

It is possible to obtain a vinylite air mattress 24 by 48 inches which weighs only 28 ounces, but it will add just that much more weight and bulk. Almost every place you camp you can make a fine mattress of balsam, spruce or hemlock boughs, or in localities where the cutting of boughs is prohibited by forest regulations, you can scrape together a good enough mattress of pine needles, moss and grass, hollowing out just shallow depressions in the ground for your shoulders and hips.

SHELTER

A very fine alpine or mountain tent, fully enclosed and bugproof, is available with many camp outfitters, but it weighs at least four pounds, and is very expensive. Our most experienced hikers have found that a tent is not at all necessary, in fact very undesirable due to its cost, weight and bulk. Instead there is a Koroseal poncho which weighs only a pound, with practically no bulk, that can be erected over your bed as a lean-to at an angle of 45 degrees, so it not only shelters from rain, but also reflects the heat of a campfire in front down on the bed, and it also serves perfectly as a raincoat, covering not only you but your pack. Exit the expensive and heavy tent. Don't try to drag civilization along with you. Half of the joy of your trip will be in getting down close to Nature.

This is what the hiker's overnight camp should look like, with a tarp lean-to instead of a heavy tent. The lean-to serves as a shelter in wet weather, and reflects heat from a fire in front.

COOK KIT

You need two kettles, one for tea or coffee, and one for cereals, boiling and stews. Camp outfitters have excellent little aluminum pots with covers and bales. Your two kettles should nest, the largest being five by six inches, and the two together weigh no more than 17 ounces. Inside the smallest you put your enamel cup and supply of tea or coffee. Also carry a little aluminum fry-pan, eight inches in diameter with folding handle, weighing no more than eight ounces. It also doubles as your plate. And then a tablespoon. This outfit will serve for two campers, with the additions of an aluminum plate apiece and another cup and spoon, and thus the total weight and bulk is divided between two packers.

There is another article you may want to take along because with the above minimum utensils—biscuits, bread and roasts are difficult to cook and these are much appreciated in the hikers' camp. The "Knapsacker" folding aluminum baker, which folds to 9¼ by 11½ by 1½ inches and weighs 26 ounces will do these jobs to perfection. So far as is

By going light, the pack's contents for a week's trip can be cut down to the bare essentials, yet still be enough to enable you to make a comfortable camp each night.

known, it can be had only from Smilie Outfits, at 536 Mission Street, San Francisco, Cal. It is well worth taking for a party of two or three, but its weight and bulk cuts it out for the lone hiker.

There are a few other necessary items for your pack. A one-pound hand ax with whetstone will suffice for up to three hikers. Each should of course have the lightest toilet kit he can get along with, which should include a small towel, and perhaps a cathartic, a few Band-Aids and one roller bandage. Each should carry a change of underwear and socks, for the end of the day almost inevitably finds the hiker in a pretty sweaty condition, and a rubdown with a change of underwear is very necessary to avoid an evening chill. So also is a very light windbreaker jacket, or a wool overshirt. Somewhere there should be a can of dry matches.

You will be tempted to add a lot of weighty and bulky gadgets. Don't do it. Don't take anything that will not pay for itself day after day in essential use. For example, a forked stick makes a good enough fork and your jackknife will do for a table and butcher knife. An electric flashlight seems necessary, although campers got along okay for hundreds of years without one. A piece of candle will supply minimum light and save on matches when it comes to lighting a fire in rain or wind.

CLOTHING WORN

No special clothing is necessary. Almost all experienced hikers wear blue denim or khaki trousers without bottom cuffs, a stout overshirt of cotton that will stand the pull of shoulder straps, any old felt hat, summer underwear and heavy wool socks. Footwear, however, is very important, and should be amply large to fit the feet when they become swollen from long walking over rough ground, as they always do from the increased blood supply drawn to them. Canvas sneakers with corrugated rubber soles and six-inch tops are fine except for sharp rock country. About the best are the light leather oiled moccasin shoes with six-inch tops and a crepe rubber, or heavily cleated rubber sole to avoid slipping in steep going.

BASIC OUTFIT

So you have your complete outfit, less your grub, which is always with you, and which you should do your darnedest to keep down to a weight of not more than 15 pounds. It will be about as follows:

	Ounces
Frame rucksack or packboard	50
Goose down mountain sleeping bag	56
Featherweight poncho and plastic tarp	20
Cooking utensils, matches	32
Hand ax and whetstone	16
Underwear, socks, windbreaker	32
Toilet kit, first-aid kit	12
Total	218

(about 14 pounds)

In your pockets you will naturally have such things as a watch, pocket compass, handkerchief, dark glasses, jackknife, tobacco and matches.

OPTIONAL EQUIPMENT

You will undoubtedly add certain special equipment, but keep this down to the very limit. Thus if you are on a hunting trip you will probably add a rifle, ammunition and cleaning kit. If you are fishing, and most of us do, you will add fish line, hooks and sinkers, and if you are not counting on cutting a pole at the stream you may not be happy without your pet rod, reel, flies or plugs. Rifle and rod are usually carried in the hand and they do not count in the basic pack weight. Then almost everyone will want a camera and films, and the little 35mm cameras have the least bulk and weight, and are very versatile. Perhaps a party of two or three will share one camera.

FOOD

So much for your basic outfit, which is always with you on your day-to-day hikes, and which will serve you from year to year. Not more than 15 pounds. So we come to the all-important item of food. You may have to carry supplies for the entire period of your trip, unless your route passes close by places where you can buy a replenishment. If you are rugged, and figure you can start out with a total pack weight of 35 pounds, then you will be able to stock up with 20 pounds of food at the start. Very long experience has shown that a man exercising hard in open air requires 2¼ pounds of water-free and nourishing food per day to maintain vigor, health and enjoyment. Thus 20 pounds will last just about 10 days, not including the meal as you start, and as you return to civilization.

Further, long experience has shown that this 2¼ pounds should be composed of the following classes of foods:

	Pounds
Cereals: Oatmeal, corn meal, hominy grits, flour, baking powder, crackers, rice, spaghetti, milk powder	.45
Sweets: Sugar, syrup, sweet chocolate	.40
Meats: Bacon, ham, Canadian bacon, dried beef, smoked salmon, cheese	.70
Fruit and vegetables: Dried prunes, apricots, apples, figs, dates, raisins, dehydrated vegetables	.35
Fats: Butter, lard, peanut butter	.15
Beverages: Tea, coffee, cocoa, bouillon	.10
Seasoning: Salt, pepper, onion and celery salt	.10
Total	2.25

You should take only those foods that you like, and that you know how to cook with your small kit of kettles and pan. Experiment at home to see how much of each food you need to make a satisfactory portion for one meal.

Note that all the above foods are water-free, or almost so. No sense in carrying water, and canned goods weigh entirely too much. You will have to use a can or two for such foods as bacon and lard. Most of the rest can go in small plastic grub sacks that you can get from camp outfitters. In recent years excellent dehydrated foods are being offered, simple to prepare, and packed in waterproof envelopes with instructions printed thereon. They are fine for economizing in weight and bulk, and some of them are precooked which is a considerable advantage. By all means investigate them, and furthermore experiment with them at home

before you include them to see that they are appetizing and nourishing.

If you are going to hike through or camp in a country where game and fish or wild fruits can be obtained your store food supply can be supplemented to last you much longer than a day for each 2¼ pounds.

All kinds of combinations suggest themselves to the backpacking camper. For example, what housewife would think of serving her man a mush made by putting salt, sugar, butter, minced dates or apricots into hot water, bringing to a boil, and then stirring oatmeal in to make a fairly thick mush. And yet mountaineers will gobble it with gusto.

And so at the end of the paved trail you leave behind you the bustle, noise, stink and expense of civilization, shoulder your pack and stride into the beautiful and unspoiled country. There is no kind of vacation that will compare with it, none that will bring you so close to peace and utter freedom.

By Col. Townsend Whelen

PACK HORSE TRIPS

The first step in preparing for a pack-horse trip is to decide what country you want to travel. Get a state map from a service station. Most oil company maps show names and boundaries of national forests, but are too small except for locating the particular forests within the general region you expect to visit.

Next, write to the Information Division, U.S. Forest Service, Washington 25, D.C., requesting available maps and pamphlets on forests in the selected locality. These will give a lot of good information for the preliminary planning of your trip. They'll aid in any correspondence with outfitters. You can almost figure out just where your camp will be and what area you'll hunt.

Names of outfitters and guides can be secured from the several state publicity or game and fish offices at state capitols. Some states put out lists of licensed guides. Or write the chamber of commerce, nearest town of size, in the area. Or write the local forest supervisor; his headquarters will be on the material you get from the USFS.

Query those outfitters who seem to offer most nearly what you would like to have in service and equipment. You can leave all planning and details to the right sort of operator. But if you know what goes into planning a pack trip, making it run smoothly, you can be more certain about preparations fitting your requirements.

A rough rule of thumb is one pack animal for each two men in the party. The acceptable outfitter has not only animals that can carry the packs but also tackle for the job. The pack-saddle with breast and breeching straps, a decent saddle blanket and stout panniers are essential to good packing. Anyone who starts to throw a pack on a stock saddle, with gunny sacks as panniers, runs a haywire outfit.

The condition of saddle tackle is a good indication of the way an outfit is operated. Riding saddles may be old and worn, but they should be in good, usable condition. The saddle you use should be long enough between pommel and cantle to furnish an easy seat but not so big it allows too much excess space. The stirrups should be just long enough so that you can raise yourself an inch or so out of the seat. The horses should be mountain-wise. They'll probably not be pedigreed but a mixture of strains to get a short-coupled, stout animal of about 1,000 to 1,200 pounds. The skittish, spooky horse has no place on a pack trip, either under a stock saddle or a pack.

Any outfitter worthy of the name will have done a thorough job of checking the shoes on his horses. If you see the stock has been freshly shod, at least a portion of the horses newly fitted, you can bank on your host knowing his trail travel. These are the four major divisions of organization in putting together an outfit for back-country camping. The camp tools, particularly an ax, gas lanterns for lights, pots, pans, dishes and eating tools are lined up to meet requirements of the party.

Any intelligent help in putting the packs together will be welcome. Even a greenhorn will know that canned foods should be packed in the bottom of the panniers and that you don't put the eggs in their productive packing at the bottom. The guest who is willing to do his share under direction is welcome. The fellow who sits around and indicates that since he paid his price, he's going to get his money's worth by letting the crew do every stitch of work, doesn't increase his popularity.

You'll have your own preferences in gun, cartridges, binocular, hunting knife, tinted sunglasses, field camera and the like. Be sure to take along a waterproof pocket match container and keep it filled. A flashlight is mighty handy in camp. Your toilet supplies can be cut down to a toothbrush and dentifrice, a bar of soap and your towels. Whatever you add above that is your choice. I'd certainly carry a colorless lipstick to prevent painful chapping of lips.

There are some important points in selecting your clothing. Several medium- or light-weight layers are warmer and more comfortable than one heavy garment. A knit, sleeveless sweater supplies a lot of warmth under an outer jacket or shirt that will turn wind. Laced boots should not be the high-legged sort; they bind the calf muscles. A 10-inch top is sufficient; you can tie pant legs over these and get by in snow of considerable depth. Make certain the boot does not pinch in on the big tendon at your heel; you can be crippled in a few hours of walking with a boot that bruises this tendon. Socks should be mediumweight wool; two pairs rather than one thick one. In zero weather, two pairs of socks, a sheepskin pac over these, a four-buckle rubber overshoe over the pac is a good combination which will fend off chilblains—but you probably will not be traveling in such weather in the West, and you'd be pretty foolish to try it.

Finally, there is the question of cost. At one end of the scale is the cheap service of the haywire outfit, slapped together to snag all the traffic will bear. At the other is the outfitter who caters to the gold-plated plutocrat who demands urban comforts in wilderness locations. The best value lies in between these extremes.

By Arthur H. Carhart

A well-ordered pack string.

THE WESTERN SADDLE HORSE

Pack trips can either be a standout experience—or they can be a pretty tough ordeal. It all depends on how much you know. The pages that follow show you how to handle the horse that will carry you.

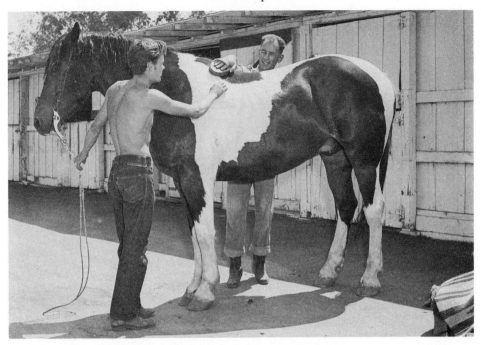

The saddle area on your horse must be brushed first, to clear it of burrs, twigs or anything that might affect the saddle horse as a wrinkle in the stocking, or a stone in the shoe, might irritate you.

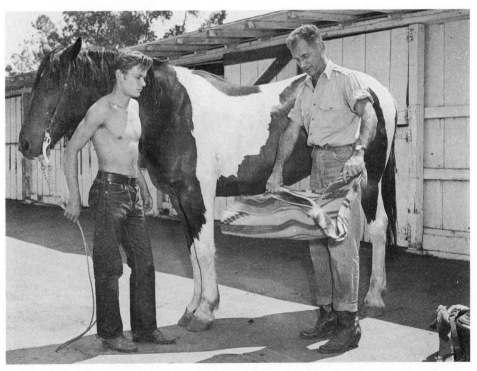

Even the hand will do to brush the horse's back before the saddle blanket is put in place. Most outfitters include a currycomb and brush as part of their inventory when on an extended trip. Shake out and smooth out blanket well before putting on back of horse.

The blanket must go well forward on the shoulders of the horse. Thus it will cushion the saddle completely and not slide to the rear. Make certain, too, that it is even on both sides, so that it cannot work out.

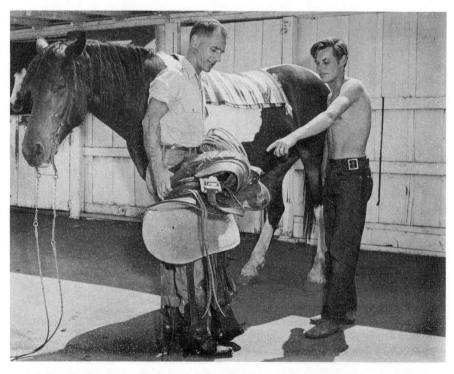

Although there are wranglers to handle the horses on any trip into mountain country, they will appreciate some aid from the "dudes" if the dudes know what they are doing. If they don't know, they are nothing more than a hindrance. Work on left side.

The saddle is put on from the left side, as is almost everything done around a horse, but it is sometimes necessary to go to the off-side to handle straps, as in this picture. Careful that the horse doesn't "suck in wind" when you start girdling him in middle!

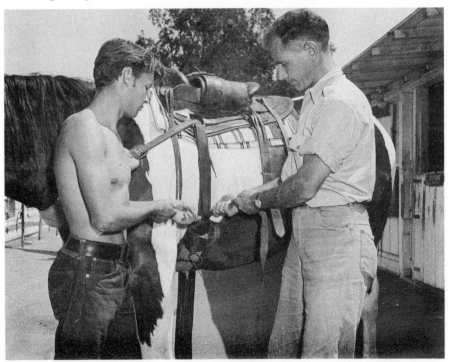

Draw the cinch strap tight under the chest, and just behind the forelegs, and pull the latigo through the left cinch ring. This is the strap that holds rider, and saddle on top of horse, and it's quite important!

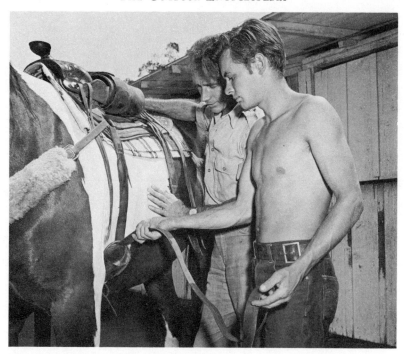

The latigo strap, the long leather one held here by the wrangler, is so long that it will go at least twice from the cinch ring on the cinch (or bellyband) to the ring on the saddle. Keep making circuits through the rings with strap until knot is all left.

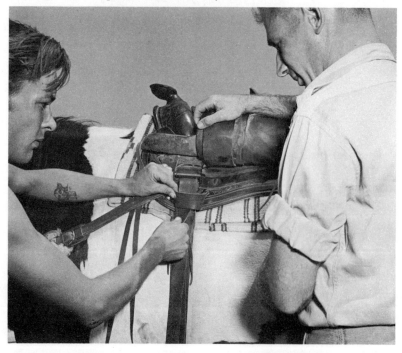

This knot is all-important, but easy to tie. It's all a matter of through the ring with the leather, around the strap on the outside, through the ring from right, and down through the loop—much like tying necktie.

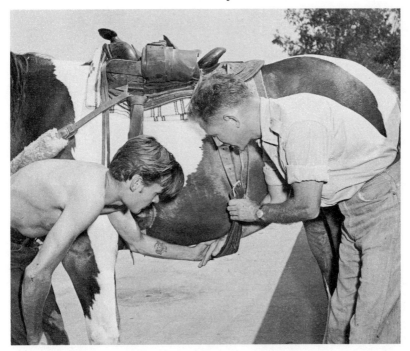

This may look too loose to you, but it's just right for purpose. It is the rear cinch strap (which is not found on all saddles), and it should not be adjusted tightly. Hand must run through easily.

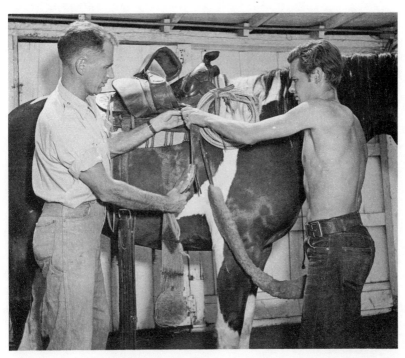

Some final adjustments of stirrup straps for length and you are almost ready to go. The lariat is coiled in place, and the cushioned breast band is put in place. These steps are in preparation for the final cinching shown in earlier pictures.

This is just about it, everything pretty much in place, lariat ready, fastened to the pommel, the bands all tightened except for breast band, and the next step is: what shall we add to the load?

Well, a rifle seems the next step if it is a hunting trip, and there are several ways of mounting the scabbard, or rifle boot, that are favored in different sections. If on the right side of horse, the scabbard usually passes through lariat.

This method of hanging the rifle from the saddle is in favor in the wooded, steep Rocky Mountain country, both in the states and in Canada. It can be on either side, but left is best for dismount hunting.

This is the high western mount so popular in open country—and, it might be added, in western movies. In wooded country it would catch on branches. It can scare the horse, too, if pulled out suddenly. Good for quick shots made from saddle.

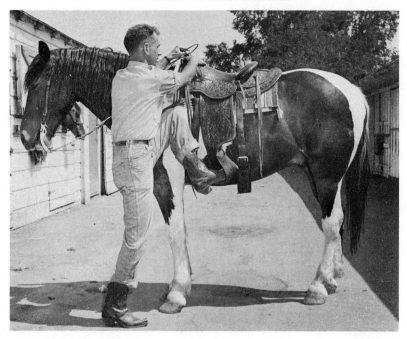

Now, you are all ready to swing into the saddle. It's somewhat like getting on a moving bus or trolley—face to rear, grab a handful of reins, mane, hair and take a graceful spring up and on.

Using the left arm for leverage, the dude pulls himself up, and over, not quite as they do it in western movies, but he gets there more or less without scrambling. At this point he will learn if his saddle is on firmly enough, or if it slips.

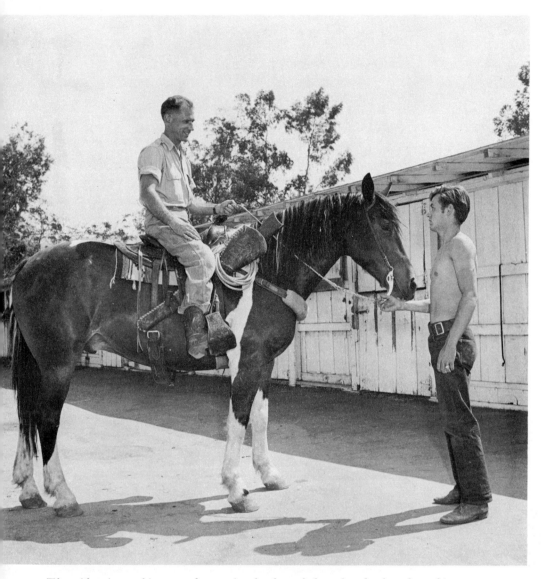

The rider is on his way, happy in the knowledge that he has done his own saddling, and that it is done right at least by his own standards. If anything happens from now on out, he has himself to blame.

CHAPTER 14

photography

To MANY outdoorsmen, the camera is simply an accessory to his favorite sport of hunting, fishing, hiking, packing or canoeing. Its chief use is probably to make a trophy record of his outings. Like his other camping equipment, it must be lightweight and easily portable and it must be rugged. There is no place for the bulky view camera and lead-heavy tripods. If the camera is to be taken afield, it must be unobtrusive enough to be stowed away in the jacket pocket, slipped into a pack or suspended from neck or shoulder within easy reach so that it can be adjusted quickly for lens aperture and shutter speed and made ready for instant trigger-finger action whenever a picture opportunity presents itself.

Tremendous interest in photography has resulted in the birth of a large number of still cameras, ranging widely in price, size, quality and ability to perform. Many have accessories and refinements which certainly must baffle the beginner trying to make his first important selection.

Which camera, he asks, should be chosen? Which, then, is best?

Most sportsmen will tell you that the ideal camera for outdoor use is yet to be born. Some manufacturers have hit close, but the needs of the picture-clicking outdoorsman are so varied and his whims so rapidly changing there is little hope that a camera ever will be built which will please all who hunt and fish and pursue wildlife.

THE CAMERA

Once considered only a toy, the miniature camera is popular among outdoor photographers because most minicam lenses have short focal lengths and consequently great depth of focus. This practically insures sharp pictures when smaller f/stops are used.

The diminutive camera also is good for filming wildlife by remote control. Housed in a substantial case, well-anchored beside a game trail, the outfit is small enough to hide from view and yet withstand considerable abuse. Some sportsmen have had excellent success with 35mm in shooting flash pictures of deer and bear at night, particularly where the animal takes his own portrait by stumbling against a hidden thread or releasing the baited shutter cord.

In addition to its lightness and portability, the 35mm is also economical to operate. Film cost per picture is low as compared with other makes and sizes, but here economy is effective only when the cameraman exercises the same care and patience in shooting a 35mm scene as he would if he were exposing a 4x5 or 8x10 plate. Because of the lower film cost per roll, the tendency is to photograph anything and everything to finish off all the exposures and get a quick glimpse at the first few frames. As a result, the ratio between well-planned, high-quality negatives and total exposures made begins to dip rapidly.

The higher-priced 35mm cameras are precision-built and offer a multitude of accessory lenses, rangefinders and other useful gadget-bag miscellany, which leads one to wonder whether the 35mm finally has begun to lose its featherweight claim for fame.

Perhaps the chief disadvantage of the 35mm is its small negative size, which requires extremely careful handling from film loading to final development. Because of the tiny postage-stamp dimension of each individual frame, cinch marks, scratches, fingerprints and even lint and dust imbedded in the emulsion will produce unpleasant enlargements. Failure to use special developer will cause graininess, and retouching has its headaches, too.

For producing 35mm color transparencies, the miniature camera is ideal, and Kodachrome and Ansco Color exposed in these outfits often permit sharp projection on large screens, and even color prints of moderate enlargement can be made.

At the other extreme are the 3¼x4¼ and 4x5 press-type or reflex cameras, which also are held in high favor by sportsmen who don't mind putting their photography ahead of other outdoor recreation. These cameras are bulkier and more costly to operate, but they will produce sharp negatives which will turn out enlargements of contact quality. The range of emulsions available in cut film sizes is great, and the advantages of developing individual sheet films immediately, rather than waiting for an entire roll to be exposed, are obvious.

The 2¼x2¼ and 2¼x3¼ offer a happy medium for price, weight and picture size. Contact album prints are big enough to show detail, yet excellent enlargements can be made from these smaller film sizes. Furthermore, the reflex camera, with its visual focusing, adds to the enjoyment of the hobby, since one can move around into position and compose or frame the scene exactly as he wishes it to appear.

With the reflex, light entering the lens is reflected to the ground-glass focusing screen by means of a mirror mounted at a 45° angle inside the camera. At the click of the shutter, the mirror ingeniously swings up out of sight and the exposure is made. Critical focusing is usually done at the widest lens aperture and then reduced down to the desired f/setting and shutter speed corresponding to the existing light. At least one manufacturer has incorporated into his camera an automatic focusing control which permits focusing with the lens wide open, yet closes down quickly to a pre-set stop as the shutter is tripped.

The twin-lens reflex camera utilizes the upper lens for viewing only, thus giving a much brighter image of the subject than the lower lens which is used only for picture-taking. In the single-lens reflex, however, both viewing and focusing are done with the lens which actually records the scene.

While it is difficult to take good photographs with cheap, inferior equipment, it does not always hold true that the more costly cameras will turn out the best results. The dollar box has been known to have taken salon pictures of prize-winning caliber in the hands of experts, but the limitations of such an outfit with its slow, uncorrected lens and its fixed 1/25 second shutter speed eliminates it from serious consideration.

Perhaps one of the handiest cameras for the beginner or occasional filmer is the folding outfit with a reasonably fast anastigmat lens, say, f/4.5 or f/6.3 up through f/32, and a moderate shutter speed ranging from 1/25 to 1/100 or 1/200 second. To insure sharp results, the camera should be of the focusing type, not fixed focus, so that the bellows can be racked in and out for varying distances.

CHOOSING THE LENS

The "eye" of the camera is without doubt its most valuable component, for the ability of this disk of glass to bend light rays and form a sharp, fully corrected, negative image on film determines the true worth of the camera itself.

Generally speaking, there are three main types of lenses—the anastigmat, found on today's higher-priced cameras; the rapid rectilinear on medium grade; and the meniscus on the cheaper outfits. Such lenses may consist of a single piece of glass, called an element, or a combination of separate components, each lens varying in focal length and usefulness.

A lens has universal or fixed focus when all objects from a designated number of feet in front of the camera to infinity are in reasonably sharp focus. The commonplace box outfit offers an excellent example of the universal focus camera, since its aperture is quite small, usually around f/16, resulting in great depth of field. By employing supplementary slip-on lenses, portrait close-ups may

be made at less than the minimum focusing distance. Convertible lenses usually have two individual elements, either of which can be removed and used separately as well as jointly, thus creating an extremely useful combination lens with three separate focal lengths.

Although outdoor pictures often must be made under poor light and sometimes in deep shade, high-speed lenses are not essential. With today's fast film emulsions, a f/4.5 or f/3.5 lens will perform even in the most adverse weather conditions, and coupled with flash its usefulness is boundless. The fast lens is particularly desirable for admitting ample light when shooting at fast shutter speeds up to 1/1000 second, covering such subjects as waterfowl in flight, surface-cracking fish or fleeing game. The big lens also is good for recording action with slow color film emulsions where underexposure would result if the faster shutter speeds were used with medium-speed lenses.

Telephoto and wide-angle lenses are available for the larger negative sizes as well as for some miniature cameras, and these fine accessories, though expensive, will add to the versatility as well as the pleasure of outdoor camera work. The wide-angle lens takes in a broad view when shooting must be done at close quarters, while the telephoto narrows down the field considerably, depending on focal length and degree of magnification, to bring far away objects up close. Most wildlife movies and stills, which appear to be taken at very close range, were in all probability clicked at a safe distance with a long-focus lens.

Coated lenses are a relatively new photographic development, yet the idea behind this discovery probably goes back more than a quarter century ago when photographers accidentally found that their lenses, which were exposed to the elements through repeated outdoor use, had a tendency to tarnish. This aging process discolored the lens surface, but instead of causing deterioration of the image, it actually improved results by creating sharper images and even increasing slightly the speed of the lens.

SHUTTER SPEEDS

How fast a shutter speed is required for general outdoor work?

Speeds of 1/100 or 1/200 second may be ample for straight scenics and average action stuff, but 1/300, 1/500 or even 1/1000 second are better where it is urgent to freeze all movement. Even at a speed of 1/1000 second, it has not always been possible to stop completely the shake of a fish's head or the flip of his tail above water.

Fast shutter speeds enable you to stop action and still retain a deep depth of field.

The angle of approaching action determines the shutter speed, too. Filming a duck flying toward you or away from you can be done successfully at slower speeds than the same subject flying past the lens at right angles or zooming by swiftly overhead. Some subjects can be halted satisfactorily at relatively slow shutter speeds when the action is filmed at an oblique angle to the camera.

Perhaps you already have found that there is a definite relation existing between shutter and lens speed. If you open up from f/4.5 to f/3.5, the amount of light admitted is approximately doubled. Closing down from, say, f/8 to f/11 halves the amount of light reaching the film.

But early photographers didn't know that. Exposure, at first, was pretty much guess-work, since nobody bothered to figure out the relation, if any, between the various lens stops. Each cameraman made his own exposure estimates and let it go at that.

Because of man's untiring efforts toward standardization, photography today has been turned into an exacting science. Thus, the progressive series of stops inscribed on your lens mount—f/1.4, 2.8, 4, 5.6, 8, 11, 16, 22, 32, etc.—was determined mathematically by experts who had found that doubling any f/number actually gave only ¼ the speed, requiring four times the exposure. Consequently, by setting up f/stops like a series of steps, each permitting the entry of only one-half as much light as the one numerically lower, exposure was greatly simplified. No longer was it necessary for the amateur to figure out with pencil and paper the stop next below f/16 which would let in twice as much light. He knew instantly that f/11 was the correct stop. Some foreign lenses, like the Leica, are inscribed with a slightly different series of stops—f/2, 2.2, 3.2, 4.5, 6.3, 9, 12.5—but relative light values remain approximately the same.

A marsh scene may require an exposure of 1/100 second at f/16. Double your shutter speed to 1/200 second, if you like, but you must use the next larger lens opening of f/11 to admit a similar amount of light and guarantee good exposure. To stop a flock of ducks winging into the scene, you might have to redouble your shutter speed to 1/400 second, but to avoid underexposure, you would open up again to the next larger stop, or f/8.

Remember that the smaller the numerical lens stop—that is, f/2 or f/3.5—the wider is the lens aperture, while a larger numerical lens stop—say, f/16 or f/32—denotes a much smaller opening. If you can grasp this, photography should hold no further terrors for you.

But why bother to close down and use a slow shutter speed at all, you might ask? Why not shoot everything fast?

As the lens aperture is opened wider, the depth of field becomes shallower. In other words, the sharpness of objects close to the lens and at some distance away decreases until there is little or no depth of field at all. This means that if distance between subject and camera is not accurately determined, the subject is going to be out-of-focus.

Where there is little movement in a scene, it would seem almost ridiculous to use a large lens opening if a smaller f/stop would lend greater sharpness and more detail, and a much slower shutter speed would halt any motion. Even the owner of an f/2 or f/1.5 lens will probably shoot most of his outdoor exposures at f/8 to f/16, but it is consoling to know that the additional lens speed is ready and waiting when poor lighting conditions warrants its use in order to get the picture.

There may be occasions, particularly in wildlife photography, where time does not permit even quick focusing before picture-clicking. Here the experts on optics have come to our aid, having prepared for us what is known as a Table of Hyperfocal Distances, recording distances in feet beyond which objects are in focus when the lens is set at infinity. This hyperfocal business, which sounds more technical than it really is, varies according to the type of lens used and the selected f/stop.

Look at your lens. Somewhere on the rim of the barrel you will find its focal length inscribed, usually in millimeters or centimeters. Since there are 25.4 millimeters to an inch (10 millimeters in a centimeter), simply divide the focal length in millimeters by 25.4, and convert the focal length of your lens into inches.

If your camera has a focal length of five inches, the hyperfocal distance at f/16, for instance, is 26 feet. At f/8, it is 52 feet. At f/2.5, it is 170 feet. In other words, if you set your camera at f/16, focused at infinity, all objects from infinity down to 26 feet will be reasonably in focus. At f/8, still focused at infinity, objects from infinity to 52 feet will be in focus, and so on.

With a two-inch lens set at infinity and stopped down to f/16, objects from 11 feet to infinity will be in focus, but with a 10-inch lens at the same lens setting and at infinity, 52 feet will be the closest working distance.

This hyperfocal knowledge is helpful in other ways, too.

If you know the hyperfocal distance of your lens and set your camera at this distance, instead of infinity, then the depth of field will run from one-half the hyperfocal distance to infinity. For example, with the above camera having a five-inch focal length, we found that the hyperfocal distance was 26 feet when set at f/16 and focused at infinity. Now you can set the camera at 26 feet, and all objects from 13 feet to infinity will be in focus. Simple, isn't it?

"f" IS NO MYSTERY

There's nothing really mysterious about the simple letter "f". Photographically, it indicates the factor of the lens, not focus as some like to believe, and it expresses a definite relationship between the focal length of the lens and the size of its opening or aperture. The f/rating or speed of a lens can be determined quickly and efficiently by means of a very simple equation:

$$f = \frac{\text{distance from lens to film}}{\text{diameter of lens opening}}$$

Let's assume that the distance from lens to film—also known as the focal length of the lens—is two inches when the lens is focused at infinity, and the diameter of the lens aperture is one inch. The lens will be f/2. This means the diameter of the opening is one-half the distance from lens to film. At the same time, f/16 means that the lens aperture has a diameter of 1/16th of the distance from lens to film. Of course, the largest f/stop always denotes the speed of the lens.

Now suppose you have acquired an uncalibrated lens of foreign manufacture. You know that its focal length is 4½ inches. You determined this by measuring the distance between the lens and a sharp image cast by it on a white surface with the lens set at infinity. If the lens is one inch in diameter, the lens is f/4½, or f/4.5. Reduce the diaphragm opening to ½ inch, and the reading will become f/9. A ¼-inch opening will give f/18, and so on. Thus it is possible to determine your own lens stops and mark the calibrations on the lens barrel for future reference.

Before the days of f/ratings, some of the early cameras bore what was called the U. S. or Uniform Scale system, denoting lens stops by means of the U. S. numbers 1, 2, 3, 4, etc. While now obsolete, this system is still found on older cameras, and compares with f/ratings, in this manner:

U. S.	1	2	4	8	16	32	64
f/stop	f/4	5.6	8	11	16	22	32

Recently, another system of lens aperture measurements, known as "T-stops" or transmission numbers, was inducted into service. Since some lenses, though similar in many respects, may differ optically because of loss of light within the lens due to surface reflection, T/stops reveal the true amount of light passed by the individual lens at a prescribed opening.

The focal length of a lens also has a definite relation to film size as well as image size. In other words, the focal length should be slightly longer than the diagonal of the film itself to prevent the corners of the picture from fading off. A 4x5 film should have a lens of at least 6½-inch focal length to cover properly.

ing red. There also are color-blind films, sensitive only to blues and violets. Verichrome and Plenachrome are popular examples of ortho-type films, while Triple X and Super-pan Press are typical panchromatic films.

Speed is usually uppermost in the minds of most outdoor photographers, and faster emulsions are receiving popular acceptance. Advantages are obvious, since high-speed film prolongs daylight shooting hours, enabling one to close down for greater depth of focus and sharpness or increase the shutter speed to halt action without causing underexposure, as might be expected with slower films.

High film speed, however, has its disadvantages, too. Fast films are more grainy, and while grain can be minimized to some extent by proper development, it is the bugaboo of every miniature camera owner, who must turn to the slower speed panatomic films which are characteristically fine grain.

For the larger negative sizes, the best general purpose film for use in the variable light encountered outdoors and for indoor flash is a fast panchromatic film. This does not mean that the slower panchromatic and even ortho stock are ruled out, for they serve a useful purpose where lighting is good.

WHICH FILM

With all the speed, sensitivity to color and exposure latitude of modern day emulsions, why is it not possible for every amateur to produce consistently fine results with the photographic materials which manufacturers have created only after long years of research? Perhaps the human element still plays an important part in the picture-clicking hobby. After all, a costly rod, a kit full of imported flies and a pair of hip waders do not make the angler. Like every cameraman, he has to acquire his lore often through trial and error and cruel experience.

There are perhaps two types of film which roll through the sportsman's camera—orthochromatic, sensitive to all colors but red; and panchromatic, sensitive to all colors, includ-

FILTERS

Every photographer who has ever pointed a camera at a cloud-billowy sky and failed to capture the fluffy stuff in the final print may have wondered why the camera did not see the subject in black-and-white in quite the same manner as it appeared to the eye. His clouds probably bleached out in a light gray-toned sky because most film is over sensitive to blue. A filter is needed to enhance the clouds in order to darken the blue sky. Of course, the filter itself does not add the clouds, but it does help to strengthen them.

The medium yellow filter, for instance, will hold back certain colors, like blues and violets, or absorb rays, producing better rendition of tones compared with other colors. This is known as a corrective filter. Sometimes late afternoon light is strong enough in yellow and red to give this same effect without a filter.

For cutting haze in mountain photography and for increasing general color contrast and improving flesh tones, the orange filter is desirable. Further rounding out of the sportsman's basic kit of colored glass is the light green filter for landscape filming to brighten foliage, bring out clouds and reduce contrast in sunlit subjects. This is called a softening filter.

For weird though interesting effects, the red filter, which absorbs blue, violet and green rays, will blacken skies and turn red objects white. In fact, the red filter is often used to create "moonlight" effects in bright daylight, and it is known as a contrast filter since it exaggerates and even changes the tonal balance. Never try to red-filter ortho film, which is insensitive to red, for you'll draw only a blank. It is intended for panchromatic and infra-red emulsions.

When the red filter is used with infra-red film, skies darken and green foliage grows bright. The density of even the medium red filter may call for an exposure increase of three stops, but the film possesses amazing ability to cut through haze. Infra-red photography requires special study and is an art in itself, since meter readings are useless and focusing differs because of the shorter color wave length. Except for occasional bizarre effects, the average sportsman will find little use for photographing by "invisible light."

Since certain filters prevent the full measure of light from reaching the film, underexposure would result if no compensation were made for this light loss. The amount of light held back by a filter depends, of course, on its color and density, and each has a filter factor which reveals the number of times exposure must be increased with films of certain sensitivity to compensate for reduced light. Orthochromatic films require more increase in exposure with filters than panchromatic stock. Some filters require no exposure change, like the sky filter, the upper half of which is yellow and lower half clear

to darken the sky without affecting foreground rendition. This is intended for use with ortho films.

Filters are available in gelatin or plastic sheets, or cemented between glass layers, or as dyed optical glass itself. The former are cheaper, but the latter will withstand temperature changes and rougher handling more readily. Some are supplied as screw-in or slip-on mounts, while others are placed before the lens in special sunshade-filter holders. Every filter maker designates his color series in his own way, and each filter serves its own useful purpose.

Obviously, any filters used for black-and-white work cannot be employed in color photography, unless for special effect, since the color of the filter naturally would give an over-all color saturation to the transparency. Kodachrome filming requires special filters—the haze filter, which looks like a transparent piece of glass, for reducing ultra-violet in distant scenes; and special filters for indoor color film used outdoors, and outdoor film exposed under artificial light. Ansco Color demands a similar filter set, and the manufacturer's instructions covering their proper use should be followed carefully.

Suitable for color as well as black-and-white photography, the polarizing filter, also referred to by Eastman as the Kodak Pola-Screen, will darken skies and subdue oblique reflections on water, glass and other shiny surfaces. Best of all, he can view his subject through the filter, rotating it to obtain the desired effect, and placing it on the lens in this exact position. As with other filters, an increase in exposure is required, depending on type of film stock used.

Haze filters help to puncture the atmospheric blanket, caused by dust and tiny water particles, which hinders successful long-distance photography. The yellow, orange and red filters are all good black-and-white haze-cutters, and even the polarizing filter can be effective when properly used. The haze filter for color filming requires no exposure change when employed. It is not always desirable to reduce or eliminate atmospheric haze, and filters should not be used if the

ize is intended to build up the mood of the
icture.

EXPOSURE METERS

Today's exposure meters probably fall
to three classes—the photo-electric, which
so includes the incident light meter; the
extinction or visual type; and the revolving
isk or sliding scale. The latter is cheapest,
asiest to operate and fairly efficient. Here
he selects type of day, direction of light,
olor of subject, film speed and other vari-
les imprinted on the face of a revolving
al or slide rule scale. By turning the disk
itil all known factors are in alignment, the
oper lens stop for a given shutter speed is
us determined. Such manually operated
ales also are available for gauging exposures
ith photoflood or photoflash as well as for
itdoor lighting. These provide a handy
ide pointing toward better exposure, but
re personal errors in judgment are bound
creep in.

The exposure meter can give correct re-
lts only when it is properly handled. For
stance, if a reading is desired for a close-
of your hunting partner, the meter should
held fairly close to the subject's face, not
camera side, otherwise the viewing angle
ay include much of the bright sky or dark
ckground, thus giving a correspondingly
gher or lower reading than the face itself.

When taking a reading from camera
sition, as in landscape photography, tilt
e meter slightly downward to exclude
ich of the brilliance of the sky, avoiding
high reading and underexposure as a result.
otographing wild game at considerable dis-
nces with long focus lenses poses another
oblem, but this can be overcome by taking
meter reading on some nearby object which
osely approximates the color, shade and
gle of lighting of the subject to be filmed.

LEAPING FISH

Today's sportsman who goes camera an-
ing will find a pulse-quickening fascination

about filming fish above water. Mid-air photography calls for a new technique. It requires patience and perseverance. While some
sportsmen may be versatile enough to shoot
stills with one hand while fighting a fish with
the other, fish filming is chiefly a two-man
job, with one partner handling the rod while
the other fellow operates the camera. It's up
to the photographer to adjust the exposure in
relation to direction of light, for the angler
will be plenty busy coaxing a fish eager for
battle to rise up and break water.

Clement Crouch

*To photograph leaping fish entirely out of
the water, the cameraman must click his
shutter as the fish starts his leap.*

Unfortunately, not all cameras are suited
for recording split-second fish action. The
ordinary box camera is far too slow, and even
outfits with shutter speeds under 1/300 of
a second may be inadequate for stopping the
rapid head and tail movements.

Speeds of 1/500 and even 1/1000 of a
second are not too great. With shutter speeds
in the lower hundredths, there is little chance
that the leaping fish may be caught entirely
motionless at the peak of his leap, but
chances are also good that slow speeds
may result in a badly blurred image. Slight

head or tail motions are not objectionable, however, but actually give the feeling of action.

This does not necessarily limit shooting to only the brightest days, for fast emulsions produce good results even in dull weather. However, the backlighted sparkle of splashing water and the gleaming sides of the fighting fish will add snap to the negative. If lighting is adequate, use a filter, but don't forget that even a K2 calls for halving the shutter speed or using the next larger lens stop.

Because of its light weight, ease of manipulation, depth of focus, compactness and economy of operation, the miniature camera is popular for fish filming, since its use does not interfere with the shouldered creel or casting technique. The ground-glass focusing reflex is also desirable, permitting the photographer to center his subject accurately and maintain pin-sharp focus up to the moment when the fish breaks water.

While acceptable results can be secured in good light on slower film, supersensitive emulsions in roll, pack or sheet film—whichever is most convenient for your outfit—are recommended. Increased film sensitivity will enable you to use a faster shutter speed or stop down the lens for greater depth of focus.

Few leaping fish make willing models. In fact, many specimens will not jump out of water even with excessive teasing. Among fresh-water game fish, the muskellunge, black bass and northern pike are the best head-shaking surface-crackers.

While not easy-to-film subjects, musky, bass and pike are more easily photographed than brook trout or pan fish, for larger fish not only jump farther but stay out of water slightly longer. Sunfish, crappies and perch occasionally do a belly-roll over the surface, but their movements usually are too rapid to try to capture.

Rainbow, steelhead, cutthroat, Loch Leven and grayling found in the West are also good bubble-water specialists. If your partner hooks a rainbow while stream-wading, have him bring the trout around within easy

camera range. This distance may vary from five to 25 feet, depending upon the type and size of the fish. Hold the camera as low to the water as possible to enhance the leap. If you film from the bank, lie flat on the ground. Your tail-wagging fish will look much better silhouetted against light sky or water rather than a backdrop of dark foliage. After sundown, negatives of the leapers exposed against water darkened by shady shorelines usually look undertimed. Although fishing is rarely good when photographic conditions are ideal, try wherever possible to shoot when the light is right. Twilight leaps can be recorded if the fish is filmed against water which reflects the afterglow of the western sky.

Clement Crouch

Shutter speeds of 1/500 or 1/1000 of a second are needed to stop wild leaping action like this.

Suppose your meter calls for an exposure of f/4.5, 1/1000 second, with a medium yellow filter on a bright day. Here focus must be critical, otherwise the leaping fish will not be sharp. You know, of course, that closing down the lens aperture to a smaller stop gives greater depth of focus, so you might use 1/500 at f/5.6, or 1/300 at f/8.

However, while gaining picture depth, you have lost considerable shutter speed, result of which could mean that the leap of the fish might show some movement.

Where both angler and fish are included in the identical scene, one or the other is bound to be out-of-focus in high-speed filming unless the photographer positions himself for a broadside view and thus keeps the fish and fisherman in the same plane.

For recording fish action in open water, the angler should sit in the opposite end of the rowboat as far away from the cameraman as possible. If a canoe is used, the angler might sit in the bow, facing backward in the usual trolling position, while the photographer manipulates both canoe and camera from the stern. This allows filming on either side of the boat, since the cameraman can swing the craft about easily if either side or backlighting is desired. The angler himself can pass his line under the bow to work his fish on port side or starboard.

The camera is kept in readiness at all times, perhaps slipped loosely into its case, stowed in a plastic bag or wrapped up in an old fishing hat for protection and stuffed under the boat seat. It must never be left in the sun for any length of time since the heat may buckle or even fog the film. If the lighting is variable, alternating between full sunlight and broken clouds, both lens setting and shutter speed must be checked occasionally so that the camera can be swung into action at the first flash of a tail.

In preparing to photograph such action, focus on the point where the line enters the water, or a predetermined spot near the angler. As soon as a strike is felt, the angler reels in rapidly before the fish exhausts most of its energy with deep-water rushes. When the subject enters the field being focused upon, the fisherman ceases reeling to coax the fish skyward by steady pumping. Let the fish rest momentarily just beneath the surface, then lift its snout slowly for a gob of air. If there is no response, tap the side of the boat, or give a slight upward jerk with the rod tip, and your prize will break water.

While the average pike is good for two or three leaps, black bass and trout often will break water many times before finally giving up. After the fish has lost its zip, wet the hands and release it, unless injured, and go casting for new filming possibilities.

The human eye is normally slow in telegraphing its messages to the brain and back to the trigger finger for action, and this time lag varies greatly among individuals. For this reason, the shutter positively must be clicked when the fish *starts* to break water, not when the specimen already is in the air. Experience has proved that if the cameraman delays even slightly in shooting the upward rush of the fish, he probably will catch only the final splash.

Fishing for leaping pictures derives most of its fun from the uncertainties. Not until the film is developed does the photographer know what odd poses he may have captured and the number of disappointing misses. If, during initial attempts, you make one good fish picture out of a dozen tries, consider yourself fortunate.

Examine first results closely. Any movement evident in the head or tail indicates that you are using too slow a shutter speed. If the entire picture seems blurred, the fault may lie with the photographer who, during the excitement, probably moved his camera as the shutter clicked, or failed to focus critically. If the negative is to thin, use a larger lens opening next time you film under similar conditions. Undertimed negatives can, of course, be intensified, but overexposure will be rare because of the fast shutter speed required.

SALT-WATER ACTION

Both tarpon and salmon provide excellent subjects, but sailfish and marlin rate highest among the salt-water favorites for cameras that ride out beyond the breakers. Here action is still more difficult to film because the water is usually rougher, making camera handling precarious, and the salt spray is forever splattering lenses and corroding exposed metal.

Strikes are often fewer and the fish more elusive than in fresh-water angling, which means that the photographer must be ever alert with camera in readiness at all times. To obtain full cooperation from boatman and angler, it should be understood well in advance that getting the action picture is far more important than landing the fish, regardless of size, and that proper background and lighting are essential to the success of the shot.

Le Roy Dorsey

Marlin are known for their acrobatics and make spectacular leaping pictures for the alert photographer.

To insure speedy camera manipulation, the filming sportsman must be thoroughly acquainted with the operation and limitations of his outfit. Above all, he must remain calm, despite the excitement which accompanies the filming of jumping fish. He must be able to gauge distances from subject to camera and make immediate allowances for changes as the fish approaches or runs away to make successive leaps.

The tarpon is an unpredictable tail-wagger but chances are that the first of his series of jumps will be the tallest. If you use a ground-glass reflex camera, focusing and centering of the subject will not be too difficult. With other types, the open viewfinder is best for following the subject, or sighting can be done over the top of the camera itself. Focusing becomes almost automatic if the readings on the focusing scale are marked with raised figures or other indicators so that the feel of the finger reveals the proper setting without glancing down at the scale itself. Even the distance of subject from camera can be determined at a glance by noting colored knots tied to the unspooled fishing line at specific intervals.

If the angler and cameraman are in the same boat, both should face aft, side by side, in the stern. Unless lighting permits a small aperture with greater depth of focus, or a wide-angle lens is used, pictures taken from the bow showing the angler in the stern and the leaping fish in the distance are rarely satisfactory. If focusing is done on the fish, the angler will be out-of-focus, while if the fisherman is sharp, the fish will be fuzzy. To get both in the same shot and add the necessary human interest, employ another skiff or motorboat and keep it abreast or parallel to the first craft so that the bent rod and the jumping fish will always appear on the same plane. Hold the camera low over the water and each skyrocket leap will seem greatly heightened. If the cautious photographer stands up in the boat, he will silhouette the fish against the watery expanse rather than the sky itself for an interesting effect.

Most sailfish and marlin go in for aerial acrobatics of a frenzied nature. While big fish stay up out of water longer than the smaller specimens, one might assume that they are easier to film. This is far from true, since the best surface cracking often is done at distances beyond one hundred feet, which calls for telephoto lenses of considerable magnification to bring the target up close. With normal lenses, the leaping fish will appear very small on the negative, but if focus is sharp and exposure is good, enlargement of only the fish itself will give a blowup closely resembling a telephoto-made shot. Of course, the cameraman always can wait until the marlin is brought closer in for boating and hope for a nearby leap, but usually by that time much of the fight has gone out of the big boy.

Good greyhounding marlin shots are not plentiful, so don't pass up an apparently half-hearted jump to wait for a better one later. If you film every burst as though it were the last, you're bound to wind up with some successful shots. Your average distance setting will be at infinity, but for closer views refer to a depth of field table and study the sharpness of your allowable shooting range for the f/stop and shutter speed used.

When shooting from a boat, it is well to remember that vibration or sudden movement of the craft at the time of shutter-clicking can ruin a well-planned picture by blurring. Never rest the camera, either movie or still, on any part of the boat, but plant yourself firmly on the deck, with knees and hips absorbing any boat motion. Since humidity at sea often runs high, check your lens surface occasionally for dots of salt spray and wipe off moisture at once.

BIRDS IN FLIGHT

Birds are usually filmed at the nest or away from it, and some of the most striking shots are made of the subjects in flight. Such silhouettes against the sky may be taken with a telephoto or the normal lens and enlarged later. Winged fellows flying past the cameraman at right angles require a greater shutter speed to halt movement than the same birds approaching the camera at a slight angle. Gunstock mounts for still cameras permit smooth panoraming to follow the bird up until the moment of shutter clicking, and are just as useful as in moviemaking.

Another type of action picture which offers a challenge to fast shutter speeds is the power dive of the pelican and similar fish feeders. Here speeds of 1/500 to 1/1000 second are needed to stop the vertical plunge, which the bird often repeats in the identical spot on the water, thus simplifying focus. The surface-skimming gull can be

brought in close by having a companion toss out dead minnows or food scraps, while cormorants and shore birds make willing and exciting subjects. You will never know the pose you have captured until the film is finally developed.

U.S. Fish and Wildlife Service

Birds flying at right angles to the camera require fast shutter speeds to stop.

FILMING BIG GAME

Big-game hunters agree that it is easier to bring down game with a high-powered rifle than to pursue it with a camera of much less effective range, yet many sportsmen claim they derive greater pleasure and satisfaction these days from filming game rather than killing it.

There is something exciting about pointing a camera at a fleeing deer or a moose feeding among lilypads, once one realizes that this striking scene will be more than merely a memory. There is indescribable excitement capturing close-ups of the antics of a wild animal after minutes or perhaps hours spent in careful approach.

In animal photography, as in bird filming, the quietly operating still camera has advantages over the more bulky and noisier reflex types, which often frighten the animal away on the first exposure, seldom permitting repeat shots. Of course, the telephoto lens is the solution to close-up wild animal work, but because of the nervousness of the subject, focusing must be fast and accurate, and even here a tripod may be necessary to calm down a camera held by an equally excited photographer who is doing the stalking.

Wildlife is often attracted by feeding grounds, salt licks, waterholes or wallows. Acorns have been used to draw deer, while honey and spoiled meat help to bring in the bear. In the north country, the upstream run of the Alaskan salmon provides a tempting lure for fishing bruins, and most big game, especially antelope, are extremely curious when a white handkerchief is waved in the air.

U.S. Fish and Wildlife Service

The use of a blind near feeding grounds or waterholes often results in exciting close-ups of big game animals.

Sudden movements which tend to frighten game must always be avoided. Any necessary motion in approaching the subject or making camera adjustments should be extremely slow. Animal vision usually is not sharp, but the power of scent certainly is. Approach a moose downwind in your canoe, and chances are you will hear him go crashing back into the timber long before you swing around the point into the hidden bay where he had been feeding. Paddle upwind when his head is submerged and allow the canoe to drift motionless with paddles frozen when he casts a bleary-eyed look in your direction. Chances are that he will resume

his feeding, unruffled, while you paddle up close to make your camera kill.

Direction of prevailing winds is as important to note in setting up blinds as the camouflage itself. Several small saplings may be felled for a hideout, interwoven with pine browse for a spruce forest backdrop. Tall grass might be suitable for a marshland layout, provided that it blends into the background. In open country, a neutral-colored pup tent or green or brown beach umbrella set up on the ground with hole cut through for lens and peepsights is suitable. Camouflage further with grass or brush. In some cases, one cannot sit and wait for approaching game, like mountain goat and sheep, but must go in search of the quarry by climbing the high country at great personal risk.

The stalking photographer must dress his part, too, but here ideas vary as to the proper garb. While clothing should blend with the background, some wildlife cameraman, who take their work seriously, have made daring close-ups of normally shy mountain climbers by dressing like a goat, with white sheet, horns and beard, and pursuing the game. Even wild animals are rarely fooled by such camouflage, but the eye-stopping ability of the costume which causes them to look in wonderment and surprise is often all that is necessary to capture otherwise elusive poses. Where game has become accustomed to seeing horses in a pack country environment, sharing the open range with them, the photographer often can approach closely so long as he remains still with camera poised and does not dismount. Where animals have been neither molested nor hunted, it is possible to walk up on them in open country by using the horse as a decoy to hide cameraman from subject. Normally, wild animals flee at the sight of man alone. Of course, the secret to success is to spot the animal before it sees you.

STEREO-PHOTOGRAPHY

Look at any outdoor scene with one eye closed. You will see the subject's width and length, but not until both eyes are opened will the brain be able to perceive depth. Three-dimensional pictures likewise can be produced if the camera itself is given another eye. Or two pictures are taken from two different viewpoints. Or two cameras are clicked, side by side horizontally, with lenses set approximately 2½ inches apart, which is the average separation of the human eyes.

Although the discovery of the principle of stereo-photography was made more than a century ago, Oliver Wendell Holmes is credited with having designed the first parlor stereoscope, which thrilled a generation past before its popularity declined. Thanks to its recent revival, today's sportsman can not only see but shoot his own three-dimensional pictures of woodland scenes and wildlife in color as well as black-and-white.

Stereo-photography is claimed to be the most beautiful of all forms of pictorial expression, and few devotees of the one-eyed camera have been known to give up stereo work once they have explored its possibilities and viewed with sheer joy the tremendous picture depth and the realities of space which the stereograph affords.

Precision-built, these specialized cameras must, of necessity, be rather costly. You can make your own stereographs with two inexpensive box cameras of identical design, mounted horizontally side-by-side, on a plywood board or metal base plate. Shutter levers are connected by a stiff wire to permit tripping both at the same time. If mounted vertically, invert one camera, so that shutter levers and film winding knobs will be on the outside for easy manipulation. Prints are made on doubleweight paper and viewed with spectacle lenses mounted about three inches apart. If the budget permits, two reflex cameras can be mounted in tandem and used in similar fashion for stereographs. The only disadvantage, outside of the extra cost of an additional camera, is the fact that separation between the two lenses might be excessive for close-up work.

Where two individual pictures are taken of the same subject by two horizontally placed cameras—or a single camera used to click two consecutive exposures from two different camera positions—the resulting prints or transparencies from each must be mounted and viewed so that the left eye sees only the left-hand picture and the right eye the right-hand picture.

Lacking a stereo attachment or dual cameras, it is still possible to shoot stereographs by clicking a still picture and then sliding the camera, mounted on a slitted or grooved base, a few inches to right or left to make another exposure of the same scene. The slot should not be longer than the 2½-inch allowance between lens positions when the camera is moved to the left for the first exposure and to the right for the second.

Another homemade gadget for shifting the camera from position to position for stereo work is the swing-over base, which consists of two pieces of wood, equipped with two metal hinges or short links on opposite sides. The lower half of the base fastens to the tripod, while the upper half is held to the camera with a tripod screw. After the exposure is made and the film advanced, the camera is raised on its hinges and flipped from left center to right center for the second picture.

Of course, where only one camera is used, the subject must hold its pose between exposures. Furthermore, the weather should be calm since motion in any part of the scene will spoil the stereograph. Obviously, water in motion cannot be filmed, nor fast-moving clouds, but there are plenty of other outdoor subjects waiting to be photographed in this unique manner.

It has already been pointed out that an average distance of 2½ inches, equal to the normal spacing of the human eyes, is required for separation of the two lens positions in stereoscopy. In close-up work, however, this distance can be decreased slightly, and for long shots, it might be widened considerably. Under normal conditions, foreground objects should be included with distant scenes so that the impression of depth is readily apparent. This calls for small lens stops of f/11 or even better, wherever possible, so that distant as well as near objects will be in focus. Sharp focus is essential, since the better stereoscopic shots will show minute detail. Best of all, no additional technical knowledge is required of sportsmen seeking three-dimensional pictures.

SELECTING A MOVIE OUTFIT

No longer is the amateur movie camera considered a luxury item among sportsmen. It's just as essential on the hunt as a box of shells or a woolly pair of long-handled underwear.

The type of camera you will need will depend a lot on your personal tastes, the amount you want to spend and the use to which the camera will be put. If you plan to show your films only before small groups or in your home, where a large screen size is not necessary, the more economical 8mm will prove quite satisfactory. It is cheaper to operate and lighter to carry afield. Even turret heads are featured on 8mm cameras, with a range of lenses and other refinements comparable to 16mm.

Having four times the size, the 16mm frame will screen up to 8x10 feet and even larger, with ample illumination. This permits public showings in theater auditoriums where the 8mm would lose sharpness over the same throw. The 16mm allows the addition of a sound track later, and the range of library film subjects available in 16mm for home or club showings is definitely advantageous.

If you are a non-movie-making sportsman, contemplating the purchase of your first cine outfit, you will have to decide whether you want to shoot 8mm or 16mm. Some amateurs start off in 8mm and "graduate" into 16mm. The disadvantage of this is that unless both an 8mm and a 16mm projector are retained, the earlier film must be shelved and cannot be shown. Buy the best camera you feel you can afford and stick to it until you have mastered all its controls and temperaments before even considering changing to another model.

There are many types of 8mm and 16mm cine cameras on the market today and most

movie makers will tell you that their favorite brand is the outfit they own. When making your decision, give preference to models produced by reputable manufacturers.

If your interest lies in getting good wildlife close-ups, you will need a telephoto or long-focus lens, since the normal ½-inch lens on the 8mm camera, or the 1-inch on the 16mm, does not bring game up close enough. Regardless of the make or model of camera you finally select, the standard lens should be interchangeable with other lenses of different focal lengths. For instance, the 1-inch, 1½-inch and 2-inch 8mm telephoto lenses—equivalent to 2, 3 and 4 inches in 16mm—will enlarge the resulting image two, three or four times the size of the image produced with the normal lens.

Now telephoto filming requires a slightly different technique. Since longer lenses greatly magnify any camera movement in the resulting picture, the camera should not be hand-held, but must be planted firmly on a sturdy tripod or other rock-steady support.

Avoid panoraming the camera with telephoto lens attached unless following birds in flight or fleeing game. Even here follow through smoothly, with the subject centered in the viewfinder at all times.

Eventually, you will probably find the single-lens system inconvenient when changing from normal lens to telephoto quickly, for during the brief seconds required to unscrew one lens and replace it with another the game itself may escape and the once-in-a-lifetime movie sequence may be lost forever. For more efficient shooting, the two-, three- and four-lens turrets evolved, permitting the amateur to mount several lenses in position on the camera and swing from one to another quickly by rotating the turret. Each camera has its own viewfinder which masks the area included by each lens.

Unless one is a patient stalker of game, with an overabundance of luck, it is almost essential to carry a telephoto or long-focus lens along in your movie kit. Although some prefer the 6-inch lens, the 3- or 4-incher will prove most satisfactory for general use. Remember that the greater the magnification, the less steady will be your results unless a tripod or other firm support is used. Panoraming to follow game in flight reduces the effect of jittery movies, while shooting at speeds of 24, 32 or even 64 frames per second, instead of the usual 16, smooths out any rough camera handling and slows down the wingbeats of birds to permit closer study of body movements.

There are other conveniences, such as magazine loading, which enables the wildlife photographer to insert a pre-threaded cartridge into the camera and continue filming without interruption. The magazine jobs have an advantage over manual threading types, since the camera is always ready for instant operation. This also eliminates possible danger of fogging leader and trailer scenes when threading film by hand. The speed with which fresh cartridge film is made ready for the camera is definitely valuable when pursuing wildlife afield or filming action shots of hunting where every second counts. The only disadvantage of 16mm cartridge films is that they are slightly more expensive, a little bulkier and heavier, and are available only in 50-foot lengths.

Compare movies taken with and without the benefit of tripod, and you are bound to become a confirmed tripod enthusiast. Not all types of wildlife, however, respond to tripod filming. Follow-up shots of fleeing game or ducks in flight are often awkward to shoot from a tripod. The homemade gunstock, however, permits one to follow veering waterfowl as well as the erratic flight of upland birds. Several commercially made camera gunstocks for 8mm and 16mm are now on the market.

Variable camera speeds greatly enhance filming possibilities. Normal silent film speed is 16 frames per second, while sound is recorded at 24 frames. When film passes through the camera at a slower speed of 8 frames per second, screen action increases considerably, while speeds of 32 or 64 frames per second produce abnormally slow picture action. Thus, a telephoto sequence in slow

motion showing a jack rabbit freewheeling over the fields or a moose or deer splashing through swampy shallows becomes a symphony of smoothness and rhythm which adds charm and beauty to amateur films.

Mere ownership of costly equipment is no guarantee of top-notch movies. Nor do increasing years of experience always insure increasing quality. Amateurs new to the hobby, who have studied movie making perplexities diligently, are often farther advanced than the fellow who has been shooting haphazardly for a decade or more.

If you can click a still camera, you can take movies. Nobody dares say how good they will be at first, but if you follow instructions, chances are they will be projectionable. Laboratory processing of black-and-white film has made possible the partial rectifying of glaring exposure faults, even on the part of beginners. Color film, however, allows less exposure latitude.

Past snapshooting experience may prove particularly helpful in movie work. Knowledge of composition, exposure, outdoor or indoor lighting, film speeds and the use of camera angles will be advantageous once you thread your initial roll.

If all scenes required the same amount of footage—that is, if they remained on the screen for the same length of time—your finished reel would be monotonous. So you learn by experience and by carefully observing the outstanding work of others when to cut and when not to cut. While most shooting will be done at normal speed—16 frames per second—there may be times when you may wish to use only 8 frames, if your camera is so equipped, to obtain super-fast exaggerated action, or 32 or 64 frames to secure slow motion for recording rapid movements.

Camera handling is quite important, and the beginner's chief fault is shooting without ample support. Another error is panoraming his camera. He pans up buildings and down streets. He pans from right to left and back to right again. Sooner or later he learns to shoot steady pictures, panoraming only to follow moving objects or swinging from one object of interest to another, and then very *slowly*. Distracting camera movement can be minimized by taking different angle shots of the same subject, and swinging from long shots to medium shots and close-ups.

There are many tricks to be learned in amateur movie making. But don't expect to absorb all of them in your first year. Perhaps that is what gives the movie hobby its zest and universal appeal.

As your film library grows, look for novel ways of editing and titling your odds-and-ends footage. To increase the enjoyment of home movies, try synchronizing reels to appropriate music and sound effects. Recordings may be had to express every picture mood, and sound disks are available, varying from the slow patter of rain to the roar of a mountain lion. With music and sound properly synchronized on dual turntables, it is possible to create effects even more realistic than if you were filming with sound camera out on location.

GUNSTOCK FILMING

If you want to shoot smoother telephoto movies of wild birds, animals or any fast-moving subjects, borrow a tip from the hunter and build a gunstock for your camera. You will quicken your trigger finger, and the combination cheek-and-shoulder grip will permit steadier camera holding and almost jitter-free pictures.

Although panoraming generally is frowned upon in ordinary movie making, sometimes it is necessary to follow moving subjects like skiers, fleeing animals and ducks in flight. A hand-held camera is none too steady, while, mounted on a tripod, it lacks the flexibility needed for rapid swings. If you revamp a gunstock for your camera, the entire outfit can be carried under your arm or slipped into a pack when not in use. By loosening the tripod screw in the bottom of the stock, the camera may be removed quickly for ordinary work.

Your camera gun should fit the shoulder comfortably. For filming purposes, however, a much shorter stock is used so that when the lens is trained on the subject, the eye will be sighting close behind the rear finder.

An old .22 rifle stock is satisfactory for 8mm, while a discarded shotgun stock or a hand-carved blank of pine, birch or walnut will suffice for 16mm. The fore part must be trimmed to fit the camera face, with a slightly raised lip along both sides to prevent slipping. Lacking a tripod screw of suitable length, buy a properly threaded bolt and solder on a knurled finger grip.

Gunstock filming is an art which can be mastered quickly. Shoot with both eyes open so that the right eye sights through the finder, while the left eye surveys the field. Face at right angles to the line of action, with body weight distributed evenly on both feet. Holding your camera to your face, follow the action in your viewfinder by turning your body at the hips rather than moving the camera itself. You will be amazed after a little practice how a two-hand grasp, with the heel of the gun steadied against the shoulder, smooths out otherwise jerky panoraming.

If you want slow-motion movies of wildfowl wings in flight, the gunstock-mounted camera is ideal. When bird filming, adjust the frame speed to 32 or 64 frames per second, and press the camera trigger as you bring the gunstock to eye level to insure capturing a full sequence. The blurred opening frames can be thrown out in editing. If you don't start shooting as you aim, you may miss out on the first part of the take-off.

TELEPHOTO

More than half a century ago—when advertisers were boasting about semi-smokeless gunpowder and advising hunters not to shoot their dogs because of mange; when pneumatic mattress makers were telling sportsmen that the ever-present root in the bed of boughs was now a thing of the past—*Sports Afield* magazine ran the following little news item in its camera department:

Nearly all amateur photographers, and more especially those who are sportsmen

Herbert Lewis

A telephoto lens is the answer when game animals are difficult to approach or when they frequent areas that offer few possibilities for concealment.

as well, will confess a desire to secure photographs of the various species of wild game in their native surroundings, yet admit that the practical range of the common view lens is too limited for work of this description, while enlargements are seldom of a satisfactory nature, only giving increased size at the expense of detail and other features of value.

The "telephoto," a recent invention, will be welcomed by both amateur and professional alike as rendering possible results in this line of endeavor heretofore quite beyond attainment. Its cost is insignificant in comparison with value, as it can be attached to any lens and has a magnifying power of from 2½ to 4 diameters. In other words, with its use, a deer or other animal photographed at 60 yards will appear as large on the ground glass as at 15 yards with the unassisted lens.

Back at the start of the century, the telephoto was being hailed as an innovation destined to revolutionize wildlife filming. It has done just that. Today the telephoto lens is used not only to produce magnified images of objects too dangerous or too difficult to approach, but it also is known to completely change the perspective of a picture and render depth of field not otherwise possible when filming closer. As focal length increases, the depth of field grows shallow, requiring accurate focusing. Such shallowness actually is desirable where a diffused background serves to accentuate the close-up.

The long-focus lens is often confused with and used loosely to refer to the telephoto lens. The actual length of the long-focus lens is equal to the distance between the lens and film when focused at infinity, while the telephoto lens of the same magnification may have a much shorter film-to-lens distance. A long-focus lens, six inches in length, will give a 6X magnification over the standard 1-inch cine lens.

In amateur movie photography, the 16mm camera has a normal or standard lens of approximately one inch, but long-focus lenses are available ranging from two to six inches and more in length. This means the 2-inch lens gives an image that looks twice as close as with the 1-inch lens, while the 3-inch lens will look three times closer, and so on. In other words, a giant elk, watching you from a distance of 60 feet, will appear to be only 20 feet away, if the 3-inch lens is used. This has definite advantages, for there are times when scent and natural obstacles prevent you from getting near enough to your prize to produce a sizable image.

If you are an 8mm owner, remember that the 1½-inch lens designed for your camera will give the same degree of magnification as the 3-inch 16mm lens. In fact, nearly everything that can be said about telephotography for the 16mm owner also holds good for the 8mm.

Amateur movie makers have a big advantage over the still camera enthusiast insofar as telephotos and long-focus lenses are concerned, for the cine lenses are faster and less bulky. Some of them have even greater magnifying power. This is apt to confuse the beginner who probably feels that the longer the lens, the better the picture.

If a sportsman can afford only one long-focus lens, experts recommend for all-around use the 1½-inch for the 8mm or the 2½-, 3- or 4-inch for the 16mm. Such lenses may be carried in the hunting or fishing coat pocket and whipped into position in short order. Nor are they quite as expensive as the longer lenses.

Some cinematographers fail to realize, until too late, that these long lenses not only magnify the subject being filmed, but also exaggerate camera movement considerably, particularly when held in the hand. Deep breathing, heartbeat or the breeze itself may give enough movement to spoil an otherwise good shot.

From the book PHOTOGRAPHY AFIELD
By Ormal I. Sprungman
Published by The Stackpole Company
Copyright 1951

CHAPTER **15**

public lands

IMAGINE A trout stream long enough to girdle the earth at the equator four times, a pad-filled bass pond half as big as Lake Erie, a stocked and specially managed shooting preserve as big as the state of Texas—*plus* the state of Maine.

Sounds unbelievable? It's not. The Federal Government still owns about one-fourth of the land in this country. Half of these 400 million-plus acres are reserved for you. They are the national forests, parks and wildlife refuges. Through the various acts of Congress that over the years instituted these vast recreational facilities, you share ownership of over 100,000 miles of streams, three million acres of lakes and nearly 200 million acres of near-wilderness country open to the hunter, hiker, camper, canoeist or to the man who just wants to share with his family the wonder of America.

For in addition to unsurpassed hunting and fishing, these lands preserve unchanged the spectacular natural phenomena that left the pioneers in wide-eyed discovery. Glacier-covered Mt. Rainier, the wilderness lakes of Minnesota, the rain forests and redwoods, the Yellowstone, the threatening beauty of Okefenokee—the list is inexhaustible.

In this chapter you will find a complete listing of all these lands and information on accommodations and facilities at each. In addition, there is a guide to the Appalachian and Pacific Crest trails and a section on the requirements and opportunities afforded by the many national- and state-owned public campgrounds.

NATIONAL PARKS

From the establishments of Yellowstone National Park in 1872, the national park system has grown to a total of 174 areas encompassing 22,569,987 acres of land.

These include 28 parks; six historical parks; 83 national monuments; 21 battlefield memorials and cemeteries; four national parkways; and the national capital park system.

It includes a new category of four national recreation areas located around federal reservoir projects and managed by the National Park Service. These cover 2,073,427 acres and are devoted to public recreational use—fishing being in top priority.

The National Park Service has constructed roads, trails and free public campsites. There are many hotels of various types and price ranges, lodges, cabins, transportation and other visitor services that are provided within the national park system by private concessioners working under contract with the Park Service.

There are fees charged to most national park system areas to cover admissions and motor permits. The park rangers not only work the year round to maintain the park areas, they also help conduct park tours along with naturalists and historians who give interpretive talks on the individual park areas.

Hunting and carrying of firearms in national park system areas is absolutely forbidden. The only exceptions are the four recreational areas—see listing—a part of the Cape Hatteras Seashore Park where waterfowling is permitted, and a special elk-hunting program authorized by Congress when Teton National Park was created.

Fishing is the sportsman's major activity. The parks include some of the finest trout streams and fishing waters. With but several exceptions, a state fishing license and state laws apply. In a number of cases the creel limit and seasons are inclined to be more restrictive in the parks than statewide rules.

These are family vacation areas with something of interest to each member of the family. In fact, one hasn't really seen America until he visits the wonders and beauty of the national parks and monuments.

NATIONAL PARKS

The name of the park, state where located, number of acres, address of park superintendent, features, number of public camp and trailer sites, number of days stay allowed at camps. (For detailed information on the park, commercial hotel and lodge concessions, address the park superintendent.)

ACADIA: Maine, (41,954). Supt. Box 690, Bar Harbor, Maine. Highest elevation on eastern seaboard, rugged coastal area on Mount Desert Island; 170 campsites, 58 trailer spaces, 30 days stay.

BIG BEND: Texas, (708,221). Supt. Big Bend National Park, Texas. Mountains and desert in the great bend of the Rio Grande. 22 campsites, 10 trailer spaces, 30 days.

BRYCE CANYON: Utah, (36,010). Supt. Springdale 3, Utah. Contains perhaps the most colorful erosional forms in the world. 40 campsites. 12 trailer spaces, 30 days.

CARLSBAD CAVERNS: New Mexico, (49,448). Supt. Box 111, Carlsbad, New Mexico. Largest underground caves yet discovered.

CRATER LAKE: Oregon, (160,290). Supt. Box 672, Medford, Oregon. Lake of deepest blue in heart of once active volcano, encircled by multi-colored lava walls 500 to 2,000 feet high. 107 campsites, 49 trailer spaces, 30 days.

EVERGLADES: Florida, (1,499,428). Supt. Box 275, Homestead, Florida. Largest remaining subtropical wilderness in United States; extensive fresh- and salt-water area. It is the newest national park.

GLACIER: Montana, (1,013,129). Supt. West Glacier, Montana. Superb rocky mountain scenery with numerous glaciers and lakes nestling among the highest peaks. 418 campsites, 133 trailer spaces, 30 days.

GRAND CANYON: Arizona, (645,808). Supt. Grand Canyon, Arizona. Most spectacular part of the Colorado River's greatest canyon which is 217 miles long and 4 to 18 miles wide. 229 campsites, 195 trailer spaces, no limit.

GRAND TETON: Wyoming, (310,390). Supt. Moose, Wyoming. Series of peaks comprising the most impressive part of the Teton range, and includes part of Jackson Hole, wintering ground of largest American elk herd. 137 campsites, 18 trailer spaces, 30 days.

GREAT SMOKY MOUNTAINS: North Carolina and Tennessee, (510,169). Supt. Gatlinburg, Tennessee. Loftiest range east of the Black Hills and one of the oldest uplands on earth. 302 campsites, 63 trailer spaces, no limit.

HAWAII: T. H., (246,748). Supt. Hawaii, T. H. Scene of impressive active volcanism on the island of Hawaii, rare plants and animals. 4 campsites, 30 trailer spaces, no limit.

HOT SPRINGS: Arkansas, (1,019). Supt. Box 859, Hot Springs National Park, Arkansas, 47 mineral hot springs. 32 campsites, 12 trailer spaces, 30 days.

ISLE ROYALE: Michigan, (133,838). Supt. 87 N. Ripley St., Houghton, Michigan. The largest forested island in Lake Superior, distinguished for its wilderness character, great moose herd.

Union Pacific Railroad

Tarner Bridge, Boyce Canyon National Park, Utah.

KINGS CANYON: California, (454,000). Supt. Three Rivers, California. Mountain wilderness dominated by the two enormous canyons of the Kings River and by the summit peaks of the High Sierras. 454 campsites, 103 trailer spaces, no limit.

LASSEN VOLCANIC: California, (105,921). Supt. Mineral, California. Lassen Peak only recently active volcano in United States proper, erupted between 1914 and 1921, impressive volcanic phenomena. 284 campsites, 61 trailer spaces, no limit.

MAMMOTH CAVE: Kentucky, (51,355). Supt. Mammoth Cave, Kentucky. Series of underground passages, 150 miles explored, river 360 feet below surface. 37 campsites, 37 trailer spaces, no limit.

MESA VERDE: Colorado, (51,334). Supt. Mesa Verde National Park, Colorado. Most notable and best preserved prehistoric cliff dwellings. 85 campsites, 12 trailer spaces, 30 days.

MOUNT McKINLEY: Alaska, (1,939,493). Supt. McKinley Park, Alaska. Mount McKinley —highest mountain in North America, large glaciers of the Alaska range; white (Dall) sheep, moose, grizzly bears and wolves.

MOUNT RAINIER: Washington, (241,782). Supt. Longmire, Washington. Greatest single-peak glacial system in the United States. 309 campsites, 91 trailer spaces, no limit.

OLYMPIC: Washington, (896,599). Supt. Box 591, Port Angeles, Washington. Mountain wilderness containing finest remnant of Pacific Northwest rain forests, active glaciers, rare Roosevelt elk. 132 campsites, 30 trailer spaces, no limit.

PLATT: Oklahoma, (912). Supt. Box 379, Sulphur, Oklahoma. Numerous cold mineral springs. 184 campsites, no trailer spaces, 60 days.

ROCKY MOUNTAIN: Colorado, (259,556). Supt. Box 1086, Estes Park, Colorado. One of the most magnificent and diversified sections of the Rocky Mountains with 65 named peaks over 10,000 feet high. 253 campsites, 54 trailer spaces, 30 days.

SEQUOIA: California, (386,560). Supt. Three Rivers, California. Great groves of giant sequoias, the world's largest and probably oldest living things; magnificent High Sierra scenery, including Mount Whitney, highest mountain in United States proper. 637 campsites, 124 trailer spaces, no limit.

SHENANDOAH: Virginia, (211,615). Supt. Luray, Virginia. Outstanding portion of Blue Ridge with Skyline Drive traversing crest, magnificent vistas of historic Shenandoah Valley, Piedmont Plains. 82 campsites, 26 trailer spaces, 30 days.

WIND CAVE: South Dakota, (28,059). Supt. Hot Springs, South Dakota. Limestone caverns in scenic Black Hills. Elk, deer, antelope, prairie-dog towns and buffalo. 8 campsites, 8 trailer spaces, no limit.

YELLOWSTONE: Wyoming and Montana, (2,221,773). Supt. Yellowstone National Park, Wyoming. World's greatest geyser area with about 3,000 geysers and hot springs; one of the world's greatest wildlife sanctuaries. 826 campsites, 348 trailer spaces, 30 days.

YOSEMITE: California, (760,951). Supt. Box 577, Yosemite National Park, California. Mountainous region of unusual beauty, three groves of giant sequoias. 3,748 campsites, 1,863 trailer spaces, 30 days.

ZION: Utah, (94,881). Supt. Springdale, Utah. Zion Canyon of the Virgin River, the best-known example of a deep, narrow vertical-walled brilliantly colored chasm readily accessible for observation. 98 campsites, 36 trailer spaces, 30 days.

NATIONAL RECREATION AREAS

COULEE DAM: Washington, (98,500). Supt. Box 337, Coulee Dam, Washington. Franklin D. Roosevelt Lake. Recreational facilities are being developed. Fishing.

LAKE MEAD: Arizona and Nevada, (1,951,928). Supt. 601 Nevada Highway, Boulder City, Nevada. Lake Mead formed by Hoover Dam. Fishing. 38 campsites, 32 trailer spaces, 90 days.

MILLERTON LAKE: California, (12,769). Supt. Box 397, Friant, California. Millerton Lake formed by Friant Dam, part of the Central Valley Project. 150 campsites, 25 trailer spaces, 30 days. Fishing.

SHADOW MOUNTAIN: Colorado, (10,231). Supt. Box 1086, Estes Park, Colorado. Shadow Mountain Lake and Granby Reservoir are part of Colorado-Big Thompson Project near west entrance to Rocky Mountain National Park.

CAPE HATTERAS NATIONAL SEASHORE RECREATIONAL AREAS: North Carolina, (28,500). Supt. Manteo, North Carolina. This is a new category within the national park system; and one of its newest additions. Some of the finest sport fishing on the East Coast is found in the waters of the Outer Banks. Deep-sea and surf fishing, also brackish-water bass fishing. There are areas open for migratory waterfowl hunting in this recreational area. At this writing, only two rough locations for campsites exist. However, there are commercial accommodations, hotels, motor courts and restaurants.

(The National Parks Association, 2144 P Street, N.W., Washington, D. C., is an old established membership organization whose main objective is to develop public understanding and support of the national parks system and to crusade to preserve this system. They publish a magazine, *National Park Magazine*, and have two books for sale, *Exploring Your National Parks and Monuments*, and *Exploring the National Parks of Canada*.)

The National Park Service is an agency of the Department of the Interior located at Washington 25, D.C. But for information about individual areas, you should write either to the park, or the regional office. A detailed check list of individual publications on the various units of the national park system which gives information on the area, features and facilities; may be obtained from the Superintendent of Documents, U.S. Government Printing Office, Washington 25, D. C. It is entitled, "C 35 Check List, National Park Service Publications." Each of the 48 states has at least one area in the NPS.

Region 1, National Park Service, 900 North Lombardy Street, Richmond 20, Virginia. This includes the states of Maine, New Hampshire, Vermont, Massachusetts, Connecticut, Rhode Island, New York, New Jersey, Pennsylvania, Ohio, Delaware, Maryland, West Virginia, Kentucky, North Carolina, South Carolina, Tennessee, Georgia, Alabama, Mississippi, Louisiana, Virginia, Florida and Puerto Rico.

Region 2, National Park Service, 307 Federal Office Bldg., Omaha 2, Nebraska. This includes Michigan, Wisconsin, Illinois, Indiana, Minnesota, Iowa, North Dakota, South Dakota, Missouri, Nebraska, Kansas, Montana, Wyoming and part of Colorado.

Region 3, National Park Service, Box 1728, Santa Fe, New Mexico. This includes Arkansas, Oklahoma, Texas, New Mexico, Arizona, Utah and parts of Colorado and Nevada.

Region 4, National Park Service, 180 Montgomery Street, San Francisco 5, California. This includes Washington, Idaho, Oregon, California and parts of Nevada and Alaska and Hawaii.

By Michael Hudoba

NATIONAL FORESTS

Since the U. S. Forest Service was set up in 1905 to manage the national forest system for watershed protection and timber, the concept of forest land resources has been vastly expanded. Under the impetus of a growing America's needs, timber, water, minerals, grazing and recreation are now all an integral part of forest management.

Recreational use of the forests for hunting, fishing, camping, riding, hiking or just plain sightseeing has become a vital element in the forest's future. The 181,567,868 acres of national forest lands in 151 forests, in 40 states, stand today as the largest unposted fishing and hunting grounds left open to the public.

National forest lands contain over 90,000 miles of fishing streams, 2,250,000 acres of lakes and an estimated one third of the big-game animals found in this country. With the exception of some areas reserved for wildlife refuges, this is all open to the public.

To take care of the visitors to the national forests, there are 4,500 camp and picnic areas equipped with 43,000 family-sized units—enough to accommodate 280,000 persons at one time. Some 700 of these are located near main U. S. and State highways and are convenient for overnight stops by tourists. The rest are located along secondary roads and are often many miles from main tourist routes. These facilities cost the government over $30,000,000 to build and more than a million dollars each year to maintain.

There are simple camp and picnic areas available in almost every one of the 151 forests. Most areas have both camp and picnic facilities. Campgrounds usually have a fire grate, table, tent site and individual parking spur at each camping site. Safe water is provided at most areas. Pit toilets are the rule.

A majority of camp areas can accommodate small trailers, but water, electrical and sewerage connections for trailers are not provided. However, access roads are frequently difficult for large trailers to negotiate. Campers using trailers must select parking spurs large enough so as not to block campground road traffic. Stores are usually not available near Forest Service camp and picnic areas and in many cases, nearest supplies are 10 to 20 miles away. It is wise to bring all necessary supplies and equipment.

There are about 50 national forest campgrounds where a charge is made for camping. These vary from 25 cents per party to 25 cents per person and 10 cents for children.

The Forest Service has established 80 areas, totaling 14,000,000 acres, in which primitive environment is maintained for those who really want to get away from it all. These are divided into primitive areas of which there are 54 totalling 9,501,922 acres; nine wilderness areas totalling 3,499,223 acres; fourteen wild areas totalling 515,665; and three roadless areas. The difference between wilderness and wild areas is that wilderness areas must be over 100,000 acres in size.

The U. S. Forest Service address is Washington 25, D. C., but for information as to individual national forest areas, it is suggested you contact the regional foresters listed.

These state listings give the name of the forest and its acreage, the town where the forest headquarters office is located, the location of the ranger headquarters, principal highways to the forest, special recreational resources, camping facilities and towns for commercial accommodations.

ALABAMA

WILLIAM B. BANKHEAD: (560,604); Montgomery; ranger at Haleyville; U.S. 31, 43. Managed deer, turkey and squirrel hunting. Bass and bream fishing in Bushy Lake. Picnic area on Sispey River. Accommodations at Haleyville, Russellville. Decatur, Cullman and Jasper.

CONECUH: (339,573); Montgomery; ranger at Andalusia; U.S. 29. Large ponds, bass and bream fishing. Deer, turkey and small-game hunting. Picnic and swimming at Open Pond. Accommodations at Andalusia.

TALLADEGA: (851,119); Montgomery; ranger at Centerville, Heflin and Talladega; U.S. 78, 241, State 6. Payne Lake Wildlife Management Area. Deer, turkey, duck and squirrel hunting. Bass, bream and perch fishing. Picnic grounds at Payne Lake and Horn and Horseblock towers. Resort hotel and cabins at Cheaha State Park. Accommodations at Centerville, Marion, Tuscaloosa, Selma, Talladega, Sylacauga, Anniston and Heflin.

ALASKA

CHUGACH: (4,809,623); Juneau; Division headquarters, Seward and Cordova. Trout fishing in Russian River. Moose, sheep, goat and brown bear; duck, grouse and ptarmigan hunting. 140 miles of roads, 285 miles of trails. Two improved public forest camps. Inquire at Cordova, Seward and Juneau offices.

TONGASS: (16,078,174); Juneau; Division headquarters at Petersburg, Ketchikan, Sitka and Craig. Direct plane service to Ketchikan and Juneau. Observatories where bear can be watched fishing for salmon. Trout fishing; also salt-water fishing for salmon and halibut. Alaskan brown and grizzly bear, goat and deer hunting.

Hiking. 210 miles of roads, 780 miles of trails. 18 improved forest campgrounds. Public camp and hotel information at Juneau office. Hotel accommodations in all southeast Alaska towns, all towns served by boat and plane.

ARIZONA

APACHE: (1,707,991); Springerville; forest lies partly in New Mexico; U.S. 60, 260, 666. Big and Crescent Lakes. Blue Range and Mount Baldy Wilderness Areas. Lake and stream trout fishing. Elk, deer, bear and turkey hunting. Horseback riding, pack trips. 33 public camp and picnic areas. Resorts, lodges, cabins. Nearby towns: Greer and Alpine, Ariz.; Luna and Reserve, N. Mex.

COCONINO: (1,999,504); Flagstaff; U.S. 66, 89, 89A; Mormon Lake, largest natural lake in Ariz. Sycamore Canyon Wild Area; more than 1,000 miles of scenic drives through timber. Deer, elk and mountain lion hunting. Horseback riding. 11 public camp and picnic areas. Arizona Snow Bowl winter sports area. Resorts, hotels, camps and dude ranches. Nearby towns: Williams, Sedona, Clarkdale, Cottonwood, Camp Verde and Winslow.

CORONADO: (1,858,265); Tucson; forest lies partly in New Mexico. U.S. 80, 84, 89. Chiricahua Wild Area. Deer and javelina hunting. Scenic drives and horseback trails in the rugged Santa Catalina, Chiricahua, Santa Rita and Huachuca mountains. Many forms of bird life including the trogon; rare species of plants such as Chihuahua pine, chilicote and madrona; rare species of animals, including coati-mundi, chiricahua squirrel and javelina. 33 camp and picnic grounds; southernmost winter sports area in the United States. Many dude ranches, resorts and hotels. Adjacent towns are Nogales and Douglas on the Mexican border; Tucson, Benson, Patagonia, Tombstone, Wilcox, Bisbee, Bowie, San Simon and Ft. Huachuca.

GILA: Safford; U.S. 60, 70, 666; State 77, 78, 88. Parts of the Gila and Superstition Wilderness Areas; Galiuro Wild Area. Coolidge and Roosevelt dams. Bear, mountain lion, deer, elk, peccary, turkey and quail hunting. Scenic drives; U.S. 60, Pinal Mt., Swift Trail and Coronado Trail. 19 public camp and picnic areas. Four dude ranches near or within boundary; hotels and auto courts. Nearby towns: Safford, Clifton, Duncan, Globe, Superior and Miami.

KAIBAB: (1,780,469); Williams; U.S. 66, 89, 64, 67. Grand Canyon National Game Preserve with the famous Kaibab Forest deer herd; wild buffalo herd; only habitat of the Kaibab squirrel. Access to both north and south rims of Grand Canyon. Thunder River, Bill Williams Mountain and White Horse Lake. Sycamore Canyon Wild Area. Hunting, including deer, elk, antelope, bear, mountain lion, turkey and buffalo. Wilderness trips; scenic drives; winter sports; fishing; riding and pack trips. Unlimited photographic opportunities in vivid coloring of geological formations. 13 public camp and picnic areas; Bill Williams Winter Sports Area. Hotels, resorts, cottage courts, guest ranches, hunting camps. Nearby towns: Williams, Grand Canyon, Flagstaff, Jerome, Ashfork, Fredonia and Cottonwood, Ariz.; Kanab, Utah.

PRESCOTT: (1,457,282); Prescott; U.S. 89. Rugged back country in the high mountains; Granite Basin Lake. Sycamore Canyon and Pine Mountain Wild Areas. Deer hunting; some fishing. Many horseback riding trails. Scenic drives. 10 public campgrounds and picnic areas; two winter sports areas. Resorts, hotels, cabins and dude ranches. Nearby towns: Prescott, Mayer, Jerome, Clarkdale and Cottonwood.

SITGREAVES: (883,919); Holbrook; U.S. 60; State 77, 173. Limited hunting of deer, turkey, antelope, bear. Saddle and pack trips. Three forest campgrounds. Resorts, hotels, cabins and guest ranches. Nearby towns: Winslow, Show Low, Lakeside and Pinetop.

TONTO: (2,793,579); Phoenix; U.S. 60, 70, 80, 89. Famous Tonto Basin, Superstition Mountains and Mogollon Rim. Superstition Mountain and Mazatzal Wilderness Areas; Sierra Ancha Wild Area. A small band of Mexican bighorn sheep in the Superstition Mountains. Apache, Canyon and Stewart Mountain Lakes on the Salt River; Bartlett and Horseshoe Lakes on the Verde River. Lake and warm-water stream fishing; fair trout fishing. Quail, deer, elk, bear and mountain lion hunting. Saddle and pack trips; winter photographic possibilities. Scenic drives. 14 public camp and picnic areas. Resorts, dude ranches, cabins, hot mineral baths, boats. Nearby towns: Payson, Pine, Young, Roosevelt and Mesa.

ARKANSAS

OUACHITA: (2,120,774); Hot Springs National Park. Forest lies partly in Oklahoma. U.S. 70, 71, 270, 271. Ouachita, Kiamichi and Winding Stair Mountains. Four major and numerous smaller artificial lakes in or near forest. Bass fishing. Deer, quail and squirrel hunting. Scenic drives, hiking and swimming. 14 improved forest camp and picnic grounds with overnight shelters at four areas. Commercial hotels, resorts and cabin camps in and near the forest. Nearby towns: Hot Springs National Park and Mena, Ark.; Poteau, Okla.

OZARK: (1,462,077); Russellville; U.S. 64, 71; State 22, 7. Three recreational lakes. Stream and lake fishing. Deer and small-game hunting. Swimming. 13 improved camp and picnic areas. Mount Magazine Lodge and cabins, White Rock Mountain cabins, commercial cabins nearby. Nearby

towns: Ft. Smith, Fayetteville, Ozark, Clarksville and Harrison.

CALIFORNIA

ANGELES: (691,052); Los Angeles; U.S. 6, 66, 99. Steep, rugged mountains adjoining Los Angeles metropolitan area. Bear Canyon Wilderness Area. Scenic drives. Riding and hiking trails; winter sports; fishing and hunting; some swimming and boating. 52 camp and picnic areas; four winter sports areas, ski lifts and tows. Resorts, cabins, pack and riding stables. Hotels and motor courts in Los Angeles and foothill towns.

CLEVELAND: (567,103); San Diego; U.S. 101, 395, 80; State 78, 94. Agua Tibia Wilderness Area. Camping. Warm-water fishing and duck hunting on the impounded lakes of the water systems. Deer season of one month; pigeon and quail hunting. The first day's ride of the Mexico to Oregon Trail crosses the forest. 24 public camp and picnic areas; one winter playground. Three resorts with cabins, and dude ranches nearby. The cities of San Diego and Santa Ana are less than two hours' drive from the forest.

ELDORADO: (885,847); Placerville; forest lies partly in Nevada; U.S. 50, 88. Rugged mountains in Sierra Nevadas. Hundreds of mountain lakes; includes south end of Lake Tahoe. Lake and stream fishing. Deer and bear hunting. Scenic drives. Highway 50 to Lake Tahoe, Carson Pass Highway 88 famous for Fremont expedition in 1844 led by Kit Carson, Georgetown to Wentworth Springs. Riding trails; wilderness trips. 27 public camps and picnic areas; three winter sports areas. Resorts, hotels, cabins, and dude ranches. Nearby towns: Sacramento, Cal.; and Reno, Nev.

INYO: (1,858,986); Bishop; forest lies partly in Nevada; U.S. 6, 395. High Sierra Wilderness Area and Minarets Wild Area. Mt. Whitney, highest point in continental United States; rugged and spectacular back country with many peaks more than 14,000 feet elevation. Lake and stream fishing. Deer hunting. Wilderness trips. Many natural lakes, some accessible by paved road up to 9,700 feet elevation. Mammoth Lakes and June Lake–Silver Lake recreation areas. 42 public camp and picnic areas; eight winter sports areas. Resorts, cabins. Nearby towns: Lone Pine, Independence, Bigpine, Bishop and Leevining.

KLAMATH: (1,564,419); Yreka; forest lies partly in Oregon; U.S. 90. Klamath River and tributaries, famous for salmon and steelhead. Marble Mountain and Salmon-Trinity Alps Wilderness Areas. High mountain lakes and streams. Deer hunting, hiking, riding and pack trips. 40 improved forest camp and picnic grounds. Commercial cabin camps, resorts and dude ranches.

LASSEN: (1,382,630); Susanville; U.S. 395, State

36, 89. Caribou Peak and Thousand Lakes Wilderness Areas. Lake and stream fishing for rainbow, Lochleven and steelhead trout. Deer and bear hunting; riding and hiking trails. Scenic road over Mt. Lassen crosses through Lassen National Park. 50 public camp and picnic areas; trailer space. Privately operated resorts, hotels, cabins. Nearby towns: Susanville, Westwood, Chester, Chico, Red Bluff, Redding, Burney, Fall River Mills, McArthur and Stirling City.

LOS PADRES: (2,007,025); Santa Barbara; U.S. 101, 99, 399; State 1, 166, 150. Primitive forest, varying from coast redwood to semi-desert; home of the California condor. Ventana and San Rafael Wild Areas; snow-capped peaks. Quail and pigeon hunting; some deer and wild boar hunting. Trout fishing. Scenic drives; wilderness trips. 67 public camp and picnic areas on roads; numerous other trail camps. Kern County Ski Lodge. Hotels, cabins and a limited number of dude ranches. Nearby towns: Santa Barbara, Ojai, Taft, Santa Maria, San Luis Obispo, Carmel, King City, Monterey, Atascadero, Paso Robles and Ventura.

MENDOCINO: (1,082,634); Willows; U.S. 99W. Middle Eel-Yolla Bolly Wilderness Area. Columbian black-tailed deer. Hunting, fishing, hiking, saddle and pack trips. 40 public camps. Local commercial dude ranches and cabin camps.

MODOC: (2,025,247); Alturas; U.S. 299, 395; State 139. South Warner Wilderness Area. Winter range of interstate deer herd; Clear Lake Reservoir migratory bird refuge. Stream and lake fishing. Mule deer and waterfowl hunting. Scenic rides; summit trail through South Warner Wilderness Area; wilderness trips. 13 public camps; one winter sports area. Hotels, cabins and hunters' camps during deer season. Nearby towns: Alturas, Cedarville, Canby, Adin and Tulelake.

PLUMAS: (1,413,022); Quincy; State 89, 24. Feather River country. Lake and stream fishing. Mule and black-tailed deer, bear, duck, geese, quail and dove hunting. Lake Almanor, Bucks Lake, Lakes Basin Recreational Area and Little Last Chance Creek. State Riding and Hiking Trail. 16 improved public camp and picnic areas; one winter sports area at Johnsville. Resorts, hotels and cabins. Nearby towns: Marysville, Oroville, Chico, Chester, Susanville and Sierraville.

SAN BERNARDINO: (812,633); San Bernardino; U.S. 18, 66, 74, 99. San Jacinto, San Gorgonio and Cucamonga Wild Areas. Big Bear and Arrowhead Lakes. Lake and stream fishing. Deer hunting. Good sites for municipal and organization youth camps. Camping and pack trips; winter sports. 45 public camp and picnic areas with space for trailers; seven winter sports areas. Resorts, hotels, auto courts, cabins at Arrowhead and Big Bear Lakes.

SEQUOIA: (1,182,589); Porterville; State 65, 180, 178, 190. High Sierra Wilderness Area with 200 peaks more than 11,000 feet. Mineral King Recreation Area; ports of John Muir Trail. Kings River Canyon; Hume Lake; Kern River Canyon. Sequoia National Game Refuge. High mountain lakes and stream fishing. Big-game hunting including California mule deer and bear. Scenic drives: Kern River Canyon, Kings River Canyon. Riding trails in wilderness area; hiking, swimming, boating. 60 public camp and picnic areas; one winter sports area. Resorts, hotel, cabins. Nearby towns: Fresno, Sanger, Visalia, Porterville and Bakersfield.

SHASTA: (1,977,159); Mount Shasta; U.S. 99, 97, 299. Mount Shasta, 14,162 feet. Shasta Lake, 365 miles of mountain shore line. Trinity Alps Wilderness Area. Lake and stream fishing, home of the Dolly Varden trout. Waterfowl, upland birds, deer, bear, small-game hunting. Riding trails in wilderness area. 29 public camp and picnic areas; two winter sports areas. Resorts, hotels, motels, and guest ranches. Nearby towns: Dunsmuir, Weed, McCloud, Redding, Callahan, Etna, Trinity Center and Dorris.

SIERRA: (1,411,935); North Fork (Madera County); U.S. 99; State 41, 168. Huntington Lake, Florence Lake, Shaver Lake, Dinkey Creek and Bass Lake Recreation Areas. High Sierra Wilderness Area and Mount Dana-Minarets Wild Area. Lake and stream fishing. Deer, bear and quail hunting. Boating; mountain climbing; pack and saddle trips; winter sports. 112 improved forest camp and picnic areas; numerous swimming areas. Commercial cabin camps, hotels, resorts and dude ranches. Mono Hot Springs, improved mineral water and mud baths.

SIX RIVERS: (1,086,785); Eureka; U.S. 101, 199, 299. Klamath, Smith, Eel, and Mad Rivers. Mild cool climate yearlong; rugged back country. Trout fishing, spring and summer; steelhead and salmon fishing, fall and winter. Deer and bear hunting. Wilderness trip riding trails; scenic drives. 68 public camp and picnic areas; one winter sports area; three organization camps. Resorts, hotels, cabins. Nearby towns: Crescent City, Klamath, Orick, Trinidad, Arcata, Eureka, Fortuna and Orleans.

STANISLAUS: (1,100,709); Sonora; State 4, 108, 120. Stanislaus and Mokelumne Rivers. Emigrant Basin Wild Area. Fishing in lakes and 715 miles of streams. Big-game hunting for deer and bear. Camping, picnicking; organization camping, scenic drives, hiking, saddle and pack trips, winter sports. 26 public camp and picnic areas; sixteen organization camps; two winter sports areas. Resorts, cabins, stores, boating areas, packer stations. Nearby towns: Sonora, Jamestown, Columbia, Angels Camp, San Andreas and Groveland.

TAHOE: (1,190,264); Nevada City; U.S. 40; State 20, 49, 89. Attractive lakes and streams, including shore line of Lake Tahoe. Lake and stream fishing. Big-game hunting for deer and bear. Riding and hiking trails. 33 public forest camp and picnic areas. Summer resorts, cabins, hotels and private club accommodations. Nearby towns: Nevada City, Grass Valley, Truckee, Downieville, Sierra City and Sierraville.

TRINITY: (1,202,675); Weaverville; U.S. 299; State 36. Extensive stands of virgin timber. Salmon-Trinity Alps and Yolla Bolly-Middle Eel Wildnerness Areas. Deer hunting. Lake and stream fishing, including steelhead and salmon on the Trinity River. Scenic drives, riding trails; wilderness trips. 23 public camp and picnic areas. Resorts, hotels and cabins.

COLORADO

ARAPAHO: (1,102,974); Idaho Springs; U.S. 6, 40. Gore Range-Eagles Nest Wild Area. Lake and stream fishing. Big-game hunting for elk, deer, bear and some small game. Scenic high-mountain routes: Mount Evans, Loveland and Berthoud Passes; Peak to Peak Highway. Riding trails, wilderness area trips. 49 public camp and picnic grounds; seven winter sports areas. Resorts, hotels, cabin camps, dude ranches. Nearby towns: Idaho Springs, Dillon, Hot Sulphur Springs, Granby, Grand Lake and Kremmling.

U.S. Forest Service

National Forestlands in Colorado

GRAND MESA: (679,810); Grand Junction; U.S. 24, 50. 250 lakes and reservoirs. Lake and stream fishing. Deer, bear, duck hunting. Scenic drives,

saddle trips, winter sports, 21 public camp and picnic grounds; one winter sports area. Commercial cabin camps, resorts in and near forest. Nearby towns: Grand Junction, Delta, Palisade and Rifle.

GUNNISON: (1,562,644); Gunnison; U.S. 50. 1,000 miles trout fishing streams; many lakes. 27 mountain peaks more than 12,000 feet. West Elk and Maroon Bells-Snowmass Wilderness Areas. Elk, deer, mountain sheep, bear hunting. Hiking, saddle trips, wilderness area trips. 21 public camp and picnic grounds; one winter sports area. Resorts and cabin camps in and near forest.

PIKE: (1,258,825); Colorado Springs; U.S. 24, 85, 285. Pikes Peak. Hunting, fishing, camping, picnicking, hiking, saddle trips, scenic drives, winter sports. 36 public camp and picnic grounds; Pikes Peak winter sports area. Commercial hotels, resorts, cabin camps in and near forest. Nearby towns: Colorado Springs and Cripple Creek.

RIO GRANDE: (1,882,825); Monte Vita; U.S. 160, 285. Mountain lakes and trout streams; Upper Rio Grande and La Garita-Sheep Mountain Wilderness Areas. Trout fishing. Deer, elk and duck hunting. Saddle and pack trips, hiking and scenic drives. 18 improved public camp and picnic areas; one winter sports area. Commercial cabin camps in and near forest. Nearby towns: Monte Vista, Creede, Saguache, Alamosa and Antonito.

ROOSEVELT: (1,085,143); Fort Collins; U.S. 287. Continental Divide with many alpine lakes; Poudre and Big Thompson Canyons. Rawah Wild Area. Trout fishing. Deer, bear, mountain lion, grouse and duck hunting. Saddle and pack trips, hiking, scenic drives. 33 improved public camp and picnic areas; winter sports areas. Commercial cabin camps and dude ranches in and near the forest. Nearby towns: Fort Collins, Denver, Loveland, Longmont, Boulder and Estes Park.

ROUTT: (1,068,630); Steamboat Springs; U.S. 40. Continental Divide with perpetual ice and snow; trout streams and alpine lakes. Mount Zirkel-Dome Peak Wild Area; Big Creek Lakes Recreation Area. Deer, elk, grouse and duck hunting. Scenic drives, pack and saddle trips, hiking. 35 improved public camp and picnic areas; winter sports areas. Commercial cabin camps in and near the forest. Nearby towns: Steamboat Springs, Yampa, Hayden, Craig, Walden and Kremmling.

SAN ISABEL: (1,287,447); Pueblo; U.S. 24, 50, 85, 87. Highest average elevation of any national forest in the United States. 12 peaks more than 14,000 feet. Lake Isabel Recreation Area. Lake and stream trout fishing. Deer, elk, bear, mountain lion and bird hunting. Scenic drives, pack and saddle trips. 29 improved public camp and picnic areas; three winter sports areas. Commercial cabin camps and dude ranches in and near the forest. Nearby towns: Pueblo, Canon City, Salida, Walsenburg and Leadville.

SAN JUAN: (2,086,474); Durango; U.S. 160, 550. Alpine lakes. San Juan and Wilson Mountain Wilderness Areas. Trout fishing. Deer, elk, bear, mountain lion, grouse and duck hunting. Scenic drives, hiking, saddle and pack trips. 24 improved camp and picnic areas; winter sports areas. Commercial cabin camps and dude ranches in and near the forest. Nearby towns: Durango, Pagosa Springs, Mancos, Cortez, Rico, Dolores and Silverton.

UNCOMPAHGRE: (1,051,292); Delta; U.S. 50, 550. Uncompahgre Wild Area and Ouray Scenic Area. Trout fishing streams and lakes. Deer, elk, bear, mountain lion and grouse hunting. Scenic drives, saddle and pack trips. 9 improved camp and picnic areas; winter sports areas. Commercial cabin camps and dude ranches in and near the forest. Nearby towns: Delta, Montrose, Silverton and Ouray.

WHITE RIVER: (2,090,170); Glenwood Springs; U.S. 24. Maroon Bells-Snowmass, Flat Tops and Gore Range-Eagle Nest Wilderness Areas. Trout fishing. Elk, deer and bear hunting. Hiking, saddle and pack trips; scenic drives. 45 improved public camp and picnic areas; winter sports areas. Commercial cabin camps and dude ranches in and near the forest. Nearby towns: Glenwood Springs, Aspen, Leadville, Eagle, Gypsum, Rifle, New Castle, Meeker, Hayden, Craig, Yampa and Steamboat Springs.

FLORIDA

APALACHICOLA: (639,736); Tallahassee. Ranger headquarters at Tallahassee and Wilma; U.S. 90, 98. State game refuge. Three rivers and tributaries of fishing waters—bass, bream, perch. Quail, deer and bear hunting. Numerous lakes and ponds. Five organization camps; one camp and picnic ground. Commercial accommodations near forest.

OCALA: (442,679); Tallahassee. Ranger headquarters at Ocala; U.S. 17, 41. Juniper Springs—flow 8 million gallons fresh water daily. Numerous lakes, streams and ponds with fishing and camping sites. Annual deer hunt. Three organization camps, 11 improved forest camps and picnic grounds. Cabins at Juniper Springs. Commercial accommodations near forest.

OSCEOLA: (161,814); Tallahassee. Ranger headquarters at Lake City; U.S. 41, 90. State game breeding ground. Bass, perch and bream fishing. Deer, turkey, quail and dove hunting. Swimming and boating at Ocean Pond. Recreation residence site on Ocean Pond.

GEORGIA

CHATTAHOOCHEE: (1,518,322); Gainesville; U.S. 19, 23, 27, 41, 76. Appalachian Trail. Deer and small-game hunting; bow and arrow hunt for deer. Trout and bass fishing. Swimming, boating. 16 improved forest camp and picnic grounds.

IDAHO

BOISE: (2,950,613); Boise; U.S. 20, 30, 95; State 15, 16, 17, 21, 22, 52. Lake and stream fishing for trout and salmon. Bear, elk and deer hunting. Scenic drives include spectacular Payette River Canyon, Boise Ridge and the edge of the Sawtooth Wilderness Area. 122 public camp and picnic areas; one winter sports area. Resorts, hotels, cabins and dude ranches, with horses, boats and other facilities. Nearby towns: Boise, Emmett, Mountain Home, Cascade, Idaho City and Horse Shoe Bend.

CARIBOU: (1,061,718); Pocatello; Forest lies partly in Utah and Wyoming; U.S. 91, 191, 30. Stream fishing; game birds, deer and bear hunting. Snake River-McCoy Road along the south bank of the south fork of Snake River. Numerous riding trails into wilderness areas. 17 public camp and picnic areas; two winter sports areas. Resort, hotel and cabin accommodations in nearby Idaho Falls, Ririe, Swan Valley, Montpelier, Soda Springs, Lava Hot Springs, and Malad City, Idaho; and Afton, Wyo.

CHALLIS: (2,468,067); Challis; U.S. 20, 93, 93A. Majestic Sawtooth Primitive Area and Stanley Basin; Middle Fork of the Salmon River in the Idaho Wilderness Area, Lemhi, Lost River and White Cloud Peaks. Salmon River and White Knob mountain ranges, headwaters of the Salmon River. Stream, lake trout and salmon fishing. Elk, deer, mountain goat, mountain sheep, antelope and bear hunting. Stanley Basin scenic drive; riding and hiking trails; wilderness boating and pack trips. 10 public camp and picnic areas. Resorts, hotels, cabins, dude ranches; commercial packers and guides. Nearby towns: Challis, Mackay, Salmon and Stanley.

CLEARWATER: (1,140,804); Orofino; State 9, 11. Selway-Bitterroot Wilderness Area. Trout and salmon fishing in back country. Elk and bear hunting; deer hunting on part of forest. Scenic drives: North Fork, Lolo Trail and Lochsa Road. Six improved public camp areas; numerous camping spots. Commercial cabins, camps and dude ranches.

COEUR D'ALENE: (802,177); Couer d'Alene; U.S. 10, 95. Many miles of fishing streams; big-game hunting for deer. Six hundred miles of scenic forest roads. Adjacent to beautiful Coeur d'Alene Lake with 104 miles of shore line. 10 public camp areas; one winter sports area on U.S. Highway 10. Resort hotels, cabins in Coeur d'Alene, Hayden Lake, Wallace, Kellogg, Mullan and nearby towns of Spirit Lake and Twin Lakes.

KANIKSU: (1,059,549); Sandpoint. Forest lies

partly in Montana and Washington; U.S. 95, 195, 10A, 2, 6. Rugged back country; Selkirk Mountain Range. Pend Oreille Lake (Lake Loop Drive, 107 miles); Priest Lake, Sullivan Lake. Lake and stream fishing; big-game, grouse and duck hunting. Boating, swimming, scenic drives, wilderness trips. 33 public camp and picnic areas; winter sports areas. Resorts, hotels, lodges, cabins. Nearby towns: Sandpoint, Bonners Ferry, Priest River, Metaline Falls, Newport, Clark Fork and Hope.

MINIDOKA: Burley. Forest lies partly in Utah; U.S. 30. Cleveland, Independence and smaller alpine lakes; exceptional panoramic views of Snake River Valley. Small stream fishing; big-game hunting for deer. Scenic drives; riding and hiking trails. 27 public camp and picnic areas; two winter sports areas. Resorts, hotels, lodges, cabins. Nearby towns having hotel and tourist cabin accommodations: Twin Falls, Kimberly, Hansen and Burley.

NEZPERCE: (1,976,046); Grangeville; U.S. 95; State 9, 13, 14. Selway-Bitterroot Wilderness Area. Big-game hunting for elk, deer and bear; lake and stream fishing. Horse trails, wilderness trips; scenic drives. Selway River, Lochsa River, Salmon River. 18 public camp and picnic areas; one winter sports area. Resorts, hotels, cabins. Nearby towns: Grangeville, Stites, Kooskia, Kamiah, Riggins and White Bird.

PAYETTE: (2,418,977); McCall; U.S. 95, 15. Idaho Wilderness Area, Grand Canyon of Snake River, Payette Lakes, Vacation Land, Seven Devils Mountains. Fishing for trout and salmon, 154 fishing lakes, 1,530 miles fishing streams. Hunting for deer, elk, goats, sheep, bear. Scenic drives; wilderness trips. 30 improved camps; one winter sports area. Dude ranches. Nearby towns: McCall, Council and New Meadows.

ST. JOE: (1,089,180); Saint Maries; U.S. 95A. Rugged Bitterroot Range of Idaho-Montana divide; St. Joe River Drainage. Canyon areas of Little North Fork of Clearwater River; Palouse River area. Big-game hunting for elk, deer, bear and mountain goat; lake and stream fishing. Scenic drives along St. Joe River from mouth to source. 30 public campground and picnic areas; two winter sports areas accessible by highway and rail. One dude ranch; Spring Creek cabins on St. Joe River. Nearby towns: Moscow, Potlatch, Saint Maries, Avery and Clarkia.

SALMON: (1,790,944); Salmon; U.S. 93; State 27, 28. Idaho Wilderness Area. Salmon River Canyon. Fishing; big-game hunting for deer, elk, sheep, goats, bear, cougar and antelope. Salmon River and Panther Creek forest roads; boat trips on "River of No Return" and Middlefork. Five improved forest camp and picnic grounds; winter sports areas. Dude ranches. Nearby towns: Salmon and Leadore.

SAWTOOTH: (1,790,356); Hailey; U.S. 22, 93. Sawtooth Wilderness Area; numerous glacial lakes, 1 to 1,500 acres in size. Lake and stream fishing. Deer, elk, bear hunting. Scenic drives: Warm Springs Creek, South Boise River, Wood River, Salmon River, Alturas and Red Fish Lakes. Riding trails; wilderness trips; boating; hot springs; mountain climbing. 28 public camps and picnic areas; two winter sports areas, including Sun Valley with 5 miles of ski lifts. Resorts, hotels, cabins and dude ranches. Nearby towns: Hailey, Ketchum, Fairfield and Stanley.

TARGHEE: (1,346,481); Saint Anthony. Forest lies partly in Wyoming; U.S. 91, 191; State 22, 29, 31. Island Park country, lakes and streams. Grand Canyon of the Snake River. Grand Teton Peaks, Big Falls, North Fork of Snake River, Cave Falls, Falls River. Lake and stream fishing; big-game hunting for black and brown bear, deer, elk and moose. Many riding and hiking trails into semi-wilderness areas. 20 improved camp and picnic areas; three winter sports areas. Resorts, cabins, dude ranches; boating facilities; pack outfits for hunting parties and one boys' dude ranch. Nearby towns: Idaho Falls, Rexburg, Rigby, Saint Anthony, Ashton, Driggs, Victor and Dubois.

ILLINOIS

SHAWNEE: (802,383); Harrisburg; U.S. 34, 51; State 1, 3, 34, 127, 144, 145, 146, 151. Fishing in larger streams. Hunting for quail, waterfowl, squirrel, rabbits, fox and raccoon. Artificial lakes in and adjacent to forest provide fishing, boating and swimming. 16 State and Forest Service camp and picnic areas. Hotels and cabins at nearby towns of Cairo, Metropolis, Harrisburg and Marion.

INDIANA

HOOSIER: (722,461); Bedford; U.S. 50, 150. Squirrel, fox and quail hunting. Fishing in the Ohio, Lost, Patoka and East Fork of the White Rivers and Salt Creek for catfish, bass and bluegill. Scenic drives for spring flowers (dogwood and redbud) and fall coloring. One public camp and picnic area with 3-acre lake for swimming and fishing. Commercial hotels and cabin camps. Nearby towns: Evansville, Jasper and Bedford.

KENTUCKY

CUMBERLAND: (1,357,085); Winchester; U.S. 25, 27, 60. Bass and pike fishing in larger streams. Picnicking, Red River gorge drive, hiking. Two picnic areas. Hotel and cabins at Cumberland Falls State Park and other places near forest.

LOUISIANA

KISATCHIE: (877,066); Alexandria; U.S. 71, 165, 167, 84; State 19, 21. Many bayous and lakes screened with Spanish moss. Fishing in lakes and bayous. Hunting for deer, quail and migratory birds. Boating, swimming, picnicking, camping, scenic drives. Two artificial lakes. Public recreational areas at Valentine Lake 20 miles west of Alexandria and Gum Springs 10 miles west of Winnifield. Commercial hotels and cabin camps nearby.

MICHIGAN

LOWER MICHIGAN: (2,074,607); (Huron National Forest); Cadillac; U.S. 23, 27. Forest easily accessible for the large population of southern Michigan, northern Ohio, Indiana and Illinois. Trout fishing in the Au Sable River and smaller streams. Deer, small-game and bird hunting. Lake Huron with excellent beaches on eastern side. 18 public camp and picnic areas; one winter sports area. A large number of resorts, hotels and cabins. Towns within and near the forest: East Tawas, Tawas City, Oscoda, Harrisville, Grayling, Roscommon, West Branch, Rose City and Mio.

LOWER MICHIGAN: (Manistee National Forest); Cadillac; U.S. 10, 31, 131. Many lakes and streams for fishing. Deer and small-game hunting. Good skiing conditions on northern part of forest. Many lakes, including Lake Michigan, have beaches for swimming, canoeing, 16 public camp and picnic areas; one winter sports area. A large number of resorts, hotels and cabins. Towns within and near the forest: Manistee, Ludington, Scottville, Whitehall, Fremont, Newaygo, White Cloud, Big Rapids, Reed City, Baldwin, Wellston, Brethren and Cadillac.

OTTAWA: (1,742,966); Ironwood; U.S. 2, 45; State 28, 35, 64. Numerous easily accessible lakes and streams. Lake and stream fishing; deep-sea trolling in Lake Superior. Deer and bear hunting. Many scenic drives. 51 Federal, state and county camp and picnic areas; two winter sports areas. Numerous hotels and cabins. Nearby towns: Ironwood, Wakefield, Bessemer, Iron River, Ontonagon, Watersmeet, Kenton, Marensico and Trout Creek.

UPPER MICHIGAN: (1,325,160); (Hiawatha and Marquette National Forests); Escanaba; U.S. 2, 41; State 28, 94, 77. Lakes Huron, Michigan and Superior. Lake and stream fishing for trout, bass, northern and walleyed pike, perch; smelt dipping. Deer, black bear, ruffed and sharp-tailed grouse hunting. Canoeing. 25 public camp and picnic areas; two winter sports areas. Resorts, hotels, many cabins. Nearby well-equipped state parks. Adjacent towns: Rapid River, Gladstone, Escanaba, Munising, Manistique, Saint Ignace and Sault Sainte Marie.

MINNESOTA

CHIPPEWA: (1,313,656); Cass Lake; U.S. 2, 71, 371. Headwaters of the Mississippi River; Leech Lake, Lake Winnibigoshish, Cass Lake and hundreds of smaller lakes. Lake fishing for walleyes, northern pike and pan fish. Water fowl and upland game-bird hunting; big-game hunting for deer and black bear. Hundreds of miles of good roads and scenic drives; swimming; boating and water sports. Winter sports including skiing, tobogganing, snowshoeing and ice fishing. 18 public camp and picnic areas; one winter sports area. 300 resorts in and adjacent to the forest. Hotels, cabins, organization camps, boys' and girls' camps. Nearby towns: Cass Lake, Walker, Deer River, Grand Rapids, Remer, Bemidji, Blackduck.

SUPERIOR: (2,873,576); Duluth; U.S. 1, 53, 61. 5,000 lakes, rugged shore lines, picturesque islands, sand beaches; million acres of virgin forest. Superior and Little Indian Sioux Roadless Areas, outstanding canoe trip opportunities. Lake and stream fishing; deer hunting. 16 unusual canoe routes. 20 public camp and picnic grounds. Resorts, hotels and cabins. Nearby towns: Duluth, Virginia, International Falls, Ely, Two Harbors and Grand Marais.

MISSISSIPPI

BIENVILLE: (382,820); Jackson. Ranger headquarters at forest; U.S. 80; State 35. Quail hunting, fishing, swimming. One improved forest camp and picnic ground.

DELTA: Jackson. Ranger headquarters at Rolling Fork; U.S. 61. Extensive areas of virgin bottomland hardwood. Deer hunting and fishing. No improved campgrounds.

DE SOTO: (1,213,740); Jackson. Ranger headquarters at Gulfport, Laurel and Hattiesburg; U.S. 11, 90. Site of South Mississippi Gun and Dog Club field trials. Quail hunting, fishing, bathing, boating. Three improved forest camp and picnic grounds.

HOLLY SPRINGS: (462,040); Jackson. Ranger headquarters at Holly Springs; U.S. 72, 78. Annual bird-dog field trials at Holly Springs. Quail and small-game hunting. No improved forest camp or picnic grounds.

HOMOCHITTO: (373,495); Jackson. Ranger headquarters at Meadville; U.S. 61, 84. Fishing, swimming, picnicking and camping with trailer facilities at Clear Springs Recreation Area. One improved forest camp and picnic area.

MISSOURI

CLARK, Rolla. MARK TWAIN, Springfield; (3,460,186); U.S. 8, 19, 21, 60, 67, 63, 66. Big springs; clear, fast flowing streams; Ozark Mountains. Smallmouth bass and other fishing; squirrel shooting, fox hunting. Hundreds of miles of streams for "John boat" float trips. Clear streams with fishing for pan fish, bass and pike; quail hunting. Scenic drives. CLARK—13 public camp nd picnic grounds. Nearby towns: Doniphan, Poplar Bluff, Van Buren, Ironton, Steelville, Salem and Eminence. MARK TWAIN—Two roadside campgrounds and one developed camping, picnic and swimming area. Resorts and hotels n nearby towns of Branson, Hollister, Cassville, Forsyth, Rolla, Willow Springs and West Plains.

MONTANA

BEAVERHEAD: (2,316,364); Dillon; U.S. 91; State 1, 41, 34, 36, 43. Anaconda-Pintler Wilderness Area. Madison, Ruby, Beaverhead and Big Hole Rivers; alpine lakes. Fishing; deer, elk, moose, antelope and bear hunting. Hot springs, scenic drives, wilderness trips. 26 public camp and picnic areas; winter sports areas. Resorts, hotels and cabins in and near forest. Nearby towns: Dillon, Wisdom, Jackson, Lima, Ennis, Virginia City and Sheridan.

BITTERROOT: (1,175,246); Hamilton. Forest lies partly in Idaho; U.S. 93. Bitterroot Valley and spectacular Bitterroot Mountains; scores of mountain lakes. Selway-Bitterroot Wilderness Area, largest in United States; Anaconda-Pintler Wilderness Area. Lake and stream fishing; biggame hunting for elk, deer, bear and riding trails; wilderness trips. 10 public camp and picnic areas; one winter sports area. Resorts, hotels, cabins and dude ranches. Nearby towns: Darby, Hamilton, Corvallis, Stevensville and Missoula.

CABINET: (1,361,209); Thompson Falls; U.S. 10, 10A; State 28. Cabinet Mountains Wilderness Area; rugged mountain ranges; numerous highland lakes and mountain streams. Mountain lake, stream and river fishing. Big-game hunting for bear, elk, black and whitetail deer. Numerous scenic drives; primitive area and trail-riding trips. 15 developed public camp and picnic areas; Lookout Pass winter sports area on U.S. Highway 10. Limited resort, hotel, cabin and dude ranch facilities. Nearby towns: Thompson Falls, Plains, Hot Springs, Paradise, Saint Regis, Noxon, Saltese, Trout Creek.

CUSTER: (1,146,569); Billings. Forest lies partly in South Dakota; U.S. 10, 12. Hundreds of lakes. Beartooth Wilderness Area. Trout fishing, biggame hunting, saddle and pack trips. 30 public camps and picnic areas; one winter sports area. Resorts, hotels, cabins and dude ranches. Nearby towns: Red Lodge, Laurel and Billings.

DEERLODGE: (1,329,841); Butte; U.S. 10S, 10A, 91; State 38. Anaconda-Pintler Wilderness Area; numerous alpine lakes. Lake and stream fishing; big-game hunting for bear, deer, elk; special moose seasons. Riding trails, wilderness trips. 25 public camp areas; five winter sports areas. Resorts, hotels, cabins and dude ranches. Nearby towns: Whitehall, Butte, Boulder, Anaconda, Philipsburg and Deerlodge.

FLATHEAD: (2,623,035); Kalispell; U.S. 2, 93; State 35, 37. Spectacular geological formations, including massive Chinese Wall and jagged Mission Mountains, hanging valleys, glaciers and scores of glacial lakes. Mission Mountains and Pentagon Wild Areas; superb Bob Marshall Wilderness Area. Fishing, hunting; big game includes elk, deer, moose, bear, mountain sheep and mountain goats. Picnicking, boating, camping, canoeing, hiking, and riding; scenic drives around Flathead Lake; wilderness trips. 12 public camp and picnic areas; two winter sports areas, including Big Mountain ski course. Resorts, hotels, cabins and dude ranches. Nearby towns: Whitefish, Columbia Falls, Coram, Belton and Bigfork.

GALLATIN: (1,699,320); Bozeman; U.S. 191, 10, 89. More than 200 lakes and thousands of miles of trout streams. Spanish Peaks and Absaroka Wilderness Areas. Lake and stream fishing; big-game hunting, including bear, moose, goat, elk and deer. Scenic drives; Gallatin Canyon, Boulder Canyon and Yankee Jim Canyon; trail riding and wilderness trips. 38 public camp and picnic areas; 3 winter sports areas. Resorts, hotels, cabins and dude ranches. Nearby towns: Bozeman, West Yellowstone, Livingston, Bigtimber and Gardiner.

HELENA: (1,156,394); Helena; U.S. 10N, 91. Continental Divide. Gates of the Mountains Wilderness Area. Lake and stream fishing; elk and deer hunting. Scenic drives: Trout and Beaver Creek Canyons; riding trails; wilderness trips. 5 public camp and picnic areas; one winter sports area. Resorts, hotels, cabins and dude ranches. Nearby towns: Helena, Townsend, Lincoln and White Sulphur Springs.

KOOTENAI: (2,053,805); Libby. Forest lies partly in Idaho; U.S. 2; State 37. Cabinet Mountains Wilderness Area; Whitfish Range; Yaak River, Kootenai Canyon and Fisher River. Lake and stream fishing; big-game hunting for black bear and deer. Scenic drives: Yaak River, Kootenai Canyon, Fisher River; riding trails. 10 public camp and picnic areas; one winter sports area. Hotels, cabins and dude ranches. Nearby towns: Libby, Troy and Eureka.

LEWIS AND CLARK: (2,031,599); Great Falls; U.S. 87, 89, 91; State 29. Bob Marshall Wilderness Area; Chinese Wall and Continental Divide. Stream and lake fishing; big-game hunting for deer, elk, grizzly, black bear and antelope. Wilderness trips; riding trails; numerous scenic drives along Kings Hill, Judith River, Crystal Lake, Sun River and Teton River. 20 camp and picnic areas; one winter sports area. Many resorts, cabins and dude ranches. Nearby towns: Great Falls and Lewistown.

LOLO: (1,726,290); Missoula. Forest lies partly in Idaho; U.S. 10, 93; State 20. Bob Marshall and Selway-Bitterroot Wilderness Areas; Mission,

Bitterroot and Swan Ranges; Continental Divide. Lewis and Clark Trail; junction Clark Fork and Bitterroot Rivers. Stream and lake fishing; hunting for native grouse, pheasant, elk, deer and bear. Wilderness pack trips; scenic drives on Lolo Trail, Lochsa River, Seeley Lake, Buffalo Park, Rock Creek. Mountain saddle trails, foot trails to a hundred lakes and peaks. 29 public campgrounds; Pattee Canyon picnic area. Resorts, dude ranches. Nearby towns: Missoula, Ovando, Superior, Alberton and Drummond.

NEBRASKA

NEBRASKA: (207,209); Halsey; U.S. 20. Largest herd of mule deer in Nebraska; entire forest in game refuge; nesting grounds of great blue heron, grouse and prairie chicken. Pheasant, migratory bird and small-game hunting in season outside the forest boundaries. Fishing; swimming. One improved public camp and picnic ground. Hotel accommodations at Broken Bow and Valentine.

NEVADA

HUMBOLDT: (1,481,094); Elko; U.S. 18, 40. Wildhorse Reservoir; Owyhee River Canyon. Fishing in streams and Wildhorse Reservoir; deer hunting. Saddle and pack trips. No forest campgrounds. Resort and dude ranch at Wildhorse Reservoir. Hotel facilities at Elko and Mountain City.

NEVADA: (1,259,528); Ely; U.S. 6, 50, 93; State 39. Deer hunting; Nevada's only elk herd. Scenic trails on Snake Division and Charleston Mountain. 20 public camp, picnic and trailer camp areas; two winter sports areas. Nearby towns: Las Vegas, Ely, McGill, Ruth and Kimberly.

TOIYABE: (2,871,780); Reno. Forest lies partly in California; U.S. 395, 50, 40, 6, 88, 108, 95; California 4; Nevada 8A, 88, 3, 22. Alpine lakes; Virginia Creek, Green Creek, and Twin Lakes; Hoover Wilderness Area. Lake and stream fishing, golden and Piute Trout. Blacktail and mule deer, antelope hunting. Scenic drives: Mt. Rose, Lake Tahoe, Ebbetts and Sonora Passes; riding trails, wilderness trips. 23 public camp and picnic areas; two winter sports areas. Resorts, hotels, cabins and dude ranches. Nearby towns: Reno, Carson City, Minden, Austin, Tonopah and Winnemucca.

NEW HAMPSHIRE

WHITE MOUNTAIN: (798,291); Laconia. Forest lies partly in Maine. U.S. 2, 3, 302. Embraces a major portion of the White Mountains. Mt. Washington, 6,288 feet, highest point in New England. Mountain stream fishing; deer and bear hunting. Scenic drives through famous notches; winter and spring skiing; mountain climbing and hiking, more than 1,000 miles of foot trails; swimming. 16 public camp and picnic grounds, including popular Dolly Copp Area. High country cabins. Nearby hotels and cabins.

NEW MEXICO

CARSON: (1,226,094); Taos; U.S. 64; State 3, 75, 38. Trout streams, lakes and hot springs. Lake and stream trout fishing; hunting for turkey and brown bear. Scenic drives; saddle and pack trips. 30 public camp and picnic areas. Nearby towns: Taos, Santa Fe and Raton.

CIBOLA: (2,275,282); Albuquerque; U.S. 85, 66, 60. Antelope herds. Deer and antelope hunting; limited fishing. Scenic drives. 34 public camp and picnic areas; two winter sports areas. Resorts, hotels, cabins and dude ranches. Nearby towns: Albuquerque, Mountainair, Belen, Socorro, Hot Springs, Grants and Gallup.

GILA: (3,053,505); Silver City; U.S. 260; State 180, 52, 78, 185, 186. Abundant game. Gila and Black Range Wilderness Areas. Stream fishing. Hunting includes black bear, mule deer, whitetail deer, antelope, mountain lion and turkey. Scenic drives: Outer Loop, Inner Loop; riding and hiking trails; wilderness trips. 18 public camp and picnic areas. Private cabins, lodge resorts, and dude ranches. Nearby towns: Silver City, Glenwood, Deming, Lordsburg and Hot Springs.

LINCOLN: (1,444,316); Alamogordo; U.S. 54, 70, 380; State 83. White Mountain Wild Area. Adjoins Carlsbad Caverns National Park and White Sands National Monument. Fishing; big-game hunting. Winter sports, scenic drives; saddle and pack trips. 8 public camp and picnic areas; two winter sports areas. Resort hotels, lodges, cabins, dude ranches and organization camps. Nearby towns: Ruidoso, Cloudcroft, Alamogordo, Carlsbad, Artesia and Roswell.

SANTA FE: (1,369,938); Santa Fe; U.S. 285, 85, 64, 84. Pecos and Jemez Rivers; mountain streams and lakes. San Pedro Parks Wild Area; Pecos Wilderness Area. Lakes and streams furnish much of the clear water for trout fishing in state. Turkey, elk, deer, bear hunting. Wilderness trips. 31 public camp and picnic areas; one winter sports area. Resorts, hotels, commercial cabin camps on Pecos and Jemez Rivers in vicinity of Santa Fe, Las Vegas and Jemez Springs. Nearby towns: Santa Fe, Las Vegas, Pecos, Espanola and Bernalillo.

NORTH CAROLINA

CROATAN: (294,610); Asheville. Ranger headquarters at New Bern; U.S. 17, 70. 3 miles from Atlantic Ocean. Deer, bear, turkey, quail and migratory bird hunting; fishing, boating and swimming. Two improved forest camp and picnic grounds. Commercial resorts and cabin camps in and near forest.

NANTAHALLA: (1,349,000); Franklin; U.S. 19, 64, 129, 23. Fontana, Hiwassee, Santeetlah, Nantahala, Cheoah, Glenville and Apalachia Lakes; Fontana Dam, Cullasaja, White Water River. Lake and stream fishing for bass and trout. European wild boar, deer, bear, turkey and bird hunting. Hiking, swimming and boating. Eight improved forest camp and picnic grounds. Tourist and cabin accommodations in and near forest.

PISGAH: (1,177,303); Asheville; U.S. 19, 23, 25, 64, 70, 221, 276, 321, and Blue Ridge Parkway. Mount Mitchell, 6,684 feet; Pisgah National Game Refuge; Boone, Mt. Mitchell and Sherwood Cooperative Game Management Areas, with annual big-game hunts. Trout, bass and perch fishing. Deer, bear and small-game hunting. Hiking; horseback riding; swimming. 18 improved forest camp and picnic grounds. Commercial resorts and cabin camps in and near forest. Nearby towns: Hot Springs, Lenoir, Marion and Pisgah Forest.

OHIO

WAYNE: (1,454,982); Columbus; U.S. 21, 23, 33, 35, 50, 52. Small-game hunting; fishing on numerous streams and lakes. Hiking; horseback riding; scenic lookout points. Lake Vesuvius Recreation Area and five other developed areas. Overnight accommodations at numerous cabin camps, tourist homes and hotels along the main highways and at the larger towns throughout the area.

OREGON

DESCHUTES: (1,927,401); Bend; U.S. 28, 97. Snow-clad peaks, ice caves, waterfalls and scores of beautiful mountain lakes; Deschutes River; Mount Jefferson Wild Area and Three Sisters Wilderness Area. Rainbow trout fishing; deer hunting. Scenic drives; saddle and pack trips; winter sports. 38 improved forest camp and picnic grounds; one winter sports area. Commercial dude ranches, cabin camps and resorts in and near forest. Nearby towns: Sisters, Redmond, Bend and Crescent.

FREMONT: (1,772,637); Lakeview; U.S. 395. Protected herds of antelope. Oregon Desert, Gearhart Mountain Wild Area. Deer hunting. 13 improved forest camp and picnic grounds. Commercial cabin camps in and near forest. Nearby towns: Lakeview, Bly, Paisley, Crescent and Klamath Falls.

MALHEUR: (1,275,913); John Day; U.S. 28, 395. Mountains; miles of fishing streams; archers' hunting reserve; Strawberry Mountain Wild Area. Stream trout fishing; elk and deer hunting. Scenic drives; saddle and pack trips. 11 improved forest camp and picnic grounds. Commercial cabin camps in and near forest. Nearby towns: John Day, Burns and Prairie City.

MOUNT HOOD: (1,183,897); Portland; U.S. 30, 99. Timberline Lodge. Mount Hood and Mount Jefferson Wild Areas. On Oregon Trail route. Stream and lake fishing. Swimming; winter sports; saddle and pack trips; spectacular auto tours. 55 improved forest camp and picnic grounds; four winter sports areas. Timberline Lodge and other commercial resorts in and near forest. Nearby towns: Portland, Hood River, Gresham, Estacada, Sandy and Maupin.

OCHOCO: (980,846); Prineville; U.S. 28, 97. Many beaver colonies. Trout fishing; deer hunting. Scenic drives. Five improved forest camp and picnic grounds. Commercial cabin camps in and near forest. Nearby towns: Prineville and Dayville.

ROGUE RIVER: (1,148,299); Medford. Forest lies partly in California. U.S. 99. Rogue River, lakes, trout streams. Mountain Lakes Wild Area. Rainbow and steelhead fishing; deer and migratory bird hunting. Scenic drives; saddle and pack trips. 24 improved forest camp and picnic grounds. Commercial cabin camps in and near forest. Nearby towns: Medford, Ashland, Grants Pass, Klamath Falls and Crescent.

SISKIYOU: (1,350,440); Grants Pass. Forest lies partly in California; U.S. 99, 101, 199. Famous fishing grounds in lower Rogue River gorge. Kalmiopsis Wild Area. Cutthroat and steelhead trout and salmon fishing. Deer, bear and cougar hunting. Boat trips; saddle and pack trips; scenic drives. 17 improved forest camp and picnic grounds. Commercial resorts, outfitters and cabin camps in and near forest. Nearby towns: Grants Pass, Powers, Gold Beach and Brookings.

SIUSLAW: (878,666); Corvallis; U.S. 20, 99, 101. Bordered by Pacific Ocean. Ocean, lake and stream fishing. Deer, bear, cougar and migratory bird hunting. Swimming, boating, clam digging; saddle and pack trips; scenic drives. 19 improved forest camp and picnic grounds. Commercial cabin camps and resorts in and near forest. Nearby towns: Corvallis, Eugene, Newport, Mapelton, Florence, Waldport and Taft.

UMATILLA: (1,192,178); Pendleton. Forest lies partly in Washington; U.S. 30, 395. On old Oregon Trail route. Elk, deer, pheasant hunting. Saddle trips and scenic drives; winter sports. 17 improved forest camp and picnic grounds; one winter sports area. Commercial hostelries in and near forest. Nearby towns: Pendleton, Walla Walla and La Grande.

UMPQUA: (1,180,908); Roseburg; U.S. 99. Umpqua River; Diamond Lake. Steelhead and rainbow fishing. Deer, bear, cougar hunting. Scenic drives; saddle and pack trips. 23 improved forest camp and picnic grounds. Commercial resorts and cabin camps near forest.

WALLOWA: (2,642,406); Enterprise; U.S. 30. Wallowa and many other lakes. Minam River, famous fishing stream. Eagle Cap Wilderness

Area. Stream and lake trout fishing; elk, deer, bear hunting. Saddle and pack trips; scenic drives. 16 improved forest camp and picnic grounds. Commercial resorts and cabin camps in and near forest. Nearby towns: Enterprise, Wallowa and Joseph.

WHITMAN: (1,568,432); Baker; U.S. 28, 395, 30. Anthony Lakes; Eagle Cap Wilderness Area. Stream and lake fishing; deer, bear, elk hunting. Scenic drives; saddle and pack trips. Eight improved forest camp and picnic grounds; one winter sports area. Commercial cabin camps and dude ranches in and near forest. Nearby towns: Baker, La Grande, Union and Prairie City.

WILLAMETTE: (1,819,967); Eugene; U.S. 20, 28, 54, 99. Most heavily timbered national forest in United States. Snow-capped peaks, lakes. Three Sisters Wilderness Area; Mount Jefferson Wild Area. Stream and lake fishing; deer and bear hunting. Scenic drives; saddle and pack trips. 51 improved forest camp and picnic grounds; two winter sports areas. Commercial cabin camps and pack trip outfitters in and near forest. Nearby towns: Eugene, Albany, Salem, and Lebanon.

PENNSYLVANIA

ALLEGHENY: (736,577); Warren; U.S. 6, 62; State 59. Allegheny Mountains. 300 miles of trout streams; Beaver Meadows Waterfowl Refuge. Trout and bass fishing; big-game hunting for bear and deer. Scenic drives. Eight public camp and picnic areas; two swimming areas; two organization camps. Hotels, cabins. Nearby towns: Kane, Bradford, Marienville, Sheffield, Tionesta, Ridgway and Tidioute.

PUERTO RICO

CARIBBEAN: (69,950); Rio Piedras. By plane: 5 hours from New York, 4 hours from Miami; by car from Rio Piedras: 1 hour to Luquillo Division, 2 hours to Toro Negro Division. For the nature lover, more than 300 tree species, 21 different orchids, 500 varieties of ferns. Forests abound with wild parrots, foot and horseback trails, and observation points on mountaintops. Scenic mountain drives over excellent highways; vivid comparison between heavy rainfall and arid sides of island. La Mina Recreation Area on the Luquillo Division—500 acres of highly developed picnic areas, restaurant, rental cabins, swimming pools. Nearby towns offer resort and hotel accommodations, with ocean beaches, surf bathing.

SOUTH CAROLINA

FRANCIS MARION: (414,700); Columbia Ranger headquarters at Moncks Corner and McClellanville; U.S. 17, 52. Bass and pan fish; deer, turkey and quail hunting. Boating, bathing, scenic drives. One improved forest picnic ground. Commercial hostelries nearby.

SOMTER: (1,008,639); Columbia Ranger headquarters at Newberry, Walhalla and Greenwood; U.S. 25, 76, 176. Walhalla trout hatchery. Trout and some bass fishing; quail hunting; scenic drives. Four improved forest picnic grounds. Commercial hostelries near forest.

SOUTH DAKOTA

BLACK HILLS: (1,325,371); Deadwood. Forest lies partly in Wyoming; U.S. 14, 85. Fishing; deer and migratory bird hunting. Swimming, hiking, saddle trips, scenic drives. 24 improved public camp and picnic areas. Numerous commercial cabin camps and dude ranches in and near the forest. Nearby towns: Deadwood, Rapid City, Belle Fourche, Custer and Hot Springs, S. Dak.; Sundance, Newcastle, Wyo.

HARNEY: Custer. Forest lies partly in Wyoming; U.S. 16, 85. Lake and stream trout fishing; deer and elk hunting. Swimming, boating, hiking, saddle trips, scenic drives. 23 improved public camp and picnic areas. Commercial cabin camps and dude ranches in and near the forest. Nearby towns: Custer, Rapid City, Belle Fourche, Edgemont and Hot Springs, S. Dak.; Newcastle, Wyo.

TENNESSEE

CHEROKEE: (1,204,102); Cleveland. Forest lies partly in North Carolina; U.S. 421, 19E, 19W, 25, 64; State 68, 67, 70. Rugged mountain country cut by river gorges. Lake and stream fishing including rainbow and brook trout. Small- and large-game hunting, including wild boar. Hiking, boating, swimming. 18 public camp and picnic areas. Hotels and tourist cabins. Nearby towns: Bristol, Johnson City, Mountain City, Elizabethton, Erwin, Greeneville, Newport, Madisonville, Tellico Plains, Etowah, Benton and Cleveland.

TEXAS

ANGELINA: (391,300); Lufkin; U.S. 59, 69. Angelina River and many overflow lakes; Boykin Lake. Bass and cat fishing in rivers and lakes; quail and dove hunting. One improved picnic and camping area.

DAVY CROCKETT: (394,200); Lufkin, Ranger headquarters at Crockett and Groveton; U.S. 287, State 94, 103. Bass and cat fishing in rivers and lakes, some deer hunting, swimming, camping and picnicking. One improved recreation area.

SABINE: (439,664); Lufkin. Ranger headquarters at San Augustine. U.S. 96; State 21. Sabine River and overflow lakes; Boles Field Fox Hunt Area. Bass and cat fishing in river and lakes, fox hunting. One improved recreation area.

SAM HOUSTON: (491,800); Lufkin. Ranger headquarters at Huntsville; U.S. 75; State 190. Numerous lakes and small streams; part of the "Big Thicket" area. Bass and cat fishing in rivers and lakes, swimming, camping and picnicking. One improved recreation area.

UTAH

ASHLEY: (1,085,587); Verna. Forest lies partly in Wyoming; U.S. 30, 40; State 44. East half of Uinta mountain range, highest range in United States extending east and west. High Uintas Wilderness Area, mostly above 10,000 feet. Lake and stream fishing. Big-game hunting for deer, elk and antelope. Riding trails; wilderness area pack trips. 20 public camp and picnic areas. Five resorts; cabins and dude ranches. Nearby towns: Mountainview and Green River, Wyo.; Manila, Vernal, Duchesne and Roosevelt, Utah.

CACHE: (953,115); Logan. Forest lies partly in Idaho. U.S. 30-S, 89, 91; State 39. Trout fishing; deer and elk hunting. Scenic drives; riding and hiking trails. 46 camp and picnic areas; two winter sports areas. Nearby towns: Ogden, Brigham, and Logan, Utah; Preston, Soda Springs and Paris, Idaho.

DIXIE: (1,936,884); Cedar City; U.S. 91, 89. Red Canyon, Panguitch and Navajo Lakes, Pine Valley Mountains, Boulder Top Plateau and its many lakes not accessible by road. Deer, elk and cougar hunting; fishing in lakes and streams. 55 public camp and picnic areas. One winter sports area. Resorts, hotels, dude ranches and cabins. Nearby towns: Cedar City, Parowan, St. George, Panguitch, Enterprise, Escalante, Boulder, and Teasdale.

FISHLAKE: (1,526,387); Richfield; U.S. 89, 91. Lake and stream fishing; big-game hunting for deer and elk. Scenic drives; Beaver Canyon, Wayne Wonderland, Fishlake-Salina and others. 20 public camp and picnic areas. Resorts, hotels and cabins. Nearby towns: Richfield, Salina, Monroe, Loa, Bicknell, Koosharem, Beaver, Kanosh and Fillmore.

MANTI: (1,312,774); Ephraim; U.S. 89, 50; State 10, 29, 31. Trout fishing; deer elk, cougar hunting. Hiking, saddle trips. 11 major, 31 smaller, camp and picnic areas. Nearby towns: Manti, Ephraim, Mt. Pleasant, Price, Huntingdon and Ferron.

UINTA: (999,214); Provo; U.S. 40, 50, 91, 189. Rocky Mountain mule deer hunting, limited number of elk, 19 public camp and picnic areas; four valley view and overlook points. Hotels and cabins at nearby towns; Provo, Spanish Fork, Nephi, Heber, Moab and Monticello.

WASATCH: (1,002,383); Salt Lake City; U.S. 91, 40, 530, 30S, 50, 303; State 152, 210, 65, 239, 168, 35. Mirror Lake; Grandaddy Lakes. Lake and stream fishing; deer and elk hunting. Riding and hiking trails; wilderness trips. 78 public camps and picnic areas; three winter sports areas. Numerous resorts, hotels, cabins and dude ranches. Nearby towns: Salt Lake City, Provo, Ogden,

Murray, Heber and Kamas, Utah; Evanston, Wyo.

VERMONT

GREEN MOUNTAIN: (629,004); Rutland; U.S. 4, 7. Lake and stream fishing; bird shooting and big-game hunting for deer and bear. Bridle trails and hiking; scenic drives. Four improved forest picnic areas, 10 high-country cabins, two camp areas; famous ski areas. Summer resorts and famous New England inns; hotels and cabins. Nearby towns: Burlington, Rutland, Manchester, Middlebury, Brandon and Rochester.

VIRGINIA

GEORGE WASHINGTON: (1,544,776); Harrisonburg. Forest lies partly in West Virginia. U.S. 11, 33; State 42, 260. Trout and bass fishing; bear, deer, turkey and grouse hunting. Panoramic vistas; 500 miles of scenic drives; Blue Ridge Parkway; 1,000 miles of foot trails. Sherando Lake Recreation Area with 20-acre lake; six small recreation areas. Hotels, resorts, and numerous cabin camps near forest. Nearby towns: Waynesboro, Staunton, Buena Vista, Harrisonburg, Covington, Clifton Forge and Hot Springs, Va.; Franklin, W. Va.

JEFFERSON: (2,364,881); Roanoke; U.S. 11, 220, 21, 52, 23, 58. Appalachian Trail; Blue Ridge Parkway. Hunting for whitetail deer. Network of good secondary roads supplementing main highways. Seven public camp and picnic areas. Resorts, hotels, cabins. Nearby towns: Lexington, Roanoke, Radford, Bluefield, Wytheville, Marion, Abington, Bristol.

WASHINGTON

CHELAN: (2,090,629); Okanogan; U.S. 97. Lake Chelan 55 miles long, between precipitous ranges. North Cascade Wilderness Area. Lake and stream fishing. Boating, saddle and pack trips, mountain climbing. 40 improved forest camp and picnic grounds. Commercial dude ranches and cabin camps in and near forest. Nearby towns: Okanogan. Tonasket, Chelan and Twisp.

COLVILLE: (736,337); Colville; U.S. 395. Roosevelt Lake, 151 miles in length and covers an area of 82,000 acres, impounded by Grand Coulee Dam. Mountain lakes. Hunting and fishing. Noted for large mule deer with a record weight of 440 pounds. Water transportation from Roosevelt Lake to Arrowhead Lakes in Canada. One winter sports area near Chewelah; three developed campgrounds, located at Lake Thomas, Swan Lake and 10-Mile Lake on U.S. Highway 44; five campgrounds with minor developments. Four resorts and cabins at Curlew Lake; one resort at Lake Thomas. Nearby towns: Chewelah and Republic, Washington; and Grand Forks, British Columbia, Canada.

GIFFORD PINCHOT: (1,421,562); Vancouver; U.S. 99, 830. Goat Rocks and Mount Adams Wild Areas. Lake and stream trout fishing. Deer and bear hunting. Spectacular auto tours, saddle and pack trips, mountain climbing. 40 improved forest camp and picnic grounds. Commercial cabin camps and resorts in and near forest. Nearby towns: Vancouver, Stevenson, Randle, Castle Rock and White Salmon.

MT. BAKER: (1,851,399); Bellingham; U.S. 99. North Cascade Wilderness Area. Trout fishing; deer and bear hunting. Winter sports; saddle and pack trips; mountain climbing. 30 improved forest camp and picnic grounds; one winter sports area. Commercial cabin camps, hotels, and resorts and experienced guides nearby. Nearby towns: Bellingham, Everett, Darrington and Granite Falls.

OLYMPIC: (689,832); Olympia; U.S. 99, 401, 101. Scores of lakes and fishing streams. Stream and lake fishing; deer, bear, cougar and elk hunting. Winter sports; scenic drives; saddle and pack trips. 28 improved forest camp and picnic grounds. Commercial resorts, cabin camps and dude ranches. Nearby towns: Olympia, Port Angeles, Shelton and Quilcene.

SNOQUALMIE: (1,538,142); Seattle; U.S. 10, 410. Snoqualmie Falls, 250 feet high. Snow peaks, lakes and miles of fishing streams. Goat Rocks Wild Area. Stream and lake fishing, including steelhead trout; blacktail and mule deer, bear and elk hunting. Scenic drives, saddle and pack trips. 43 improved forest camp and picnic grounds; one winter sports area. Commercial cabin camps and outfitters locally available. Nearby towns: Seattle, Everett, Tacoma, Yakima and Cle Elum.

WENATCHEE: (1,552,860); Wenatchee; U.S. 10, 97. Snow-capped peaks, lakes. Many miles of fishing streams; Lake Wenatchee. Stream and lake trout fishing; deer and bear hunting. Scenic drives, saddle and pack trips. 32 improved forest camp and picnic grounds; two winter sports areas. Commercial cabin camps and dude ranches in and near forest. Nearby towns: Wenatchee, Leavenworth, Cashmere and Cle Elum.

WEST VIRGINIA

MONONGAHELA: (1,641,981); Elkins; U.S. 33, 219, 220, 250. Southern Appalachian and Allegheny Mountains. 11 wildlife management areas; beaver colonies. Trout and bass fishing; deer, bear, grouse, turkey and small-game hunting. Swimming, hiking, horseback riding. Scenic drives. Eight improved forest camps and picnic grounds. Commercial tourist homes and highway cabins in and near forest.

WISCONSIN

CHEQUAMEGON: (1,035,408); Park Falls; U.S. 2; State 13, 63, 64, 70, 77. Hundreds of large and small lakes. Lake and stream fishing, particularly for muskellunge. Deer and small-game hunting. Canoe travel on Flambeau and Chippewa Rivers. 26 public forest camp and picnic grounds; two winter sports areas. Organization camp, resorts and cabins. Nearby towns: Medford, Park Falls, Ashland, Washburn and Hayward.

NICOLET: (988,853); Rhinelander; U.S. 17, 32, 55, 64, 70, 139. Northern Wisconsin lake region; trout streams and scenic rivers. Lake and stream fishing for muskellunge, pike, bass and trout. Deer, bear, grouse and duck hunting. Swimming, boating, canoe trips, nature hikes, snowshoeing and skiing. 16 public camp and picnic grounds, five of which have swimming beaches; one ski area. Numerous resorts and cabins are located on private lands within and near the forest.

WYOMING

BIGHORN: (1,121,541); Sheridan; U.S. 14, 16, 87. Bighorn Mountains. Over 300 lakes. Cloud Peak Wild Area. Trout fishing. Elk, deer, bear and duck hunting. Saddle and pack trips; scenic drives. 77 public camp and picnic areas; winter sports areas. Commercial cabin camps and dude ranches in and near forest. Nearby towns: Sheridan, Buffalo, Lovell, Greybull and Worland.

BRIDGER: (1,710,220); Kemmerer; U.S. 89, 189, 187. Wind River Mountain Range. Bridger Wilderness Area. Lake and stream fishing. Big-game hunting for bear, moose, elk, mountain sheep and deer. Pinedale Skyline Drive; wilderness trips. 25 improved public camp and picnic areas; two winter sports areas. Resorts, hotels, cabins and dude ranches. Nearby towns: Pinedale and Afton.

MEDICINE BOW: (1,398,288); Laramie; U.S. 50. Snowy Range Natural Area. Many lakes and fishing streams. Numerous beaver colonies. Fishing and deer hunting. Saddle and pack trips. Scenic drives. 35 improved public camp and picnic areas; two winter sports areas. Commercial cabin camps and dude ranches in and near the forest. Nearby towns: Laramie, Cheyenne and Encampment.

SHOSHONE: (2,458,644); Cody; U.S. 14, 20, 287. Hundreds of lakes. North and South Absaroka, Popo Agie, Glacier, and Stratified Wilderness Areas. Fishing. Mountain sheep, elk, moose, deer, bear and game-bird hunting. Saddle and pack trips. Scenic drives. 55 public camps and picnic grounds. Commercial cabin camps and dude ranches in and near the forest. Nearby towns: Cody, Lander, and Dubois, Wyoming; Red Lodge and Cook City, Montana.

TETON: (1,729,306); Jackson; U.S. 89, 187, 287; State 22. Unspoiled scenic back country famous for big-game herds. Teton Wilderness Area. Stream, lake fishing. Big-game hunting for moose, elk, deer, mountain sheep and grizzly bear. Winter sports. 11 public camp and picnic areas. Winter sports area. Resorts, dude ranches, cabins.

NATIONAL WILDLIFE REFUGES

The 272 individual national wildlife refuges were set up for the conservation restoration of various species of wildlife. These 17,409,968 acres administered by the Fish and Wildlife Service have also become an important recreational resource. Since many of the refuges are for waterfowl, ponds and dikes for water impoundment are an important part of refuge management and also provide good fishing.

Public waterfowl hunting was permitted on parts of 32 refuges in the United States under a program approved by Congress. This raised the price of the duck stamp and provided that refuges acquired with duck-stamp funds may be opened to waterfowling when duck populations are up, although no more than a fourth of the refuge can so be opened at any one time.

Upland and big-game hunting was allowed on parts of 23 other refuges.

Other uses of the refuges included camping, boating, picnicking, photography and nature study, and, of course, observation of birds and animals in their native habitat.

On most of the refuges, except during periods of waterfowl concentrations, fishing is allowed in accordance with state laws and regulations. On some of the larger refuges, public shooting is allowed on limited parts of the refuge in cooperation with state game departments.

The Fish and Wildlife Service owns a lodge, operated by a concessioner in the Mattamuskeet National Wildlife Refuge, North Carolina, for public waterfowling.

Recreational facilities have been developed on a number of refuge areas; some are provided by the Fish and Wildlife Service, others are developed in cooperation with local governments or civic groups or by commercial concessioners.

The Fish and Wildlife Service, Department of the Interior, is located at Washington 25, D.C. But information pertaining to individual national wildlife refuges may be obtained from the following regional offices.

Region 1: California, Idaho, Montana, Nevada, Oregon, Washington. Fish and Wildlife Service, 600 Weatherly Building, Portland 14, Oregon.
Region 2: Arizona, New Mexico, Oklahoma, Texas, Utah, Wyoming. Fish and Wildlife Service, Box 1306, Albuquerque, New Mexico.
Region 3: Illinois, Iowa, Michigan, Minnesota, Missouri, Ohio, Nebraska, South Dakota, Wisconsin, North Dakota. Fish and Wildlife Service, 928 Plymouth Building, Minneapolis 2, Minnesota.
Region 4: Alabama, Arkansas, Florida, Georgia, Kentucky, Louisiana, Mississippi, North Carolina, South Carolina, Tennessee, Virginia. Fish and Wildlife Service, 316 Glenn Building, Atlanta 3, Georgia.
Region 5: Delaware, Maine, Maryland, Massachusetts, New Jersey, New York, Vermont. Fish and Wildlife Service, 1105 Blake Building, Boston, Massachusetts. Region 6: Alaska. Fish and Wildlife Service. Box 2021, Juneau, Alaska.

State, name of refuge, acreage—(WF) waterfowl; (F) fishing; (H) hunting permitted. Although refuge lists waterfowl, many also contain big game, upland game and birds. For information on individual refuges, write to the regional office of the Fish and Wildlife Service.

ALABAMA: Petit Bois (also Mississippi), (134). Wheeler, (34,044), (WF).
ALASKA: Aleutian Islands, (2,720,235), (WF), brown bear, caribou, sea otters. Bering Sea, (41,113). Bogoslof, (390). Chamisso, (641). Curry Bird, Game and Fish Refuge, (8,960). Forrester Island, (2,832). Hazen Bay, (6,800). Hazy Islands, (42). Kenai National Moose Refuge, (2,057,202), Kenai moose, brown bear, Dall's sheep, mountain goats. Kodiak, (1,957,002), (WF). Nunivak, (1,109,390). Pribilof Islands Reservation, (50,163), fur seals. St. Lazaria, (65). Semidi, (8,422). Tuxedni, (6,439).
ARIZONA: Cabeza Prieta Game Refuge, (860,-041). Havasu Lake (also California), (26,656), (WF). Imperial (also California), (28,711). (WF). Kofa Game Refuge, (660,041). Salt River, (21,060), (WF), upland game birds.
ARKANSAS: Big Lake, (9,522), (WF), (F). White River, (116,390), (WF), (F).
CALIFORNIA: Clear Lake, (34,616). Colusa,

(2,385), (WF). Colusa National Wildlife Management Area, (1,095), (WF). Farallon, (91). Havasu Lake, (also Arizona), (19,105), (WF). Imperial (also Arizona), (18,080), (WF). Lower Klamath (also Oregon), (21,460), (WF). Merced National Wildlife Management Area, (2,562), (WF), (H). Sacramento, (10,776), (WF), (H). Salton Sea, (38,887), (WF), (F), (H). Sutter, (1,278), (WF). Tule Lake, (37,337), (WF), (F), (H).

DELAWARE: Bombay Hook, (13,810), (WF), (F), (H). Cape Henlopen, (212). Killcohook (also New Jersey), (580), (WF).

FLORIDA: Anclote, (194). Brevard, (12). Cedar Keys, (379). Chassahowitzka, (11,016), (WF), (F), (H). Chinsegut, (2,033), quail. Great White Heron, (2,151), Key deer, (F). (WF), (F), (H). Passage Key, (36). Pelican Island, (3). Pinellas, (91). Sanibel, (2,474), (F). St. Marks, (65,100), (WF), (F), (H).

Key West, (2,019), (F). Loxahatchee, (141,336), GEORGIA: Blackbeard Island, (5,618), (WF), (F), (H). Okefenokee, (329,110), (WF), (F). Piedmont, (31,192), (F). Savannah also South Carolina), (5,460), (WF), (F). Tybee, (100). Wolf Island, (538).

HAWAII: Hawaiian Islands, (623). Johnston Island, (100).

IDAHO: Camas, (10,535), (WF). Deer Flat, (10,267), (WF), (F), (H). Minidoka, (22,123), (WF), (F). Snake River, (355), (WF), (F), (H).

ILLINOIS: Batchtown, (4,140), (WF). Calhoun, (3,565), (WF). Chautauqua, (4,471), (WF), (F), (H). Crab Orchard, (44,000), (WF), quail, (F), (H). Flannigan Island, (668), (WF). Henderson, (352), (WF). Keithsburg, (1,448), (WF). Upper Mississippi River Wildlife and Fish Refuge (also Iowa, Minnesota and Wisconsin), (3,016), (WF), (H).

IOWA: Louisa, (3,890), (WF). Union Slough, (2,075), (WF), upland game birds, (F), (H). Upper Mississippi River Wildlife and Fish Refuge (also Illinois, Minnesota and Wisconsin), (20,406), (WF), (F), (H).

KENTUCKY: Kentucky Woodlands, (64,829), (WF), (F), (H).

LOUISIANA: Breton, (7,512), (WF). Delta, (48,789), (WF), (F). East Timbalier Island Reservation, (337). Lacassine, (31,125), (WF), (F). Sabine, (142,717), (WF), (F). Shell Keys, (77).

MAINE: Moosehorn, (22,526), (WF), (F), (H). Widow's Island, (12).

MARYLAND: Blackwater, (11,216), (WF), (F). Chincoteague (also Virginia), (95). Patuxent Research Refuge, (2,679), Experiment Station. Susquehanna, (16,410), (WF).

MASSACHUSETTS: Great Meadows, (210), (WF). Monomoy, (2,946), (WF), (F). Parker River, (6,417), (WF), (F).

MICHIGAN: Huron, (147). Lake St. Clair, (4,200), (WF). Michigan Islands, (12). Seney, (93,835), (WF), prairie chickens, (F), (H).

MINNESOTA: Mille Lacs, (1). Mud Lake, (60,744), (WF), (H). Rice Lake (15,240), (WF), (F). Tamarac, (29,108), (WF), (F), (H). Upper Mississippi River Wildlife and Fish Refuge (also Illinois, Iowa and Wisconsin), (26,710), (WF), (F), (H).

MISSISSIPPI: Noxubee, (38,933), wild turkey deer, quail, doves, (F), (H). Petit Bois, (596).

MISSOURI: Mingo, (21,609), (WF), (F) Squaw Creek, (6,809), (WF). Swan Lake (10,675), (WF), prairie chickens, (F).

MONTANA: Benton Lake, (12,235), (WF) Black Coulee, (1,480), (WF), sage hens. Bowdoin, (15,437), (WF), (H). Creedman Coulee (2,728), (WF), prairie chickens. Fort Peck Game Refuge, (946,944), sharp-tailed grouse antelope, deer, mountain sheep, elk, (F), (H) Hailstone, (2,664), (WF). Halfbreed Lake (3,097), (WF). Hewitt Lake, (1,360), (WF) Lake Mason, (6,433), (WF). Lake Thibadeau (3,508), (WF). Lamesteer, (800), (WF). Medi cine Lake, (31,457), (WF). National Bison Range, (18,541), buffalo, elk, deer, bighorn sheep. Nine-Pipe, (2,020), (WF), (F). Pablo (2,868), (WF). Pishkun, (8,195), (WF). Re Rock Lakes Migratory Waterfowl Refuge (40,008), trumpeter swans, Shiras moose, (F) (H). Willow Creek, (3,119), (WF).

NEBRASKA: Crescent Lake, (46,540), (WF) (F). Fort Niobrara, (19,122), buffalo, prairi chickens. North Platte, (5,107), (F). Valentine (70,401), (WF), (F).

NEVADA: Anaho Island, (248). Charles Shel don Antelope Range, (548,373), antelope, (WF (F), (H). Desert Game Range, (2,204,201) (WF), bighorn sheep, mule deer, Gambel quail, doves, (F), (H). Fallon, (17,902), (WF) Ruby Lake, (35,618), (WF), (F), (H). Sheldo National Antelope Refuge, (34,091), antelope (WF). Stillwater National Wildlife Manage ment Area, (204,633), (WF), (F), (H). Win nemucca, (9,806), (WF).

NEW JERSEY: Brigantine, (12,094), (WF (F), (H). Killcohook, (905), (WF).

NEW MEXICO: Bitter Lake, (23,923), (WF (F). Bosque del Apache, (57,191), (WF), (F Burford Lake, (1,845), (WF), (F), (H). Sa Andres, (57,215), bighorn sheep, mule dee white-winged doves, quail, (H).

NEW YORK: Montezuma, (6,174), (WF (F). Wertheim, (1,799), (WF).

NORTH CAROLINA: Mattamuskeet, (50,178 (WF), (F), (H). Pea Island, (5,880), (WF (F). Swanquarter, (15,501), (WF), (F).

NORTH DAKOTA: Appert Lake, (1,163 (WF). Ardoch, (2,761), (WF). Arrowoo (15,934), (WF), prairie chickens, (H). Billing Lake, (760), (WF). Bone Hill, (640), (WF rumba, (1,977), (WF). Buffalo Lake, (2,085), WF). Camp Lake, (1,225), (WF). Canfield ,ake, (453), (WF). Charles Lake, (800), (WF). Chase Lake, (375), (WF). Clearwater, (144), WF). Cottonwood Lake, (1,048), (WF). Dakota Lake, (2,768), (WF). Des Lacs, (18,841), WF), (H). Flickertail, (640), (WF). Florence ,ake, (669), (WF). Half-Way Lake, (160), WF). Hiddenwood, (568), (WF). Hobart ,ake, (1,840), (WF). Hutchinson Lake, (477), WF). Johnson Lake, (2,007), (WF), prairie hickens. Kellys Slough, (1,620), (WF). Lac aux Mortes, (5,882), (WF). Lake Elsie, (635), WF). Lake George, (3,119), (WF). Lake Ilo, 3,139), (WF), (F). Lake Moraine, (320), WF). Lake Nettie, (1,800), (WF). Lake Zahl, 3,561), (WF). Lambs Lake, (1,287), (WF). ,egion Lake, (1,038), (WF). Little Goose, 359), (WF). Little Lake, (480), (WF). Long ,ake, (22,732), (WF), (F). Lords Lake, (1,915), WF). Lost Lake, (960), (WF). Lostwood, 26,107), (WF), (H). Lower Souris, (58,571), WF). Maple River, (1,120), (WF). McLean, 480), (WF). Minnewastena, (144), (WF). ainted Woods, (2,181), (WF). Pioneer Lake, 640), (WF). Pleasant Lake, (1,001), (WF). rairie Lake, (320), (WF). Pretty Rock, (800), WF). Rabb Lake, (261), (WF). Rock Lake, 5,587), (WF). Rose Lake, (1,280), (WF). chool Section Lake, (680), (WF). Shell Lake, 1,678), (WF). Sheyenne Lake, (802), (WF), rairie chickens. Sibley Lake, (1,087), (WF). ilver Lake, (3,348), (WF). Slade, (3,000), WF). Snyder Lake, (1,550), (WF). Springater, (640), (WF). Stewart Lake, (2,230), WF). Stoney Slough, (1,908), (WF). Storm ake, (687), (WF). Stump Lake, (27). Sullys Iill, (994), buffalo. Sunburst Lake, (495), WF). Tewaukon, (4,710), (WF). Tomahawk, 440), (WF). Upper Souris, (32,045), (WF), F), (H). White Lake, (960), (WF). Wildfang ake, (560), (WF). Wild Rice Lake, (779), WF). Willow Lake, (2,848), (WF). Winterg River, (399), (WF). Wood Lake, (280), WF).

HIO: West Sister Island, (82).

KLAHOMA: Salt Plains, (31,129), (WF), F). Tishomingo, (13,449), (WF), (F). Wichita Iountains Wildlife Refuge, (59,099), buffalo, k, antelope, Texas longhorned cattle, deer, ild turkey, quail, ducks, (F).

REGON: Cape Meares, (139). Charles Shelon Antelope Range, (627). Cold Springs, ,618), (WF). Hart Mountain National Antepe Refuge, (240,664), antelope, mule deer, H). Lower Klamath (also California), (1,340), WF). Malheur, (165,276), (F), (H). McKay reek, (1,813), (WF). Oregon Islands, (21). hree Arch Rocks, (17). Upper Klamath, ,140), (WF).

UERTO RICO: Culebra, (3,000).

SOUTH CAROLINA: Cape Romain, (34,016), (WF), (F), (H). Carolina Sandhills, (40,518), (F). Santee, (78,364), (WF), (F). Savannah, (7,225), (WF), (F).

SOUTH DAKOTA: Bear Butte, (436), (WF), (F). Belle Fourche, (13,680), (WF). Lacreek, (9,442), (WF), (F), (H). Lake Andes, (443), (WF), (F), (H). Sand Lake, (21,451), (WF), (F), (H). Waubay, (4,651), (WF), (H).

TENNESSEE: Lake Isom, (1,850), (WF), (F). Reelfoot, (9,273), (WF), (F). Tennessee, (49,-510), (WF), (F).

TEXAS: Aransas, (47,261), whooping cranes, (WF). Hagerman, (11,429), (WF), (F). Laguna Atascosa, (38,759), (WF), (F). Muleshoe, (5,809), (WF). Santa Ana, (1,981), (WF).

UTAH: Bear River Migratory Bird Refuge, (64,899), (WF), (F), (H). Locomotive Springs, (1,031), (WF). Strawberry Valley, (14,080), (WF).

VERMONT: Missisquoi, (1,941), (WF).

VIRGINIA: Back Bay, (4,589), (WF), (F). Chincoteague, (8,827), (WF). Presquile, (1,250), (WF).

WASHINGTON: Columbia, (9,761), (WF). Columbia River, (8), (WF). Conconully, (933), (WF). Copalis, (5). Dungeness, (235), (WF). Flattery Rocks, (125). Jones Island, (179). Lenore Lake, (6,201), (WF). Little Pend Oreille, (42,716). Matia Island, (145), (WF). Quillayute Needles, (177). Smith Island, (65), (WF). Turnbull, (15,964), (WF). Willapa, (7,123), (WF), bear, black-tailed deer, raccoons, (H).

WISCONSIN: Gravel Island, (27). Green Bay, (2). Horicon, (20,683), (WF), (F), (H). Long Tail Point, (103), (WF). Necedah, (39,672), (WF), (F), (H). Trempealeau, (707), (WF). Upper Mississippi River Wildlife and Fish Refuge (also Illinois, Iowa and Minnesota), (67,141), (WF), (F), (H).

WYOMING: Bamforth, (1,166), (WF). Evanston, (360), (WF). Hutton Lake, (1,969), (WF). National Elk Refuge, (23,648), elk, (F). Pathfinder, (46,341), (WF).

By Michael Hudoba

TRAILS

THE APPALACHIAN TRAIL

This is a footpath extending for 2,050 miles from Mount Oglethorpe in Georgia to Mount Katahdin in Maine. It crosses the wilderness areas along the crests of the Great Smoky, Blue Ridge, Allegheny and Catskill Mountains, through the Berkshire Hills, the Green and White Mountains, and finally the lake and mountain country of Maine at its northern terminus.

One recent "feeder" path is the Horseshoe Trail which starts at the Valley Forge battlefield and joins the main Appalachian Trail at Manada Gap, Pennsylvania. Unlike the main trail, this is a riding trail as well as a footpath.

There are many motor roads that cross the summits of these mountains, thus tapping the trail, and providing easy access to it from any of our eastern states. It runs for the most part through high wooded mountains at elevations from 2,000 to 5,000 feet, with many open crests and magnificent panoramas, and through a well-watered country. There are campsites with fireplaces, a number of lean-to shelters along it for those who do not pack their own shelter and many camp spots for the more experienced.

It is at its best as to climate and trail conditions from mid-June to late September. The climate at its high altitudes offers a relief during these months from the swelter of the lowlands, and the smell and grime of the cities. Winter camping and hiking under almost arctic conditions is possible for the more strenuous.

Here and there along the Appalachian Trail will be found an occasional lodge or small summer resort, but as a rule it is all wilderness, and those who plan to enjoy the country must pack shelter and food on their backs as it is a foot trail, not a horse trail.

The Appalachian Trail is a volunteer recreational project. It is supervised and maintained by the Appalachian Trail Conference with headquarters at 1916 Sunderland Place, N.W., Washington 6, D.C. This is a federation of organizations, mainly outing clubs and individuals interested in the trail, and its objectives and activities are entirely voluntary. It has no salaried employees. It disseminates complete information about the trail by means of its pamphlets, guide books and maps, for which a small charge is made. The funds derived from these sales are used to republish the literature. The data contained in them is complete, and no other information is available. On receipt of 35 cents in coin the conference will mail a pamphlet, "Suggestions for Appalachian Trail Users,"

which gives general information and which lists the other necessary pamphlets and guide books. Do not write the conference and ask for other information, as they have neither funds nor facilities with which to answer correspondence. All the information anyone needs is contained in their publications.

THE PACIFIC CREST TRAILWAY

This extends from Canada to Mexico along the crests of the Cascade, Sierra Nevada and Sierra Madre Mountains for a total of about 2,156 miles, passing through many of the national forests and national parks of the Pacific slope, and skirting the most famous mountains—Rainer, Adams, Hood, Shasta and Whitney. It passes through the Yosemite and Sequoia parks, and trails of many names are incorporated in its system, including the famous John Muir Trail. It has been built and is maintained by the U.S. Forest Service and the National Park Service. In fact only 160 miles of it are outside of national forests and national parks. This is not a trail for picnic parties; it is a wilderness trailway for expert backpackers. It is "a true nature trail."

To publicize it the Pacific Crest Trail System conference with headquarters in Pasadena, California, was organized. The Sierra Club, 1050 Mills Tower, San Francisco 4, California, is the organization that has done the most work in bringing the Trailway to the attention of the public and in fostering all it stands for.

Much of the trail, where not too steep or alpine, is suitable for animal transport—horses, mules and burros—as well as for backpackers and hikers. Most of it passes through very wild country, with considerable distance between possible supply points; to traverse many of the long stretches animal transport becomes necessary, since the backpacker cannot carry more than about two weeks of grub.

It is a rougher trail, steeper in spots, than the Appalachian Trail, and some of it is at altitudes of 5,000 to 12,000 feet. Because of snow in the high country parts of the trail are not passable until mid-July, but then the

Pacific Crest Trailway

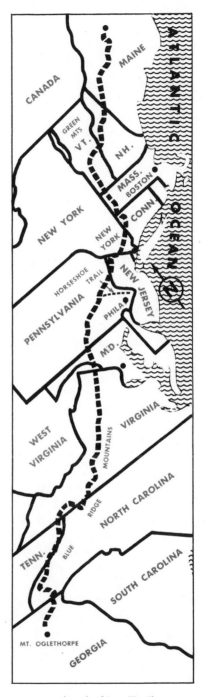

Appalachian Trail

higher passes can usually be crossed until late in September. Only those capable of mountain travel at high altitudes should undertake trips in these rough places without a guide or some companion familiar with the conditions that may be met. But many portions of the trailway, particularly in California, are entirely feasible even for families with young children.

The best general information on the Pacific Crest Trailway is found in the booklet of the same name published by the Pacific

Coast Trail System Conference, Pasadena, California, price $2.25, and the "Starr's Guide to the John Muir Trail" published by the Sierra Club, price $2. The best maps are those published by the U.S. Forest Service, Washington 25, D.C. Mention the particular section of the trail you are interested in, and they will give you the names and prices of the maps. The supervisors of the various national forests can suggest to you the names of outfitters for the region you wish to penetrate.

By Col. Townsend Whelen

PUBLIC CAMPGROUNDS

The campground capacity of our public lands varies in different areas from just a few all the way up to 3,000 (Yosemite) individual campsites, and, in most most places, camping is free on application to the caretaker when you arrive. And scattered in these parks and forests are individual campsites with fireplaces where you may camp on application to a local forester.

As a rule, camping is allowed in parks only on these prepared grounds. But in some of the more remote wilderness areas in national forests, you may camp anywhere by notifying the local forester and obeying the forest regulations.

Practically none of these grounds have electrical connections, but all have pure water, frequently piped, and toilet facilities. Some even have showers. You can get detailed information on the location and facilities from the superintendent of the park or forest. During the height of the tourist season these camps are often filled to capacity, and prospective campers must be pre-

pared for such an eventuality. Access to the grounds is usually by automobile, although a few can be reached only by canoe.

In addition, dotted all along our main motor highways are other campgrounds usually run in connection with municipal authorities, filling stations or motels. Such campgrounds have similar accommodations and only a nominal charge is made for overnight camping. You can find their location at filling stations en route.

In many respects, camping on such grounds differs from wilderness camping. Usually there is little privacy, as individual campsites are sometimes as near as five yards to each other. So closed tents are very desirable. The cutting of trees and brush is not permitted, so you must bring your own tent poles, stakes and mattresses. When firewood is provided it is usually in large pieces, so an ax and buck-saw are desirable to reduce the wood to a size for cooking.

Sometimes, but not always, you can park your car right alongside your tent. Then you can use a portable electric light with a connection to your battery circuit. But it is advisable to carry a lantern. Always include a wash basin and two buckets, one for fresh water and the other for a slop-jar. It is not permissible to throw wash water or garbage on the ground.

You don't have to have prior experience for this kind of camping. All you need to know is how to put up your tent (practice in your back yard). Someone in your party should know how to cook simple meals.

In these public camps you will find a lot of congenial people, many of them experienced campers who will be glad to give you a helping hand.

By Col. Townsend Whelen

CHAPTER 16

shooting

THERE IS a unique kind of exhilaration in walking up to a target and discovering you have placed five straight shots in the 10-ring or in powdering two clay pigeons as they come roaring simultaneously out of the skeet houses. Shooting at targets of one kind or another has always been a popular American sport since the pioneer families gathered to test their abilities with the long rifles against each other. The statistics released by the many shooting organizations in the country today prove that the sport of shooting is still immensely popular and growing all the time. In this chapter there is the full history of both rifle and handgun shooting as it has developed through the years as well as similar stories on the refinement of the sports of trap and skeet shooting. You will also find information on how to organize and build your own gun club and a section on miniature clay pigeon shooting which any club would want to include. Another section shows in pictures exactly how to keep your guns in top-notch condition.

RIFLE SHOOTING

Rifle shooting gained favor as a sport immediately after the Civil War. There was a conviction that what this country needed was high-class marksmen, with the long-barreled guns, and, because this was so, most men with such weapons began to practice shooting to a greater degree than ever before.

Prior to the war, the major part of shooting had been in rural communities on Saturday afternoons and Sundays. The shooting matches usually took place in the neighborhood of the country stores. Targets were of various kinds. Many were placards with an "X" to indicate the bull's-eye. In other instances, some tree or post, similarly marked, was the target.

The men in the pre-war era shot from three positions: standing, on one knee and flat on the ground with the gun resting on a log or across the top of a small rock. Any shooting method had its merits, so long as accuracy resulted.

When the war was over the city folk, who previously had ignored rifle shooting as a sport, took it up, going to some open space, erecting crude targets and blasting away in the effort to determine who was the best shot. A great assortment of rifles was called into action, each marksman having his favorite. Some clung to the old type, others preferred the new, which had been created for war purposes.

The early guns generally were muzzleloaders, black powder being the propellant. The projectiles were of various kinds, the round ball being the most popular. The loading of such guns, of course, was important, it being done according to the ideas of the individual. If the shooter hit or came close to the bull's-eye, it meant that his method of loading must be all right. If he missed often, he changed loading methods and, perhaps, the shape of the missile.

In those early years England, like the United States, also felt that expert gunnery was much to be desired. In the 1850's and into the 1860's the Englishmen were encouraged to practice rifle shooting. As early as 1860 targets were erected at Wimbledon and the range became world famous. The English and Irish assembled shooting teams and shot it out to determine which was the superior. While many Americans were gaining rifle practice in actual warfare, the men of Great Britain were having regular shoots of greater and greater importance.

As rifle shooting gained in popularity in the late 1860's in the United States and shooting matches were arranged in many places along the Atlantic seaboard as well as in the interior as far west as the Mississippi River, there were repeated demands for a governing body.

In 1871 a group of officers in the National Guard felt that the sport had advanced to a point where some executive control must be exercised. This suggestion led to the formation of the National Rifle Association, which ever since has ruled the sport.

The first act of the organization was to standardize the targets and distances and to take the sport from chaos to steadiness. The N.R.A. has held it to such lines in all the years since.

The association arranged for the first championship matches in 1871, supplanting the impromptu shoots which had been the vogue throughout the country for many years. Its plan brought the greatest rifle shots of the nation into competition with each other, under standardized contest rules, and the matches provided great advances for the sport.

The highlight of the 1871 matches at Creedmoor, Long Island (New York), was brought about by the invasion of a team of rifle shooters from Ireland, representing the Ulster Rifle Club and reputed to be made up of the most accurate shots in the world. The Americans put together a team, but there was no guarantee, at the time, as to its greatness. Men were chosen who, in some other matches, in the old days, had done well. Yet the selection was so good that the United States defeated the invaders by a margin of three points.

So great was the interest in the championships at the national range at Creedmoor in 1872 that over 100,000 persons were spectators. They were taken to the ranges in special trains, or by any form of vehicle that was available. When it is recalled that very few sports events in the 80-odd years since then have attracted greater crowds, the appeal the rifle folks made in so early a time is remarkable.

A new team of Irish rifle shooters in 1872 took rank as the greatest in the British Empire and it hurled a challenge at the men of the United States. The result was the naming of an American team, which journeyed across he Atlantic. The impending match was of great interest to Americans. So keen was the excitement over it that newspapers, which previously had refused to spend as much as a dollar in the cabling of sports news, ordered that complete coverage be given to the practice activities of the American team. The match itself was spot news, and there was great exultation in the United States when word was flashed that the Americans had beaten the Irish, and thus gained international supremacy, by a margin of 957 to 921.

The success of the Americans in 1871, against the Irish sharpshooters, was regarded as "one of those things that occasionally happens." The success in 1872 was different. It put the Americans in the forefront in a sport which was international, and the Americans were determined to hold the heights. Therefore, there began intensive search and development of the best type of weapons for high-class shooting, and Americans proceeded with experiments, as to different rifles and the way of firing them, designed to keep them champions.

Metallic cartridges had been known before that time, but had not been generally used because they were not regarded as dependable. Little shooting had been done with other than lead for bullets. But the rifle manufacturers began to make better weapons, using a higher grade of steel, and, thus, it was possible for marksmen, equipped with such guns, to put metal jackets on bullets to increase their velocity. The higher speed flattened the trajectory and lessened the effects of wind, drift and atmospheric conditions.

All of this meant to the man who shot both at targets and moving game that absolute accuracy was not so vital as it had been, and that estimating the distance from gun to target was not required to the ultimate degree, as had been the rule in the old days.

When black powder was used as the explosive, the velocity of the bullet was between 1,000 and 1,500 feet per second. As early as 1900, the lighter bullet, plus smokeless powder, had increased the velocity to 2,000 feet per second. Since then, bullet velocity has increased steadily to 4,100 feet, or faster, per second.

A great rifle shooter of the 1870's was as much a public idol, in ratio, as were Babe Ruth, Ty Cobb, Jack Dempsey, John L. Sullivan and other athletes of later eras. He was lionized wherever he went. He was recipient of dinners, of trophies, of huzzahs and wild acclaim. He was regarded as a "magnificent type of American," and no honor was too great to be showered upon him.

When the National Rifle Association came into existence the affiliated clubs were few and the membership was not of great consequence. Amazing progress has been made since its formation. At this time there are thousands of senior and junior clubs identified with the organization and its individual membership numbers hundreds of thousands. A vast number of tournaments are put on annually under its auspices—among senior units, veterans' organizations, colleges, high schools, Y.M.C.A.'s, Boy Scouts and many other groups. The best appear in the national championships, staged each year at various locations throughout the country.

The champions of the pioneer shoots are among the forgotten men of history. Little attention was paid in the records as to who were outstanding. History really begins in 1875, when cup matches became popular. The Leech Cup was great at the time. The first winner was Col. John Bodine. The Marine Corps Cup, inaugurated in 1909, was next in importance, with the Member's Match preceding it, in 1901. In the international field one of the leading current competitions is the Dewar Trophy tournament.

The President's Match also began in 1901. Before this contest there was the Wimbledon Cup, pioneered in 1875 and of international significance. A great many other contests came into existence later. They called for matches with different bores. There were competitions, indoors and outdoors. Pistols gained recognition under National Rifle Association auspices for the first time in 1904.

Many years ago Congress became aware of the importance of the organization and to encourage the sport because of its great value in warfare appropriated funds to continue its existence and to encourage marksmanship.

Both rifle and pistol shooting are organized through the medium of the N.R.A. in this country, as well as the International Shooting Union, for international competition. In addition, the International Olympic Committee has a rifle section and a pistol section and other international events are arranged directly between the N.R.A. and similar national bodies in other countries.

The many tournaments sponsored today under the auspices of the National Rifle Association offer prime testing grounds for competitive shooters.

The N.R.A. conducts the annual national championships. Regional affairs, held under the supervision of the governing body, are a step below the title contests. Then come the state championships, district championships and local tournaments, in that order.

The entire competitive program is divided into sections for the smallbore (.22 caliber) rifle, the high-power rifle, and pistols and revolvers. The high-power section of the program is subdivided into events limited to the Army rifle and events open to match rifles

with match sights. The pistol section of the program is similarly divided into matches for the .45 service pistol, matches for center-fire revolvers (.32 caliber or larger) and matches for the .22 caliber rim-fire pistols and revolvers.

Service rifle shooters are automatically classified by their Army qualifications. All smallbore rifle shooters and all pistol and revolver shooters are classified on the basis of scores made in registered tournaments. The classifications are Master, Expert, Sharpshooter and Marksman.

The standard ranges for smallbore rifle shooting are 50 feet (indoor and junior), 50 yards, 50 meters, 100 yards and 200 yards. For high-powered rifle shooting the standard ranges are 200 yards, 300, 500, 600, 800, 900 and 1,000 yards. For pistol and revolver shooting, the standard ranges are 50 feet (indoors), 25 and 50 yards (outdoors).

HANDGUN SHOOTING

The pistol was invented by Caminello Vitelli about 1540 in the town of Pistoia in the Florentine Province of Italy, where he lived. The weapon derives its name from that of the town.

Vitelli's creation was the answer to the demand for some sort of gun that was not of tremendous weight and could be handled and fired by one man. In an earlier era, the weapons were huge affairs, on the order of cannons. The pistol continued to be the only hand-weapon until some centuries later when Samuel Colt of the United States, improving upon a crude English design, devised the revolver.

The pistol in its original design fired only a single shot, whereas the revolver, having a chamber, that turned, could project from five to seven bullets in one loading.

The pistol was not a real success during the lifetime of Vitelli. Those who succeeded him and worked on his principle made the pistol far more effective. Since the pistol was created to succeed the sword in close fighting, it meant that the gun had to function to perfection, else the man, exploding his one shot, left himself to the mercy of his enemy if he missed fire.

The English, more than the Italians, became aware of the value of the pistol and experimented through many generations toward making it a useful weapon for soldiers. The English Army was well equipped with improved pistols in the middle of the 18th century and placed a great deal of dependence upon the weapon.

Interest in handgun shooting has grown every year. National pistol championships are held annually by the National Rifle Association.

Historians generally ignore that "the shot that was heard around the world" was fired from a pistol—not a musket, as is generally supposed. The Revolutionary War actually was started at Lexington, Massachusetts, on April 19, 1775. British Maj. John Pitcairn had ordered the patriots (he called them rebels) to disperse. They ignored him. In rage, Pitcairn whipped out his pistol and fired into the group; the act precipitated the warfare that led to America's independence.

In the early frontier days of the United States, the weapon in use was the pistol. Since it fired only one shot at a time, it meant that men who called it into action had to be deadly in their accuracy. Among the great shots was William F. (Buffalo Bill) Cody, who put on shooting exhibitions in the 1860's, using the pistol, as well as the revolver, which at that time was just coming into general use.

Ira Paine, ranked in his day as the greatest pistol and revolver shot in the world, popularized the pistol as a means of sport and directed attention, especially in Europe, to the value of the revolver, which had not been subjected to much use beyond warfare. The revolver had been useful for soldiers during the Mexican war in the 1840's and was of worth during the Civil War. Paine made Europe aware of its effectiveness as he demonstrated what could be done with a pistol, during exhibitions with both types of guns.

Early in the 1880's, Paine made an exhibition trip into New England, which at the time was interested only in the rifle. Paine's shooting mastery with pistol and revolver influenced the Massachusetts Rifle Association to put targets for both pistols and revolvers on its range and the members thereafter engaged in contests with both weapons.

Yet the interest in those guns was so scant that not until 1900 did riflemen in other states give them recognition by building targets and arranging pistol and revolver programs. Most riflemen opposed the use of the small guns in contests involving marksmanship for the reason that the range of the guns was short, and the assumption was by riflemen, who fired from a greater distance, that it would be the simplest thing in the world to hit a target with a pistol or revolver "from just a couple of steps away."

However, when the rifle shooters were influenced into trying to hit targets with pistols or revolvers, they found that the accomplishment called for marksmanship as great as that needed with rifles. And so pistol and revolver shooting grew in favor, and matches for the United States championship were added to the program of the National Rifle Association of America for the first time at the "shoot" at Sea Girt, New Jersey, in 1900. Today national pistol championships are staged annually by the N.R.A.

TRAPSHOOTING

English huntsmen in the early part of the 19th century devised the sport of trapshooting because they had been deprived of the chance to shoot at wild birds.

Throughout the 18th century there had been greater and greater use of guns for hunting, and, as time went on, the supply of birds grew smaller and smaller. When this situation came about, members of the nobility and aristocracy in England made deals which gave them possession of much of the wide open spaces, which had been favorite public hunting grounds. An old Roman law, which was still in force in England, forbade any private shooting grounds, but the wealthy class chose to ignore the law and set up their own game preserves. This ruled out the commoners.

The huntsmen, who were denied their sport, made protests, but it gained them nothing. The wealthy continued to use what previously had been public hunting ground as places where they and their guests alone might shoot, and there the matter ended.

Gunners, thus shut off from their annual hunts, began to experiment in search of a substitute sport. This brought about the formation in 1832 of a shooting club in England known as the "High Hats." It was so called because members placed live birds under their hats and, upon signal, lifted the hats, clamped them back onto their heads and then—and only then—took a shot at the birds, which usually were well on wing.

Soon the supply of birds became exhausted, and the gunners, looking about for a substitute, hit upon a glass ball. This was the first real method of shooting at objects zipped out of a trap. The balls had a diameter of 2½ inches. They were placed in a cup, which had a spring inside. When the spring was released, the ball flew out. To make things more realistic, the pioneer trapshooters often glued feathers to the ball and when it was hit, they flew in all directions.

Later came the revolving trap, which sent the glass ball in different directions, the shooters not knowing in advance which way the object would fly. This made hitting the target more difficult but it increased skill in handling the gun and resulted in greatly improved marksmanship.

Eventually there was demand for a more difficult target, and this brought about the creation in the 1860's of the first type of clay pigeon. The target was made of regular clay, baked into the shape of a saucer. A tip of cardboard was glued to the edge, perhaps to cause eccentric flight and make shooting more intriguing. It was thrown from a trap, which had a clamp on the end fixed in a sidewise position, so that the target would fly with only the edge exposed.

Such "pigeons," it soon developed, were baked too hard, it being difficult to break them with gunfire. So a cardboard ring, with a rubber balloon some two inches in diameter in dead center, was invented. The idea was for the gunner to shatter the red balloon, as the target was sent out of a trap almost identical to that used for clay pigeons. This target was not popular, but by that time trapshooting had firmly established itself as a sport and its enthusiasts experimented vigorously in the hope of perfecting a superior target and trap.

In 1880 a new and lighter type of clay pigeon was tried. This was easier to smash than the earlier ones. Just when the gunners were about to accept it as standard, an Englishman named McCaskey perfected a target made of a mixture of river silt and pitch—an ideal combination. This became known as the famous "Blue Rock" target. McCaskey later introduced a revolutionary trap, which he named the "Expert," and with this satisfactory target and a well-functioning trap, the sport neared standardization and quickly came into world-wide popularity.

There have been certain improvements on the McCaskey target since then, and many changes of the trap, but McCaskey's creations remain basic. Rotary motion was originated after McCaskey's time, and this solved the last of the trapshooters' many original problems. The big difference between trapshooting and shooting at game birds is this: the clay target has its maximum speed at the start of its flight, whereas the bird starts slowly and increases acceleration.

Trapshooting as a sport was introduced to the United States late in the 1870's. By the early 1880's it had quite a following and this led to the creation of the Interstate Association of Trapshooters, which purchased land on Long Island and conducted both live bird and trapshooting tournaments there under direction of Elmer E. Shaner. It was on these grounds that the Grand American Handicap trapshoot first was conducted. The winner of this annual contest, beginning then and in all the years since, is regarded as the American champion.

In 1900, the Interstate Association was succeeded by the American Trapshooting Association, which became the national governing body. Until 1924, the A.T.A. was controlled by manufacturers of guns and ammunition. In that year it was decided by the trapshooters to divorce it from all "subsidy" and to have the association go on its own as strictly a sports organization. The severance was made and the name changed to its present one of Amateur Trapshooting Association.

The organization now has magnificent quarters at Vandalia, Ohio, and its shooting equipment is without peer in the world. The plant cost over $200,000 and there are about 50 traps. The membership is made up of 48 state trapshooting organizations, with allied membership in Canada.

More than three decades ago, women took up trapshooting and became enthusiasts. The feats of some of them are on a par with the ranking men. They once were limited to competition among their own sex, but the organization now puts on a mixed-team championship match.

The custom is to hold annual state championships in the four outstanding classes. Such state champions, men and women, and others of ranking ability, later go into action in the nationals at Vandalia.

There are championship tests for men, women, juniors, sub-juniors and professionals at Vandalia. The events include the blue-ribbon Grand American Handicap, North American Clay Targets, National Doubles, All-Around, Champion of Champions, High-Over-All and the Preliminary Handicap. In addition, there are class title tests, father-and-son, husband-and-wife, brother-and-brother and others.

In 1900 there were about three or four thousand trapshooters in the United States. The total now is well over 100,000. The first trapshooting tournament, in 1900, attracted fewer than 100 contestants. Over two thousand took part in the 1956 Grand American.

The Grand American Handicap calls for shooting at 100 targets from distances between 16 and 25 yards, as the rules may require. The National Doubles contest requires 100 shots; the North American Clay Targets, 200; the High-Over-All is a 1,000-shot affair and 400 shots are taken in the All-Around championship.

Trap shooting at the Greenbrier Club in West Virginia.

SKEET SHOOTING

Skeet shooting is a sport devised wholly by American trapshooters whereas trapshooting originated in England.

The newer sport came into existence in 1910, and, for some time, was known as "Round the Clock Shooting." It was decided the game rated a distinct name, and a contest to find one was instituted by the *National Sportsmen* magazine. The winner was Mrs. Gertrude Hurlbutt of Dayton, Montana, who won the $100 prize in a field of 10,000 with the name by which the sport now is known.

Mrs. Hurlbutt chose "skeet" because it is a Scandinavian word meaning "shoot."

Henry E. Ahlin of Boston, one of the pioneers of the sport and for many years secretary of the governing organization, the National Skeet Shooting Association, explaining skeet, states:

"In skeet shooting, guns are used and fire is directed at targets, the same as in trapshooting. But from there on the technique is radically different, and the sports are not really related.

"Skeet shooting, a purely American and fascinating form of the clay target shooting sport, had a following of 25,000 in the United States before the first World War and many thousands in foreign countries.

"The seed from which the sport of skeet grew was planted on the grounds of the Glen Rock Kennels, Andover, Massachusetts, in 1910. A small group of New England upland game gunners, including the late C. E. Davies, proprietor of the kennels, his son, Henry W. Davies, and William H. Foster, used standard clay targets and clay target throwing traps as a means of obtaining wing-shooting practice with their favorite guns.

"There was nothing unusual about this form of practice shooting, since similar attempts to stimulate actual shooting conditions with animated targets in one form or another had been tried before. But this form of practice shooting was enjoyed at the Glen Rock field between 1910 and 1915.

"As time went on, a friendly rivalry among members of this group led to the establishment of a more definite program of competitive shooting. This gave each contestant the same series of shots, and, thereby, made competition as equitable as possible.

"This form of shooting, with definite rules governing, was enjoyed between 1915 and 1920. The shooting arrangement at that time was a complete circle of 25 yards radius, with the circle marked off like the face of a clock. The trap, or target-throwing mechanism, was set up at '12 o'clock' and adjusted to throw the clay target directly over 'six o'clock.'

"The program of shots consisted of two from each of the 12 stations. The 25th shell to complete the round-off then was shot from a position directly in the center of circle, with target representing a direct incomer. This later developed into what is now termed the 'station eight shot.' It was purposely made a part of the program as excellent training for snap-shooting and fast gun-handling, and now is the most talked about one in the entire shooting course.

" 'Shooting around the clock,' as it was informally referred to in 1920, had many of the elements of the present day skeet program. It soon became popular, and the enthusiastic acceptance of this style of shooting soon indicated that it had possibilities as a new and separate form of sport.

"In 'shooting around the clock' shots were fired to all points of the compass. A farmer, owning land adjoining the shooting field, started a hen farm, to put a stop to shooting in that direction. W. H. Foster, a member of the trio responsible for the invention of skeet, met that problem. He produced a second trap and placed it at the six o'clock station marker and adjusted it to throw targets over '12.' This revision produced the same shooting problems as were present in the original clockface setup.

"Between 1920 and 1926, the same small group, augmented now and then by a few interested visitors, continued to shoot clay targets for wing-shooting practice during the closed season on game. Occasional changes in the rules were made to give a closer parallel to game shooting. Important among these changes was the elevation of one of the traps in order to obtain a target more level in flight, and in contrast to the rising target from the other trap. A new set of rules was drawn and the sport was introduced to the shooting public in February, 1936. These rules govern the game today."

Jimmy Robinson, Skeet and Trapshooting Editor of SPORTS AFIELD, and one of America's leading authorities on both forms of sport, advises:

"Skeet uses the same clay birds that have so long been standard for trapshooting, throwing them in the same way, with the same style of powerful spring catapult, called a trap. The targets—actually molded of filler and pitch and devoid of clay—are saucer-shaped and thrown with their convex side up. The trap gives the target a horizontal rotary motion, which causes it to plane. In flight this animated target approximates the swift, steady flight of a quail.

"A standard target is 4½ inches in diameter, weighs about 3¼ ounces and breaks or pulverizes when struck with bird shot. Guns used are 12, 16, 20 and 28 gauges and .410 bore. In match shooting there are gauge classes. The standard skeet load for a 12-gauge is 3 drams of powder and 1⅛ ounces of No. 9 chilled shot.

"Two traps are used, each in a separate small house. The houses face each other 40 yards apart. Each trap throws its target at and over the house of the other trap—always in the same line, at the same elevation. Seventeen out of each 25 are thrown one at a time, the rest in pairs.

"Incidentally, if you are a game shot, your first reaction to skeet pairs is liable to be hostile. You try it for a while. Then you are a skeet shooter.

"Skeet shooting, in comparison with trapshooting, is comparatively new, but it has had a remarkable growth. Before World War II about 50,000 Americans were devoted to skeet shooting, of whom about two per cent were women. But the sport was moving along into remarkable popularity when the war, which had dried up the supply of ammunition and limited the supply of new guns, halted the progress.

"Skeet, only a little more than 20 years old as a standard sport when war broke out, was the one which the Army and Navy decided to draw upon chiefly for instructors in small arms gunnery. Some of the greatest skeet shooters in the United States went into action early and schooled millions of boys in the proper use of a gun. It was a remarkable tribute to skeet that its marksmen were preferred as tutors over those of shooting sports that have been in existence for a great many years.

"Since the war many trained shooters used their instruction to good advantage in professional and amateur shoots all over the country. Today, 11 years later, a whole new crop of shooters has reached skeet shooting age and the popularity of this sport is still on the increase."

By Frank G. Menke
From the ENCYCLOPEDIA OF SPORTS
A. S. Barnes and Company
Copyright 1953

BUILDING A GUN CLUB

Gun clubs are not as hard to come by as you may think. The first hurdle is the hardest. It's location.

Before you begin to look around for a location you will first have brought together a group of shooters who are willing to lay out a little effort and funds to have a club. There should be 12 or more to get the club started. The number of members and the amount of funds available will determine the kind of club you are going to have. You can build one costing anywhere from $250 to $10,000. Build the best one that you possibly can.

When the group is organized, go after a location. Here are the factors to be considered: First you want a location where the shooters face north or northeast. Next you must be at least 300 yards in every direction from the nearest building—and a half mile is better. The location must have access to a fair road and there should be water available. Electricity should also be

Finding a suitable location is the hardest part of organizing a gun club. For safety's sake the range should be 300 yards from the nearest dwellings.

available but this isn't a must. Traps can be operated with batteries or by hand if necessary. The land should be available for lease, a long one if you are going all out on your club. The land should be level so that no expensive ground-leveling operations are needed. Bulldozer rentals run into money.

When all of these conditions have been met you are going to have to consider noise. Shotguns make a considerable racket which can become annoying to people living within hearing distance. Remember that everybody except shooters hates shooting. Talk to the folks living nearby to get their reactions. Get agreements if possible. Perhaps members of neighboring families could be invited to use the facilities of the club when it is ready, thus forestalling objections when the shooting starts.

Once the site has been chosen you will go to your county authorities and apply for a permit. The local law enforcement agency will inspect your location for compliance with existing laws and safety measures and, if everything is in order, you are ready for the next step.

At this point you should incorporate the club. Probably one member of your group is an attorney who will do the necessary legal work gratis. If not, employ a good lawyer to handle it. Incorporation is important in protecting individual members in the event of injury or accident even from the start of building operations. Don't wait till too late.

Two buildings are essential. They are the high house and the low house from which skeet targets are fired. If you include a trap range a shedlike covering for the target trap will also be needed. You can go as far as you like in the way of a clubhouse. Buildings don't make the shooting. You will need a mall four-by-four-foot building to house the release mechanism for electrically operated skeet traps but beyond this and the trap houses any buildings you add are luxuries.

If members do the work, the two trap houses should cost approximately $100 for materials. The small house for the trap-shooting range is easy to build but the trap located there must set in cement since it is pulled by cable from nearly 85 feet away. Any slight change in its alignment would cause faulty operation. Complete, detailed plans for all the buildings needed, plus graphic drawings for the field layout are available without change from the major arms companies.

When you start planning the field layout you will need a width of at least 150 feet and a depth of not less than 45 feet for skeet, a depth of 90 feet and a width of 60 feet for trap. Shooting station distance from point of release varies from 16 to 26 yards.

As soon as your club is in operation you must consider insurance. Liability insurance is a must. Should a nincompoop member use a defective weapon and be injured by it or injure bystanders the club can be held responsible if it happens on club grounds.

The operation and maintenance of the club can be placed in the hands of competent hired help or handled by members. When skeet shoots are in progress there must be some one in each house to load the traps and a third person for releasing and scoring. At least two are required for trapshooting; one in the house to load, one at the release to pull and score. A third person to do the scoring makes for more efficient and faster operation.

By Shep Shepherd

MINIATURE
CLAY BIRD SHOOTING

Miniature golf was a success, even though it didn't replace the greater sport. There is a miniature low-cost shotgun game that has been with us many years, yet we hear very little of it. Most gun clubs have never even given it a try.

The miniature game is known by various names—Mo-Skeet-O, Targo, clay dove shooting and Skrap. The small-size clay pigeon has a diameter of 2⅜ inches and is made very nearly to the same shape and proportions as the larger regulation clay pigeons. They also appear to be made of the same fragile black substance. Traps are used from a mounted position on a bench or counter or block of wood or concrete base.

On the market are light traps, designed primarily for occasional back-yard or picnic use. It is cocked by pulling the carrier arm back against the main spring tension until it catches. Other throwing mechanisms are more sturdily built for constant operation and are faster to use. The carrier arm swings back and catches all by itself and the trap is cocked by simply hauling back on an easily operated cocking lever. Both traps are released by a trigger on the right-hand side. The trigger can be released by the touch of a finger or, if you are operating as your own trap boy, you can mount the trap on the ground and release the trigger with your foot. The traps are made of light alloy and are easily transported.

The trap, gun, clay doves and cartridges constitute the basic equipment. You must do some fast shooting in order to get a good score with the little birds. They must be hit before they get 35 feet beyond the muzzle of the gun in order to assure breakage even with the best pointing. If you can get your shots off within 30 feet, so much the better. Straightaway shots aren't too difficult, but when it comes to angles you've really got to swing fast and you've got to develop some lead on the angles. Not much lead—it's all relative with the big bores on the clay pigeons. Shorter range and smaller patterns make the shooting sporty.

Most commercial setups throw straightaway targets from a counter with the trap mounted 30 inches above the floor. An operator is required at each trap to load it, trip the trigger and see that inexperienced shooters handle the guns safely. This also makes a good setup for clubs. Most clubs can find a safe place to put a range of this type. It is possible it may be placed quite near the clubhouse. For that matter, the straightaway layout can go inside if you have a space about 45 feet long and about 12 feet wide. It is not unlikely that a number of visitors and others who do not participate in other shooting events, because of the expense or lack of interest, will get a big kick out of this setup.

If the game becomes too easy you can set up a miniature skeet field. This involves building two skeet houses and a field layout, but it is practically the same as regulation skeet on a small scale.

By Pete Brown

SHOT SHELL RELOADING

During the past three decades, shot shell reloading came near being a lost art. The past year or two, however, has seen a new surge of interest in this skill.

Shot shell handloading is not a difficult job once you get the hang of it. The first time one sits down with a set of tools, and with no instructions, it is somewhat confusing. But if you know what is to be accomplished, it all becomes a simple mechanical operation. Here are the steps from an empty fired shell to a reload.

1. *Selecting or sorting shells.* This is done by brand name and height of base wad. Manufacturers produce shells with a base wad height to suit the powder and wad column they are loading. Base wad height, therefore, varies with loads used by the manufacturer. For your loading, you must select a batch of shells which all have the same base wad height.

2. *Decapping.* This is merely removing the old and spent primer. Spent primers may be thrown away. Don't throw any live primers away loosely or in trash. It is a good idea to drop them in oil, let them soak and burn them a few at a time in a safe place and at a safe distance.

3. *Resizing.* Standard in any reloading procedure is resizing the case or shell body to the proper outside dimensions. With most of the power tools, resizing is done in the same die which holds the case while the wads are seated. In this case, recapping is done before resizing.

4. *Recapping.* This is simply seating a new primer in the base of the case. *Note:* All manufacturers do not use the same size primers. Western, Winchester and Federal use one size while Remington and Peters use another. Foreign shells may use still another size.

5. *Powder charge.* A charge of power is weighed, measured in a scoop or dropped from a mechanical powder measure into the case.

6. *Seating wads.* From loading instructions in handbooks, or as determined by experiment, a proper combination of wads is selected to fill the shell to proper height. With the correct height of wad column, the shell will crimp properly in the final crimping operation. Before putting wads in all your shells, carry one or two shells through to the crimping operation to make sure you have the correct wad combination.

    A. *Over-powder-wad.* A hard card wad (at least one) must go directly over the powder. These wads are usually about ⅛-inch thick.

    B. *Filler or sealing wads.* At least one of these wads, made from felt or soft fiber, is pressed on top of the over-powder-wad or wads. These serve to seal the powder gases and cushion the load. These wads can be purchased in ¼-inch, ⅜-inch or ½-inch thickness.

Note: Different powders require different wad seating pressures. The pressure used in seating the wads is an important factor in the performance of the load. The power presses have a scale from which you can gauge the pressure being applied.

Suggested wad seating pressures	
Hercules Red Dot	70 lbs.
Dupont Bulk	40 lbs.
Alcan Acapnia	10 lbs.
Alcan Nike	25 lbs.
Alcan M-B	25 lbs.
Hercules Herco	70 lbs.
Alcan No. 5	30 lbs.
Alcan No. 7	40 lbs.

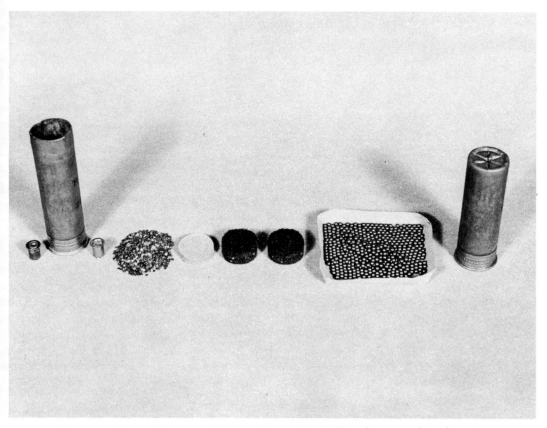

These are the components which go into a shot shell load, arranged in the order of their loading. Next to the fired case is the fired primer which has been removed, and the new primer. After recapping, a powder charge is dumped into the case; the card wad is seated over the powder, the felt wads are seated. The shot charge goes over the felt or fiber wads and then the shell is crimped. The finished shell shows new-style folded crimp.

7. *Shot charge*. Shot charges can be weighed or measured in a scoop. A mechanical powder measure can be used to throw shot charges. In any event, it is a good idea to check a few shot charges on the scales.

8. *Crimping*. There are two types of crimp, the rolled crimp and the new-style folded crimp now used by most of the loading companies. If the rolled crimp is used, a thin over-shot-wad must be placed over the shot before crimping. The folded crimp closes the end of the shell with the end of the paper-case tube. All of the modern tools are equipped to give the folded crimp, but special rolled crimp equipment is available.

The cost of loading, like anything else, depends on how you do your buying. If you are careful you can load a box of shells (25 rounds) for very close to half the price of a new box. You can buy components through a few dealers. If you don't have a local dealer in components write directly to the factory or importer and ask for information on the nearest one. Most dealers in shells have the price of components put out by the large loading plants.

A few last words of advice: If you are going to load shotgun shells get yourself a handbook for guidance. Don't try to soup up your loads by going above the recommended specifications in the handbooks. The light loads are usually the best performers and a souped-up load will usually give you poor patterns.

By Pete Brown

CARE OF FIREARMS

Guns seldom wear out, yet each year thousands become almost unusable—chiefly through neglect. Rust, the principal enemy of guns, does its damage when the sportsman thinks his guns are safely stored away. That's just when rust gets in its corrosive licks on an improperly protected gun.

The cleaning and care of a gun seems so elementary that it should be unnecessary to remind anyone to do it. But this reminder is far more necessary than the average gun owner thinks.

Just about every type of gun is included here: bolt, lever and slide-action as well as semi-automatic. The cleaning tips were photographed under the direction of one of America's foremost marksmen and shooting instructors. He is Jack Lacy, top gun tester of the Winchester Repeating Arms Company of New Haven.

To make it easy to follow, these pictures have been divided into three main sections: barrels, actions and magazines. The barrel-cleaning pictures show you which guns should be cleaned from the muzzle and which from the breech.

Particular caution should be exercised in the selection of the gun preparations that you use. For example, don't use just any kind of machine oil when you oil a gun to be stored. Many light oils evaporate rapidly and provide only a short-lived protection. Use well-known brands of gun oil, grease and so on. They cost a little bit more than the wrong kind but they will be worth more than the difference because they will save your guns.

Here is one final tip to shooters: with your gun clean and functioning properly, be sure your ammunition is also clean and dry.

If you have always cared for your gun in the proper manner, these instructions will serve as a fine refresher course for you. If you are a novice, then you will learn the best way—from the start. Read all of the instructions carefully.

For gun care: Cleaning rods, patch, gun oil, pad, cloth, gun grease, rust remover, screw driver, light oil, brush, furniture polish and waxed paper.

GUN BARREL CLEANING. BARRELS SHOULD BE CLEANED BEFORE AND AFTER
FIELD TRIPS, GREASING FOR STORAGE.

*Barrels cleaned from breech: heavy bolt-action, Model 73; double-barrel shotgun,
Model 21; take-down pump-action shotgun, Model 21; some semi-automatic .22s,
Model 74; light bolt-action, Model 43; single-shot bolt-action, Model 47.*

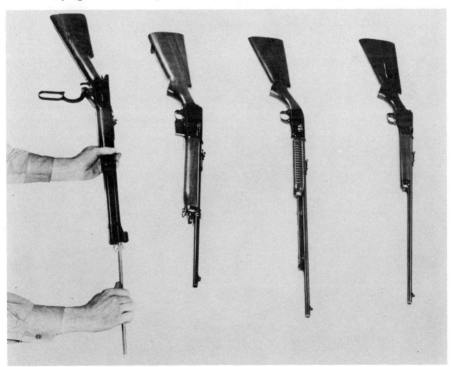

*Barrels cleaned from the muzzle include (left to right): the lever-action, heavy
semi-automatic action, light and heavy pump-action and the light semi-automatic
action.*

GUN ACTIONS. LIGHT FILM OF GUN OIL ON SURFACES OF ACTIONS
INSURES GOOD WORKING, AND LESSENS WEAR.

*Black line shows where to apply oil film on these guns (left to right): heavy bolt-
action, double-barrel shotgun (must be taken down as indicated here), heavy
pump, light pump, light bolt and single-shot bolt action.*

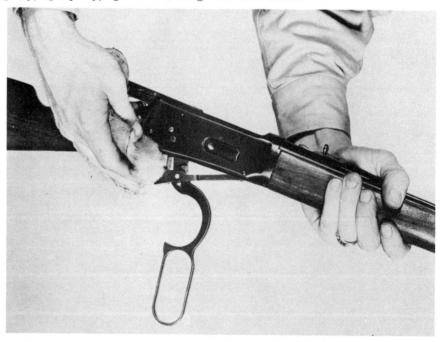

*Here you can see that the lever should be opened to apply oil film to the action
of levers. A small amount of oil and clean cloth or pad are only tools you need.*

HOWEVER, THESE HEAVY AND LIGHT SEMI-AUTOMATIC GUNS REQUIRE AN OIL BATH, RATHER THAN A FILM OF OIL.

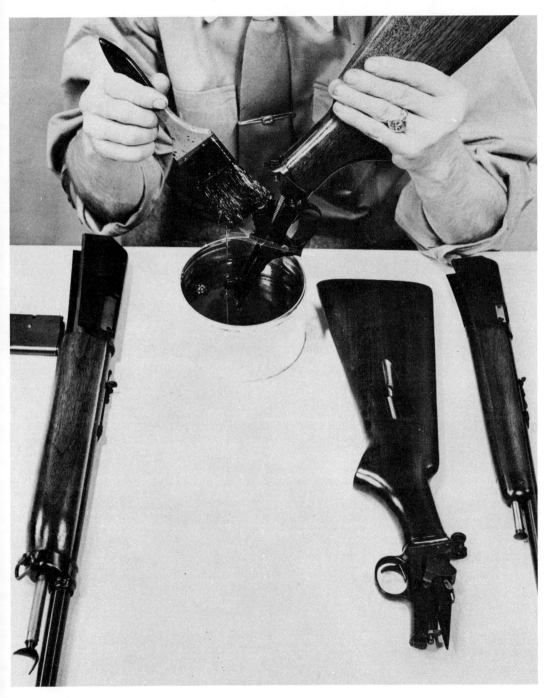

First you apply oil freely with a brush to all parts of the firing mechanism. You drain oil thoroughly before reassembling.

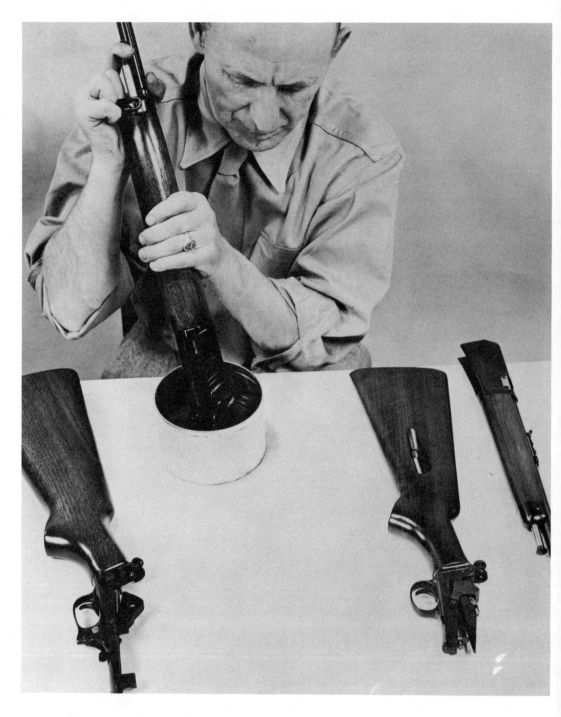

Immerse receiver end into oil; work cocking rod and piston plunger—up and down. Drain oil thoroughly before reassembling.

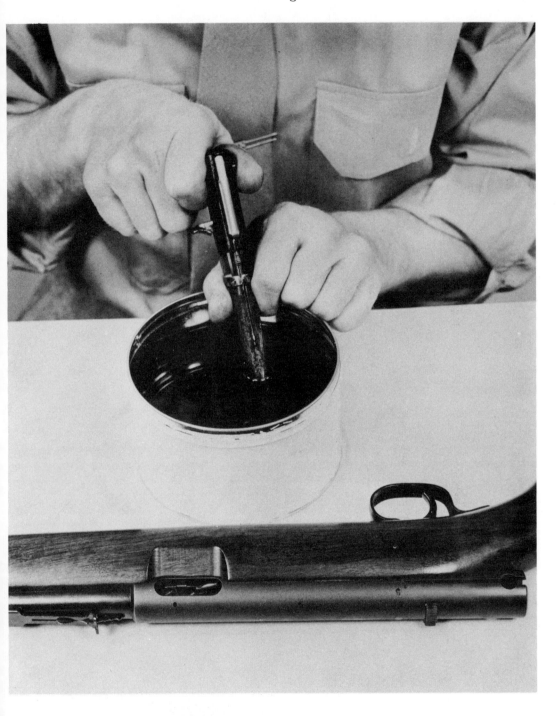

Semi-automatic action with removable bolt cleaned by immersing entire bolt in oil and working bolt up and down. Drain off oil.

GUN MAGAZINES, TUBULAR AND BOX TYPE, SHOULD BE CLEANED, TOO.

Tube holders of tubular-type magazines should be cleaned with rod and patch. Loading port of lever (second from right) must be depressed; and patch and thin wire used.

With rod and patch clean tubes of automatic, pump-action rifles—compressing plunger.

Clean box magazines with an oily cloth. Black line shows location of magazines.

Principal moving parts—as cocking gams, bolt guides, rubbing surfaces —should get small amount of gun grease. The black line shows location of parts to be greased.

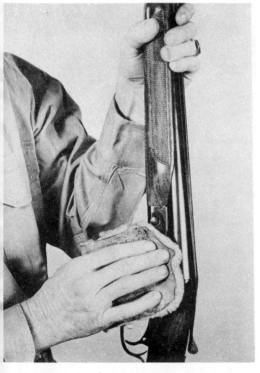

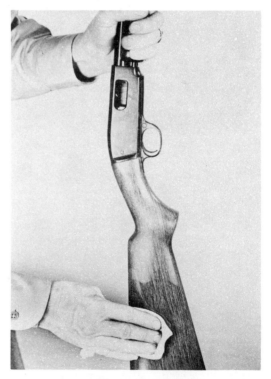

Perspiring of your hands is chief cause of rusty exterior surfaces. It can be avoided with light film of oil on the metal parts before you take your gun into the field.

If you'll use a good furniture polish on the stock and fore end of your gun, you'll keep it like this.

Piece of pointed wood guides your oiling cloth in cleaning crevices between raised or ventilated ribs of your guns, as here.

GREASE YOUR GUNS FOR STORAGE.

Coat the barrel of your gun, all interior metal parts, thickly with good gun grease. Store gun in a cool, dry, high, safe place.

After you have given a generous coating of gun grease to all the exterior metal parts, use good furniture polish on wood.

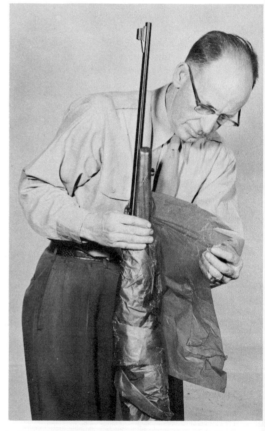

Wrapping the gun in waxed paper prevents grease from rubbing off. If you store a gun for a long time, check at least once a year to renew your storage precautions.

tanning

FEW THINGS can add a more authentic touch to the outdoorsman's home or cabin than the cured skins of game or fur-bearing animals. In addition to their decorative effect, skins of both large and small game can be put to practical use in the form of such things as fur-lined garments and warm rugs. Anyone who has ever owned a buckskin shirt knows the superb qualities clothing made from this material possesses. In this chapter you will find information that will enable you to do simple yet effective tanning and curing furs and to make that time-honored do-all of the wilderness—rawhide.

RAWHIDE

Each fall the returning deer hunters among my friends like to tell about their success. They bring back a lot of fine venison, and occasionally a nice rack of antlers. But 90 per cent of them throw away the skin. To an old outdoorman this is a sinful waste.

It is true that the skins of the deer tribe, including both moose and caribou, when tanned with the hair on, do not make very satisfactory rugs or robes. At first they are attractive to look at, but the hair is very brittle. It breaks off and for years you have hair all over everything.

Did you ever hunt in the cold North where caribou hides are often used for bedding, or for insulation under sleeping bags? Hair is constantly all over everything—including in your tea and soup. On the other hand, the skin of the Rocky Mountain goat, tanned with the hair on, makes a most attractive

This is the setup you use for dehairing. Clamp the skin, hair side up, between log and tree trunk. Then you sit on log and with scraping blade remove hair.

couch cover so long as you keep it clean.

But there are other uses for the hide of any animal. A number of firms will convert it into buckskin for you and make it into most attractive hunting shirts and gloves.

Or you can take the skin yourself and make it into rawhide, a material that has a dozen useful applications for any outdoorsman. Rawhide is simply the skin of any animal, with the hair removed, that's been dried without any preservative.

You can use rawhide for making strong

containers or boxes such as panniers, saddle holsters for rifles, pistol holsters, knife sheaths and so on. It is also most useful for strong repairs to any broken article such as a broken gunstock.

How do you make rawhide? It's really quite simple.

After you have skinned the animal, the first thing to do is to flesh the skin; that is to cut or scrape off *all* pieces of meat, muscle and fat that adhere to it. You can do this with your knife, if you are careful not to cut the skin. Or you can use any tool with a scraping instead of a cutting edge.

Then stretch the skin tight by nailing it on the shady side of a building, or lacing it on a frame. Or you can even peg it out on a clean piece of dry ground, cutting little holes every six inches along its edge through which you drive thin wood pegs into the ground.

Let the skin remain stretched in the shade until it is dry. Use no salt or other preservative for skins to be made into rawhide or garments (without hair), although you may find it necessary to use salt, and sometimes alum, or arsenic soap in warm weather for skins to be tanned with the hair or fur on to keep them from spoiling.

When the fleshed and stretched skin is dry, it is ready to be used. For rawhide the stretching and drying are not absolutely necessary, but the fleshing is. The skin must also be dehaired.

To remove the hair, immerse the skin in a tub of water, preferably slightly warm (not hot) into which you have thrown and stirred a couple of shovels of wood ashes. Let the skin remain in this water, stirring every now and then, for one to three days until the hair loosens.

As soon as you can pull a tuft of hair out with your fingers, take the skin out of the water and put it on a dehairing or fleshing log. This is simply a log about eight or nine feet long and at least six inches in diameter, one end stuck in the ground, and the other leaned against a tree about four feet above the ground. Slightly lift the log where it contacts the tree, and place the edge of the neck of the skin in between, lowering the log. This

clamps the skin for dehairing. The skin now drapes down over the log, hair side up.

For scraping off the hair, use any piece of steel with a scraping edge, not a cutting edge, such as an old flat file with one edge ground like a skate blade, and handles on each end, or a drawknife with scraping edge ground on it.

Straddle and sit on the log below the skin, and with the scraper, scrape off the hair and the epidermis or grain under the hair, taking care not to cut the skin proper. Work *with* the hair, not against it.

Loosen and move the skin where it is pinched tight at the top of the log, so you're always working and scraping against the slanting log. If the hair is very difficult to scrape off, it probably hasn't been soaked long enough. Simply return it to the water for a few more hours.

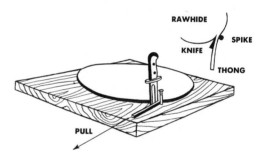

To cut a rawhide thong, here's all you do. You drive spike and sharp knife into board with a ⅛" space betwen them. Cut from round piece.

When the hair has all been removed, wash the skin again to clean it, and then stretch it on a very strong frame, punching little holes about every three inches in its edge, and lacing it on the frame with strong fish line (cod line) or leather thongs.

Pull up on the various strings until the skin is drum tight on the frame. Then let it dry in the open air, preferably in sunlight, until it is thoroughy dry. It will then be as hard as a board. This is rawhide.

Rawhide will keep indefinitey so long as you keep it dry and away from insects and animals.

You must make a wood form or pattern of the article you wish to make of rawhide. On this form you stretch, lace, shrink and dry the hide. For a pannier this form may be a wood crate of the inside dimensions of the pannier you want, and for a scabbard or holster, it should be a wooden replica of the gun, only just very slightly larger so the gun can be easily withdrawn from the final holster.

As it dries, the rawhide is going to shrink terribly tight on these forms so that the forms must be constructed so they can be taken apart inside the dry rawhide. Thus the box-like crate may be constructed with its parts fastened together with screws accessible from the top.

And the form for a holster should be made of three pieces of wood, the center piece in the form of a wedge so it can be knocked or pulled out when the hide is dry, allowing the whole form to.collapse and be withdrawn.

When the form is ready, cut out a piece of the dry rawhide big enough to cover it correctly. If you're in doubt, practice with a piece of wrapping paper.

Soak this piece of rawhide in water; stretch, pull and work it until it is soft and pliable. Then while it is wet, stretch it very tightly on the form. Punch holes at the edge of the opening, and lace it on the form as tightly as possible with leather laces. Pull it up very tight, and so form it as to eliminate any wrinkles, much like wrapping a parcel very neatly in paper to go by mail.

Let the hide dry thoroughly, in the sun if you like, and the article is finished.

The leather thong lacing that binds the rawhide will remain a part of the article. So since it will probably show, it should be neatly done.

For lacing the edges of scabbards and holsters, it's a good idea to assure equal spacing of the lacing holes by using a pair of dividers, making just a barely discernible punch hole where the lacing hole is to come. Then you can punch the holes with a ⅛-inch leather punch that you can get from most any hardware store.

To make sure that the holes line up through the two edges of the hide, I hold about two inches of the edges together with a hand vise while punching through the two thicknesses.

The vise also is used to pull the hide up very tight on the form.

For the leather thong lacing, you may use leather shoe laces. You can often get them as long as six feet from dealers in high-topped boots, or use rawhide belt lacing that you can get from most hardware stores. Or better still, and with no expense, make your own thongs from your rawhide. The Indians call this rawhide lacing *babiche*.

Take a piece of rawhide, roughly circular in shape, about eight inches in diameter, and of uniform thickness. With your sharp knife, cut along one edge of it about ⅛-inch wide to form the start of a thong. Do this for about six inches along the edge. The end of the thong where you start is free, but let the other end remain on the circular piece of rawhide.

Now, drive a spike into a board so that about an inch and a half of the head extends above the board. Drive a very sharp knife into the board alongside the spike, so there is ⅛-inch between the spike and the knife edge. This forms your die for cutting the thong.

Place the circular piece of rawhide on the board, and start the thong attached to it through the opening between the nail and knife edge; then pull on the thong. Your die will continue to cut a thong neatly off the edge of the piece of rawhide until you have six or seven yards of it.

Then put the thong in a can, cover with neat's-foot oil, and let it soak overnight. Then drain off the oil, work the thong soft with your hands, and you have babiche, an exceedingly strong form of leather lacing.

If you have the bad luck to fall and break the stock of your gun at the grip, lace some wet rawhide around it, pulling it up tight with thongs, and let it dry in the same way that's already been described. The repair will be nearly as strong as iron.

In fact all these rawhide articles, completed this way, will be very strong and almost as hard as iron.

Things like panniers are probably all the better for being left hard. But if you want to make scabbards and holsters a little more flexible and more attractive, just paint them once a day for several days with neat's-foot oil, with just enough animal lard mixed in to make it a little thicker. Then rub the holster with an oily cloth, smoothing and softening it a little, and making it quite water resistant.

For some scabbards and holsters the ordinary deer hide does not make rawhide that is quite thick enough. For these use a heavy bull hide. The hide is almost an eighth of an inch thick.

On the other hand, you can easily thin down rawhide with sandpaper, while the rawhide is stretched flat on a small piece of board. Extremely heavy rawhide can also be planed thinner with a regular carpenter's plane.

By Col. Townsend Whelen

SMALL-GAME FURS

Maybe you like your cottontail simmered down in a thick stew gravy, or cooked brown in a hot, buttered skillet. But chances are you're missing out on half the fun a cottontail can give you—as well as a lot of good practical items that you can make from a rabbit's fur. The same thing holds true of all small game. Whether you like to pot shot squirrels under a big oak or chase over the countryside behind a pack of hounds and a running fool of a fox, the hunt doesn't have to end for you when you hang up your gun.

Nothing will stir up pleasant memories quite like putting on a pair of fur-lined slippers, when you can remember exactly which ridge that particular fur came from. Even your wife will take a brighter view of those early morning rounds with the pack when she sinks her hands into warm furry mittens.

Most anyone can think of a couple of new uses for a piece of fur. An inexpensive pair of house slippers can be made over simply by stitching yor own fur into the lining. By matching home-tanned fur to material already cut and patterned for mittens, the fur will make a soft warm lining when the mitten is sewed around the seams and the fur turned inside. You can make your own squirrel-lined earmuffs from any dime store variety. Boys

who would like a coonskin cap can make their own, given one fresh coon and a few chemicals from the drugstore. And a soft tanned wildcat hide or big red fox can look mighty good tacked up on the wall in a den or over the mantle—or it will feel good underfoot on a cold morning.

But the trick is to get your fur tanned well enough so the hairs won't begin shedding as soon as you proudly hang it up on the wall. To tan a fur is a simple process, but you must carry out each step carefully.

It is always advisable to have the more valuable fur skins, such as mink, done by a commercial tanner. The standards of the fur trade and the perfection of tanning technique are what make these furs especially valuable in their finished state. An amateur might unknowingly destroy much of the value of a really fine skin.

But don't think that because you're working with rabbit or squirrel that these furs are no good. Remember that in the fur trade many fancy trade names are only a social register for your cottontail friend. And Alaskan sable in a furrier's is the same wood pussy you let pass as a skunk.

(A list of tanners who will tan leather or furs for you will be sent on request by the Eastern Regional Research Laboratory, Bureau of Agricultural and Industrial Chemistry, Chestnut Hill Station, Philadelphia 18, Pennsylvania.)

The first step in the tanning process is to cut away all loose flesh from the pelt while skinning. Cut the skin along the belly and split it open the full length of the tail, so that it may be spread out flat. The skin should be spread out on poles, trestles or a clean floor to cool out.

If you want to delay further treatment, the pelt should be thoroughly salted on the flesh side. Store the skin rolled up while still damp, fur side out, in a cool place. This way the skin will remain in good condition for a week or more. It may be kept for even longer periods before tanning if it's tacked onto a flat surface with the flesh side turned up and coated with a layer of salt. Left in a cool, dry place, it will then keep for several months.

But completely drying the skin makes the later soaking and removal of grease more difficult. In tropical or semi-tropical lands, it's often wise to add alum or an arsenical compound to the salt.

The second step is to clean and soften the skin, and to completely remove all remaining fleshy tissue and grease from its surface. First soak the skin in several changes of clear, cool water. Ordinarily this will require no more than two hours, and less for a lighter, thinner skin. But if the skin has been dried, you may have to soak it thoroughly, then roll it with the fur side out and let it soften in a cool place overnight. Do not leave the skin submerged for prolonged periods (for example, overnight) or it will become *too* soft and the hair may tend to slip. Knead the skin occasionally while soaking and test the hair by pulling to see that it has not begun to slip.

After soaking, stretch the skin—flesh side up—across a narrow surface such as a sawhorse, a fence rail or a rounded beam or pole. Then proceed to scrape and score the fleshy tissue with any blunt tool. A fish scaler or dull saw tooth will do. Be careful not to cut the firm true skin in which the fur is embedded. Alternately scrape the skin firmly with a flat, dull edge such as the back side of a kitchen knife. This will help clean away the scored tissue and remove the grease from the skin. It's not a very hard job.

All grease must be removed from the skin for the tanning liquor to produce the desired effect. Wash the skin frequently while scraping as you cover the entire flesh side until it is free of fleshy tissue and grease.

When the skin seems clean, douse it in a solution of warm soapy water mixed with one ounce of borax to each gallon. Knead the skin in this solution to further clean it and remove surface grease. Then stretch the skin, flesh side up, over the narrow surface that you used before, and scrape it again with the blunt back side of a knife. After scraping, rinse the skin in warm water and squeeze partly dry—*do not wring!*

Now wash the skin thoroughly in gasoline, squeeze out and suspend it to let the excess gasoline drain off. *Naturally, smoking, sparks and flames are taboo during this operation.*

Keep the flesh side of the skin moistened with water, but dry out the hair side by rubbing sawdust, cornmeal or bran into the fur. This will prevent the hair from matting while tanning and will give a better finish to the fur.

The pelt should now be ready for the third step, the actual tanning. There are a number of methods by which this may be done, but only one, a combination tannage technique, will be described here. This combination of mineral and vegetable tanning is advantageous for home tanning.

The tanning liquor to be applied to the flesh side of the skin consists of the following: mix one pound of aluminum sulfate and one pound of ordinary salt into one gallon of water. Dissolve three ounces of either gambier or Terra Japonica in a small amount of boiling water. Then combine these two solutions and add more water until the combined mixture equals two gallons. This completes the preparation of your tanning liquor.

Now spread the skin, flesh side up, over a flat surface and tack it into place. If the skin has dried out, it must be dampened evenly with a wet rag before you apply the tanning liquor.

Mix a portion of tanning liquor with flour in a separate container until it forms a thin, watery paste. (The amount to be mixed will depend on the size of the skin.) Then paint the pasty liquor onto the flesh side, covering it with a coating about an eighth of an inch thick. The skin should be left coated with this liquor for 24 hours. During this time it should also be kept covered with sacking or paper so that it remains moist.

Then the first coating should be scraped off and a second application of the pasty tanning liquor painted on. For thin pelts such as rabbit and squirrel this is the last coating, and the skin should be left uncovered and the liquor allowed to dry slowly. For thicker pelts such as wildcat and fox, an extra coating and covered period of 24 hours must precede the third and final coating of liquor.

This last coating may require several days o dry depending on local conditions of umidity. When it is almost dry, but preferably before hardening, wash off the thick-aked mixture. Then rinse the skin in a solu-on of water and borax mixed as before with ne ounce of borax to each gallon of water. fter this, rinse the skin in plain water and queeze partly dry. Stretch the skin once nore over the narrow ledge (sawhorse, rail r pole) with the flesh side up.

Now draw the blunt back of a knife over he skin slicking it out, removing the water ith an action like a squeegee. When you ave rubbed out all excess moisture, but while he skin is still damp, tack it smoothly onto flat surface with the flesh side up. Then pply a very thin coating of animal fat or ondrying oil. Butter, neat's-foot oil, castor il, glycerin or soap may be used.

Usually faint white spots will begin to orm on the skin when it is ready to be oftened. Or you can make a test by folding he skin. If it is ready, a light streak should ppear along the fold.

Softening is best accomplished while the kin is still just slightly damp. Stretch and raw it in all directions—flesh side down— ver a hard, blunt surface. A board with he sharp edges rounded off and clamped, nd up, in a vise makes a serviceable stake r softening skins.

If the skin is not soft enough after first retching and drawing it over the stake, it tay be repeatedly dampened and worked ver again until you are satisfied with the esults. The skin may be further softened nd smoothed by working the flesh side riskly but lightly with sandpaper.

If the skin seems to have a greasy texture, r if it retains an unpleasant odor, dip it in asoline for a quick bath—but don't let it ak.

Then to brighten the fur and get the best nished appearance, "tumble" the skin in arm, dry sawdust. (Cornmeal or bran will

also do.) You can do this tumbling by enclosing the sawdust and skin in a heavy paper bag and shaking vigorously. For larger skins, not so easily tumbled, you can rub the sawdust into the fur by hand.

Brush out the sawdust and the tanning process is now complete. The fur should be well preserved and ready for use. Spread out on a wall or underfoot, it will wear surprisingly well. And it will always be a source of pleasant memories to the hunter.

The entire process for home tanning is outlined below to be used as a check list to insure that no part of the process is omitted. All the ingredients for the tanning liquor can be purchased either from a local drugstore, or the druggist can furnish the address of a chemical supply company that sells them.

1. Remove all loose flesh from skin.
2. Soak skin in fresh water, scrape, score and scrape.
3. Wash skin in a solution of borax and soapy water, then scrape again.
4. Rinse skin in warm water and squeeze dry.
5. Wash thoroughly in gasoline, drain and dry out the fur side of skin. (*Watch out for fire!*)
6. Paint tanning liquor onto dampened flesh side of skin and leave covered under paper or sacking for 24 hours.
7. Scrape off first coat and paint in a second coat of tanning liquor (and a third coat for thicker skins), leaving this last coat uncovered to slowly dry.
8. Wash off the last coat when almost dry and rinse skin in a solution of borax and water.
9. Rinse skin in plain water, wring dry and scrape.
10. Apply thin coating of animal fat or non-drying oil.
11. When almost dry "soften" skin.
12. Tumble skin in warm, dry sawdust.
13. Brush out sawdust and tanning is complete.

Note: Other formulas for tanning liquors can be found in Farmers Bulletin No. 1334, a Department of Agriculture publication, 15 cents per copy.

By McGregor Smith, Jr.

CHAPTER **18**

trapping

PROBABLY MORE than any other group, the solitary trappers of the early West did more to roll back the wilderness and plant the seeds from which our civilization grew. It was the trappers who crossed the unmapped plains traced the unnamed rivers to their sources and found the mountain passes Their camping places became sites for present-day towns, their trading posts became cities. From this colorful beginning, the trapping industry today has grown into a billion dollar business with trappers annually collecting an estimated 100 million dollars for the furs they catch. This chapter tells you how to trap the important fur bearers and prepare and process pelts for commercial use. Whether your interest is professional or purely for pleasure, trapping with its requisite wisdom in the ways of the wild is a fascinating sport for any outdoorsman.

TRAPPING TODAY

One of the most attractive things about trapping is that it does not require any great amount of capital to start into business. The "equipment" necessary for even a long trap line in the Far North, costs less than a milk-separator. a plow or a peanut vending machine—and yet the trapper can make for himself several thousands of dollars during a few weeks' interesting work On the other hand, many a good farmer has little fur-bearing animals running around on his land, and entirely taking care of themselves, the prime pelts of which are worth more in dollars and cents than he can get for the best domestic stock he owns and which he has spent a good many months of careful effort and considerable expense in raising. But the unfortunate part of the whole situation is that far too many folks fail to look upon these fur bearers and trapping as a serious business. What farmer would let dogs chase his sheep or his hogs to some unknown place; or would go out and willfully try to kill every last one of his breeding stock? And yet how many farmers and ranchers try to do just that with the valuable fur-bearing animals on their land. If the landowner will look upon the mink, beaver, skunk, muskrat and other fur bearers that make their homes on his property in much the same way he looks upon, protects and fosters the other livestock he possesses, he will have more money in the bank at the end of each year.

Farmers have been known to have "cleaned out" all the skunks on their place, in midsummer when the hides were without value, merely because the "varmints" killed one of their chickens. It would have been more profitable, in many such cases, to have "cleaned out" the chickens and taken care of the skunks! And more than one farmer has drained a swampy area, or cleared a wooded section on his place, that would have proved more profitable to him if the land had been left as it was, or improved for the benefit of the fur bearers. In many instances it is better to put in a dam or two, and plant some feed, to make waste land so attractive that the fur bearers will stay and thrive, rather than chase them away.

The remuneration from trapping, both in financial returns and the fascinating enjoyment of the great out-of-doors, does not necessitate one going deep into the wilds. The farmer and farmer boy who runs his trap line through the woods on his own place, or down through a nearby river bottom or foothill, sometimes gets as much out of it as the person who winters in a crude log cabin in the remoteness of the far northwest.

There are also many who through the circumstances of life are compelled to spend their days at a work bench or in an office building, but whose hearts are really in the winter woods. Many such persons have trap lines a considerable distance from the towns in which they work and which are reached a certain number of mornings or evenings each week by automobile. There are also others who work in town during the summers and spend the entire trapping season in the wilds.

The amount and value of fur caught by farmers and part time trappers throughout rural America runs into a fabulous total—and the health and real pleasure which these men and boys enjoy, is even greater.

It is sometimes surprising what wild sections may exist within reach of the town or even the city in which you live; and not all of the wilderness in the United States is in the Far North or the Far West. There are sections along the East Coast, particularly in the Carolinas and Georgia, as well as the Appalachian and Adirondack Mountains and the Gulf Coast, which are but seldom visited and are about as wild as anyone might hope to find. In some of these sections the native white inhabitants have been isolated so long that they still retain customs and speak dialects of hundreds of years ago.

To the average person, Louisiana is not generally thought of as an important fur producing state; and yet, Louisiana furnishes approximately 75 per cent of the entire muskrat catch of North America. Southern Louisiana is considered the greatest furproducing area of the entire continent. Not only are muskrats plentiful, but also mink, otter and raccoon; and they provide an annual income of six to 10 million dollars. What is even more surprising is the fact that this rich fur industry has only been realized during recent times—less than two generations.

The most interesting sections of North America today, from the standpoint of the trapper and the lover of virgin wilderness, is the Northwest. In western and northern Canada, and Alaska, there is an area almost half the size of the entire United States that is still to a large extent wilderness; and throughout this vast area are hundreds of men who spend the trapping season just about as they might have if they had trapped there 100 years ago.

The famous Alaska Highway, up to Alaska through western Canada, has made a vast area of good trapping grounds in the north-west more accessible than ever before; and it will see many a new pioneer heading north, with his auto packed with provisions, warm clothing and steel traps.

BEAVER

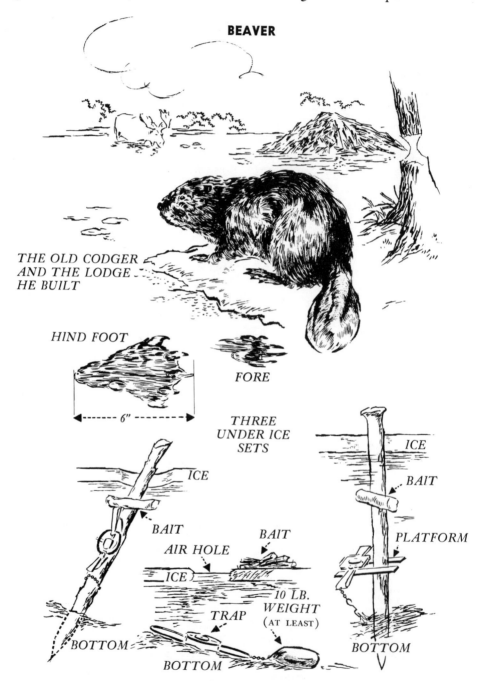

THE OLD CODGER AND THE LODGE HE BUILT

HIND FOOT

FORE

6"

THREE UNDER ICE SETS

ICE

BAIT

BAIT

AIR HOLE

BAIT

ICE

TRAP

10 LB. WEIGHT (AT LEAST)

BOTTOM

BOTTOM

ICE

BAIT

PLATFORM

BOTTOM

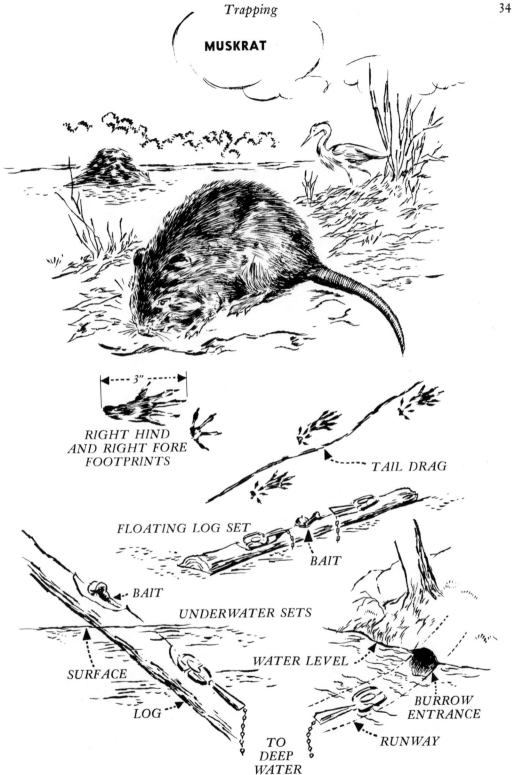

MUSKRAT

3"

RIGHT HIND
AND RIGHT FORE
FOOTPRINTS

TAIL DRAG

FLOATING LOG SET

BAIT

BAIT

UNDERWATER SETS

WATER LEVEL

SURFACE

LOG

BURROW
ENTRANCE

TO
DEEP
WATER

RUNWAY

WOLF AND COYOTE

FORE FOOTPRINTS

WOLF   *COYOTE*

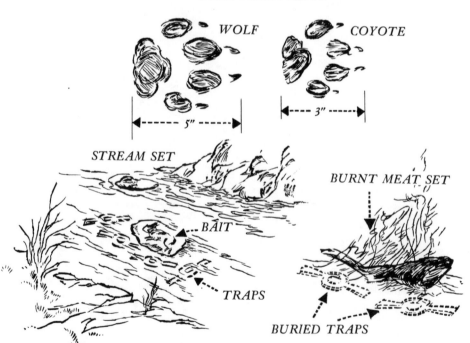

STREAM SET

BURNT MEAT SET

BAIT

TRAPS

BURIED TRAPS

RED FOX

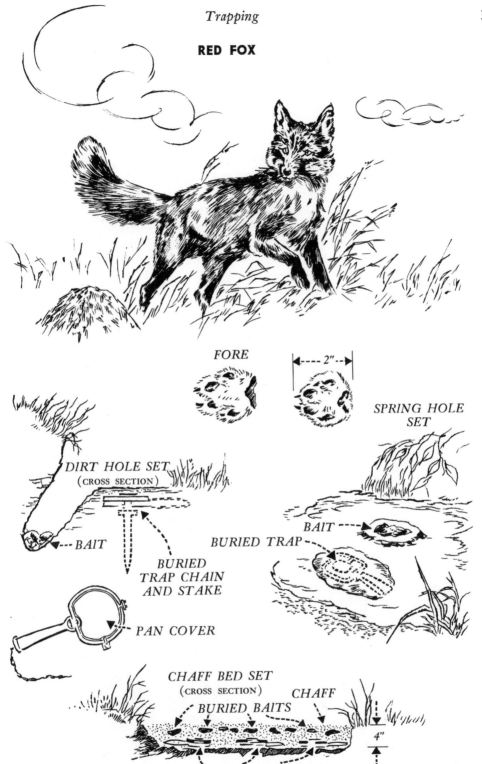

FORE

2"

SPRING HOLE
SET

DIRT HOLE SET
(CROSS SECTION)

BAIT

BURIED
TRAP CHAIN
AND STAKE

BAIT

BURIED TRAP

PAN COVER

CHAFF BED SET
(CROSS SECTION)

BURIED BAITS

CHAFF

4"

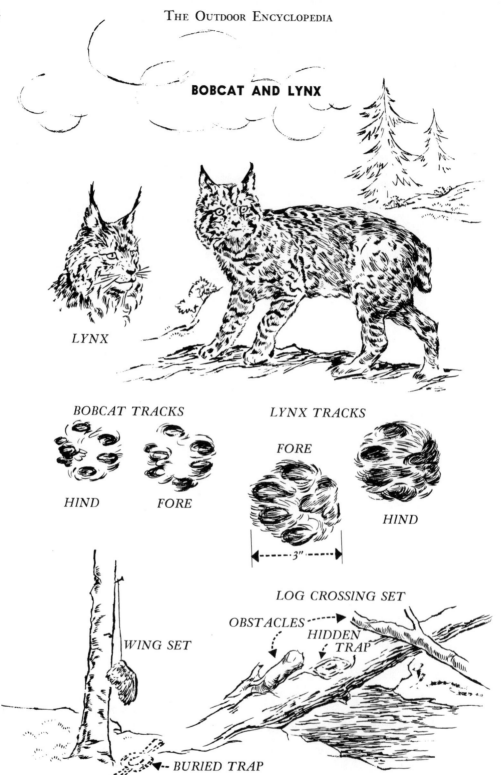

BOBCAT AND LYNX

LYNX

BOBCAT TRACKS

LYNX TRACKS

HIND   *FORE*   *FORE*   *HIND*

←----3"----→

LOG CROSSING SET

OBSTACLES

HIDDEN TRAP

WING SET

←-- BURIED TRAP

RACCOON

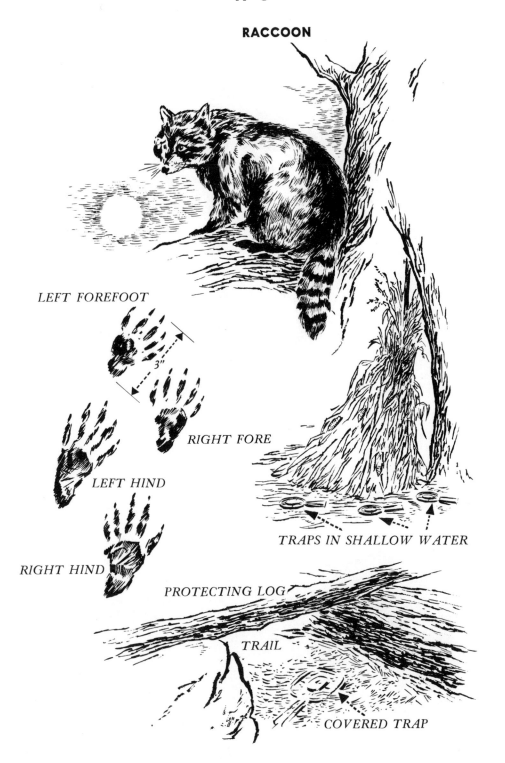

LEFT FOREFOOT

3"

RIGHT FORE

LEFT HIND

RIGHT HIND

TRAPS IN SHALLOW WATER

PROTECTING LOG

TRAIL

COVERED TRAP

SKUNKS

HOGNOSED SKUNK

LITTLE SPOTTED SKUNK

COMMON SKUNK

FORE

2½"

HIND

RUNNING TRACKS

CUBBY SET

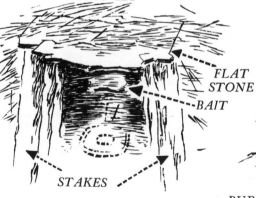

FLAT STONE

BAIT

STAKES

ROCK PILE SET

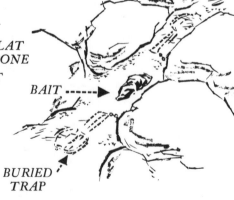

BAIT

BURIED TRAP

Whether you do your trapping in the snow and ice of Alaska or the marshlands of Louisiana, however, the most important requirement for success is to have a thorough knowledge of the animal being sought. The trapper must be a naturalist, as well as an expert in the art of setting his trap.

The printed page can only be an elementary guide. Real knowledge of wild life is something which comes only from first hand experience. To some people, with a keen sense of observation, this comes quickly; but there are other folks who can wander through the woods or fields year after year and still miss the many little tell-tale things which seldom escape the naturalist-trapper.

One of the best ways to assure a successful winter trapping season, if circumstances permit, is to spend your summer holidays quietly observing the locations where you plan to set your traps. Train yourself to see and analyze all the little evidences left by the fur bearers. You'll be surprised how they can be pieced together and give you ideas for your winter program.

Never trap or kill fur bearers until the fur is prime. When you do this you only cheat yourself of top prices for the pelts.

THE CARE OF PELTS

Hundreds of thousands of dollars are lost to trappers annually because pelts are improperly skinned, fleshed, stretched and dried. This is a great economic loss, not only to the trapping fraternity but to the raw fur trade, and can be prevented if trappers would exercise greater care in selecting equipment and would learn the correct technique of skinning and preparing pelts.

Wilderness trappers usually whip off the pelts of captured fur bearers on the trap line, or on the spot, so to speak. The pelts are rolled or wrapped and carried back to camp for the finishing touches.

Trappers in settled areas usually maintain comparatively short trapping lines and travel back and forth, either by foot, horseback, canoe or automobile. These trappers some-

times bring the animal carcass back home for skinning.

In either event most trappers maintain a headquarters camp and can procure or make proper pelting and finishing equipment.

Pelt drying boards. First in importance is an ample supply of properly made drying boards. Too much emphasis cannot be placed on the vital need for providing the proper sizes and shapes of pelt drying boards, or, as they are commonly called, stretching boards. Unfortunately the word "stretching" is too often taken literally by trappers. Boards that are out of proportion or skins that are stretched out of proportion always result in misshapen pelts. These are an eyesore and are materially disqualified by the raw fur buyer. Your goods are on display when you show them to the buyer, and otherwise good pelts are certainly shown at a disadvantage if improperly dried. They not only lack trimness but, if overstretched, invariably show up natural thin spots that should be pinched and covered with underfur and guard fur.

Most trappers prefer to make their own drying boards and here is where the skill and workmanship of the individual trapper comes into play. Drying boards should be smooth and as finished as possible. It is just as easy to make a thing right as it is to make it in a slip-shod fashion and this axiom certainly applies to trapper's equipment. Many trappers use formed wire or cut steel stretchers. Good results can be obtained by proper care both in selecting the right size and keeping the edges free from corrosion or rust. If this is not watched carefully, damaged pelts will result. Fine furs, such as mink and fox, should be handled only on wood drying boards.

Skinning knives and appliances. The trapper's prime requisite for the actual work of pelting is a good trapper's knife. The right kind of knife is equipped with a slitting blade, a skinning blade and a small blade for general use. Each blade should be kept keen and sharp. A dull blade will cause more damage to pelts than a sharp blade that does its work smoothly and without friction.

Small, medium and large fleshing boards should be provided. These are best made of two- by eight-inch material, four feet long and tapered from eight inches at the upper end to two inches. Smaller sizes can be provided for animals smaller than a fox. The upper side should be slightly rounded to fit the curve in the fleshing knife.

The fleshing knife has a large, curved knife edge with a handle on each side. The edge should be dull so as not to cut the pelt. If preferred, a complete set of fleshing instruments can be made, or secured, of wood.

Another appliance that comes in handy is a tail slit guide. The manufactured guides are metal troughs tapered to fit the tail. An old umbrella rib also makes a good tail slit guide. A tablespoon is also handy for scraping and removing excess fat.

In addition, the trapper should also provide himself with a tack hammer and tacks and split sticks for removing tail bones, a pair of nippers for cutting toes and plenty of clean hardwood sawdust to absorb fat and dirt and give a good gripping surface on the pelt.

The stretched open or open-handled method is used almost universally for beaver, badger, raccoon, bear and wild cat, although some fur buyers prefer to have the full-furred northern type of coon cased. Open skins are taken off by cutting the skin straight down the belly, from the lower jaw to the vent, then slitting the front and hind legs to the body cut, after which the skin is carefully removed from carcass.

The case-handled method is used for such furs as wolf, fox, coyote, marten, fisher, mink, otter, lynx, skunk, opossum, muskrat, ermine and civet cat. Cased skins are taken off by cutting down the back of the hind legs to the vent and then peeling the skin off carefully toward the head.

Care must be taken to keep the skin as free from flesh as possible. Use a sharp knife but guard against cutting into the skin. Peel the skin from the front legs, cut the ears close to the head and use great care in skinning around the eyes, nose and mouth.

Feet and tails. It is the customary practice to cut the tails off the muskrat, beaver and opossum. The feet should be cut off the following animals: muskrat, beaver, opossum, skunk, raccoon, badger, civet cat and coyote. The feet of the other animals should be left on and properly skinned and dried.

Fleshing. There are certain mineral elements in fresh blood that tend to stain fur so it is advisable to wipe blood from the pelt as soon as possible after skinning.

Fleshing is one of the most important operations in preparing the pelt. It is not only essential that all surplus flesh be removed but as much fat as possible. The layers of fat and muscle can be worked loose with the thumbnail and sawdust.

Place the pelt over the fleshing board and work down with the knife, using plenty of sawdust. Be careful not to scrape too hard. Overscraping will result in cutting the hair roots and cause the hair to fall out. Work the fat off carefully around the ears. If this is not done, the fat will very likely burn the fur and cause it to slip. Every trapper should accumulate a supply of hardwood sawdust. Use this freely when scraping off the fat.

Sawdust not only absorbs fat and grease but makes it possible to keep a firm grip on the slippery pelt. Sawdust can also be rubbed into the fur and then shaken out. By this means much of the dirt and grease can be eliminated from the fur and it will give it a fresh, sparkling appearance.

Placing the pelt on the drying board. Select a proper-sized board for each pelt. Your supply should include appropriate sizes to accommodate various sized pelts. When fitting the pelt to the board, be sure the belly is on one side of the board and the back on the other. Slip the pelt onto the board gently. Don't stretch it but pull it down to full length and tack. A pelt that shrinks a little on the board is better than one that is stretched a little. Fleshed pelts dry quickly so it is important that they be placed on drying boards as soon as possible. Just before hanging the board straighten out the ears, tail and legs.

Drying the pelt. Drying is also an important process in the preparation of the pelt. Pelts should not be allowed to freeze nor should they be hung in a heated room. They should never hang where exposed to the sun. Pick a dry, dark space, keep flies away, and, if possible, provide for a circulation of air.

A small number of skins can be hung from nails in rafters or ceiling. If a large number of skins are to be dried, a frame can be made of two by four's or small, split logs. This frame slanted against a wall and studded with nails will hold a large number of skins. It is advisable to inspect the legs of pelts occasionally and make sure they are drying properly. If tails and legs are not hanging straight, they should be pinned down. Pelts of foxes and other animals that are to be shipped "fur out" should be dried leather-side-out in a comparatively warm place for 24 hours; then the pelt should be turned fur side out.

After drying, pelts should be removed from the boards and be given a final cleaning. Wipe the grease off pelts leather-side-out and if fur-side-out proceed as follows: Lay the pelt out on a clean table or bench and rub the fur full of clean hardwood sawdust. Be sure and rub the sawdust in gently otherwise the guard hairs will be damaged.

Rub the fur until the grease is cleaned out. Shake the pelt out well and hang in a well-ventilated place. Commercial skins should never be washed, nor should alum, salt or other preparations be used.

Packing and shipping. Many dollars are lost to trappers annually because of improper packing. Green furs or furs that have not been stretched and dried should never be shipped. Skins should be properly packed in cloth or burlap and they should be laid leather side against leather side or fur side against fur side. Fine furs should be wrapped individually in absorbent paper or cloth before being packed into the bundle. Do not wrap in newspaper or any printed paper. The ink is apt to color pelts.

Pack the skins flat and sew bundles tight. Make the package big enough so the skins can be laid out, otherwise they will come out of the bundle rolled up and creased and their full beauty will be lost. Your pelts will look much more valuable to the fur grader if they come out of the bundle flat and free from creases or rolling.

If you are selling your furs to a local buyer, take them to him or show them to him unpacked, as it is almost impossible to pack furs in a bundle and have them come out after shipping in as good an appearance as they were before being packed. When shipping furs, be sure to have your name and address both on the inside and outside of the package.

From the book TRAPPING
By Harold McCracken and Harry Van Cleve
A. S. Barnes and Company
Copyright 1947

CHAPTER 19

travel

Outdoorsmen are a traveling bunch today, quite unabashed at setting out weekends with the family for a drive to the mountains, the seashore or wherever their inclination takes them. Naturally, when they go, they like to take the implements of their sport along. A select few even hitch their home on the back of the family car and it, too, goes along. In this chapter you will find information on choosing and using a house trailer and the best ways by which to transport your boat. Also included is a section on that delightful little traveler of the sandy regions—the beach buggy.

HOUSE TRAILERS

The small house trailer, or as it is often called "camp" or "vacation" trailer, has been growing slicker and slicker year by year. Today it is one of the world's most delightful, ingenious and amazing wheeled gadgets. It is a home in miniature. With it a sportsman can painlessly take all the conveniences of home right into the woods.

It has everything in a single cleverly compact package. It goes practically anywhere a car can go; it is trouble-free; it's easy to tow, soundly engineered, built to "take it" and priced right. Best of all, it is on the market in such variety that there is a model certain to suit every customer.

Available are: build-it-yourself trailer kits; tiny, bare-necessity units costing little more than a tent; fully furnished slip-on models to slide into a pickup truck; slick, fold-up tents-on-wheels; stripped-down standard models at rock-bottom prices; dozens of fine fully furnished models in the middle price bracket; last-word trailers built like fine airplanes, expensive but with the reasons plainly showing in anatomy and interior.

Here are tips on choosing the trailer tailored exactly to your particular needs and purposes.

Select your general price range first. But buy for quality in direct proportion to proposed use. An expensive trailer that is to travel 10,000 miles annually may be a better buy than a cheap one. Conversely, a cheap trailer may do just as well for the sportsman who pulls it only a few hundred miles in two weeks each year.

Size—length. Contrary to popular opinion, a 23-foot trailer doesn't necessarily tow harder, or place more weight on car hitch, than a smaller size. Conceivably, the reverse may be true. Your choice of how big a

trailer to buy should depend entirely upon how many persons will use it, how much money you want to spend, how many conveniences you wish and how much room you require for comfort. Any good car will take any sport trailer on decent roads over any U.S. mountain.

Size width. Sport trailers are built in widths from six to eight feet. In mountains and on back-country trails, a width of seven feet or less is advantageous. Height and axle clearance are about the same on all models.

Folding tent-on-wheels, and like types serve well the outdoorsman who wishes to go "back-of-beyond" with a car. So do the various pickup truck body models. A fine plan, where money is not a barrier, is to use pickup with one of the slip-on body models as a tow vehicle for your standard trailer. Gives more room. Also, haul in the trailer as far as you can, then use it as a base camp

Today's trailers offer luxury accommodations for all kinds of outdoor living.

while the truck goes anywhere there's a trail.

Don't underbuy, regarding size and equipment. A trailer bought for one trip, or for short vacations, soon gives one the bug, maybe even turns into a summer cottage.

Is this a once-in-a-lifetime purchase, or will you trade every few years? In the first instance, high-quality construction, higher price may be the best investment.

Wheels, rims and tires. All truck-types are best in general, especially for the larger models, or if you expect to subject them to heavy loads. Cutouts over wheels are important so the wheels are easily removable in case of a flat. Tires should be six or eight ply.

Frame. Three-inch or four-inch high-quality steel channel, with adequate cross members are needed here, this is no spot to tolerate skimping.

Undercarriage. It should be of standard, top-grade make, not homemade throw-together. Never buy a trailer whose undercarriage is made of used materials.

Rear bumper. All trailers should have one; the best kinds are formed channel welded to the frame extension.

Exterior. Metal is best, aluminum preferable because of its lightness and inexpensive upkeep.

Fasteners. Rivets, screws and bolts are a necessity. Look out for models in which nails or screw nails are abundantly used.

Roof. One piece aluminum is preferable, or, if the roof is built with seams, make sure they are properly engineered and sealed so they cannot leak. More than one roof vent is preferable in larger models. It should be large, screened and with a sturdy lifting mechanism. The outside seams should be leakproof.

Windows. Any trailer needs plenty of them. The split type are preferable with aluminum frames, aluminum (or copper) screens. Look out for models with windows that don't open. In single-door models, look to see if the rear window is built to serve as an emergency escape hatch. It is a good feature. Front and rear windows that are built for complete see-through-trailer vision when looking in your car's rear-view mirror are an extremely desirable convenience and safety feature.

Door. It should be hinged on its leading edge and equipped with a top-grade catch and lock, leakproof and screened.

Signal lights. Good trailers have two or four running lights on sides, plus top-quality tail, stop and directional lights. If the latter are not standard equipment, by all means install them.

Brakes. Surprisingly enough, these are not always standard equipment on all models. However, they should be, even on the smallest, lightest trailers, regardless of opinions to the contrary. You can have them installed as an extra. Either electric or hydraulic systems are good, electric is currently more often installed.

Incidentally, the newer cars with 12-volt wiring systems must have a resistor installed to be able to operate six-volt electric trailer brakes. The signal light bulbs on the trailer must be changed from six to 12 volt.

Luggage-space door. A small outside door to "trunk space" beneath a bed or elsewhere is a good feature and one to look for. You'll be amazed how it simplifies storing and removing long items such as fishing rods or skis.

General construction. It is difficult to check, but most important. If you can do so, go through the factory of your chosen trailer. Otherwise, hold out for detailed information on construction you can't see. Aluminum ribs with aluminum panels riveted to them are excellent. Where wood frames are used, good glued, mortised side-wall construction, with laminated oak bow structure bolted to side wall and floor (of at least ⅝ inch ply with covering) makes a sound combination.

Insulation. This is another important, but often overlooked, feature. Check to see that insulation is thicker under the floor than on the side walls. Material used should be fixed in place or of a kind that cannot shake down. The trailer should have a vapor barrier so it absolutely will not sweat. Make certain on this.

Wheel housing. This should be made of metal and waterproofed. Make sure the distance from the top of the tire to the top of the wheel-well exceeds the distance from the top of the spring to the bottom of the channel. Then you'll have no housing breakage on dips, or with heavy loads.

Hitch. Any standard brand with an automatic spring lock is all right.

Balance. This you can check with several thorough trial runs. Balance makes all the difference between an easy or hard pulling trailer, a trailer that sways or one that stays in line even at high speeds.

Interiors. What is best in interior appointments, arrangements and equipment depends entirely on your individual tastes. Purposes and uses vary so widely only you know exactly what you want and need. However, there are a few general things to look for.

Don't be dazzled by slick interiors. Sort each over carefully for conveniences—and faults—for *you.* Are there plenty of closets and storage space for your particular needs? Are all doors in line, none warped and with smooth-working secure catches that will hold when traveling? Are closets and cupboards secured to the wall by screws (or rivets if interior is metal), not nails or screw nails? Curtains or blinds of some kind should be at the windows? Are they there? Is there a fuse box for safety and is all the wiring of top quality?

Floor plans usually are offered in several choices. Comb each for its highest comfort and convenience qualities, its best utilization of limited space. Aesthetics are secondary. Relate your choice of interior to what you will do with the trailer, where it will be most of the time, how much of your time will be spent in it, and doing what.

Aside from these general considerations, there are specific ones you should keep in mind. But remember always that the prime reason for trailers on a camp trip is comfort, so get all you can for your money, and in the space you buy!

Cooking. Long trips or poor digestion lend importance to having a full stove with an oven and broiler. An over-wheel-housing stove with burners and a small oven but minus broiler saves space. A simple burner plate will do for only short camp trips. Having a vent and blower above the stove is a good way to keep the cook happy.

Refrigeration. Large gas refrigerators are too heavy. Small ones will work for one or two people, but will cramp more than that. An icebox saves weight, but ice doesn't last except for short trips. Extended stays off the beaten track prove that gas is best for this. However, there are hundreds of trailer parks, state and national parks that furnish electricity. An electric-ice combination refrigerator with a four-cubic-foot capacity is therefore perhaps your best all-round bet.

Lights. Electric standard. See that there are plenty of them and that they are well placed. A couple of auxiliary gas lights to run off your gas bottle make excellent added equipment.

Heating stove. It is a toss up whether gas or fuel oil is best. Make sure, either way, that the heater is well vented. Don't use one that isn't. Having a blower on the heating unit is a good idea.

Hot-water heater. In a fairly big sport trailer, where space permits, by all means pack in a hot-water heater. You'll want it in trailer parks, or when traveling. Electric seems to be the most popular. Gas is also available.

Bathroom. The extra cost is well worth it to have comfort and privacy in this department. You'll find it wonderful when in trailer parks. Hookup is simple and quick. The railroad-type toilet can be used when you're backwoodsing it, by digging and covering a dry well, and running the sewer hose to it. You fill the toilet bowl from a bucket.

Here are a few more random suggestions on interiors. Foam rubber mattress and dinette seats are expensive, but comfortable, and great weight savers. A dinette may not be the best bet for you. A folding, free-standing table and light, comfortable folding chairs, may be better. Consider having a bunk bed in back. Or twin beds to give "runway space" between, and a single bunk cross bed above them, if necessary to sleep three. Or you may need a dinette that makes into bed, this arrangement sleeps five. Make sure the dinette, if you get one, will seat all the people who are to use the trailer.

Check to see that there are ample electric outlets, well placed. Remember that a double sink is better than a single, where space permits. Formica or comparable material makes a fine, sturdy counter and table top. If you plan to use gas for refrigeration, heat, cooking and lights, two gas bottles in a double rack will be mandatory. (Only one is usually furnished.) They're a good idea anyway except where hitch weight is crucial. A full standard-size gas bottle weighs roughly 40 pounds, cooks three meals a day for from four to six weeks.

What about mirrors? Are there towel racks? Will the closet (or bathroom) door swing back to close off the bedroom from the dinette when you wish? Is there a place to sit comfortably after meals, or in the evening? Are the seats too high or too low for comfort when eating, writing a letter or repairing a reel at the table? All these little things count after a trailer is yours!

Here are some tips on extra or optional equipment. Chemical toilets that work very well are nowadays available. Adequate interior lighting can be run from the car battery, or from an extra battery in the car trunk. Built-in water tanks are available, with marine-type hand pumps over the bowl in the bathroom, and by the sink. Generator units mounted on pickup track, or on the trailer tongue are available. These supply full electric power for refrigeration, lights and appliances. They're fairly heavy. At least one sport trailer may be had nowadays with a complete extra built-in hot- and cold-water pressure system (in addition to regular plumbing) which works off built-in tanks. This system is run by a generator unit, mounted on the trailer tongue as a rule. The unit also furnishes lights and power. Such a system (or full gas operation) plus chemical toilet makes a trailer wholly self-sufficient anywhere.

Make certain of what is and is not furnished with the particular model you are buying. Ask the salesman to describe the equipment in detail, right down to light cords, hitch ball and the wiring plug for the signal lights. An uncommonly low price quote may mean the interior is almost barren, with most equipment considered optional extras. Nothing wrong with this—just so you know it when you write the check.

By Byron W. Dalrymple

BOAT TRAILERS

Today's skipper has added a new dimension to his boating needs. Along with traditional qualities like seaworthiness and speed, the modern skipper wants mobility in his boating. If his boat is easy to launch and recover, he can save boatyard fees by storing her in his backyard. If he tires of one lake, another beckons. On family vacations, the boat comes along. Mobility adds to the potential of any boat and it isn't hard to come by. No matter what kind of boat you own, there is a way you can transport her. Here are some tips that will make for better trailer boating and safer hauling of the outfit.

There are two schools of thought on transporting the small boat. One group of people say the only way to haul a small boat is on top of the car. Another group will like the less cumbersome loading and launching features of the trailer, being content to go more slowly, and to keep an eye peeled for the "extra car in the train."

It is true that slightly higher road speeds can be maintained with auto-top carrying. But there is a limit to length and a limit on weight that can comfortably be carried this way.

The best length for auto-top carry is between 12 and 14 feet. The lighter the boat, the better. Usually 150 to 175 pounds is top limit. Anything longer, or anything heavier, calls for special security in fastening the boat down, and will call for lower over-the-road speeds. An unusually large boat will be heavy, and the metal in the car's dome may buckle on bumps. Also, longer boats are prone to get loose in higher winds, and to give trouble.

Auto-top carry has the advantage of no trailer cost, no trailer license, no trailer stowage or theft problem, higher general road speed and no backing problem. Disadvantages are: hard loading, especially after the boat has been used and has soaked up weight, the need for help in loading and unloading, possible scratching of the hull in overhead brush, proneness of the hull to open in long exposure to the sun.

If your outfit is big, say from 15 feet up, and weighs the usual 250 to 750 pounds, a trailer is the only answer. For one thing, the tires on your car are not burdened by other than normal weight. Then too, one man can haul and launch a much heavier boat and engine than the fellow who hauls atop his car. The hull of the boat itself becomes extra toting space for gear the car can't haul, and more adequate excursions and cruises can be taken. For instance, what better place to stow your tent and camp stove than in the hull of your boat when she is cradled on a trailer?

Advantages the trailer will give are many:

Ball of hitch must be perfect for socket.

Make pads straddle channel properly.

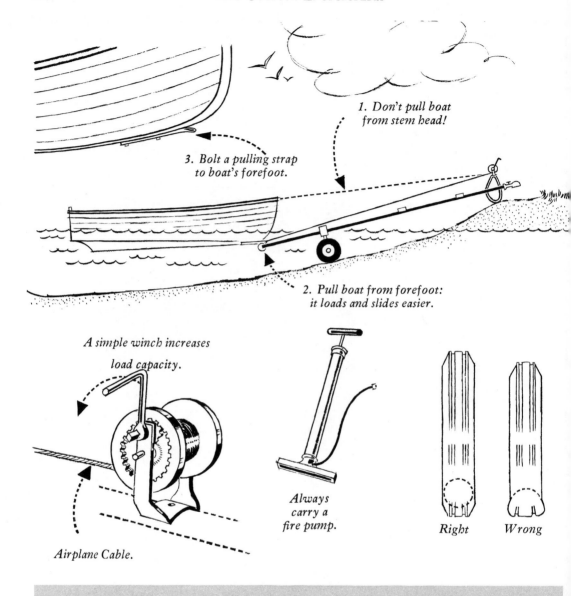

1. Don't pull boat from stem head!

3. Bolt a pulling strap to boat's forefoot.

2. Pull boat from forefoot: it loads and slides easier.

A simple winch increases load capacity.

Always carry a fire pump.

Right   Wrong

Airplane Cable.

greater load capacity, easier launching, much easier hauling. Your load may be "broken"—that is, you can leave the boat and trailer behind for side excursions once you have reached your vacation area. Aside from the disadvantages of cost, license, backing problems and a mite less general mobility, one must also consider the ever-present hazard of mechanical failure at the hitch, and subsequent insurance costs.

It all boils down to the size of the outfit you need. Light boats on an auto top give generally greater freedom, but you're going to get wet in them and they don't carry much. Bigger boats need a trailer.

Let's look at auto-top carrying first. Nearly all auto-top carriers are crossbars to which are secured rubber suction cups of some sort. In addition, these crossbars will invariably be clipped to the car's rain gutter by canvas straps attached to stamped metal clips. When buying a carrier, examine these clips most closely to make sure they have not been fractured in the punch press when bending. Also see that the canvas straps are rugged, and that the webbing is well fastened.

When installing a carrier on top of the car, keep an eye on two things: Spread the carriers as far forward and as far to the rear as you can. Also, you will find under the dome of your car, concealed by the fabric, little cross channels welded across the top. Try to locate the pads of the carrier so that they straddle the channel at about this location. Installed in this manner, over the dome channels, any carrier will carry a much heavier load without denting the top. This buckling action will eventually fracture the metal in the car dome through fatigue, if the boat is too heavy or the roads too rough. The paint also has a tendency to flake if much of this action persists.

On a two-footed suction cup, four to a beam, or eight to a set, bear in mind that the local pad load on each cup is an eighth of the total. Thus if your boat weighed 200 pounds, you can see that each cup would be holding a 25-pound load. This is why a lighter boat is recommended.

Once you have minimized buckling by properly locating the channels, the next problem is adhesion. The best stuff to use in rendering the pneumatic cups tight is glycerine, or brake fluid. Any filling station will be glad to saturate a rag for you by which you can jam the cups down airtight.

Oil or grease will rot rubber. Soap will dry out, and usually contains hydroxides which discolor the paint. Since this paint is sprayed on, it is always pebbly in texture. While pure water will work on an initial sealing, it soon dries, and the air seal is broken. You'll be without the holding power of pneumatic grip.

Once the straps are pulled up tight, a good dodge in a new carrier outfit is to wet the canvas thoroughly with water. This shrinks the webbing. When it dries after this treatment, it can be taken up again, and wet again until the stretch is largely removed.

It seems needless to say that a boat toted atop a car should be hauled bottom up. If you haul right side up and run into rain, the accumulated water in the boat will render the car unstable.

Although boats longer than 12 to 14 feet, such as canoes, are often carried this way, make sure that the bow or stern, whichever hangs over, is crosstied to the bumpers. You'll be traveling above the burble point of air— that point at which it "takes hold"—and any sudden gusts of wind will put a real wallop into side thrust. It is best to have the overhang crosstied, or "X'ed" to the bumper for this reason. A very good safety precaution for top carrying is to loop and tie the hull thoroughly over the rear windows, then to lower these just a fraction, and loop the auto top itself with rope, passing it through the windows.

Auto-top carriers cost about $7.50 for the average outfit up to $25 for custom made jobs.

Trailers, of course, will cost more money. They are available in all sizes and shapes to transport boats ranging in size up to 24-foot cruisers. You can choose either a full trailer that supports the boot at the bow, aft and amidships or a three-quarter model that supports the boat at the bow and two, rather than three, other points. Though some people do not mind the inconvenience, the bobtailed model is harder to retrieve a boat on, and to haul out with. The more popular models are those having a rear tongue on which there is a roller. This is a lot of help in launching, and highly helpful in hauling out.

A good winch forward near the ball hitch is wanted by many. This winch is more effective if the forefoot or underside of the boat's keel is provided with a strap eye, so that the hauling cable pulls from *under* the boat. Hauling from the stem *top* doubles the work, increases the strain on both boat and trailer.

Most hitches are ball-and-socket type. There are several sizes. *Be absolutely certain that the ball of the hitch is the correct size for the socket.* Just because the lock on the socket, or tongue end, closes over the ball and seemingly prevents the tongue from coming off the ball is no sign the outfit is safe. As a matter of mechanical fact, this condition is the most dangerous of all. The loose-fitting tongue on a too small ball will "cam" itself off, invariably. The only safe hitch of this type is where the ball and socket are exactly mated. Then the lock will really hold.

A chain is required in most states by law. This must lead from the tongue to the chassis of the car to prevent wild runaways in the event of hitch failure.

Properly mated ball-and-socket joints seldom give any trouble.

Occasionally, with home-made trailers, a lip with a hole in it is connected to a double strap on the trailer tongue by dropping a bolt through it. If the head of the bolt is big enough, and the nut beneath is safety wired, this system will be safe. You can't count on it over great distances otherwise. It is very prone to work loose.

In all events, don't shove off without the added safety of a chain between tongue and chassis, no matter what type of hitch you use. That imagined accident can happen and if it does it will seldom be in the manner you anticipate it.

Most stock and mutual company insurance policies cover trailer use and some public liability and property damage policies are voided if the car is towing a trailer. You should check with your insurance agent on this. No use letting a faulty trailer hitch result in either an accident, or in your losing a court decision.

With trailers, most states require licenses. The license fee varies according to the particular state.

Most modern trailers come equipped with sealed bearings so that water will not enter the wheel sockets. Even so, particularly if you launch in salt water, periodic inspection of the bearings is a must. Salt water will emulsify the oil into a nonlubricating sort of soap.

Tongue loads should come to about 75 to 150 pounds at the ball hitch. If the boat is loaded correctly, the center of weight will be about a third the tongue length forward.

Keep a tire pump in the car. After using the boat, she will be heavier. Inflate the tires of the trailer so there is no bulge in the side wall. Bear in mind that with a little wheel and tire such as the 4.00x8 size, which is standard, the wheel revolves about twice as fast as the car's wheels, so the bearing speeds are about two times as great. This is another reason why it is advisable to drive at moderate speeds with trailers.

By Weston Farmer

BEACH BUGGIES

If you've ever struggled through loose beach sand, loaded down with fishing, camping or picnic equipment, you can appreciate why the beach buggy came into being.

But beach buggies are far more than mere sand taxis. They have developed into self-propelled camps with galley, full-length bed, numerous compartments for stowage and a water supply. The extent of these facilities is limited only by your ability to fit your requirements for comfort into the restricted amount of space.

With a bit of wise conversion even a regular automobile will ride along the beaches and sand dunes of our coasts. Light vehicles of short wheel base will take to the sand somewhat easier than the larger models.

The one departure you must make from normal road equipment before you try sand travel—and it's an absolute must—is to replace your tires with low-pressure sand tires such as the 8.20x15 size.

Used tires with nearly no tread (or completely bald) are preferred over new tires for two reasons. First, they pack down the sand so your car can get proper traction. Second, the cord and rubber of the older tires are soft, pliable and more inclined to "float" on top of the sand.

You'll need an accurate tire pressure gauge, for tires must be deflated when you leave the hard-top road to cruise the sand. The usual deflation is to eight or 10 pounds of pressure. It takes trial and error to find where the individual automobile operates best.

In general, an 8.20x15 may be dropped as low as five pounds, if necessary, but it should not be deflated that much immediately after a long, hot drive. For later when the air in the tire cools and contracts, a flat may result.

There's a kit on the market that is handy for inflating tires when you leave the beach. One spark plug is unscrewed and momen-

With minor modifications almost any car can be run on sand. But the all-out beach buggy is light, equipped with oversized tires and comes in as many different shapes and sizes as there are owners.

tarily replaced by a small valve which connects to the tire by a hose. You merely start the engine and compression actuates the valve, blowing air into the tires, and inflating them to normal road pressure.

Lacking this unit, you can inflate your tires by hand pump or drive *slowly* (a precaution against rolling the soft tires off the rims) to the nearest garage. In most localities, garages now leave their air hoses out 24 hours a day. Thus, with these choices, reinflation of the tires presents no great problems. Gas mileage and control on the highway are not noticeably altered by these big tires.

There are numerous refinements on many beach cars that increase their functional ability. But oversize tires are the only must.

Among the additional improvements you'll see are the four-wheel drive, dual cooling system, low-speed gears for the rear end, dual tires (both front and rear), dual rear ends set one behind the other and the built-in winch for use if you get stuck.

If you drive on the sand, you'll likely get stuck occasionally. So carry a small shovel in your gear. Getting stuck, unfortunately, is not completely avoidable. But there are a few tricks which help prevent it.

Ease your clutch pedal out gently when you start. *Do not spin the wheels.* And if your car bogs down, avoid the temptation to try to force your way out. The wheels will almost instantly churn their way deep into the soft sand. It is far easier to remove a few shovels of sand right away than to dig the whole running gear of your car free later.

When you're stuck, be sure the front wheels are directed straight ahead before you try to break free. If they are turned at even a slight angle, the drag is immeasurably increased.

A couple of hundred pounds of ballast in the rear provides excellent traction, and helps reduce wheel spin. Passengers or sandbags are fine for this purpose.

Beach buggy operators often go all out for installing the comforts of home into the narrow confines of their cars. Scarcely a square inch of space is wasted. You'll find bed, stove, icebox, cupboards, water tanks and most of the articles commonly used by fishermen or campers. In the vehicles used solely for beach cruising, these fixtures are permanent.

Prospective beach buggyists often ask if sand driving isn't too rough on a car. There's no denying it's harder than highway driving. But if you use common sense, there's no reason your car should suffer. And if you wash off your car with the garden hose after each beach trip, you should have no trouble from the salt air.

By W. L. Searle

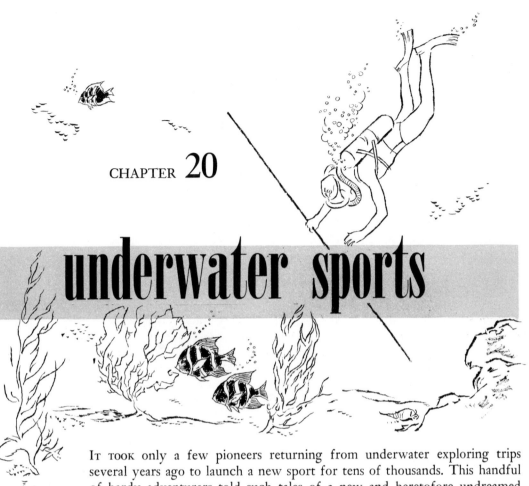

CHAPTER **20**

underwater sports

It took only a few pioneers returning from underwater exploring trips several years ago to launch a new sport for tens of thousands. This handful of hardy adventurers told such tales of a new and heretofore undreamed of world under the sea that it was almost impossible to deny the urge to investigate this new world personally. Seemingly overnight, skin diving clubs were organized all over the country, sporting goods dealers were harassed to get the latest equipment on their shelves and the door to another phase of outdoor living was opened. Interest in skin diving is still booming. Last year's equipment, techniques and fishing grounds are outmoded this year. The basic instruction for the beginner remains the same, however, and this is what you will find on the pages that follow.

EQUIPMENT

SPEARS

The essential problem underwater fishermen have to face is to substitute some method of long-range projection of the spear for the greatly restricted range of the human arm. There are today countless variations of the same weapon but in essence there are only two main types.

The first is the method for propelling the spear by an ordinary sling or catapult. The spear is shot toward the fish by stretching a piece of rubber which holds the blunt end of the spear and then releasing it. The other method is release of spear by a metal spring. The spear is pressed down the muzzle of a gun, inside of which there is a spring. Shooting consists of simply releasing the spring which then sends the spear along its way toward the fish. In the course of development there have been all sorts of other models working on the principle of the explosive release of compressed air or carbon dioxide, but guns worked by means of the catapult and guns working with a steel spring are the two most common underwater weapons.

The Hawaiian or Polynesian sling. This is the simplest and cheapest of all and is only a refinement on a most primitive instrument. It consists usually of an aluminium, plastic or wood tube held in the hand. A strong elastic rubber band is fixed at one end of this tube so when you insert the spear through the other end you can stretch the rubber by pulling out the spear. The blunt end of the spear is held by the thumb and the first two fingers of the right hand together with the rubber band. The tube is held as near as possible to the right eye in order to achieve the best aim and the spear is suddenly released by letting go with the right hand. The spears in this case are usually very light in weight since your arm cannot stretch a long elastic rubber band far enough to gain reasonable momentum with a heavier spear. These spears are usually not connected with the holding tube by a line, so when you release your spear and miss you have to dive down again to retrieve it. If you spear a fish you must also dive down again to get it. This weapon should thus not be used at depths over 15 feet as it involves frequent diving to the depths.

Other Sling Models. These are all developments of the original sling or catapult model which is the lightest in weight. The simplest consists of a nonrusting metal muzzle about two feet long. The spear is inserted in it. The rubber band has been replaced by a solid piece of elastic rubber, circular in section, divided into two parts by a small V-shaped wire joint. The base of the spear has a groove which can be fitted on to this joint. When the spear is forced down the muzzle the elastic rubber is stretched until a click

indicates that the gun has been cocked. The stretching of the stronger rubber is thus achieved mechanically in these models. The spear is released by pulling a trigger on a handle resembling an ordinary pistol or revolver handle. Some models have been strengthened by the use of three, four or even more rubber pipes in the same manner. Although all parts of the gun itself as well as the spear are made of nonrusting metal, the disadvantage of these models is that the rubber sooner or later begins to rot as a result of contact with salt water. They are, however, easily replaced and do not cost a great deal, but even before salt water has had its rotting effect the rubber usually becomes over-stretched by use. These guns are easy to handle and they do not weigh very much. They can be held in one hand for long periods of time so that the other hand is free for swimming.

Metal Spring Guns. The power of this gun depends on the length and strength of the spring which is compressed in the muzzle. In this model, too, the spear is pressed down the muzzle until a click indicates the gun is cocked. The spear is released by pressing the trigger fitted to the handle in much the same way as on the sling-type guns. These models are usually heavier, and therefore more difficult and tiring to handle. The longer and more powerful the spring is the longer must the muzzle be. Therefore the stronger must be the force to compress the spring when inserting the spear down the muzzle. This makes loading the gun in water a more difficult and more tiring job.

Spear fishermen discovered very early that it was not enough simply to spear a fish. A speared fish will manage to wriggle off the spear quickly unless there is something to hold it on. That is why the spear itself has developed varying systems of barbs. An old-fashioned trident is one of the simplest models. The next development came about when it was found that taking a live fish off the spear and swimming at the same time was an extremely difficult business. A movable barb was therefore developed. This consists of one or two wings fitted about two inches

Cruising just below the surface the top of the breathing tube is just out of water. The gun is held ready for use as the fisherman propels himself by his flippers. The loaderpin may be seen suspended from the neck and the handle of the knife is just visible.

from the point. These wings cannot move higher up towards the point than at right angles to the spear itself. They may be U-shaped in section so that when pressed down parallel to the spear they are flush with it, or they can fit into the body of the spear to achieve complete streamlining. A well-timed spear shot at a fish from a fairly short distance will usually pierce it beyond these movable wings. When these are pressed down parallel and flush with the spear the fish can be slipped off it fairly easily. The wings can be held down by the fingers of one hand or they may be pressed on to the spear by means of two small pins.

Most fishermen have found to their regret that a good number of their shots miss the fish and their spears hit rocks. Even if steel spear points are used, these blunt fairly quickly. Many spears therefore have removable points which can be screwed on and off easily. It is well for the beginner to have a good supply of spare points.

The beginner should also keep in mind that the density of water has a sharp effect on his shooting. For example, the speed of a spear in the last nine feet of its trajectory is so slow that by the time it reaches its target in many cases the target is there no more. In practice you should try to approach fish so the point of your spear is at most not more than five or six feet away. If you have a powerful gun, your chances of spearing fish are increased considerably, but even with the weakest gun you have an excellent chance of hitting your target from a distance of three to four feet.

Exposing the metal parts of your gun to salt water causes them to rust very quickly. It is therefore advisable every day after using your gun, even if it is claimed to be made of nonrusting metal, to wash it in ordinary fresh water and then to grease it.

The muzzles of all guns have dozens of small holes all along the surface of the cylinder. As the metal spring is released up the muzzle, water is expelled through these holes. Care should be taken that these are not blocked with sand or dirt.

GOGGLES AND MASK

Goggles are indispensable for spearfishing. Your view of underwater life when wearing goggles is exactly the same as your view of fish in an aquarium. Your eyes will never tire of admiring the beauties under the sea, and even if you never succeed in catching a fish you will have had an experience you will never forget.

The simplest goggles are made of rubber with two ordinary glass lenses. If worn very tightly they should not let any water come to your eyes.

When you put on your goggles and put the breathing tube into your mouth you will feel extremely clumsy and the odds are you will think that you will never overcome all the difficulties in your way. The first thing to remember is that, using all types of goggles except the mask type, you must breathe only through your mouth. This is a rather difficult job for those who have learned to swim using both the mouth and the nose for breathing. If you use a mask face plate it does not matter whether you breathe through your mouth or your nose, because the breathing tube which forms part of your mask is connected with the whole space inside the mask. Your entire face is covered.

You will find that very soon a mist will form on the inside of your goggle or mask. This is especially true of the mask where, in addition to the heat of your face on the inner surface, there is also your breath. To prevent this you should either spit on the inside of your goggle or mask or spray some anti-mist liquid on the inside surface. Another good hint is to breathe hard into it while you are still out of the water. All goggles and masks should be washed thoroughly in fresh water and dried after use.

FLIPPERS

Equipped with a pair of goggles and some form of breathing apparatus and with the gun cocked in your hand, you are ready to go skin diving. By using your one free hand and your legs, you can move quite freely along the surface of the water, and you can dive below the surface in order to approach your quarry. Even if you are an excellent swimmer, you will find, however, that you are far too slow for most fish. Moreover, it will take you some time to be able to go down to a depth of 10 or 12 feet. The effort of doing so will tire you, so that you will be able to stay very little time at that depth in order to pursue your fish or stalk it in any manner likely to be successful.

Some years ago rubber flippers which can be attached to your feet were developed. These will give you, through the use of the crawl stroke with your legs, a tremendous increase in your surface speed. You will even be able to swim at a quite respectable speed by using your legs only. If, when you are lying horizontally along the surface you take a deep breath and double up your body as though making a deep bow, you can get yourself to a depth of about six feet in the space of a second. If you continue to point almost vertically downward with your head and then begin using your feet in the crawl stroke, you will find that you will shoot downward at a speed you hardly thought possible. Within a second or two you will find yourself at a depth of about 15 to 20 feet. By changing the position of your body under the water at that depth so that your head points upward, and by keeping your body quite straight, and again using the crawl stroke with your legs, you will find that you will shoot up toward the surface just as quickly as you came down.

You must get a pair of flippers that fit your size of foot exactly. There are several types on the market, but with most of them you will be able to achieve results that have been described above. They should also be washed in fresh water and dried after use.

THE FISH RING

This is a ring about eight inches in diameter made usually of steel wire. This ring can be attached to the belt of your bathing trunks. When you have had a successful shot and you have taken your fish off your spear you can save yourself a trip to the shore or your boat by threading the fish on your ring. You should lead the point of your wire through the gills so the wire comes out through the mouth. If the fish is attached in this manner, even the liveliest of them will be unable to move very much and the rest of your fishing day will not be much disturbed.

THE KNIFE

It is useful to carry a knife. Stainless steel is the best material for knives as it does not rust. There are some on the market with cork handles that float.

EAR PLUGS

Every spearfisherman will find his ears begin hurting when he goes below a certain depth. To stop this, you will find ordinary rubber ear plugs very useful. There are also on the market various types of ear wax, usually sold to people who cannot sleep if there is any noise. To prevent these falling out you may find it useful to use a rubber cap.

GLOVES

Even when you use the loader for loading your gun, wearing a glove on your right hand will prevent cuts. Golfing leather mittens are most useful, as they leave the fingers entirely free.

GETTING ADJUSTED

With all this equipment available you are now ready to start spearfishing. It will take you some time to conquer your clumsiness. Breathing may prove the most difficult task to master. At the beginning something is wrong all the time; either you can't breathe because water has entered your mask, or you can't see because the additional pressure below the surface has caused your mask to change position. By pressing on your eyebrows or on the skin of your temples the goggles can distort your vision.

You have to learn to put your mask on properly and you will have to learn to swim holding the gun in one hand. You should also learn to swim with your legs only. It is helpful sometimes to hold heavy guns in both hands when cruising along the surface.

Unless you have a very long holiday, you will find that many days will pass before you can begin enjoying your spearfishing, and you will have very little time left for the sport.

It is fortunately possible to do most of your preparatory work and your training at home. You can go through all the preliminary stages in a swimming pool. The first thing to do is to learn to use your mask. You must accustom yourself to movement in every direction at varying speeds just below the surface and under the surface of the water with your goggles on. When you are comfortable with your goggles over your eyes, you can begin to use whichever breathing apparatus you have chosen. You can then practice using the flippers until you feel they are a natural extension of your legs. When you feel completely at ease in the water—with all your equipment—you are ready for the actual test.

You will find that everything under water is enlarged and distorted. A useful way to accustom yourself to movement and judging distances and angles under water is to drop coins to the bottom of the swimming pool and then try to pick them up.

Construct a target in the form of a fish not longer than eight inches. This fish can be made of wood, or of cork, and should be attached by a string to a heavy object such as a stone or a piece of metal. You then drop your practice target in the middle of the pool. Try shooting at it from all sorts of angles and at all sorts of distances. If you can get a friend to help you, you will probably be able to invent a kind of moving target by using a tin fish suspended from a line and a pole with your friend walking along the side of the pool. You must, of course, use some kind of padding over the point of your spear in order not to damage the swimming pool.

THE TECHNIQUE

ENTERING THE WATER

You must not forget to bring a towel and spare bathing trunks with you. You may find that after you have spent only an hour or so even in the warmest water you will be quite cold when you come out. It is advisable to wear trunks which have a belt as will be made clear later.

If you are swimming in a sunny climate, don't start spearfishing unless you have become tanned. As you swim along the surface of the water your back is exposed constantly to the sun, and at times it is partly submerged and partly above water. This is the surest way of getting a burn—five minutes exposed to the sun in such circumstances is equivalent to a quarter of an hour of sunbathing on the beach.

Even entering the water is a different problem when you are wearing skin diving gear. Choose, if you can, a place where you can wade in the water without having to dive. If you have to dive, your mask will probably come off, you may lose your gun, or you may make a splash which will frighten the fish that happen to be near. Before you go in load your gun and apply the safety catch. Check your reel and check the position of your line. Then place the gun as near the edge of the water as you can. (You pick it up on your way in.) Put your ear plugs in and put your rubber bathing cap on if you have one. The next thing to do is sit down as close to the water as you can get, and put on your flippers. You will find it best to wet the flippers before you put them on. Then tie your fish ring to your belt. When you have done that, put your glove on and then you are ready to prepare the mask or the goggles by making sure a mist will not form on the inside of the glass. Once the goggles are on and your breathing tube is in your mouth you are ready to go.

At all times when you are handling the gun, out of the water, or in the water, be extremely careful not to point it at anybody. Your gun is a lethal weapon.

You should, at the beginning, try to avoid diving too often. The effort of going down to a depth of about 15 to 20 feet, spending a few seconds under water and coming up again is tremendous. The strain on the heart and on the lungs is considerable. The human body will withstand easily the change of pressure experienced at a depth of between 15 and 20 feet, but one should avoid straining one's system too much.

The beginner should avoid trying to go to greater depths than 20 feet and he should be satisfied with the kind of fish he finds in shallow waters.

It is useful at the beginning to take frequent rests at the surface of the water in between your dives. If you haven't got a friend with a boat, the next best thing is a life belt or perhaps an inner tube which you can anchor with a line and a stone. You can rest your gun on it, and by holding on with one hand you can relax for a few minutes.

The first thing to do on coming out is to fire your gun into the water to avoid struggling out of the water with a cocked gun. The next thing to do is to take off your mask, then your flippers and take the ear plugs out of your ears. Get yourself dry and warm as quickly as possible.

FRESH WATER

Rivers present a special problem for the skin diver. Where there is clear water it is usually very shallow, in which case swimming is extremely difficult and diving impossible. Other times the depth of water permits free movements, but the current is very strong. Most of the time, however, you will find that organic matter in rivers impede visibility beyond perhaps a foot or so. All large rivers are far too dirty for fishing under the water. Mountain rivers and torrents are too fast and the temperature of the water is often below 45° F. This makes fishing impossible, since even the most experienced and strongest swimmer could not stay in such water for any length of time or hope to have a fair chance at any fast moving fish he may accidentally meet. Most lakes are also too cold, and experience has shown that, except for the smaller ones, most fish in lakes stay in the depths.

ESTUARIES AND DELTAS

The great problem at the mouths of rivers is again visibility. Wherever large quantities of fresh water intermingle with salt water there is a tremendous movement of organic matter in the water and visibility is restricted at best to a few feet only. Here again, you have the problem of cold, and if you go farther out into the sea then, of course, with every yard you move, fishing conditions approach those in salt water.

ALT-WATER FISHING

Wherever you go in the world and you find the sea clear enough to see with your goggles at a distance of more than about 10 or 12 feet and wherever the sea is warm enough to enable you to stay in the water for about half an hour or so, there are fishing grounds. There are, however, two major problems which you will have to face. The first is that you must be careful of rough sea and the second is that you must be careful of dangerous fish, such as sharks and barracuda.

If you see that the water is blue up to the very shore it means the water is clear below the surface and that visibility is good. If the first 50 or 60 feet of the water are brown or grayish in color, you will immediately know that even with goggles you will be able to see very little once you are below the surface. Many sandy beaches will thus be immediately eliminated from your choice.

The next thing to examine is the shore itself, because the kind of bottom that you are likely to encounter depends very much on the kind of shore on which you are standing. If the coast is rocky and steep, you will find the water becomes deep immediately. If there is little vegetation within the first few yards of the coast this means the situation below the water level will be very much the same. You will encounter rocks and only occasional vegetation. This means that though the sea is likely to be crystal clear, most of the quarry you are after will be at considerable depths, except for very small fish immediately along the coast. If you find large stones lying along the shore, you will probably find that many large stones are also immediately under the surface of the water. You will probably be able to wade into the sea and you will be able to walk along the

One of the fascinations of skin diving is meeting the strange underwater world and the strange creatures that live in it. This is a manta ray, found in most tropical waters. They are huge but not particularly dangerous to the skin diver if unmolested.

rocks underwater for a little bit before you plunge in. You may find hilly country or dunes reaching all the way down to the sea, and in such a case you will probably find that within a few yards out from the shore there will be banks or bars or other signs of shallow water farther out. If there is much vegetation along a coast where there are sand dunes you will probably find the same kind of vegetation continuing also under the water and the sea will be shallow for quite a while.

In all of these localities you are likely to find fish. You may catch a large fish in places where hundreds of other fishermen have come away empty handed. On the other hand, you must realize that there are considerable differences between various types of shores.

Let us first of all examine the situation where there are rocks underwater or shallow places farther out. This is the ideal fishing ground for the beginner. You may well find a rocky plateau about 10 to 20 feet under the water rising up from the sea-bottom and surrounded by water going in depth down to, let us say, 50 or 60 feet. It is as though there was just too much water for it to become an island. This is usually the place where rock fish establish their home. It is also the sort of place where passing fish stop for food and refuge. Fish of all kinds gather round these rocks at different times of the day and go about their business. At certain times such places have the characteristics of a water hole on the edge of an African jungle, only fish gather to feed and not to drink. Bigger fish coming in from the greater depths find plenty of opportunity to make their raids for food. It is almost impossible to encounter bigger fish in shallow water except in places like this. If you are not yet ready to go for the bigger fish there are plenty of little and medium-sized fish passing in their search for pasture. You will soon begin to look upon the medium-sized fish as cattle or sheep quietly grazing in a field. If

Around the mouth of a cave is a good place to lie in wait for big fish that may make their home in its dark inner recesses. Exploring such caves is for advanced divers only. The beginner will do well to steer clear of them.

you swim quietly among them, the fish appear not at all frightened by your appearance and will continue at their occupation. You can come quite near them. You soon discover, however, that though the fish seem to be quite unconcerned at your presence they are fully aware of the stranger in their midst. They see far better than you do and they are much quicker than you are. Their very timidity is their greatest defense. If you make any kind of quick movement, they move away with lightning speed.

The next best ground for the beginner is where you find large stones near the shore, and large stones immediately under the surface. As you swim quietly over the rocks, round corners and promontories, you can surprise quite large fish.

If you choose to fish in waters where there is much vegetation, your greatest chance is to swim quietly along the surface and hope that you will surprise one of the fish quietly grazing among the submarine flora. Unless you are quick, you will probably find the fish will disappear in the vegetation. It is almost useless to remain over the spot hoping the fish will come back. This is, therefore, very chancy ground, and it is not to be recommended for the beginner because he will very soon be disappointed.

The same applies to sandy bottoms where you will rarely find fish, and if you do, they have so much room to maneuver they will simply run away.

Next comes exploring at great depths, and essentially it is very much the same as fishing the rocky shores. Your chances of finding fish are smaller in deep water because you have to take frequent deep dives, look round and come up again for air. This is a very exhausting business. Here is, however, where you can achieve the greatest element of surprise with your sudden dive to the depths. You may find quite large fish quietly cruising near the rocks on the sea bed never expecting you to come along.

Where the coast is very steep and rocky

you may find underwater caves. If you approach the mouth of a cave very carefully, you may encounter fish that use the cave as

Coral is found in all warm waters and grows in weird twisted shapes. It is a natural home for many kinds of fish and is a most productive grounds for the spear fisherman.

a home. The best thing to do is to lie in wait hidden from view and wait for fish coming in or going out. When you have become more experienced you may venture to dive down and even enter caves, but the thing to remember in such a case is to be very careful that the entrance to the cave is big enough so that you can turn round and come up for air again, without the danger of hitting the rocks with your head or any other part of your body. You should avoid entering a cave so deeply that you cannot make a quick and efficient turn.

From the book SPEARFISHING
By Ivan S. Ivanovic
A. S. Barnes and Company
Copyright 1955

CHAPTER 21

weather

WEATHER has a profound effect on everyone and few are more vitally concerned with it than those who follow the out-of-doors. The rain that ruins a family picnic can also improve chances on a trout stream; the same high wind that keeps the wise sailor in the harbor will send the duck hunter into his blind. The snow that discourages driving fills the skier and deer hunter with delight. In this chapter you will find a layman's guide to understanding the conditions that cause our weather. Included are how to read weather maps and use a barometer and what causes such things as wind, clouds, rain, snow and fog, and violent storms such as hurricanes and tornadoes.

Not everyone can be a meteorologist; but it is easy to be weather-wise.

Our forefathers and the men of ancient times had no weather maps, but they were, in the actual sense of the word, far more air-minded than we are.

Many people are surprised when it is pointed out that in Chapter 16 of Matthew there is a favorite of sailormen, a familiar weather saying first spoken by Christ: "When it is evening, ye say, It will be fair weather; for the sky is red. And in the morning, It will be foul weather today; for the sky is red and lowering." Few appear to be acquainted with that bit of weather lore in the Bible; but most of us know some version or other of the sailor's rhyme:

Red sky in the morning
Is a sailor's sure warning;
Red sky at night
Is the sailor's delight.

Folklore is generally frowned upon by scientific men, but many of its sayings and predictions have found scientific backing. The red sunset mentioned by Christ, for example, was a view of the sun through dust-laden air.

Even scientific men are impressed by the accurate weather observations made by primitive people. Ancient Navajo blankets and pottery show cloud designs, with correct anvil tops and flat bottoms, as accurate as a trained meteorologist could devise today.

Here is an old rhyme that is so crowded with weather lore evolved from accurate observation that reading it, you can almost feel the rain gathering and getting ready to come down:

SIGNS OF RAIN

The hollow winds begin to blow:
The clouds look black, the glass is low,
The soot falls down, the spaniels sleep,
And spiders from their cobwebs peep.
Last night the sun went pale to bed,
The moon in halos hid her head:
The walls are damp, the ditches smell,
Closed is the pink-eyed pimpernel.
Hark how the chairs and tables crack!
Old Betty's nerves are on the rack;
Loud quacks the duck, the peacocks cry,
The distant hills are seeming nigh.
Low o'er the grass the swallow wings,
The cricket, too, how sharp he sings!
Through the clear stream the fishes rise,
And nimbly catch incautious flies.
The glowworms, numerous and light
Illumined the dewy dell last night;
And see yon rooks, how odd their flight!
They imitate the gliding kite,
And seem precipitate to fall,
As if they felt the piercing ball.
'Twill surely rain; I see with sorrow,
Our jaunt must be put off tomorrow.

All these signs and portents can be sensed and observed before a rainfall, and although the poet did not know the scientific explanation of them, he recognized them as reputable weather signs. Let us take the old rhyme apart meteorologically, line by line, and find the reasons behind its uncanny accuracy.

The hollow winds begin to blow refers to the hollowness of sound before a rain; this can be noticed particularly with boat horns, the droning of planes and the hoot of train whistles, all of which seem unusually clear and like they were sounded down a long corridor. This happens when the cloud ceiling and bad weather inversion lower to earth, the sounds then echo back against the meteorological sounding board of the heavens. In fair weather, sound radiates outward and dissipates into clear space.

The clouds look black, the glass is low is elementary; dark clouds are dark because they hold more precipitation and because they reflect the darkness of a dull-colored earth, rather than refracting the light of the sun, as the ceiling of a weather front moves in. The "glass," means the barometer which measures atmospheric pressure.

The soot falls down indicates a lowering of air pressure. Delicate soot is often kept in place within the chimney simply by the high pressure of good weather air; when the atmospheric pressure lowers (and the soot becomes heavy with humidity) chunks frequently fall into the fireplace below.

Last night the sun went pale to bed has already been commented upon in the explanation of Christ's words.

The moon in halos hid her head means that a mass of rain-bringing warm air has flowed in overhead, causing ice-crystal cloudform. When the sun or moon shines through ice-crystal clouds, a halo results.

The walls are damp, the ditches smell indicates humid air and a lessening of the atmospheric pressure that has held in much of the odor of swamps and wet places during the high pressure of good weather; when that pressure lowers, captive odors are released and things "smell more." Sailors who can "smell an approaching rain really are simply sensitive to the odors of the floating seaweed and tiny marine life that exudes captive smells when the barometric pressure lowers.

Hark how the chairs and tables crack hardly needs explanation, for we all know how wood "breathes," swelling and contracting with humidity and dryness.

But *Old Betty's nerves are on the rack* indicates more than the obvious mental depression of pre-storm atmosphere. A drop in air pressure affects the nerves instantly by causing greater dehydration of the tissues; old wounds begin to ache, corns and bunions are felt the minute the barometer drops.

The distant hills are seeming nigh is an often-noticed weather sign of sailors. When the Connecticut shores appear unusually near to a Long Islander, rain is usually less than a day away. Marine air is always rich with salt haze from evaporation during good weather, but becomes clear with the mixing action of unstable atmosphere. When the instability of pre-storm air invades the coast, the clearing-away of salt haze results in great visibility.

Low o'er the grass the swallow wings is a weather sign that to my knowledge has never been researched. Yet we know that bats and swallows have extremely sensitive ears which they use as a sort of radar mechanism during flight, to avoid hitting obstacles and to locate insects in the air. When pre-storm air pressure lowers abruptly, the pressure difference between the inside and outside of their heads becomes irritating, possibly painful. Therefore, bats and swallows will be seen seeking the relief of the highest pressure air, which of course is always found closest to the earth. When you see swallows flying so close to the water that their wings occasionally touch the surface, you may usually predict a lowering barometer and a rainy spell ahead. Likewise, very high-flying bats and swallows would foretell fine weather.

The cricket, too, how sharp he sings indicates that the old-timer observed the effect that weather has upon insects, especially crickets, which are astoundingly accurate atmospheric instruments. It has been recently learned that the cricket's reaction to temperature is often more immediate and accurate than that of the average thermometer, which has considerable lag and variation. If the chirps of the black cricket are counted for 14 seconds and the number 40 is then added to that figure, you will get the exact temperature of the air (where the cricket is) in degrees Fahrenheit. You will also find the katydid a responsive insect-thermometer, its call lengthening with warmth, and shortening—and finally ending completely—with colder atmosphere.

Birds imitating the *gliding kite* would simply indicate an unstable condition in the atmosphere. Strong noonday thermals soon build into towering afternoon storm clouds, so that an unstable morning atmosphere might well indicate an afternoon shower. Also when the air pressure lowers or the air becomes thin, birds must fly harder and faster in it in order to say aloft; so much so, in fact, that before a hurricane or a stormy cyclonic atmosphere you will frequently find birds roosting or resting rather than staying aloft to face the strenuous flying conditions of the thinning air.

All these observations are of the kind that make being weather-wise a pleasure. When you know what they mean they cease to be folklore weather prophecies and become science. For example, almost everyone has heard that "when the leaves show their backs" rain is on the way, and has probably thought that, if this be true, leaves of trees just naturally curl upward before a storm. Any schoolboy can explain that leaves are designed to grow in a pattern according to the prevailing good weather wind; therefore, a nonprevailing or stormy wind turns them over. It's that simple.

Today when we build a house we usually regard the land plot as flat, and we place our house ornamentally rather than meteorologically. The old houses were more often placed with great consideration for prevailing winds and sun exposure. A small hill or a grove of trees was not regarded only decoratively, as it is today, but as an atmospheric mechanism that insured the working of fireplaces, the elimination of mildew, freedom from snow-drifts and protection from unfavorable winds. The fact that many old barns still stand is a tribute to the air-mindedness of the pioneers who built them. You can usually remodel an old barn into a pleasant and comfortable home, but not even livestock could live well in some of our modern homes if they were remodeled into barns.

The effects of weather upon humans have been studied much too little. While it is ridiculous to infer that all quarrels occur during high humidity or barometric depressions, it is not ridiculous at all to state that such weather changes affect mental conditions and that quarrels do occur more often during such a period.

Moods can be changed by atmospheric changes and it wise to take this into consideration. The actions of drunken people are often overlooked and forgiven; but people can be drunk with humidity or heat, too. Many people even become extremely irritable in dry warmth.

It is definitely established in medical and criminal reports that heat induces anger and that more crimes are committed during hot weather than in cold. It is not the heat alone that causes irritation, however, but either the dryness or the larger water content that the expanded warm air contains. In wise but plain words, *it ain't the heat, it's the humidity* that often irritates.

There are people who insist that the financial market moves in rhythm with the barometer. There are wives who watch for the barometers to rise before asking their husbands for any special favor. But there is no point to definite rules of human behavior in relation to the weather, because we all respond differently to pressure changes. Although weather does affect us physically and mentally, we do not all generally react in the same way.

Of all body necessities, oxygen is both the most important and the least stored. Man stores in his body energy and material of all kinds, but he has no storage place for even the smallest amount of oxygen. Therefore, the instant his oxygen supply is lowered or he is deprived of it he instantly experiences marked effects.

Although most people believe that high altitude is marked by a lack of oxygen, the oxygen proportion of upper air is practically the same; what differs mostly is density and pressure. It is the pressure of all the air above

us that squeezes oxygen into our bloodstream to give us life; as soon as that pressure lowers, our life process slackens and anoxia (lack of oxygen) begins to take its course. No matter how a man dies, whether it be from disease, shock, drowning or another cause, the actual and final reason for death will be anoxemia, failure of oxygen to reach the bloodstream fast enough. The low pressure of pre-storm air sometimes makes one sad; at other times, drowsy, irritable or even gay; there is no set rule. But one is never so *alert* as during the high pressure of fine weather.

Ben Franklin advised that we "do business with men when the wind is in the northwest." He knew that when the wind is from that direction anywhere in the temperate zone of the Northern Hemisphere, the weather is likely to be buoyant, dry and hopeful—the best state for quick decisions and for bold enterprises. So the barometer and wind-vane can be regarded as instruments for forecasting man's mood.

ANATOMY OF AIR

Air is so much like a transparent, filmy nothingness; it can hardly seem to have any anatomy. Yet it has body and shape and density just like water or any part of the earth. A fish cannot be aware of water pouring from one place to another. He lives within the element; he can't even see it. We cannot picture our air flowing, either; but if air were poured out from a big pitcher in space, it would flow by its own weight, exactly like water, envelop the earth and seek its own level.

The fact that cooled air shrinks, or packs denser and becomes heavier, is one of the secrets of weather lore. The changes in weight (caused mainly by heat differences) cause air to flow this way and that, and new weather to evolve.

One of the reasons that we find it hard to visualize air having weight is because atmospheric weight is always referred to as pressure. (The weight of a gas *presses* out in all directions.) The pressure of air is caused by the weight of all the air above that presses down on whatever air there is below. A barometer is no more than a scale that weighs the mountains and valleys of air that pass overhead. When the barometer is high, it reveals that a mountain of good-weather density is pressing its weight down on us and all the surrounding atmosphere is flowing downhill toward some outlying rainy low-pressure area.

Here is something important to remember: the actual reading on a barometer is often very little indication of anything. The thing one really wants to know is if the barometer if rising, falling, steady or unsteady. In this way one can tell whether the present outside weather is liable to change and, if so, whether for better or worse.

Barometers are delicate things and difficult to use for weather prediction unless they are used along with other information. For example, if one uses the barometer with wind-direction information, one has a fair prophecy. A chart of this nature should be kept alongside the barometer to make it more valuable throughout the United States:

WIND DIRECTION	PRESSURE	WEATHER
E to N	Low, falling fast	Severe gale, rain
E to N	Low but rising	Cold wave
S to E	Falling	Storm, clearing in 24 hours
S to SW	Rising	Clear soon, several good days ahead
SE to NE	Falling	Rain for one or two days
E to NE	Falling	Rain in 24 hours
S to SE	Falling	Wind, rain in 18 hours
SW to NW	Steady	Fair for two days
SW to NW	Rising fast	Fair, rain in two days
Going to West	Rising	Clearing, colder

WEATHER MAPS

Most weather maps look to the uninitiated like a complicated mess. Most people look at them thoughtfully only to look away uninformed. Sometimes you will find it raining right smack in a high-pressure area or the sun shining right in the middle of a low. But the weather map is the basis of all forecasting, and it demands the greatest respect from all weather prophets. It still provides the beginning for any intelligent weather forecast, followed next by the wind direction.

In the middle of Drawing No. 1 you will find an average weather-map design. Dotted lines lead from the various features of the map to a thumbnail explanation of each one. This will take a bit of studying and comparing with your current map, but with some effort the reader will find he can read a weather map from it.

You see a high over the Northwest, and a low toward the middle East Coast. The winds in and around New York are probably high (close isobars) and the rain is fairly heavy (strong low there). But by tomorrow it will all pass out to sea and clear weather will have set in. There is one of each kind of front in this diagram, and you can easily visualize the actions of each. Note, too, how the winds flow clockwise out of the high and counterclockwise into the low.

The cold front has caught up with the warm front near Cleveland and the whole cyclonic machine at this point will wind itself into a whirlpool-like occluded front of wind and rain within a matter of 10 or 20 hours, and wind itself into nothingness within another day or so.

After studying this chart for a while, look at your daily newspaper map and see what features you can pick out. If you really want to be a weather-map student, snip out a series of maps and chart the course of the weather patterns. The map, remember, is not a static thing but like a still picture taken from a rather fast-moving set of camera pictures. You need a whole set to conceive the action.

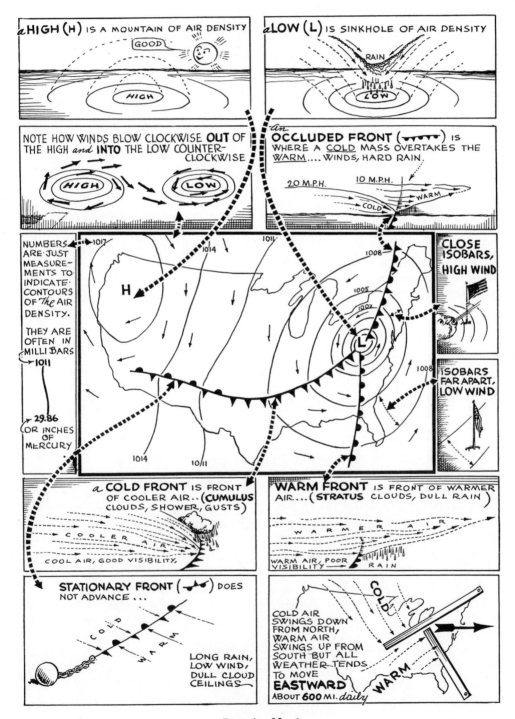

Drawing No. 1

Finally comes a dismaying note. Almost everyone who looks at a weather map forgets that he is looking at a picture of *yesterday's* weather. Or maybe he never even knew it. Frequently he believes that he is looking at tomorrow's weather! If you look at the date on the map you will find that it was compiled some time the day before; the weather picture at the moment will be quite different and the weather tomorrow will be still more different. But as long as you realize that you are looking at yesterday's weather, and if you know the tendencies of weather movements, you can all the better predict what tomorrow's weather (the map of which will be prepared the day after tomorrow) will be like.

It all sounds quite complicated but you can see why the weather map is still the basis for a forecast and also why sometimes the cloud or folklore type of observation (when complemented by your map report) can be very valuable in reaching a decision when the map reading is indefinite.

WINDS

What a machine is global weather! Squint your eyes and Drawing No. 2 looks not unlike a radial motor; each circulatory cell operates like a separate cylinder, and with mechanical perfection.

It is important to understand that although the sun heats the air, it does so very indirectly. Atmosphere is like a pane of glass; the sun shines right through it without heating it. For example, the sun will shine through an icy windowpane and make a warm spot inside your room without giving the least bit of heat to the glass. But, in turn, the glass is heated by the warmed room. Just so in nature: it is the sun-warmed earth that heats the air. That is why, by flying just a short way aloft—above thermal circulation—you will find the atmosphere a constant and year-round winter temperature.

Of course, if there are imperfections in atmosphere, such as dust, the sun will heat the dust particles and, in turn, the air around them will become warm. But for all general purposes of wind and circulation, the thermals of rising warm air from the earth are the heat machines.

Most thermals form over land, where the sun's heat saturates the soil and great heat canopies accumulate. For instance, all sailors know how cumulus clouds frequently form continuously over an island, and they are familiar with the old shipwreck rule about rowing toward the part of the horizon where the cumulus clouds are gathered. Land is usually under them. But thermals do form over open water too, wherever the sea takes on more heat than its surrounding area. As soon as the sun's heat is diminished by a cloud a differential is caused and an immediate thermal circulation occurs. Shallow bodies of water become warm during summer and thermals may be found rising from covered shoals. In calms the sailboat-racing sailor may find light flows of air moving toward such shoals, to take the place of the rising warm air. Thermals over warm land can suck in so much surrounding air that midsummer breezes become well developed wind systems, such as the summer sea breezes on Lake Michigan and in Long Island.

The land breeze, of course, is the antithesis of a sea breeze, resulting from aftersunset cooling. Land breezes, however, seldom reach 10 miles an hour and are restricted to the immediate coastline. They achieve their maximum velocity at about sunrise. In general the land breeze is just an interesting wind, with little practical sailing application because of its weakness and its propensity to be overcome by coastline wind systems. The only exceptions seem to be such as are found on the shores of Lake Erie between Buffalo and Cleveland where land breezes occur almost regularly each night and early morning.

The sea breeze can be seen to depend upon the sun's heat upon the land. If the sun is partially or totally obscured for a few hours, the breeze to shore will often give way to a calm or to a weak gradient wind. A cloudy day, therefore, will not produce a steady sea breeze. A sailing man can anticipate a diminishing sea breeze when the sky becomes threatened with clouds.

And now a word about thermal winds, or winds that are actuated by rising warm currents. *Webster's Dictionary* says *thermal* means "pertaining to heat" and meteorology textbooks call it "a cell of rising warm air." The flier knows the thermal as a bump of

rising air that pushes him down into his seat. It is more accurate to think of it as a circulatory aerial machine in which as much comes down as goes up. A thermal is a big doughnutlike arrangement, as shown in Figure 5 of Drawing No. 3, where the updraft is forced through a small center chimney while the same amount of air falls slowly all around.

This drawing is a set of sketches which de-

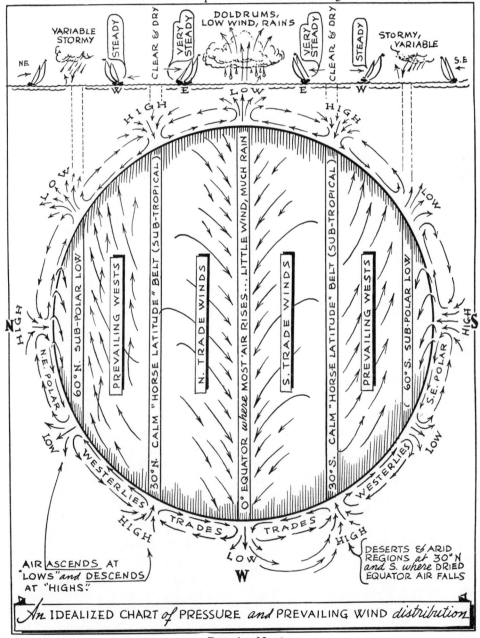

Drawing No. 2

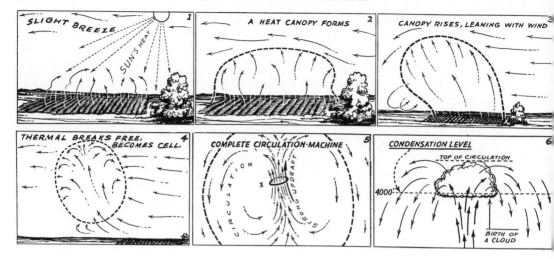

Drawing No. 3

picts the general machinery of a common thermal, from heat canopy to free cell and then to its final dissipation, or if the air is that moist, to the birth of a cumulus cloud. The cumulus cloud, by the way, would be better named the *thermal cloud*, for it is really the visible head of a thermal machine, as shown in Figure 6.

When you think of a thermal you usually think only of rising air. But the old saying that whatever goes up must come down still holds true. With a thermal cell, the same amount of air goes up as comes down but, because of the doughnut shape, the ascending air squeezes necessarily very rapidly through the doughnut hole and dissipates slowly and downward all around it. Therefore an airplane hardly notices the thermal's downdrafts but is jarred uncomfortably by the fast updrafts.

Any small variation in a light wind, or a light wind that breaks a calm, is known as cat's-paw. Sailors have learned to call the resulting flurry on the water's surface a cat's-paw, watching eagerly for them in order to detect an occasional gust. Gusts are characteristic of all winds from the sea and land breezes to the hurricane. But because we are discussing sea-level thermals, we will consider the relationship between gusts and thermals.

Ordinary winds have a velocity variation of about 50 per cent and a direction variation

of about 25 per cent. Gustiness is more prevalent when a strong horizontal wind is penetrated by many thermal cells.

CLOUDS

Clouds sometimes seem to come from the air and go back again without having accomplished any purpose. Yet they do function importantly to affect weather since they reflect back much of the sun's rays and thereby set up a machinery of weather that keeps circulating horizontally in small areas.

Clouds may not seem to be much of a parasol between you and the sun on a fine day because daylight can be so indirect that we don't notice their shade. When next you go up in an airplane, look down and you can readily see the landscape mottled with big splashes of shade from more clouds than you thought were up there with you. When you realize that each area of shade is a circulation machine moving over the earth even faster than low-level winds, you can see what a maze of circulatory machines combs the earth. Each circulatory cell becomes a potential machine for making another cloud, so we have the picture of one cloud dropping eggs of shade to give birth to other clouds in its wake.

The obvious utilitarian purpose of clouds, of course, is to be giant watering pots that

Drawing No. 4

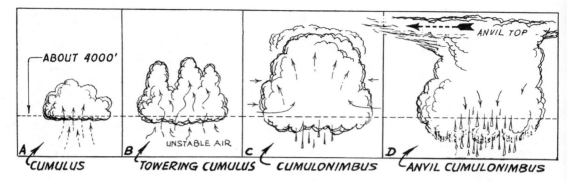

Drawing No. 5

pick up moisture from one place and deposit it at another. They take water up from very wet places, then rain where the earth most needs it. Dry land has an almost human capacity to reach its thermal arms upward and loosen the rain trigger of low passing clouds.

The world of clouds is a very precise one. Although many of us think of them as shapeless white puffs that occur spasmodically, each cloudform has its own anatomy, its own height, its own reason for being and, of course, its own name. Everything, it seems—even nebulous wisps of cloud—has its place in place in this orderly universe.

Anatomically, there are only three kinds of clouds to remember: lumps (*cumulus*); layers (*stratus*); and icy (*cirrus*). You puff a cigarette cloud of cumulus shape; if you smoke enough there will be a stratus cloud shape hovering in the room. If you open the deep-freeze, you will see wisps of cirrus curl out. These shapes can be seen in the upper part of Drawing No. 4. Notice that the names cumulus, stratus and cirrus are further qualified by Latin words like *alto* for high, *nimbus*, for head, and so on. Their average heights are shown on the left side in thousands of feet, and each cloud name is followed by a two-letter weather-map designation. The heights of clouds depend upon latitude, as we have already mentioned, but also upon the time of year. Summer clouds are higher, because the earth then radiates more heat and the atmospheric circulation rises to greater heights.

Clouds are presumed to be white. At least they certainly look white. A frequent ques-

tion is not why clouds are white but "why do they sometimes appear dark?" The truth is clouds are as colorless a water—as colorless as the water which they are composed of, as colorless as glass. Yet grind glass up, or sandblast it and it becomes pure white. Take clear ice, also, crush it and it too becomes white. Actually our whitest of white, the snow, is colorless, too; it is composed of clear ice shapes. It is just the matter of complicating a surface so that it scatters light in all directions; then the effect is white. The individual droplets of cloudform are transparent but, like billions of tiny glass beads, they scatter sunlight to give the illusion of whiteness. A sailor may shake his head in wonderment at all this, yet he knows well that the whitecaps of the sea can be made of nothing but clear water.

Clouds become dark when the sunshine is blotted out from their vicinity, but frequently they reflect back the darker colors of earth. Most interesting to the artist or photographer is the reversal of the earth color-theory as it exists in the sky. On earth, as with mountains, nearby things have red hues while distant objects become bluer. Faraway mountains, for instance, are almost lost in their blue haze. But in the sky it is different: nearby clouds are bluest, distant clouds are reddest. You will often see thunderous cloud mountains looming sullenly over the horizon like sultans with large red turbans. In fact, the whole horizon is marked by a tinge of distant reddish hues.

You might think that, because a cloud is wet and white, the air around it is dry. The secret is that moisture can be visible or invisible; when it is gas you *can't* see it; when it is liquid you *can* see it. And cloudbirth is the process of changing moisture from gas to liquid. Evaporation changes moisture back from liquid into gas.

A cloud is the air's moisture gone from invisible gas to visible water droplets.

When warm, wet air arises away from the heat of earth to become cooled in the cold heights, it becomes chilled and condenses into visible cloud droplets. All clouds are the result of some sort of cooling. The wetter the air, the less cooling is needed. Dry air produces no clouds, or else very high ones.

The lowest form of cloud is ground surface air cooled into aerial pools of water known as "fog." There are three ways that fog can form, or three ways that ground surface air can be cooled. First is advection fog, which is caused by warm air flowing over and being cooled by cold ground. Second is radiation fog, usually caused by the earth losing heat into the night air, thereby cooling the air directly above it. Cooled air becomes heavier and flows downhill like water, to settle into valleys as fog. When you fly over a countryside of warm wet atmosphere at sundown you will see white patches of radiation fog that look like hundreds of little ponds; these are the cool valleys.

Fogs are more frequent on the Pacific Coast than on the Atlantic, due to the prevailing west-to-east wind. On the East Coast the prevailing wind sweeps off the land and is therefore less humid. However, the moist winds from the Gulf Stream areas do frequently blow upward to the Labrador current in the vicinity of Newfoundland to create a great fog-breeding place. Again, prevailing eastward winds over England carry moisture to soot-laden air and make the thick London fogs.

The third kind of fog is called precipitation fog. This is caused by relatively warm rain or snow falling through cold air. When a storm moves in on very cold and wet air the precipitation falls into chilling air, raising the dewpoint and causing fog.

Sailors have little comment about fog but landsmen have some:

> *A summer fog for fair,*
> *A winter fog for rain,*
> *A fact most everywhere,*
> *In valley and on plain.*

and:

> *When fog goes up the rain is o'er,*
> *When fog comes down 'twill rain*
> *some more.*

A New England saying goes:

> *Evening fogs will not burn soon,*
> *Morning fog will burn 'fore noon.*

and:

> *Fog that starts before the night*
> *Will last beyond the morning light.*

Aircraft weather maps indicate the present temperature along with the dewpoint of the present air, such as "Temp. 80°, dewpoint 70°." This would indicate that the present air contains that much moisture so that it needs exactly 10 degrees cooling before it will become saturated and close to precipitation. Of course, the greater the spread between temperature and dewpoint, the farther away is rain.

Many people think that "dewpoint" is a term referring to the dew instead of being a humidity and forecasting measurement, so they need to get clear in their minds what dew is. Dew does not fall. It collects on objects colder than the air itself. The moisture that runs down the side of an iced drink is a perfect example of dew. The cold glass has collected water directly from the air in the room.

Because warm air can hold in suspension a larger quantity of moisture than cold air, the cooling of air with the fall of night makes some of its moisture condense in the form of dew. If the temperature is below freezing, however, this collection will be frost rather than dew.

Dew forms more rapidly when the air is calm than when it is in motion. It forms on cloudless nights because there are no clouds to hinder heat radiation. Hence when dew collects there is a clear sky and the morrow will be without rain. A dewless night or early morning is a forerunner of rain.

Few sights are more ominous than that of a glowing thunderhead over the horizon. Even a hurricane gives a warning, with a cirrus canopy sign a day or so ahead of its whirlpool center, but thunderheads can appear quickly in a clear sky. They move faster than a sailing ship, and the higher they build up the harder will be the rainfall beneath. They are the air pilot's forbidden territory and the yachtsman's invitation back to port. The thunderhead's only blessing is its concentrated area. It is small enough to fly around by air and its path is so narrow that it may miss you by land or sea.

All clouds of the cumulus type are convective, which means they are formed by vertical air currents. Their flat bottoms indicate the altitude at which the air's moisture became cold enough to condense into visible droplets. The higher the cumuli, the drier is the atmosphere and the less possibility there is of rain. Drawing No. 5 shows several stages of cumulus forms.

Because "cumulus" suggests "accumulation," it is easy to remember that all lumpy clouds are cumulus types. Fair-weather cumulus clouds as in Diagram No. 5 (A) are simply the visible heads of thermals which form over heated land or sea to become aerial circulation machines lasting for about a half-hour. But in very unstable air these machines often become a factory of circulation that refuses to dissipate, building up into a towering head known as "cumulonimbus" or "thunderhead." It is possible with practice to forecast summer weather for a few hours ahead by looking at the cumulus clouds and observing their development, particularly the upper parts. If there are no towers on cumulus clouds like those shown in (B) there is less chance of storm. This towering effect is also likened to turrets or castles, hence the name *cumulus castellatus*.

The cumulonimbus in its mature stage (D) develops a flat "anvil" top that usually spreads out into the storm path. By observing this cirrus-like spread, you can forecast the storm's direction. When an anvil top approaches you it spreads overhead like a cobwebbed ceiling, and you know then that it is only a matter of less than a half-hour before the wind shift and downpour.

It is difficult to describe a thunderhead without including lightning, for it is only within these aerial machines of violent updrafts that the atmosphere's electrical charges become scattered and in a position to equalize themselves again by discharging from one area to another.

First of all, lightning is the child of violent updrafts. Warm sultry air, when thrown aloft into cold heights too quickly to dissipate its electrical differences, will overcharge its cloudform slowly, yet discharge it with an instantaneous bang. The cumulonimbus or thunderhead cloud is always the powerhouse. Watch for it looming over the horizon from the west or northwest (because thunderheads usually move eastward). In the temperate zones, lightning from anywhere but the west or northwest will most likely pass you by.

You've often heard of timing thunder to tell how far away the lightning occurred, but may have forgotten the formula. Simply count the interval between flash and report in seconds, then multiply by one fifth to get the answer in miles.

So-called "heat lightning" is just plain lightning that is occurring too far away for you to hear its thunder. Thunder cannot be heard more than 25 miles away, usually not more than 10 miles. Small flares of lightning sometimes happen with no apparent thunder. Their power is negligible, having no destructive force whatsoever. The noise of thunder results from the sudden expansion and contraction of the air as the lightning bolts heat it. Thunder is similar to the expansion and contraction of air at the muzzle of a gun when it is discharged. Echoes from the initial explosive discharge continue for a half minute or more, constituting the rumbling of thunder.

A boat, if alone on a flat stretch of water, is an invitation to the heavenly discharge, but the chance that she will be struck is about one for every hundred years of such exposure. The chance that a bolt might take a personal interest in you is close to one in a million.

Lightning does strike water, so swimming during thunderstorm should be avoided. This brings up something of importance. Seldom are struck swimmers burned. Rather, they are paralyzed by the shock. Therefore immediate application of artificial respiration, until the paralysis of the diaphragm ceases, can save the life of many a person struck by lightning. If this chapter has any message at all, let it be this: *Learn artificial respiration, for lightning lifesaving as well as for first aid in drowning.*

The most dangerous places to be during a lightning storm are in the bathtub, between two metal objects or under a large tree. A convertible automobile is an invitation to danger, but an all-metal car becomes a Faraday cage which surrounds you with absolute safety. All-metal airplanes are also safe vessels; they are very frequently struck without any damage being done to them.

Hail is another child of the cumulonimbus. Perhaps you've noticed that the first drops of a thunderstorm are always the biggest. The reason is simply that only the heaviest drops can fall through the powerful storm updraft. In fact many drops are carried aloft and quick-frozen into hail. Hail must be carried aloft several times and re-frozen to larger size before it is heavy enough to fall through the violent upward winds.

STORMS

It's an ill wind that blows no good. Take, for example, the hurricane. It has probably had more articles and books written about it than any other weather phenomenon. Yet if someone asks you what a hurricane is, can you tell him? It is a compact piece of atmospheric machinery, made in several inconvenient sizes, and designed to do an expert job of destruction during its destined course.

Called "typhoons" in East Asia and "hurricanes" in the West Indies, these storms are more correctly known as tropical cyclones. "Cyclone" is, no doubt, the most misunderstood word in the layman's meteorological vocabulary. Any little, rainy low-pressure area is really a cyclone. The word comes from the Greek *kyklos*, meaning a circle, and the dictionary says a cyclone is nothing other than "a wind blowing circularly," or "a circular wind system."

On your daily weather map you will see any number of highs and lows. Each high is an *anticyclone* and each low is a *cyclone*. This simply means that in the Northern Hemisphere the winds blow clockwise around one (the high) and counterclockwise around the other (the low).

Cyclones and anticyclones travel from 200 to 500 miles a day in summer and from 500 to 700 miles a day during winter. Lows or cyclones move faster than highs or anticyclones, but both follow more or less defined paths. Most people confuse the word "cyclone" with tornado (twister) or with tropical cyclone (hurricane). The dread tropical cyclone is a simple cyclone, but, born in the heat of the tropics, instead of wearing itself out by friction, it has fed upon the latent heat associated with the warm, flat stretches of water and has become there an uncontrollable global whirlpool on a rampage. When you explain this to a youngster, you might fill the tub with water, then take the stopper out. Let him observe the whirlpool and then tell him a hurricane is a whirlpool in the sea of the air. If he wants to know how the storm goes only 10 miles an hour, yet has winds over a hundred miles an hour, start your portable victrola. Show him how you may walk about from room to room slowly or even stop completely, yet the record always goes around steadily and just as fast. That is exactly how the hurricane works.

The eye of the hurricane might average from three to 15 miles across; because the whole storm revolves around it, this area is calm. The rain there may cease and the sky may clear overhead almost completely.

Notice in the cutaway in Drawing No. 6 how the upper clouds mushroom outward into a flat ceiling of cirroform. This sheet

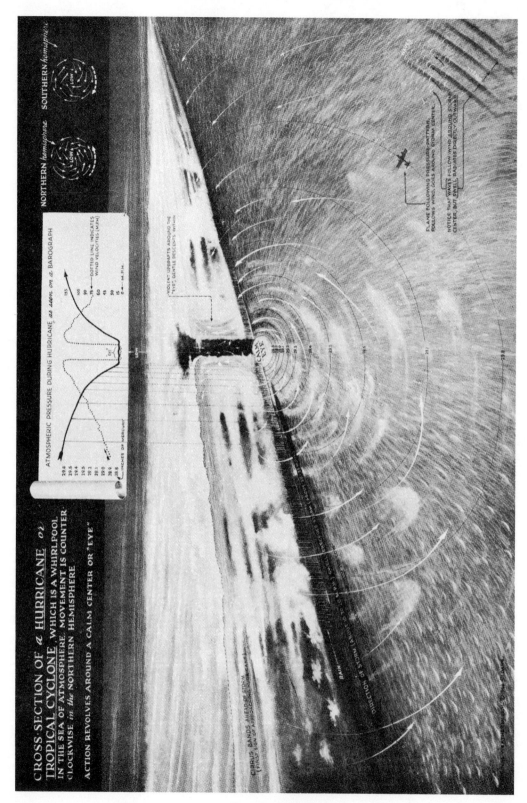

Drawing No. 6

of chaotic and weblike cloud is ample warning of winds to come. Even more positive a warning is the sea swell that radiates outward from the storm center. A hurricane may loaf along or stand still, yet the swells radiate outward at considerable speed.

Tornadoes are often called cyclones and hurricanes. Actually they are concentrated twisters, short-lived but most vicious of all. They are the most compact low-pressure machine in the whole atmosphere. Few of us connect pressure with wind, yet the two are closely associated. The most interesting thing about cyclones, hurricanes and tornadoes is the low pressure that feeds their machinery. Most people think that when a tornado passes over a house it blows it down; actually, it *sucks* it down. The sudden low pressure on the outside of the house leaves normal high pressure inside, enough to blow the house outward. Probably you have seen pictures of cattle untouched within a barn that has been blown outward from a tornado. Automobile tires in the path of such low pressure will burst outward, and watches, bottled goods or any air-filled articles will explode outward.

You'd think that a fast stream of air would cause a great deal of outward pressure, but it doesn't. If you suspend two ping-pong balls close together and then blow between them, they don't blow apart. Believe it or not, they are pulled together!

The most awesome weather sight at sea, yet the least understood, is a waterspout. Most sailors think it is a column of water sucked up from the sea. But if there is water within the spout at all, it is fresh water and not sea water. When a waterspout ceases, a torrent of sea water does not fall back into the sea; the funnel simply passes silently back into the atmosphere from where it came originally. There it is just a dark cloud.

The waterspout is a cloud that marks a tornado whirlpool in the sea of air beneath a line squall or cumulonimbus. The winds are around and not upward, as you may think. When a tornado vortex occurs over the water, its low-pressure core may suck sea water eight to 10 feet upward, but this is very unusual. With an average diameter of 20 to 60 feet, these seagoing tornadoes last for about 10 minutes and actually do very little damage. Thousands occur yearly.

Tornadoes and waterspouts usually move parallel with a squall line traveling east or northeast at from 20 to 50 miles an hour. While every meterological textbook defines a "waterspout" as "a tornado at sea," there seems to be no written mention of why the land storm often lasts for as long as an hour while the seaspout version averages five or 10 minutes.

Although very rare, aerial whirlpools, such as those that whisk newspapers around a windy street, will occur over open water with enough force to condense a cloud from the water level instead of from the storm cloud above. These vortexes are similar to the "dust-devils" seen whirling in 10- to 50-foot columns over dry deserts.

According to old legends, tornadoes and waterspouts can be broken by firing a gun into them. Could a cloud be broken by firing at it? The legends can be marked off as inaccurate folklore.

ATMOSPHERIC ANTICS

A sailor with Columbus once wrote, "And at the height of this foule weather the storme did settle upon our vessel in strange manner. A ghostly flame danced among our sails and later stayed like candle lights to burn brightly from the masts." This eerie phenomenon called St. Elmo's light occurs as often on land as it does on sea, but the loneliness and darkness of night on the water, along with the convenient playground of masts and spars at fair height from the ground, have helped to make it one of the haunting legends of the sea. Get a few old salts talking about the supernatural and you'll always hear a few words about St. Elmo's light.

In reality a "brush discharge" or "corona discharge," St. Elmo's light was really unmasked and researched in all-weather airplane flights during the war. It was a frequent occurrence during Atlantic flights, when entire wings and protruding parts of airplanes were at times enveloped in this orange and bluish light. Propellers often became pinwheels of flame so bright that the uninitiated would be prepared to jump from the "burning plane."

The process is very similar to that which occurs when you walk over a thick rug during a crisp winter day: you collect current that will jump from your fingertip whenever you come in contact with a light switch or person that can use the overload. Your plane, too, bursting with the overload which now is spilling over with visible glow, is ready to discharge into the nearest cloud which is low in positive current. Such is the capering of St. Elmo's light aloft; but a boat at sea may also sail through fog or snow patches, picking up unequal current and glowing wherever it discharges the overload into the surrounding atmosphere.

Phosphorescent water is not a phenomenon of St. Elmo's light, although the atmosphere and oxygen mechanics are involved. Most of us have been swimming during a rain when each raindrop hit the water's surface with a little sparkling light.

Many seamen swear that phosphorescent sea is caused by minute jellyfish being turned upon their backs. That, of course, is far-fetched. All of us have seen the glow of jellyfish when they are walked upon or struck after being cast up on shore. Jellyfish do secrete bacteria which glow during exudation, causing a phosphorescent effect, but jellyfish themselves do not cause the phenomenon. The crest of a wave, or any agitation which might throw active water into a spray that mingles with atmosphere, will cause sufficient oxidation to give the startling and beautiful effect of phosphorescent sea.

Many of the weird "spook lights" that occur are explained simply. When open burials were common or rotten pine coffins were involved, the low pressure of bad weather often loosed from decaying bodies the phosphorus which floated in the damp air of graveyards. Recently someone found out that even wintergreen Life Saver candy,

if broken in a pitch-black room, made a tiny spark.

Few of us have missed the thrill of seeing "northern lights" or the aurora borealis. In reality this magnificent nighttime display does not originate from the northern seas or from the reflection of sun or polar ice—as often supposed—but directly from the sun. It occurs beyond the stratosphere, in the outer stretches of atmosphere called the ionosphere, about 70 miles up. Whenever the sun has a volcanic eruption (as evidenced by a large sunspot) great streams of electrified particles rocket through space toward the earth at terrific speed. These collide with the rarefied gases of the upper atmosphere and make a disturbance which blazes into a brilliant battleground of fire and flashes. Actually there is always an overload of electrified particles sent to us, but after the 93 million miles and 24 hours between the sun and the earth, they have become very much affected by our world's magnetic field. Instead of penetrating any part of our air, they flow toward the regions of the North and South Magnetic Poles where the heavens glow eternally with solar overcharge. The aurora at the northern magnetic field is called aurora borealis, the one at the southern field aurora australis. Auroras have been said by sailors to indicate good weather, and there is at certain times some truth in this. When a great mass of polar air comes in, visibility is keen through the dry cold atmosphere, so that auroral lights become brighter. Polar air, of course, means a weather purge and a few days of crisp good weather.

Possibly the most widely publicized atmospheric antics have been our own doing, the experimental research into "man-made rain."

Because of local variations in rainfall it is nearly impossible to evaluate cloud-seeding operations, but in many instances "rain-making" has proved its worth, particularly in the high elevations of the mountainous West.

Man cannot compete with Nature's atmospheric antics when it comes to color. It is not only one of our hackneyed expressions that

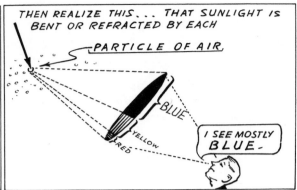

Drawing No. 7

"a sunset is a picture no artist can paint"; it's a known fact. Light is so transparent and paints are so opaque in quality that direct sunlight, even when it shines through the translucence of dust and haze, is impossible to reproduce. Sunlit clouds around the sunset become possible and very interesting subjects—and, by the way, much more exciting than the sunset itself. The most magnificent "sunsets" are not in the West at all, but in the East! When you are in the open and viewing the sun going down, watch the deep and sullen clouds on the opposite eastern horizon as they reflect the setting western light. The changing colors are as thrilling as a symphony. You will also hear about "unusual" sunsets at various places, but you can discount many of them as having occurred on occasions when the viewer was on vacation or relaxed enough to find the time to look upward and behold what goes on constantly, but what was unnoticed before. Some of the most wonderful sunsets occur right in New York City or around large towns, because the sun's light shining through dusty air creates hues that are close to deep purple and geranium lake.

You will remember our discussion about snow not really being white. Well, we can continue that theme by remarking that the sky is not really blue. Space is jet black and air is really colorless, but the many particles of air refract the light of the sun so completely that they divide sunlight into its true body of colors and we see color more than

light. Try this refraction business with a glass of water (as shown in Drawing No. 7) and you will find that sunlight is not only light but color too. Notice that the predominant color (because it refracts most easily) is blue. All the rest of the colors are in the sky too, but there is so much blue that it crowds the other colors out. We see only blue and say, "The sky is blue." Dust refracts red, which causes things near the horizon to appear redder, such as the far clouds, the setting sun or the moon. But high above, where the air is dust-free, the sky begins to be a deeper blue—as Southey described it, "Blue, darkly, deeply, beautifully blue." Above the troposphere, the sky is gun-metal blue; and presently it becomes the blackness of stellar space.

The formation of a rainbow depends upon the passage of light through water droplets much in the same manner of our glass-of-water demonstration. Because the sun must be less than 42 degrees above the horizon, you will not see a noonday rainbow except in higher latitudes. There is a saying:

A rainbow in the morning, shepherds take
warning;
A rainbow at night is the shepherd's delight.

Which is quite logical, when you observe that weather patterns usually move from the west to the east. If you see a rainbow reflected by the morning sun you will be looking at moist air toward the west that will later reach you. But if you see a rainbow reflected by a late-in-the-day sun, you will be seeing it against the rain backdrop that is already on its way eastward—and good weather is with you. A jingle more to the sailor's liking is:

> Rainbow to windward, foul fall the day;
> Rainbow to leeward, damp runs away.

The justification of this is that, if the rainbow is to windward, the shower is approaching, while if it appears to leeward, no rain can come from that moist curtain because it is already receding.

It usually takes a rainbow, a thunderstorm or some other kind of atmospheric antic to make us look upward and take note; but if that gives us the habit, it is worth while.

From the book:
"ERIC SLOANE'S WEATHER BOOK"
Duell, Sloan and Pearce, Inc.
Copyright 1947

CHAPTER **22**

winter sports

EXCEPT FOR a few pioneers who knew better, a generation ago the idea of having a good time outdoors in winter was unheard of. To say that all that has changed is quite an understatement—as any week-end visitor to a popular ski resort will quickly attest. Today the outdoors beckons in all seasons and many a winter sports fan looks with real regret on the coming of spring and subsequent loss of precious ice and snow. In this chapter you can see why this change has taken place. Included is all the necessary information you need to try such sports as winter camping and fishing, iceboating, curling, skating and, of course, skiing. On this subject you will find a complete listing of the major ski areas in this country and Canada.

WINTER CAMPING

It might surprise newcomers to the outdoors that many experienced woodsmen, especially in the north country, actually prefer camping when winter unlocks the woods. Contrasted against the thick tangle of summer foliage, the winter woods are open, easy to travel through and easy to see through. Then it is good to be out when there is no thawing, when the woods are hushed with the deep quiet of midwinter. The bite of dry, cold air puts a snap into your exercise. It is an off season for most hunting, but a fine time to take along a .22 and listen to its friendly crack as you train the sights on a target.

There will be tracks on the white blanket that covers the ground—small lines of footprints and sometimes a detective story with an ending of torn fur and bloodstains on the snow.

Camping at this time of year has its rewards, but it is a careful business. An omission or a mistake can cost far more than it would in summer. The summer camper keeps dry for comfort. The winter camper must keep dry for safety. He may pitch his tent on snow, provided the snow is cold enough to squeak underfoot, but he must be careful not to melt it with the combination of body heat and pressure. He should have either a layer of boughs under the tent floor or an air mattress above it, and preferably both. In addition he should fluff up his bed to make the most of its insulating quality. If a man feels cold in his bed, the chances are five to one that the cold is crawling in from underneath.

A tent in the winter camp needs ventilation. If it is the waterproof kind that doesn't breathe, ice crystals will tend to form on the roof. They do no harm so long as they stay there, but in the process of getting up, you will brush some of them off on your clothes and down your neck, and if there is a midday sun they will melt and drip on the beds.

A wise winter camper cleans his tent of these crystals and any snow that comes in with him. The job is made easier if you assemble a mat of boughs or throw down a ground cloth outside, then with a small whisk brush work over your clothes and boots.

Clothes must be kept dry from the inside too. If you exercise in them be careful to guard against becoming overheated. You can either slow your pace below the perspiration point or cut down on the clothing. For the latter purpose the best combination to wear is a tight-woven windbreaker outside with removable sweater layers under it. A single heavy coat such as you might wear to sit in a frosty duckblind is too much of an all-or-none proposition.

When clothes become moist they should on no account be worn at night. It is safer to sleep with no clothes on than with wet ones; in fact, there are some who sack out raw in cold weather by preference.

Dry footwear is a prime need. You should take a change of socks along even for a one night stand, and if you want the ultimate in bedtime luxury, have a pair of Adirondack boots in your sleeping bag to put on when you roll in. It's hard to feel cold anywhere else with your feet cradled in their thick, dry fleece.

Each night out puts moisture in a sleeping bag. It should be dried on the outside where your breathing has formed frost and then hung up wrong side out, preferably where sunlight or a breeze gets to it.

For drying clothes you will more likely use the fire. It's a good way but the process shouldn't be hurried, especially with woolen things. If they are hung too close they can scorch in one spot and be wet in another, only inches away. The same is true of leather, which becomes worthless when it is maltreated with excess heat. For boots the best treatment is to pack the insides with paper as soon as you take them off. The paper holds out the chill while it does the work of absorbing the moisture; its use will make them more pliable and easier to put on in the morning. In a two-layer sleeping bag, boots and clothes can be put to bed between the inner and outer layers.

The one piece of equipment that an old woodsman would rate first in importance for winter camping is a full-sized, sharp ax. An axman need never be cold in woods country.

Food for a cold-weather trip should be planned carefully. It is best to keep away from things that have a high water content. Fresh fruits and fresh or canned vegetables that can freeze are a nuisance to keep insulated from the cold. Dried fruits, meats, cheese and the dehydrated varieties of soups and vegetables are not hurt by it.

Cooking should be simple. It is enough to produce a one-pot meal twice a day. This and the hot coffee, tea or soup that goes with it will be plenty of work, especially when conditions are rugged. But hot food is your morale booster, and no amount of weariness or weather should stampede you out of preparing it properly.

Clean snow makes perfectly good cooking

With the proper equipment and technique a winter camp becomes a comfortable affair.

water, but if you drink it you should add a pinch of salt to kill the flatness. Melting it down is tricky. It has to be stirred at the start or it will merely sublimate and let your pot burn on the dry side.

A small liquid-fuel stove is very useful. It

keeps you independent of the campfire and even when you do build one it cuts down the meal-getting time. In a blizzard your outdoor fire may not be worth the struggle it takes to maintain it; you can pull your stove into the tent and cook there. You have to be careful of your movements and careful to provide ventilation, but the heat it gives off and the warm chow it provides will take care of your basic needs.

Winter outings, especially where camping is involved, will never be a sport for large numbers. It would be disastrously unsafe if it were. But if you have a taste for adventure, winter camping will give you a taste of the real thing. Little things like match cases and snow glasses become vitally important, and the decisions you make spell not merely convenience but survival. Even in familiar terrain your problems are those of a first-time visitor. The great white blanket makes a new and beautiful world.

By Robert M. Ormes

WINTER FISHING

Fishing through the ice is lawful in most waters throughout the country and hundreds of cold-weather anglers enjoy taking game fish during zero weather. Lake trout and walleye pike are two of the favorite species taken by northern fishermen, as these fish are willing strikers under the ice.

Most fish taken through a hole in the ice are attracted by live or cut baits, such as minnows, cut herring, fish gullet or belly, liver or beefsteak. Lake trout fishermen prefer strips of fresh herring or minnows, while the pike fisherman selects minnows as his first choice and particles of raw meats as a second choice. Winter-caught fish are usually found hungry and on many occasions they strike almost any kind of bait lowered to them.

Winter fishing is not a sport cherished by timid folks. It takes a red-blooded northerner to really like the fun of handling an icy line in zero weather. To many, the sport of fishing through the ice holds little appeal, while others manage to get a great kick out of dancing around on the cold ice, chopping holes here and there, handling wet lines and baiting hooks with chilly, stiff fingers. Of course, there are some ice fishermen who ply their trade in a deluxe fashion, having a gasoline or oil heater all set to warm a cozy fishing shack that can be moved about on runners. A comfortable seat is built inside and the fisherman is as snug as a bug in a rug even when the northern winds whistle around the shack.

But the majority of ice fishermen must pick a fairly warm winter day and face the ordeal in the open. However, warm clothing helps to keep them warm so the day may be comfortable even in zero weather.

A method of ice fishing which is universally popular is via the "tip-up" way. Two sticks are joined together in an X form, one stick being a trifle longer than the other. The long stick is placed directly over the hole, while the other stick serves as a signal for the fisherman. A small white flag is placed at one end of the stick and the fishing line attached to the other. When the fish strikes, the stick is pulled upward at the end which carries the flag, warning the fisherman that a fish is ready to be pulled from the deep waters. Several similar sets are placed at different locations, all of which can be watched by a single fisherman. This is an excellent method to use when the fish are hard to locate, as a wider range can be covered.

Jigging for lake trout is also popular among fishermen of the Great Lakes region and in large waters where these silvery fish are known to inhabit. In this instance the fisherman busies himself around one or two holes in the ice, keeping the line jigging up and down to attract the fish. In many waters it is necessary to fish very deep, anywhere from 50 to 150 feet deep.

All days are not good fishing days, even in the wintertime. A warm, sunny day is usually best for walleyes—and we know such a day is the most comfortable and enjoyable for the fisherman. However, many lake trout have been taken when the thermometer reg-

Henry Zeman

Dress for it and you'll find ice fishing an exciting sport.

stered several degrees below zero and a small blizzard was blowing across the ice. The "lakers" seek deep waters and are not affected by weather conditions, whereas walleyes are nearer the surface.

By Cal Johnson

ICEBOATING

Iceboating, like water boating, has undergone a great change in the past 25 years. Formerly a rich man's sport, with boats costing thousands of dollars and professional skippers and crews the order of the day whenever an important trophy was at stake, the sport today is confined almost entirely to small, light, but extremely fast boats, often built by their owners, and costing from $500 to $1,500 apiece.

These are so easily carried on top of a car that fans no longer wait for ice on their home waters, but travel far afield to regattas. It is possible for today's iceboater to sail from early December until late March in a normally cold winter.

In a severe winter, when long-frozen lakes are snowed under, there will be ice on the

Hudson, Navesink and Shrewsbury rivers, as well as Great South Bay on Long Island. Similar variations of conditions are possible in the midwestern iceboating region, comprising roughly the states of Wisconsin, Michigan, northern Ohio and northern Illinois, as well as the province of Ontario.

Between these two areas, stretching roughly from Buffalo to Newburgh, New York, there is a wide belt which suffers severely from snow, and does not get sufficient rainy or warm weather to cut the snow down. As a result, throughout this region, the sport never has prospered, though a few boats will be found on almost every sizable lake.

As a sport iceboating started about 1790 when Dutch settlers along the Hudson revived their old-country sport. However, the sport did not become widely popular until after the Civil War.

The Poughkeepsie Ice Yacht Club was formed in 1869, followed within a few years by the formation of the New Hamburgh and Hudson River Ice Yacht clubs, the latter organization located at Hyde Park, New York.

The development of the sport at Long Branch and Red Bank, New Jersey, followed a similar pattern and the boats were similar to those of the Hudson. From 1883 to 1902 the North Shrewsbury Ice Boat and Yacht Club of Red Bank sent its best boats to the Hudson for the Ice Yacht Challenge Pennant of America.

However, iceboating on the Hudson died after 1902, and the centers of activity shifted to the Jersey rivers and the Midwest, where the sport became active in Kalamazoo, Michigan, and Madison and Oshkosh, Wisconsin. The boats in use were still almost all of the basic Hudson River pattern, consisting of a single fore-and-aft stick or spar, called "backbone" or "keelson," mounted just ahead of its midpoint on a broad, flexible wooden plank called the "runner plank," which had a runner mounted at each of its extremities. The third running blade was pivoted through the after end of the backbone and controlled by a tiller. The helmsman and crew man (only two men sailed these huge boats as a

rule) clung precariously to a shallow, elliptical tray just ahead of the steering runner. The mast was stepped on the backbone several feet ahead of the runner plank. The rig, almost without exception, was jib-and-mainsail.

Although the modern boats are usually equipped with a single sail and more refined to the credit of the older boats go the speed records. In 1885, Commodore James Weaver sailed the *Scud* at 107 miles an hour on the Navesink River at Red Bank; in 1907 Commodore Elisha Price sailed the *Clarel* at 14 miles an hour on the Shrewsbury River at Long Branch; in 1908 the *Wolverine* of Kalamazoo, Michigan, sailed the fastest 20 miles to windward and return recorded to 1953, covering the course from a standing start in 39 minutes, four seconds. There is a record of four yachts sailing together down the Hudson from Poughkeepsie to New Hamburgh (nine miles) at an average speed of 84 miles an hour!

Speeds of these magnitudes are not commonplace in iceboating, but they have been repeatedly accomplished by well-rigged and well-sailed boats when conditions were favorable—plenty of room, clear, hard ice and a strong wind. To the uninitiated, sailing faster than the wind is hard to believe, yet it is by just this means that such speeds are made. As far as experiments show, about the best the iceboat can accomplish is approximately four times the speed of the wind that is blowing at the time. This speed is not a simple phenomenon to explain, but if it is borne in mind that (1) the boat is sailing *across* the wind and is not being pushed along by it and (2) by her very motion the boat creates an increase in the velocity of the wind she sails with, it may become more understandable. The truth of the matter is that the boat *never* sails faster than the wind which is driving her.

On a day with a gentle breeze of eight to ten miles strength, a well-handled iceboat can sail 35 to 40 miles an hour and her occupants will feel a regular gale in their faces as she does it. The limit to this process is set by the fact that the faster the boat moves, the more the wind tends to strike her from straight ahead. The boat whose sail can develop driving power at the smallest wind angle off dead ahead is the boat that will develop the greatest speed.

By Frank G. Menke
From THE ENCYCLOPEDIA OF SPORTS
A. S. Barnes and Company
Copyright 1953

CURLING

Just who originated curling, where and when is not known. It is a game played on ice, and thus a product of the cold countries. But which cold country is a matter for debate that has continued through the centuries the sport has endured.

Scotland claims credit for its creation. So does Flanders. But there is no evidence that anything similar to curling existed in any part of the Netherlands before Scotland elevated curling to the status of a major sport. So the honor appears to belong to Scotland.

The sport was introduced in Canada about 1807 and the United States about 1820. For the first 70 years it made infinitely more progress in this country than in Canada. The original United States club was the "Orchard Lakes" of Pontiac, Michigan, and the members influenced the creation of many other organizations along the Canadian border.

While players in New York State kept the game alive in the East, it spread in popularity to states around the Great Lakes and on the Canadian border, where there was a reasonable assurance of ice for steady play. Wisconsin became an important curling state and developed many outstanding rinks.

There are now three major organizations in the United States; the Grand National Curling Club of America, the Mid-West Curling Association and the United States Women's Curlers Association, the latter now having a membership of over 1,000 players.

BASIC RULES

In curling, players push a huge stone along the ice toward a tee, or fixed object. The game gets its name from the right or left spin given a played stone which causes it to proceed in an arc to the right or left. This change in direction of a played stone is known as the "curl" of a stone.

The stones used now are standardized at 38 pounds, 36 inches in circumference and 4½ inches in height (maximum measurements). If a stone is broken during a game, no substitution is permitted. The player continues with the largest fragment.

Curling is played on ice, usually in an indoor rink. Each team is made up of four men. The tee lines are 38 yards apart; the total length of the rink is 42 yards. At each end is a hack, or foothold, imbedded in the ice from which each player delivers his stones. Each player curls two stones alternately with his opponent.

B. J. Paulson of the Wauwatosa Curling Club of Wisconsin, describes the technique of play as follows:

"The curling stone is dished on both top and bottom. One side is sharp, for keen ice, the other side is smooth, for slow ice. A hole is broached through the center of the rock with a square countersink at either end to receive the square head of a bolt which passes through the stone and is screwed into a gooseneck handle. The stone is delivered by means of this handle.

"Bolt and handle can be removed and replaced quickly when it becomes necessary to turn the stone, depending upon ice conditions.

"The player swings the stone back, clear of the ice much in the same manner as one who is delivering a bowling ball and skims the surface of the ice with a smooth follow-through. At the instant he releases the stone, the player gives the handle either an in-turn or an out-turn, which is accomplished by a twist of the wrist that gives the stone a one-quarter turn and imparts the curling action, nothing more than a long curve. The amount of force put into the shot depends upon the condition of the ice and the orders of the skip.

"Each team comprises the lead man, who is usually the novice; the No. 2 man, who plays second; the No. 3 man, next to the skip in proficiency and the skip, or captain.

"The skip always figures out the plays and designates with his broom where he wants the stone laid which is being played by his team member. He then calls for either an in-turn or an out-turn, a running shot, a guard, etc. The skip holds his broom on the ice to designate the mark at which the player shoots. He also calls for whatever weight he thinks the play requires—that is, the amount of force to put into the stone as it is delivered, in order to stop at the point where the skip wants it laid.

"The broom has a two-fold purpose. In addition to being a pointer, in the skip's hands, it is used by supporting players to sweep frost or moisture from in front of the moving stone, permitting it to carry farther.

"After all 16 stones have been played, that end is completed and the score is counted. The scoring side receives one point for each stone inside the house that is not canceled by reason of an opponent's stone lying closer to the center. The house is the designation given to the target, embracing the entire area inside the outer ring. If a stone is lying on the outside of the outer ring, with the edge of the stone barely overhanging the ring, this stone is called a hanger and counts the same value as any stone inside of the house, provided it is not canceled by an opponent's stone. Sometimes a long hanger is the only count in cases where each side has been cleaning house. That is, taking out opponent's stones with running shots.

"The customary game consists of 10 or 12 ends, although 14 or more ends are frequently played. In case of a tie score an extra end is played to determine the winner.

"The ice is kept scrupulously clean and should be as level as a billiard table, free from humps, bulges and cracks. Before a game is started the players get out their brooms and wide-blade steel scraper, scrape down the ice to remove all inequalities, then sweep off every particle of scrapings and then pebble the ice. This last is a very important operation and consists of spraying warm water on the ice, accomplished by means of a special sprinkler with a straight handle at the bottom of it. The pebbler, accompanied by a player carrying a bucket of warm water, walks backward down the rink, and swings the water-filled sprinkler over his head in a wide rhythmic arc to throw the water uniformly across the ice, from side to side. Usually the sprinkler has to be filled half a dozen times in pebbling the length of the rink.

"At temperatures of around 25° F. above zero, the pebble will set within five or 10 minutes and the ice is then ready for play. The pebble is accurately descriptive, as the drops of hot water, sprinkled on the ice, raise tiny ice knobs on which the stones ride. Without this pebble, it would be impossible to control the stones."

By Frank G. Menke
From THE ENCYCLOPEDIA OF SPORTS
A. S. Barnes and Company
Copyright 1953

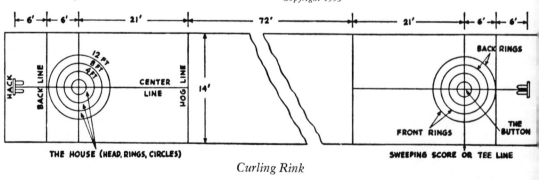

Curling Rink

SKIING

EQUIPMENT

Skis. Today it is almost an art to select a good pair of skis. The buyer is confronted with hundreds of pairs of skis made by a battery of manufacturers. Usually the buyer doesn't know what type of ski he wants. Usually he knows only the amount of money he can spend.

In order to obtain skis of the correct length for safety in all snow conditions and all slopes, you should purchase skis that measure nine to 12 inches over your height.

Composite skis made of a combination of wood, aluminum and plastic are the best skis on the market today. Other materials used in ski-building are fiber glass and laminated woods. Hickory is the best wood to make skis out of. Most good skis today come with steel edges which give you a good grip on the snow and wear well. Reject all skis made of ash or maple as these woods are too light. As in all things else too much attention paid to price and not enough to quality results only in headaches and not in fun on the slopes and hills.

Bindings. A good pair of bindings is important. Easily adjustable toe irons are necessary to hold the boots firmly. Steel cable or leather straps with a Bildstein clamp are the most used tightening means. The so-called "down pull" will help you to master control over your skis.

Poles. When you select poles, don't be influenced by their appearance. They must be well balanced and not too thick nor too heavy. Today they are used not in braking, but rather as a help in walking and climbing, increasing speed and maintaining balance.

The ring should be three inches from the tip, and the leather grip must fit the hand well so you won't lose them. The ends should reach no higher than your chest. The most commonly used poles are made of tonking, steel and aluminum.

Boots. Few skiers realize how important it is to wear a good boot. The soles should be absolutely rigid with a built-in piece of steel to prevent buckling in tight bindings. A deep groove should start high on the heel and continue almost all the way around. The upper leather should not be too stiff and it must be waterproof. A deep-cut tongue is advisable. The lacing should reach almost to the toe of the boot to allow a snug fit. Ankle straps are not absolutely necessary, but the lacing should reach down to the beginning of the toes so that the boot can be laced tight around the foot.

Selecting the right dressing is also important. Be sure not to use too much oil or grease on the boots or the leather will lose its waterproofing. Wax containing polish, applied not more than once or twice a week, is sufficient. It is important that the soles never be brought in contact with a hot stove or radiator, and that the boots not be dried out too quickly if they are wet through.

Clothing. The style of ski clothing changes so often it is almost impossible to recommend a certain type of outfit. However, it is necessary that the trousers, wind-jackets, sweaters, etc. keep you warm and allow free movement. Ski clothing should not be too heavy, but snow- and waterrepellent qualities are a must.

To prevent your ears from freezing, a very painful matter, wear a head band. This can be put in your pocket when not required.

BEGINNING TECHNIQUE

To enjoy skiing it is important that you get the right start. Your first hours should be spent doing exercises only on the level. First practice sidestepping. Hold the poles back and well above the snow. Step straight sideways with the right ski, shift your weight over to it and follow with the left, bringing it close to the right one and parallel. Keep on practicing until you can sidestep to both sides. After you have acquired fairly good control over your skis, you may put the poles into action. Place them at least a foot away from the skis in the snow and move your left pole with the left ski and vice versa.

Now practice turning around. The simplest turn is made by moving the tips of your skis around, or by turning the rear ends. Hold the poles back and up. Lift the tip of one ski, turn it away from the other, shift your weight to it and bring the other one parallel. Always keep the rear end stationary. Repeat the process until you have made a complete turn. To reverse this exercise, keep the tips in place and shift the rear ends around.

THE WALKING STEPS

Now it's time to attempt walking. Hold the skis close together and parallel. With the knees well bent, push one ski forward and at the same time push with the pole on the opposite side and slide as far as you can. Then straighten the body, bring the relaxed back leg forward, glide and push with the pole on the other side. After a few practice steps you'll feel the rhythm. Always advance the right ski and the left pole together and vice versa. Place the poles not too far ahead and close to the skis.

Gliding Step

CLIMBING

When you have mastered the walking steps, climb to the top of the practice slope. If it is at all steep, don't try to climb straight up but traverse the hill in a gradual ascent. Stamp your skis down on the slope to make them stick better.

Depending on the steepness of the slope you are crossing, you will have to edge more or less. On a gentle slope, in soft snow, just hold your legs and ankles straight and the edging will take care of itself. If the hill is steeper, or the snow hard and icy, you will have to edge more. Here you must guard against a common error. Many skiers bend their ankles to get more grip with the upper edges of their skis, a method that is not only incorrect, but quickly tires the legs. Keep your ankles straight, but push your knees inward toward the slope, at the same time leaning away from the slope with your body. Thus you force your edges to hold against the slope with your weight in a vertical line over the skis.

The poles play the most important part in climbing. It should be imprinted in every beginner's mind to keep one pole in the snow at all times, no matter how gradual and harmless a slope appears. Skiers in a hurry too often push with both poles simultaneously. That means both are in the air at the same time. That moment is usually the one chosen by the skis to slide sideways or backwards. Laboriously gained altitude is lost, and a spill is inevitable.

Suppose, however, the hill you want to climb is too steep to go straight up and affords no space for traversing. In this case you must sidestep.

The most important thing to do is to keep your skis always horizontal to the slope. Sidestep directly uphill, and place the skis on their upper edges, as you did in traversing. Again, remember to keep your ankles straight, press your knees toward the slope and lean outward for edging.

The sidestep can be modified for even steeper ascents. As you lift the upper ski, move it forward instead of straight upward and bring the lower ski up parallel to it. Thus you move upward and forward, instead of straight up, and relieve yourself of some labor over very steep spots. Handle your skis in the same way you do for straight sidestepping, but use your poles as you would in walking, left ski and opposite pole, etc. The shorter your steps, the easier your climb.

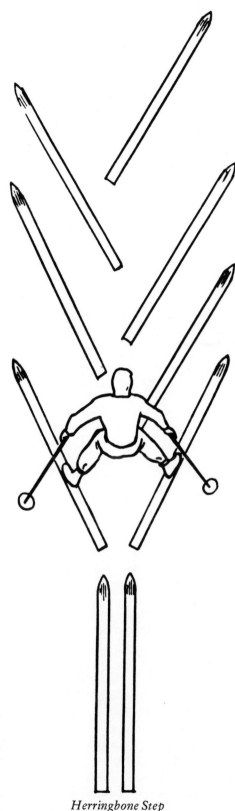

Herringbone Step

There is still another way to outwit a hill or narrow trail which cannot be traversed, in case you weary of continual sidestepping. This is the famous herringbone. The best way to get your skis into position for this step is to ski straight for the hill in regular walking formation. As soon as the slope steepens your skis will go into V position automatically. Keep your skis in the V position, widening it as the slope becomes steeper. Throw your weight well forward, and drop your knees forward, in a somewhat knock-kneed position to give your skis the necessary edge. The steeper the slope, the more you will have to bring your knees together to increase edging. Then, with your poles behind your bindings, swing one ski ahead, and put it down with the rear end in and the tip out. As you swing the left leg, the right pole goes forward, so that your left pole supports much of your weight. A swing of the shoulders helps you to relax and swing your weight up the hill.

THE KICK TURN

There is a good reason for learning the kick turn along with the climbing steps. So long as you spend your time on a gentle practice slope, you can always find a level spot for stepping around to change direction. As you become more proficient you will adventure into steeper terrain, and stepping around will be impossible.

Practice first on the level. Start with your skis together and parallel. Then face sideways, and plant both poles behind you, not too far apart and about a foot from the skis. If you are turning to the right, both poles will be by your left ski. Now put all your weight on your left leg, bending it slightly, and support yourself on your poles as you swing your right leg forward and up so you can rest the rear end on the snow beside the upbend of the left ski. That is half of the complete swing on the right ski. To complete it, turn the right ski outward and downward until it rests on the snow, parallel to the left ski, and heading in the opposite direction. The poles are still in the same place. To get out of this twisted position and complete the

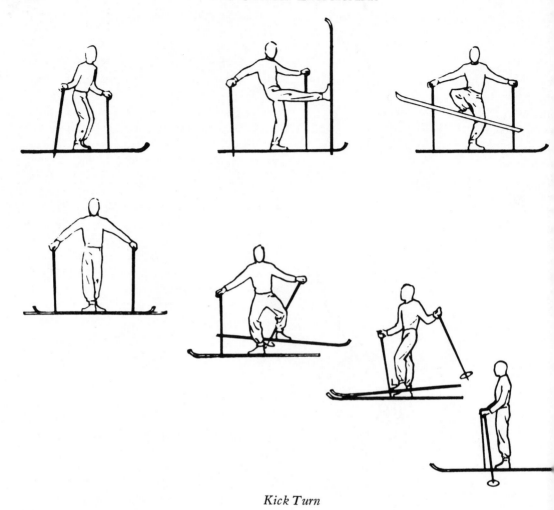

Kick Turn

turn, shift your weight to your right ski, and lift the tip of the left one well up, swing it around and put it down parallel beside the right. As you swing your left ski around, the left pole follows. There you are, ready to head in exactly the opposite direction.

The swing of the right leg as you go into the ski upright position is the key to the turn. In turning to the right, as above, you will do well to move your right leg back a little to increase the momentum of the swing. Soon you should be able to use this momentum to carry your right ski all the way up and around, without stopping to rest the rear end on the snow halfway over. Another thing, be sure to keep your poles in the snow until the final motion of the turn. Otherwise

you may lose your balance for lack of sup port or find yourself unable to get around vagrant pole to complete your turn.

DOWNHILL RUNNING

Presumably you can walk, climb and re gain your feet after a spill. If you can, you are ready for downhill skiing. Select a smal practice slope with a long level outrun, and not too crowded. Other skiers will not only seem to be in your way all the time, but may disturb your balance just by watching you

When you start, keep your skis parallel and one about six inches ahead. Press you knees forward, with your weight equally on both skis. Carry the body relaxed and ben slightly from the hips. Push with the poles a

he same time, and let your arms, after your
kis have started to slide, hang loose with the
ands forward above your knees. Hold your
oles above the snow, parallel to your skis.

Now the real fun is going to begin. It may
ake several tries before you are able to nego-
iate a "no-fall" run, but don't give up. After
ou have gained some confidence, try differ-
nt running positions. For example, the half
rouching position, which brings your body
loser to the skis, is mainly used for trail ski-
ng. The skis are more nearly abreast, and the
nees must be farther forward. Before you
et too far along on your straight running
ositions, you had better learn how to slow
own and stop. The "sit down halt" in front
f an obstacle is probably the most common
vay for a beginner to avoid collision, but
here is a better way.

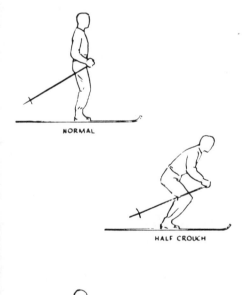

NORMAL

HALF CROUCH

CROUCH

Running Positions

RAKING AND TURNING

Go back to the little hill to practice brak-
ng, or snowplow. In fairly low running
osition, push the rear ends of the skis wide

apart, keeping the tips abreast, almost touching. Hold your ankles absolutely straight. Of
course you will have to look where you are
going, but keep one eye on the tips of your
skis so you can keep them from crossing. It
sounds simple, but your first attempt will
show that it is not. However, if your weight
is distributed equally on both skis, and the
bindings fit snugly, you should not have
much trouble getting the knack.

To control your speed in snowplow on
any hill or trail, edge the skis into the slope
by bringing your knees toward each other,
and put more weight on the back of the
bindings. If you want to stop, edge the skis
still more sharply and push the rear ends
farther apart.

In this braking position it is imperative that
your knees be pushed well forward. Never
use the poles as a help in stopping. It is most
dangerous. Keep them back where they belong, and the possibilities of a serious injury
are cut down to zero.

The snowplow turn is the most important
way for a beginner to change the running
direction of his skis. A novice derives as
much thrill from the perfect execution of
several fine turns as does an expert from
slipping several seconds off the record time of
a breathtaking run.

Start from the snowplow position and keep
the ski tips almost in contact throughout the
turn. If you want to turn left, shift your
weight over to the right ski, or vice versa for
a right turn. Both knees must be bent well
forward throughout the turn. The hips and
shoulders swivel in the new direction, inward
toward the turn, with a rotary motion. The
poles, held down above the knees, follow
around behind the body, parallel to the skis.
When you finish, equalize your weight and
you are still in snowplow position, as when
you started, but facing another direction.
That's all there is to it, and you'll be surprised how nicely you swing around.

But while you are admiring your progress,
be on guard for the mistakes all beginners
seem destined to make, mistakes which must
be corrected at once. In the first place, don't
stiffen your outside leg when you put your

weight on it for the turn, but keep it limber, and well bent. You will have to fight a tendency to straighten your leg as though you had no knee joint. Remember you have joints in your arms and shoulders, too. Don't hold them so stiffly that your arms and poles sail around as though they were cut from one piece of wood. Correct "vorlage" or forward lean cannot be acquired either if you are stiff. Your knees, pushed well forward, carry most of your weight, though your heels must stay pressed down on your skis. If your weight is forward, over limber knees, you will not have to bend from the hips at right angles, poker stiff, but can maintain an almost erect position with the upper part of your body. And never get your poles ahead of you. It is always dangerous.

A few turns to the left, a few to the right and you can link them together. First, keep your skis in snowplow position as you equalize your weight after a turn, but make it a moderate snowplow, with only a little edging, so that you will not come to a dead stop. Then shift your weight to the other ski and turn in the other direction.

Later you can bring the skis parallel between turns, for a traverse or schuss before you swing back the other way. Be sure to flatten your skis on the snow when you bring them parallel for a schuss, or the edges will catch and throw you. Even more difficult to remember is the change of edges for a traverse between turns. As you complete your snowplow turn, your skis are somewhat on their inside edges. When you go into traverse position, the lower ski remains the same, but the upper one must be turned onto its upper edge by the action of the knee. At the same time practice on different hills, and do not hesitate to tackle slopes with all kinds of snow conditions, even deep powder.

TOURING

If you have hiked or camped in your skiing areas in the summer months you will find your familiar haunts transformed and enchanted by the snow. Wander over hills and follow your skis up deserted trails for a while. You will love the quiet winter symphony and derive from it a satisfaction deeper than any you have experienced on the beaten tracks.

You will soon find that skiing on mountains or trails which are not polished by hundreds of skis requires more careful selection of the routes and turns. The snow conditions are changing almost from slope to slope, thus forcing the skier to adjust his technique to the snow. This is the technical value in touring. On a practice slope or a well-known trail, a skier often uses the same turns all afternoon, swings in the same places and repeats the same mistakes over and over again. Not only that, he wears himself out, the motions become less and less exact and instead of improving his technique, he looks worse. In touring, however, you must unpack the whole repertory of turns to reach the bottom and that is what makes a skier out of anybody.

By Walter Prager
From the book SKIING
The Ronald Press Company
Copyright 1939

A SURVEY OF NORTH AMERICAN SKI AREAS

INTRODUCTION

A quarter of a century ago there was plenty of skiing in this country—skiing of a sort. You could go touring through farm country, ski along wagon roads and even slide downhill occasionally over steep pastures or sparsely wooded land. If you were good enough at it, you might even do some ski mountaineering, or try one of the jumps the Norwegians built wherever they settled in the snow belt. Yes, there were places to ski, but there were no "ski areas" as we know them today. No lifts, of course. No uphill transportation at all, except in rare spots like North Creek, New York, or Teton Pass, Wyoming, where trucks and buses could carry you to the start of downhill runs. It was hard even to find a hill where skiers had packed down the snow firmly enough to make turning easy. Without packed slopes to learn the fundamentals on, it's no wonder that so few skiers of that day were at all proficient in downhill skiing—by modern standards. And of course they had to spend most of their time climbing up, instead of skiing down.

American skiers' first answer to this problem was the rope tow—a loop of rope driven by a motor and rigged so as to pull you up the hill when you grabbed onto it. The first rope tow in the United States was erected on Gilbert's Hill, Woodstock, Vermont, early in 1934. It was inspired by the successful operation of a similar tow at the Laurentian Club Lodge, Strawbridge, Province of Quebec, which may have been the very first rope tow. Questions of priority aside, the new gadget caught on swiftly and was widely copied: before two more seasons had gone by, rope tows could be counted in the hundreds. For the thrill of downhill skiing, rather than the charm of cross-country touring, was the magic that lured first hundreds, then thousands and millions of Americans to the sport.

The lowly rope tow was the world's first uphill conveyance designed specifically for skiers. Although Europeans had made use of everything from street cars to aerial tramways to get to the top of a hill, they had not yet built a ski lift. So the rope tow has this distinction, plus that of outnumbering all other kinds of lifts: there are over 1,000 of them in North America. The tow is a democratic institution, a true child of the depression. In the thirties the usual rate was a nickel a ride, 50 cents for an all-day ticket, and the tow remains the most economical form of uphill transportation for skiers. But Americans, like Europeans, are now insisting on comfort as well, and rope tows are gradually being replaced with fancier contrivances —at a whopping increase in rates.

The first "overhead cable" or "alpine" type lift in the country was probably the one erected by Dartmouth College on Oak Hill in 1935, although several other areas claim priority. In this modification of the rope-tow principle, a hook of some sort, suspended from a cable, pulls the skier along. Most common types are the T-bar, J-bar and platter-pull (so called because of the rubber disk on the end of the bar which the skier places between his legs). On a T-bar, two skiers ride on the same stick. On the Pomalift—a kind of platter-pull—the hangers are stored at the bottom and clamped onto the cable as needed. Still more luxurious, the chair lift whisks you through the air on chairs suspended from a cable; if the seats are wide enough for two, it is called a double chair lift. The aerial tramway or cable car usually has two enclosed cabins which counterbalance each other and transport a group of skiers at once. The gondola lift, latest creation, has a number of smaller enclosed cabins seating two or four persons each; the cabins are stored at the base station, Pomalift-style, and are clamped onto the moving cable after loading.

The first chair lifts were built in 1936 as part of that winter sports surprise package, Sun Valley. The Union Pacific Railroad—or rather, its chairman of the board, W. Averell Harriman—had decided to create a complete ski resort in the West, the peer of anything Europe had to offer. His agent, Count Felix Schaffgotsch, picked a site in the middle of nowhere, next to a town called Ketchum in Idaho. Nobody expected the project to pay for itself other than through promotion of train travel on the deluxe Union Pacific streamliners. But then, nobody could have predicted how popular a sport skiing was to become. The outcome is significant. Today easterners usually fly to Sun Valley instead of taking the train, while the railroad tries hard to keep the resort from making money instead of losing it. Consistently expanding its facilities, Sun Valley is still unrivaled in North America as a ski resort—unless perhaps by Aspen, Colorado.

Sun Valley brought in Austrian instructors, too, at about the same time that Austrians, Swiss, Italians and Bavarians began to teach skiing in the East. With increasing technical ability came the demand for longer and steeper runs, longer and faster lifts, and more of them. Before World War II a number of chair lifts had been built at places other than Sun Valley—at Mont Tremblant, Province of Quebec, Stowe, Vermont, Sugar Bowl, California, Alta, Utah, Timberline, Oregon, and elsewhere. After the war, the growth in lift facilities was little short of fantastic, and the boom has not let up yet.

Who built these lifts? Some of them were built by people with money who loved skiing enough to devote their lives and fortunes to it—people like the late Joe Ryan at Mont Tremblant and Fred Pabst at Big Bromley in Vermont. Other areas have enjoyed the patronage of financial angels—Harvey Gibson at his home town of North Conway, New Hampshire, C. V. Starr at Stowe and others. Today, the angels supply only a small percentage of the money used in ski area development and expansion. Most of it comes from banks and out of profits; from hardheaded investors who have learned that ski areas can be lucrative; from interested skiers; and from people who live in the community where the area or future area is located. In the past few years, more areas have been financed locally than in any other manner.

While the capacity of ski lifts has been stepped up enormously during the past 20 years, the greatest improvements in modern ski areas have been made on the trails and slopes proper. Area designers have learned to choose sites and lay out lift lines and trails in such a way as to provide the greatest possible variety and extent of downhill skiing. The old trails have been widened to handle more traffic. The new runs are cut hundreds of feet wide and constructed with banked turns so that less snow is scraped off to the sides. They are provided with drainage systems to carry off troublesome surface water, graded to exact specifications with dynamite and bulldozers, raked and seeded to rye or other cover crop, or covered with hay where this is impossible—all in order to provide good skiing on a minimum of snow. During the season, the snow itself is constantly treated to make it wear-resistant. Sno-Cat tractors pack new snow before wind and skiers waft it away, and flatten the bumps or "moguls" inevitably formed on the steeper pitches. At ski areas where snowfall is unpredictable, a new process of making artificial snow by means of water and compressed air is rapidly coming into favor. At some areas the snow base is preserved by spraying with ammonium chloride. All techniques undreamed of 20 years ago!

A ski area may be anything from an isolated hill with a tow to a complete skiing community. In the following survey of ski areas, as a general rule, only those possessing lifts will be mentioned. For lack of space, discussion of other facilities offered by many ski areas—ski schools, shops, rentals, lodging and the like—will be omitted. Areas offering such facilities in abundance and catering to vacationing as well as week-ending skiers may be designated as "resorts." Our survey separates North American ski areas into four regions analagous to our time zones: the Pacific Coastal, Rocky Mountain, Central and Eastern regions. The states in each region are taken up in north-south order.

PACIFIC COASTAL REGION

Here we are dealing with four different mountain ranges and four different sorts of climate. Fog, mingled with occasional snow, settles on the Olympics of western British Columbia and Washington during the winter. At the southern end of the Coastal Range, the mountains around Los Angeles have the least reliable snow of any high peaks in the West. Just the opposite is true of those farther inland. The Cascades (extending north-south in Washington and Oregon, 50 to 100 miles inland) and the Sierra Nevada (extending north-south in eastern California and including the highest peak in the continental US) have annual snowfall measured in the hundreds of inches. In the Cascades, wet snow and fog are the rule early in the season, changing to powder and sunshine later on. The timber line is low, and ski developments lie at elevations between 4,000 and 7,000 feet. Above that, skiing is often possible the year round. In the Sierras, most lift-served terrain is situated between 6,000 and 9,000 feet. The season lasts as long as you are willing to climb high, but is usually reckoned from the beginning of December to the end of April.

The entire Pacific Coastal Region enjoys relatively moderate winter temperatures, and in many spots the transition between citrus groves or rose gardens and the snowfields is a matter of only an hour's drive and a few thousand feet of altitude. Warning: many areas, particularly in the Cascades, operate only on week ends, and lodging is often scarce.

BRITISH COLUMBIA

The only major ski areas in the Olympic Mountains are located in the northern part of the range, in British Columbia. Grouse Mountain and Hollyburn Ridge, both chair lift areas, (Grouse's double chair lift is in two sections) lie directly across the harbor from the city of Vancouver and are quickly reached by car or bus via Lions Gate Bridge. These well-developed areas are dotted with the private and club cabins of Vancouver skiers, who number in the many thousands owing largely to the activity of newspaper-sponsored ski schools.

WASHINGTON

Mt. Baker is the northernmost (150 miles from Seattle) ski area in the state of Washington and the one with the longest ski season (November through July, minimum). Sheltered from prevailing winds by the mountain and massive Shuksan Arm, Heather Meadows has been a popular tow-skiing and touring area for many years. The surrounding slopes afford limitless descents. A double chair lift on Panorama Dome takes you to the top of some of the finest powder snowfields above the timber line.

Next longest season is claimed by Stevens Pass, 80 miles east of Seattle, equipped with a mile-long double chair lift in addition to a dozen tows. The third high-altitude chair lift area in Washington's Cascades is White Pass, near Yakima, now being developed.

Potentially the greatest ski area in Washington is the Paradise Park face of 14,408-foot Mt. Rainier, highest mountain in the state, whose glaciers afford skiing all during the summer. Two portable rope tows have been operated at Paradise Park during the season, and the US Park Service not long ago authorized a T-bar. However, installation of a big permanent lift, such as a chair lift, appears out of the question in the light of current federal policies.

The earliest developed and most popular region with Washington skiers is that centered around Snoqualmie Pass, 63 miles from Seattle. Here the newspaper ski schools hold forth, and Seattle snowbunnies scamper in droves. There are two main ski areas. Snoqualmie itself has a double chair lift, a Poma-lift and a dozen rope tows to handle the heavy week-end traffic. One half-mile to the east, Ski Acres is also equipped with chair lift and tows.

Mt. Spokane, near the city of that name in the extreme eastern portion of the state, lies on the edge of the Rockies rather than in the Cascades. This extensive area is provided with a double chair lift. Among lesser Washington areas, Leavenworth, an important center for jumping tournaments, and Walla Walla in the southeastern portion of the state, deserve mention on account of their perennial sponsorship of nordic events in skiing.

OREGON

In isolated grandeur, 60-odd miles east of Portland, rises a familiar landmark: the snow-topped cone of 11,245-foot Mt. Hood, tallest peak in Oregon. To this mecca Portland skiers flock by the thousands every week end during the long season. Center of ski activity and terminus of five trails cut through the wooded slopes of the lower mountain is Government Camp on Highway 50, which among other facilities maintains the largest rental shop in the country. Now, there are various ways and places to go skiing at Government Camp. If you are a beginner, you may join the other bunnies at the adjacent Summit Area with its seven tows. If you are broke, you can hitch a ride up the highway to the top of the trails. If well-heeled, you may ride the unique tramway to the top, a conventional highway bus suspended from a cable which rises 2,500 vertical feet from the highway. If an expert skier, you can head out to nearby Tom-Dick Mountain on the slopes of Mt. Hood, for some of the most fabulous skiing anywhere in the country. In addition to rope tows, you will find two chair lifts: an access lift and a double chair serving the steep sides of the bowl itself. Tired? Hop over to Multorpor to watch the jumping or ride the T-bar. Is it comfort you're after? Simply run up to Timberline.

Timberline Lodge, at the 6,000-foot level, is the only major ski resort in the Cascades. The lodge itself is an imposing chunk of rustic architecture, a product of FDR's WPA. In addition to the other nearby facilities, it has its own ski areas. The pre-war chair lift built by the US Forest Service rises above the lodge. Below it, a new double chair lift serves a network of intermediate slopes and trails. In summer the management provides Sno-Cat transportation to the high snowfields, where it operates a jig-back cable lift, primarily for the use of youngsters enrolled in the summer racing school.

Other Oregon areas of note are Hoodoo Bowl, with a double chair lift, in the Willamette National Forest at the southern end of the Cascades; Tomahawk Ski Bowl at Klamath Falls, with a new Pomalift; and Bend, site of the National Ski Association's summer training camp for promising downhill and slalom racers.

CALIFORNIA AND NEVADA

California has not only the mildest climate and most advantageous mountains of all the main skiing states in the union, but also a population of skiers large enough to support new development on a big scale. As a result, California has more lifts than any other state. There are more chair lifts within two hour's drive of the city limits of Los Angeles than in the entire state of Vermont—and this in a region reputed for its sunshine and bathing beaches!

The concentration of ski areas around Donner Pass and Lake Tahoe is familiarly dubbed the "Sierra loop" by San Francisco regulars. Along a 20-mile stretch of Highway 40, from Cisco to Donner Pass, lie Tunnel Mountain with its Pomalift, platter-pull and

ski jumps maintained by the Auburn Ski Club; Soda Springs, with double chair lift, J-bar and tows on Beacon Hill; Donner Ski Ranch, with double chair and tow transportation; and famed Sugar Bowl. Just northwest of the lake, near Tahoe City, lies Squaw Valley, projected site of the 1960 Olympic Winter Games. Northeast of the lake, near Reno, lie the Mt. Rose T-bar area and Reno Ski Bowl on Slide Mountain, with two double chair lifts in tandem—a long access lift (rendered superfluous by a new paved highway to the top of it) and a somewhat shorter lift serving the ski bowl proper. To the south on Highway 50 in Nevada is the Spooner Summit T-bar area. Main California areas on Highway 50 south and southwest of Lake Tahoe are Heavenly Valley at Bijou, with its double chair lift and steep expert runs; Edelweiss Lodge, also with double chair lift; and Sierra Ski Ranch, with Pomalift facilities. Reno and Bijou are both potentially great resorts needing longer lift-served runs —the former primarily expert runs, the latter primarily novice and intermediate slopes and trails.

Sugar Bowl and Squaw Valley are the major resorts in the Sierra loop. At Sugar Bowl the original chair lift (since replaced with a modern double chair lift) was built before the war on Mt. Disney. In addition to the luxurious main lodge, many private chalets were put up by San Francisco and Los Angeles skiers. In recent years access from Highway 40 has been provided via the "flying carpet" tramway, and a giant double chair lift has been constructed. This lift runs from the valley to the summit of Mt. Lincoln and serves a great variety of intermediate and expert runs, including the famous Silver Belt race course.

Squaw Valley is located in one of the most beautiful valleys of the Sierra Nevada. At present the resort is equipped with three lifts: a long double chair lift; a unique double chair tramway in tandem with that, serving steeper terrain; and a Pomalift that whisks you up the precipitous mountain called KT-22. The long, gentle descent provided by the main lift may not constitute the ideal Olym-

A P Photo

The Squaw Valley slopes mean thrills and excitement.

pic downhill course, but it is certainly popular with beginning skiers—who all too often must struggle with rope tows, while the experts ride in comfort. The main Squaw Valley Lodge, destroyed by fire in July of 1956, has been replaced with an even more luxurious structure. By 1960 Squaw is slated to have additional lifts, two jumping hills, a bobsled run, complete Olympic village, ice arena and other buildings, vast parking areas and other facilities. The California state legislature has already appropriated five million dollars and will undoubtedly appropriate more; the highway department has allocated millions to improve the access road and make a four-lane highway out of US 40 from San Francisco to Reno; individuals have donated funds—all in order to prepare the resort for the 1960 Olympic Winter Games. Quite likely, Squaw will become a state park, and the best equipped winter resort in America.

Farther south in the Sierras, at Sonora Pass near Pinehurst, lies Dodge Ridge, another favorite of Bay Area skiers. Dodge has a double chair, Pomalift and T-bar and plenty of tows to handle the week-end crowds. Badger Pass in beautiful Yosemite National Park, one of the oldest developed areas in California, has two T-bars. Mammoth Mountain, budding resort in the Inyo National Forest near Bishop, has a new double chair lift which, though providing wonderful skiing, does not begin to tap the massive mountain's potential as a great ski area.

In southern California, lift towers, like oil derricks, have mushroomed in recent years. The first chair lift was built before the war at Mt. Waterman, 43 miles north of Los Angeles. It is still going strong, and the steep, tricky runs are popular with expert skiers. The experts also enjoy plenty of challenging terrain at nearby Mt. Baldy. This magnificent area is equipped with three double chair lifts and a T-bar. The really difficult and steep gullies are located on the lower reaches of the mountain; unfortunately they are all too often unskiable, owing to insufficient snow. Close by, Kratka Ridge also has a double chair lift as well as tows. The Los Angeles businessman is pretty lucky. When there is snow—and that, unfortunately, is unpredictable—he can work some marvelous skiing into his schedule as easily as a round of golf.

In the Big Pines-Wrightwood section of the Angeles National Forest, east of Baldy, three areas are to be singled out from among the flock of lesser facilities. These are Blue Ridge, with its new double chair; Table Mountain, with a Pomalift; and Holiday Hill, a major area with two single chair lifts and a mile-long double chair lift, plus the inevitable tows.

Still farther east of the city, in the San Bernardino National Forest near Big Bear Lake, Snow Valley—with a mile-long chair lift, new Pomalift, ski jumps and 11 tows—is the largest and most popular area. Snow Summit, with double chair lift and seven tows, runs a close second; and nearby Big Bear has a chair lift and alpine lift as well as tows. At Green Valley Lake, we have witnessed the first self-service lift operation in ski history. There the Pomalift, serving open slopes, is rigged so that the passengers themselves can pull the lever which clamps the hangers to the cable and sends them on their way up the hill—leaving the attendant free for other jobs. Someday, perhaps, we will have coin-operated lifts with safety devices so foolproof that no attendants are necessary at all.

Of all the San Bernardino Mountains, the prize peak is 11,485-foot Mt. San Gorgonio. So far, however, all attempts to build a lift there have been defeated by the Sierra Club and other conservationist groups. Maintained as a wilderness area, this mountain offers magnificent downhill runs for those who are willing to climb.

What about the northern half of the Sierras, where all the really high peaks are—including 14,495-foot Mt. Whitney, highest point in the United States? Here there are two main obstacles to development: lack of access roads to remote peaks, and avalanche danger at the higher altitudes. Nevertheless, a start is being made. A T-bar has been erected as the first step in developing the lower slopes of Mt. Shasta, reached by a brand-new highway. Elsewhere in the north, a new platter-pull has been installed at the Sulphur Works rope tow hill in the Mineral area of Lassen Volcanic National Park.

Finally, no survey of California ski areas would be complete without mention of Mineral King. Because there are so many mountains, it is natural to think that perfect sites for ski areas should be easy to find. This is not the case, however. The ideal site—if it may be said to exist at all—is a great bowl walled in on three sides by mountains, just south of Sequoia National Park in central California. Here, a radial lift system could provide the optimum variety of downhill runs with a drop ranging up to 3,400 feet. The season is long, yet avalanche danger is not excessive. Unfortunately our ideal is 25 miles—that is to say, two or three million dollars worth of highway—removed from civilization. Yet there are California skiers who fervently wish the state of California were spending its millions of dollars on Mineral King instead of Squaw Valley.

ROCKY MOUNTAIN REGION

The climate of the Rocky Mountains is different from that of the peaks farther west, and this difference is reflected in the location and characteristics of the ski areas. By and large, snowfall is appreciably less in the Rockies at any given elevation. This circumstance has pushed Rocky Mountain developments to higher altitudes than their counterparts in the Sierras and Cascades. The other important factors are generally lower temperature and humidity, resulting in dry snow. So while the flatlander skier may huff and puff a bit more in the Rockies, he will ski more powder for his pains. As you go northward in the range, the timber line recedes and the mountains get balder on top, and in Canada treeless terrain is the rule. As everywhere in the West, most of the ski areas are located on national forest land, wherever the mountains are conveniently accessible from population centers.

ALBERTA

The Canadian Rockies are as remote as they are glorious, and ski development is naturally limited. Because of the decline of interest in ski touring and mountaineering, some areas—such as Assiniboine and Skoki— are probably less frequented by skiers today than they were 10 or 20 years ago. Banff, on the Canadian Pacific Railway line, is the principle resort and a deservedly famous one, its chair lift serving wide-open terrain on Mt. Norquay. Nearby Sunshine's T-bar area offers higher altitude skiing and somewhat more reliable snow conditions. Whistler's Mountain in Jasper Park is acquiring a Poma-lift. To the West, just over the border in British Columbia, lies the Red Mountain chair lift area.

MONTANA

The main spot is Big Mountain, a T-Bar area and resort near Whitefish that is popular with midwestern as well as local skiers. Yellowstone Ski Bowl on Lion Head Mountain has a convertible T-bar chair lift. Other areas equipped with alpine lifts are Bridger Bowl, near Bozeman; Grass Mountain at White Sulphur Springs; and Elkhorn Springs. New Pomalifts are operating at Snow Park, Missoula, and King's Hill at Great Falls.

WYOMING

The Grand Tetons are perhaps the most wildly beautiful mountains in the country. Jackson Hole, a ski-crazy town for decades and still the state's main chair lift area, has lagged behind other western regions in development and is now perhaps better known as a summer than as a winter resort. Other chair lift areas in Wyoming are Barrett Ridge and Libby Creek in the Medicine Bow National Forest.

IDAHO

In the heart of the Sawtooth Mountains, in south central Idaho, lies Sun Valley, the country's greatest resort. Sun Valley has seven chair lifts: two on Dollar Mountain, the novice area; one on Ruud, the slalom and jumping hill; and four on Baldy Mountain, the three tandem lifts rising over 3,000 vertical feet. With its many wide trails and steep, open bowls, Baldy offers more skiing variety than any other developed mountain in North America. Without first having trained and raced on the downhill courses at Sun Valley —or those at Aspen—our racers would not stand a chance in international competition. Here the Harriman Cup, one of the three most important US events, is held annually. The ski school is one of the largest in the country. Apart from facilities in the nearby town of Ketchum, Sun Valley is a self-contained village with luxury hotels, skating rink, heated swimming pools, shops, restaurants, etc., etc. Sun Valley is unquestionably the American ski resort *par excellence*.

The other Idaho areas are much smaller and cater primarily to local skiers. Bear Gulch, near Ashton, Bogus Basin, near Boise, and Magic Mountain near Twins Falls have T-bar lifts. Lookout Pass, near Wallace, has a new Pomalift.

UTAH

Utah is justly famous for its magnificent powder-snow skiing, perhaps even more so than Colorado. The powder paradise of the US is Alta, nationally famous resort, dramatically situated between steep avalanche slopes at the head of Little Cottonwood Canyon in the Wasatch Mountains, 25 miles southeast of Salt Lake City. Alta's three chair lifts include a new double chair to Germania Pass, which lets you ski the race course and other long, exciting runs as well as the Rustler, Collins and Peruvian faces served by the original lifts.

More popular with local—and beginning—skiers is Brighton, at the head of nearby Big Cottonwood Canyon. There a double chair lift and single chair provide wonderful powder-snow skiing on relatively gentle terrain.

Another important chair lift area in Utah is Snow Basin, 18 miles from Ogden.

COLORADO

Aspen is the great Colorado resort. Like Sun Valley, its lifts—two tandem chair lifts to the summit of Aspen Mountain plus two new auxiliary double chair lifts—serve a great variety of runs dropping well over 3,000 vertical feet. It boasts a crack ski school, and is renowned as a center for training and competition—the world ski championships were held there in 1950. Unlike Sun Valley, Aspen was not "built"; it just "growed." What is now a resort was, 15 years ago, a semi-abandoned mining town. With the exception of that Victorian restoration, the Hotel Jerome, it has many small lodges rather than one or two big ones, plus an accumulation of restaurants, night clubs, ski shops, etc. Under the patronage of Walter Paepcke, Aspen has become a cultural center as well, and in summertime music festivals, conferences on the humanities and other highbrow affairs are conducted in the pleasant mountain atmosphere.

The highest ski lift in the country is at Arapahoe Basin on the west side of Loveland Pass, 68 miles from Denver. In two sections, the chair lift reaches 12,500 feet and affords descents up to 3,000 vertical feet. A Pomalift auxiliary operates on the lower slopes. Flatlanders are well advised to acclimatize themselves at slightly lower altitudes before attempting the tougher runs—and rarified atmosphere—at Arapahoe.

The concentration of ski areas west of Denver is the heaviest in the Rocky Mountain Region. Winter Park, with its three T-bars and trail-slopes similar to those at better eastern areas, is both a resort and a favorite week-end area of Denver skiers. The Berthoud Pass area, with double chair and ropes, is also extremely popular. Loveland, the new double chair lift area, is particularly convenient for Denver skiers.

Other Colorado T-bar areas are Cooper Hill and Climax, both near Leadville; Tenderfoot Hill on the south slopes of Pike's Peak; and Stoner, near Cortez, in the south-west corner of the state. Hidden Valley, near Estes Park, has two platter-pulls. There is a double chair lift at Glenwood Springs, and a combination T-bar-chair lift at Steamboat Springs, a town which has produced many outstanding skiers and jumpers. New Poma-lift areas are located at Wolf Creek Pass, near Monte Vista, and at Grand Mesa, near Grand Junction, in the uranium country.

ARIZONA AND NEW MEXICO

Arizona Snow Bowl, a tow area just north of Flagstaff, and some skiing in the mountains above Tucson are about all Arizona can offer. But New Mexico is another story. In the mountains rising abruptly from the desert, there are three ski areas with lifts: Santa Fe Basin, with chair lift; the La Madera T-bar area near Albuquerque; and the new Hondo Lodge area near Taos, which employs Ski-Kuli shuttle T-bars for uphill transportation. Increasing numbers of Texas and Oklahoma enthusiasts are finding the New Mexico areas mighty convenient.

THE CENTRAL REGION

Midwest skiing had two strikes against it from the start: no big hills, and not much snow. But the Midwest did have skiers—increasing hordes of them—who insisted that any sort of skiing was better than no skiing at all. And, considering the disadvantages of the region, it is truly amazing what has been accomplished. Tow areas were built on most of the promising hills and some of the not so exciting ones (it is sometimes difficult to tell whether the tows run uphill or downhill), and on week ends these areas are jammed. Now some of these tows are being replaced with lifts, and at a few areas, snow-making machinery provides skiing in almost any weather.

Boyne Mountain at Boyne Falls, Michigan, the sole resort, has a chair lift, T-bar, J-bar and seven tows operating on its 500-vertical-foot alp. The other chair lift in the region (although the Black Hills belong to the Rockies, we are putting them in the Central

Region) is at Terry Peak, Lead, South Dakota. The T-bar at Rib Mountain, Wausau, Wisconsin, rising over 600 feet, is probably the biggest lift in the Midwest. There are now T-bars at Porcupine Mountain, Mt. Mancelona and Brule Mountain, Michigan (Brule is near Iron Mountain, the famous ski jumping center). There are Pomalifts at Sylvan Knob, Gaylord, Michigan, and at Sheltered Valley, Wisconsin. There is a platter-pull at Mt. Normandale near Minneapolis, a J-bar on Muskellunge Hill, Woodruff, Wisconsin. A new Pomalift has been installed at Ontario's most popular area, the Blue Mountain Resort near Collingwood.

But Midwest skiing is still primarily dependent on rope-tow areas, and in order not to slight the region we ought at least to name a few of the bigger ones. In Minnesota: Buena Vista, Comet Skiways, Lutsen, Mont du Lac, Moon Valley, Wirth. In Michigan: Michigan Tech Ripley, Pine Mountain, Holiday Hills, Manistee, Caberfae (with no less than 16 tows!). In Wisconsin: Trollhaugen, Mt. Telemark, Lockhaven, Ski Mac, Pinehurst, Hardscrabble, Deepwood, Potawatomi, New Munster, Wilmot, Mt. Atalanta. In Illinos: Fox Valley. Unless you happen to live in the Midwest, you have probably never heard of any of them. But they have introduced thousands of people to the sport who now swell the ranks of America's skiers.

THE EASTERN REGION

In the eastern United States and Canada, ski areas are strung out along the foothills and mountains of the Appalachian chain and the Laurentians of Quebec. The northern Appalachians include the Catskills and Adirondacks of New York, the Berkshires of Massachusetts, the Green Mountains of Vermont and the White Mountains of New Hampshire and Maine—mountains old in geological time, worn down to mere stumps of their former selves. All the developed skiing in this region lies at altitudes under 4,000 feet. And where it is possible to go appreciably higher than that, as on Mt. Washing-

ton, the weather is the world's worst and skiing is possible only in late spring. Temperatures run colder than in the West, and run to extremes. Thus it is quite possible for snow to fall one day, be chilled to 30 below zero the next, and be melted away in the following day's thaw. In contrast to the West, most eastern ski areas are located near villages and towns providing lodging, food and other necessities and comforts. Most eastern ski areas are resorts as well; and a few, particularly in the Laurentians and New York State, are primarily resorts and secondarily ski areas.

Typical eastern ski terrain today is a far cry from the narrow, twisting trails of 15 and 20 years ago. Wide-open trail-slopes are the rule, and the layout of many eastern areas is indistinguishable from that of below-timber-line areas in the West. The big three in eastern resorts—those capable of holding blue-ribbon competitions—are Mont Tremblant, Stowe and Franconia, while Mt. Snow threatens to make the big threesome a foursome before long. These resorts all have a great variety of lifts and trails with as much as a 2,000-foot drop and rank among the finest ski areas in the country—regardless of location.

QUEBEC

As you drive north from Montreal on Highway 11, you pass through what must be one of the most intensively—if not extensively—developed ski regions in the world. Every hill of any size has a ski slope and some sort of tow on it—and likely as not a lodge at its base, complete with a good bar, continental atmosphere and French cuisine, and possibly even a swimming pool, curling rink, outdoor ice pavilion and sleigh with jingle bells. Going north, the areas with alpine lifts in addition to rope tows are: St. Sauveur, T-bar, J-bar; Morin Heights, T-bar; Mont Gabriel, four T-bars; Ste. Adèle, platter-pull, the Chantecler's T-bar and Pomalift, and the new Sun Valley T-bar; Ste. Marguerite, Chalet Cochand's T-bar; Ste. Agathe, Pomalift at Mt. Kingston and platter-pull on Mont Chevreuil. From Ste. Agathe you can either branch off to Jasper at St. Donat, which has the second best hill and the longest T-bar in the Laurentians; or you can continue north to St. Jovite, with T-bar at Gray Rocks, and on to Mont Tremblant, the apex of Laurentian skiing. All these areas are so close together that it is actually possible, if you hustle a bit, to visit all of them in a single day.

Tremblant is a mountain of considerable size and a ski development of considerable scope. Two mile-long chair lifts, on the north and south sides of the mountain, are linked to the summit and thus to each other by means of two T-bars. You can easily ski and ride back and forth from one side of the mountain to the other. The south side trails of the original area terminate at Mont Tremblant Lodge with its chalets, shops and auxiliary buildings. The newer north side system of wide trail-slopes converges at Devil's River Lodge. Tremblant is a luxury resort, with an exceptionally fine ski school and all the trimmings. Scene of many important competitions, Tremblant annually holds the Quebec-Kandahar downhill and slalom, Canada's biggest prestige race.

Elsewhere in the province, the city of Quebec itself offers skiing as well as old-world charm. Chateau Frontenac is a winter sports resort in the old tradition, while Manoir St. Castin, just north of the city at Lac Beauport, maintains a modern ski area with parallel T-bar lifts, a Pomalift and tows. Quebec's third Pomalift is at Green Timber Mountain, North Hatley, not far from Newport, Vermont. In the Gatineau district, near Ottawa, there is a T-bar at Camp Fortune, and a practice-slope J-bar at Mountain Lodge, Chelsea.

MAINE

Maine has lagged behind neighboring New England states in ski development, largely because its mountains are remote from population centers. However, just during the past two years, three modern ski areas have sprung up. Pleasant Mountain, near Bridgton, has a double chair lift and T-bar. Near Kingfield, two tandem T-bars take you over two-thirds of the way up Sugarloaf Mountain; when fully developed, this mountain will offer magnificent lift-served skiing above the timber line. Newest Maine area is Farmington, where a Pomalift serves open slopes.

NEW HAMPSHIRE

Franconia, one of the two state-operated developments, actually has three ski areas: Cannon Mountain proper, with aerial tramway to the summit and auxiliary T-bar; the Roland Peabody Memorial Slopes, served by two T-bars; and the Mittersill (private) ski area with a T-bar lift. The tramway is the only true European-style funicular (*téléphérique* or *Luftseilbahn*) in operation at a ski area in North America. In addition to novice and intermediate trails and slopes, Cannon Mountain offers difficult, steep skiing for the expert. While the area sponsors no big annual race, the national championships and other important competitions have been held there repeatedly. Lodging and other facilities are abundant in this region.

Franconia lies adjacent to the so-called Eastern Slope region of the White Mountains, which on a good week end counts more skiers per square mile—or sometimes, it seems, per square foot—than any other area in the East. At Cranmore Mountain alone, as many as 7,000 skiers have been counted on a Sunday. This North Conway area was made famous by the late Hannes Schneider, former head of the ski school. The Skimobile, a unique conveyance of cable-mounted kiddie cars in two sections, provides transportation up the face of Cranmore. A new Pomalift assists a battery of tows in handling weekenders. On the back side of Cranmore, a new double chair lift serves runs mapped out by Hannes Schneider himself, just before his death.

To the north, Intervale has a Pomalift slope, and Jackson has two ski areas: Black Mountain with T-bar and J-bar; and Thorn Mountain, with two chair lifts. Pinkham Notch, starting point for skiing on the Wildcat trail and Mt. Washington, is the site of a projected one and a half million dollar ski development. Backbone of this area would be

Brother and sister throng the Laconia Belknap ski area in New Hampshire.

a mile-long gondola lift up Wildcat Mountain, a type of tramway with cabins seating four people.

Farther south in New Hampshire, there is a T-bar area at Waterville Valley. Mt. Whittier, at West Ossipee, and Snowcrest, near Lebanon, have J-bars. Belknap Recreation Area, near Gilford, and Mt. Sunapee (the other state-operated development) each have a chair lift and T-bar serving well-built trail-slope systems; the runs at Sunapee are particularly challenging. Dartmouth College now operates, in addition to the Oak Hill J-bar at Hanover, a beautifully laid-out Pomalift area at Holt's Ledge, near Lyme, called Dartmouth Skiway. The four trails range from a gentle, intermediate run to a downhill racing trail with steilhang and artificial bumps.

VERMONT

Thus far, Vermont has held the lead in eastern ski development, and Stowe is generally conceded to be the top resort on its side of the Rockies. Whereas the hotel business is divided up among a good many smaller lodges, the ski facilities are all owned by a single company under the farsighted management of Sepp Ruschp. There are five lifts, including two giant ones. A T-bar serves the Toll House practice slope, another T-bar the open slopes of Little Spruce, and a longer lift the Mt. Mansfield T-bar area. The original Mt. Mansfield chair lift, built before the war, rises from the state parking area to the Octagon hut at the starting point of the trail system. The Spruce Peak development is entirely separate, with its own parking areas and luxurious new base lodge and restaurant. The wide-open, more gentle slopes of Big Spruce are served by a double chair lift. Stowe is a major center of ski competition and training, and sponsors its own event, the American International races, every other year.

The other two chair lift areas in Vermont are Mad River Glen, near Waitsfield, and Mt. Snow, near West Dover. Mad River has excellent trail skiing served by the mile-long lift, including difficult terrain on the lift line and other routes. Mt. Snow has four double chair lifts of unique design. Instead of being suspended from cables, the chairs ride on greased rails and are conveyed by chain drive. The area has been growing at the rate of two such lifts per year; a full dozen is the goal envisioned by the management. Thus far, a generous area of intermediate trail-slope has been constructed, plus a longer and steeper run which permits the experts to "open up." Another high-capacity area in southern Vermont is Big Bromley at Manchester Center, with five J-bars and Pomalift. The slopes at Bromley are possibly the smoothest and best maintained anywhere in the East.

Only a short hike from the top of Spruce Peak at Stowe is the summit of a new ski area on the back side of the mountain: Smuggler's Notch Ski-Ways, accessible via Jeffersonville, Vermont. This development employs two Pomalifts in tandem to service a trail system of moderate extent. The first such Pomalift system was constructed on Okemo Mountain, Ludlow, Vermont. There, the upper lift is all of 6,200 feet long—the longest Pomalift in North America. At both areas, the lower lift serves a practice hill for beginning and intermediate skiers, while the upper section takes you to more challenging terrain. Other Pomalift areas in Vermont are Jay Peak, near North Troy, northernmost area in the state, where a start has been made toward developing a vast horseshoe of peaks; Burke Mountain near Lyndonville; Middlebury College Snow Bowl, near Middlebury; and Suicide Six at Woodstock, Vermont. Pico Peak near Rutland, Snow Valley near Manchester and Dutch Hill at Heartwellville

are all T-bar areas; High Pond at Brandon has a platter-pull; and Hogback, popular area near Brattleboro, Vermont, has two developments, one with T-bar and the other with Pomalift.

NEW YORK

Why is the Empire State so far behind in ski development? A special committee of the New York state legislature is currently trying to find the answer to this question. Doubtless, part of the answer lies in the state constitution's "forever wild" clause restricting development in the Adirondack State Park. Actually, many of the state's ski areas are comparable in every way to smaller areas in the New England states. What New York needs most of all is one really big area with long runs and steep skiing as well as slopes for intermediate and novice skiers. That is to say, a big mountain is needed—and all the big mountains lie behind the "paper curtain" in the Adirondack State Park.

A fine all-around ski area is Snow Ridge, near Turin, with T-bar and Pomalift and a snowfall reputed to be greater than that of any New England area. The Whiteface Ski Area has proved something of a disappointment to the many skiers who campaigned for the constitutional amendment that made it possible. Unfortunately, the state chose to ignore skiers' advice on where to locate the expensive T-bar development, with the result that skiing there is often poor or impossible owing to insufficient snow. In addition to Whiteface, Lake Placid—site of the 1932 Olympic Winter Games (nordic events only)—has the Lake Placid Club T-bar area on Mt. Whitney and two Pomalift slopes: Scott's Cobble and Fawn Ridge. Gore Mountain at North Creek, Hickory Hill at Warrensburg and Oak Mountain at Speculator are all T-bar areas, while Alpine Meadows near Saratoga Springs operates two platter-pulls.

In the Catskills of southern New York, state-operated Belleayre—with its chair lift, two T-bars and sporting runs—is a boon to metropolitan skiers. Nearby Highmount, and Roxbury Ski Center, near Roxbury, both have T-bars. The state has recently installed

A P Photo

This idyllic spot at Mount Washington offers ski enthusiasts sporting adventure as late as June.

a Pomalift at Allegany State Park in southwestern New York. Best known of rope tow areas is Bear Mountain, the ski jumping center.

MASSACHUSETTS AND CONNECTICUT

Most of the old Massachusetts ski areas have been slow to modernize and expand, and the projected development of Mt. Greylock—the state's highest and most suitable mountain—with an aerial tramway and extensive trail system has been delayed. Three areas in Massachusetts now have lifts: Bousquet's, near Pittsfield, a T-bar; Jiminy Peak, a platter-pull; and Otis Ridge, a Pomalift. All of course have rope tows in addition, and rope-tow areas elsewhere continue to operate. In Connecticut the Mohawk Mountain tow area provides good fun—given the necessary snow.

PENNSYLVANIA, WEST VIRGINIA

Not counting the numerous tows in the Poconos, there are three lifts in Pennsylvania: a T-bar at Big Boulder near White Haven; a Pomalift at Camp Soles, Somerset; and a combination T-bar and chair lift at Laurel Mountain Slopes, Ligonier, which area has also installed extensive snow-making equipment to keep its surprisingly good trails skiable. At Davis, skiers' headquarters in West Virginia, the first lift has appeared on Weiss Knob—a Ski-Kuli T-bar shuttle-type lift.

Unfortunately, that is about as far south of the Mason-Dixon line as ski developments go. Contrary to general superstition, skiers do not like the cold. They merely love snow and mountains enough to put up with it.

CONCLUSION

In the foregoing article we have mentioned no less than 238 lifts—platter-pulls, Pomalifts, T-bars, J-bars, chair lifts and aerial tramways—now operating at ski areas in the United States and Canada. These lifts themselves are worth anywhere from two thousand to two hundred thousand dollars apiece. The expense of lift-line and trail cutting, bulldozing, drainage, seeding, etc., usually exceeds the lift cost and often comes to two or three times as much in the East. Add to that the outlay for auxiliary rope tows, trucks and Sno-Cats, maintenance equipment and buildings, first-aid facilities, restaurants, shelters, parking areas, access roads, etc. Then take into account the cost of the even greater number of rope-tow areas in the country. Fifty million dollars would be a fair estimate of the total capital investment in North American ski areas alone—excluding lodges and hotels, retail shops and other resort facilities. During the past two years the number of lifts has been increasing at the rate of about 15 per cent per year. If this furious pace in development continues—as appears likely—more than 30 new lifts will go up this year—from China Peak, near Fresno, California, to Ragged Mountain, near Plymouth, New Hampshire.

These figures are significant not so much because they reflect the prosperity and ambitiousness of ski area operators, but because they are concrete evidence that the sport of skiing is growing by leaps and bounds. All these developments are possible only because more and more Americans are taking active part in a healthful, exciting outdoor sport.

By Fred Springer-Miller

ICE SKATING

In many parts of the country all that is needed to draw crowds of people into the outdoors is enough of a drop in temperature to freeze the small ponds and lakes. Then, even the smallest body of water becomes an oasis of fun to ice skaters. Certainly one of the main reasons for the popularity of ice skating is the minimum amount of equipment that is required for the sport, and the ease with which anyone with normal balance and coordination can learn to become a fairly proficient skater.

SELECTING SKATES

Unfortunately many skaters begin their ice career on someone else's hockey skates. These are often cheap and, for the most part, unmanageable. That floundering about on contraptions of this sort has not cooled the ardor of more skaters is a rare tribute to the appeal of the sport.

In general, skates are made for three specific purposes: hockey, figure skating and speed skating. And a skate specifically manufactured for one purpose is practically no good for any other. It is no more sensible to purchase hockey skates with no intention ever of playing hockey than it would be to purchase speed skates with no intention of ever speed skating. In fact, most authorities agree that both figure and speed skates are much more practical for general skating than hockey skates.

Hockey skates are designed with a short, highly-rocked blade, suitable for quick starts and fast turns. Speed skates are manufactured with a long, nearly level blade for maximum speed with minimum effort. Figure skates are made with highly-rocked, hollow-ground blade and a saw-tooth toe for a variety of graceful movements on ice. Beginners buying skates should bear in mind the type of skating toward which they intend to direct their attention.

Not having any special desires on the subject, many beginners have bought hockey skates. However, it is just as simple to learn to skate on either speed or figure skates.

Whatever type of skate you eventually decide to purchase, it is wise to avoid cheap skates. As in most other purchases, you get just what you pay for. Skates should be purchased with these factors in mind: weight of skate (in general, the lighter the better), durability, design of blade and quality of steel in the blade. Because they have been produced in large quantities for many years, hockey skates are today less expensive than either the speed or figure skating types.

LEARNING TO SKATE

The vast majority of skaters learned how by putting on a pair of skates and sliding about on the ice. They take their falls, look hopelessly at their sagging ankles and wonder how anybody could possibly make any sense out of the whole thing. In short order, however, the ankles *do* stiffen up, a feeling of the rhythm of the blades somehow comes alive and the beginner is no longer a beginner but is suddenly intent on joining a hockey game or teaching himself to skate backward.

In all skating the body should be relaxed, leaning slightly forward, with knees slightly bent. The toe should point out slightly at the beginning of the push, care being taken to thrust with the whole blade of the skate, and not just the toe. After the thrust, the blade should be carried back to its original position near the other foot, with the blade pointing down only slightly. Speed skates should be carried back almost parallel with the ice, but the toe is permitted to point downward more with figure and hockey skates. The chief advantage in bringing the blade back parallel to the ice is that it is ready at any time for the next stroke, and there is no danger of the tip of the blade catching in the ice and throwing the skater.

When leading with the right foot, the right shoulder should be lowered slightly over it. The body rolls in a smooth motion with each alternate stride.

CARE OF SKATES

Good skating is not possible without sharp skates. No matter what type of blade you are using, every attempt should be made to keep the edges as sharp as possible. Expert speed skaters sharpen their skates about every other time they go on the ice. Hockey stars sharpen them at least as frequently, because their edges are not accorded the tender treatment a speed star gives his blades. But often amateur skaters go for months and sometimes years without ever sharpening their skates.

If your blades are narrow enough purchase a holder and sharpen your skates yourself. If not, you can have them machine ground as often as occasion demands, but insist upon an oil-stone finish.

Once skates are sharpened any skater should exercise due caution to keep his edges in good condition. Such care not only makes skating more enjoyable, it is a necessity for serious skating. Leather, rubber or wooden guards are available for any type skate and should be used religiously.

Figure skaters are partial to the wooden guards which are carved with a rocker effect. These greatly simplify walking. Leather guards are satisfactory when attached securely to the skate. The chief advantage of the rubber guards is that they can be folded up and put in your pocket while skating, being much smaller than any of the other types.

Walking on the toes of your skates is better than walking on the entire blade, but it dulls the edge along the most important section of the blade. Guards are so inexpensive toe-walking should be used only in an emergency.

By Harold Putnam
From THE DARTMOUTH BOOK OF WINTER SPORTS
A. S. Barnes and Company
Copyright 1939

SKATE SAILING

Skate sailing is a sport just beginning to come into its own in the United States, yet it is almost as ancient, in Scandinavian countries, as skiing. In those nations, sailing on skates continues to be practiced, for sport or other reasons, when the rivers and lakes are frozen solid and a human being wishes to get somewhere in a hurry. It does not call for any muscular effort, and greater speed is possible than while on skis.

W. Van B. Claussen of the National Red Cross, Washington, D.C., an authority on skate sailing, describes his favorite sport as follows:

"Skate sails may be triangular, rectangular or kite shaped, and from 50 to 70 square feet in area—roughly, 10 feet high and 14 feet long. The cloth sail is stretched to drumhead tightness on a cross-frame of light spars which is held in a vertical plane with the middle spar resting on the sailor's shoulder. It is manually controlled depending upon the angle it presents to the wind. Ordinary cruising sails may be made of unbleached muslin, with bamboo spars, but the present-day racing sail is of fine balloon silk or nylon and duraluminum or rattan spars give it a true airfoil form.

"The most satisfactory ice skate for sailing is the long tubular racing skate—preferably the special 18 inch length, with the heel end of the blade ground to a parabolic rocker and provided with teeth for quick stopping.

"The skate sail is held on the shoulder, between the sailor and the wind, in such a manner that the wind strikes at an angle and the sailor leans comfortably against the sail to counteract the pressure. Sailing into the wind, or away from it creates speeds from a comfortable cruising rate of 15 miles per hour up to racing speeds of 50 and 60 miles.

"To standardize competition, the racing rules of the Skate Sailing Association of America permit only skates 18 inches and under in length of blade. Sail areas for racing are limited to one square foot for each 2½ pounds weight of the sailor. Thus a man weighing 150 pounds (in street clothing, without an overcoat) would be permitted to carry a sail of 60 square feet."

By Frank G. Menke
From THE ENCYCLOPEDIA OF SPORTS
A. S. Barnes and Company
Copyright 1953

THIN ICE

Ice travel should at all times be treated with caution. Especially toward the end of the cold weather does it become extremely hazardous to trust any frozen surface. Most of the ice accidents that occur could be prevented by application of these Red Cross rules for ice travel.

First of all, don't venture alone on ice at all questionable. If an accident does happen, your chances are far better if someone is nearby to give or get assistance.

Second, beware of thin ice. A pat rule is— one inch, keep off; two inches, use caution; three inches, safe for small groups; four inches, okay. But watch out for weak spots; the character of the ice may not be the same all over.

During a midwinter thaw or near the end of the season when hot sun and warm winds affect the ice, even as much as two feet of apparently firm ice may become crystalline or honeycombed so that slight pressure will break it, leaving open water thick with floating mush in place of ice.

Ice on small flowing streams, on large rivers with fair current and on tidewater is always subject to constant wear or strain. In late winter it is particularly treacherous. Have a healthy respect for ice—its hazards are varied.

However if, in spite of your precautions, a break-through does occur, hope is not lost if you keep your head and follow the suggestions in the accompanying drawings.

Remember this, too: Even if you fall on cracked ice, you can prevent a break-through by remaining prone and rolling away from the danger area. If there is a break-through, all other people should be warned away from the scene.

From The American Red Cross

If you break through the ice, don't try to climb out by pressing on the edge of already weakened ice. Extend arms forward, kick feet to an extended and nearly level swimming position and work way forward on the ice. A large nail or pocket knife, when driven into ice at arm's length from hole, gives you anchorage to draw yourself out to safety.

*Smart skaters carry 50 feet of line in case a rescue, like the one shown
becomes necessary. A pole, ladder or plank can be used for this purpose. Tell victim to extend arms and kick to the surface. Place ladder
flat on ice and slide one end of it to him. Rescuers should wear skates
or ice creepers to anchor themselves and thus avoid being pulled
toward the hole. Keep other people well away from the hole area.*

A human chain can also be used for a rescue. But this method can be dangerous and it should only be used as the last resort. Four or five men lie prone on ice, gripping each other by the feet. They hold their bodies rigid so that two men on shore end of chain can push them within the reach of victim. The last two men must be firmly anchored by skates or by some hold on shore for pulling the chain back.

index

FIRST AID

FISHING

SHOOTING